MOBILIZING THE INFORMATION SOCIETY

Mobilizing the Information Society

Strategies for Growth and Opportunity

ROBIN MANSELL
and
W. EDWARD STEINMUELLER

OXFORD

UNIVERSITY PRESS

OXFORD

UNIVERSITY PRESS

Great Clarendon Street, Oxford OX2 6DP

Oxford University Press is a department of the University of Oxford.
It furthers the University's objective of excellence in research, scholarship,
and education by publishing worldwide in

Oxford New York

Athens Auckland Bangkok Bogotá Buenos Aires Calcutta
Cape Town Chennai Dar es Salaam Delhi Florence Hong Kong Istanbul
Karachi Kuala Lumpur Madrid Melbourne Mexico City Mumbai
Nairobi Paris São Paulo Shanghai Singapore Taipei Tokyo Toronto Warsaw

and associated companies in Berlin Ibadan

Oxford is a registered trade mark of Oxford University Press
in the UK and certain other countries

Published in the United States
by Oxford University Press Inc., New York

British Library Cataloguing in Publication Data

Data available

Library of Congress Cataloging in Publication Data
Mansell, Robin.
Mobilizing the information society: strategies for growth and opportunity / Robin
Mansell and W. Edward Steinmueller.
p. cm.
Includes bibliographical references.
1. Information society. I. Steinmueller, W. Edward (William Edward) II. Title.
HM851 .M363 2000
303.48'33—dc21 00-061118

ISBN 0-19-829556-1

1 3 5 7 9 10 8 6 4 2

Typeset by Best-set Typesetter Ltd., Hong Kong
Printed in Great Britain
on acid-free paper by
Biddles Ltd., Guildford and King's Lynn

For Esmee and Glen
Dee and Milton

Acknowledgements

The research underlying this book was supported by the European Commission, Information Society Directorate-General, formerly Directorate-General XIII, over an extended period throughout the FAIR (Forecast and Assessment of the socio-economic and policy Impact of advanced communications and Recommendations) project, which was funded as a horizontal action within the Fourth Framework Programme on Advanced Communication Technologies and Services (ACTS). We are grateful to the Commission for funding this research and to our colleagues, especially Peter Johnston and Jean Millar, who were active promoters and critics of our efforts. Nothing that we say in this book should be construed to represent the viewpoints of these individuals or the European Commission.

Since the political flux of the European Commission is often as intense as the 'white heat of innovation' that its representatives are seeking to promote, we are not sure about the reception of this book. It represents a more synthetic and critical analysis than the reports and the set of fifty FAIR project working papers that provided the initial basis for the research. Our intention throughout, however, is to offer a constructive assessment of the development of the European information society. We largely share and agree with the goals of the European Council, the European Commission, and the European Parliament of promoting progress towards an equitable and sustainable information society. This book is intended to be a contribution towards that goal.

Without the active collaboration of our colleagues in the FAIR project, this work would not have been possible. The project's co-ordinator, Gabriella Cattaneo, Databank Consulting, Milan, played a critically important role in stimulating the team to address a number of key issues, including the problems of disparities between northern and southern Europe and the importance of assessing the economic significance of information society developments for employment, for small and medium-sized firms, for the non-profit sector, and for public sector organizations. She recruited very talented researchers to work on the project, including Marco Farinelli, Enrico Grazzini, Peter Hounsome (Welsh Development Agency), Stefano Kluzer, Guido Lucchi, Silvia Melloni, Lucia Passamonti, Laura Sisti, and Teresa Tardia. Annaflavia Bianchi, then at the Centre for Urban and Regional Development Studies (CURDS), University of Newcastle, contributed to the research on regional development undertaken by Databank Consulting. We also benefited from the advice, insights, and contributions of Professor Franco Morganti, Databank Consulting, who, together with Gabriella Cattaneo, reinforced a very productive collaborative relationship between Databank and SPRU (Science and Technology Policy Research, University of Sussex) that stretches back over many years.

Jacques Bernard, the principal in Technology Investment Partners, Paris, a FAIR project partner, provided a continuous flow of information about the development of new technology and its significance for the social and economic issues that we examine.

Throughout the life of the project at the University of Sussex, Professor Roger Silverstone played a key role in the FAIR project, provoking us to examine more deeply the role of social exclusion issues. His colleague, Dr Leslie Haddon, provided further important empirical and theoretical insights into the processes of social exclusion, some of which are incorporated in Ch. 2. Silverstone has now moved to the London School of Economics and Political Science where he is leading a flourishing interdepartmental programme of research and teaching in the new media and communication studies field.

Over the life of the FAIR project, the Maastricht Economic Research Institute on Innovation and Technology (MERIT), at the University of Maastricht in The Netherlands, was an institutional partner in the project. Professor W. Edward Steinmueller was very fortunate to be able to work at this outstanding institution from 1995 to 1997, the beginning years of the FAIR project. He would like to express his gratitude to Professor Luc Soete, MERIT's Director, for encouraging and supporting the work underlying this book. Soete's own contributions on the fiscal impact of the Internet are but a small part of the contribution that he has made to our work in other connections, such as his service as Chair of the High Level Expert Group (HLEG) whose viewpoint we largely share. At MERIT, Steinmueller was able to draw upon the research work of Huub Meijers, Parantha Narendran, Gert van de Paal, Karin Kamp, Bas ter Weel, and Aldo Geuna (who has subsequently joined SPRU). Wilma Coenegrachts provided the key administrative support for the project at MERIT, making it possible to focus on the research without fear, uncertainty, or doubt about the financial consequences.

Professor Robin Mansell directed the work of the SPRU team on the FAIR project and a substantial portion of this book reflects its contributions. During the life of the project other SPRU members included Dr Andreas Credé, Dr Richard Hawkins, Dr Willem Hulsink, Emma Jansen, Pantelis Margaris, David Neice, Lara Srivastava, Ingrid Standen, and Uta Wehn de Montalvo, all of whom made major contributions to the empirical base of research that has contributed to this book. David Sayers, Independent Consultant, Brighton, was extremely helpful in establishing contacts with key industrial players and people in the policy community and helped us to amass considerable information, especially with respect to our discussion in Chs. 7 and 8 on technological solutions, electronic payment systems, and cryptography. We thank Professor Michael Gibbons, Director of SPRU at the time the FAIR project was designed, for his insistence that it was indeed feasible to generate reasonably long-term finance for a creative programme of independent research in the fast-moving field of information and communication technological policy. Our commitment to research on both the socio-political and the techno-economic dimensions of transformations accompanying developments in information and communication technologies has been championed throughout the project by Professor Chris Freeman. We are grateful to him for his support of all our endeavours in this area. Peter Morris of Business Training, Brighton, contributed many of the graphics and the design of FAIR project reports over the years and he must take full credit for the special logo that helped to bring our work to the attention of a large number of readers. Jackie Fuller and Steff Hazlehurst played important roles in ensuring the smooth running of the administrative side of the FAIR project in SPRU. During the production of this book, Dr Michèle Javary played a key role in our research and we were also assisted by Ana Arroio and Dr Jane Millar. Lastly, Cynthia Little, Programme Administrator for the SPRU Information, Networks & Knowledge research centre, not only withstood all the pressures of reporting deadlines for the project, but also contributed her excellent editorial skills to improve the quality of the manuscript for this book.

As can be surmised from the above, the material underlying this book was very much of a team effort. It is important to understand, however, that this material can be used in a multiplicity of ways. In most cases, the main purpose of the original working papers produced by the FAIR project was to support a factual account of emerging developments in the European information society. A substantial amount of this material has been integrated into the text of this volume and each of the chapters notes the individuals most responsible. In the case of two chapters, however, the analytical basis of the studies directly complements the architecture and purposes of this book. As a result, we have included Richard Hawkins as a co-author (Chs. 5 and 6). This reflects Dr Hawkins's contribution not only to the factual basis of each of these chapters, a contribution he shares with the other contributors noted above, but also to the analytical theme and purpose of the chapters.

We are indebted to the network of some forty-five experts throughout Europe in the academic, policy, and business communities who agreed to comment on the FAIR project research outputs and supported the FAIR project team throughout. To the very substantial number of individuals within the private and public sectors who were contacted for information through the life-cycle of the FAIR project, we can finally only say thank you, and hope that you will be provoked into visionary thinking and action by our work. To David Musson, our editor at Oxford University Press, we express our gratitude for his patience and confidence in this book. We accept full responsibility for all the viewpoints and arguments in this book and the normal disclaimers of all institutional and organizational responsibility apply.

R. M.
W. E. S.

Brighton
April 2000

Contents

List of Figures

List of Tables

Acronyms

ACTA	America's Carriers Telecommunication Association
ACTS	Advanced Communication Technologies and Services
ADAGP	Société des auteurs dans les arts graphiques et plastiques
ADSL	Asymmetric Digital Subscriber Line
ADSL-F	Asymmetric Digital Subscriber Line Forum
AIN	Advanced Intelligent Network
AIW	Advanced (peer-to-peer networking) Implementers Workshop (IBM forum)
ALCS	Authors' Licensing and Collecting Society
AM	Amplitude Modulation
AMPS	Advanced Mobile Phone Service
ANSI	American National Standards Institute
API	Application Program Interface; Applications Programing Interface
APNIC	Asia Pacific Network Information Centre
APPI-F	Advanced Peer-to-Peer Internetworking Forum
APPN	Advanced Peer-to-Peer Networking
ARIN	American Registry for Internet Numbers
ARPANET	Advanced Research Projects Agency Network
ASIC	Application-Specific Integrated Circuit
ASMO	Advanced Storage Magneto Optical
ASV	Average Sales Volume
AT&T	American Telegraph and Telephone
ATDM	Asynchronous Time Division Multiplexing
ATM	Automatic Teller Machine
ATM	Asynchronous Transfer Mode
ATM-F	Asynchronous Transfer Mode Forum
ATM-JIG	Asynchronous Transfer Mode Forum—Japan Interest Group
ATM UNI	Asynchronous Transfer Mode User Network Interface
ATSC	Advanced Television Systems Committee
ATSC-TV	Advanced Television Systems Committee—Television
BA	Broadband Access
BBS	Bulletin Board Service
BCS	British Computer Society
BEUC	Bureau Européen des unions de consommateurs
BGP	Border Gateway Protocol
BHEs	Busy Hour Erlangs
BIEM	Bureau internationale des sociétés gérant les droits d'enregistrement et reproduction mécanique
BIPE	BIPE conseil (French consultancy)
BISDN	Broadband Integrated Services Digital Network
BNL	British National Laboratory
BPI	British Phonographic Industry
BPR	Business Process Re-engineering

BRI	Basic Rate Interface
BSA	Business Software Alliance
BUMA/STEMRA/CEDAR	The Dutch authors' rights societies
CA	Certification Authority
CAGR	Compound Annual Growth Rate
CALS	Computer-Aided Life-cycle Support
CAMEL	Customized Applications for Mobile Enhanced Logic
CBDS	Connectionless Broadband Data Service
CBR	Continuous Bitrate (Services)
CCITT	International Telegraph and Telephone Consultative Committee of the International Telecommunication Union
CCTV	Closed Circuit Television
CD	Compact Disc
CD-E	Compact Disc—Erasable
CD-i	Compact Disc Interactive
CDMA	Code Division Multiple Access
CD-R	Compact Disc—Recordable
CD-ROM	Compact Disc—Read Only Memory
CD-RW	Compact Disc—Rewritable
CEMA	Consumer Electronics Manufacturers Association
CEN	European Committee for Standardization
CENELEC	European Committee for Electrotechnical Standardization
CERN	European Laboratory for Particle Physics
CESG	Communications Electronics Security Group
CHAPS	Clearing House Automated Payment Systems
CIR	Committed Information Rate
CITADEL	Citoyens et internautes tous associés pour la défense des libertés
CIX	Commercial Internet Exchange
CLA	Copyright Licensing Agency
CLARCS	Copyright Licensing Agency Rapid Clearance System
CLI	Calling Line Identification
CNCA	National Co-ordination of Sheltering Communities, Italy
CNRI	Corporation for National Research Initiatives
COCOM	Co-ordinating Committee for Multilateral Strategic Export Controls
COG	Collaborative Open Group
CommUnity	Computer Communications Association
CORBA	A standard for ensuring portability of software
COTS	Commercial Off The Shelf
CPE	Customer Premises Equipment (US usage)
CPSR	Computer Professionals for Social Responsibility
CPTW	Copyright Protection Technical Working Group
CRS	Cell Relay Services
CSELT	Centro Studi e Laboratori Telecommunicazioni
CSMA CD	Carrier Sense Multiple Access with Collision Detection
CSPS	Community, Social and Personal Services sector
CSU	Channel Service Unit

CTI	Computer Telephone Integration
CUG	Closed User Group
DAB	Digital Audio Broadcasting
D-AMPS	Digital Advanced Mobile Phone Service
DSL	Digital Subscriber Line
DSU	Data Service Unit
DAVIC	Digital Audio Visual Council
DB.NL	Digitale Burgerbeweging Nederland
DBRW	Development Board for Rural Wales
DBS	Direct Broadcast Satellite
DCS 1800	Digital Cordless System 1800
DCS	Digital Communication Service
DECT	Digital Enhanced Cordless Telephony
DES	Data Encryption Standard
Divx	Digital Video Express (brandname)
DMMS	Digital Media Management Systems
DNS	Domain Name System
DSA	Digital Signature Algorithm
DSL	Digital Subscriber Line
DSRM	DAVIC Systems Reference Model
DSU	Data Service Unit
DTI	Department of Trade and Industry
DTMF	Dual-Tone Multi-Frequency
DVB	Digital Video Broadcast
DVD	Digital Versatile Disc
DVD-R	DVD-Recordable
DVD+RW	DVD-Rewritable
DVD-RAM	DVD Random Access Memory
DVD-ROM	Digital Video Disc Read Only Memory
DVI	Digital Video Interactive
DXI	Data Exchange Interface
EARN	European Academic Research Network
EBLIDA	The European Bureau of Library and Information and Documentation Associations
EBU	European Broadcasting Union
EC	European Commission
ECAC	Electronic Commerce Advisory Commission United States
ECMA	European Computer Manufacturers Association
ECMS	Electronic Copyright Management Systems
EDI	Electronic Data Interchange
EDIFACT	Electronic Data Interchange for Administration, Commerce and Transport
EEA	European Economic Area
EFF	Electronic Frontier Foundation
EFT	Electronic Funds Transfer
EGP	Exterior Gateway Protocol
EIA	Electronics Industry Association
EIS	Electronic Information Services

EITO	European Information Technology Observatory
ELSPA	European Leisure Software Publisher Association
EPG	Electronic Programme Guide
EPIC	Electronic Privacy Information Centre
ESF	European Security Forum
ESP	Enhanced Service Provider
ESPRIT	European Strategic Programme for Research and Development in Information Technology
ETNO	European Telecommunication Network Operators
ETSI	European Telecommunications Standards Institute
ETUC	European Trade Union Confederation
EU	European Union
EURIM	European Informatics Market
EWOS	European Workshop for Open Systems
FAC	Feminists Against Censorship
FACT	Federation Against Copyright Theft
FAIR	Forecast and Assessment of Socio-Economic Impact of Advanced Communications and Recommendations
FAST	Federation Against Software Theft
FCC	Federal Communications Commission
FDDI	Fibre Distributed Data Interface
FEDIM	Federation of European Direct Marketing Associations
FEI	Federation of the Electronics Industry
FhG-ISI	Fraunhofer-Institut für Systemtechnik und Innovationsforschung
FPLMTS	Future Public Land Mobile Telecommunication System
FREE	Fronteras Electronicas España
FTP	File Transfer Protocol (most commonly referred to as ftp)
FTTC	Fibre to the Curb
FTTH	Fibre to the Home
F-UNI	ATM Forum's Frame-based User of Network Interface
G7	Group of Seven countries
GATS	General Agreement on Trade in Services
GATT	General Agreement on Tariffs and Trade
GCHQ	Government Communication Headquarters
GDP	Gross Domestic Product
GEMA	German mechanical copyright protection society
GESAC	Groupement européen des sociétés des auteurs et compositeurs
GII	Global Information Infrastructure
GIM	Global Information Market
GMPCS	Global Mobile Personal Communication Systems
GNP	Gross National Product
GPRS	General Packet Radio Service
GSM	Global System for Mobile Communication
GSTN	General Switched Telephone Network
GVU	Graphic Visualization and Usability
HDSL	High (bitrate) Digital Subscriber Line

HDTV	High Definition Television
HEI	Higher Education Institution
HFC	Hybrid-Fibre Coaxial (cable)
HIV/AIDS	Human Immunodeficiency Virus/Acquired Immune Deficiency Syndrome
HLEG	High Level Expert Group (European Commission DG V—Employment and Social Affairs)
HTML	Hypertext Markup Language
HTTP	Hypertext Transfer Protocol
IAB	Internet Architecture Board
IAP	Internet Access Providers
IBC	Integrated Broadband Communication
ICCPR	International Covenant on Civil and Political Rights
ICI	Information and Communication Infrastructure
ICO	Satellite company name
ICRT	International Communications Round Table
ICSAC	Confédération internationale des sociétés d'auteurs et compositeurs
ICT	Information and Communication Technologies
IDC	International Data Corporation
IEC	International Electrotechnical Commission
IEEE	Institute of Electrical and Electronics Engineers
IESG	Internet Engineering Steering Group
IETF	Internet Engineering Task Force
IFLA	International Federation of Library Associations and Institutions
IFPI	International Federation of the Phonographic Industry
IFRRO	International Federation of Reproduction Rights Organizations
IIF	Image Interchange Facility
IIOP	Internet Inter-ORB Protocol
IISP	American National Standards Institute—Information Infrastructure Standards Panel US
IITF	Information Infrastructure Task Force
ILO	International Labour Organization
IMA	Interactive Multimedia Association
IMPACT	Information Market Policy Actions
IMT-2000	International Mobile Telecommunications-2000, formerly FPLMTS
IMTC	International Multimedia Teleconferencing Consortium
IN	Intelligent Network
INFOSEC	EC framework set up for consideration of security of information systems
INRA	International Research Associates
InterNIC	Internet Network Information Centre
IP	Internet Protocol
IPA	International Publishers Association
IPR	Intellectual Property Rights
IPX	Internetwork Packet Exchange

IRD	Integrated Receiver-Decoder
IRISI	Inter-Regional Information Society Initiatives (and RISI)
IRs	Internet Registries
ISAN	International Standard Audio-Visual Number
ISBN	International Standard Book Number
ISDN	Integrated Service Digital Network
ISO	International Organization for Standardization
ISO/IEC-JTC1	International Organization for Standardization/International Electrotechnical Commission—Joint Technical Committee 1
ISOC	Internet Society
ISP	Internet Service Provider
ISPA	Internet Service Providers Association
ISRC	International Standard Recording Code
ISRN	International Standard Recording Number
ISSN	International Standard Serial Number
ITSEC	IT Security Evaluation Criteria Scheme
ITU	International Telecommunication Union
ITU-R	ITU Radio Communication Sector
ITU-T	ITU Telecommunication Sector
IVF	International Video Federation
JAVA	Sun Microsystem programming language
JIT	Just-in-Time
JPEG	Joint Photographic Experts Group
JTC1	Joint Technical Committee 1
KDD	Kokusai Denshin Denwa Co.
LAB	Legal Advisory Board, European Commission
LAN	Local Area Network
LANE	Local Area Network Emulation
LEAF	Law Enforcement Access Field
LEO	Low Earth Orbit (satellite)
MAN	Metropolitan Area Network
MAOSCO	Multi-Application Operating System Consortium
MARS	Multimedia Archive and Retrieval System
MASE	Mobile Application Support Environment
MATs	Multimedia Access Terminals
MCI	Microwave Communications Incorporated
MCPS	Mechanical Copyright Protection society
MEO	Medium Earth Orbiting satellite
MERIT	Maastricht Economic Research Institute on Innovation and Technology, University of Maastricht (The Netherlands)
MHEG	Multimedia/Hypermedia Expert Group
MHP	Multimedia Home Platform
MIDI	Musical Instruments Digital Interface
MIME	Multipurpose Internet Mail Extensions
MIPS	Million Instructions per Second
MIT	Massachusetts Institute of Technology
MMCD	Multimedia-CD
MMCF	Multimedia Communications Forum

MMVF	Multimedia Video Format
MO	Magneto Optical
MoU	Memorandum of Understanding
MPC	Multimedia Personal Computer
MPEG	Motion Picture Experts Group
MPLS	Multiprotocol Label Switching
MSAF	Multimedia Services Affiliate Forum
MSDOS	Microsoft Disc Operating System
MULTOS	Multi-application Operating System (for smart cards)
NA	Network Architecture subcommittee
NADG	North American Digital Group
NETS	Norme européen de télécommunication services
NHS	National Health Service
NI	Network Level Interoperability
NIC	Network Interface Card
NII	National Information Infrastructure
NIST	National Institute of Standards and Technology
NMF	Network Management Forum
NSA	National Security Agency (US)
NSF	National Science Foundation
NVoD	Near Video-on-Demand
NVPI	Netherlands subsidiary of the International Federation of the Phonographic Industry and the International Video Federation
ODA	Open Document Architecture
OECD	Organization for Economic Co-operation and Development
Oftel	Office of Telecommunications
OMG	Object Management Group
ONP	Open Network Provision
OSF	Open Software Foundation
OSI	Open Systems Interconnection
OSP	Open System Protocol
OSTA	Optical Storage Technology Association
OSTC	Optical Storage Technology Conference
PABX	Private Automated Branch Exchange
PBX	Private Branch Exchange
PC	Personal Computer
PCN	Personal Communication Network
PCS	Personal Communications Services
PDA	Personal Data Assistant
PDC	Personal Digital Cellular
PGP	Pretty Good Privacy
PHP	Personal HandyPhone
PI	Privacy International
PICS	Platform for Internet Content Selection
PIN	Personal Identification Number
PKP	Public Key Partners
PLS	Publishers Licensing Society
POP	Points of Presence

POS	Point of Sale
PPP	Point-to-Point Protocol
PPV	Pay per View
PREMO	Presentation Environment for Multimedia Objects
PRS	Performing Rights Society
PSI	Policy Studies Institute
PSTN	Public Switched Telecommunication Network
PTO	Public Telecommunication Operator
PTT	Post Telegraph and Telephone administration
PVS	Permanent Virtual Switch
PWT	Personal Wireless Telecommunication
QR	Quick Response (time)
R&D	Research and Development
RACE	Research and Development in Advanced Communication Technology for Europe
RAM	Random Access Memory
RES	Radio Equipment and Systems technical committee
RFC	Request for Comments
RIAA	Recording Industry Association of America
RIPE	Reseaux Internet Protocol Européen (Internet registry for Europe)
RISI	Regional Information Society Initiatives
ROME	Remote On-line Member Enquiries
RRO	Reproduction Rights Organization
RSA	Rivest Shamir Adleman (Public Key Algorithm)
RTD	Research and Technology Development
RTD&D	Research, Technology, Development and Demonstration
SACD	Société des auteurs et compositeurs dramatiques
SACEM	Société des auteurs, compositeurs et éditeurs de musique
SAP R/3	Systems, Applications and Products (the company SAP AG) product named R/3
SCAM	Société civile des auteurs multimèdia
SCMS	Serial Copy Management System
SD-DVD	Super Density Digital Video Disc
SDH	Synchronous Digital Hierarchy
SDLC	Synchronous Data Link Control
SDO	Standards Development Organizations
SDSL	Single (line) Digital Subscriber Line
SEPP	Secure Electronic Payment Protocol
SET	Secure Transaction Standard
SGML	Standardized General Markup Language
SID	Source Identification; Source Identification Code (depending on context)
SIGCAT	Special Interest Group on CD Applications and Technology (Foundation)
SLIP	Serial Line Interface Protocol
	Serial Line Internet Protocol
	Service Link Internet Protocol
SMDS	Switched Multi-megabit Digital Service

SME	Small and Medium-Sized Enterprise
SMG	Special Mobile Group
SMPTE	Society of Motion Picture and Television Engineers
SMS	Short Message Service
SNA	System Network Architecture
SNI	Subscriber Network Interface
SOHO	Small Office Home Office
SONET	Synchronous Optical Network
SOS TDP	Security in Open Systems Technology Demonstrator Programme
SPA	Software Publishers Association
SPADEM	Société des auteurs des arts visuels
SPRU	Science and Technology Policy Research, University of Sussex, United Kingdom
SSL	Secure Sockets Layer
STDM	Synchronous Time Division Multiplexing
STET	Società Torinese Exercizi Telefonici
STM	Scientific, Technical and Medical Publishers
STOA	Scientific and Technological Options Assessment Programme, European Parliament
STP	Shielded Twisted Pair
STT	Secure Transaction Technology
STU-III	Secure Telephone Unit—III
SWIFT	Society for Worldwide Financial Transactions
SWMAN	South Wales Metropolitan Area Network
TAP	Telematics Applications Programme
TAPI	Telephony Applications Programming Interface
TCP	Transport Control Protocol
TCP/IP	Transport Control Protocol/Internet Protocol
TDMA	Time Division Multiple Access
TE	Terminal Equipment technical committee
TECs	Training and Enterprise Councils
TERENA	Trans-European Research and Education Networking Association
TIA	Telecommunications Industry Association
TIIAP	Telecommunications and Information Infrastructure Assistance Programme, US Department of Commerce
TINA-C	Telecommunications Information Networking Architecture Consortium
TIS	Trusted Information Systems
TMD	Telemetadata
TMN	Telecommunications Management Network
TNO	The Netherlands Organization for applied scientific research
TRIPS	Trade-Related Aspects of Intellectual Property Rights
TSB	Trustee Savings Bank (now LloydsTSB)
TTC	Telecommunication Technology Committee
TTP	Trusted Third Party
UDP	User Datagram Protocol

UK	United Kingdom
UMTS	Universal Mobile Telecommunication System
UNESCO	United Nations Educational, Scientific and Cultural Organization
UNICE	European confederations of employers associations
UNIX	Portable, multi-user operating system
UPT	Universal Personal Telecommunication
URL	Universal Resource Locator
US	United States of America
USAC	Universal Service Administrative Company
USAT	Ultra Small Aperture Terminal
USDC	US Digital Cellular system
USTP	Unshielded Twisted Pair
VAT	Value Added Tax
VAX	Digital Equipment Corporation mainframe computer
VBR	Variable Bitrate Services
VCR	Video Cassette Recorder
VDSL	Very High (bitrate) Digital Subscriber Line
VEMMI	Videotex Enhanced Man/Machine Interface
VESA	Video Electronics Standards Association
VHS	Video Helix Scan (video cassette format for half-inch tapes)
VLAN	Virtual Local Area Network
VLSI	Very Large Scale Integration
VMS	Virtual Multiprocessing System
VoD	Video-on-Demand
VPC	Virtual Private Circuit
VSAT	Very Small Aperture Terminal
W3C	World Wide Web Consortium
WAN	Wide Area Network
WDA	Welsh Development Agency
WDM	Wave-length-Division Multiplexing
WIPO	World Intellectual Property Organization
WIS	Wales Information Society project
WPR	Dutch Data Protection Act
WTO	World Trade Organization
WWW	World Wide Web
X.25	Public Packet Switched Data protocol
X3	American National Standards Institute SDO
XA	Extended Architecture
xDSL	x Digital Subscriber Line (generic reference; an instance is ADSL)
XML	eXtensible Markup Language

In recent years it has been the practice of consortia applying for EC RTD&D funding to abbreviate the title of their project as if it were a true acronym. In practice, the use of a theme word is customary even though this often includes only a selection of the words making up the name of the project, for example MORE: Mobile Rescue Phone.

Prologue

This book provides a critical assessment of progress towards a specifically European vision of the 'information society'. The features of this vision include an expected contribution of information society developments to European economic growth, employment increases, and social and economic cohesion across the European Union, which eventually will extend eastwards from the present boundaries of the Union. Transformations in the social order, the economy, and the governance systems accompanying efforts to achieve the information society vision provide the focus for our analysis. Our view is that the European information society that evolves in the coming years should be for *all* Europeans. We consider key features of information society developments with the aim of enabling the reader to conclude more than that 'profound changes are underway'.

Our analysis begins in Ch. 1 with an examination of competing visions of the information society that have emerged since the publication in 1993 of the European Commission's *White Paper on Growth, Competitiveness, and Employment*. The authors of the White Paper took the view that information society developments were inevitable. Broadly accessible information and communication infrastructures were expected to create new opportunities for beneficial and progressive change. Progress towards the information society was expected to yield some negative effects, but these were to be mitigated by policy action. The early vision of the information society was conceived as the outcome of a single evolutionary pathway. We argue that there are many possible European information societies depending on the rate and implementation of technological developments, how these technologies interact with their users, and the actions of those in other parts of the world. The pathway to the European information society involves choices by a host of actors, many of whom are highlighted in this book.

The consequences and the implications of information society developments for policy and strategic action are analysed using a framework that we set out in Ch. 1. The interests of actors in these developments are formulated as alternative forms of strategic action. The first is represented by incumbent strategies that involve efforts by firms to control non-reproducible or difficult to reproduce assets. The second is represented by insurgent strategies. These emerge from the peculiar economics and social features of networks and the potential for widespread adoption of new technologies and services that can allow a firm very rapidly to capture a major share of the market and to retain it through continuous innovation. Finally, virtual community strategies involve deep, persistent, and intense relationships between members of a community who may include customers, clients, or members of another form of voluntary association. The virtual community strategies receive particular attention in our analysis because such strategies offer opportunities for the development of an information society reflecting uniquely European aspirations and interests. We devote considerable effort to discovering the extent to which interactions between all these strategies are favourable to commonly held European social and economic goals. Our aim in this book is not simply to recount events, but to offer an interpretative social and economic account of the changes that have taken place during the 1990s with a view towards the changes in the next decade.

Worldwide changes in the information and communication technology and service markets parallel the formation of the European Union. For example, the international momentum towards market-led development of the telecommunication industry through liberalization and privatization by January 1998 resulted in the official opening of the European telecommunication market to competition. By then, the main directives promoting this change were being transposed, implemented, and enforced by the Member States. In the audiovisual sector, in the same year, there were major initiatives to launch digital broadcasting. There were moves to encourage a wide range of 'information push' technologies and services as well as to promote the diffusion of electronic commerce applications. The popular press and media, consultancy firms, and technology and service suppliers had been forecasting enormous potential for European markets, but the promise continued to be for the future.

Success was expected to be visible in a strong position for European-based firms in globally competitive markets for the supply of information and communication technologies and services. At the end of the 1990s, some observers still believed that the positive implications of the information society for European citizens and consumers were foregone conclusions. Wealth creation and improved living standards for everyone were expected to follow from the increasing scale and scope for the generation and distribution of socially and economically useful digital information. By the end of the decade, however, concerns were being expressed as unemployment remained high in many European countries while it declined in a few others. Financial crises created new uncertainties and the damaging effects of social exclusion from the information society began to become more apparent. Our analysis illustrates the uneven and circuitous pathways towards the information society that are accompanying these social and economic developments in Europe.

Three main analytical arguments are developed in the chapters that follow. These arguments concern the principal issues that we believe are at the heart of the adjustment processes that are currently underway in Europe (and globally). The first of these arguments focuses on uncertainty about the extent to which expectations for the radical 'dematerialization' of social and economic activity are likely to become a reality. For this process to occur as the outcome of the continuous spread of networks it is necessary to assume a very significant capacity for 'digital intermediation', that is, a capacity that resides within complicated software-driven networked systems. We argue that some aspects of intermediation will continue to require a degree of physical presence, associated intermediary organizations, and support services. This requirement offers major opportunities for economic growth and employment in Europe, but it also creates an enormous task for skills development and accumulation that has yet to be fully appreciated by many of Europe's stakeholders in the information society.

The second argument concerns emergent patterns of interactive service use especially among consumers and citizens and the implications of these patterns for the social ordering of society. The successful use of many of the new information and communication services depends upon whether uncertainty about citizen and consumer preferences can be reduced and whether the preferences of users are being adequately embedded within the design of new service offerings. It also depends fundamentally upon the extent to which citizen and consumer groups engage in resisting the deployment of certain services, especially those requiring them to pay for information or to invest in hardware and software, as well as in skills and training, themselves. We suggest that many business models for electronic business are predicated on assumptions about these matters that are not borne out in the practices of many European citizens and consumers. The issues in this area are closely related to the pace of construction of the new information and communication infrastructures, their accessibility, and their affordability.

The third argument concerns the uncertainty associated with the development of demand for services supported by the information and communication infrastructure and the unpredictability of the spread of new 'platform' technologies. The deepening involvement of some users of the Internet, intranets and extranets, and the growing familiarity of some consumers and citizens with World Wide Web resources and multimedia personal computers, is giving rise to divisions between the members of both local and geographically dispersed communities. The consequences of these divisions for information access and use, and for the generation and application of new knowledge, are substantial for the achievement of the economic and social goals of the European Union.

The issues raised by all three of these arguments are related to the emergence of new forces of social inclusion and exclusion in Europe and they are all remarkably little understood. A primary reason for this is that user engagement with the process of building information societies is essential and it has received much less attention in the literature than producer interests in economic growth and the structure and operation of markets. In fact, investigations of the social dimensions of the many new forms of engagement that can be supported by the information and communication infrastructure are often relegated to the end of, or omitted entirely from, considerations of the technological and economic parameters of emerging information societies.

In Ch. 2 we take up the issues of the social dimensions and consequences of voluntary or involuntary exclusion from the information society. We believe that these are profound. Non-participation in cultures that are becoming defined by, and articulated through, electronic networks and the information they convey, has major consequences for all citizens. Our focus is on the ways in which electronically mediated social communities are being forged and on the alternative arrangements that may be introduced for accessing the new network environments. Issues relating to the formation of users' capabilities for living and working in environments that are intensively mediated by information and communication networks and digital sources of information are central to our analysis. We argue that the best antidote to social exclusion from the information society in Europe is participation. Therefore, we consider how skills are being acquired and the ways that the symbols of engagement in virtual environments are informing changing perceptions of social status within the information society. We suggest that these developments have significant consequences for employability and for effective participation within social communities of all kinds.

The next three chapters (Chs. 3, 4, and 5) provide an integrated study of the major trajectories in the use of network technologies to construct information society resources. These chapters examine how the design of the information and communication infrastructure is emerging from the growth of specific markets and the interplay of insurgent, incumbent, and virtual community strategies. These chapters document the basis for our specific concern with the relatively weak development of virtual community interests in the European context. They also present our assessment of the likely near-term outcomes of information society developments.

Chapter 3 examines how the diffusion of local area networks has come to have a major influence on the development of a high-capacity infrastructure and the effects of this influence on technological innovation and service development. The spread of high-capacity and flexible infrastructures has implications for the way people access information and communication services. The conditions of access to networks and information and communication resources are being shaped by the processes of technological 'convergence' that enable electronic signals to be converted into interconnected digital 'bit streams'. By examining the patterns of diffusion for the deployment of local area networks and the Internet, we provide insights into the processes that are influencing demand growth and imbalances in the evolution of markets in Europe. The interactions between the formation of technological trajectories and the central role played by business demand for new services are shown to be the primary features governing the pace of the upgrading of the infrastructure and capabilities for its use.

Chapter 4 analyses network and optical disc methods for the distribution of multimedia as alternative 'channels' of distribution, a contest that has major implications both for European multimedia producers and for users of multimedia applications in countries where the information and communication infrastructure is only very slowly being improved. One reason for uncertainty and chaos in the market-place in this area stems from uncertainty about the extent and nature of demand given the lack of experience in the use of the new services for communication and information access. There is enormous variety in the possible network configurations for delivering new services. This threatens to fragment the market and discourage the scale of investment that is needed to bring an advanced infrastructure into the home and to push forward Europe's leadership in mobile data communication.

Chapter 5 examines views about electronic commerce in order to trace patterns of continuity and change as business transactions and customer relationships develop in 'virtual' environments. Many observers regard electronic commerce as the beginning of a new paradigm for interactions between service suppliers and their customers. We suggest, however, that most of the opportunities and challenges created by electronic commerce relate to changes in the structures and processes of transactions between experienced trading partners. We argue that building an electronic commerce environment is likely to bring public and private stakeholder agendas closer together.

The need to co-operate to facilitate a productive migration to the new trading environments and to ensure that electronic commerce developments do not disadvantage European firms is producing incentives for policy actions to encourage a more open electronic market-place.

In the next three chapters (Chs. 6, 7, and 8) we examine five of the key institutional issues underlying the growth of the information society, that is, regulatory developments related to liberalization and universal service, technical standardization, intellectual property rights, personal privacy, and electronic payment systems. The first two are examined in Ch. 6, intellectual property rights are examined in Ch. 7, and the last two issues are considered in Ch. 8. The emergence of information societies involves a re-examination and re-configuration of familiar and traditional institutions in the virtual environment. The virtual environment imposes new constraints and opens new opportunities for institutional definition and the processes that are encouraged by these institutions. Just as Chs. 3, 4, and 5 indicate a set of technological trajectories that is emerging in the formation of the European information society, Chs. 6, 7, and 8 identify and analyse a set of institutional or regulatory trajectories that are the principal focus of attention in the movement in Europe towards the information society.

Specifically, in Ch. 6, we examine the European institutional developments that are intertwined with the technological development and diffusion processes of the information and communication infrastructure. These include regulatory intervention and the promotion of European interests in the development of technical interface standards for the infrastructure. This examination indicates the extraordinary difficulty of mobilizing European interests in shaping the development of technology, even when many of the relevant institutions are nominally democratic and open to international participants. The *de facto* exclusion of virtual community interests from these processes raises numerous questions about the appropriate strategy of governments given the strength of the insurgent interests in the creation of such standards. Advocates of an exclusive focus on market-led developments tend to assume that competition will reduce the price of access to the infrastructure and services. However, our analysis shows that there already are substantial gaps in the accessibility of new services. We suggest that these are likely to grow due to increasingly widespread access to advanced services by professional people in their business, academic, and government settings. We argue that issues of interconnection, interoperability, and universal access are the most basic elements of the 'new regulation' for the information society infrastructure and services.

Chapter 7 examines the issue of intellectual property rights in terms of both social and economic interests and our focus is on the copyright of software and content. Incumbent and insurgent interests in 'strong' intellectual property rights are having a major influence on how the information and communication infrastructure is utilized and this has important ramifications for the evolution of information society institutions. We argue that the movement towards strong intellectual property rights can have potentially adverse consequences for certain social actors. There is no easy resolution of these issues, as we indicate in a review of the technological and institutional frameworks of copyright protection. Nevertheless, we outline a strategy that encompasses a greater range of interests. We examine the predominant rationale that is influencing policy and legislative action, that is, that networked information is a commodity that is best transferred through explicit contracts. This rationale is rendering copyright a universal feature of information creation. Although remedies for the infringement of copyright are limited by the ability to detect and prove that an offence has been committed, finding an appropriate balance between those who seek to use information and those who seek greater protection continues to be a difficult challenge. Greater emphasis on copyright enforcement and implementation could dampen the growth of markets for applications targeted at small firms and consumers because they do not have the economic resources to verify whether their intended uses of information contravene the law. We suggest that a strategy for the cultural exchange of information would enhance the social and educational value of information society developments.

In Ch. 8 we examine the social and economic issues involved in the governance of privacy and the establishment of a market framework for achieving electronic commerce applications. Individual privacy is a potential battleground between libertarian and social order interests, but it is also one of the key institutional uncertainties that will define the character of the information society. The effective governance of privacy is essential if the information and communication infrastructure is to be maintained as a vehicle for interpersonal community and as a medium that encourages the formation of virtual communities. The design of electronic payment systems is essential for supporting the growth of some types of virtual community activity. The potential emergence of insurgent actors with dominant positions in electronic payment systems indicates a need for a regulatory preparedness to act on behalf of all users.

In the last substantive chapter (Ch. 9), we reassess questions about the economic and social effects of the information and communication infrastructure at this stage in the development of the European information society by presenting three case studies. The first examines approaches to assessing how the Internet generates employment and economic growth through the process of diffusion. The second case study demonstrates how the implications of virtual community development can be pursued through an examination of non-profit Internet activities in the 'third sector' of the European information society. The third focuses on the controversy surrounding the taxation of Internet activities as an illustration of the unfinished agenda of reproducing institutions from the 'real' into the 'virtual' environment. The analysis in this chapter shows that despite the growth of industries whose principal outputs are services, and the increasing interdependence between manufactured outputs and services, it is extraordinarily difficult to assess the employment consequences. Estimates of the net impact of investment in the new technologies and services are predicated upon a vast number of questionable assumptions and suffer from many inadequacies in the data. Our analysis of the roles of the 'third' or non-profit sector and the contributions of local civic and city web sites to regional development initiatives suggests that the third sector represents considerable potential for future employment in

Europe. It also provides locations for the development of virtual community strategies and for enabling much needed training and skills development for people who may otherwise have few opportunities to acquire the skills for participating in the information society. The fiscal consequences of continuing growth in electronic commerce are discussed to highlight the emerging stresses and strains in governance regimes that are accompanying the move towards the information society in Europe.

In the final chapter (Ch. 10), we recapitulate the major themes of the book and argue the need for a new agenda for socio-economic research if we are to understand and effectively respond to information society developments in fruitful ways. Among our main conclusions is that virtual community strategies will need substantial support within the wider framework of information society developments if opportunities to deliver social, cultural, and educational content using the information and communication infrastructure in Europe are to be exploited fully. Another conclusion is that, although the determinants of innovation for a technological system are important considerations, the problems of reshaping social and organizational customs and practices and institutional rules and norms to take advantage of these possibilities are of even greater importance. We contend that much greater attention will need to be given to the determinants and consequences of the evolutionary pathways of the information society if the three principal goals of European policy—liberalization, harmonization, and cohesion—are to be achieved within the new social, technological, and economic framework for growth and development.

1

Competing Interests and Strategies in the Information Society

1.1 Introduction

This is a book about how visions of the information society are interacting with the profound technological changes in information and communication technologies. These interactions will shape our lives and work in the opening decades of the twenty-first century. Our primary attention is devoted to Europe, the place where *we* live and work, but neither visions nor technologies stop at border crossings. European developments are powerfully influenced by understandings of the visions of other societies, notably the United States, and by the global character of technological developments. Distinguishing the European character of the information society[1] vision from other visions is one of the major themes of this work. In making this distinction, we are guided not only by the public expressions of policy-makers in Europe, but also by the objective distinctions of Europe, in social, cultural, technological, and economic development, from other areas of the world. While these distinctions highlight the differences between Europe and the United States or Japan, they also emphasize important similarities between Europe and many other areas of the world. Within Europe there are major disparities in economic development, populous as well as small countries, and a diversity of political economies and social orders. Thus, while we expect this work will interest American and Japanese readers, we hope that readers in other countries and regions will find the European experience particularly relevant to their own situations.

The profound technological change that is our subject is also known as the information revolution which had its origin following World War II in the innovation of the modern digital stored-program computer. A reasonable date to assign to the

This chapter draws upon research that was summarized in Bernard *et al.* (1997; 1996); Cattaneo *et al.* (1998).

[1] Throughout this work we utilize the term 'information society' to refer to statements about the use of information and communication technologies and the related social, economic, political, and cultural developments linked to the growing availability of new forms of information and means of communication. In some instances we use the term to highlight statements about the European information society originating from the European Commission, the European Parliament, or the Information Society Forum. The first two of these institutions are politically accountable while the third has a broad membership and considerable linkage to political process. The statements of these institutions therefore are taken to represent a measure of policy consensus about a specific vision of the information society in Europe.

beginning of this revolution is the summer of 1946.[2] Much has been written and remains to be written about the progress of this revolution over the past half century from the viewpoints of technological and business history. This book is, however, about the *use* of information and communication technologies rather than about the history of their *production*. Moreover, our concern is with relatively recent times during which that use is becoming widespread. The process through which information and communication technologies are becoming ubiquitous artefacts follows the widespread commercialization of the personal computer during the 1980s. Yet, it is only during the last decade of the twentieth century that the cascades of innovations in information and communication technologies accumulated to yield the complex social and economic interrelationships that are the principal subject of this book. Most of our attention is devoted to this last decade, a decade marked by new beginnings in western Europe with the formal establishment of the European Union, and in eastern Europe, by a transition towards market economies.

A decade of new beginnings inevitably will produce new visions of where those beginnings might be leading. One such vision is that of the 'information society'; the idea that the information revolution opens a path to new opportunities for sustainable growth and development, new potential for social inclusion and representation, and new ways to achieve social and cultural expression. This vision, and our analysis, cannot be separated, however, from the course of social, economic, and technological developments that make these new opportunities possible. The course of these developments need not be, nor is it, a smooth and easy passage. There are many obstacles, blockages, rapids, whirlpools, and waterfalls in the stream of developments. These are providing the potential for catastrophe, for contests over control of the journey, and for all of the other dramas of travel. Throughout this work, we identify many of these hazards and their consequences and we indicate where the course of the journey appears to be smooth and rapid. Although we are convinced that every journey, including the journey towards the information society, is certain to have unpleasant moments, we acknowledge at the outset that this is a journey that will be undertaken; we can only benefit by charting the troubled waters as well as the smooth. Every journey, and every vision, has a beginning. Although the journey towards the information society has many such beginnings, a good place to commence our analysis is with the vision articulated by the European Commission shortly after the

---

[2] This date is chosen because a summer school at the Moore School of Electrical Engineering entitled 'Theory and Techniques for the Design of Electronic Digital Computers' was attended by twenty-eight individuals from the United Kingdom and the United States and both countries were also represented on the lecture staff (M. R. Williams, 1985: 303). British attendees and their colleagues at their home universities were the first to construct working machines at the University of Manchester in 1948 and Cambridge University in May 1949 (ibid. 334). The American effort at the Moore School was slowed by departures of key individuals as a result of disputes over patent rights and opportunities to pursue corporate careers. The Moore School team did not complete the machine initially envisaged as the first stored program digital computer until 1952 while two of those who had left, John Mauchly and Pres Eckert, achieved the first North American machine late in the summer of 1949 (ibid. 1985: 353, 363). Although the idea of the stored program computer predates the summer workshop, a considerable amount of information about war-time developments and ideas remains secret and the whole subject of the invention of the stored program idea continues to be controversial.

implementation of the Maastricht Treaty and the inauguration of the European Union.

1.1.1   A Vision for the Future

The 1993 European Commission White Paper *Growth, Competitiveness, Employment: The Challenges and Ways Forward into the 21st Century* has proven to be the most influential and enduring policy statement articulating the vision of the information society yet produced (European Commission, 1993*b*). Its influence is indicated by the extent to which it is referenced by subsequent policy documents.[3] Its endurance can be partially explained by its timing. It was issued in December 1993, one month after the Maastricht Treaty came into force and was, therefore, the European Commission's first high-level statement of policy for the European Union subsequent to the Treaty. While this timing assured the historical significance of the White Paper, its continuing influence stems from the way that it articulates the relationships between pressing policy concerns and builds a case for a specific set of policy actions. The centrality of information society issues in the analysis contained in the White Paper served to highlight the particular significance attributed to these issues by policy-makers as well as the priority of actions responding to the opportunities and challenges of the information society. From this perspective, the White Paper's influence and endurance reflect the persistence of the central policy issues that it addresses.

The opening question of the White Paper is 'Why this White Paper?' The answer is succinct: 'The one and only reason is unemployment. We are aware of its scale and of its consequences too. The difficult thing, as experience has taught us, is knowing how to tackle it' (ibid. 9).

In the text that follows the heading 'There is no miracle cure', the Commission dispenses with protectionism, Keynesian deficit spending, reduced working hours and job sharing, and widespread wage reductions as possible solutions. A brief analysis highlights how the coincidence of cyclical, structural, and technological influences acts to exacerbate the extent of the unemployment problem.

The White Paper linked reducing unemployment to building the information society by noting the significance of information and communication technologies for stimulating growth and employment. Indeed, the 'dawning of a multimedia world (sound—text—images)' was seen as a 'radical change comparable with the first industrial revolution' (ibid. 13). This bit of hyperbole clearly was meant to convey the dynamism and excitement of technological developments rather than to stand as an

---

[3] Many of the major European Commission reports following the White Paper refer to it, usually as a 'touchstone' or starting-point, see European Commission (1995*f*; 1996*m*; 1997*e*; 1997*f*). For example European Commission (1997*f*: 16) characterizes the White Paper in the following terms: 'A range of Community initiatives have attempted to give a concrete form to the impact of the social and societal implications of the information society following the landmark White Paper in 1993, and the Bangemann Report published the following year.' The latter is discussed below.

opening to a precise historical analogy. A more insightful explanation of the expected linkage appears in the supporting (preparatory) work to the White Paper:

The competitiveness of the European economy will to a great extent depend both on the conditions of utilization and on the development and application of these technologies. Since they are amongst the highest growth activities in industrialized countries, and they are also highly skilled labour activities, their potential for employment creation is considerable, in particular for the creation of new services. At the same time, potential drawbacks of widespread use of these new technologies, such as the risk of non-skilled people being left behind by progress in information technologies, should be combated through positive policies.   (ibid. 197)

The last sentence of this paragraph links the promotion of the information society to the very strong commitment that the White Paper makes to issues of solidarity between the employed and unemployed as well as between the genders, generations, regions, and the poor.[4]

The motives for promoting the stronger development of information and communication technologies in Europe in the White Paper, therefore, are apparently straightforward. Within a context of fiscal discipline and stringency, the potential for information and communication, and other new technologies (biotechnologies and eco-technologies are also mentioned), to enhance European growth and competitiveness, is seen as central. Job creation is expected to follow the enhancement of growth and competitiveness. The White Paper vision of the information society is, therefore, in the first instance, an invocation of improved growth and competitiveness through technological progress that pledges to seek mitigation for any negative impacts of the technology that might threaten a broad commitment to social solidarity. Although information society developments have failed to provide the engine of growth that is contemplated, this has not yet led to a rejection of their value. For example, the unemployment issue was to persist throughout the 1990s and unemployment remains the defining European public policy issue.[5] Instead of disappointment with information society developments, citizens and policy-makers have attributed responsibility for slow employment and output growth to the barriers to change within European society. These barriers include factors such as the inflexibility of employment contracts, the difficulties of establishing new enterprises, and the persistence of market power in the European economies.[6]

---

[4] With regard to the poor, the White Paper specifically highlights the 50m. Europeans subsisting below the poverty line (European Commission, 1993*b*: 15–16).

[5] The UK and The Netherlands made substantial progress in reducing unemployment during the years following the White Paper. Two-thirds of the EU countries that had substantial unemployment in 1994 (ten of the fifteen; Denmark, Luxembourg, and Austria are the three other exceptions) have continued to suffer from unemployment rates exceeding or approaching 10% of the total labour force.

[6] For economists, market power is, in the first instance, the ability to raise prices above the level that would prevail in a fully competitive economy. Price increases are possible when there are effective arrangements for restricting competition or output such as implicit or explicit cartels, restrictive distribution arrangements that limit entry, or government regulations that limit competitive behaviour. A more general understanding of market power is the existence of the ability to establish arrangements that will influence the perceived profitability of potential entrants and thereby affect their behaviour or limit the willingness of financial markets to provide capital investment.

The information society vision presented by the White Paper, however, is considerably more detailed than the basic argument that appears in its opening pages. Two further sections, one within the body of the White Paper and one in Part B (which reports on supporting work), develop richer foundations for the information society vision.

The White Paper visualizes an information society in which the advance of new technology is inexorable: 'it would be fruitless to become embroiled in a fresh dispute about the "machine age", as was the case with the first industrial revolution. Worldwide dissemination of the new technologies is inevitable' (ibid. 23).[7] Yet, it is also one in which some form of social regulation may have a role: 'The aim must be not to slow down this change but, instead, to control it in order to avoid the dramas which marked the adjustments in the last century but would be unacceptable today' (ibid. 23).[8]

The positive features of the inexorable movement towards the information society are emphasized. The information society means new methods of production involving changes in the organization of companies, in managers' responsibilities, and in the relations with workers. In particular, changes are anticipated in work hours, the growth of remote working relationships (teleworking), and the terms of labour contracts and compensation. For enterprises, possibilities for 'forging forms of partnerships and *co-operation* on a scale never possible before' (ibid. 22, emphasis added) are anticipated. And 'it is in Europe's interest to meet this challenge since the first economies which successfully complete this change . . . will hold significant competitive advantages' (ibid. 23). Indeed, these advantages may be reinforced by the fact that 'Europe holds comparative advantages from the cultural, social, technological and industrial points of view' (ibid.) in comparison to its leading competitors.

The White Paper attempts to weaken the case for negative outcomes from information society developments, either by making them seem uncertain, that is, 'concern has been expressed about employment, but it is difficult to assess this factor precisely' (ibid.) or by emphasizing the necessity of making changes to the existing order. With

---

[7] In this respect, the White Paper echoes the sentiments of Ricardo (1821: 271): 'The employment of machinery could never be safely discouraged in a state, for if a capital is not allowed to get the greatest net revenue that the use of machinery will afford here, it will be carried abroad, and this must be a much more serious discouragement to the demand for labour than the most extensive employment of machinery; for while a capital is employed in this country it must create some demand for some labour; machinery cannot be made but with the contribution of their labour; by exporting it to another country the demand will be wholly annihilated.'

[8] From the historical perspective, however, Ricardo (ibid. 266) observes that the introduction of new machinery may also reduce demand for labour. While Ricardo was primarily interested in the general principle of whether labour reduction was possible, Babbage (1835: 229) followed the process of adjustment in a way familiar to contemporary economists: 'One of the most common effects of the introduction of new machinery into manufacture is to drive out employment of the hand labour which was previously used. This, for a time, produces considerable suffering among the working classes . . . It is almost the invariable consequence of such improvements ultimately to cause a greater demand of labour; and often the new labour requires a higher degree of skill than the old; but, unfortunately, the class of persons who have been driven out of the old employment are not always qualified for the new one; and in all cases a considerable time elapses before the whole of their labour is wanted.'

regard to the latter issue, 'Europe's main handicaps are the fragmentation of the various markets and the lack of major interoperable links. To overcome them, it is necessary to mobilize resources and channel endeavours at [the] European level in a partnership between public and private sectors' (ibid.). This approach to potential shortcomings or problems with information society developments takes the progressive qualities of these developments as given. The view is not that information society developments are necessary, but they are likely to create deep shocks and displacements that we must anticipate and move to ameliorate. It is, instead, that information society developments are necessary and their disruptive influence will create new opportunities for progressive change as well as some negative effects that must be mitigated to preserve social solidarity. Identifying information society developments as part of the solution to long-standing European economic and social issues rather than as another source of problems, increases the priority that can be attached to information society policies and provides a positive view of future European prospects.

The White Paper fully embraces the American metaphor of the 'information highway' with suitable adjustment of vocabulary. Thus, the communication networks of the information society will have 'motorways with several lanes, and access roads and service areas allowing motorists to drive wherever they choose' (ibid. 25). The White Paper endorses the paramount importance of infrastructure development as the enabling feature for new service development.

What will be the new services in the information society? A major focus of the White Paper is its emphasis on the role of information and communication infrastructures in overcoming distance. Of the seven services emphasized as providing the basis for diversification and growth, three are principally concerned with remote access—teleworking, telemedicine, and teletraining. The centrality of these applications is surprising given the historical development of information and communication technologies in which workplace, medical, and educational applications are first implemented at the local level. The emphasis on the 'distance' feature of these applications serves an important purpose, however. If cast only as local developments, the case for European-level programmes rather than initiatives at the Member State level is much weaker. Overcoming boundaries between organizations is emphasized by two more of the services, electronic mail and links between administrations. With electronic mail it is the need for 'interoperability' to support the initiatives of smaller firms that is emphasized while electronic services of administrations promise smoother operation of the single market and easier access by the public to the administrations' information. Finally, two services (which appear first on the list) emphasize the potential of scale in collective endeavour, that is, the development of electronic images and databases for widespread access.

Conspicuously absent from this list are the development of information services that seek to provide new forms of interaction among individuals sharing common interests, the role of communication networks in creating new markets for goods and services (electronic commerce), and the implications of such networks for creating new data resources.[9] The absence of these three applications that were to become quite significant in driving subsequent developments is puzzling if no account is taken of the difficulties of arguing for European versus Member State initiatives. In each of these applications, there is the problem of the level of government at which initiative should be taken. The services that *are* listed transcend Member State boundaries and provide a basis for European-level action. Those that are not listed are, arguably and in their initial development, examples of actions that can be undertaken on a smaller scale, within Member States or within groups of states sharing common or similar languages.[10] Substantial progress has been made since the publication of the White Paper in constructing a case that electronic commerce is a European-wide issue and substantial attention has been devoted to directives for a common European framework on electronic commerce (European Commission, 1999*a*).

This interpretation of what is included and what is omitted from the information society vision is reinforced by a consideration of the actual initiatives proposed. These fall into four categories: (1) information highways, (2) interconnected advanced networks, (3) general electronic services, and (4) telematics applications (European Commission, 1993*b*: 27). In each area, the proposed initiative involves the development of enabling technologies. A budget of 67 billion ecu (becu) is proposed for supporting these developments, more than half of which is assigned to networks—a high-speed communication network (20 becu) and consolidation of the integrated services digital network (15 becu). These items are followed by telematics applications with collective proposed expenditure of 20 becu. For general electronic services, 10 of the 12 becu of proposed expenditure was to have been devoted to electronic images and interactive video services with electronic mail and access each accounting for 1 becu. The proposed expenditures are, of course, indicative of relative priorities.

The proposed funding levels for enabling technologies are loosely related to an action plan that was produced for the European Commission's March 1994 meeting in Corfu. Subsequently, it has been referred to as the Bangemann plan.[11] The priorities suggested for that action plan were: (1) promoting the use of information technologies, (2) providing basic trans-European services, (3) creating an appropriate regulatory environment, (4) developing training on new technologies, and (5) improving industrial and technological performance. Promoting the use of information and communication technologies was linked to fostering teleworking, public service uses of telematics applications, and closer involvement of users in

---

[9] The service entitled 'electronic access to information' specifically contemplates 'bringing together information (administrative, scientific, cultural or other data) in databases to which all users in the community should have access' (European Commission, 1993*b*: 25–6).

[10] England and Ireland, France and portions of Belgium, Germany, and Austria (the last was not at that time part of the European Union), and to a lesser extent the Scandinavian countries and the countries sharing stronger Latin influences in their languages such as France, Italy, Spain, and Portugal.

[11] Martin Bangemann was the chair of the 'High-Level Group on the Information Society' which included nineteen other members with senior standing in government and industry.

drafting and implementing technology policies. The items detailed in the second and third priorities are straightforward and generally consistent with the aims of market liberalization for telecommunication services. The more difficult issues of the fourth and fifth priorities included little guidance as to how they might be implemented except through Research, Technology, Development and Demonstration (RTD&D) policies of the Fourth Framework Programme that ran from 1994 to 1998.[12]

Hastening the advance of the technologies supporting the information society remains the principal theme of the more detailed discussion that appears in Part B of the White Paper. The principal features of the information society are the use of information and communication technologies to restructure the production of goods and services and to support the growth of new services. To make this structure possible, a complex techno-social infrastructure is envisaged. Within this infrastructure, a community of users who are 'not only trained in operation of the applications, but are also aware of the potential of ICTs [information and communication technologies] and of the conditions required for optimum use thereof' (ibid. 109) are seen as complements to the networked technological components. This view of users as the extension of the technological network is problematic as it strongly supports the view that technology can lead the process of change.

The issue of the global versus European character of the information society is also raised. The White Paper sees the development of the information society as a global phenomenon in which widespread co-operation, openness in standards for constructing technical infrastructure, and genuine reciprocity are to be pursued. The 'system' characteristics of the information society should, however, also be those which 'take due account of European characteristics: multilingualism, cultural diversity, economic divergence, and more generally the preservation of its social model' (ibid. 110). How these goals might be accomplished is not stated and the statement holds no specific implications other than a recognition of the need for mitigating actions to prevent social exclusion.

The human or user side of the issues is specifically examined in the section that underlies the setting of a priority for developing training on new technologies. The White Paper makes it clear that this area is a challenge, noting that 'the competitive pressures on European industry require from all staff an increasingly high level of skills and an ability to use new technologies effectively' (ibid. 113). This challenge is carried forward to each of several groups:

---

[12] The Fourth RTD&D Framework Programme (1994–8) had a total budget including the Euratom Framework Programmes that amounted to 13,215m. ecu. This amount is far smaller than the estimated 67b ecu required for priority projects between 1994 and 1999 in the European Commission's White Paper (White Paper, 1993*b*: 26). The Fourth Framework followed two previous programmes: the Second Framework Programme ran from 1987 to 1991 and the Third Framework Programme from 1990 to 1994. The Fifth Framework and Euratom Programmes (1998–2002) have a budget of 14,960m. euro, 4.6% higher in absolute terms than the Fourth Framework Programme, see Community Research and Development Information Service (CORDIS) at www.cordis.lu/src/I_006_en.htm and www.cordis.lu/src/I_005_en.htm, accessed 19 Oct. 1999.

Managers need specific training to make them aware of the potential of ICTs and their organizational and socio-professional implications. Technicians and other workers need to have specific ICT-related aspects better integrated into the training for their basic trade. Schoolchildren and students should learn to use ICTs, in particular in order to resolve general education and training problems. Educating potential ICT users to enable them to make effective use of ICTs entails training as many people as possible in the basic skills and providing specialist training for some of them.   (ibid.)

This statement of a widespread need for training is coupled to a specific criticism: 'Europe has made a big effort to develop basic training in computer science, but it does not have sufficient qualified staff, and *insufficient attention has been paid so far to the application of new technologies in training and education systems*' (ibid., emphasis in original).

A similar problem is identified at the level of companies: 'the introduction of computer systems must go hand-in-hand with the identification of companies' strategic objectives, the functions and support to be provided by the system, and appropriate work organizations. This is an area where the awareness of the user companies must be raised' (ibid. 112).

These passages suggest that users are a major constraint to the expansion of the technology and the benefits that use might bring in terms of growth and competitiveness, and the ultimate pay-off in increased employment. While the training requirements necessary to meet the challenges set out in this section might themselves be a significant source of employment growth, these initiatives, if undertaken, would have to occur at the Member State level. All of this puts those within the European Commission in the rather frustrating position of being convinced that a key solution to the most urgent political priority is being blocked by the failure of private-sector decision-makers and education authorities fully to realize the potential of the new technologies. This frustration is voiced in the conclusions to the section: 'Devising a policy to promote a common information area [the socio-technical network described above] requires in particular the setting-up of an *efficient system for co-operation* between the parties concerned. Because of the Community's political structure, this is much more difficult than in the USA or Japan' (ibid. 115, emphasis in original).

The White Paper's vision of the information society can therefore be summarized as follows:

• The process of technological change bringing networked information and communication technologies and multimedia information into greater utilization throughout the industrialized world is inexorable and irreversible.
• Advancing to the forefront of this process of change will bring benefits in economic growth and competitiveness that will translate into lower levels of unemployment.
• To advance to the forefront, proactive policies are required in regulation, technology policy, and investment to construct the information and communication

infrastructure supporting the exchange of information and the creation of new services.

• There are problems with the massive process of change implied by these processes that will require attention and mitigation to preserve the inclusivity of the information society and to reflect its European character.

• The recognition of the scale and importance of these developments is too narrow in Europe and substantial efforts must be made to convey their significance at all levels of society.

The human features of the information society are largely unarticulated in the White Paper. In this respect, the information society vision is clouded. The technologies are expected to bring major changes to the conduct of business, easing the process of globalization, corporate restructuring, and the redefinition of work at all levels of the enterprise. They are also expected to bring productivity improvements that will be beneficial particularly to small and medium-sized enterprises. Individuals, of course, will be affected by these developments. They will face a higher level of expectations with regard to their mastery of the new technologies and the identification of how to harness it to the best advantage in their social situations. They may expect to benefit from the emergence of new services generally, and tele-services in particular—telemedicine, teleworking, teletraining—and from improvements in transportation and access to public information services. Of course these are all significant issues. They do not, however, provide a very complete picture of life in the information society.

The processes of organizational and institutional change as well as changes in market structure and the position of existing companies in the information society are also not articulated in the White Paper. Some elements that are mentioned include the growth of international commercial partnerships, the support for globalization, and the evocation of change within organizations in the processes of production. The broad outlines of change contemplate a liberalized telecommunication sector and the emergence of new companies that will be active in providing new service offerings. It is assumed throughout the White Paper that improvements in the use of information and communication technology will strengthen the competitiveness of individual enterprises. Increasing competition is expected to strengthen the position of European firms in global markets and, because of the challenges in these markets, failure to reach the forefront will bring negative consequences. It is also the case, however, that the changes contemplated by the White Paper will influence the horizontal and vertical structure of production within Europe. This process will create structural adjustment issues, perhaps similar to those faced by Europe during the 1950s or at other points in history. Since the move towards the information society is seen as inexorable, these changes may be regarded as inevitable and, therefore, as ones that may have to be dealt with through policies of mitigation and adjustment as they emerge, particularly when they have untoward social effects.

Is there one information society for Europe defined by a technical infrastructure and human skills base that together operate as a system for the competitive production of goods and services and innovation in services? Alternatively, are there many possible European information societies according to the rate at which new technological developments occur and are implemented, how these technologies are mediated and transformed by interaction with their users, and the actions taken by societies in other parts of the world of their own volition, or as a response to the developments in Europe? We believe that the answers to these questions are no and yes, respectively. There are many different configurations of the European information society. These configurations involve different industrial structures, different roles of users, and different approaches to policy in both the private and public sectors. The information society vision of the White Paper and subsequent articulations of policy by the European Commission are strongly influenced by the scope of action that the Commission is allowed and by prevailing views of the potential contribution of information society developments to important policy priorities. It is essential, therefore, to examine critically the features of the information society as it is developing in Europe and to compare and contrast these features with the information society vision offered by the European Commission and other policy-making institutions.

1.1.2　Expanding the Vision: Many Paths and Purposes

The European Commission has established a vision for the development of the European information society and has sought to reinforce this vision by funding RTD&D programmes whose magnitude is relatively small compared to private investments in research and development or in information and communication technologies. It would be highly unrealistic to assume that the European Commission could, through these actions, co-ordinate or lead all the activities that are needed to turn this vision into reality. This is one of the reasons why the Commission's vision is premised upon private-sector leadership of the actual building of the information society. The centrality of the private sector may be problematic because of the importance of the contributions from the educational, non-profit, and public sectors. It is, nevertheless, an area where initiatives are likely to be relatively rapid and on a large scale. The centrality of private-sector interests makes it necessary to analyse their interests and their interactions with other stakeholders. The importance of these dynamic relationships gives rise to our conceptualization of a threefold partition of countervailing and strategic interests which is outlined in the next section and applied in subsequent chapters of this book.

　　The vision of the European information society is built not only upon the idea of a better society but also upon a competitively fit society. It is therefore an open question as to what configuration of the countervailing and competing interests will best serve *both* goals, or for that matter, either of them when considered individually. We must look at the implications of developments in the market for the specific interests and the outcomes for stakeholders. It is also necessary, however, to consider these developments from the perspective of creating a socially better information society, one that is cohesive, inclusive, diverse, and competitively fit, that is, an information society that promotes initiative, wealth generation, and employment.

These are the themes of our work in this study—the standing of interest configurations, the effectiveness of social, economic, and technological developments for both a socially better and a competitively fit information society, and the specific contributions of the European Commission in sustaining the vision and reinforcing it through RTD&D efforts. Our thesis is that the path to the European information society is still being built, that it involves choices between many possible paths, and that several distinct paths may be followed simultaneously. An active and informed debate about the process may enhance the viability, the distinct value for Europeans, and the contribution to the 'rest of the world', of the path that eventually emerges.

Information and communication technologies are shaping the future path of social and economic development in Europe. It is not our thesis, however, that a single path has been set or that technologies are the prime movers of the process of development. The European information society is to be supported by advanced information and communication technologies and services and it will embrace (or exclude) many different groups of users. A consistent vision of a European information society that is compatible with the social and economic goals and aspirations of private citizens and corporate actors is only discernible from a great distance, a distance that obscures many of the conflicting aims and purposes of actual developments and policies. When initiatives are translated into practice, they have unanticipated and unintended implications for unemployment, working conditions, and the social fabric of everyday life. They are as likely to stimulate as to reduce the competitiveness of European industry or any of the other desirable features of the information society. There is, nevertheless, a considerable sense of urgency and purpose in taking initiatives that will support information society developments.

At the highest levels of government and industry in Europe it is now being recognized that the transition to an information society that is fully responsive to the aspirations of all Europe's citizens is not easy. Disparities in all aspects of the economy, and especially in the resources devoted to innovative technology development, are substantial in Europe. However, the reality of the mismatches between the capacity for innovative technical development and deployment, and the institutional (legal, regulatory, and organizational) foundations of the European information society, is an even more serious problem. These mismatches will need to be mitigated or aligned if the potential benefits of the spread of information and communication networks and services are to accrue to all Europeans.

Resolving these mismatches involves an extension and reconstruction of social institutions as well as technological systems since these institutions provide the starting conditions and the initial alignment of producer and user interests. The differences in the development and use of information and communication technologies across the European Union, and between different social, cultural, economic, and political groups, do matter considerably. This is because they influence wealth generation potential and the extent of inclusion within new networking communities that is likely to occur locally, regionally within Europe, and globally.

The information and communication technologies and services that are being developed within and outside the European Union could support many *different* paths towards a European information society. The supplier and user communities have different needs and interests, and, therefore, will push for different outcomes in the construction of the information and communication infrastructure. The contests between many of the actors involve incumbent firms in the telecommunication and established media and information publishing industries, a host of newer companies in the personal computer and software industries, and an even larger array of potential communities of 'virtual' information producers and users.

Our interest in constructing a social and economic account of change arises from the belief that analyses of issues of market restructuring and control, and the potential social and economic implications of these developments, matter for people in their varying capacities as citizens, employees, and consumers. Developing understandings of where we are heading can have an influence on the choices made both by policy-makers and those involved in creating and using the tools and institutions of the information society. We are particularly concerned with articulating some of the possible viewpoints of those who do not have ready access to the levers of opinion formation. They include citizens, consumers, and those running small businesses—whom we term 'virtual community' members—who will be the most numerous users of the tools and institutions of the information society. These individuals and small organizations have a smaller voice in the determination of outcomes about how technology is designed, deployed, and governed than the larger incumbent or the new insurgent producers of new technologies and services. Nevertheless, the capacity and will of the users of the new technologies and services to resist or transform developments favoured by larger interests are also influencing the path that is chosen and the outcomes achieved in the process of change. Some of the meeting-grounds for those with different interests occur within the institutions and processes leading to decisions taken in public policy and regulatory domains, in the standardization process, through measures to protect intellectual property, and in building trust in the security of advanced information and communication networks and services. We return to these issues of governance in later chapters.

Advanced information and communication technologies are being developed and used within a particular context of policies and business strategies. This context is strongly influenced by the trend towards market liberalization and the role of competitive entry that began in the United States and has extended at an uneven pace to other industrialized countries. Our analysis in this chapter suggests that there are reasons to be concerned about whether the outcomes expected from liberalization and market entry will stimulate the same degree of innovation and experimentation in Europe that is characteristic of the United States. In the United States, market changes appear to be creating a pluralistic information society in which the virtual communities of small businesses, individual citizens, education institutions, and other nonprofit institutions have a major role. Despite major co-ordination problems, 'users' are assuming an active role in information society developments.

In Europe, the plurality of initiatives and interests that provide a foundation for the interests of these virtual communities appears to be attenuated. As the Interim Report of the High Level Expert Group (HLEG) put it in 1996, the information society discussion 'has been dominated by technological issues and more recently the appropriate regulatory economic environment, neglecting by and large, some of the broader issues in the "society" notion' (European Commission HLEG 1996: 1, fns. omitted). Their call for greater attention to social issues received support within the European Commission and they announced in their final report that the task of increasing the attention given to these issues had been achieved.

> Since the publication of our interim report, the Information Society Forum (ISF), a broad-based user expert group also set up by the European Commission, has produced its first annual report, arguing along similar and complementary lines. . . . At the end of 1996, the Commission adopted its own action programme 'Europe at the forefront of the global information society', pointing to the many social challenges brought about by the emerging IS [Information Society]. In other words, the field has expanded rapidly, with the social aspects of the emerging IS moving to the top of the policy agenda. We very much welcome this shift of priorities, and hope the HLEG interim report and the ensuing debate may have made a modest contribution to bringing it about. Perhaps somewhat presumptuously, we conclude that one of the first tasks we set ourselves has thus been achieved.   (ibid. 1997: 14, fns. omitted)

There are several problems with this conclusion. First, the participation of high-level experts, regardless of where they are drawn from, is not the same as the widespread development of citizen and community initiatives and the active involvement of these communities in the processes affecting them. It is not clear that forums, however constituted, are likely to be effective in reshaping or redirecting technological developments. Second, when the proposals of the High Level Expert Group and the European Commission are examined, they prove to be largely expressions of concern or they are 'framing' ideas for action, rather than specific policy proposals that have the possibility of being implemented. The third problem, and the most severe from our viewpoint, is that these discussions occur largely apart from concrete analysis of technological developments and their deployment.

There are many very detailed discussions of technological developments in this book. The reason for our attention to technological detail is that we believe that social issues, with which we are also concerned, cannot be isolated as requirements or specification orders that are issued to the developers and users of technologies. Our view is that the social usefulness and value of technological developments evolves concurrently with the research responsible for new ideas and the processes of implementing these ideas in new products and services. This viewpoint has important implications for the members of a number of the communities who are involved in decision-making. It involves achieving a greater degree of integration between the technological communities and the socio-economic tradition of analysis that often stands apart from technological developments and assesses their social implications. We argue that the realization of socio-economic consequences lies in the ways that technologies are designed, deployed, or evolve according to the 'logic' of the incremental search for better ideas and approaches. These processes of decision-making may or may not include a wide range of different stakeholders. The effectiveness of many of these stakeholders, and particularly those representing some virtual communities, in voicing their concerns would probably be very different if they were aware of the contexts and trajectories of the technological developments in which they have an interest. One of our main purposes, therefore, is to illustrate how, with a relatively modest level of resources, we and our colleagues have analysed important socio-economic processes that are influencing the European information society taking the technological dimension fully into account.

Our concern with the interactions between the process of technological development and its social and economic implications has led us to develop a tripartite analysis of incumbent, insurgent, and virtual community strategies and the various social and economic interests in the information society. The players who develop and implement alternative strategies and their probable successes in achieving expected outcomes are analysed, drawing upon insights developed within the framework of studies of the economics of technological change and innovation, the political economy of information and communication technologies, and the social dynamics of network formation and development. Our more particular concern is with enlarging the contributions of virtual community users, that is, the interests of those who are often depicted as 'users' from the perspective of the producers of new products and services. These users are also the *producers* of a major, if not the dominant, share of information content and communication within the information society and their interests in the path selected in the coming decades is substantial.

1.2   Dynamic Players and Emergent Communities

To . . . stimulate the creation of new markets, the Commission proposes to identify strategic TransEuropean projects. . . . The strategic projects would be carried out at each of three interdependent 'levels' that make up the telecommunication networks: the carrier networks for transmission of information, generic services and telematics applications. . . . With regard to the networks which serve to carry the information (voice, data, images) the objective would be to consolidate the integrated services digital network and to install the high speed communications network using advanced transmission and switching techniques (asynchronous transfer mode: ATM), which will help digitized multi-media services to make a breakthrough. (European Commission, 1993*b*: 95)

The European Commission's White Paper on growth, competitiveness, and employment called for economic and employment growth through the creation of seamless access to information and to interactive information and communication services providing a foundation for the Commission's Fourth Framework RTD&D programmes which encompassed the information and communication infrastructure and its applications. These programmes were expected to support and encourage the formation of a distinctively European information society embracing many different kinds of users. The visions of an information society that the White Paper and numerous other policy documents of this period embraced were compatible with the social and economic goals and aspirations of most private citizens and corporate actors only at the level of the expression of broad policy initiatives. In practice, if the deployment of the new technologies and services was to contribute to alleviating unemployment and to improving working conditions and the social fabric of everyday life, far-reaching changes in social institutions would be needed alongside the evolution of new markets.

European policy-makers and industrialists argued at the start of this Framework Programme that differences between the Member States in the development and use of information and communication technologies were jeopardizing the competitiveness of companies operating in the European Union. The seriousness of these differences in the telecommunication segment of the market was emphasized by the European Round Table of Industrialists when Mr C. Benedetti argued in the Foreword to the Round Table's report that:

Europe today is a patchwork of incompatible communications networks marked by high costs, low quality of services, and very limited interoperability between systems. European communications costs are up to ten times higher than in the US and present a major obstacle to the introduction of new applications. National monopolies still persist in most European countries, restricting innovation and competition, whereas deregulation has brought about a dramatic development of the markets in the US and Britain. The European Union has launched a process of liberalisation, but it is too slow, and in many countries is being applied inadequately or not at all. (European Round Table of Industrialists, 1994: 5–6)

As the Round Table members pushed for the liberalization of telecommunication markets, they did so in the face of accumulating evidence that the information and communication infrastructure and the new applications were developing within and outside the European Commission's RTD&D programmes along many *different* trajectories. The principal reason for these different trajectories in the evolutionary paths towards the European information society is that the various producer and user communities have very different needs and interests. They therefore push for different outcomes in the construction of the information and communication infrastructure and in the ways in which this infrastructure supports social and economic activity.[13]

1.2.1   Strategic Design Configurations for the European Information Society

Three relatively distinct configurations of interests in the outcomes of actions leading to the organization of the information and communication infrastructure and related

---

[13] It is difficult to draw clear distinctions between 'infrastructure' and 'services' because of the way digital technologies are becoming intertwined in innovative architectures where hardware, software, and content are combined in various ways to support functionality that may be provided as a 'service' that is accessed by users. For a discussion of this issue see Hawkins (1996). In this book, we use the terminology 'information and communication infrastructure', or 'information infrastructure', to refer to hardware and software that comprise various kinds of networks that support electronic communication and information appliances including personal computers. These may be used to support services that include various types of content and various types of interaction.

markets are emerging as the markets for information and communication technologies and services expand.[14] Distinct economic incentives and social motivations can be shown to define these interests. These incentives and motivations arise from the specific and changing features of advanced information and communication technologies and the content and services that these technologies enable. The first and second clusters of interests are around the perception that the information infrastructure represents a new resource that will be controlled by a limited number of dominant players. The strategies of players that hold this perception tend to be differentiated by their respective approaches to controlling resources or assets.

One set of players, which we call the incumbents, is likely to adopt business strategies focused upon the control or ownership of key assets within the information and communication infrastructure. The most obvious of these assets is the communication network. While it is no longer possible to construct a monopoly in the control of telecommunication networks in Europe, it *is* possible to construct a dominant position in key access paths to the communication networks, such as the local telecommunication network or the high-capacity links over which long-distance communication flows. It is also possible to view emerging parts of the information and communication infrastructure, such as the Internet and compact discs, as new media for the mass distribution of content and services and to construct a dominant position in the ownership of content or the provision of specific services. Thus, incumbents may pursue strategies similar to those of major publishers or other media companies. They may engage in building stocks of content that will appeal to a mass audience or in constructing services that will interest participants in a mass market. The key point to bear in mind about the incumbent strategy is that it is built upon 'ownership' of irreproducible and difficult to imitate assets and 'scale' in the grouping of users into relatively homogenous communities that can be served by common products and services.

The second strategy is based upon the perception that the new information and communication infrastructure represents a resource that is subject to control. This is a strategy of 'insurgency'. Instead of seeing the information and communication infrastructure in terms of predefined resources or assets, the insurgent strategy is to create new resources or assets that can be controlled by a limited number of actors as the result of specific actions. These actions include efforts to stimulate a rapid pace of innovation, sophistication in anticipating or responding to user needs, and building networks of alliances that can substitute for exclusive ownership or control of

---

[14] Membership in these categories is fluid in the sense that firms and users of information and communication technologies and services may adopt different strategies depending upon the market. The actors may shift their predominant strategies as a result of their changing economic, political, or social interests over time and they may actively pursue different strategies within different institutional contexts at the same time. This framework was initially developed in Bernard *et al.* (1996) and Mansell and Steinmueller (1996c). It has been reworked substantially for the present analysis to serve as an analytical framework that helps to articulate the strategic interests of the firms and other stakeholders within the European information society. This approach is in contrast to its original presentation as a taxonomy for classifying the players in the market.

the assets necessary for success. The prospects of the insurgent are greatly aided by the speed at which innovation is progressing in the evolving infrastructure; what Cusumano and Yoffie (1998) have referred to as 'Internet time'.[15] They are also aided by the technological opportunities afforded by the convergence of telecommunication and computing applications which is (after considerable delay) proving to be a fertile source for innovation and growth. An insurgent is an aspiring incumbent, and, if successful in achieving a dominant position is likely to differ from the incumbent only in the extent to which the company adopting this strategy will appreciate from experience the possibility of displacement and therefore will seek to maintain a rapid pace of technological advance.[16] In many cases, however, insurgents will not achieve a persistent dominant position because the assets that they control may be reproduced or imitated. The key point about the insurgent strategy is that it is based upon 'rapid mass adoption' and that it involves control of assets that potentially may be reproduced or imitated by maintaining a rapid pace of technological innovation.

The interests that incumbents and insurgents share, mass adoption and scale of use, are the basis for differentiating a third set of interests and its accompanying strategy. Virtual community interests lie in individualized and customized content and services. There are many ways in which individualization and customization can be expressed. As a business strategy, the aim of a virtual community participant is to build a sustained relationship with customers or to offer specialized services that satisfy a niche demand that is difficult to address with mass-produced content or with services aimed at a mass market. Virtual communities also emerge as a result of the non-profit motivations of their members such as the aim of exchanging better teaching materials, information about specific health care options, or publicly available research findings. Virtual community strategies involve approaches to solving the problem of building networks of interested people and preserving the individualized and customized character of the community if it attracts substantial interest. These strategies include measures to improve the quality of engagement of the user with the content or services available within the virtual community. A virtual community may have a prime mover or owner but its growth generally will be limited by the strategy of

---

[15] Internet time is running at a faster pace than ordinary clock time because of the pace of change and the rate at which adoption of new innovations can occur due to the distribution capabilities provided by the Internet. As Cusumano and Yoffie (1998: 5) conclude, 'For companies competing in the new information economy, the Internet is forcing managers and employees to experiment, invent, plan, and change their ideas constantly *while* they are trying to build complex new products and technologies. The Internet also requires companies to face the reality that competitive advantage can appear and disappear overnight. This is because the Internet makes it possible to organize your business in new ways, to offer new products and services, and to distribute those products and services to tens of millions of people *almost instantaneously* via telephone lines, cable TV networks, and wireless communications. It was the electronic distribution capability of the Internet that allowed Netscape to burst onto the scene in 1994 and, in only a few months, emerge as one of the most serious threats Microsoft had ever faced. This sudden rise to prominence of new companies can and will happen again.'

[16] e.g. Microsoft was once an insurgent in the operating systems market where, after contributing to the initial success of the IBM personal computer, it faced the efforts of IBM to capture control with the development of a rival operating system, OS/2.

deepening involvement with a specific group of users. Of course, the experience and knowledge gained through the construction of a virtual community may provide a basis for the definition of an insurgent strategy. The accumulation of resources within a virtual community eventually may make it possible to adopt an incumbent strategy. In terms of the social and economic implications for the way we live and work, however, virtual community developments are much more likely to have an impact due to their growing numbers than because of their transformation into incumbents or insurgents. Virtual community enterprises and institutions are less likely to have a voice in the discussion of policy and in the design and implementation of the information and communication infrastructure due to their relatively small size as compared to most of those companies pursuing incumbent and insurgent strategies.

It is important to observe that in our analysis, 'interests' are not synonymous with the actors who produce or use the information and communication infrastructure. It is possible to find citizens and those within public or private organizations as well as consumers embodying each or all of the interests that motivate the different strategies or any combination of the three strategies. For example, a major telecommunication network operator may be simultaneously an incumbent in its ownership of key components of the network, an insurgent in the market for Internet service provision, and a virtual community participant in encouraging its research workers to participate in international scientific and engineering communities. It is reasonable for our analytical purpose to consider the relative importance of each of these strategies and to identify the major telecommunication network operator, for example, as principally an 'incumbent' at a given point in time as a means of indicating that an operator's motives and behaviours will be shaped primarily by the relative importance of this strategy within the organization.

In the following subsections we develop the idea of a tripartite division of interests further and apply this framework to consider the strategies of some of the specific groups of stakeholders in the information society in Europe. Each of our configurations suggests a different institutional and market arrangement for the supply of the information and communication infrastructure and alternative prospects for stakeholders in meeting their goals and aspirations within the European information society.

1.2.1.1 *The Incumbent Strategy*

Many of the corporations pursuing an incumbent strategy have inherited the control of key assets from the historical activities of their organizations. The assets of the former European public telecommunication operators may have been privatized and their markets may have been fully open to entry since January 1998. Nevertheless, they retain enormous stocks of fixed assets that may constitute an effective barrier to new entrants. At a minimum, these assets allow the operators to choose from a diverse set of strategies in meeting competitive threats and exploiting competitive opportunities. A similar position has been inherited by broadcasters due to the allocation of the radio frequency spectrum through the licensing policies of Member States and the relatively recent arrival of a new group of incumbents, that is, the satellite broadcasters and cable television operators. There are continuing uncertainties about the competitive opportunities available in the broadcasting area.[17]

Many large publishing and media companies also have achieved a significant incumbent position through a long history of building market reputation and controlling intellectual property rights to their stock of titles. All the types of organization mentioned so far have been aided in achieving their incumbency by specific government policies, which have served to limit entry. In some cases, these decisions may have been unduly restrictive as, for example, in delays in regulatory decisions enabling the entry of cable television companies in certain countries. In other instances, it is difficult to imagine the development of an effective market without the existence of government intervention to limit entry. For example, without copyright, it is highly unlikely that a successful publishing industry would have emerged. We do not take a normative view of the decisions that may have contributed to incumbent positions. We simply observe that these positions with respect to the information and communication infrastructure arose historically from specific forms of protection and, in many cases, have created additional opportunities to control key assets.[18]

The incumbent strategy need not be confined to situations where historical developments combined with specific forms of protection have led to the control of key assets. In the personal computer operating system market, Microsoft has achieved an incumbent position due to the enormous range of software that requires its operating system products. The case of Microsoft illustrates that the incumbent strategy is not the same as the strategy of a company that has achieved (or been granted) a monopoly. While Microsoft has achieved significant market power in the personal computer operating system market, this power is largely exercised for the purpose of protecting its position of incumbency rather than for raising prices. Although a conventional economic view of monopoly and market power may be appropriate for some markets in the information society, firms that have achieved a dominant position are unlikely to prevail for long if their strategy is confined to maximizing profit on their existing position. Instead, the strategies of these firms must involve retaining control of their dominant position through increasingly creative strategies for meeting competitive threats. Many responses to such threats will require substantial investment and reconfiguration of assets that in the past have proved to be stable sources of competitive advantage.

In European markets, the most important European incumbent players include public telecommunication operators, audiovisual companies (broadcasters and media companies), cable operators, and their international partners. Most of these companies traditionally have controlled or influenced the evolution of the

---

[17] The pattern of cable installation is remarkably diverse in Europe, largely as the result of the history of policy decisions. Some countries, such as The Netherlands, have a very high percentage of cable households while others, such as Italy or Spain, have a very low penetration of cable television subscribers.

[18] e.g. a concerted refusal by major publishers to deal with distributors and retailers who stocked 'pirated' versions of published works would be likely to create a *de facto* copyright system even in the absence of laws establishing and protecting copyright.

information and communication infrastructure. They have defined new services and installed new capacity within the frameworks of policy and regulatory systems in the Member States that are intended to serve a variety of public policy objectives including the promotion of cultural production, the achievement of universal telephony service, and new opportunities for employment creation.

Measures introduced via European Union directives and through the initiatives of the Member States have sought to encourage competition in the markets for these companies' services. The incumbent companies have had to develop new strategies to ensure that they can continue to play a central role in the design of the information and communication infrastructure for the information society. There are substantive differences between the strategies these companies are adopting to respond to the challenges presented by companies developing insurgent strategies. Incumbency, nevertheless, means that companies have substantial, and perhaps even unique, capabilities for extending and deepening the physical infrastructure for the information society in Europe. For example, such organizations as the British Broadcasting Corporation have moved aggressively to establish an Internet presence and British Telecom is seeking to become a major player in the Internet service provision market. Incumbent publishers and other media companies in the private sector have sought strength through alliances and mergers, and the former monopoly (or dominant) public telecommunication operators, to varying degrees, have acknowledged that more competitive markets bring the challenge to deploy aggressive strategies to retain market share in those aspects of their businesses that they chose to retain.

1.2.1.2   The Insurgent Strategy

One of the most dramatic developments in the information and communication technology and services industry in the last decade has been the increasing use of the personal computer as an information terminal for access to networks. The Internet revolution, which has proved to be the next stage of the personal computer revolution, is being supported by the growth of local area networks and the construction of on-line service networks including Internet–Intranet–Extranet services. The personal computer itself is a robust engine for the generation of a new market in multimedia information, distributed using Compact Disc–Read Only Memories (CD-ROMs) as well as the Internet. The personal computer is also the basis for a continuously expanding desktop publishing and image processing market as well as more traditional uses of the machine as a word processor, numeric analyser, and database manager. All of these applications are made possible by software and some involve the growth of new markets for peripheral devices.

These developments are only a small part of the future possibilities offered by access to networked information and the continuing growth in the personal computer's capability as an information- and communication-processing device. Each of the markets generated by the personal computer is a resource of the information society over which there is an active contest for control and domination and this applies also to the market for personal computers. We characterize the strategy by which companies achieve a dominant position in these markets as an 'insurgent' strategy.

An insurgent strategy may involve the innovative definition of a new technology or service for the purpose of achieving mass-market acceptance. It also may involve a redefinition of an existing technology or service in a way that makes it possible to over-turn established incumbent positions or to open new market opportunities, again with the aim of mass-market acceptance. In addition to the significance of the rapid pace of technological change in the information and communication infrastructure, many products and services that are the subject of the insurgent strategy offer positive network externalities—their value increases with the number of adopters. Positive network externalities are a more precise formulation of the mechanism often referred to in business circles as the 'virtuous cycle'.[19] For example, the capacity to receive word-processor files from other users increases the value of choosing a software package that is able to read and edit such files. In other words, the value of choosing a software package may be increased by the size of the network of other users of the product. Similar principles apply with respect to the selection of other types of files and per-sonal computers and peripherals due to the greater ease of finding parts or service. An insurgent strategy involves achieving a strong lead in the adoption of a particular domain of application and retaining that lead through innovative improvement and service to the adopting users.

An insurgent strategy gives those companies that select it an enormous forward momentum. Such companies as Microsoft, Netscape, Sun Microsystems, and Oracle, for example, have actively sought to become the architects of the global information society. Their strategies are predicated upon a model of innovative initiative and mass-market creation that has become identified with companies from the United States. American-owned firms do not necessarily have a unique technological capability with respect to their European or Japanese rivals, but they do appear to have an advantage in the speed at which they construct mass markets for new technologies and services due to the size and integration of their domestic market. As a product or service achieves mass-market success in the United States, the process of localizing it for other markets is often able to overwhelm domestic competitors and extend the advantage gained within the United States market on a global basis.

Those companies following the insurgent strategy appear to have unlimited aspirations and they design their technologies and configure their market presence in distinctive ways. These frequently depart from the previous generation of communi-cation network architectures and from the organizational forms and tactical alliances of many of the incumbent firms in the telecommunication, broadcast, or computer industries. European companies are largely absent from the ranks of those companies that are adopting an insurgent strategy although there are some exceptions. Sweden's Telia, for example, has considerable aspirations and the company has adopted business

---

[19] In the general formulation, intangible issues such as the effect of reputation or user expectations (bandwagon effects) may also support the growth of a leader's dominance.

strategies that bear many of the hallmarks of the insurgent strategy. In some instances, this strategy produces alliances with information and communication infrastructure and equipment suppliers, but, in most cases, it implies their subordination. The vision that underpins the insurgent strategy is playing a very major role in influencing the deployment of new information and communication technologies and services in European markets.

1.2.1.3   The Virtual Community Strategy

The virtual community strategy is simultaneously both the oldest and the newest of the three strategies that are vying for success as the means of organizing the new resources of the information society. It is old in the sense that it reproduces the practices of merchants and craftsmen from time immemorial in building communities of customers or users or in assembling groups of people with common interests to participate in the creation and use of common resources. What is new about this strategy is that the medium for constructing these communities no longer requires physical proximity. Those who gain membership within these communities can, in many cases, be serviced from any location at any time of the day or night. The elimination of time and distance as the most significant features in building networks of interested customers or citizens is not the defining characteristic of the virtual community strategy. The same opportunity is available to organizations developing incumbent or insurgent strategies. What enables and strengthens the virtual community strategy is the capacity to address the variety of interests and needs of users *in depth* and to specialize and customize products, services, or resources that address these issues.

The basis for the virtual community strategy is the Internet. The Internet, now the dominant mode for achieving internetworking, is a vast system of interconnected computers and telecommunication links that rivals the complexity of the public switched telecommunication network and differs from the traditional implementations of local area networks. The Internet has been constructed with the aid of a simple, and now somewhat aged, standard for inter-computer communication and process control (Transport Control Protocol/Internet Protocol or TCP/IP) and funding of the initial key backbone capacity by public authorities and the defence sector is rapidly being displaced by private-sector investors.[20] These companies may provide portal services, enable access to the Internet, or provide services and content, and they range in size from the smallest entrepreneurial or social services organization to those, such as e-Bay, Yahoo!, Amazon.com, and a host of others, that receive head-

[20] The Internet originated from the work of Licklider and Clark at the Massachusetts Institute of Technology who envisaged a global interconnected network accessible from any site. Davies and Scantleberg at the British National Laboratory are said to have been the first to use the term 'packet' for the type of switching that enables the new networks. Paul Baran at the RAND Corporation in the United States played a major role. The computer network concept was proposed in 1964 at RAND and the first installation commissioned by the Department of Defense, ARPANET, was hooked up at the University of California at Los Angeles in September 1969. A second node was established in October at the Stanford Research Institute. The electronic mail application was introduced in 1972. The TCP/IP was developed by Cerf and Kahn, see Leiner *et al.* (1998); Kizza (1998); and Zakon (1999).

line news attention because of their market capitalization. Within the ranks of these companies there are many that aim to become insurgent strategy leaders. As yet, however, the size of their user base combined with the vigour of technological innovation has limited the extent of their dominance. An exception may be Yahoo!, a search engine (for finding sites on the Internet) and portal service provider (a point of entry to regularly initiating connection to World Wide Web resources) that has achieved a very strong position in relation to its rivals. It would be premature to describe this company as dominant. Yahoo!'s experience, however, does demonstrate the potential for the insurgent strategy in the Internet service market. The large number of its users raises significant advertising revenues, allowing greater investment in services than some of its competitors, and the attraction of yet more users. This is the virtuous cycle associated with the insurgent strategy.

A predominant strategic goal on the supply side of this configuration is the formation of new virtual groupings or communities that are attracted to the Internet to engage in some form of electronic commerce, to gather public information, or to be entertained or educated. Although until recently the members who comprise these communities have been drawn from the education, government, and research communities rather than from the public at large, the numbers of the latter are growing as are the commercial uses of the Internet. In fact, Internet users are assembling themselves into virtual communities that are expanding as the amount of reference information and the number of available services multiply. In this process, their strategies are uniting members of supplier and user communities into common constituencies. Some of the users who adopt a virtual community strategy are indifferent to the technological principles of the Internet's operation, but others are highly technologically sophisticated. In addition, the suppliers and users of this strategy have been the most innovative with respect to creating new business models for the information economy that are not based upon direct sales or subscriptions. These new business models involve advertising support, indirect sources of revenue (such as subscriptions to organizations associated with the Internet services), and shareware (the purchase of software or information content after trial use with the encouragement of distribution of trial copies to other users). In the non-profit sector, support for an organization's Internet activities may occur as a by-product of other activities, for example, the funding for an Internet presence may be part of the organization's promotion or dissemination budget.

1.2.1.4 Summary
A social and economic account of information society developments requires an analysis of the relevant actors and interests. The tripartite division of interests into incumbent, insurgent, and virtual community strategies identifies the distinct economic incentives and social motivations involved in developing information society resources. Certain actors may be tightly or loosely associated with these specific strategies. A relatively tight identification is possible when the behaviour of the organization can be described unambiguously as being aligned with a specific strategy especially when the significance of that alignment with the organization's basic

purposes and goals is clear. Looser identifications are necessary for organizations that are pursuing multiple strategies including those organizations that are attempting to move their activities from one strategy to another. For example, in recent years, Microsoft has adopted an incumbent strategy in the personal computer operating system market but continues to pursue an insurgent strategy in dozens of other markets in which it operates. Similarly, Yahoo! originated in a virtual community context and has attempted to move towards the insurgent strategy.

The profit motive associated with incumbent and insurgent strategies is a powerful force of attraction for the companies. The competitive outcome of these strategies is, however, one in which the 'winner takes all' or achieves a dominant position in a mass market. Many virtual community participants are inherently unable to construct a mass market because the source of their appeal is specifically in the specialization and customization of the products, services, and resources that they offer. Other virtual community participants would like to target mass markets but are prevented from moving towards an insurgent strategy by the competitive vigour of similar communities and the fluidity of movement of the participants within these communities.

We do not assign normative values to any of the strategies in our tripartite division; each is capable of providing major social and economic benefits if it is tempered by the continuing growth of effective competition. However, we will not ignore the possibility that effective competition is in many cases unavailable or the reality that the incumbent and insurgent strategies are inherently anti-competitive. Movements towards greater levels of competition are often confused with the achievement of a competitive market when, in fact, substantial market power persists and may create adverse social and economic outcomes. We are also concerned with the potential exclusion of European (and other) companies from participation in the insurgent strategy due to the structure of the United States market, which provides large-scale and rapid reinforcement of successful insurgent initiatives. This concern prompts us to devote particular attention to virtual community interests and strategies throughout this book. Such strategies may provide the best, although not the last, hope for European leadership in implementing important information society resources reflecting uniquely European aspirations and interests.

1.2.2   *Technological Trajectories, Institutional Evolution, and Interests Co-ordination*

The future dominance of any one of the three strategies, and therefore of the groups of players and the network and service architectures they champion at any given time, matters because the health of information society developments hinges on an active contest between them. The absence of virtual community interests would pit two 'winner take all' strategies against one another with the probable outcome that accommodations and mergers would be arranged to produce an oligopoly composed of allied insurgent–incumbent interests. The deployment of the information and communication infrastructure would create another medium that would call for a substantial regulatory structure that would face an uphill battle to preserve public interests and inveigh against exclusionary forces. The absence of an incumbent strategy would lead those developing insurgent strategies to mobilize blocks of user communities around their infrastructures and services creating potentially severe interoperability problems and the marginalization of virtual communities. The absence of an insurgent strategy would encourage accommodations and mergers between the incumbent firms that are proceeding with incumbent strategies, producing an information society dominated by multimedia broadcasting in which virtual community members would be marginalized. This, in turn, would produce potentially severe problems in generating localized content and innovative technological approaches. In the case that only the virtual community strategy prevailed, no player would have the scale of resources to construct cohesive information and communication infrastructures or general-purpose tools.

The tripartite division of interests and strategies, therefore, is desirable relative to the alternatives. The contest between firms with incumbent and insurgent strategies can draw upon the experimentation and variety of virtual community participants and it is in the interest of both to promote the development of virtual community initiatives to enlarge the potential market for their products and services. This is so as long as virtual community activities do not interfere with incumbent or insurgent interests or threaten to favour either one of these players' interests. All these developments are strongly apparent in the development of the Internet, largely because the rate of Internet technological and market developments highlights the actions and the short-term advances and retreats of actors with identifiable interests. The Internet is not the only place where these processes are occurring, however. The development of other elements of the information and communication infrastructure, such as broadcasting, telephony, or intelligent transportation and logistical systems, is occurring more slowly and often involves the attenuation of the influence of the adherents of one or more of these three interests and strategies.

The reason to argue that these changes are occurring throughout the industries involved with the information and communication infrastructure is that they are all influenced by a common technological trajectory, the improvement of microelectronics technology generally, and microprocessor hardware and software systems in particular. Improvements in microelectronics technology are the principal engine driving the insurgent strategy and frustrating the extension of incumbent strategies. The effects of this technological trajectory are most apparent in the use of the personal computer as an information appliance. A decade ago, personal computers were only able to display crude graphic diagrams and their capabilities were strained by the requirements of graphic user interfaces. Today, a suitably networked personal computer is able to display, for instance, an intimate and high quality photographic view of the monastery cloister garden at Mont-Saint-Michel accompanied by an appropriate musical score, as well as millions of other images and sounds.[21] Although many technological changes are responsible for this advance, the increase in the complexity and speed of microelectronics plays a central role.

With the rapid pace of advancement along the technological trajectory of increasing speed and complexity, the creation of an effective information and communication infrastructure also requires institutional evolution. In our example of the cloister of Mont-Saint-Michel, it has been necessary to agree the standards by which visual and audio information can be decoded by the networked personal computer. These standards involve the operation of standards-making institutions and the rapid response of hardware and software companies to the new opportunities provided by standards. Access to this information, which resides on a server in France, from Great Britain requires institutional arrangements for international communication of data outside the traditional arrangements for international telecommunication traffic. The provision of this information by the Office de Tourisme de Dol-de-Bretagne, a department of the regional government of West France, indicates that it is not only international institutions that are evolving in response to new technological opportunities, but also local institutions.

Analysing the contest between those developing the three strategies for their place in the European information society involves an assessment of the relative position of the organizations employing these strategies. It also calls for the alignment of technological and institutional issues with the interests of the actors. Any snap-shot of technological or institutional position is but a fleeting impression of a rapidly evolving process. It is necessary to take into account the rate and direction of technological and institutional changes as well as the current position. The theoretical framework of diffusion analysis (the study of the pattern and determinants of the adoption process in the deployment of new technologies and services) provides a *partial* solution to the problem of organizing observations and analyses of the processes of technological change. For the analysis of institutional evolution, the available theoretical apparatus is less satisfactory and we employ case studies and comparative approaches as the principal tools in our analysis of institutional evolution. Our analyses of both technological and institutional changes are, of necessity, impressionistic given the scope of the developments that we examine. We believe that the broad perspective we adopt is necessary to convey the importance of the interactions between the different social and economic, as well as technological, developments.

Many of the assessments of trends in the development of the emerging information society focus predominantly either on the choices of users or on the components of the advanced information and communication infrastructure that key players appear to be selecting.[22] This leads to projections of the demand for individual pieces

---

[21] See http://www.asteria.fr/mont.htm, accessed 6 April 2000.

[22] The methodology of market forecasting varies, but it generally employs the development of consensus estimates of the CAGR that is expected by major participants. Examples of such market forecasts include Aderton and Delaney (1995) and Barling and Stark (1995). A guide to many other such studies is Oxbrow, Kibby, and While (1997).

of technology or speculations about the future use of specific services. Such projections can be helpful in examining the diffusion of specific technologies and services, but the pathways for their diffusion are influenced by the choices of a wide range of actors and institutionalized actions in addition to those of the individual user. For example, the decisions taken by those active in the standards and regulatory arenas, as well as those who develop and implement legislation with respect to intellectual property, security, and privacy are equally important in setting the context in which the diffusion process occurs. Changes in the social practices, cultural values, and the organizational routines of the people who use the information society infrastructure and services are also vitally important for the outcomes that we analyse in this book.

1.3   Conclusion

One of our aims is to provide a social and economic account of movement towards the European information society since this vision was articulated in the European Commission's 1993 White Paper on *Growth, Competitiveness, Employment*. Another is to define, by example, an analytical approach to the issues presented by this movement that has important policy implications and provides an agenda for the socio-economic research that is needed to support this movement in a way that supports both diversity and especially the interests of the members of virtual communities who generally have a smaller voice in the decisions that are shaping the information society and that are affecting their lives. Our claim is that policy relevance requires an intimate involvement in the examination of the interactions between actor interests, technological change, and institutional evolution. Defining the socio-economic research agenda in terms of idealizations such as 'competition' or through a political process in which 'wise men' define the social needs to which technologists should respond appears to us to fall short of the mark. The European information society is in the process of being born through the contests of interests as they are shaped by technological opportunities and constraints and by the evolution of institutions supporting or discouraging particular lines of development. There are numerous studies that have taken up this agenda and many are cited throughout this book. Much more work is needed particularly on the interaction between technological and institutional developments and on the social and economic processes governing market development and strategy. What follows is not a beginning. It is an account of a journey that is underway and on which we are accompanied by many fellow-travellers.

In Ch. 2 we develop the basis for an account of information society developments by identifying and elaborating several sources of social exclusion. We emphasize the way the emerging information society is being experienced by people as citizens and consumers, and highlight some of the applications of the information and communication infrastructure that are being devised in a bid to ensure that the European information society is responsive to social and cultural aspirations and to efforts to use the tools of the information society to devise innovative forms of governance and access to relevant information. We also consider the value of proactive policies designed to combat exclusion and the role of virtual communities in bridging the powerful forces supporting exclusion.

2

Social Communities: Access and Users' Capabilities

2.1 Introduction

Progress towards the information society depends fundamentally upon the degree and nature of user engagement with the process. There are many dimensions to such engagement, but an essential prerequisite is the development of skills by users. Skills are much more than the knowledge about how to 'launch' software applications on a personal computer or to operate a browser to access URL (Universal Resource Locator) addresses. Skills must also encompass the judicious use of networked information and communication technology resources for particular purposes and the development of reflective capacities for the use of technologies. The acquisition of skills relevant to participation in the information society cannot be separated from the processes by which one learns to acquire information through critical reading or to master tools, such as the use of a library catalogue. For these skills to become widely available, actions such as provision of Internet and World Wide Web services in schools and libraries throughout Europe must be considered.

Improvements in skills and in the accessibility of new web-based information also must be accompanied by the emergence of new norms and understandings of the processes of establishing social status and ordering by which social inclusion or exclusion are perceived. Fostering broader user engagement also means acknowledging that the 'user' is an enormously variegated category and that sensitivity to people's motivations, or lack thereof, for engaging with the new virtual or 'cyber' environments is a prerequisite for the evolution of economic and social processes that contribute to well-being (Steinmueller, 1999). As Silverstone and Mansell (1996: 224) argue, the consequences of both voluntary and involuntary exclusion are profound.

While societies as a whole become progressively more dependent on electronic media and information and communication services, then those who find access, for financial or other reasons, increasingly difficult or just simply impossible will become progressively marginalized and excluded. Isolation can take many forms. In an information age, where technologies themselves are reasonably seen as the instruments of social and economic inclusion, then non-

This chapter draws substantially upon original research by Dr Aldo Geuna, Professor Robin Mansell, David Neice, and Professor W. Edward Steinmueller, all of SPRU. At the time his research was undertaken, Dr Geuna was at MERIT, University of Maastricht. Dr Leslie Haddon was Senior Research Fellow at the Graduate Research Centre in Culture and Communication, University of Sussex, at the time his research was undertaken, and the authors gratefully acknowledge permission to draw on his material.

participation in a culture defined and articulated through electronic networks of one kind or another will have profound cultural as well as political and economic consequences.

As these processes unfold they need to be accompanied by public discussion and consensus around the levels and types of security and privacy needed to establish trust in the uses of computer-mediated communication. These issues range from the inter-personal understandings reached about the use of electronic mail to the means of institutionalizing appropriate regulation of electronic commerce. At the most abstract level, and, therefore, the most difficult level to achieve, broad participation in debate and consensus is needed to achieve resolutions of issues about standards, intellectual property protection, and the institutional and regulatory arrangements needed to encourage competition. These issues are taken up in the ensuing chapters. In this chapter we set the stage by considering what it means to talk about 'access' in an information society, how changes in access might influence the formation of new kinds of social communities, and how these issues are linked to the accumulation of user capabilities and skills.

At the centre of our critique of many of the existing conceptions of the information society is the idea that rapid changes in technological capability alone will suffice to meet the needs of people in that society.[1] This chapter aims to develop a more stimulating and engaging vision of the role of the user or, better, the participant, in the European information society than is the case when the user is seen as a 'node' in the information and communication infrastructure. To accomplish this we must move beyond relatively conventional discussions about skills and access to new technologies and services.[2] We need to understand more deeply how the alternative visions of the information society are borne out and experienced by the participants through their engagement with the social and cultural environments of their everyday lives. An assessment of both prevailing and minority visions is necessary to interpret the drama of technological change.

It is important to bear in mind that the full implications of new technologies are rarely well understood during their formative years (Marvin, 1988). As Rosenberg (1976) has noted, new technologies are neither robust nor obvious replacements for those that are already employed. New technologies encounter difficult hurdles since their early acceptance often stimulates the improvement of existing methods that become more competitive as a result. The study of new information and communication technologies and services has blossomed over a half century of

---

[1] See e.g. Gilder (1994); Leebaert (1998); Tapscott (1995).

[2] e.g. the chapters in Dumort and Dryden (1997) devote only a few lines to the issue. In Dumort and Riché-Magnier (1997: 167): 'The introduction of advanced services will require the combination of new skills and qualifications, including adaptability, polyvalence, critical thinking, communication, conceptualisation, technical and intellectual processing of information and the ability to acquire new skills and know-how on a life-long basis.' These authors define this list as the social capabilities and argue that they will 'progressively gain momentum over technical and specialized qualifications' (ibid.). This is the end of the story until we reach the conclusions where Dryden (1997: 274) presents skills issues as questions: 'Which skills will be most in demand, and how will they be supplied? How are such skills and knowledge developed and transferred?'

research.[3] Even with a more sophisticated understanding of the interactions between social and technological developments, new and unanticipated implications are emerging because the processes of learning and social interaction are continuously producing novelty.

A deeper analysis of the experiences of information society participants involves reflecting upon the empirical evidence on the distribution of Internet access at public sites and education institutions in Europe and upon the critiques of prevailing concepts of 'universal' access to networks and information. The latter are beginning to emerge as perceptions of consumer and citizen rights change with the accumulation of experience with European 'cyberspace'. Both inclusive and exclusive forces are manifest in the design and implementation of new convergent networks such as the Internet. They are also visible in emerging patterns of communication and information exchange within social networks in the 'cyberspace' environment.[4]

The emphasis on generating bits and bytes, whether in the context of electronic commerce or in public service initiatives to provide electronic information, is creating new processes of social stratification that are only beginning to be understood. These new processes have substantial implications for future opportunities to acquire and develop skills and to engage in lifelong learning. They also influence the kinds of capabilities that increasingly appear to be needed to sustain participation in the European cyberspace in ways that are perceived by consumer and citizen participants as being effective.

Policy-makers are recognizing that access to, and participation in, the information society are important political issues. Policy attention, however, tends to focus on the idea that building information societies, or more commonly in the 1990s, building knowledge societies, means fuelling growth and consumption through achieving equality of consumer access and getting more people plugged in and wired up as if these were self-evidently good things to do.[5] Participation in the consumer culture and

---

[3] See e.g. earlier work by Innis (1951); McLuhan (1964); Melody (1977); and more recently Dutton (1996; 1999); Kling *et al.* (1999); Melody (1994); Silverstone and Haddon (1996a); Silverstone and Hartmann (1998); Steering Committee on Research Opportunities Relating to Economic and Social Impacts of Computing and Communications (1998).

[4] The term 'cyberspace' was coined by William Gibson, a science fiction writer, to describe a dystopian information infrastructure vision (Gibson, 1984). Gibson's vision is of access to a global information resource achieved through neurological interfaces with the user and global information network containing malevolent artificial intelligence agents capable of action in the virtual reality experienced by users with additional implications for what happens in the 'real' world. We use the term with the somewhat more limited meaning of complex social interrelationships occurring on the Internet in which social interactions and the architectures of virtual meeting-places influence one another, see Mitchell (1996). Gibson's world is one in which a relatively small élite has the capacity to make full use of network resources.

[5] A relatively early contribution outlining the transition from the view that information is another input in economic activity towards the view that information resources are an integral part of the knowledge-based organization of economic activities is Institute for Information Studies (1993) and early accounts by Lamberton (1971; 1984) and by Melody (1981). Recent popular accounts of the 'new economy' implications of these developments include Kelly (1994; 1998); Leadbeater (1999). Academic contributions to this viewpoint include Boisot (1998); Eliasson (1990); K. Smith (1995). A consideration of these issues from the viewpoint of developing countries is given in Mansell and Wehn (1998).

equality of purchasing and transaction access are important, but are also intimately linked with issues of citizenship and the emergence of new dynamics that generate social inequalities.

Citizenship may be seen as a special legal relationship between individuals and the modern democratic state (Marshall, 1973). Certain rights and entitlements are enshrined in acts and statutes. The exercise of these rights, however, is manifestly uneven across society. In addition, other rights and entitlements are not legislated but adhere to individuals by virtue of their social status and position. Citizenship is linked to social privilege and social class and the condition of citizenship refers to a baseline of societal participation and inclusion. Citizenship is not a static social relationship among individuals, or between the individual and the state, in which individuals are locked into fixed positions. Instead, the perception of the link between an individual's position and the 'rights' of inclusion and participation are subject to change. Correspondingly, the perception of exclusion can foment demands for inclusion and participation that are inconsistent with social position or class, setting off processes of resistance, accommodation, and change in what is defined as the baseline.

A dynamic conception of the issues of inclusion and participation is therefore a necessary counterpart of any consideration of the opportunities for, and the implications of, participation in cyberspace. Individuals are unlikely to begin with clear or strong views about what is meant by inclusion or exclusion without a familiarity with the interactions defining participation. With experience, however, they develop a view as to their position and status as well as to their entitlements to inclusion and participation. A smooth working-out of how privilege and position generate entitlement to participation and inclusion is unlikely. It becomes even more unlikely if there are marked and visible gains to be had from inclusion and participation (ibid. 65). Efforts may be taken, nevertheless, to mitigate exclusionary processes at both the technological and institutional level. We begin our analysis of the possibility of mitigation with an examination of those social groups that are most at risk of exclusion and proceed towards a more general discussion of exclusionary processes with even more widespread effects.

2.2   Social Processes of Exclusion

The potential for social exclusion is fundamental to the deployment of advanced information and communication technologies and services that create or sustain the information society. Freeman and Soete's comprehensive survey of the *Economics of Industrial Innovation* emphasizes particularly the deeply divisive trends within the emerging information society.

The advent of the information society has thus been accompanied by a reversal of all those trends towards social justice and improved welfare services, which were such a characteristic feature of the quarter century following the Second World War. It seems probable that some features of the information society will exacerbate these trends even further. In particular a division is taking place between the 'information rich' and the 'information poor'. A fairly large number of people, even in the richest countries, are unable or unwilling to use the new technologies or to gain access to facilities where they might be used. 'Information poverty' corresponds fairly closely to material (income) poverty but is not identical. However, it can easily lead to material poverty in the labour market conditions generally prevailing. Social exclusion and the growth of a large underclass are thus becoming characteristic features of the information society, reinforced by the decline of the welfare state and the growth of regressive taxation. (Freeman and Soete, 1997: 410)

More often than not the developers of new technologies and services find it difficult to involve users at an early stage in their design and it is especially challenging to draw such users from excluded groups (Haddon, 1998). Many of the European Commission's Research, Technology, Development and Demonstration (RTD&D) programmes that are concerned with designing technical systems to support engagement with the European information society explicitly encompass the goal of taking account of the 'social and cultural implications' of the new systems. Many of these projects in the Commission's Fourth Framework Telematics Applications (TAP) and Advanced Communication Technologies and Services (ACTS) programmes have been identified to provide a starting-point for our analysis of these implications.[6]

The ACTS programme was charged with the goal of taking into account the social and cultural implications of the funded activities (European Commission, 1995*i*). In presenting examples of how new technologies might affect everyday life, the outline for the programme observed that emerging trends 'have a social dimension (appropriately used communication can improve social cohesion and overcome isolation)' (ibid. 12). It also stated that 'the two major European social challenges in the 1990s are in the areas of employment and European cohesion. Advanced communications are an essential part of the responses to both of these' (ibid. 13). It is, however, very difficult to reconcile these statements with the more immediate goals of realizing products that can be readily commercialized and that will improve European economic competitiveness. The result is a division between projects that have an explicit social aim and, therefore, can be assessed in relation to their social contribution and other projects whose aims are in accord with the commercialization and competitiveness agendas. This practical outcome is rather removed from the view that technology developers and users should look beyond the immediate aims of moving towards marketable service applications to examine the implications of the technologies they are developing for social cohesion and for its counterpart, social exclusion (Silverstone and Haddon, 1997). In effect, there is a failure to embed social considerations in the design of new technologies. One reason for this is the view that advanced information and communication technologies inherently have the potential to help overcome some forms of exclusion. What is ignored, however, is that they also have the potential to create new, or to reinforce existing, forms of disadvantage (Haddon, 1998).

---

[6] For a review of the goals and initial outcomes of the European Commission's Fourth Framework Programme, TAP projects, see ASSENT (1999*a*).

For example, the basic telephone has become such a routine part of daily life that to be without a telephone in the 1990s is to be socially disadvantaged (Häußermann and Petrowsky, 1989). If some services or types of information become mainly or exclusively accessible on-line there is the risk that those without the appropriate access and skills—as well as the physical ability—will be unable to work in a virtual environment. If many of the new networks under development are, for sound commercial reasons, located in urban regions then this has prima facie consequences for those living in rural areas. In the field of higher education, it is increasingly required that students utilize word-processing software and network skills in their work and those who lack access to a computer are becoming educationally disadvantaged. By no means do all of these issues have purely 'technological fixes'. They also require the evolution of institutions with mandates providing incentives for people to become prepared and motivated to seek ways of mitigating the issues of exclusion.

Technological mitigation of exclusion requires more than pronouncements about the nature and extent of the problem. It requires the adoption of a new rationale or ethos in the design process, much as considerations of safety or usability are incorporated in design because of their perceived contribution to product or service commercialization. A particularly important feature of non-exclusionary technologies is their flexibility. Flexibility involves anticipating how technologies and services that are designed for one expected pattern of adoption or for the early stages of a product's diffusion path or 'career' can be adapted and used in different ways by different user groups, for example, the elderly or the disabled (Haddon and Silverstone, 1996). The analysis of flexibility involves asking questions such as, 'Are the design parameters that are being set at an early stage so rigid that they will impose limits on how and by whom the technologies might be used in the future?' This approach is essentially proactive, but it can be effective only to the extent that it becomes embedded in the processes of engineering and business decision-making.

Developing a proactive approach requires a concrete view of the potential user who is at risk of exclusion. One starting-point for considering the scope of social exclusion is the social group of the 'homebound'. The homebound include the disabled, the elderly, and others who are isolated because they are confined to home for other social and physical reasons, for example, carers or those with a long-term illness such as chronic heart disease (Haddon, 1998).[7] Many women and a few men may be considered as homebound because of their domestic responsibilities. The needs of these users can be explicitly addressed on a targeted basis[8] or customized human interfaces geared to particular end-users can be developed.[9] Adopting a proactive approach, however, requires incorporating into the ordinary design process considerations about the consequences of design choices.

---

[7] See ASSENT (1999*b*) for a review of recent developments in applications for the disabled and elderly.

[8] e.g. RISE (Caring for the Elderly in the Information Society Era), aimed to provide new means of communication for the elderly, the disabled, and those with special needs so that they can form 'social groups of common interest' but also receive telemedicine and home-care services.

[9] e.g. MORE (Mobile Rescue Phone) and HOME (Home Applications Optimum/Multimodal System for Environment Control).

Following through with the analysis of the implications of exclusion for this group entails examining all of the processes involved in the use of a particular technology to identify those that require mobility. It also requires assessment of whether potential alternatives to mobility are available. Most obviously, visiting the local office of the service provider is either not an option or quite costly for this group. Less obviously, but still well within the domain of market research that might provide an input into the design process, are questions about the specific group's interests in the use of products and services. For example, an information service that gives a high priority to news about mobility (the state of motorways, rail service, and underground or metro) would appear to be, at best, a waste of this group's time. Even less obvious is the fact that some members of this group may attach a greater priority to such information than the typical user due to the discomfort or danger of travel. Others within the group may want at least as much of this information as the typical user because it creates for them the feeling of participation in the rhythms of ordinary life. Conventional market research will not capture the latter two needs of these users.

The variety of users that should be considered will differ depending upon the value attached to the potential exclusion. Exclusion might also encompass those individuals whose participation in society is restricted by income, for example, the unemployed or low-income families. In cases where the aim is to provide a product or service designed to complement an affluent lifestyle, the decision to ignore these users has already effectively been made. The designer of a product or service for lifelong learning who assumes that the users will pay more for convenience rather than investing their own time is making a decision that will have exclusionary effects. A similar analysis can be applied to those who are isolated because they are geographically remote, mainly those in rural communities, those who are marginalized through language and, to some extent, culture such as migrants and ethnic minorities, and those who are marginalized for other reasons, for example, drug addicts.

Drawing boundaries around groups of people who are actually or potentially excluded from the information society is difficult. An example suggests a reason for this. With respect to the elderly, those campaigning for changes in the design of artefacts to take into account the deterioration—to a greater and lesser extent—in strength, dexterity, and sensory acuteness that comes with advancing age, tend to treat the elderly as if they collectively face some form of disadvantage. It is important to differentiate within this group in order to understand the different situations and problems that are faced by individuals.

For example, there are marked differences between elderly people based upon the extent of economic independence they have achieved. Increasing numbers of the elderly have contributed to occupational pension schemes and, as a consequence, have incomes well above the poverty line and high enough to satisfy their aspirations. Many are sufficiently physically fit to accomplish what they wish. In other words, many are not excluded through problems of wealth or health. By contrast, many others, by virtue of being unemployed or receiving low pay, face poverty in retirement, with the consequence that they cannot afford to participate in the social and cultural activities of their peers or other people. Still other, or sometimes coincident, groups of elderly people have a degree of physical disability that makes it difficult to get out of the house to participate in the social life of the community.

Therefore, it is important to be clear about which elderly people are being addressed and to be precise about both the dimension and the degree of their social exclusion. In relation to some dimensions of social exclusion, it may be appropriate to consider the whole of a group (such as the elderly, *tout court*). In relation to others, the group may need to be defined more specifically. Some service applications will be designed to target a specific form of social exclusion affecting a group. This also has implications for measuring the extent of social exclusion. It is difficult to provide absolute numbers of the total number of the socially or physically marginalized, though it is possible to define the extent of the specific dimensions of exclusion.

Disadvantage is always relative. Identifying priorities is a difficult matter especially in the light of what a particular form of disadvantage might mean for a group's overall life chances. Identifying priority groups according to a hidden or half-hidden judgement of worthiness can also be a problem. There is, and consistently has been, a hierarchy of sympathy in judgements about exclusion and whether it is deserving of public attention. In the United Kingdom, for example, distinctions were sometimes made between the poor who were 'worthy' or 'deserving' and those whose poverty was deemed to arise from their own choices.[10] In other words, there was more sympathy for those who could be portrayed as victims, or perhaps 'victims of circumstance'. Some of this thinking still exists. For instance, it may be easier to mobilize support for the obviously disadvantaged disabled as the focus for new electronic services than for the homeless.[11] In Europe, some RTD&D projects have been funded to address those individuals whose social exclusion might be seen to be controversial such as those with HIV/AIDS, drug addiction, and the homeless.[12] RTD&D that is aimed at the socially excluded tends to use one or more of the following strategies: designing telematics for their use; customizing a service for particular groups; providing skills and training through telematics; and/or providing access to information and services. Each has a role to play both in tailoring design solutions to the needs of the socially excluded and in enabling them to approach, and participate in, what would otherwise be beyond their reach.

[10] Schumpeter (1954: 272–3) describes the evolution of this view from the Middle Ages to the 20th cent., concluding 'a great many writers on the poor laws argued on the explicit or implicit "theory" that, barring misfortune, and especially sickness, the destitute unemployed was personally to blame for his fate. In appraising this view, contempt for its inadequacy as a theory of the social phenomenon to be explained, and indignation at the callousness of which it may be the symptom, must not blind us to the element of truth in it which has come to be as much underrated in our own time as it was overrated then. It was at the basis of the argument of the defenders of the workhouse system and survived, in various nuances, until 1914 [in the United Kingdom].'

[11] The HORIZON programme of the European Social Fund was aimed at the disadvantaged and it has been noted how very few projects target this group (Employment Horizon, 1996).

[12] For an overview of RTD&D projects, see Silverstone and Haddon (1997). In this case, SEAHORSE (Support, Empowerment and Awareness for HIV/AIDS, the On-line Research and Self-help Exchange); EPITELIO (Excluded People Integration by the use of Telematic Innovative Opportunities); and PERIPHERA (Telematics Applications and Strategies Combating Social and Economic Exclusion).

2.2.1   *Designing Telematics for Use by the Socially Excluded*

Inclusive or barrier-free advanced information and communication technology and service design raises a number of issues including, for example, whether all technologies and services need to be constructed so that they do not unnecessarily exclude some people from their use.[13] A particular strategy aimed at overcoming barriers to the use of electronic services lies in the attention that is given to the design of the human interface. Even if aimed at the general public, these interfaces need to take into account the less able-bodied as well as the able-bodied. Sensory impairments are the most obvious, but not the only, characteristics to take account of in such designs.[14] Inclusive design strategies are ones that allow the desired interaction to occur even if at a slower rate or with higher levels of guidance, for example, multiple presses of any key, rather than the entry of a specific number.

There are further barriers to use which need to be considered, including knowledge, competencies, and, potentially, linguistic difficulties. The process of mapping potential impairments and tracing their implications to the design as well as confronting concept and prototype designs with 'what if' questions can be useful in achieving the goal of inclusive design. It is possible to extend the principle of inclusive design to address whether different ways of financing services, establishing billing procedures, and implementing pricing structures cause problems for certain social groups.[15] Inclusive design is an aesthetic outlook or perspective that extends the idea of social solidarity to the engineering design process. This aesthetic perspective values novelty in the design of new applications. It recognizes the specific potential of some applications to overcome the barriers that others will face in using the new applications and seeks to engage such people in the innovation and creativity of the new design.[16]

2.2.2   *Providing Skills and Training through Advanced Service Applications*

Training may involve distance learning, the use of information and communication technology applications with specialized human interfaces, or interactive software

---

[13] e.g. VISTEL (Visually Impaired Screen-Based Telephony), aimed to design new services and facilities by modifications to existing text displays and screens on telephones so as not to disadvantage those with visual impairments; HOMEBRAIN had an explicit 'design for all' theme focusing on the needs of the elderly and disabled in the development of general home automation products.

[14] e.g. TASC (Telematics Applications Supporting Cognition) and PCAD (Portable Communication Assistant for People with Acquired Dysphasia).

[15] e.g. SPECIAL (Service Provisioning Environment for Consumers' Interactive Applications). Collins and Murroni (1996) argue that tariffs, and knowledge about them, have significant consequences for the participation of economically disadvantaged groups in the provision of telephone services.

[16] e.g. ARIADNE (Access, Information and Navigation Support in the Labyrinth of Large Buildings), used applications in the form of information for navigation in buildings and lighting and door control to allow the disabled and elderly more access to, and movement around, existing large buildings. BARRIER (development of a multimedia database providing information on the accessibility in public buildings for people with handicaps to their mobility), aimed to provide information for those with mobility problems to gain access to various parts of urban environments.

that provides new ways of learning. It may involve providing resources for learning, such as on-line libraries. The majority of training projects involving advanced service applications are aimed at providing various socially excluded groups, for example, unemployed women, young people, and the disabled, with the skills to help them enter the labour market.[17] A number of RTD&D projects have specifically focused on the potential of using services for delivering teleworking skills.[18] Not all training programmes are concerned, or exclusively concerned, with developing skills for work purposes. For example, a project in the European Commission's Telematics Applications Programme was aimed at training intellectually disabled adults with skills for personal life as well as professional skills,[19] while another project aimed to empower the disabled through using a service application to train them how to make independent informed choices about appropriate enabling technologies.[20]

2.2.3   *Providing Access to Information and Services*

Innovative service applications in Europe are being developed to provide access to local government and other community organizations. Often these are directed to local (or visiting) citizens in general but they may also be seen as being of specific benefit to some socially excluded groups. Such RTD&D projects may include providing access to information that can enhance the ability to participate, improve employment prospects or the general quality of life,[21] provide access to services, for example, local council services for the elderly,[22] or otherwise facilitate contact with council employees. They may provide access to new forms of remote transactions or support the political/community participation of disadvantaged groups.

2.2.4   *Redressing Social Exclusion*

When actions are being developed to redress social exclusion it is helpful to ask a series of questions. Which groups are excluded from what? What are the mechanisms or reasons for that social exclusion? How widely or narrowly can the boundaries of such groups be drawn? To what degree are they excluded? Are there multiple forms of marginalization? How temporary or permanent is the exclusion and what are the chances of a change in circumstances? In addition to the proactive technological approach outlined in the previous sections, mitigating social exclusion through institutional development is also a possibility.

Advanced information and communication technology applications can benefit

---

[17] e.g. EMPLOY for young people (European Multimedia Pedagogic Local support network organizations for the social integration of unemployed young Europeans).

[18] The issues were addressed in IRDSS (Integrated Regional Development Support System) and TELEINSULA (Telematics Services for Islands).

[19] e.g. MULTIPLE (Multimedia Education and Training System).

[20] e.g. EUSTAT (Empowering Users Through Assistive Technologies).

[21] e.g. ATTACH (Advanced TransEuropean Telematics Applications for Community Help).

[22] e.g. INFOSOND (Information and Services On Demand).

the socially excluded indirectly as well as directly. Services can be offered directly to end-users or via non-governmental organizations and local authorities that deal with the socially excluded. It is important to consider the social context in which applications are introduced as understanding the context may help to enhance their usefulness. For example, in the United Kingdom, the Warwickshire Rural Enterprise Network provides free childcare to give women in rural areas the opportunity to be trained in information technology skills, creating as it does so the atmosphere of a social and advice centre. The socially excluded may be represented in applications development at one remove, that is, through reliance on an organization's past experience of working with or for such groups. Such knowledge may be substantial, as in the case of the feedback gained over the years by suppliers of equipment for the disabled. Research on innovating companies has shown, however, that this knowledge can often be partial, based upon industry folklore and, as a result, inadequately representative of target end-user needs (Cawson, Haddon, and Miles, 1995).

Consultation with the socially excluded can take place in a variety of forums, sooner or later in the innovation process, or on a regular or occasional basis. There will always be problems in creating a fully representative group of the socially excluded, even within a given category of disadvantage. For example, in the case of the disabled, which is a significantly heterogeneous group, a person with one particular disability may be able to speak with only limited knowledge of the problems of other disabilities. In practice, many developers will consult with, or have as partners, agencies and advocacy groups representing the interests of different socially excluded groups. While such groups may have more awareness of the range of issues affecting various individuals in such communities, there is scope for differences between how such agencies define problems and how the socially excluded, were they to voice their concern directly, might elect to do so. The choice of a particular group to represent the socially excluded can have significant political consequences. In some cases, applications initiatives may originate from the socially excluded themselves, or as a result of a tie-in between their initiatives and the applications being developed by firms.[23]

In many cases, a particular information and communication technology application is regarded as being of no relevance by the members of a group. For example, a British study of lone parents indicated that many single mothers living on state benefits alone were so busy coping with day-to-day pressures that the information society was, by and large, an irrelevance. They were so preoccupied with the demands of everyday life that new technologies received little if any consideration (Haddon and Silverstone, 1995). It is important to ask from the perspective of the socially excluded whether other policy initiatives might be more desirable than those promoting the use of new information and communication technology applications. In this case,

---

[23] e.g. in EPITELIO, Manchester Metropolitan University had existing projects involving two youth groups and a local community based on a housing estate. This project allowed its extension to provide online communication and information. The Manchester-based Women's Electronic Village Hall was an agency run by women for training women returning to work. EPITELIO was able to involve this initiative in its wider programme.

improved childcare provision or changes in social benefit rules to make returning to work more attractive might be more appropriate initiatives. Even when an application is appreciated as being of some help, how important or salient are the technological design solutions that emerge for the socially excluded? For example, in a French trial of home automation for those living in social housing, the participants showed some interest in the technology. They noted, however, that it was more important for them to have repairs made to access facilities within the building and to have better sound-proofing than to have access to the new applications (*Intelligent Home Newsletter*, 1993).

The role of advanced information and communication technologies and services in improving the lives of excluded groups in society, and in remedying their exclusion, is complex because of the major problems that are encountered in integrating technological development with participation in, and access to, the information society.[24] These problems arise not only because of the variety of social circumstances and the difficulties of involving users early in the design process, but also because of the complex relationship that technologies have with exclusion. Technological innovation is only one part of a necessarily wider strategy to counteract exclusion.

Embedding consideration of social inclusion and exclusion in broader policies offers a particularly important means of realigning incentives and signalling the social intent to address these issues. For example, policies on universal access to the more advanced components of the information and communication infrastructure differ across the European member states. It will not be easy to extend them for commercial and political reasons into the converging information and communication services environment of the information society. Yet, as the information society increasingly is embodied in technological innovation and the electronic delivery of services replaces older forms of delivery, the need to formulate policy is even more acute. As social and commercial institutions increasingly come to favour electronic services over conventional ones, such as face-to-face, post services, or conventional telephony, then issues of participation, access, and inclusion become paramount.

Policies must be developed to enable the provision of the information and communication infrastructure to distinct and identifiable marginal or potentially excluded user groups. These policies need to be both flexible and sensitive to the different needs of very heterogeneous marginal groups. Among the range of possible policy options are targeted subsidies for marginal or disadvantaged groups, sensible and flexible network connection charges and light-user schemes, the provision of public access in public spaces and institutions, and the use of taxation to stimulate companies to supply technologies and services that would otherwise be commercially unsustainable. As Silverstone and Haddon (1997) suggest, the development of access technologies to obviate the need to provide expensive physical infrastructure for specific user groups, and sustained public information campaigns

---

[24] See Gann, Barlow, and Venables (1999) for an analysis of the many factors that must be considered in constructing the modern 'smart' home.

within the European Union and nationally are also crucial considerations for policy in this area.

2.2.5 New Dimensions of Social Exclusion

Sometimes the fear of new forms of exclusion evokes the image of two substantial groupings with different relationships to technologies and services. For example, 'The main risk lies in the creation of a two-tier society, of haves and have nots, in which only a part of the population has access to the new technology, is comfortable using it and can enjoy its benefits' (High Level Group on the Information Society, 1994: 5).

However, Haddon (1998) and other observers such as Claisse (1997) argue for a rejection of simplified dichotomies between information 'haves' and 'have nots'. They suggest that it is necessary to examine specifically what technological and other resources are available to people who want to participate in the information society.

The processes of social differentiation are much more complex and cannot simply be explained away by a model of dualisation. Between households with only telephone and television and the 'super-equipped' households there is a high degree of diversity and diversification of equipment combinations. . . . Rather than talk about 'haves' and 'have nots', as most official reports do, it would probably be better to talk about the distinction between individuals and households who are 'with it' and will have all the equipment and services, those who will only have part of them, and those again who will only have basic services (television and telephone). We must add those who have nothing at all to these three groups—even if they are few and far between. (Claisse, 1997: 135, 41)

This is not to argue that disadvantage does not exist, nor that there are not different ways of discussing the emergence of potentially new forms of disadvantage (Haddon, 1998). For instance, the concept of 'relative deprivation' was promoted in the 1960s as a way of conceptualizing poverty and Townsend (1987), for instance, has argued that people should not be excluded from acceptable styles of living and social activities practised or approved by the majority of the national population. Deprivation can be partial, it can be specific, involving the lack of some options open to the majority of the population but not of others. This approach to poverty focuses on its social and cultural dimensions because as Townsend (ibid. 35) suggests, 'It is through social relationships and social roles that needs arise. This comes from being parents, partners, neighbours, friends and citizens, for example. People are not only consumers, therefore, but leaders, active participants and producers.' While there may be some degree of consensus about material deprivation, it is around social and cultural minimum rights that there is scope for considerable disagreement.

With their increasing roles in everyday life, information and communication technologies and services might be added to a list of deprivations. Exclusion may be associated with the absence of connection to conventional telephony, mobile telephony, or the Internet (Ling, Julsrod, and Krogh, 1997). Awareness of what is possible, what is available, what is taking place—through access to information at various levels and in various senses—is important for participation in society and as a basis for new forms of advantage and disadvantage. As Haddon's (1998) research shows, being able to maintain contact with families, to afford the costs of reciprocal group relationships, and to take part in local events and activities is meaningful to people and provides a motive for action.

Taking action is necessary because, important as access is, the competence to make use of the information and communication infrastructure is a prerequisite for participation in the information society. Competency is itself complex, however, and it is not straightforward to prescribe a set of actions that will achieve the goal of information and communication technology competence for a particular user. In the early 1980s, 'computer literacy' was the term used to refer to awareness of what tasks computers were able to perform. For a brief period this term applied to being able to program, but 'keyboard literacy', as it is now called, refers now mainly to the operational skills involved in using software packages. 'On-line literacy' appears to be the next stage in the effort to provide a readily identifiable goal for accumulating new skills. Each of these labels for information and communication technology competence connotes a set of skills that may be mastered at many different levels. For example, it is possible to use modern word-processing programs to produce a reasonable facsimile of typeset text. This does not mean that every user should achieve this degree of proficiency with the application program.[25]

It also is possible to define competence as Haddon (1998) suggests in terms of levels of abilities to make choices and to take action. A first level would be awareness of what exists, of what is possible, and also what the significance of new services might be for an individual or a household. A simple example is using the World Wide Web to check product specifications and reviews before making a purchase possibly at a local shop. This level of competence implies an appreciation of the implications of using new applications and of the effort that is involved and the potential problems that could arise. It entails a critical appreciation of advanced information and communication technologies, for example, the possibility that product reviews may not be entirely objective or complete. The next level may be the technical and intellectual skills involved in operating technologies or using services that involve coping with human–computer interfaces, such as search engines, discussion groups, or technical support call centres. Here there is a question of how much technical capability individuals need in their particular social circumstances. A third level of competency involves knowing when an application is 'useful' or how to achieve what is desired. This level of competency may entail locating and dealing with people who have the appropriate expertise rather than developing that expertise. All of these issues involve *intermediation* as a complement to the use of information and communication technologies and the differences in the inter-

---

[25] It may be far more effective for a user to acquire the appropriate tool, a desktop publishing package, than to devote the time needed to achieve similar results with a word-processing package.

mediary services required depend upon the experience and knowledge of the individual user.[26]

The ability to develop the appropriate competence with information and communication technologies depends crucially on the 'free' time available to people (Silverstone and Haddon, 1996b). People's disposable time may be analogous to disposable income. Individuals and households have different amounts of 'temporal capital' after commitments to work, or to finding work, to children, to the extended family, or to other social networks, have been met. Developing competency requires time; time to learn, time to experiment, and, ultimately, finding the time to stop and think. While many benefits offered by new information and communication technology applications may be welcomed, the new options and possibilities these technologies bring mean that the mechanisms and nature of deprivation or inequality—and what resources, competencies, and cultural values are involved—are in a constant process of change.

Any analysis of social exclusion in the use of the information and communication infrastructure must consider how mechanisms of social differentiation confer advantage, and simultaneously disadvantage, on some people and not others, forming a basis for new inequalities to emerge. A particular group might be disadvantaged in certain respects relative to some people but not to others, especially where there is competition for positions or for limited resources. For example, an electronic service or training programme may help the return to work of those women who may live in households that are not particularly poor, but who, without the appropriate skills, may be disadvantaged personally in the workforce, relative both to men and to other women with those skills. The problem of defining an effective plan for the acquisition of skills is a major issue in this example. The social exclusion of being outside the social context of paid employment disadvantages such women in their attempts to identify what skills to acquire. Those offering training courses may regard their offerings as relevant but may be unable properly to assess or advise an individual who is not already in a position that requires certain skills or a work context that defines what additional skills might be usefully acquired.

The uneven distribution of the new applications of the information and communication infrastructure plays an important role in these processes of social differentiation. Such processes may be based upon the possession of, or access to, resources as in the case of the personal computer, which enables some schoolchildren to win greater credit by completing word-processed, instead of hand-written, essays. The outcomes of the process of social differentiation also may be influenced by the distribution of technical competencies as, for example, when Internet searching skills give an individual an edge in a particular labour market.

The symbolic dimension of the information and communication infrastructure

---

[26] See Hawkins, Mansell, and Steinmueller (1999) for a discussion of the role of intermediation. This issue has been discussed and developed as well by Baldwin, McVoy, and Steinfield (1995); Fulk and Steinfield (1990).

also needs to be considered. Bourdieu (1986) suggested that when classes reproduce themselves, passing on advantage from parents to children, 'taste' plays a role as a social differentiator. He argued that parents invest in the 'cultural capital' of their children, developing tastes in such areas as music, food, and art, which later translate into economic advantage (economic capital) by facilitating success in the education system (Bourdieu, 1977*b*) or in acquiring more remunerative employment. There is an ongoing symbolic struggle for the legitimization of some cultural forms and the discrediting of others. But once certain tastes are construed as having a higher symbolic cultural value, the possession of them is a means by which a class structure is perpetuated.

Bourdieu did not include tastes and values about the advanced forms of the information and communication infrastructure in his analysis, but his argument can be extended to include them. Work on the determinants of consumption in recent years has drawn attention to the symbolic nature of all goods (Miller, 1995) and the symbolic nature of the infrastructure and new media has been receiving increasing attention (Silverstone and Hirsch, 1992). A British study, for example, showed that teleworkers are sometimes concerned that outsiders may think that they are not really working or that they are unemployed precisely because they are based at home. These workers took opportunities to display their equipment to family and friends in order to convey the message that they had been working and, in some cases, doing high-status work (Haddon and Silverstone, 1993). When we turn to a consideration of social differentiation involving the symbolic nature of the technical tools of the information society, it is not only having equipment, or access to services, that matters. The features of the type of equipment or the specific arrangements for access that are possessed are also important, as Neice (1998*a*) suggests.

2.3   Status Differentiation, Social Exclusion, and Virtual Engagement

In this section we take up the issue of the interrelationships between appreciation of, and orientations to, the acquisition of new information and communication technologies and services from the perspective of whether some of these relationships confer advantage in certain aspects of life because of their practical usefulness and because of their symbolic value.

2.3.1   *Transformations in the Status Order*

The exclusion of the socially or economically disadvantaged from the information society represents one facet of a much more broad-based transformation of the social structure and organization of European society. These trends are also discernible in the societies of other regions that have been adopting the tools of the information society on an increasingly widespread, albeit uneven, basis.

As we have seen in the preceding section, leading observers of global developments in information and communication technologies as well as scholars of the economics of industrial innovation routinely point to the economic and social divides that digital technologies are thought to generate and exacerbate.[27] Recognition that this process is multifaceted and multilevelled, however, complicates assessment and analysis of exclusion and access. Is it access to hardware; to silicon-chip technology, personal computers and modems, and new communication devices such as cellphones, pagers, and satellite television that matters? Or is it accessing the information they carry; the information that courses about as an endless bitstream flowing through various conduits? Or, indeed, is it access to digital networks and the social communities (virtual communities) that are using new applications? Quite routinely, access refers to all of these and many more.

Until relatively recently, knowledge of a person's occupation, gender, and ethnicity, as well as various well-ordered perceptions attached to the ownership of specific types of property and styles of conspicuous consumption, positioned most people somewhere on the 'map' of social status (Neice, 1998a). The status map that gave hierarchical meaning and order to life in market societies today seems very incomplete. The internal status maps that we carry no longer seem to fit with emerging and shared perceptions of what is important and socially valued. The principal issue is whether the growing deployment and use of the information and communication infrastructure is simultaneously being accompanied by new patterns of social inclusion and exclusion that are demarcated by a newly defined status order. Are the acquisition and use of new networks and applications being accompanied by a redefinition and reallocation of social status and social honour, and a reshaping of community (such as occupational community) prestige hierarchies?

2.3.2   Contributing Factors

The growing application of the information and communication infrastructure is expected to lead to a dematerialization process, that is, a process that is popularly described as one whereby economies and societies might be said to be 'lightening up' (Herman, Ardekani, and Ausabel, 1989; Wernick *et al.*, 1996). This term is being used to characterize the views of those who suggest that the main axis of economic value is shifting towards the increased valorization of 'weightless' configurations of bits as distinct from, and contrasted to, configurations of material atoms. Negroponte (1995: 12), for instance, contends that we are witnessing a redefinition of economic value, commerce, and work wherein bits (or information content) are gradually becoming more valued than atoms (or material forms): 'The information super highway is about the global movement of weightless bits at the speed of light. As one industry after

---

[27] Commentary on the structural transformations associated with the rapid adoption and spread of digital information and communication technologies comes from diverse fields including management studies (Drucker, 1993; Handy, 1990), economics (Freeman and Soete, 1997; Lipsey, 1995; Romer, 1993a; 1993b), policy studies (Reich, 1991; Rifkin, 1995), and media and communication studies (Collins and Murroni, 1996; Garnham, 1994; Lanham, 1993; 1995; Tremblay, 1995). Most now agree with forecasts by sociologists two decades ago (Bell, 1973; Gouldner, 1979) that the penetration of information and communication technologies into contemporary life would produce large-scale social and economic change. Specific interpretations vary widely, however.

another looks at itself in the mirror and asks about its future in a digital world, that future is driven almost 100 percent by the ability of that company's product or services to be rendered in digital form.'

Cars, cauliflower, and cod will be needed for many decades and they are not likely to be rendered digital. What seems to be occurring is that for every object or service we develop or utilize, the information density and knowledge inherent in it is rising.

Others who identify dematerialization as a central feature in the modern economy are more restrained. For Quah (1996), for example, a dematerialized economy represents an extreme polarity where infinitely replicable commodities congealed in software or gene sequence codes become the stock of trade. This is contrasted with the materialized polarity where atoms and molecules hold sway. Neither polarity exists at present; there are always blends and valences. Quah argues that dematerialized economies display specific dynamics especially involving income polarities. Dematerializing processes may increase meritocracy within society, but they may also enhance social closure at the high and low ends while hollowing out the middle. Another feature involves the concept of infinite expansion. Bit-based or codified ideas and knowledge can be infinitely replicated, challenging the perception of scarcity. Idea networks are expansive stocks, opening the possibility that everyone can be 'plugged into' and contribute to knowledge-based growth and social development.[28] Quah (ibid. 9) suggests that in an emergent 'weightless economy', 'subgroups in societies form knowledge-based coalitions; a class [*sic*] structure endogenously emerges. Over time, small differences across social groups magnify. Depending on initial circumstances, patterns of polarisation and stratification appear.'

Complementing Quah's work within economics, Castells's (1996; 1997; 1998) influence upon sociological and geographical research is significant. Castells contends that a new model of socio-economic organization, the informational mode of development (or 'informationalism'), characterizes the international economic and social system of the late 1980s and the 1990s.[29] Increased use of new information and communication technologies is said to be increasing the rate of profit, supporting the domination and accumulation functions of the state, and allowing for the internationalization of the economy. However, Castells does not argue that the technologies themselves somehow preordain a new social order. As he suggests:

New information technologies *are not in themselves the source of the organizational logic* that is transforming the social meaning of space: they are, however, the fundamental instrument that allows this logic to embody itself in historical actuality. Information technologies could be used, and can be used, in the pursuit of different social and functional goals, because what they offer, fundamentally, is flexibility. However, their use currently is determined by the process of the

---

[28] Other approaches to the potential implications of knowledge economies are based on the increasing returns associated with the 'learning economy' (Lundvall and Johnson, 1994), 'Mode 2' activity (Gibbons *et al.*, 1994), and the 'experimentally organized economy' (Eliasson, 1991).

[29] This has three dominant characteristics: (1) The appropriation by capital of a higher share of surplus from the productive process; (2) state intervention moves from political legitimization and social distribution to political domination and capital accumulation; (3) the accelerated internationalization of all economic processes to increase profitability and open up markets.

socio-economic restructuring of capitalism, and they constitute the indispensable material basis for the fulfilment of this process.   (1989: 348, emphasis added)

The outcome of the dynamics of the informational economy is characterized by:

the differential reassignment of labour in the process of simultaneous growth and decline [which] results in a sharply stratified, segmented social structure that differentiates between upgraded labour, downgraded labour, and excluded people. Dualism refers here both to the contradictory dynamics of growth and decline, and to the polarising and exclusionary effects of these dynamics.   (ibid. 225)

Perez (1983) has argued that these transformations in the economic and social order are the outcomes of the close interdependence of technical innovation with human beliefs and practices. Each successive techno-economic paradigm, she argues, requires many decades of gestation, and involves massive numbers of small experiments (both successes and failures) while building a base of advocates. Perez uses the term 'techno-economic paradigm' to designate large and widespread configurations of complementary technology that influence a major share of economic activity. During the industrial revolution, the techno-economic paradigm was shaped by mechanization and the intensive use of inanimate power sources (coal and water power) while a distinct and more modern techno-economic paradigm is based upon the economic activities depending upon petroleum and electricity. It is only after a long process of evolutionary selection and reinforcement that a new techno-economic paradigm arises and matures.

The newest techno-economic paradigm, that began to gather force in the 1970s, involves the widespread deployment and use of information and communication technologies (Freeman, 1994; Freeman and Perez, 1988; Freeman and Soete, 1994). This ascendance and replacement of what came before involves the slow construction of a new social, cultural, economic, and political institutional regime that is constructed by individuals and their coalitions. The new paradigm is based on human agency; on choices, design decisions, and the construction of perceptions and values, but always within certain constraining structures (Mansell, 1994; 1996a).

Routine practice, or common sense, rests on dispositions of both people and organizations, and these cluster to form what Bourdieu (1977a) called the 'habitus'. The existence of institutional mismatches, gaps, and disconnects in technical design and implementation together with institutional evolutionary processes provide room (or degrees of freedom) for new social interpretations and the active construction of meaning and the application of new technologies. These processes are documented in the flourishing literature that attempts to chronicle the social transformation arising from the emergence of the information society.[30]

Such diverse views suggest an evolution of new patterns of social and economic activity that derive from the processes of dematerialization and their interactions with the material world. The new patterns involve income polarities, new categories and strata of occupations, new status group configurations, and technical and socio-

---

[30] See e.g. Lyon (1988; 1994); Miles (1996); Miles and Thomas (1995); Webster (1995).

institutional mismatches of many different kinds. These processes are destabilizing or disruptive to previous patterns of social organization. The increasing centrality and embeddedness of knowledge that is associated with the dematerialization of information exchange, economic transactions, and other forms of human exchange, occurs in the context of a capitalist market society and, therefore, associates the dematerialization process with economic value. Such an association, which may be due to perception as much as fact, has implications for social structure and for social conceptions of property, wealth, status, social honour, and prestige. While each of the writers discussed in this section predicts fundamental shifts in the social and economic hierarchy, none has a clear prescription for avoiding the process of 'creative destruction' that each believes is imminent. This suggests that we need to pursue the process of change to more disaggregated levels of society in order precisely to identify the nature of the process and how to reckon with its effects.

2.3.3   Reordering Status Hierarchies in the Digital World

The social stratification of society refers to 'its internal division into a hierarchy of distinct social groups, each having specific life chances and a distinctive style of life' (Scott, 1996: 1). Hierarchical divisions that mark identifiable status groups are subject to enormous cultural and interpretative variability. Their social importance derives from their reproducibility and transmission through recurrent patterns of social distinctiveness and social closure. These processes involve powerful forces of social inclusion and exclusion; specific moments where self and society meet and intertwine. Status processes mark out relevant social distinctions, ordering these distinctions hierarchically to reflect the allocation of prestige. They produce social closure to reinforce status group boundaries. To be social is to be marked and ranked both through and by distinctive features.[31]

Fundamental shifts in shared perceptions of status ranking and social honour, their flexible firmness, result from largely hidden processes. A key aspect derives from interpenetration between material and technical processes and symbolic and cultural processes (Harris, 1979).[32] The challenge is to analyse the emerging perceptual changes in status orders that are associated with the growing spread of access to the information and communication infrastructure. Of particular interest is the formation of new virtual communities and this directed our interest especially to earlier studies of community-based processes of status ordering undertaken initially in the United

---

[31] See Neice (1998a; 1998b) for further development of this argument.

[32] Max Weber distinguished between three elements of social stratification—class, status, and party. Social classes are collectivities that accrue from similarities in the market positions of actors. Social classes by and large are coincident with market economies. Status groups are marked by their allocation of prestige and social honour within a community that shares common perceptions. Social status is distinguished from economic class because it involves community judgements about social ranking, independent of market position. The party reflects the mobilization of a society's resources by a class or status group or a combination of both to take and exercise control of a collectivity, usually a society. John Scott has recast this dimension into the concept of 'command' (Scott, 1996).

States,[33] and to more recent studies of the formation of scientific communities and of the operations of scientific laboratories (Latour and Woolgar, 1986).

A common feature of many community field studies (at least those done in market societies) is their intense preoccupation with shared community perceptions of the allocation of social honour. This is usually indexed by community status and prestige rankings of families and geographic areas. These rankings often have nuances that involve very high levels of discriminating detail and differentiation. In the community field study tradition, status constructions also involve broad perceptions of the worth of labour, or of the lack of worth associated with idleness. Skills are part of the mix, but the acquisition of skills is also influenced by social perceptions of these skills.

In the context of studies of scientific communities, Latour and Woolgar found evidence of cycles of credit and credibility management exemplified by scientific activities and careers. They argued that scientists work with a kind of quasi-investment model of personal and career behaviour, that is, they engage in a quest for credibility. A careful reading of their work on 'cycles of credit' sees scientists engaging in a process of credibility management for the purpose of refining and enhancing their prestige within their reference community. And, as Neice (1998a) suggests, credibility management processes may be a manifestation of deep processes of social ranking and prestige allocation and accumulation.

Any analysis of changes in social status perceptions accompanying the spread of today's technologies and services therefore depends upon the core processes involved. The new status markers and descriptors as well as status process differentiators need to be understood in emergent virtual communities and in situations where technology and people interact and construct meaning. Status markers may be physical features or social distinctions based on socially defined categories. Status differentiation is likely to involve institutionally embedded processes whereby a marker is given widespread collective validation, assent, and reinforcement through its social reproduction.

Evaluating social status and position in the emerging knowledge-based economies is not easy precisely because of the multifaceted and multilevelled nature of skills and, therefore, the capacity for interaction in these economies. Access to particular information resources and to digital technology, even to such services as electronic mail, may have symbolic value within the status order. The significance of these markers is, however, likely to be highly dependent upon a particular context and not readily transferable to other organizations or even within a single organization. The ownership or lease of digital resources by individuals or by institutions, the ability to develop and produce digital information, or the skills to interpret complex data, establish a loose hierarchy of sophistication in the use of information and communication technologies. The translation of these levels of capabilities into clear markers of social status

---

[33] See e.g. Lynd and Lynd (1929); for Canada, Seeley, Sim, and Loosley (1956); and for the UK, Young (1961). Although the functionalist perspective of these sociological studies is largely discredited, in the anthropological literature functionalism was less prone to endorsement of prevailing inequalities.

TABLE 2.1. *Trends producing potential shifts in status consciousness*

- Trajectories in which the use of information and communication technologies is emerging as a dominant mode of development
- A general perceptual shift towards the valorization of information and knowledge work
- Displacement and adjustments involving a reordering of the meanings of phrases such as 'laid off', retrained, contingency worker, contractor, part-timer, home-based teleworker, and flexible worker
- Growing—though uneven—access to, or ownership of, information and communication technologies and digital resources, often aided by institutional support
- Specific behaviours and orientations towards a range of services and applications involving digital technologies and resources
- Advanced skills that allow work at various degrees of efficiency and productive complexity
- Values and lifestyles that reinforce patterns of social closure based on status distinctions through the expansion of digital work cultures, linkages with new forms of cyber-leisure

Source: Adapted from Neice (1998a).

or even effective job specifications is very difficult. Effective social positioning within the new forms of knowledge-based economies appears increasingly to rest on three types of access: (1) material and physical access to infrastructure, networks, hardware, and support resources; (2) access to related occupations and specialized technical training, skills, and competencies (including the skills to produce valued input) while keeping abreast of accelerating developments in computer-mediated communication; and (3) access to social groups and communities that reinforce formal skills and facilitate an accumulating and relevant knowledge base.

Some of the major trends that appear to be influencing potentially far-reaching changes in social status as a result of the salience of new social markers and processes of differentiation are summarized in Table 2.1.

These trends are being experienced in the forms of labour adjustments and skill and competency mismatches; fears of displacement and new patterns and categories of adjustment and adaptation; new languages to describe interactions with technology; and new occupational definitions for who does what and why. They entail new strategies of management control and reinforcement of hierarchy, new rules for the governance and use of technologies, and new policies for organizations to provide some basis for managing widespread changes in how, why, and when social groupings communicate with each other. The derivation of social status may, as Neice (1996) suggests, be an emergent property of this complex pattern of interaction and change. A new vocabulary may be needed to describe the processes of alignment, coincidence, and complementarity that collectively are coming to define social status.

For example, the collection of attributes associated with individuals' relations to the information and communication infrastructure are increasingly coming to be seen as constituting a 'status estate' resting upon, and derived from, digital cultures (Neice, 1998*a*). Status estates result from clusters of status situations where social propinquity stemming from overlapping roles and other features of interaction combine to re-inforce social closure. Labels associated with status estates that have emerged for individuals most deeply immersed in the information culture, include 'hacker' and 'digerati'. The former has achieved a sufficient degree of closure to support exclusive, invitation-only cultures while the latter remains a broad description for individuals with substantial knowledge and interest in digital culture developments. The emer-gence of new terms and ones that have a particular European context will be an indi-cation that the processes described here are working as predicted. As Scott (1996: 33) comments, 'Separate status situations may also be clustered together [in addition to occupational overlaps] as a result of leisure-time interactions, residential patterns, and other forms of intimate and informal interaction that result from the exercise of social closure.'

Social estates have been defined as 'communal groups which, through various means, enjoy certain forms of privileged access to scarce resources, especially where those scarce resources are of a cultural, moral or symbolic character' (Turner, 1989: 139–40). Table 2.2 suggests some of the potentially significant status markers and status differentiators for Internet users.

The evolution of a digital culture is a complex and prolonged process involving the emergence of status markers connoting the skills and interests of individuals in their use of information and communication technology resources. The process is complex because, as in fashion, clothes do not make the man or woman. The ownership of particular technological resources or access to them does not ensure that the individual will make creative or complete utilization of their potential. Because the 'clothing' of a sophisticated user of information and communication technologies is an unreliable indicator of his or her capabilities or interests, other social markers around which cohesive groups may form are developed. The process of closure in the formation of groups is particularly important because it serves to strengthen the cohesion or solidarity of the group and to support the formation of collective objectives. During the 1990s the closure process has been more pro-nounced for groups whose members are most intensively involved with the use of information and communication technologies and, specifically, for those who are involved in modifying and extending these technologies and their applications. This situation is not unusual. The technology is complex and a high level of mastery requires considerable arcane knowledge that must be acquired through enormous investment in time.[34]

The prolongation of the process of group formation and closure in the information

---

[34] Knowledge about information and communication technologies is unusually particularistic due to the enormous flexibility of the underlying technology which presents innumerable decision points in the design of any system or application. Although experience aids in 'anticipating' the range and variety of choices that a designer might have chosen from, there is no general or abstract 'model' by which a user may anticipate particularities. The consequence is that to achieve a high level of sophistication, the user must master innumerable particularistic details, a process that takes considerable time.

TABLE 2.2. *Status markers and differentiators for Internet users*

Physical Differentiators
- Bandwidth: more is better
- Specific types of connections and links: from hot-wired to dial-up; SLIP/PPP
- Types of platforms and servers: MIPS account for further gradations, as do the skills in manipulating these information interfaces
- Access Locations: large institutional settings are preferred due to their physical connectivity and local data and network resources
- Ownership of equipment: less important relative to leasing or accessing very advanced capabilities such as videoconference suites or boardroom multimedia capabilities

Information Service Differentiators
- Encrypted services: access to what is deemed secret conveys status
- Password protected services: access conveys inclusion but is being diluted by the variety of access modalities
- Extent of service functionality: the expectation that the user is someone who will fully and responsibly use the functionality
- Hard firewalls and functionality restrictions: define lower status and regulated use of resources as well as concerns about opportunism
- FreeNets and community Nets: convey relatively low status

Occupational Differentiators
- Application architects: the highest status within the programmer community
- Coders and programmers: moderate status within programmer community but may be viewed as knowledge workers by others with higher status within organizations
- Operators and technicians: lowest status within the technical community with exceptions for highly specialized capabilities (e.g. maintenance of globally distributed network systems)
- Symbolic workers: effective use of computers and/or networks is an essential part of job
- Information retrievers and modifiers: assist the symbolic workers
- Document formatters and viewers: lower in the hierarchy, female dominated
- No Internet connection at work: lowest status level

Skill Markers
- Codifiers and architects: top of hierarchy, produce proprietary value, gradations possible based upon the techniques employed
- Value-added producers: routine symbolic analysts at work
- Basic and more complex consumers: emphasis on downloading with gradations between novices and more sophisticated users
- The 'unconnected': lowest status level

Symbol Markers
- Domain name: type
- Domain name: ownership
- E-mail: addresses and aliases (some have extra cachet)
- Preferences: for an ISP and suppliers (such as browsers)

Subculture Markers
- Gurus and hackers: non-corporate, a defining subculture
- 'Flamers': individuals passionately involved with virtual communities
- Technophiles: early adopters and cyber-toy collectors

Source: Adapted from Neice (1998*a*).

society *is* a problem. Without group formation and at least the beginnings of the closure process, the user community is an amorphous construction that has little meaning other than to designate people who use information and communication technologies and services. Since virtually all people in industrialized countries use these technologies, including the telephone, the user community is practically indistinguishable from mass culture.[35] The interim position in this evolutionary process is that the more cohesive and closed communities of the highly sophisticated information and communication technology users, many of whom are involved in production, confront an undifferentiated and incoherent mass of general users. This is an unhealthy situation from the viewpoint of social inclusion. Absence of cohesion in the user community makes for ineffective, incoherent participation in the design and implementation of new applications and services. The result is an overemphasis on the initiative of the élite and their particular needs and interests that may become self-perpetuating.

Fortunately, there are some countervailing processes at work. A segment of the élite users has been charged with the responsibility of increasing the usability of information and communication technologies and they have had to devise means to test user response and incorporate this knowledge into design processes. Even more encouraging is the development of virtual communities of users defined by computer-mediated communication (see s. 2.5 for greater detail). Many virtual communities are defined by common interests that, with sufficient experience, are likely to congeal into coherent interest groupings that are capable of collective advocacy. The formation of virtual communities is, however, a prolonged process and it is not yet apparent that it has had a major impact on the effective exclusion of users from the design and implementation of new technologies and services. Thus, while substantial optimism is warranted for the long-term development of user involvement, the short- and medium-term is likely to be characterized by substantial user exclusion. Even in the longer term, the barriers to participating in virtual communities are likely to prevent a significant share of the members of society from effective inclusion in the design decisions shaping the information society. The next section reviews the evolution of policies to deal with this problem. Many of these policies focus largely upon extending the user base. Very little consideration is given to how the formation of coherent groups or communities within this expanding population might be encouraged. The remainder of the chapter reviews developments supporting the broadening use of the Internet, a network that appears to be the best platform for extending participation and inclusion yet devised. We also give more detailed consideration to the processes shaping virtual community formation.

---

[35] Defining the information and communication technology user community to include people who use telephones may seem a specious argument in the context of discussions of cyber culture and the information society. This is not the case, however, if we recognize that the telephone is increasingly the user interface to an ever more complex hierarchy of information processing services. Telephone access to automated messaging systems, pre-recorded messages, and voice menu systems may not be multimedia services but they are information services. These services will continue to evolve in parallel with others and are due for substantial augmentation as voice recognition techniques become more widely deployed.

2.4   Joining the Information Society

There is a widely held belief that the take-up of information and communication technologies will eventually assume the shape and penetration patterns of other technologies that have become ubiquitous.[36] Commentators point to the telephone or the
television as examples of technologies with near-universal penetration, at least in the
industrialized countries. However, the spread of the new digital technologies and services does not necessarily support the conclusion that mass use *per se* is consistent with
the effective development of the information society which is generally believed to
require more active user involvement. As we saw in the previous sections, there is a risk
that their use may be wedded to very specific social and economic characteristics and
aspirations.

2.4.1   *Conventional Approaches to Communication Access*

By the end of 1996 in Europe, *people*, with their concerns and expectations for the
European information society, had become a central focus in the European Commission's efforts to ensure that the emerging society will bring social and economic
benefits to all. The Commission's Rolling Action Plan was intended to put 'Europe
at the Forefront of the Global Information Society'.[37] One of the four priority areas
for action (including improving the business environment, education and training,
and global co-operation), was to take measures to put 'people first' in considering
the implications of the information society for citizens (European Commission,
1996*m*). The European Commission's 'Green Paper on Living and Working in the
Information Society: People First', stated explicitly that 'the benefits, in the form of
prosperity, and the costs, in the form of the burden of change, are unevenly distributed
between different parts of the Union and between citizens' (ibid. 1). The overriding
concerns were employment, democracy, and equality. It was clearly recognized that
advanced information and communication technologies and services will be at the
core of new social and economic developments. The interaction between producers
and users was expected to influence the development of new business models that
would lead to the provision of new services. While 'People First' reiterates several times
the need for affordable services, it does not explicitly deal with the issue of the availability of content. At about the same time, the Information Society Forum issued its
report 'Networks for People and their Communities' (European Commission, 1996*n*)
which *did* take up the issue of content availability. The Information Society Forum saw
the public sector's move into the information society as 'giving a valuable stimulus to
the creation of both content and software' (ibid. 17). In particular, the forum stated
that 'public access to basic electronic service (such as public information, education
and health) must be universal and affordable' (ibid. 12). The Information Society

---

[36] See Department of Trade and Industry (1996; 1997*a*; 1998*a*); European Commission High Level
Expert Group (1997); Industry Canada (1997); United States (1993).
[37] See European Commission (1996*h*; 1994*e*; 1996*b*).

Forum confronted the need for public-sector action squarely. It described the need for public-sector initiative and investment and for 'using public procurement to stimulate software production and new services, notably in the areas of education and training and provision of public information and services based on public data bases' (ibid. 29).

The definition of universal service and access, and the rights and expectations of consumers and citizens, are at the centre of the deliberations surrounding the development of a more 'user-focused' action plan for developing the European information society. As noted in both 'People First' and the Information Society Forum documents, without access to networks and to certain types of information, the European information society will mean very little to a great many people. Their exclusion could disrupt their capacity to participate effectively in European society.

The traditional universal service obligations that must be met by telecommunication service operators have been addressed by the European Commission and a minimum set of services that should be offered at affordable prices has been defined (European Commission, 1996e). However, the ability of European citizens to experiment and to learn about the potential benefits of advanced information and communication services continues to depend upon the creative use of policy, regulation, and the market to bring access to services and content closer to becoming a reality in the lives of many people.

The consensus on what people 'need' in the information society is changing. There is widespread support for the view that people do need access to the telephone service. Do they also need access to the Internet? Do they need access to electronic health services, libraries, museums, and interactive multimedia content? Do they need access to electronic bulletin boards to participate in the civic culture of their villages, cities, or countries? Some argue that there is a need for these services, but that their provision should be driven mainly by the market. Others have suggested that 'Citizens must have the possibility of enhanced participation in democratic structures as well as access to a wide variety of public information, entertainment, retail, education and health services. *These should be provided for all*' (European Commission, 1996o: 21, emphasis added). Arbitration of a new consensus on the needs that should be reflected in universal service and access provisions within and outside the traditional telecommunication regulatory framework is essential for shaping the way consumer and citizen rights and expectations of the European information society will be met.[38]

The European Commission's communication on universal service issued in 1996 began with the observation that 'to be able to communicate and interact whether by telephone, fax, e-mail or electronic media is a crucial and decisive factor for

---

[38] A widely circulated report on 'The Consumer in the Information Society' stressed the need for 'consumer empowerment' to ensure that informed choices about the selection of services in the information society can be made by consumers and citizens: Graham *et al.* (1996). The need for early involvement in the design and implementation of new services was stressed as was the need to ensure open access to networks and services. In Europe a growing number of organizations represent consumer interests in the provision and use of information and communication technologies and services.

every citizen and business' (European Commission, 1996e). The Commission recognized that universal service must be a dynamic and evolving concept and that the liberalization of Member State telecommunication markets would have implications for how the concept evolves. In 1999, the scope of the definition of universal service had not changed substantially, that is, the provision of voice telephony service via a fixed connection that also allows a fax and a modem to operate, as well as the provision of operator assistance, emergency and directory enquiry services, and public payphones. This definition does embrace Internet and on-line service access in so far as it ensures technical access to all services that can be provided over the telecommunication network. Nevertheless, the principal objective remains to ensure that a basic level of affordable voice telephony service is available throughout the European Union. Debates as to whether the scope of universal service or access targets should be modified continue.[39]

The focus of the debate from the telecommunication perspective on universal service is on access to networks and affordability. The elements that are commonly considered to be within the remit of the telecommunication regulator include issues about the legal status of universal service obligations expected of telecommunication operators, the services covered, the uniformity of price regardless of geographical location, the affordability of services, the deposit required for services, the availability of low-volume (telephony) user schemes and discounts for the disabled as well as the right of the operator to disconnect users for non-payment (Analysys Ltd., 1997b). Affordability of services is dealt with at the national level in Europe. Financing of any financial burden under the current definition is guided by principles for costing and arrangements for interconnection. The presumption is that access to networks will stimulate use of advanced information and communication technologies and services that have reached a substantial number of people under normal commercial conditions.

In the United States, the Telecommunications Act of 1996 produced an ongoing debate on the scope and delivery of universal telecommunication services. The definition of universal service enshrined in this legislation extended the concept to services for schools, healthcare institutions, and libraries.[40] Judgements about the affordability of services are left to the state jurisdiction creating the potential for uneven interpretations of the concept (Federal Communications Commission, 1996b) and there is ongoing debate about how revenues should be generated to support universal service objectives. In both Europe and the United States, Internet, software, and com-

---

[39] See e.g. Analysys Ltd. (1995b; 1997); Blackman (1995); Borrows, Bernt, and Lawton (1994); Hart (1998); Huart (1996); Milne (1990); OECD (1995; 1996b); Office of Telecommunications (1995a; 1995b); Peha (1999); Xavier (1997).

[40] Elementary and secondary schools and classrooms, health care providers, and libraries, should have access to advanced telecommunication services (Federal Communications Commission, 1996a). A USAC handles funding support for schools and libraries that qualify based upon judgements about their relative economic disadvantage. Funding mainly supports external connections although some funding is available for internal networks. In 1999, a cap of US$ 2.25b. was established for schools and libraries support and US$ 12m. for rural health care support, see Federal Communications Commission (1999c; 1998a; 1998b) which find that ISPs should not contribute to universal service funds. This viewpoint continues to be the subject of discussion. See Mansell (1998) for further analysis of this issue.

puting service providers have argued that they should not be subject to universal service charges. They claim that any such charges would damage the development of the Internet and risk distorting the development of the technology.

2.4.2 *Alternative Access Modes and Realities*

While the telecommunication-based understanding of universal service and access remains deeply embedded in European Commission documents, there are signs of a growing appreciation that new modes of networking such as the Internet may call for novel arrangements for access as well as innovative partnerships between public- and private-sector players. From 1996 onwards the numbers of such arrangements have been growing. For example, the British government's Green Paper on the Electronic Delivery of Government Services proposed mechanisms to improve the accessibility of public information as well as services for electronic vehicle licence renewal, skills training information, tax returns, benefit claims and the possibility of checking personal information. In late 1998, the government was calling for 25 per cent of government services to be accessible electronically by 2002 (Department of Trade and Industry, 1998b).

Telecities projects were being implemented in numerous cities throughout the European Union aimed at supporting local industrial and service sectors and citizens. Some observers claim, however, that these initiatives simply reinforce inequality, injustice, and conservatism by virtue of the fact that they are initiated and controlled by local, national, and/or regional élites (Eurocities, 1996; Treanor, 1996).[41] Internet enthusiasts often promote visions of enormous opportunity. However, change will need to be radical if it is to deliver the ubiquity of the information and communication infrastructure. One of the most important areas of change is in the roles played by individuals and organizations in facilitating access to networks and services and to relevant skills and training.

Gaining access to the new networks and services continues to require considerable technical expertise. Much of this expertise is embedded in organizations making extensive use of information and communication technologies, such as universities, government offices, and large enterprises. These organizations are able to fund the acquisition of the specialized skills and knowledge that are necessary for accessing the information and communication infrastructure. Some employees make an effort, with or without their organization's assistance, to extend their skills into their homes. Yet others independently develop enough expertise to be able to gain access to these services.

What will be involved in extending access more broadly outside the structure of large, information and communication technology-intensive organizations into other organizations? The answer to this question requires an understanding of the social and economic determinants of the evolution of the new networks and services. It requires detailed knowledge of the problems of user familiarization and skill acquisition that

---

[41] See Ch. 9 for discussion of the development of telecities in the context of regional development.

are prerequisites for broadening public access to the commercial and non-commercial uses of the new services.

Issues of user skills lead us directly to consider the challenge of 'deepening the value of access', which involves building the skills for using advanced information and communication technologies and services. To analyse this process of skills deepening we need to identify 'trajectories' of user familiarization and skills building that contribute to obtaining higher value from the use of the Internet over time. For some users, deepening will lead to more intense involvement and Internet use will substitute for other forms of information acquisition. For other users, the process of deepening value will represent more rapid and effective access to desired information or services during the limited time they spend in using this medium.

The Internet is an innovation both in interpersonal, that is point-to-point, communication and in broadcasting and publishing using point-to-multipoint communication. As a broadcast medium the Internet has the unique character that it can accumulate content from its users. It is the first medium with broadcast capabilities that is able to provide a tight 'feedback loop' between users and producers of information. This characteristic differentiates both the Internet and on-line services from existing media. By comparison, 'letters to the editor' or 'subscriber contributions' are features of print media while 'public access' television programmes are common in the United States and Canada. In both these cases, the user contribution is marginalized by problems inherent in the design and organization of the particular medium. In the case of the print medium, publication delays and hierarchical relationships between subscribers and editors, for example, letters *to* the editor, render contributions peripheral to the principal editorial content. In television, high production costs make it difficult for a public access channel to approach the state-of-the-art in production quality. All these problems are present in the case of the Internet and on-line services, but they are not yet as significant because of the newness of these services. Very low costs of access (low entry barriers) and the widespread availability of content creation tools mean that individuals with specialized interests or knowledge can compete with commercially financed content offerings. As a result, entirely new opportunities exist for individual expression, though it is not clear that institutional arrangements will favour radical 'democratization' of expression.

The growth of the Internet, which we examine in detail below, is making it possible for individuals with very specialized interests, for example, the preservation of Roman ceramics, to share knowledge and experience. As a communication and information publication method, the Internet is also able to serve commercial interests, for example, the sale of Roman ceramics; educational interests, for instance, the role of Roman ceramics in ancient commerce; and hobbies, such as the means for reproducing the glazes used in Roman ceramics.

We can identify three possible styles of access to the Internet (Geuna and Steinmueller, 1997). The first is organizational access. This is an arrangement in which the user is part of an information and communication technology-intensive institution that provides its members with a connection (generally through a local area network), a personalized set of services (ranging from basic electronic mail and file transfer to Intranet services) and technical support for the use of these services. Organizations have different policies concerning their members' use of Internet services and they are establishing and revising policies at a rapid pace. Most commonly, these policies restrict the individual's use of the Internet for non-work-related purposes. Enforcement of these policies requires monitoring of communication and may violate the basic principles of personal privacy.

Second, there is individual access whereby information services are accessed from the home through a connection with an Internet Service Provider or an on-line service offering Internet access. The services available depend on the type of service contract. Usually no training or in-depth support is available although, in some cases, there are 24-hour telephone helplines. Third, there is community access which allows information services to be accessed using a connection made available at public institutions, for example, libraries, city halls, museums, and Internet cafés. In the cases of both on-line services and public institutions, access to basic Internet services, for example, World Wide Web access, may be available as an adjunct to other information.

The costs of individual access are relatively high although commercial availability of information appliance-type approaches may reduce these costs in time. Another approach is a public access model in which information terminals are provided in schools and libraries along with the training and familiarization necessary to make use of such services. This approach was strongly endorsed in 1996 by the Information Society Forum (European Commission, 1996n: 16) which called for 'local access points at public libraries, schools and other community meeting places for people who cannot access from home'. It was noted that this would approximate universal access. An even stronger statement was made in the 1997 Annual Report when the Information Society Forum stated that the European Commission needed to take a 'clear approach' to universal and public access (European Commission, 1997g). If a public access model is to be deployed effectively it will require a new class of technical support providers so that both information suppliers and users can focus on services rather than on infrastructure technology. There are issues of culture and context that influence whether people are willing to interact with such devices in public places that also must be considered (Wessels, 1999).

A crucial distinction is that between access to the network and access to the service. Research has shown that the former does not guarantee access to information services (Computer Science and Telecommunications Board (CSTB), 1994). The former depends upon the development of the information and communication infrastructure and, in particular, on the development of the 'last mile technology', that is, the type and cost of a connection into a user's home or workplace. As the Information Society Forum concluded, 'popular demand for on-line services is unlikely to emerge unless they are affordable and respond to actual needs. Their potential benefits must also be better understood. It will take even longer if we maintain the present slow pace of installation of wide band networks whose technical "muscle" is needed for rapid, good quality transmission of sound, pictures and text' (European Commission, 1996n: 29).

Technological capabilities for high-capacity access must, however, be aligned with the *availability* of access to such an infrastructure. Availability will depend not only upon the terms and conditions of access markets, but also upon the willingness of potential users to invest in the skills needed to use the access opportunities that do emerge.

Taking these considerations into account when assessing the size of the Internet user community is very difficult. The number of hosts connected to the net, the most commonly used indicator, yields some insight into the trends of growth and diffusion of the system. This indicator has technical shortcomings, however. For example, a computer can be connected full- or part-time to the Internet, it can be used by more than one user, and it can be used for different purposes. None of these differences is represented in currently available statistics. In addition, the market for Internet access providers has developed in different ways between the European Union Member States. This has implications for the distribution of service provision and for the future use of the Internet. An assessment of Internet access issues must also take into account the representation of educational, research, cultural, medical, and public information within the Internet. Addressing these issues is the task of the following subsections.

2.4.3   Information and Communication Infrastructure

Currently, there are two main distribution systems with the potential to access the Internet. The first and most broadly diffused is the use of a telecommunication connection (telephone, Integrated Services Digital Networks (ISDN), or leased line) with a communication device, a modem or more specialized data communication device.[42] Regardless of the telecommunication connection method that is used, a personal computer is also required.[43] Although ordinary voice connections are capable theoretically of supporting 28.8 kbps, the reality is often that this speed is unattainable—how often is unknown. It is unknown even to the public telecommunication network operators until service complaints are received from users attempting to use this capacity.

In addition, the cost of the telecommunication infrastructure depends upon the distribution of service 'points of presence' which influence the costs of making a dial-up connection to establish modem communication. In Europe, metered calling raises the costs of access compared to the United States where non-metered local calls are the normal practice. If the service point of presence to the network is outside the local call area, connection to the Internet may become extremely expensive. This is often the case for rural areas, mountainous areas and, more generally, the less-favoured

---

[42] ISDN service is defined around a number of 64 kbps channels for data and a signalling channel. Basic rate ISDN has 2 data channels (allowing data communication at 128 kbps) while primary rate ISDN in Europe has 30 data channels. A leased line is a dedicated telecommunication link offering various levels of transmission speed (e.g. E1 is defined as 2.048 Mbps or 32 channels of basic rate ISDN, E2 is 8.448 Mbps or 4 E1 channels, E3 is 4 E2 channels, E4 is 4 E3 channels, and E5 is 4 E4 channels or 565.148 Mbps). See http://www.whatis.com/ under 'E1 through E5' Carriers and ISDN, last accessed 6 April 2000.

[43] For telephone access, there are technical issues with respect to line noise and reliability for which no comprehensive data are available.

European regions although the availability of local access tariffs for services mitigates this problem in some European countries.

The second of the main systems for gaining access to the Internet is based on the cable television system. The first issue here is the extent of existing development of the cable network. In the United States, cable television services have achieved penetration of 62 per cent of households with television (Computer Science and Telecommunications Board (CSTB), 1996). In the European Union, except for The Netherlands, Belgium, and Sweden, with respectively, 101, 106, and 57 per cent household penetration,[44] cable service is not as broadly diffused. This is both a problem and an opportunity. It is a problem because of the costs of establishing rights of way and construction and an opportunity because new systems may be built with advanced capabilities available from the outset or at less expense for future upgrades. In any case, the combination of low diffusion and the nascent state of development of the cable television networks to support advanced services means that this type of network is not well positioned at present to offer a substitute in many geographical areas for the telecommunication network (Geuna and Steinmueller, 1997).

Table 2.3 gives indicators for the availability of several components of the information and communication infrastructure in the Member States of Europe. A combination of telecommunication connections and personal computers is the main method used to access the Internet. The number of personal computers per 100 inhabitants may be used to quantify the information technology intensity of a country although no distinction between business and home is available. There has been a substantial increase in the number of personal computers per 100 inhabitants over time. Greece, Italy, Portugal, and Spain remain conspicuously below the median represented by Austria at 20.6 computers per 100.

A survey has been conducted over the past few years by INRA (International Research Associates) in the EuroBarometer project which allows data on the number of personal computers to be related to patterns of use.[45] Table 2.4 provides the basic data for examining the situation in 1998.

According to Table 2.4, the European average was that roughly one-quarter of home personal computers and about one-third of personal computers used in work were connected to the Internet in 1998. This share varies significantly between countries. Those countries with the highest level of personal computer use have a much higher share of connections. For example, in Sweden nearly two-thirds of personal computers used at home and in work are Internet connected with

---

[44] Higher than 100% penetration in Belgium and The Netherlands is the result of the division of total subscriptions (which include business and other institutional subscriptions) by the number of households with televisions. Finland, Germany, and Ireland also have significant (around 45%) penetration of cable television.

[45] The significance of the survey is augmented considerably by its large and statistically representative sample size of 15,900 respondents and by the fact that the interviews were conducted in people's homes in the national language of their country. The project is organized and managed by European Commission DGX for DGXIII, see INRA (International Research Associates) (1999) and http://www.ispo.cec.be/polls/Specs.htm accessed 6 April 2000 for further details.

Social Communities

T A B L E 2.3. *Indicators of the information and communication infrastructure*

	Households served by residential main lines 1996 (%)	Digital switched lines 1996–7 (%)	ISDN subscribers 1997 (000s)	Inhabitants with PCs 1997 (%)	Cable TV subscribers 1996 (000s)
Austria	n.a.	82.0	86	21.06	897
Belgium	85.0	73.1*	99	23.56	3,658
Denmark	>100.0	86.0	58	36.02	1,383
Finland	88.3	100.0	58	31.09	842
France	>100.0	96.0	599	17.44	1,477
Germany	n.a.	100.0	2,887	25.55	16,700
Greece	98.1	47.1	1	4.47	n.a.
Ireland	72.2	92.0	8	16.55	900
Italy	91.1	85.1*	335	11.30	n.a.
Netherlands	94.9	100.0	310	28.03	5,842
Portugal	90.5	88.3	45	7.44	171
Spain	94.7	80.8	86	12.21	425
Sweden	>100.0	96.0*	64	35.04	1,875
United Kingdom	96.0	92.6*	600	24.23	2,068

Note: n.a. = not available.

* 1996 figures.

Source: Compiled from International Telecommunication Union (1998; 1999).

home connection exceeding that of the personal computers used in work. At the other extreme, France, Portugal, and Spain have markedly lower rates of Internet connection. In the case of France, the significance of the legacy of the Minitel system may be responsible.[46]

Table 2.4 indicates that the propensity for Internet use, to some extent, may have sociocultural origins. In the case of Austria, Finland, and Spain, each has markedly higher rates of connection to the Internet for the use of work computers than for home use. While this may be explained by the costs of infrastructure access or quality problems in the case of Spain, this is not a likely explanation for Finland.[47] Sociocultural factors may also play a role in those countries with very similar rates of connection to the Internet for home and work use. These countries can be divided into two groups: those with a high level of personal computer use such as Luxembourg (home 14.0%,

[46] Home use is lower in France than all countries except Greece and Portugal while office use is comparable to Germany, the United Kingdom, and Italy. See Mansell and contributors (1988); Schneider *et al.* (1991) for an analysis of Minitel deployment. The low home use result for France suggests the need to examine policies for promoting access by French children to computers in the home.

[47] In the case of Spain, it is important to note that the share of computers used in work that are connected to the Internet is approximately equal to that of the United Kingdom. Far fewer individuals use personal computers in their work, however.

TABLE 2.4. *Patterns of use of personal computers, 1998*

Country	Location Home Work	PC (%)	CD-ROM connected to PC (%)	Internet connection to PC (%)	Modem or fax- modem connection to PC (%)
Austria	H	30.8	24.3	6.8	9.6
	W	49.2	42.4	24.8	29.8
Belgium	H	33.0	19.1	8.2	10.1
	W	47.9	25.5	15.9	20.4
Denmark	H	56.7	44.8	24.6	24.5
	W	62.2	40.6	33.0	34.9
Finland	H	38.6	27.3	17.2	17.7
	W	51.5	31.3	31.3	28.6
France	H	22.8	17.1	3.9	5.5
	W	39.1	18.9	8.9	16.7
Germany	H	30.5	22.9	7.1	10.2
	W	39.0	28.4	12.2	17.2
Greece	H	12.2	7.0	2.9	2.4
	W	20.7	9.9	5.0	5.3
Ireland	H	26.3	16.6	8.4	9.0
	W	30.6	20.4	12.7	16.3
Italy	H	26.6	16.8	6.1	7.0
	W	39.2	23.7	10.9	15.8
Luxembourg	H	42.5	34.5	14.0	15.0
	W	63.2	45.0	23.5	30.3
Netherlands	H	58.8	39.5	19.6	24.7
	W	71.2	42.6	30.7	39.8
Portugal	H	18.4	10.9	3.4	4.2
	W	22.7	9.7	5.1	8.2
Spain	H	28.4	17.9	5.0	4.6
	W	28.4	18.9	8.9	9.3
Sweden	H	59.8	49.5	39.6	34.3
	W	74.4	49.7	46.1	42.3
United	H	35.2	19.7	10.7	9.3
Kingdom	W	42.3	21.4	12.9	17.1
EU 15	H	30.8	20.8	8.3	9.3
	W	40.5	24.7	13.3	17.8

Source: INRA (1999: 10) for home use and http://www.ispo.cec.be/polls/EB98.htm for home and office use, accessed 15 September 1999.

work 23.5%), Sweden (home 39.6%, work 46.1%) and the United Kingdom (home 10.7%, 12.9%) and those with a relatively low level of use such as Greece (home 2.9%, work 5.0%) and Portugal (home 3.4%, work 5.1%). In these countries, it seems probable that those who use personal computers in their work are likely also to be users in the home. France and Italy also appear to follow this pattern which has implications for the accessibility of the Internet for family members.

Table 2.4 also shows that there is a very high potential for Internet growth. This is indicated by the number of personal computers that have compact disc-read only memories (CD-ROMs) connected to them. A CD-ROM connected to the personal computer means that the personal computer's 'vintage' is relatively young and that it will support the addition of Internet access capability at a relatively modest incremental cost. If all computers equipped with CD-ROMs were connected to the Internet, the number of Internet users in Europe would roughly double. If we consider only those computers that already have a modem there is a potential for a 50 per cent growth in the number of Internet users. The costs of connecting computers already equipped with a modem (except those few that are of older vintage) is the time that it requires to acquire and apply the knowledge. Software costs are negligible.[48]

A final observation with respect to Table 2.4 concerns the comparison between these data on personal computer use with the penetration of personal computers reported in Table 2.3. The data in Table 2.3 are based on the number of personal computers installed divided by the population, which yields the number of personal computers per 100 inhabitants statistics. The data in Table 2.4, in contrast, are based upon a statistically representative survey of Europeans who were asked about whether they use a particular technology in their home or work. For example, there were 21.06 computers per 100 inhabitants in Austria in 1997 according to the data in Table 2.3. When Austrians were asked in 1998 if they used a personal computer in their home or work, 30.8 per cent replied that they used a computer in their homes and 49.2 per cent of those replying about work use replied that they used a computer in their work.[49] At first glance, it might be concluded that these data sources are inconsistent. This would be true if there was one computer for each individual. However, if each computer is assumed to be shared, on average, by two users then the difference between these sources is reconciled. It is of interest that the extent of sharing of personal computers that can be inferred from these data is consistent across the countries.

2.4.4   Internet Use Patterns

The Internet is composed of a set of utilities that allows the transmission of data, images, video, and voice. The seven principal components are: File Transfer Protocol, Telnet, Netnews, e-mail, Gopher, and the World Wide Web. Until March 1995 when NSFNet discontinued its support for the backbone of the network, it was providing statistics on data sent over this network. The most common way to quantify the size of

[48] A small charge may be involved for modem driver software to establish an Internet Protocol connection and World Wide Web browsers are available for the cost of a computer magazine.

[49] There was a dramatic decline in the number of respondents who replied about their use of all types of technology in their work. This is not indicated as a problem in the interpretation of the data by INRA (1999) or in the technical description of the sample procedure at http://www.ispo.cec.be/polls/Specs.htm accessed 6 April 2000.

Internet is a count of 'hosts'.[50] This indicator does not give the exact size of the Internet and it does not allow an estimate of how many users are connected. It can, nevertheless, be used to highlight the dynamic trends in the system.

To estimate the extent of European presence on the Internet, the high-level domain name of known server addresses can be used. Although it is possible for European institutions to be classified with a top-level domain name such as *.com*, *.edu*, *.net*, and *.org*, we use the sum of these four domains plus the domains *.gov*, *.mil*, and *.us* as an estimate of the United States dimension.[51] The European dimension is given by the sum of the hosts with a top-level domain name of European nationality. A share of the domain names referring to European countries may be located outside Europe. This procedure is likely to produce a lower-bound estimate of European presence since the number of organizations designating their addresses in the *.com*, *.net*, or *.org* domains is likely to be far greater than the number of non-European organizations providing a European domain address.[52]

The growth of hosts seems to be declining over time in both Europe and the United States although this decline in the growth has been more pronounced in Europe (see Table 2.5). Even if the United States were to stop growing altogether, at the rate that Europe has been growing on its 1995 base (57% CAGR), it would take more than seven years for it to catch up with the United States. This rather low number is a measure of the modesty of Europe's performance over the past three-and-a-half years. If we take the much higher short-term growth rate as an annual rate (123%, or about equal to that of the 125% of the United States) and again assume the United States were to stop growing, it would catch up in less than two years. Put another way, at the current rate of growth, Europe will be where the United States is today in less than two years. Given that the European and the United States short-term growth rates are similar there is no foreseeable prospect for Europe to catch up with the United States in the level of hosts. In the category 'others', 80 per cent is comprised of Japan, Canada, and Australia, and these host domains have a faster rate of growth than either the United States or Europe.

The spread of the Internet in the European Union is characterized by strong national heterogeneity as shown in Table 2.6. On the one hand, the southern European countries, with less-developed information and communication infrastructures (Greece, Italy, Portugal, and Spain) have relatively low levels of Internet diffusion. They have experienced growth rates, however, that are higher than the European

---

[50] A host is a domain name that has an IP address record associated with it, that is, any computer system connected to the Internet, see http://www.isc.org/ds/rfc1296.txt accessed 6 April 2000. The combinations of name/IP address are managed by the DNS.

[51] Traditionally, most European organizations in all these classifications identify themselves by their country rather than by the functional purpose of their site. This is subject to change and, given the very large number of organizations, it will prove extremely difficult to determine nationality without devising new estimation techniques.

[52] Of course, multinational companies are among those that choose such designations. Many of these, however, should be regarded as European organizations given their investment and contribution to economic growth and job creation in the European market.

Social Communities

TABLE 2.5. *Number of hosts by top-level domain, 1994–1998*

Domain	Jan. 1994	Jan. 1995	Jan. 1996	Jan. 1998	July 1998
USA dominated	1,475,422	3,178,266	6,053,402	20,623,323	25,739,702
.com	567,686	1,316,966	2,430,954	8,201,511	10,301,570
.edu	605,402	1,133,502	1,793,491	3,944,967	4,464,216
.net	12,608	150,299	758,597	5,283,568	7,054,863
.gov	129,134	209,345	312,330	497,646	612,725
.org	50,544	154,578	265,327	519,862	644,971
.mil	103,507	175,961	258,791	1,099,186	1,359,153
.us	6,541	37,615	233,912	1,076,583	1,302,204
Europe	587,135	1,106,077	2,284,750	4,343,988	5,361,444
Other	154,443	567,657	1,133,848	1,076,098	1,265,371
TOTAL	2,217,000	4,852,000	9,472,000	26,043,409	32,366,517

Source: Figures adapted from Network Wizards, http://www.nw.com; RIPE NCC, http://www.ripe.net, both accessed 6 April 2000, and OECD (1999d: 86).

Union average. On the other hand, Sweden, Denmark, Finland, and The Netherlands have a high level of Internet penetration. For the first two countries the Internet phenomenon is part of the broader development of the information and communication infrastructure, while for the latter two the level of Internet diffusion is higher than might be expected from the level of development of their infrastructures. Particularly in the case of Finland, the high number of hosts per 100 personal computers may be the result of policy initiatives favouring the rapid growth of Internet usage in higher education and more generally throughout society.

Throughout Europe, the rate of growth in the spread of Internet access appears to be slowing. The slowdown is most pronounced in those countries that have achieved a relatively high level of Internet penetration with the exception of Ireland, Italy, Portugal, and Spain whose annual increase in the 1998–9 period falls well below their more rapid pattern of growth between 1995 and 1999. Nevertheless, with the exception of Portugal, these countries all experienced higher annual growth rates in the 1998–9 period than the European average. Among the countries with high Internet penetration, the growth rates during 1998–9 for Finland, Germany, and Sweden have been much slower than their long-term experience while Austria, France, Greece, The Netherlands, and the United Kingdom have come close to equalling their long-term rates of growth. Belgium is the only country where the single year growth rate from 1998 to 1999 exceeded its annual growth rate from 1995 to 1999. These patterns are to be expected in a process of growth that begins on a relatively small base. It is important to note that the slowing pace reinforces our earlier conclusion that Europe will catch up to the level of Internet use presently experienced in the United States in about two years. There is, however, no indication at the individual country level that this gap will be closed.

TABLE 2.6. *Number, growth, and intensity of Internet hosts, 1994–1999*

Country	Jan. 1994	Jan. 1995	Jan. 1996	Jan. 1997	Jan. 1998	Jan. 1999	CAGR 1994–9	Annual Change 1998–9	Hosts per 100 PCs 1997
Austria	16,274	30,157	59,595	99,354	133,811	206,767	66.3	54.5	7.87
Belgium	8,459	20,885	38,206	77,858	137,557	264,427	99.1	92.2	5.73
Denmark	11,131	25,335	65,739	132,339	230,912	396,789	104.4	71.8	12.15
Finland	33,878	70,244	220,046	321,464	504,411	573,568	76.1	13.7	31.53
France	62,042	104,050	196,504	313,332	538,788	908,782	71.1	68.7	5.28
Germany	124,011	229,825	542,239	806,328	1,407,274	1,906,119	72.7	35.4	6.70
Greece	1,952	4,070	9,111	18,784	33,048	60,736	98.9	83.8	7.03
Ireland	2,886	6,912	16,559	32,164	52,529	79,002	93.8	50.4	8.75
Italy	21,077	40,330	101,580	192,071	360,520	578,794	94.0	60.5	5.55
Luxembourg	427	838	2,608	4,746	7,695	12,334	95.9	60.3	n.a.
Netherlands	48,796	98,554	199,396	317,115	503,235	814,155	75.6	61.8	11.44
Portugal	3,819	5,771	13,347	26,132	48,817	68,827	78.3	41.0	6.60
Spain	19,386	40,669	80,139	161,606	312,675	488,948	90.7	56.4	6.51
Sweden	46,911	89,037	177,651	293,165	481,596	638,271	68.6	32.5	15.54
United Kingdom	127,090	266,573	528,475	868,951	1,347,322	2,025,824	74.0	50.4	9.42
European Union Total	528,139	1,033,250	2,251,195	3,665,409	6,100,190	9,023,343	76.6	47.9	8.26

Note: Estimates vary considerably between sources and should be treated with caution.

Source: Adapted from International Telecommunication Union (1999).

The extent and rate of growth of computer servers supporting the Internet in the European market strongly suggests that the Internet is likely to become as pervasive in the European market as it is in the United States. In Europe, the growth of Internet access is, nevertheless, marked by significant regional disparities and distinctly different rates of development. The leadership of some countries (for example, Finland and Sweden) appears to be related to proactive government policy as well as, in the case of Sweden, to a distinct interest in the use of the Internet at home. Relatively high growth rates in other countries (the United Kingdom and Germany) seem to be more related to the level of user interest although the availability of relatively low local telecommunication usage charges in the case of the United Kingdom and the spread of ISDN in Germany may also play a role. The potential for a particular configuration of personal computer ownership (in business rather than in homes) and the existence of competing information providers, for example, the Minitel system in France, may explain the slower rate of Internet diffusion in several European countries.

2.4.4.1   Internet Service Providers

During the early period of Internet diffusion there were three clearly distinguishable categories of Internet providers: Internet Access Providers (IAPs), Internet Service Providers (ISPs), and On-line Service Providers (OSPs). The first specialized in selling an Internet Protocol (IP) connection, while the second sold access plus basic services. OSPs, such as CompuServe and the British company On-line, began from a position of offering their own user interface and a range of specialized services such as access to on-line databases, chat lines for simultaneous user interaction, electronic magazines, and various kinds of user forums. With the rapid growth of the Internet, all the major OSPs have added Internet access as a feature of their service and differences between the first two categories of provider have largely disappeared as IAPs have begun to offer additional content and services. Although the distinction between ISPs and OSPs is blurring, there remain distinctions in the user interface, service bundles, and identification of the two types of service. OSPs retain a distinct sense of identity and provide a 'home base' from which users venture into the larger and more chaotically organized Internet and tend to charge for this service by metering the connection time of users. ISPs generally take their subscribers' interests to be focused on the Internet, and try to augment or enhance the use of the Internet rather than to offer substitutes or a 'sheltered' environment for the user.

No consistent data on ISPs are available. In the World Wide Web, different sites offer lists of ISPs but none is sufficiently comprehensive to serve as a census for the purpose of cross-country analysis.[53] In Europe, local Internet Registries are operated by ISPs that offer Internet Protocol (IP) registration services to their customers. Major ISPs receive IP address identification directly from the Regional Internet Registry for Europe (RIPE) Network Co-ordination Centre rather than from an upstream

---

[53] The site http://thelist.internet.com/ accessed 15 September 1999 claims to provide listings for 7,800 service providers throughout the world as of Sept. 1999.

provider.[54] ISPs that register directly with RIPE become the local Internet Registries. Thus, it is possible to assume that all important ISPs operating in a country are local Internet Registries as well. An analysis of registrations at the Internet Registries conducted in 1997 found patterns similar to those exhibited in the growth in the number of hosts by country (Geuna and Steinmueller, 1997). In addition, it found that in some of the countries with the highest level of Internet use, the Finnish, Swedish, Dutch and, to a lesser extent, Danish markets, Internet access tended to be more concentrated than in the markets of the other member states.

2.4.4.2 *Educational, Research, and Cultural Aspects of the World Wide Web*

The 'public' part of the Internet is recognized as an area where the implications of access policies are very important.[55] Education, research, cultural, medical, and public information form the 'public' part of the Internet, and we focus in our analysis on sites that offer educational, research, and cultural information. The presence of sites accessible through Telnet, Gopher, or the World Wide Web indicates the availability of information for potential users. It also indicates the existence of a physical location where it is possible to access the Internet and where, in some cases, technical support may be available for Internet use. The World Wide Web has played a dominant role in recent Internet developments. We assess the participation of libraries, schools, Higher Education Institutions (HEIs), and museums with web sites as an indicator of the level of potential for public access to the Internet that was available when this analysis was undertaken in 1996.

Three different types of access are available for libraries. A user can access the library catalogue via the Telnet section, Gopher service, or World Wide Web. Usually, the access method for a library is the service offered by the library to connect with other institutions. For example, if the library makes its catalogue available using Telnet, it is also likely to have Telnet services for accessing other libraries, but is less likely to have a web presence, or to have only a very limited web connection. In other words, the pre-existence of electronic library catalogues is a barrier to the growth of web-based library services since a 'good enough' solution exists for many users, the costs of changing the interface are substantial, and the change would make obsolete many existing user skills.[56]

---

[54] The network co-ordination centre for Europe and adjacent areas is RIPE, http://www.ripe.net/; the western hemisphere is co-ordinated by ARIN, http://www.arin.net/, the successor to InterNIC, http://www.internic.net/, and the Asia Pacific region is co-ordinated by APNIC, http://www.apnic.net/ all accessed 6 April 2000.

[55] Due to the fast growth of the web and the difficulty of identifying new servers the figures given here should be considered as an indication of the possible dimension only and not as definitive values.

[56] In principle, little substantive difference in the user interface and search methods would be necessary to implement a web version of many library systems. In practice, however, many of these systems are of proprietary design and were sold to libraries as 'turn-key' systems with upgrading and maintenance performed by the original supplier. Restructuring the databases and reintegrating the database with web server software is a non-trivial system design task in which some delay is to be expected. The issue of access rights is of minor significance as the addition of password protection to a web site is an easy task assuming that user response for searches is already part of the system.

According to UNESCO, there were 27,000 libraries with 41,000 service points in the European Union in the 1990–2 period.[57] Of these, only about 300 had some kind of connection to the Internet in July 1996,[58] of which more than two-thirds were university libraries.[59] With respect to public libraries, four countries, Finland, The Netherlands, Sweden, and the United Kingdom, with respectively, 20, 16, 14, and 28 institutions, accounted for about 80 per cent of the public libraries on the web. Less favoured regions, and, in general, the southern European countries, showed a very low penetration of the Internet into the public library system.

The main and most reliable source of information on the diffusion of the web in schools, both elementary and secondary, is the International World Wide Web School Registry.[60] In August 1996 there were about 4,600 schools with a web site. Of these, 3,350 were located in the United States and 403 in the European Union.[61] As of September 1999 there were 11,003 schools in Europe and the United States with web sites listed in the Registry. Europe accounted for 1,990 of these while the United States had 9,013. The compound annual rates of growth over this three-year period are 39 per cent for the United States and 70 per cent for Europe. If Europe were to reproduce the last three years of its growth experience over the next three years, it would have approximately the same number of schools connected to the World Wide Web as the United States has at present. Even with this almost fourfold increase, only about 2.5 per cent of all European primary and secondary schools would have a World Wide Web address. The current level of European Union connection is only 22 per cent of that of the United States, which has achieved the connection of 9,000 schools.[62] There are, however, important differences between countries. For example, when we considered the number of web sites per 1,000 schools (see Table 2.7), Denmark, Finland, The Netherlands, and Ireland had a comparatively high number of schools with web sites, while France, Spain, Greece, Portugal, Italy, and Germany had a relatively low number.

In the European Union, the definition of Higher Education Institutions (HEIs) is inconsistent across the Member States. To define a benchmark for the analysis of the HEIs with World Wide Web sites, we start from the institutions listed in the *International Handbook of Universities*. This estimate suggests a lower bound of the number

---

[57] In the count of libraries, national, non-specialized, public, and higher education libraries are included. For Italy and Ireland, data were available only for the administrative units, the actual number of service points, therefore, is higher, see United Nations Educational Scientific and Cultural Organization (1994).

[58] The sources of this and the following figures are lists and directories available on the web. Particularly useful are: http://sjcpl.lib.in.us/homepage/ and http://sunsite.berkeley.edu/Libweb/europe.html both accessed 6 April 2000.

[59] For libraries with an Internet presence see Cattaneo *et al.* (1996: 52).

[60] This resource is organized and maintained by the University of Minnesota College of Education and Human Development, Office of Information Technology and Center for Applied Research and Educational Improvement at the site http://web66.coled.umn.edu/ accessed 6 April 2000.

[61] In the European Union, there were about 370,000 schools, therefore the schools with a web site accounted for about 0.1% of the total population.

[62] Projects such as Tele-School Online in the UK, Digischool in The Netherlands, and the international Web for Schools have been stimulating schools to become connected to the Internet.

TABLE 2.7. *European primary and secondary schools on the World Wide Web*

Country	Schools with web sites 1996	Total schools 1996	Web sites 1996 (per 1,000 schools)	Schools with web sites 1999	Web sites 1999 (per 1,000 schools)[1]
Austria	17	n.a.	n.a.	77	n.a.
Belgium	18	6,000	2.8	87	14.50
Denmark	24	3,300	7.3	135	40.91
Finland	25	5,400	4.6	66	12.22
France	9	74,200	0.12	140	1.89
Germany	70	89,700	0.78	322	3.59
Greece[2]	5	16,800	0.29	37	2.20
Ireland	16	4,100	3.9	91	22.20
Italy	25	67,600	0.36	122	1.80
Luxembourg	n.a.	n.a.	n.a.	13	n.a.
Netherlands	48	10,400	4.6	230	22.12
Portugal	5	14,000	0.35	31	2.21
Spain[2]	6	39,800	0.15	69	1.73
Sweden	61	n.a.	n.a.	212	n.a.
United Kingdom	74	33,168	2.2	358	10.79
TOTAL	403	364,468	1.11	1,990	5.46

Note: n.a. = not available.

[1] These figures are based on the number of schools in 1996.
[2] Corrections for Greece and Spain, http://wfs.vub.ac.be accessed 17 July 1997 discontinued by 6 April 2000; and National Statistical Yearbooks.

Source: Geuna and Steinmueller (1997) and http://web66.coled.umn.edu/ accessed 6 April 2000.

of HEIs in the European Union.[63] In the 1990–2 period there were about 1,500 HEIs, of which 30 per cent were universities. Analysis of a comparable list of colleges and universities with a web page indicated that in July 1996 about 580 had an active web site, and universities comprised the majority of these institutions.[64] Nearly all universities in Europe had a web site at this time, while only some of the equivalent institutions had one. When we analysed the institutions with a web site relative to the total, Finland, Sweden, The Netherlands, and Austria had a very high number of sites. The other countries had lower shares, but none could be characterized as being excluded from this development. However, if we had included all institutions offering tertiary-level programmes, the situation would have been much less positive.

[63] Some university directories include all post-secondary institutions, both universities and small organizations granting specialized degrees, as HEIs. In some Member States the definition of 'university' includes all universities and other education institutions that are equivalent to a university while omitting some of the smaller or more specialized institutions categorized as HEIs in other listings.

[64] See list compiled by Christine DeMello, http://www.mit.edu:800/people/cdemello/univ.html accessed 6 April 2000.

Another aspect of the Internet is its capacity to provide access to content that is of cultural significance to potential Internet users across Europe. Searching the web using the term 'culture' produces a list of sites with content ranging from classic art to the new cyber-arts, from classical to avant-garde music, and literature in antiquity to modern poetry. Our interest was in the presence of public places where citizens can access and learn how to use, or at least to become familiar with, the Internet. We focused, therefore, on the presence of museums offering a web site. There were about 9,000 museums in the European Union in 1996 (United Nations Educational Scientific and Cultural Organization, 1997) of which about 200 had an active web site. This number had increased to 280 by 1999 according to a directory maintained by World Wide Arts Resources.[65] Thus, about 2 per cent of European museums appear to have World Wide Web connections. Comparing the individual country museums with web sites with the total number of museums, France, Germany, Italy, and the United Kingdom have the highest share. Of the other countries, only Sweden (with 21 in 1999) had more than 15 museums listed in the World Wide Arts Council directory.

Three conclusions can be drawn from this analysis. First, in all the European Union Member States the education and cultural domains of the Internet, measured in term of libraries, schools, institutions of higher education, and museums with web sites, are relatively poorly represented as compared with equivalent developments in the United States. This was true at the time of the original analysis in 1996 and remains true in 1999. The comparatively rapid growth of European primary and secondary schools with Internet addresses since the 1996 analysis is an encouraging development, but there continues to be considerable potential for further growth.

Second, within this general profile, there are strong regional variations. Cultural institutions in France, Germany, Italy, and the United Kingdom have overtaken the initial leadership of Sweden, The Netherlands, and Finland in the number of web-connected museums. Sweden and The Netherlands, however, have continued to have a very high participation in the number of schools connected in proportion to the population, ranking third and fourth behind the leaders, the United Kingdom and Germany. The United Kingdom, in particular, has made the connection of schools a national priority. In a partnership with the private sector and with investment of £1b., the Prime Minister, Tony Blair, announced that 'virtually all secondary schools are now connected to the Internet' (Blair, 1999). France, Denmark, and Italy, the next three in the ranked list, are the only other countries with more than 100 schools connected to the Internet in 1999. Greece, Portugal, and Spain were at the lower end of the distribution of participation on both measures. Universities generally have achieved a similar pattern of connection with their counterparts in the United States while other European HEIs appear to be lagging behind.

Third, with respect to all these measures there is substantial room for expansion. Connecting as many schools as are currently listed in the United States as having

---

[65] The count of the number of museums was taken from http://www.wwar.com/museums.html 12 July 1996, and for the increased number noted in the text, 19 Sept. 1999. At this latter date the number had increased to 280. In 1999, the United States had 945 museums with Internet addresses.

Internet addresses would mean that only 2.5 per cent of all European primary and secondary schools had an Internet connection. Doubling the number of museums connected would increase the share of European museums with an Internet address to 4 per cent. These levels are attainable. The current low levels are an indicator that there are substantial issues yet to be dealt with by policy-makers and the business community not only in terms of the cost structure of Internet access but also with respect to the skills and interests of Europeans in participating in the World Wide Web environment.

2.4.5   Internet Access Cost Structure

Increases in Internet access are related to three main factors that influence the structure of demand. First, the variations in the level of development of the available information and communication infrastructure and the costs of upgrading it are related to the number of potential users of various levels of Internet service.[66] Second, the skills available, including computer or network literacy, facility in using computer interfaces, and the level of support provided, influence the number of interested consumers or citizens. Third, the costs of obtaining Internet access including skills acquisition and individual, or in some cases organizational, perceptions of the value of access, influence the number of people who will become users. It is inappropriate to estimate demand in this market in terms of 'fixed' preferences because changing skills and knowledge sets have marked implications for user preferences and, at the margin, are probably more influential than the price of access in influencing demand.

   Opportunities for skills and knowledge development are closely related to the type of access that individuals may be expected to have, that is, organizational, individual, or community as we described in s. 2.4.2. Each of these types of access has a distinct 'style' for acquiring knowledge and skills.

2.4.5.1   Organizational Access
The typical Internet connection used by a large organization is based on a leased line, usually a line operating at 2.048 Mbps, and a Local Area Network (LAN) that links terminals and personal computers distributed throughout the institution.[67] The management of the system, the supply of services, and the technical and training support generally are run by a specialized department or team within the institution which may, in turn, outsource parts of its responsibility to contractors. Internet access costs are composed of: (1) the subscription to the service provider, (2) the rent of the leased line, (3) a fraction of the infrastructure costs for the LAN, personal computers, etc., and (4) a fraction of the management and training costs such as the costs of the specialized department or team or the costs of outsourcing these functions. The final user, the employee, is unlikely to bear any of these costs directly but may have to comply

---

[66] Infrastructure here includes home personal computers, digital plant, ISDN connections, and FTTH, HFCC, FTTC facilities, etc.

[67] See Ch. 3 for an extensive discussion of the role of LANs as a 'driver' of network development.

with restrictions on use. In some cases, employees will invest independently in up-grading their skills to secure a better position or to improve their performance. In any organization, the costs of providing Internet access including skills and knowledge development are substitutes for other investments and, in particular, the use of personnel who are sufficiently knowledgeable about information and communication technologies to provide Internet access is a substitute for using these individuals to perform other functions in the company.

In larger organizations there is a trend towards providing services to business units based on the provision of budgets that can be deployed across different types of service inputs. In the allocation of these budgets, 'free-rider' problems often emerge. A business unit might, for example, refuse to allocate a portion of its budget for certain types of services in the belief that others will make such a contribution. The result can be a systematic reduction in the number of common resources available in the organization. This trend may be strengthened by efforts to downsize organizations. In such cases, common services are often disassembled because support for them is diffuse relative to other services that have strong 'local' support. The result is often a patchwork of services, including those using information and communication technologies, with little connecting or supporting activity, a situation that reduces the overall quality of service within the organization.

In the case of the Internet, however, a new and important development is emerging from the growing need for organizations to create, maintain, and distribute information in electronic formats. The growth of the Internet has induced substantial investment in the creation of new software including browsers, content creation tools, and specialized tools for accessing audiovisual information. The result is a portfolio of 'off the shelf' solutions to the problems of networked information management within the business enterprise. The growth of Intranets, that is, private networks using tools and techniques similar to those used on the public Internet, has been very rapid.[68] With this growth has come an increased familiarity with the tools and methods of Internet use and a growing potential for spill-over to the use of the public Internet. Since private networks very often operate at higher speeds than many of the links on the public Internet, Intranet growth tends to create a 'bottom up' demand for better performance on the public network. These developments are reasonably robust. They seem to counteract downsizing efforts as well as free-rider problems because of the benefits that can be derived from consolidation of enterprise information in a single, easily accessible format and the potential for decentralization of content creation and maintenance.

As the result of these developments, large organizations may be expected to make a significant contribution to the development of Internet-related skills and knowledge over time, even though such organizations are making major structural changes in their other data-processing activities. From a social viewpoint, this contribution to a common pool of skills for using the Internet is valuable, but it raises

---

[68] See Chs. 3 and 5 for discussions of the roles of Intranet and Extranet systems in supporting demand and network development.

questions about growing imbalances in the acquisition of these skills in the wider community.

2.4.5.2   *Individual Access*

Both home and small enterprise use of the Internet via dial-up access involves telephone, ISDN, and other forms of connections supplied by telecommunication operators. These connect the user to an Internet or on-line service provider offering access to the Internet and to other services depending on the type of contract. Internet access costs in this case are composed of: (1) a subscription to the service provider (that may be 'free'); (2) the usage costs for the public telecommunication network connection; (3) a fraction of the hardware costs, usually for a personal computer; and (4) skill acquisition and support costs. Subscription and telecommunication costs vary considerably between countries and where infrastructure competition exists, charges are about one-third of those in countries with a low level of competition (OECD, 1996*a*).

An often forgotten, but extremely important, component of the cost structure facing the individual user is the personal investment he or she has to make to learn how to use the system. Compared with the use of such artefacts as the telephone or television, using the Internet is very complicated. These costs differ in relation to the age and education of the user and they depend on the availability of a support structure. The existence of an education system that familiarizes students with the new technologies would be expected to reduce the incremental costs that must be paid to achieve access to the Internet.

2.4.5.3   *Community Access*

The cost structure of community access is similar to that for individual access, but the various components have different weights. Only the larger public schools and libraries generally are in a position to consider the use of a leased line as a means of acquiring service. The clearly identifiable costs of telecommunication access make a 'piece by piece' upgrading of public access to the Internet difficult for many institutions. The school, library, or museum of average size is likely to access on-line services using a voice telephone link or an ISDN connection and store its web content on a server maintained by an ISP that is continuously connected to the Internet. Since schools and libraries have the highest use of communication networks during the peak daytime hours, the usage costs of connections represent an extremely important element in the cost structure.

One approach to reducing imbalances and disparities in Internet access across Europe would be to promote access to public Internet services as a criterion for the goal of universal access. The costs of achieving this goal would be substantial and there are three major categories of cost that would need consideration. The first is the cost of equipment, which could decline dramatically with the development of personal computers dedicated to Internet use. The second cost component is telecommunication access, which would be significantly reduced by establishing lower prices for public ISDN connections, or by a major shift in Europe towards the introduction of non-metered prices for local usage of the telephone network for education and cultural institutions. The third cost component is the development of skills and knowledge. Including this component as part of basic education would reduce private training costs and also create substantial spill-overs as employers would find it easier to hire people with basic computer skills.

Specific cost estimates for achieving access as well as debates on the merits of this goal from a social viewpoint are needed. These must encompass assessments of the potential of the Internet for improving the social, cultural, quality of life, and wealth-creating implications of a growing capability to use the new communication medium of the Internet. This section has examined and quantified the issues involved in joining the information society. We have measured the extent to which Europeans and their institutions are taking steps to gain access to the information and communication infrastructure. Taking this assessment further to chart the costs and value of accelerating the pace of educational, social, and cultural access to Internet resources is, in our view, an urgent priority. Any such examination should also include a qualitative and quantitative examination of emerging features of virtual community formation in Europe and internationally.

2.5   Virtual Community Formation

The development of the information society involves experimentation and implementation of new technologies and services across a broad frontier. The term 'virtual communities' encompasses the social and interactive processes that occur when people utilize computer-mediated communication. Computer-mediated communication is any person-to-person communication that employs computer *and* telecommunication technologies. This is a broader definition than that adopted in some sociological studies. For example, Overby (1996) introduces ideas about distance and content to further limit the definition. It is a narrower definition than that adopted by some contributors to the communication studies literature where human–computer interaction is conceived as a form of communication (Strate, Jacobson, and Gibson, 1996a; 1996b). The word 'community' is intended to encompass a much broader variety of meanings than the formation of networks of friends as suggested by Rheingold (1993: 1).

My seven-year old daughter knows that her father congregates with a family of invisible friends who seem to gather in his computer. Sometimes he talks to them, even if nobody else can see them. And she knows that these invisible friends sometimes show up in the flesh, materialising from the next block or from the other side of the planet.

It includes, for example, the entire gamut of social interchange that may arise from interpersonal interactions in electronic commerce, in education, and in scientific research. Computer-mediated communication, therefore, involves a very wide variety of motives and rationales beyond the formation of new friendships.

The members of virtual communities employ certain technologies that support their social functions and ignore others. As a means of accelerating the adoption of new technologies, virtual communities, therefore, may serve either as a catalyst or as a retardant. Virtual communities rarely spring to life fully formed and mature and someone must bear the costs of their development. There is a substantial role for risk capital and venturing in new profit-making opportunities where the potential is not fully developed. The problem in the case of virtual communities is that much of their value stems from the voluntary contributions of their members, contributions that ultimately may become an asset that is owned by someone else. If an economic return is to be earned from an information asset, it is necessary to impose a charge for access. This creates a paradox in which those people who volunteer to aid a virtual community's development with the expectation of sharing in the gains from their efforts, may later have to pay for their own contributions.

The difficulties that arise from financing the establishment and supporting the early growth of virtual communities suggest a role for public investment. The justification for this role is greatest when it involves traditional public or not-for-profit activities in the early stages of accumulating skills and building the value of the virtual community. A second criterion for public investment is that a major share of the value of the virtual community be generated by the use of information created or maintained at public expense by local, regional, or national governments. Public investment may be justified when private investment would provide incentives to allocate the provision or use of information according to an ability to pay *and* where a public policy decision is taken that such allocations would interfere with public value.

For example, a local government authority might choose to provide tourist information in competition with the growing array of private companies offering such information on the basis that its listings are more representative of the community's cultural values or inclusive of its citizens. Such a choice might be taken even if private investors promised similar levels of representation and inclusion. The choice to spend public resources in this way ultimately is an issue over which voters can take their own decisions. Public investment may also be justified in supporting the growth of specialized communities of interest that otherwise would have difficulty mobilizing the resources to gain the skills needed to establish themselves and to support their early growth.

It is important to examine the pattern of evolution of needs for technological capabilities in various types of virtual communities and to assess the congruence between these needs and available or potential technologies and services. The demand for technologies and services by virtual communities is an evolutionary and adaptive process. Many healthy virtual communities have been built with extraordinarily primitive technological tools.[69] These same communities, however, were highly specialized to

---

[69] One example is the Usenet bulletin board system, which allows users to subscribe to particular areas of interest and to read and post simple text messages. The Usenet system was designed by two graduate students at Duke University and one at University of North Carolina in 1979 who distributed the code in the public domain through Usenix (a UNIX user's group) (Rheingold, 1993: 117). The University of North Carolina, at the time, was not connected to the Internet. The three students devised a way to create the world's largest computer conferencing system even though they could not achieve person-to-person e-mail connection outside their own campuses!

individuals who were willing to engage in computer-mediated communication despite its severe technical limitations.

Other virtual communities are based upon common interests that involve very high technological and service requirements. Examples include the research and medical communities where the need to transfer and display vast amounts of data provides an important impetus to new technology and service development.[70] The potential for electronically mediated interpersonal communication for encouraging the evolution of virtual communities can be assessed by examining how computer-mediated communication has been evolving within relatively stable communities of users.

2.5.1   The E-Mail Legacy

Computer-mediated communication emerged as an early feature of computer networks and has played an important role in their evolution. Largely due to inter-operability considerations, this form of communication began with real-time and time-delayed text messaging features. The latter capability required the development of a means for reviewing, printing, and replying to such messages that are collectively called electronic mail, or e-mail. Throughout the history of e-mail services, a persistent problem has been determining the 'address' for a potential recipient. Despite substantial efforts at standardization of address formats and directories, address conventions remain relatively unfriendly for the novice computer user.

The development of e-mail was influenced by the continuing division between its use on local computer systems and its use as a general communication method. For example, as of September 1997, Inteco estimated that e-mail was used by 5m. people in the United Kingdom with 3.9m. able to send information outside their companies (Steinmueller, 1998). This means that almost 40 per cent of e-mail users used e-mail only within their own companies. Access is growing for these intracorporate users and a new wave of internal users is expected from the continuing development of Intranets.

E-mail systems are closely related to a very basic characteristic of modern computers, the capability to transfer information files. As e-mail expands to involve more diverse capabilities than text messaging and a higher degree of global connectivity, it raises significant problems of confidentiality, appropriate use policies, and security. For example, the extension of e-mail to include word-processing file attachments is a major mechanism for the transfer of computer viruses. Attachments that incorporate executable code further increase the risk of harm and are a significant barrier to achieving universal e-mail connectivity.

Particularly within established user communities, e-mail using both text messaging and file attachments has established a foundation for computer-supported co-operative work involving the transfer of word-processing, graphics data, and presen-

---

[70] e.g. the EMERALD project in the Commission's ACTS programme involved the use of 34 Mbps data links connecting sites in Paris, Cologne, Milan, Barcelona, and Madrid for medical imaging exchanges (European Commission, 1997f: 96–7).

tation files within and across organizations. Based upon projections by the Electronic Messaging Association, the 3.9m. British users who were able to send e-mail across companies accounted for some 280m. messages annually.[71] Within high e-mail activity communities, individual users may receive upwards of 50 messages *per day* or over 18,000 per year. A population of 10m. active e-mail users might therefore receive 180,000m. messages annually. Such estimates indicate the potential severity of information overload. A single user might devote 150 hours annually or one work-month per year to e-mail management if she or he is successful in spending an average of 30 seconds on each e-mail received. For this level of effort to be justified, a high level of productivity must be achieved in the use of e-mail.

The potential contribution of e-mail to the problem of information overload suggests that the means for managing information flows will have to be improved substantially in the coming years.[72] Within virtual communities, the World Wide Web is increasingly used as a means to constrain the growth of message traffic. By providing information updates and current information it is possible to avoid notifying the community participant of every news item that might be of interest.

Although the information overload problem is growing, e-mail remains an important mode of information distribution. A significant source of e-mail growth is the formation of list-servers and mailing lists by which a single e-mail information is distributed to multiple users.[73] Mailing lists and list servers account for the discrepancy between the number of e-mails that an individual can reasonably be expected to compose over a given time and the much larger number that he or she will receive.

Although e-mail is a medium that contributes to problems of information overload and absorbs significant amounts of user time and attention, it also is a medium for the rapid, personalized, and specialized transmission of messages and work-in-progress to connected users. The use and volume of e-mail traffic is likely to continue to expand. Significant modifications to the use of e-mail can be expected over time involving the means employed by users to organize the 'filtering' of information messages and the management of attachments, including the wider use of file transfers to encompass other forms of data such as video messaging. As a medium for establishing virtual communities, e-mail has distinct limitations due to the information overload problem. As a result, e-mail is likely to remain a complementary tool in virtual

---

[71] For Electronic Messaging Association results, see http://www.nua.ie accessed 10 September 1999, in their technical features index under e-mail which indicates a projected use rate of 70 messages per year per user (the distribution of use is of course likely to be highly skewed). Applying this projection to the number of UK users results in the estimate.

[72] The issue of information overload has received considerable attention in the business and academic literature, see Strassmann (1985).

[73] A list server is an automatic system for distributing e-mail messages on a one-time basis or at periodic intervals. Users address an e-mail with a specified string in either the message header or body indicating their interest in receiving e-mail transmissions from the list-server. There are no reliable estimates of the number of e-mail list servers in existence although the two dominant list server companies believe that there are 187,000 lists employing their products, see Bennahum (1988: 108). Bennahum's electronic newsletter MEME is distributed to 4,400 subscribers monthly and thus generates 52,800 messages per year, based on 12 messages per subscriber.

community formation and maintenance. It is, however, likely to become less important over time as other techniques for maintaining dialogues between virtual community members are developed and more broadly adopted.

2.5.2   Using the World Wide Web for Computer-Mediated Communication

The World Wide Web is used for an enormous variety of purposes. There is an indistinct demarcation between the use of the web and e-mail list servers as a 'publishing' medium. While web pages are not 'transmitted' in the sense that e-mails are, their location can be communicated to those users seeking to form a virtual community.[74] What differentiates the web from e-mail is that it is several generations more advanced in the tools it offers for content creation. Web-page creation tools allow the composition of rich graphic images and, if desired, multimedia and interactive content. As a medium of communication, the web can be employed within a virtual community to expand substantially the variety and quality of information exchange between members. There are costs involved in achieving this higher-quality level of content transmission. While an e-mail application program is one of the easier applications for the novice to master once she establishes a network connection, the creation of web pages is considerably more difficult. Although new applications programs reduce the level of required skills, these same tools continue to raise the standard of what is regarded as a high-quality web page.

   This overview stresses the boundary between the legacy systems of e-mail and the emerging applications of the web. These developments are strongly linked to the sub-community of the information society that has achieved a relatively high degree of computer literacy. Many of these people use information and communication technology applications regularly as part of their working lives. They bring to their families a set of skills and knowledge that extends the utilization of new technologies and services. This subcommunity will evolve and add new members as the use of these technologies becomes more ubiquitous. Other members of society with interests in the use of these technologies are likely to play a growing role as the applications become more user-friendly.

   The technical features of the Internet have been used to construct a number of advanced services. The earliest of these was the development of a global bulletin board system called USENET, which, along with IRC (Internet Relay Chat), provides the basis for global piazzas. We use these here as a case study to illustrate some of the fea-

---

[74] A web page is the term used to describe the image displayed as the result of entering a URL address in a web browser. Many users do not enter these addresses directly but cause them to be entered automatically by using a pointing device (e.g. a personal computer mouse) to 'click' on one of the browser control buttons or on a hyperlink appearing within a displayed document. The composition of hyperlinked documents in a coherent architecture is the source of a new generation of 'legacy' problems that arise from the difficulty of managing the 'universal resources' to be located. The removal of content at a URL creates 'dead-links' that are cul-de-sacs in the information motorway. By the time that content at a particular URL address is eliminated, there may be hundreds or even thousands of references to it. If it is a publicly accessible URL address, there is no way for the user to control all the references that may have been made to it as the address itself is easily incorporated in other documents (such as the references in this book to URLs).

tures of virtual community formation. Our second case study concerns the linking of virtual to physical communities. In this example, we focus on the trade-offs between local community sites as information resources and other applications including the construction of virtual communities. Finally, we examine the growth of virtual communities based upon the emergence of virtual realities for both entertainment and social interaction.

2.5.2.1 Global Piazzas: USENET and IRC

The Internet provides the means to construct public and private spaces for people to meet with one another (Mitchell, 1996). The development of demand for advanced information and communication technologies and services depends, in part, upon how these virtual structures are constructed and utilized. The evolution of two non-web-based Internet services, USENET and IRC, suggests the potential of these communication media for the information society and problems that emerge in the design and use of such virtual spaces.

USENET provides a means of 'posting' (recording) messages to a publicly accessible file and reading these messages in various ways including following the threads of particular conversations between groups of users. The list of interest groups, or newsgroups, in USENET is extensive, with titles such as de.soc.politik.deutchsland and alt.music.trombone. Within each of these groups, it is possible to read and post text messages. Since the origins of USENET in 1979, it has grown in availability so that now over 2.5m. individuals throughout the world can access its services (Overby, 1996). A graphic description of the potential and the reality of this service is conveyed by the following.

Usenet is a place for conversation or publication, like a giant coffeehouse with a thousand rooms; it is also a worldwide digital version of the Speaker's Corner in London's Hyde Park, an unedited collection of letters to the editor, a floating flea market, a huge vanity publisher, and a coalition of every odd special-interest group in the world. It is a mass medium because any piece of information put onto the Net has a potential worldwide reach of millions. But it differs from conventional mass media in several respects. Every individual who has the ability to read a Usenet posting has the ability to reply or to create a new posting. In television, newspapers, magazines, films, and radio, a small number of people have the power to determine which information should be made available to the mass audience. In Usenet, every member of the audience is also potentially a publisher. (Rheingold, 1993: 130)

A key element in the process of community formation over the history of the USENET has been the development of more interest groups. There are approximately 20,000 groups represented under various group headings that offer some guidance about content. The group headings are relevant for European users because they are organized by country code and provide a means of locating material for, and about, a country and signal the predominant language employed within a group.[75] While representing only a small part of the world's diversity, growth in the number of

---

[75] e.g. the code .de for Germany contains news groups such as de.soc.politik.deutchsland where there may be as many as 600 messages posted, all of which have their subject headers in German.

newsgroups creates a major navigation problem for which a solution has yet to be found. The navigation problem is, in itself, a means of reducing the size of the piazza in which people congregate for exchanges of information and viewpoints.

Another feature of USENET is the emergence of social norms of control for regulating discussions. A large number of newsgroups have a moderator who filters the messages. Only those that are deemed by the moderator to have content relevant to the specific group are admitted. The moderator function initially was introduced as a means to control antisocial behaviour and to discipline the novice who would inadvertently or naïvely post messages of no interest to the particular newsgroup community, exacerbating the information overload problem. It has become more essential as a variety of opportunistic uses of USENET have emerged including the posting of commercial advertising material and the promotion of web sites that may or may not be relevant to a particular newsgroup.

USENET illustrates the problems of social control that arise when virtual spaces are completely public. As the result of being public, they attract both antisocial and opportunistic behaviour.[76] USENET is now nearly 20 years old. It provides a useful forum for people to meet and discuss ideas and exchange information. It remains one of the simplest ways for new users to actively participate in the exchange of views and is likely to continue to be a useful part of the Internet. It does, however, have shortcomings as an architectural model for constructing public spaces on the Internet.

A second well-established approach to the architecture of public spaces is organized under the IRC service. Chat facilities are similar to an open conference call in which those who know the location can achieve connection and either listen (the somewhat sinister term 'lurk' is employed to describe listening-only behaviour) or engage in exchanges with others who are connected. Unlike USENET, connections are made in real time so that several line-text exchanges contributed by participants at a particular moment are rapidly retransmitted to others who are simultaneously connected.

The providers of Chat facilities and the participants must take a different approach to social control due to their real-time operation. In general, antisocial users are disciplined by group displays of hostility. In addition, when two or more users determine that they would like to exit a public space, they may convey messages to each other and the system allowing them to define a private conversation that cannot be monitored by the casual user. The transformation from public to private space offers a particularly important lesson in the design of computer-mediated communication. People use the public spaces to meet others, but once a social connection is established, they often prefer to develop the connection more intensively in private.

There are, of course, important technical limits to what can be exchanged through the format of the IRC facility because of its text basis and real-time operation. Some of these limits have been mitigated by modifying alphanumeric entries to reflect graphic content, for example, the smiling face represented by the character sequence :-) or its opposite :-(. More advanced service providers have developed IRC interfaces

---

[76] See Agre and Rotenberg (1997) for an edited collection of papers that considers various aspects of social behaviour in public and privates spaces and also Samarajiva (1994).

using the web to include more sophisticated means of user representation through virtual reality applications. These limitations both define the medium and influence its potential for social interaction.

The piazza characteristics of both USENET and IRC provide a means for people to meet and become acquainted on the Internet. Both are services that are defined using the most basic capabilities of the Internet and which emerged at a relatively early stage in the Internet's growth. The fact that they have continued to survive and grow for almost twenty years indicates their continued value to Internet users. At the same time, the growth of the Internet has made the unregulated piazza a place that is visited with a degree of care. In the case of IRC, the real identities of participants are shielded and, in the case of USENET, postings are often made by individuals through intermediaries or from computer accounts that do not provide a means to access information about their real identities.

As a method of establishing virtual communities, these virtual piazzas have some disadvantages over their physical counterparts. The virtual piazzas of the USENET and IRC do not provide the depth of social connectivity or the fluidity of social groupings of their real-life counterparts. In this respect, their social characteristics are limited and may be incapable, even with further technological improvements, of supporting some of the kinds of social development that might be desired in Europe or elsewhere. The formation of limited membership communities is common, indicating the limitations of the inclusive virtual piazza despite its widespread use.

2.5.2.2 *Virtual and Physical Communities: Is Relocalization Desirable?*
A means of 'relocalizing' virtual communities and re-engaging the richness of their social contexts involves enhancing the capabilities of people in particular locales to interact with one another. The concept of 'locale' is elastic and depends upon the interests that may draw people together. For instance, a rural population from the Perigord region in France may find common interests even though the people are distributed over a much more extensive area than the citizens of Paris who may wish to distinguish themselves by means of much smaller virtual communities. Although the Internet is a global means of communication, virtual communities evolving through the use of its services do not need be global. Despite the potential for globally dispersed communities to form, it does not follow that this is a desirable outcome for most people most of the time. The European High Level Expert Group has given specific encouragement to the place of local developments in the information society.

A vital step towards reinvigorating the spatial community is to promote cultural production and consumption at the local level. This is important as part of helping to reassert a sense of place and pride, to develop people's natural creativity (especially in remote and peripheral areas), and as an educational process. It is important, therefore, that cultural services be designed so they counter, rather than reinforce, the forces of centralization. Once again, the natural place for cultural expression is in the public sphere, and policies for the information society should be expressly committed to developing public arenas and the shared celebration of culture (European Commission High Level Expert Group, 1997: 59).

The 'relocalization' of physical communities is being conducted through the development of municipal web sites, the ISPs, and 'citynets', which we consider in more detail in Ch. 9. A major driving force in the development of municipal web sites is the widespread belief of public administrations that they should take responsibility for representing their communities to the rest of the world in ways that reflect the diversity of local social and cultural resources. The term 'municipalities' is used here to encompass all jurisdictions in which there may be a degree of local identity, for example, villages, communes, cities, and counties. In many communities there is a strong interest in portraying the desirability of the community for business investment, tourism, or as a locale that is attractive for commerce. In addition, some administrations are interested in providing access to municipal services using the Internet including the potential to apply for permits, query municipal databases that are meant to be publicly accessible, and provide information about the availability and conditions of municipal services of all types.

All these goals are based on the desire to facilitate either a one-way broadcast of information to interested users or a two-way exchange of information between the municipality and a particular person seeking municipal services. In general, these goals do not encompass the enabling or facilitation of communication between citizens in their communities. This is to be expected since municipalities, like businesses, would find it difficult simultaneously to enable open forums for current users about the shortcomings of existing services and to promote these same services to the world at large.

Accompanying the development of municipal web sites is the growth of ISP businesses that are often localized within a particular area. This may be a temporary condition arising from the tariff structure of telecommunication services in Europe and the advantages of local control in the management of marketing and service operations. Although there is considerable evidence of market consolidation, local providers may persist if certain ISPs are able to distinguish themselves from ISPs offering services on a national or global basis. A similar contest between local and national service providers in the United States has had mixed results. Some communities have continued to have viable local service providers while most users are served by national services (Downes and Greenstein, 1998). The advantage of a local ISP is that the business revenue of providing a telecommunication service is bundled with, and able to finance part of, the costs of the provision of local content.

The third model is the development of citynets. These are web sites that are identified with a particular place but not officially sponsored by the local community. These sites operate under a wide range of models, from non-profit organizations such as local chambers of commerce to profit-oriented sites operating under the business model of advertiser-supported content. Regardless of how these sites are funded, they share an interest in providing useful local information that will attract viewers and justify their costs either to the sponsors or to those paying for advertising. Many ISPs and virtually all citynets face the issues that confront other advertising-supported media. The potential exists for a conflict between the purposes of the advertisers and the interests of the community as a whole. In some cases these issues have a clear outcome. For example, it is rare to find a citynet sponsored by a chamber of commerce that hosts a community group focusing on the environmental non-sustainability of retail packaging. In other cases, commercial interests may coexist with various types of virtual communities.

A common understanding of the web is that it is a means to broadcast information. As a result, its potential for establishing and building virtual communities is often overlooked. This is unfortunate because as Steinmueller (1992*b*) has observed, the value that users assign to the provision of electronic connections may stem precisely from their ability to establish social connections with other users.

2.5.2.3 *Virtual Communities in Virtual Reality*
Many of the developments discussed so far involve virtual reality in the sense that users must use their imaginations to engage in social relationships using mediated communication, much as the reader of a novel may visualize its places and people. The cooperative processes involved in establishing and building virtual communities can also be facilitated by more explicit technologies for visualization. Just as the USENET and IRC create global piazzas where people may congregate by interest or relocalized web sites may draw individuals with an identification and need to know about the particularities of a physical place, virtual communities may be built based on other 'architectural' models.

Techniques in computer graphics and data communication allow for an infinite array of new architectural models for devising imaginary places or simulations of real places. It is possible to journey through a virtual representation of a real town or one that has never existed and, in so doing, to meet other people and interact with them. Virtual reality applications are presently associated with MUDs (Multi-User Domains), a term that evolved from the interactive computer game community where they were known as multi-user dungeons. MUDs provide an architecture in which users can navigate, encounter other users, and interact socially. When used for interactive games, the social interactions may be relatively unsophisticated and involve tasks such as slaying dragons or discovering treasures. The medium, however, does not constrain the possibilities for innovation in its use for more complex social purposes, such as computer-supported collaborative work.

Virtual reality applications for virtual communities combine computer-mediated communication as a social process with the capabilities of advanced information and communication technologies. Providing an engaging virtual graphic environment and portraying the movements and actions of dozens, or even hundreds, of users within this space is a process requiring substantial computational and communication resources. The use of virtual reality in interactive computer games is providing an important testing-ground for new ways of utilizing the full technological capabilities of the Internet despite the fact that the use of virtual reality techniques for building virtual communities is in its infancy.[77]

---

[77] Despite this, a major European software company has been built on the new medium, see http://www.blaxxun.com/main.html accessed 6 April 2000.

2.5.3 *Metaphors for Virtual Social Communities*

There is a widely held notion that 'the net' is a kind of new frontier. This notion is expressed in descriptors about the Internet and in the wider cyber-culture it is said to nurture and spawn. It is promulgated by journalists and academics and it is present within specific organizations devoted to developing the Internet, including one of its designers, Vincent Cerf (Gilster, 1993). This metaphor holds that new and uncharted territories are ripe for exploitation and that they offer greater potential for personal freedom of thought and expression. It implies a levelling of opportunity such that those who arrive at the frontier will find themselves among equals.

Melbin (1978) has described the social features that characterize frontiers, arguing that as uncharted geography in the United States declined and settlements spread, the geographic frontier might transfer into the time frontier through an increase in wakeful activity. For Melbin, the gradual occupation and appropriation of the night was a new frontier. He showed that night-time social life in urban areas resembled social life in the former territorial frontiers. Table 2.8 illustrates how the 'frontier' hypothesis has been translated within the context of the Internet within the United States (Neice, 1998a).

TABLE 2.8. *Common features of geographical and Internet frontiers*

Geographical frontiers	Internet frontiers
Advance is in stages involving successive steps in the colonization of regions	Many steps preceded the World Wide Web
The population is sparse and also more homogeneous	Initially used by academics and researchers; now by many young males, with emergence of the *.com* domain
There is welcome solitude, fewer social constraints, and less persecution	Computer-mediated communication invites seclusion
Settlements are isolated	Net nodes are often distant from each other
Governance is initially decentralized	Initially not governed or 'owned' by any formal legal apparatus
New behavioural styles emerge	As in newsgroups, fetishes are catered for in abundance
There is more lawlessness and violence	Viruses, spamming, and flaming abound
There is more helpfulness and friendliness	Novices usually receive a helping hand from the more experienced
Exploitation of the basic resource finally becomes national policy	Government initiatives to promote infrastructure development and services such as electronic commerce
Interest groups emerge	The Electronic Frontier Foundation, and many others, have emerged

Source: Adapted from original compiled from Melbin (1978: 6–18) and extended by Neice (1998a).

The 'frontier' metaphor masks the social characteristics of different kinds of frontiers and it is a metaphor that resonates much less with the social perception of the Internet and its use in Europe even among relatively sophisticated users (Neice, 2000). To understand these emergent characteristics we need to delve more deeply into the intertwined dynamics of co-evolutionary technical and social systems; a challenge that we set for ourselves in subsequent chapters.

2.6   Conclusion

Many of the discussions about access in the information society, the emergence of new social communities, and their users' capabilities and skills are dominated by economic considerations or by debates about the psychological or attitudinal characteristics of users. We have argued that the basis for understanding information society developments cannot be based exclusively upon the economic mapping of user preferences to user demand, the generation of supply, or the meeting of demand and supply in the market. The processes of social development and community formation are institutionalized within both 'élite' and popular cultures that play important roles in generating the preferences and social motivations for individuals to participate by using the information and communication infrastructure. These processes, along with the problems of acquiring the skills and pertinent knowledge, influence the willingness and interest of individuals to participate in the information society. They are the basis for the evolution of new preferences, new demands, and, ultimately, the supply of new technologies and services. The development of an interest in joining in the new activities of the information society represented by Internet use must precede the variety of investments that are required to become a member.

The figurative and literal architectures and designs of the new infrastructures and services interact with these social processes to create paths or trajectories of social evolution. The path that any particular society takes in developing the new information and communication resources may be self-limiting, embracing only the élite who are already deeply enmeshed in the use of these technologies to create new symbolic structures, and rejecting those whose interests, expressions, and capabilities differ. The most basic test of a commitment to an inclusive approach to the development of the information society is the extent to which it encompasses the needs and aspirations of people whose physical or mental capabilities differ from those of the predominant designers, implementers, and users of new technologies. Incorporating the ethos of inclusion as a design principle is an important goal that will gauge the effectiveness of a society in meeting its goals of solidarity as well as its aspirations for competitiveness in world markets.

Patterns of use of the technologies associated with the information society indicate that over one-third of all Europeans have an active involvement with information and communication technologies. The extent of the use of these technologies varies considerably across Europe, particularly as one proceeds from the Scandinavian north towards the Mediterranean. These differences reflect disparities in economic development as well as in the negotiation of valued uses for these technologies. Shortcomings

in the quality of infrastructure and the costs of access appear to be particularly important constraints to the movement towards creating the physical networks by which
information appliances are used to access a growing array of resources available
through the use of the Internet.

The growth of Internet use throughout Europe is, nevertheless, very rapid.
Europeans have not joined the Internet bandwagon with the fervour or conviction
of Americans. Their patterns of use and access are, however, developing at very rapid
rates, surpassed only by the even more rapid growth of cellular telephony, another
channel for enriching interpersonal communication which appears to be a central
feature of the information society. In Europe, the pattern of Internet usage is strongly
oriented to use at work. This pattern is reflected in the relatively modest connection of
European educational (except for universities) and cultural institutions to the Internet. Clearly, a central issue influencing how advanced information and communication technologies and services will come into broader use involves establishing their
value to the user.

The role of virtual communities is central to understanding the evolution of
the social path or trajectory of the use of information and communication infrastructures. At the broadest level, the information society is a system of interacting
(human) individuals, technological artefacts, and institutions that embody the communities of interest we described in Ch. 1. Virtual communities can be viewed as all-
encompassing, much as the idea of the information society itself can become imbued
with whatever features are desired. Our perspective is that the effective individual and
social use of information and communication technologies requires the evolution of
an information society that draws its dynamism and vitality from much smaller and
more focused communities of interest than constructions like the 'user' or the 'citizen'.
Understanding the structure of these smaller communities, the ones that we can
readily identify ourselves as belonging to, and their engagement, or lack of engagement, with the processes of information society development is a primary basis for
comprehending the evolution of the information society. This is why we have focused
upon the seemingly narrow technical issue of whether educational and cultural institutions are connected to the Internet or with the architecture of interpersonal interaction in the use of the Internet for e-mail, chat rooms, USENET, or virtual reality
applications. It is at these levels that the skills and knowledge are accumulated that will
assure or discourage people's interest in utilizing the resources that are being developed and, ultimately, in contributing to these resources.

We accept that, in addition to the social processes that may motivate the individual
to develop active interests in the new resources of the information society, there are
powerful forces at work at the level of the individual. In our view, many of the existing
approaches to these issues focus upon the barriers to participation arising from
immutable processes that are outside the influence and control of those who might
use technologies for their own purposes. For example, people may be classified as
'technophiles' and 'technophobes' or 'the enthusiasts' and 'the alienated'.[78] It has been

---

[78] On the use of the former practice in the psychology literature, see Neice (1996) while the latter
dichotomy is drawn from Department of Trade and Industry (1996; 1998a).

argued by authors such as Gandy (1993) and Lyon (1994) that digital devices enhance people's feelings of inadequacy and challenge their senses of mastery or induce fears of control and surveillance. However, it is also the case that psychological dispositions can be influenced profoundly over time by the changing institutional contexts of experience, use, expectations, and support. In this chapter, we have begun the process of examining how these institutional contexts interact with the construction of social status and the individual's own feelings of entitlement or interest. There can be little doubt that individuals who are confronted with the prospect of a global information infrastructure that has come into existence without their participation, but which requires their participation, will have feelings of inadequacy, alienation, and phobia.

Neither an analysis of the virtual communities in which we are now, or will be, engaged, nor our individual efforts to construct meaning and purpose in relation to the growth of the information society is sufficient for our social and economic account. There is a vast difference between the development of an interest in empowerment or the desire to participate in making critical choices and the exercise of power through actual participation. The capacity for the effective involvement of individuals is constrained by the interaction of individuals with organized interests. People may ally themselves or resist the outcomes of these interactions, but the development of institutions to serve those interests and their interplay with technological and market forces are essential components of our analysis.

What we seek to preserve throughout the discussion in the ensuing chapters is the significance of the experiences of people, the potential for their exclusion, inadvertently or by design, in the building of the European information society. It is our view that the best antidote to exclusion is participation. Despite the potential *noblesse oblige* of these sentiments, the reliance of the economic and political interests promoting the information society on the active participation of individuals and their creation of a rich 'virtual society' composed of many virtual communities is real. The journey towards the information society is one that will be turbulent and that will produce contradictory outcomes. As argued by Ferge and Miller (1993: 298),

affluence arises from economic growth and growth in turn is an unsettling, uneven process. While many gain, others are threatened and new forms of inequality appear . . . the cultural and skill capital of some may be devalued or devalourised . . . [and] new bureaucracies demand new understanding of how to deal with them . . . it is the upheaval in society—the disutility of old patterns, the barriers to and disadvantage in adapting to new demands—which produce and maintain poverty.

To this we would add that the changes in economic growth also bring opportunity for the restructuring of economic, social, and cultural life in ways that will be more fulfilling and complete for those who succeed in seizing the opportunity.

3

Transforming the Infrastructure Supporting the Information Society

3.1 Introduction

The conditions for, and the nature of, user access to the information and communication infrastructure are shaped by the evolution of the underlying technologies. The central theme of discussions about the evolution of this infrastructure over more than a decade has been 'convergence'. Convergence conveys two ideas. The first is the technological potential of rendering all electronic communication signals as digital 'bitstreams' that can be interconnected. The second is the industrial and market implications of this technological potential. For example, the process of convergence between information and communication technologies creates opportunities for defining new advanced telecommunication capabilities and services.

Our perspective on the convergence process differs from that of many other writers in the extent of emphasis we place on the imbalances in the growth of demand, the evolution of specific convergent markets, and the institutional problems of achieving interoperability and interconnection. Interoperability is the construction of effective interfaces between data flows, software applications, users, and the supporting data communication infrastructure. Interconnection is the construction of vertical and horizontal business relationships implemented through interoperable technological linkages in the information and communication infrastructure. Addressing each of these issues requires resolution of the conflicting interests of companies with incumbent and insurgent strategies. The first two of these issues influence the nature and extent of conflicting interests. This is why we examine the process of demand growth and imbalances in the market evolution accompanying the realization of convergence.

In this chapter, the principal focus is on the formation of technological trajectories governing the evolution of the information and communication infrastructure in the near-term. Chapter 4 examines the demand issues that are raised by multimedia applications and Ch. 5 considers the specific role of electronic commerce. Each of these chapters has a parallel relationship with institutional developments in areas of interoperability and interconnection, intellectual property rights, privacy, and electronic payment systems that we examine in Chs. 6, 7, and 8. Our analysis emphasizes the

This chapter draws substantially on original research undertaken by Parantha Narendran, Gert van de Paal, and W. Edward Steinmueller.

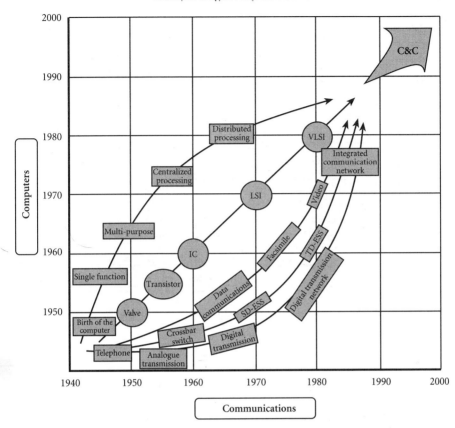

FIG. 3.1. *The computer and communication perspective on convergence, 1990*

Source: Adapted from Irwin (1984: 46) citing Kobayashi (1980: 80).

importance that we attach to the co-evolution of demand and the institutional framework for building markets.

Our purpose in structuring the explanation of information and communication infrastructure growth along these lines is a response to the intellectual cul de sac that supply-led approaches have produced. This problem can be explained concisely by referring to three diagrams, Figs. 3.1, 3.2, and 3.3.

Figure 3.1 summarizes developments in the computer and telecommunication industry in relation to the trajectory of microelectronics improvements. This is the 'technological' view of the convergence process. From the mid-1980s it was widely believed that the distribution of computing and the integration of communication networks were on an intersecting path that would result in a convergent network structure. Figure 3.2 depicts how these developments appeared during the European Commission's Research and Development in Advanced Communication Technology for Europe (RACE) programme around 1986. Europe's telecommunication network

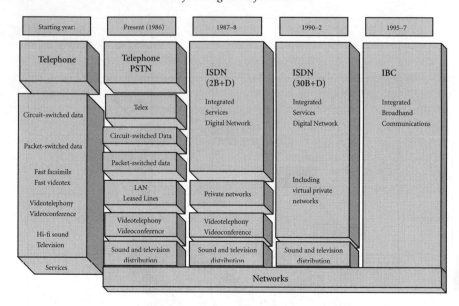

FIG. 3.2. A European perspective on convergence, *c.*1986

Source: As reported in OECD (1992*a*: 86).

operators, as well as the information technology companies who were most active in the mainframe computer business, had a well-defined plan for implementing techno-logical convergence. This was based upon the development of the standards and tech-nology for the Integrated Services Digital Network (ISDN). The plan was based upon the progressive development of ISDN-based standards, first at the 128 kbps level during the late 1980s, then at the 2.048 Mbps level at the beginning of the 1990s, and, finally, with 'broadband' ISDN, whose speed was nominally defined in the 10 Mbps range, providing a foundation for a convergent communication infrastructure by the mid-1990s.

The plan was not executed. What did happen is told in the story that unfolds in this chapter. Instead of implementing a progressively higher performance ISDN network, those constructing the infrastructure in Europe have continued with a combination of circuit-switched telephony, leased-line, and packet-switched networks based upon het-erogeneous technological standards.[1] One of the reasons that this plan or widely held set of common expectations was not realized was that the 'convergent markets' that were expected to develop (see Fig. 3.3) have not been large enough to support the investment costs of upgrading the entire network. The convergent markets that were expected to develop have been dominated by the development of the Internet and by off-line multimedia applications. In effect, what was a perfectly reasonable

[1] Additional reasons for this are discussed in more detail later in this chapter and in David and Steinmueller (1990).

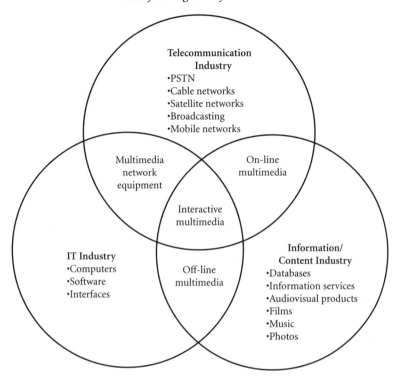

FIG. 3.3. OECD vision of converging markets

Source: Adapted from Spectrum Strategy (1996: 4) and originally from OECD based on Devotech, 'Développement d'un environnement multimedia en Europe'.

technological plan was disrupted by the rapid pace of technological developments and by the incremental development of demand.

Our focus on the evolution of demand is complementary to, but distinct from, views that emphasize the strong links between telecommunication liberalization, the convergence process, and the articulation of demand for advanced information and communication services. The preparation for European telecommunication liberalization that culminated with a suite of legislation that came into force on 1 January 1998 is a large topic and one that has been extensively examined in the existing litera-ture.[2] The intentions of liberalization of the European telecommunication market are to hasten the process of technological change as well as to open individual Member State telecommunication markets to the potential for new entry. The combination of technological innovation and entry is expected to bring a proliferation of new services and a market discipline to telecommunication prices that will simplify the regulatory task in line with the interests of the industrial players as well as consumers and citizens.

[2] See e.g. Lips, Frissen, and Prins (1998); Skouby (1997); Tyler and Joy (1997); Vaitilingam (1998). Several issues arising from the implementation of this legislation are taken up in Ch. 6.

Liberalization is not necessarily a force for strengthening the process of technological or market convergence. The problems of co-ordination involved in deploying a high-capacity information and communication infrastructure are likely to be more complex in a market characterized by active competition for the heaviest users of the new services provided by such networks. At the same time, the telecommunication network operators did not act during the 1980s to realize the necessary network upgrade to achieve the vision represented by Fig. 3.2.

To the extent that liberalization is successful in achieving the aims of innovation and price control through competitive market forces, Europe will have achieved a major goal of the liberalization process. Although there are some encouraging signs that price reduction and new entry are following on from liberalization, it is too early to offer a comprehensive assessment of the results.[3] A pessimistic viewpoint is that the price reductions experienced to date are a strategic response of the formerly monopolistic public telecommunication operators to discourage alternative infrastructure investment by reducing the economic returns on such investments. This is not in contradiction to all of the goals of market liberalization. Price reduction and innovation, even if undertaken for strategic reasons by the dominant competitor, still serve the primary goals of liberalization. Entry constraints may, however, prevent a competitive market structure from emerging. Over a longer span of time, an absence of effective competition may prove troublesome for the Member State regulatory bodies, requiring broader and more active regulation than is presently expected.[4] The market structure implications of liberalization depend upon how technological change combines with market developments to meet the growing demand for an upgraded information and communication infrastructure.

A central technological development in the convergence process that has emerged over the past several decades has been the computerization of public telecommunication networks. Not only is the network infrastructure itself now managed and controlled with the aid of sophisticated computer-based algorithms, but the network now provides support for a host of computer applications that are inter-networked using a variety of software applications. In consequence, the voice telephony networks of the past are increasingly interwoven with data networks and the distinctions between networks capable of transmitting voice, data, and visual images are rapidly becoming irrelevant.[5] In this sense, the technological convergence process can be said to have occurred during the 1990s. However, it has not been based upon the extension of high-capacity telecommunication services to all customers. Instead, it has focused on business applications where greater willingness to pay and more geographically

[3] Although 1998 was the agreed date by which all European Union Member States with the exception of Greece, Spain, and Portugal would implement telecommunication market liberalization, many Member States enacted legislation before that date and Spain accelerated its plans to do so as well.

[4] In the UK, despite a deliberately proactive regulatory policy aimed at enabling non-dominant telecommunication providers to establish themselves in the market, the former public telecommunication operator, British Telecom, retains an 80% share of the market for local telephone connections, an 85% share of the domestic long-distance voice telephony services market and an approximately 72% share of international long-distance voice service (Office of Telecommunications, 1999: 3).

[5] See Mansell (1993) for a discussion of the history of the computerization of telecommunication networks and Bernard (1998) for recent developments.

concentrated demand in urban areas has made investments in network upgrading more feasible.

An explanation of the role of demand and technological competition in disrupting the plan for a European ISDN infrastructure involves a better understanding of the factors influencing the rate of market development. The ways in which the technological opportunities suggested by Fig. 3.1 are realized are subject to considerable uncertainty. Because of this uncertainty, there are many different 'paths' or directions along which demand may be articulated and markets developed. Moreover, the roles played by companies adopting incumbent, insurgent, and virtual community strategies in sponsoring particular technologies, or in arranging particular configurations of market competition and co-operation, are very important. The choices made by these actors are either supported or rejected by processes of market competition. Thus, while it is possible to describe innumerable company choices and strategies and the particular outcomes resulting from these choices, a theoretical approach is needed to organize these experiences into a coherent account of the technological evolution of the information and communication infrastructure.

The theoretical approach employed here is the theory of market diffusion, modified in ways that support a qualitative analysis of experience. The following section provides an introduction to the theory and its limitations, an extension to the problems of 'system markets', and an application of the theory. It is in the application that we will explain more fully how the plan for an ISDN infrastructure was disrupted by the emergence of alternative technologies, including voice-line modems and IP devices.

3.2   What is Technology Diffusion?

Other things being equal, it is desirable that European information and communication infrastructure construction proceeds along a smooth path that opens opportunities for delivering new information services and applications. As we have stressed in Ch. 2, there are many reasons for concluding that 'other things' are not equal. For example, the time required for users to become accustomed to new technological opportunities and to develop the skills to exploit them makes it unlikely that precise technical specifications for the infrastructure will ever be available in advance. The unevenness of technological advance is the result both of the uncertainty of discovery processes and the myriad details of 'reducing to practice' ideas that may be sound in principle, but remain untried. Technological progress is also uneven because of the different rates at which new technologies are adopted and deployed and because of the varied processes of acceptance and resistance to alternative service designs and architectures. The construction of a European information and communication infrastructure is, therefore, unlikely to be a smooth process.

The uncertainty involved in the process of technological change produces a number of human responses. For some, it is preferable simply to ignore the process and to act as if a current vision of the next step is the only appropriate response. For others, it is important to identify and map the broad paths of various alternatives and to seek an understanding of the factors that are likely to be influential if a particular path emerges as the most likely course of development. This chapter is based upon the latter response to technological uncertainty. It must also be acknowledged that entirely unforeseen developments may occur that would dramatically alter our analysis and conclusions.[6]

3.2.1 Introducing the Theory and its Limitations

An analysis of the factors influencing the diffusion of new technologies is essential for understanding the alternative paths of technological development. In both sociology and economics, the diffusion of new technologies is analysed by examining the adoption behaviours of those who employ them. For both sociologists and economists, technology diffusion is the aggregate outcome of individual choices to adopt new technologies.[7] In what follows we use the term 'technologies' to include all forms of innovation including new ideas that are not embodied in products (whether these ideas are sold or transferred by other means) as well as products that do embody innovations. Market, technological, and institutional considerations, as well as the particular needs and preferences of individual adopters, shape the adoption choices of individual actors and organizations. Both economists and sociologists recognize that social processes—individual and collective or institutional—influence adoption behaviours. Economists prefer to analyse social processes in terms of their effects on the individual decision-maker, while sociologists are more likely to view the 'decision-maker' as a problematic conception for the social processes defining adoption behaviour.[8] Correspondingly, economists are more likely to focus exclusively on relative profitability as the criterion determining the likelihood of individual adoption while

[6] e.g. an effective means of delivering broadband data communication through the use of the electrical power distribution network or through wireless technologies that make much more efficient use of the radio frequency spectrum than do currently available technologies, could fundamentally alter the dynamics of the diffusion process. Efforts to develop this particular technology have encountered recurrent problems, see Taaffe (1999).

[7] The method of technology diffusion studies draws upon sociological and economic analysis. A more detailed presentation of this method from these two different disciplinary backgrounds can be found in Rogers (1983); and Stoneman (1983). For Rogers, 'diffusion is defined as the process by which (1) an *innovation* (2) is *communicated* through certain *channels* (3) *over time* (4) among the members of a *social system*' (Rogers, 1983: 10, emphasis in original). An innovation is 'an idea, practice, or object that is perceived as new by an individual or other unit of adoption' (ibid. 11). In this form of analysis, Rogers is not concerned with how or why an innovation is perceived as such. Communication, for the most part, is understood as information-exchange relationships between pairs of individuals which set the conditions under which a 'source will or will not *transmit* the innovation to the receiver, and the effect of the transfer' (ibid. 17). Therefore, this analysis is situated within a rather conventional understanding of sender–receiver models of communication even if there are allowances for recursive learning.

[8] e.g. Rogers, a leading scholar of diffusion from the sociological perspective, identifies eight types of diffusion research, none of which centres upon the economic incentives to adopt a particular innovation. They are: (1) earliness of knowing about innovations, (2) rate of adoption of different innovations in a social system (which includes economic incentives as one aspect), (3) innovativeness (which includes the incentives to innovate as one component), (4) opinion leadership, (5) who interacts with whom in diffusion networks, (6) rate of adoption in different social systems, (7) communication channel usage, and (8) consequences of innovation (which include economic effects) (ibid. 85).

sociologists regard innovation as an 'uncertainty reduction' process that is influenced by cognitive processes and the availability of information for these processes to operate upon, among other factors.[9]

The distinctions between sociological and economic views are particularly important for the prospective analysis of the diffusion of new technologies. The preference of economists to limit their analyses to the observable implications of profitability of the adoption of innovations ensures that technologies that are likely to have widespread disruptive effects (dramatically increasing and diminishing the relative benefit from different activities) will be difficult to assess. Unfortunately, in these circumstances, sociological approaches often require even more data and evaluation of the social processes to assess the likely rate of diffusion. An *ex ante* sociological assessment of the prospects for a new technology can be either much more optimistic *or* pessimistic than an economic assessment depending upon the assumptions the researcher is willing to make. The limitations in predictive power of either economic or sociological analysis for the prospects of particular information and communication technologies suggest that research needs to begin with a clear identification of influential factors and a specification of their possible interrelationships. It is important to keep in mind that an analysis based upon a limited selection of factors may provide a satisfactory and quantitative *ex post* account. If one is to take into account the broader spectrum of issues arising from design, implementation, absorption, and reshaping of applications, a qualitative approach rather than a quantitative approach will almost certainly be necessary. The former approach is adopted in this chapter.

In recent years there has been considerable criticism of perspectives on social and technological change that focus on diffusion. The reasons are many. They include a tendency for diffusion studies to examine the impact of existing technological systems on users with little regard for the interactive relationships that are forged through time between technology and service developers, producers and suppliers, and different types of users. There is also a tendency within the literature on technology diffusion to neglect the fundamentally important processes of learning and negotiation and those through which asymmetrical power relationships are developed, maintained, and, in some cases, modified, as technological systems achieve more widespread use by individuals and organizations. At the micro level of analysis it has now been recognized that the differences in the ways that users appropriate or reject technological innovations are as important (and complex) as the structural relationships that influence the formation of new markets for products and services.

Although E. M. Rogers's (1983) work on the diffusion of innovations provides a bridge between the issues that are given priority by economists and by sociologists of

---

[9] As Rogers (ibid. 214–15) observes in discussing Griliches's (1957) pioneering economic work on hybrid corn diffusion, 'Market forces undoubtedly *are* of importance in explaining the rate of adoption of farm innovations. For some innovations (such as high-cost and highly profitable ideas) and for some farmers, economic advantage may even be the most important single predictor of rate of adoption. But to argue that economic factors are the sole predictors of rate of adoption is ridiculous.'

technological change, it does not fully account for the contextual features of different sites of innovation that influence diffusion patterns. These contextual features include the influence of the broad characteristics of institutionalized systems of governance (policy and regulation) and the culturally specific styles of learning (by doing, through interaction, etc.) that are essential features of a more complete analysis of the diffusion process.[10] In our analysis, we have chosen to adopt the language of the more traditional approaches to the diffusion of innovations because our principal application of this approach is confined to a relatively well-bounded case of technological competition between ISDN and IP technologies in the context of business applications. If, however, we take the broader approach suggested by the criticisms of the diffusion approach, it is possible to see this entire book as being about the diffusion of information society technologies and institutions. We have chosen not to describe our account in these terms because we believe that the narrower concept and approach continues to have analytical value. Labelling the broader approach as 'diffusion analysis' adds very little and is liable to be confusing.

The broad outlines of economic and sociological methodologies are employed in business forecasting analysis as well. A basic tool for business forecasting as it is applied by leading market research is the process of developing consensus estimates of the compound annual growth rate. These are then compared against past rates of growth to characterize markets as experiencing either accelerating or slowing rates of growth. Like economics and sociology, business forecasting analysis begins with the observation that technologies have followed similar historical *patterns* of adoption. This pattern is typified by an 's-shape' or sinusoidal path relating time to the total level of adoption as in Fig. 3.4.

This stylized representation of the historical experience has several features that reflect experience with a considerable range of technologies in several different historical periods.[11] For discussion purposes, the entire time path has been divided into three periods that may be referred to as (I) the period of early adoption, (II) the 'take-off' period, and (III) the maturity phase. The relatively long period of early adoption is characteristic of many historical technologies. Its length is prolonged due to the time-consuming processes required to adapt the innovation to particular applications

---

[10] See Sørensen (1998) for a comprehensive overview of the various criticisms of conventional diffusion theory from the perspective of more recent approaches to social learning theories. Issues of power and conflict resolution with respect to technological change are discussed by Nelkin (1992), and with respect to the contributions that social science analysis can make to policy by Jasanoff (1987). Theories of learning and the evolution and selection of innovative technologies draw to a substantial degree on work by Lundvall and Johnson (1994); Nelson and Winter (1982); Rosenberg (1994), and within the sociological tradition on work by Bijker and Law (1992); Callon (1992); Woolgar (1996). Broadly based analyses of the intersections between micro-level and institutional analysis of innovation and use of information and communication technologies have been developed by Mansell and Silverstone (1996). In this work, Silverstone employs concepts of appropriation and the 'domestication' of new technologies and Mansell employs concepts of institutional design to examine the evolution of information and communication service markets. A recent compilation of research that embodies many of these perspectives on the problematique posed by issues of technology diffusion in the information and communication technology field is found in Dutton (1999).

[11] See David (1975); DuBoff (1967; 1983); Griliches (1957); Mansfield (1963); Nishiyama (1982); Romeo (1975).

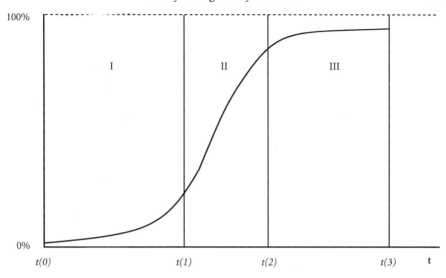

FIG. 3.4. The diffusion curve

Source: Authors' elaboration.

and by the adaptations that users must, themselves, make in order to become adopters of the new technology. An important 'adaptation' in many technologies is a decline in their cost. So long as a technology remains relatively specialized and expensive it will attract relatively few adopters. The relatively long time interval that virtually every technology spends in the 'early adoption' phase is significant for assessing technological prospects. The technologies of the near future that are likely to displace existing technologies are most likely already present in the market, albeit in some specialized and high-cost applications.[12]

The 'take-off' period is marked by much more rapid adoption as the technology comes into widespread use. In Fig. 3.4, the technology becomes very attractive to users, and the cumulative number of adopters rises from around 20 per cent to over 80 per cent in a relatively short interval of time. Finally, during the maturity period, the technology has little further prospect for adoption as virtually all the individuals likely to adopt the technology will have done so. The fact that the curve describing cumulative adoption never reaches 100 per cent reflects the fact that, for virtually any technology, there will be some non-adopters. The period of 'maturity' depicted in Fig. 3.4 is relatively long. This need not be so, particularly for information and communication technologies, as they are often displaced by substitute technologies and related services. The main controversies about the use of a diffusion curve in prospective analysis stem from the considerable variance in the

---

[12] e.g. although Internet adoption grew very rapidly during the 1990s, the basic technology had been in use since the 1970s in the specialized and publicly subsidized environment of the research community.

lengths of the three periods depicted in Fig. 3.4 and the slope of the diffusion path during period II.[13]

At a deeper level of analysis, there are two important observations to be made about the diffusion curve. The first is that there are many possible mechanisms or processes responsible for accelerating or slowing the adoption process. Identifying what these may be is likely to make an important contribution to the assessment of a particular technology's prospects. For example, rapid adoption may reflect a trajectory of price reduction that occurs as companies compete with one another for market share in a rapidly growing market. Alternatively, and following a more sociological approach, rapid adoption may be the consequence of information about the technology becoming widely available so that a very large share of adopters with potential interest in the technology become aware of its existence simultaneously. Yet another possibility is that the individual value of adopting the technology is influenced by the extent to which others have adopted it, a process or mechanism that economists refer to as positive network externalities.[14] An example of a barrier to diffusion is the unavailability of skilled labour necessary to implement a particular technology since the development of skilled labour takes time and, therefore, tends to lengthen the time before a technology can be brought into widespread use. Individual factors can be classified according to whether they serve as 'barriers' or 'drivers' to the adoption process and this language will be employed in discussing a number of the technologies examined in this chapter.[15]

3.2.2   Technology Diffusion and Technology Systems

In the case of advanced information and communication technologies and services, the 'system features' of these technologies complicate the choice of an appropriate unit of analysis for the technology diffusion process.[16] Much of the Research, Technology

---

[13] In examining numerically controlled machine tools Romeo (1975) found substantial differences between industries in their rates of adoption. Correspondingly, in Nishiyama (1982), consumer electronics adoptions in Japan varied dramatically between different products. The audio tape recorder had a much more protracted growth period than either the colour television or home videocassette recorder. The latter shared a similar pattern of adoption with a relatively short early adoption period followed by five years of rapid growth, during which the number of households with the technology grew from around 20% to approximately 80%.

[14] Positive network externalities are a general feature of communication and transportation networks. The larger the network the more value that it is likely to have for users (assuming that they can efficiently navigate to their desired location), see Rohlfs (1974).

[15] Many of the barriers or drivers of the adoption process are, from, a sociological perspective better conceived as social processes of interaction that involve the negotiated outcomes of power relationships. When these negotiations occur either wholly or partially in electronic environments, the participants within these communities may experience and perceive the barriers and drivers differently to how they regard them in conventional physical places. For a recent exploration of the differences and similarities in the social processes at work in cyber and physical places, see M. A. Smith and Kollock (1999). The importance of human interaction and the social and cultural context is especially evident in Turkle (1999).

[16] The diffusion framework raises three issues for analysis of advanced information and communication technologies and services: (1) the selection of appropriate units of analysis that define the boundary between, and interaction among, specific technology applications and cultural, social, economic, and

Development and Demonstration (RTD&D) in this area involves research into system components or subsystems that must fit into and interoperate with other technologies. This feature has two implications. The first is that the relative maturity of particular parts of the system must be considered in assessing diffusion prospects. The prospective diffusion of a particular technology will be limited if the part of the system in which it fits is relatively immature. Maturity is defined not only by technological considerations; it is also influenced by institutional and social considerations. These considerations include the extent of the users' prior experience, the availability of skills, the adaptation of social customs and practices to the use of specific technologies, and the ways in which these customs and practices shape perceptions and outcomes for technological design and use.

The second implication of systemic interrelatedness of technologies is that they may be either complements or substitutes in demand relationships. If a technology is a complement in demand with another, the quantity of one technology purchased will depend upon the price and characteristics of the other. A higher price for one technology will reduce demand for the other and, conversely, a lower price will increase demand for the other technology. Technologies that are substitutes follow exactly the opposite relationship; price increases in one will *increase* purchases of the other because customers choose the relatively lower-priced technology in preference to the one that is more expensive. Declines in price of one will discourage customers from purchasing the other, *reducing* the quantity demanded. Information and communication technology systems are typically composed of components that have a complex pattern of substitute and complement relationships in demand. A decline in the price of a particular software product may increase the sales of personal computers while reducing the sales of a competing software product. In this example, software and personal computers are complements, while the two software products are substitutes in demand.

The existence of complementary and substitute relationships between information and communication technology products is often reinforced by the existence of positive network externalities affecting particular groups of components. Positive network externalities exist when the value of a technology increases as the result of the decisions of *others* to acquire the same, or a related, technology.[17] Positive network externalities can be realized through a variety of mechanisms. The most straightforward is that the collective effect of others' acquisitions increases the usefulness of a product because there is a direct connection between an individual and others. Thus, if many individuals acquire the means to send e-mail it is likely that the value of acquiring a means to send and receive e-mail will be higher to an individual. Complementary relationships can also be reinforced by network externalities and may arise from a more indirect connection between individuals. If many individuals acquire software for creating

political developments embedded within the process of technology diffusion; (2) the identification of relevant actors and the determination of their interactions; and (3) the role of 'complementary developments', some of which are complementary or competing technologies, while others are institutional developments.

[17] See e.g. Katz and Shapiro (1985; 1986).

World Wide Web content, the value of an individual acquiring a World Wide Web browser is increased. Finally, the relationship generating the positive network externality may be relatively indirect. Companies considering a choice of a word-processing package are likely to benefit by choosing one in which potential employees can be expected to have skills. The positive network externality is generated collectively by the prior accumulation of skills of potential employees.

Information and communication technologies are likely to be technologically inter-related as components within systems. For this reason, the existence of complementary and substitute relationships is particularly important in evaluating the diffusion prospects of a particular technology or cluster of technologies. These complementary and substitute relationships are likely to be reinforced by the existence of positive network externalities that raise the value of acquiring a technology as a consequence of others' decisions to acquire the same or related technology. The concepts explained in this and the earlier section are used in the remainder of this chapter and the two succeeding chapters to examine the course of development of the technologies supporting the development of the European information and communication infrastructure.

3.2.3   Applying Diffusion Analysis to the Competition between ISDN and the TCP/IP

The push to undertake the latest round of infrastructure upgrading stems from two key factors. First, exploding volumes of data are being exchanged between computer systems that benefit from permanent or dial-up connections across Local Area Network (LAN)/Wide Area Network (WAN) and global infrastructures to exchange 'packet data'. Packet data transmission involves the deconstruction of a bitstore or bit-stream into distinct parcels that can be independently forwarded through the complex lattice of a data communication network and reassembled in their original form. The reasons for this increase in the volume of exchanged data stemming from the growth of Internet technologies are examined in this chapter. Second, the same infrastructure designed for data telecommunication is becoming more effective in supporting voice traffic, raising issues as to the future of the circuit-switched architecture of the entire telecommunication infrastructure.

Computer networking infrastructures are increasingly interchangeable with circuit-switched network infrastructures at least for some applications. The process of interaction between telephonic and data communication has been a gradual development. For many years it was widely believed that the telephone network's advantages of widespread (even ubiquitous) reach to physical locations was offset by technical limitations stemming from the architectures of circuit-switching and the 'local loop' or the facilities linking the customer's premises with the main parts of the network. These limitations supported the development of specific data communication networks that were, in many respects, independent from the global public switched telecommunication network. During the 1970s and 1980s, it became increasingly apparent that this was an unsatisfactory state of affairs for many reasons. These included the increasing costs of maintaining and extending two architecturally distinct networks, both of which were growing, and the declining justification for the initial support of independent developments.

Reintegrating telephony and data communication became a major pursuit of the technical and business communities. A plan emerged to introduce ISDN, with a suite of technical standards facilitating the development of digital interoperability.[18] Telecommunication operators and information technology companies throughout the world broadly endorsed this plan. ISDN would offer progressively higher digital bandwidth (higher rates of bit transmission) connections for business, and, ultimately, for consumer applications. ISDN was the primary strategy of the dominant telecommunication operators and was supported by the telecommunication policy community. The telecommunication engineering community regarded the construction of an ISDN infrastructure as the most appropriate and systematic reconfiguration of the existing telephone network to achieve a reintegration of telephony and data communication services. In many respects, ISDN offers substantial advantages for building a broad, accessible infrastructure for the data communication needs of the information society.

ISDN has, however, been challenged at several levels as the dominant technology for achieving widespread data communication interoperability. At the most elementary level, modem equipment was devised to employ telephone circuits for data communication.[19] The quality and speed of these connections was not nearly as satisfactory as what was planned even for the lowest level of ISDN connection. However, delays in offering the most basic ISDN configuration on a widespread basis allowed a modem-based telephony data communication infrastructure to develop.[20] The early advance of this network has led to substantial price reductions in voice-line modems that provide partial solutions to quality and reliability issues. The principles at work are a combination of network externalities accelerating the diffusion of this equipment and economies of scale that reinforce the speed of diffusion by reducing the prices of such equipment.[21] These 'principles' also include the waxing and waning of enthusiasm for

[18] See Wallenstein (1990: 22) who notes that as early as 1968 the study of digital systems had been undertaken by the ITU whose aim was to develop a plan for eventual development of the ISDN. Basic-rate ISDN consists of two 64 kbps channels carrying information as B Channels devoted to data communication and one 16 kbps D Channel carrying signalling information, a configuration also referred to as 2B+D. The Primary Rate Interface operates at 2.048 Mbps in Europe and uses 30 B Channels and 1 D Channel. In the US to preserve compatibility with the North American T1 standard, 23 B Channels are employed, yielding a speed of 1.544 Mbps.

[19] Modems translate digital data bitstreams into the constrained frequency range of the human voice employed by telephony circuits and transmit continuous (*mo*dulated) signals to their destination. At the destination, these signals are (*dem*odulated) into digital bitstreams.

[20] Delays were attributable in part to the variations in implementation standards which led to increased costs of achieving interoperability between national networks and between the networks operated by Bell Operating Companies, and later Bell Regional Operating Companies in the United States. There were also variations between the implementations undertaken initially by the public telecommunication operators in Europe, see Mansell (1993).

[21] The term 'economies of scale' is used here to refer to price reductions associated with a larger market. A more precise economic explanation of price declines involves the cost reductions available from integrated circuits which are the result of both 'static' and 'dynamic' economies of scale, see Steinmueller (1992*a*), and the existence of a competitive market that translates these producer cost savings into price reductions.

ISDN on the part of the public telecommunication operators and policy-makers. In Europe, particularly, the early phases of implementation coincided with political pressures to open markets to competition and, therefore, with changes in investment strategy by the operators.

At the high end of the market, companies were dissatisfied with the speed at which high-capacity ISDN connections were becoming available (David and Steinmueller, 1990). The consequence was that they became increasingly eager to buy high-speed equipment suitable for use on leased lines or other point-to-point connections that allowed them to construct their own intra-company or closed user group data communication networks. Again, these solutions were, in principle, to be addressed by the ISDN infrastructure. As with the low-end applications, however, the early growth of the market contributed to equipment cost reduction, creating many business networks that reduced the demand for high-end ISDN services. In defence of the public telecommunication operators, the evolution of demand for both low- and high-end applications was complex and it was difficult, therefore, for these operators to respond by deploying ISDN or setting prices that would strengthen ISDN in competing with available alternatives. The facts, however, are not completely exculpatory. Even after the preponderance of the added technological value of ISDN had evaporated due to advances in dial-up modems and other technologies, network operators tended in most countries in Europe to establish prices as if there was no effective competition.

These developments have been reinforced by the extension of the TCP/IP which offers an alternative suite of standards for achieving data network construction. The IP allows the creation of networks composed of highly heterogeneous equipment that can serve dial-up equipment and is scaleable to high-speed data communication applications. The extension of the Internet from its origins as a research and academic network infrastructure to general public and business use has again provided a 'first mover' advantage for companies offering equipment employing IP standards.

The driving technological principle that has allowed the TCP/IP to advance is its capability to support the construction of heterogeneous data communication networks. The technologies that feed demand for packet switching include bridges, routers, LAN/WAN switches, and other hardware/software products. These represent an increasingly large percentage of procurement and United States companies adopting insurgent strategies dominate the market.[22] In the latter half of the 1990s, the European telecommunication industry focused on Asynchronous Transfer Mode (ATM) technology as a means to improve packet switching within the core of the networks maintained by telecommunication operators and paid relatively less attention to the IP. Perhaps they regarded the IP as an *ad hoc* and naïve approach to the problems of creating a 'proper' telecommunication network. There is much to be said for this view. The IP does not offer essential characteristics such as packet transmission priority that would facilitate real-time communication or an addressing scheme

---

[22] In the United States and Canada, the innovative technologies came not from established players such as Lucent or Nortel, but from start-up companies like Cisco and Bay Networks.

that offers proper support for billing or security. Nevertheless, the dynamism of IP expansion has disrupted a number of plans for the orderly (and, therefore, possibly slow) upgrading of the telecommunication infrastructure. ISDN has not been entirely bypassed by these developments. It remains a technically viable means for defining dial-up access for small and medium-sized businesses. Higher-level services for businesses combining TCP/IP and ISDN are still viable. ISDN's future has, however, been clouded by the TCP/IP and the proliferation of non-ISDN equipment at virtually all levels of the network.

This example is one of the most important cases of how network externalities can influence the diffusion process. Completely viable technological alternatives that fail to win adequate adoption early in the process can be bypassed entirely or in part. The key lesson is that diffusion processes matter in selecting which technology is likely to prevail in the development of a system of interconnected components. Ignoring the diffusion process because of a belief in the technological superiority of a particular solution is a dangerous strategy.

3.3 Market Drivers for the Diffusion of Advanced Information and Communication Technologies

A key question in assessing the prospects for advanced information and communication technologies and services is the identification of a market that would be sufficiently large to justify the relatively high costs of higher-capacity infrastructure deployment. The traditional market drivers for paying these costs include broadcast entertainment services, multimedia applications, and data telecommunication services. Figure 3.5 summarizes the four sources of revenue that are currently available for financing the costs of infrastructure upgrading. Data telecommunication services related to the development of LANs and their role in driving business use of data communication is the first theme of this section. The development of the Internet in strengthening business use and contributing a consumer demand component to data telecommunication is the second theme. The theme of consumer applications is continued in Ch. 4 where the contest between various forms of multimedia application delivery systems is discussed and Ch. 5 returns to the theme of the evolution of data communication services with a consideration of the role of electronic commerce.

We do not suggest that fixed and mobile services will play a major role in infrastructure upgrading. With respect to the fixed telecommunication network, the post-liberalization telecommunication network providers are unlikely to receive substantial additional revenues from telephony services that could be applied to upgrading data communication and other advanced services. Competition arising from the liberalization environment may, however, provide an incentive for telecommunication network operators to make network upgrades that will improve their competitive position. Most of these potential changes are intimately connected with the more rapidly increasing demand for data communication services and the

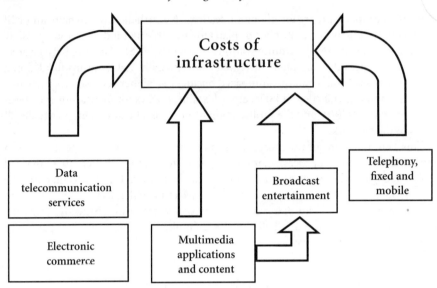

Fɪɢ. 3.5. Sources contributing to the upgrading of the information infrastructure

Source: Authors' elaboration.

opportunities offered by the various types of packet-switched network architectures discussed in this chapter.

Mobile telecommunication plays an important role in the convergence between data communication services and telephony applications, an issue that is considered in Ch. 4. The mobile telephony network is one of many sub-networks that are emerging to improve access to communication services, both voice and data. At the same time, however, mobile telecommunication is a fertile area for new service development and for extending access to information and communication services in ways that are different from the fixed-line infrastructure. These new types of access may involve very different patterns of competition between technologies than the issues discussed in this and the following two chapters. Uncertainties about how this will work in practice would dominate any present-day discussion of the topic. We have decided not to reproduce speculations about the future market potential of Universal Mobile Telecommunication System (UMTS) or other technologies supporting wireless information and communication infrastructure applications. Readers interested in these topics may wish to consult existing basic technical references or speculative discussions on this topic.[23]

Significant price competition resulting from liberalization will make it possible to upgrade the mobile telecommunication network only in ways that support either cost saving or revenue increases. Increased revenue for telecommunication network

---

[23] See e.g. Amendola and Ferraiuolo (1994); Calhoun (1992); Comparetto and Ramirez (1997); de Gournay, Tarrius, and Missaoui (1997); Mansell and Hawkins (1991); Steele (1993); Wood (1993).

operators is likely from data communication services and may arise from multimedia content provision. Significant real revenue increases are unlikely in fixed telephony either because of competitive pressure or regulatory oversight. In mobile telephony, most of the additional revenue will be absorbed by the costs of extending and upgrading the cellular radio portion of the network. Although it is possible that technological advances will allow substantial advances in mobile data communication, it seems unlikely that these will make a major contribution to extending the availability of the information and communication infrastructure to large numbers of the population.

Data communication services (including electronic commerce), and multimedia content services (including broadcast entertainment) are the principal candidates that we consider as 'drivers' of the diffusion of advanced information and communication technologies and services. Each has limitations. The expansion of data communication is particularly dynamic, but suffers from the problem of extending access to the consumer and citizen and, as this chapter and Ch. 5 make clear, is likely to be influenced in the short- and medium-term mainly by business applications. Multimedia content services, including broadcast entertainment, have considerable potential for accelerating the development of the information and communication infrastructure by creating a mass market for broadband telecommunication services. Entertainment services involving broadcast entertainment, however, can be expanded at relatively low cost using available unidirectional systems such as broadcast television and cable television. Even the greater expansion suggested by high-definition television or some forms of delivery of on-demand services can be implemented without establishing high-capacity return paths for accessing individual users. In our view these are necessary features of the information and communication infrastructure in an information society that involves the extensive use of computer-mediated communication for building democratic 'cyber-institutions', virtual communities, educational applications, and other applications in which users play an active role in contributing to content.

Data telecommunication services often receive less attention than broadcast entertainment and multimedia as a potential source of demand for broadband capacity. This is largely because many traditional data telecommunication applications (for example, e-mail or file transfer) can be implemented effectively using lower-capacity networks such as basic rate ISDN or even voice telephony switched circuits. Those who believe that distance learning, teleworking, video telephony, and other services will require much higher-capacity technologies often challenge the pessimistic conclusions suggested by this view.

Rapidly falling costs in some of the technologies that would support near-broadband access, new methods for using existing infrastructure, such as cable television, and new wireless technologies appear to offer a model for the extension of services requiring high bandwidth. In this new model, growth in high-bandwidth access would occur incrementally. Markets with customers having a high willingness to pay would receive such access capability earlier than other segments of the market. This approach substantially complicates the issue of universal service or access and the problems posed by new divisions between those with and without the opportunity to participate in the information society. This approach is, however, the most likely short-term source of market development. It is a particularly important feature of developments in inter-LAN connectivity. The high capacity of modern LANs permits implementation of desktop videoconferencing and other high-bandwidth using services. Interconnection of these LANs with private networks of leased lines, public network provision of primary-rate ISDN,[24] and other network services is extending what are, in effect, broadband services.

An examination of the chain of competing technologies that supports the information and communication infrastructure demands of inter-networking is, therefore, where we begin. As the sources of demand for inter-networking are traced, the specific role of the Internet and the technologies supporting the growth of the Internets, such as LANs and the IP, are considered (s. 3.3.1). The growth of the Internet is not only about inter-networking demand. It is also about the growing number of users of data communication services. The considerations about users that we first raised in Ch. 2 are applied in an examination of Internet access in s. 3.4.1. The specific role of business information services arising from Intranet and Extranet services are considered in s. 3.4.2. In s. 3.4.3 we extend the discussion on users to consider questions of inter-country differences in the development of web sites and the claim that the Internet's dominant language is English.

3.3.1   The Diffusion of Local Area Networks as a Market Driver

Introduced in the United States in the late 1970s as a means of connecting terminals and printers within companies or company-departments, the importance of LANs has increased dramatically. The need for workstation and personal computer connectivity is not restricted to business enterprises. Many government organizations and academic institutes have also installed LANs. LANs can be defined as 'a group of computers and associated input/output and storage devices, within a limited geographical area, such as an office block, connected by a communication link, so that any device on the network can interact with each other'.[25]

3.3.1.1   The Strategic Importance of LANs
Although LANs originated as a means to share peripherals and thus to reduce the per-user cost of acquiring peripherals, the potential of LANs for creating a local information infrastructure for data-processing applications was recognized at a relatively early stage in their development. The growth of LANs is intimately connected with the diffusion of the personal computer. Many organizations recognized that the personal computer was a mixed blessing. On the one hand, the personal computer extended and confirmed movements towards decentralized information-processing operations within the company. Applications such as word processing that previously had been

---

[24] See n. 18 for definitions of basic- and primary-rate ISDN.
[25] LANs are local in the sense that their installation does not require the use of public easements for their installation.

done clumsily on mainframe and minicomputer systems or spreadsheet analyses, a technology that originated with the personal computer, could be performed locally by the user. On the other hand, the personal computer was an inappropriate application platform for corporate applications that required high-capacity data storage, multi-user capabilities, and systematic data back-up and security procedures. These applications often included the core or 'mission-critical' functions of the company and involved ordering and invoicing, accounting and cost control, and production scheduling and quality control. These applications, as well as others, continued to be maintained on mainframe or minicomputer systems that were accessed typically from remote terminals and from personal computers that emulated terminals through various types of connections. The rapid diffusion of personal computers in business applications, therefore, was not only attributable to their ability to perform decentralized data-processing applications, but also because of their capacity to be integrated into the existing information-processing network. As a result of this latter application, personal computers benefited from, and contributed to, the creation of network externalities in information processing. Their value was enhanced by the pre-existing network of terminals and their unique capabilities for downloading information and independently processing it, contributed to the value of this network. LANs are a means to improve the connectivity in such data networks. They increase substantially the speed at which data can be transferred and they simplify the process of adding new or reconfigured paths of communication between terminal equipment. These applications provided a strong foundation for the diffusion of the technology.

LAN growth was accelerated by developments in the late 1980s and 1990s that supported further migration from centralized computing towards decentralized architectures and distributed computing. This trend is especially relevant to large organizations where the change in business strategy towards more decentralization and flatter organizations has resulted in more responsibilities at the departmental level, including managing the computing infrastructure and decisions about what software to use. These developments were supported and further stimulated by the growth of client-server technology. Client-server technology became possible when improvements in the capacities of workstations and personal computers as well as in the extension of back-up and security applications, allowed these smaller computers to serve as the central computer for multi-user and medium-sized database applications. During the 1990s many mission-critical applications still required the computational or storage capacities of the mainframe or large minicomputer. In many companies, however, the focus of new applications development shifted to the client-server network and the performance requirements of the LANs supporting these networks increased dramatically.

Throughout this process, terminal-based applications continued to be a fundamental design strategy for engineering the user interface to software applications. A terminal-based application transforms a general-purpose microcomputer into a dedicated data entry and query platform controlled by the software application. A particularly significant feature of the growth of the World Wide Web has been the burgeoning use of web pages as interfaces for database systems. A central feature of popular search engines, on-line bookstores, and many other general- and special-purpose web information applications is their use of simple data schemes to generate customized information displays for the user. The principle of the terminal-based application, therefore, has been extended and deepened by the development of the World Wide Web. The diffusion of the web as a common interface platform for the rapid prototyping and design of user interfaces for these types of applications has accelerated and reinforced the use of the Internet infrastructure. Given the dynamism of Internet developments, the rapid speed at which the packaged software browser applications for accessing content can be upgraded and distributed, and the potential for plug-ins and add-ons to the basic browser package, there is no reason to believe that the pace of development will slow. Unless fundamental errors are made in upgrading the security of Internet applications or in failing to improve performance, Internet-based applications will gradually replace every other system for database access.[26]

In short, LAN developments are marked by the emergence of a local information infrastructure, the emergence of competing technological standards for developing this infrastructure, and the acceleration and reinforcement of these developments by the creation of a common platform for accessing information resources. These developments could not, and do not, occur without substantial change in the organization. The moves towards 'flatter' organizations, more rapid response times for all organizational functions, and widespread accessibility of information resources are essential elements promoting and reinforcing the role of the LAN. As these networks are extended across the organization, they generate rapid growth in the demand for data telecommunication capacity. The increasing focus on Internet applications is shaping the form that this demand takes.

The supply of LAN equipment has, unfortunately, largely bypassed European information and communication technology companies. It has not, however, bypassed European users. LANs entered Europe with some delay and one explanation for this delay is the view that United States manufacturers first sold their LAN products in their own market. Once they faced a mature domestic market, they started marketing more aggressively in Europe. A second explanation is the fact that prices for LANs and LAN equipment were initially considerably higher in Europe than in the United States, impeding widespread diffusion, but this situation has improved. Table 3.1 illustrates the pattern of growth in LAN-related technology investments.

These investments are distributed across Europe in a pattern that illustrates the significant differences within Europe in the pattern of information and communication technology diffusion (see Fig. 3.6).

Figure 3.6 illustrates the rapid pace at which northern European countries have been adopting the LAN. A comparison of this figure with Table 3.1 illustrates that there are important distinctions between level and intensity in the development of LAN

---

[26] The database 'engine' operating behind the scenes will, of course, be subject to vigorous competition and there is no particular reason for any specific technology to become universal in performing these functions other than through one company, such as Oracle, gaining sufficient market share to dominate purchase and development decisions.

TABLE 3.1. *Market value of LAN hardware in European Union countries, selected years (m ecu)*

Country	Year					Growth Rates (%)			
	1996	1997	1998	1999	2000	1996/7	1997/8	1998/9	1999/00
Austria	81	94	115	127	138	16.2	21.9	10.6	8.8
Belgium and									
Luxembourg	145	167	194	218	231	15.3	16.1	12.3	5.6
Denmark	115	134	151	169	187	16.7	12.3	12.1	10.5
Finland	117	135	152	170	186	15.7	12.4	12	9.3
France	531	622	729	788	851	17.1	17.1	8.2	8
Germany	776	1,016	1,199	1,379	1,517	30.9	18	15	10
Greece	13	15	17	19	21	11.8	12.5	12.5	11.5
Ireland	16	18	21	23	24	12.5	15.1	10.6	6.3
Italy	258	310	346	378	404	20.5	11.5	9.1	6.9
Netherlands	298	342	372	403	426	14.6	9	8.4	5.7
Portugal	13	15	17	19	21	14.7	12.5	12.5	7.1
Spain	165	204	231	254	274	23.7	13.4	10	7.7
Sweden	245	283	322	355	375	15.5	14	10.3	5.5
United									
Kingdom	1,329	1,552	1,862	2,032	2,118	16.8	20	9.1	4.2
TOTAL	4,102	4,907	5,728	6,334	6,773	17.29	14.70	10.91	7.65

Note: Market values are expressed in constant 1997 ecu and reflect the revenues paid to primary vendors, and the value added across distribution channels for sale to the final customer; LAN hardware is restricted to the equipment for multi-user systems, PCs, or workstations required to implement a LAN; it does not include software. LAN connections that come bundled with a system and/or integrated on the motherboard (e.g. Ethernet in workstations) are excluded.
Source: European Information Technology Observatory (EITO) (1999: 352–67).

applications. For example, while France and Germany have been investing significantly less per employee in LAN equipment, the *level* of both of their investments substantially exceeds the total investment of Denmark, Finland, and Sweden combined. Correspondingly, while German investment per employee is slightly smaller than in France, the *level* of German investment is substantially higher than that of France. Collectively, demand for LAN applications is a very significant information technology market. It is also one in which European suppliers, unfortunately, have played a relatively minor role. The following section on the development of LAN technology illustrates some of the reasons why this is so.

3.3.1.2 *The Technical Evolution of LANs*

In the evolution of LANs, roughly four phases or generations can be distinguished.[27] Each is marked by a distinctive pattern of technological competition.

[27] For a more extensive overview of LAN evolution, see Christensen *et al.* (1995).

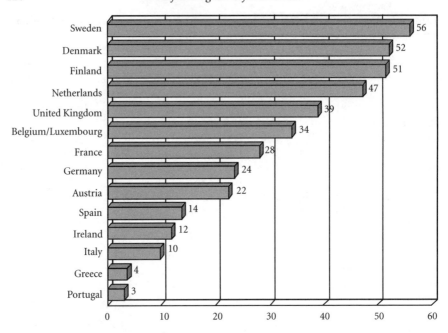

F<small>IG</small>. 3.6. Spending on LAN hardware per employee in the European Union, 1997

Note: Ecu in constant 1996 exchange rates.

Source: Adapted from Databank Consulting (1997); European Information Technology Observatory (EITO) (1997).

The first LAN to operate as a true network (rather than a dedicated wiring scheme) was the Ethernet, introduced in the late 1970s with a data rate of 10 Mbps. Ethernet employs a packet data communication technology[28] to control network transmission access in which all network transmissions are commonly available to all devices on a network connected using coaxial cable. Individual devices detect and receive packets while 'collision detection' provided a means to deal with the moments in time in which a particular packet cannot be received because the receiver is engaged in processing another packet. The packet frame size (64 bytes) and the length of the coaxial cables that could be installed limited the data rate of the first-generation Ethernet offering. The length limit of cables had the effect of limiting the size of the network in terms of the number of terminals and square footage given that terminals are spread about an office or other installation. Other first-generation systems included IBM's R-Loop and PC Network LANs. All the first-generation systems were proprietary implementations although the standards developed for the first Ethernet system implementation were later incorporated in the Institute of Electrical and Electronics Engineers' standard—IEEE 802.3.

---

[28] The technical term is Carrier Sense Multiple Access with Collision Detection (CSMA/CD).

The second generation of LANs, introduced in the mid-1980s, was driven by a cabling war in which IBM and AT&T adopted insurgent strategies in an effort to capture market share in the installation of 'upgradeable' wiring systems. These systems could serve larger installations and take advantage of improvements in the 'active electronics' of the LAN.[29] The IBM and AT&T approaches competed with a wide variety of proprietary systems in this period, all of which had the effect of 'locking' users into a particular choice of wiring. User resistance to these developments as well as the growing awareness that internal data communication would be a characteristic of modern business facilities led to the definition of generic standards for shielded and unshielded twisted pair, coaxial, and fibre that were linked to building standards. While these standards preserved the wiring rivalry between IBM (the sponsor of shielded) and AT&T (the unshielded sponsor) they also allowed a number of companies to develop alternative electronic systems and to use the standardized wiring scheme to construct LANs. The market for the active electronics portion of LANs was thus decoupled from the cabling network. During the second-generation phase, two new methods of solving the problem of simultaneous packet arrival were devised, creating further technological differentiation in the LAN market. The sponsors of these new methods, however, made them available to other market competitors through the adoption of IEEE Standards.[30]

The third generation of LANs is characterized by the use of intelligent wiring closets, the interconnection of LANs to build enterprise networks, and the rationalization of large LANs into smaller LAN segments in order to improve efficiency. The existence of the three suites of IEEE standards has improved the interoperability of equipment and allowed a measure of competitive entry. Many enterprises, however, retain a single supplier, providing an advantage for companies that can ensure smooth upgrade paths from smaller to larger networks. The rationalization of existing LANs and the construction of extensive corporate networks have led to a more extensive use of interconnection devices such as routers, bridges and hubs, and gateways. These developments have been accompanied by moves to improve LAN performance in terms of speed and throughput. In recent years, the market for LAN equipment has become diversified as illustrated in Table 3.2.

The developments set in motion in the second and third generations, as well as the ongoing progress in integrated circuit technology, make it possible to construct systems that operate well above the original Ethernet and Token Ring standards, without the necessity of installing new cabling. A key development in LAN architecture is the introduction of switching and packet technologies into the LAN. This development makes it possible to upgrade existing systems to 100 Mbps performance by changing the electronics in the wiring closets that emerged during the third generation. In addition, optical cabling systems are beginning to be deployed widely. These developments indicate the emergence of a fourth generation in LANs.

---

[29] The 'active electronics' of a LAN are the equipment that processes transmitted and received signals as distinct from the cabling system, which is only responsible for maintaining signal quality level.

[30] The CSMA/CD of first-generation Ethernet was supplemented by token bus and token ring standards that became technical standards with the adoption of IEEE 802.4 and IEEE 802.5.

TABLE 3.2. *Worldwide market sales of networking equipment (US$ m.)*

Selected product revenues	1994	1995	1997	1998
Low-speed LAN cards	3,057	3,944	n.a.	n.a.
High-speed LAN cards	240	432	n.a.	n.a.
Servers	12,995	16,000	30,617	35,854
Shared media hubs	3,259	4,771	3,360	2,068
LAN switches	390	1,300	4,446	5,135
Wiring	2,539	2,996	4,250	5,120
Network operating systems	2,046	2,332	4,176	4,927
Computer telephony integration	246	649	1,289	2,479
Network security	122	193	877	1,490
Network management	800	952	5,400	6,480
Diagnostic and test equipment	509	611	815	905
Routers	2,350	3,549	5,896	6,394
Modems	2,861	3,871	4,985	5,183
PBXs	4,063	4,444	6,986	8,677
CSU/DSUs	383	423	900	973
PRODUCT TOTAL*	43,357	55,560	101,946	119,973

Note: Only selected market segments reported; CSU = Channel Service Unit, DSU = Data Service Unit, PBX = Private Branch Exchange.

* Includes excluded categories.

Source: Data Communication Market Forecast for 1996 and 1999, http://www.data.com/cgi-bin-keyindex accessed under Market Forecast 15 September 1998 and 6 April 1999.

New applications, such as multimedia and videoconferencing, as well as the increased use of client-server architectures all have something in common; they require an increase in bandwidth or a more efficient use of available bandwidth. At the same time, enterprises are confronted with faster data rates due to an increase in the amount of data to be transferred and the need to enhance the speed at which these data can be transmitted. Due to the complexity of enterprise networks, network management is also very important.

One of the biggest disadvantages of conventional LAN technologies is that they are shared networks. This means that traffic passes every node in the network either simultaneously or sequentially. As a result, processors within the LAN are always 'competing' for bandwidth. This can be solved by a more efficient way of routing data traffic called switching. A LAN switch is a new inter-networking device that determines the destination of a particular message and sends it only to that address, thereby using the available bandwidth more efficiently. In addition to increasing available bandwidth, switching also can be used to segment LANs thus improving individual LAN performance and creating flatter networks. The concept of switched LANs has given birth to another type of LAN called a virtual LAN.

Virtual LANs (vLANs) can be defined as 'the possibility of interconnecting remote

LANs and [the workstations and personal computers of these LANs over data telecommunication channels] to create a single "logic-defined" LAN. Such LANs are capable of sharing resources and providing real interoperability by means of software, without any drastic reconfiguration or changes in wiring closets' (European Information Technology Observatory (EITO), 1996: 111). The introduction of similar approaches to network development (packet switching, fibre, the combination of voice and data on the same network) raises the possibility of technological convergence between LAN and telecommunication network technology. At a minimum, these trends suggest the integration of LAN and WAN technologies into a single infrastructure.

3.3.1.3 The Impact of LAN Developments on Data Telecommunication Traffic

The need to interconnect LANs led to the introduction of a variety of inter-networking technologies and architectures. We do not develop the history of these schemes here.[31] These inter-networking solutions began with the use of public switched telecommunication network telephone (dial-up or leased) lines in combination with modems to create links outside a single site of the organization. Because information is sent in analogue format, error detection and correction must be performed at a higher level, reducing the efficiency (and hence effective bandwidth) of transmissions.[32] Digital facilities and services overcome this disadvantage since there is no longer the requirement to translate the information for purposes of error correction or data recovery. Therefore, the modem becomes superfluous. Instead, a connecting device (Data Service Unit) is needed to connect the computer and the digital link. The main advantage of digital facilities is the transmission speeds they offer. A major drawback is that a dedicated connection (permanently assigned) is needed.

The introduction of ISDN addressed this problem by offering a non-dedicated digital connection. Basic-rate ISDN (64 kbps) is suitable for transmitting both voice and data. Basic-rate ISDN falls short of the longer-term goal of constructing a European high-capacity information and communication infrastructure. Although the technical standards have been defined and it is a straightforward matter to combine two basic-rate channels to increase capacity to 128 kbps, this still falls far short of many higher capacity requirements even with the continuing advance of compression technologies. Filling the 'gap' between 128 kbps and some speed (constantly changing) benchmark that could be defined as 'broadband' access is the task in which an entire range of technologies is competing. This gap, and the vigorous competition to fill it, is the predominant reason for the disruption of the orderly transition to an ISDN infrastructure for the European information and communication infrastructure.

The evolution of higher-capacity network services for business began with public

---

[31] A common terminological distinction in the literature is between Metropolitan Area Networks (MANs) and Wide Area Networks (WANs). Practically speaking, the main distinction involves opportunities to employ a more heterogeneous collection of technologies such as direct microwave links in the MAN while WANs are more bound to the services provided by public switched telecommunication networks.

[32] Although analogue channels can be highly reliable, they do not have equivalents for procedures such as the digital check sum for packets which provides a means of detecting data transmission errors and initiating correction (e.g. usually retransmission) procedures.

packet-switched data networks (X.25) and leased-line services, both of which have evolved to higher capacities over time with regard to speed and functionality. The X.25 packet-switched data networks are examples of parallel data communication networks constructed alongside the telephony network. In terms of functionality, the leased-line concept has evolved from dedicated transmission paths towards virtual connection paths of which Switched Multimegabit Data Service (SMDS) is one manifestation in the United States. An SMDS connection retains several characteristics of a leased line even though it is, in practice, a service quality definition for a data connection achieved using a telecommunication operator's network (which, increasingly, is likely to be based on packet-switching technologies). The nearly technically identical European service is called Connectionless Broadband Data Service (CBDS). The development of fully digital high-speed connections is closely related to the spread of fibre optics. Fibre optics are the basis for Frame Relay Services (FRS),[33] Cell Relay Services (CRS), and Asynchronous Transfer Mode (ATM)[34] as well as for many implementations of high-capacity ISDN.

The technologies for constructing ever faster networks appear to offer the capabilities for meeting virtually any level of capacity demand. The problem is the cost of these technologies when they are translated into services. Having the means to extend LANs across widely separated sites, especially spanning international boundaries, is still a major problem for small and medium-sized enterprises and an expensive proposition for large organizations. Nevertheless, it is clear that substantial demand exists for data communication services that can support inter-networking of LANs and this can only be expected to grow as the quantity and quality of information resources (based both on traditional and newer, Intranet, approaches) within LANs improves.

More sophisticated networking will pose challenges to existing LANs in terms of speed requirements. The market for commercial network services continues to be dominated by leased lines. However, their market share is dropping rapidly, partly due to the use of Internet backbones to carry traffic. Traditional packet-switching networks are gradually losing position in the market and are being replaced by fast packet-switching services. The next step in the evolution of LANs is the virtual LAN which brings with it a need for more co-ordination and the further development of virtual offices and telecommuting.

---

[33] Frame Relay Services were introduced at the beginning of the 1990s. The idea is that permanent virtual circuits are brought together in a larger virtual network. This network is operated and maintained by a network operator and can be shared by other customers. Since only one access line is needed to establish the connection between the customer and the virtual network, companies can more efficiently use the available bandwidth 'on demand' rather than using multiple dedicated leased lines. Major drawbacks are that Frame Relay Services support only data transmission and switching technology is often proprietary.

[34] ATM is a fast packet technology that is cell-based, meaning that data are divided into cells with a fixed length of 53 bytes and then switched through the network. A similar technique is used with CRS. Cells are switched through public or private networks. The switching techniques differ between ATM-CRS and Frame Relay. Whereas the latter uses proprietary switches, the former uses ATM switches. ATM and CRS have two important advantages over Frame Relay Services: they support data and voice, image, and video transmissions and they use cells with a fixed format, which enhances speed. These distinctions are, however, subject to revision as technological improvements shift the relative positions of these technologies.

3.3.2 Friction at the Interface: An Uneasy Relationship

The evolution of effective inter-networking strategies for the connection of LANs presents a paradox for telecommunication network operators. On the one hand, the data communication revenues available from inter-networking are substantial and high-volume sites can be very profitable due to the relative simplicity of connecting them to the high-capacity spine of the telecommunication network. On the other hand, LANs are capable of completely integrating voice and data traffic so that the network operator's voice telephony revenues from its customer's intra-company calls disappear. With the embedding of some processing intelligence in the company's network management system, a substantial share of telephony traffic will bypass the telecommunication network operators' intended tariff structure.[35]

This paradox creates difficult strategic choices for the telecommunication network operator. One strategy is fully to embrace data telecommunication. The main disadvantage of this strategy is that it encourages companies to accelerate their development of inter-networking solutions and then to shop for the lowest priced 'bulk' networks operator, which, with market liberalization, may not be the incumbent telecommunication network operator. Thus, a strategy of fully embracing data communication developments may prove catastrophic in the longer term. A second strategy is to devise a means simultaneously to slow the pace towards some forms of data communication while devising services that will tie customers more tightly to the telecommunication network operator's services.

This latter strategy is the one most commonly being adopted in Europe. It has several distinct elements: (1) promotional pricing and short-term price discrimination eroding the competitive environment for newer services; (2) migration costs or switching costs from legacy networks to newer networks; and (3) discrimination against equipment suppliers preventing the deployment of the 'best available' network technologies for public infrastructure. The first two are interdependent since incumbent telecommunication operators face the problem that new technologies are likely to threaten their existing portfolio of services. The easy solution is to introduce a pricing strategy that protects major revenue streams and directs market developments along a predefined trajectory. Along with premium prices, early adopters also bear 'uncertainty costs', further discouraging the diffusion of new technologies.

Promotional Pricing: In the monopoly era of telecommunication, tariffs levied by public telecommunication operators were often set according to the market being served, i.e., the general public or the corporate sector. In the latter sector, the main revenue earner was leased-lines services and billing was by regular payment for each line. With the advent of new technologies, the pricing structures of public telecommunication operators are changing. The proliferation of billing data, along with the advent of virtual circuits and least-cost-networking allow more complex billing models to be used. In business markets, there is substantial opportunity to

---

[35] These possibilities also create some friction within telecommunication network operators where data communication and telephony are commonly organized as separate business units.

negotiate packages of telephony charges that reduce the costs of high-volume traffic. These forms of price discrimination may, in some cases, be difficult to reconcile with principles of 'cost based' pricing, but they provide an important instrument for reducing the customers' efforts to invest in inter-networking based bypass. Network technology for corporate users has been based on fixed leased lines, but newer technology allows virtual private circuits or networks to be set up. These 'group service' definitions avoid the problems associated with cost-based pricing and serve the same purpose of discouraging customer investment in bypass technologies.[36]

Migration Costs: In Europe, the Open Network Provision (ONP) Directive and subsequent legislation calls for harmonized technical characteristics for network interfaces and the availability of information on the supply (including delivery and repair times), usage, and access conditions (European Council, 1990). The intention of ONP is to reduce the costs of migration and thus to increase competition. The Directive, however, is oriented towards transparency rather than regulation and incumbent telecommunication operators retain substantial latitude in setting the terms, conditions, and pricing of particular services. The construction of large-scale private networks requires considerable co-operation with the network operator because competitive conditions vary considerably. While high-speed connections within a particular metropolitan area may be priced very competitively, the same competition may not apply in other locations that the customer wishes to make an integral part of its corporate network. It is possible, therefore, for the incumbent telecommunication operator to influence the overall costs of upgrading, making it a less attractive option than purchasing a more heterogeneous collection of services which implies a continuing dependence on the incumbent operator.

Technical Barriers: The diffusion of new technologies into the network infrastructure is influenced by the evolution of demand for advanced information and communication services. At the centre of recent developments is the demand for business data communication services and the upgrading of the network using advanced packet switches such as ATM. What is done within the telecommunication network in terms of technology need not be directly or immediately translated into new service offerings. Moreover, the pricing of services reflects the strategic aims of telecommunication operators who are influenced by the emergence of competition under market liberalization. Thus, because equipment is available for implementing a technology does not mean the smooth or easy translation of this investment into a service.

The purpose of noting these issues is not to make an argument about how extensively they are being employed by network operators in any particular European Member State. Rather it is to call attention to the friction that can arise in the integra-

---

[36] Cost-based pricing issues are discussed in Bigham (1997); Cave (1997); Garnham (1997); Trebing (1997). For a discussion of bypass of the public switched network by leased-line configurations see Bethesda Research Institute (1984); General Accounting Office (1986); Mansell (1986) and for the potential of bypass by IP networks see Kiessling and Blondeel (1999: 26).

tion of a common information infrastructure. The incentives for its construction are not completely aligned and potential, or actual, friction between telecommunication network operators and their customers is likely to have an important influence on the evolution of the European information and communication infrastructure. It is possible, however, that the speed and intensity of the movement towards creating an upgraded infrastructure that can support Internet traffic will surmount technological and artificial or strategic barriers to network integration. Assessing this possibility is the purpose of the next section.

3.4   TCP/IP: The Dominant Networking Technology for the Twenty-First Century?

As noted in s. 3.2.3, the TCP/IP emerged from efforts to define a standard for inter-computer communication that could be used in a highly heterogeneous network.[37] The standard for network connectivity defining the Internet is the IP. The IP has evolved into one of the most flexible networking protocols available. Despite its flexibility, the IP network has characteristics that have given it the reputation of being difficult to use in corporate networking environments. This reputation arises from two principal sources. First, many corporations have made substantial investments in data communication networks that follow protocols different from those of the TCP/IP. There are concerns that integrating these networks with the TCP/IP-based networks may create substantial performance problems. Second, proprietary protocols often provide a variety of tracking and security features that are not available in the IP. This raises questions about the soundness of committing confidential data (and corporations regard most of their data as confidential) to IP networks.

Internet service providers, equipment vendors, and software developers argue that they can offer the security, performance, availability, and multi-protocol support of a private network using the cost-effective and global Internet.[38] With respect to performance, there are converter technologies available for virtually all the legacy protocols that permit multi-protocol operation of complex networks with very little or no degradation in performance. In addition, many of the remaining performance issues can be dealt with by contracting with ISPs who have direct feeds into Internet

---

[37] The original research objectives for the Internet also stressed the development of a network that would be robust to the disruption to particular links. By employing a standard by which individual packets could be routed flexibly, a communication system that 'detoured around damage' was created. Internet performance is an emergent property of a very complex and heterogeneous system. So far, this system has proved to be remarkably robust, although Robert Metcalfe, the inventor of the Ethernet in May 1973 and founder of 3Com Corporation in 1979, has warned that there is a substantial probability of major network malfunction, see Metcalfe (1995; 1998).

[38] In the United States, attractive pricing of IP networks is resulting from IP network providers offering flat rates for each network connection. This includes all communication facilities (circuits), terminal equipment or customer premise equipment (CPE) necessary for IP access, site routers, and external modems for remote out-of-bandwidth access. Ongoing monitoring and management support are also included, providing a full end-to-end managed service. Additionally, the vendor will provide on-site installation; 7 day, 24 hour, on-site field-support; equipment maintenance; and detailed usage reports.

backbone services operating at much more rapid data rates than the majority of the legacy systems. Performance can still be an issue for some types of application, but it is not a major issue for the majority of corporate data communication needs.

Security is addressed by advances in encryption techniques and firewall technology. Encryption technology was, for a time, relatively controversial due to national security concerns about the availability of 'strong encryption' (encryption that could not easily be overcome by national security or police agencies). These concerns have faded with the growing commercial availability of encryption methods that are likely to resist even determined efforts at decryption. We take up this issue again in Ch. 8.

Firewalls are becoming an important component of any organization's network security architecture. The best firewalls provide security controls without making Internet access prohibitively difficult for the end user. Some firewalls even improve upon those solutions by adding detailed audit trails and accounting information. State-of-the-art firewalls offer management control over secure Internet and Intranet resources, logging usage and charge-back reports, intrusion detection capabilities, and graphical administrative interfaces to provide secure and managed network access solutions. Today's TCP/IP networks can provide this advanced level of security, accountability, and manageability. However, network-wide mutual authentication and centrally controlled access authorization are also required in a distributed environment. Once the connection is established, unique site-to-site data encryption at the customer LAN level is necessary to ensure confidentiality of all network traffic, making it unintelligible and unalterable by unwanted visitors. TCP/IP network providers can protect data by offering end-to-end network-based data encryption, where the traffic is protected before it leaves the customer site.

Advances in TCP/IP technology together with the increasingly widespread use of TCP/IP-based applications and a growing body of experience in the management of TCP/IP networks, mean that IP-based networks are now appropriate and robust enough for the majority of today's corporate networking needs. The issues of IP performance and security may be addressed specifically and resolved to the majority of users' satisfaction. The ability to share information across a single, multi-site enterprise that crosses international boundaries is now regarded as a strategic necessity in business. Connecting these locations securely and reliably requires significant ongoing capital investment and evolving expertise. As service-level demands increase, in-house resources become strained, jeopardizing overall network reliability and diminishing effectiveness. By using IP, companies can choose the telecommunication medium best suited to their needs while keeping the corporate infrastructure stable and flexible. This strategy protects investment in the network while keeping open options for future transport technologies.

This relatively positive assessment of Internet technology is offset by three significant issues: (1) the possibility of a performance gap in TCP/IP as companies develop faster LANs and the need for higher data communication performance; (2) the specific problems of managing dial-up Internet access on the public switched telecommunication network; and (3) the particular demands that the rapid growth of Internet

TABLE 3.3. *Comparison of data communication technologies*

Feature	X.25	IP	Frame Relay	ATM
Frame/cell length	Variable (64–2,000 bytes)	Variable (64 to several thousand bytes)	Variable (64–9,000 bytes)	Fixed (53 bytes)
Switching mechanism	Software	Software	Software	Hardware
Typical user port speed	4.8–64 kbps	64–128 kbps	64–2,048 kbps	155 Mbps
Maximum user port speed	2 Mbps	10 Mbps	45 Mbps	622 Mbps
Transmission medium	Twisted pair Coaxial cable	Twisted pair Coaxial cable	Twisted pair Coaxial cable Untwisted pair	Coaxial cable Fibre Untwisted pair
Cost per kilobit of user data switched	High	High	Moderate	Low

Note: This ignores new developments in compression techniques.
Source: Adapted from Narendran (1997) and Greenstein (1995).

data communication places on the telecommunication network. Each of these issues is subject to mitigation by technological means. The first, however, requires an upgrade of the current TCP/IP standards and the possibly substantial costs of retrofitting existing systems designed around current standards.

The positive assessment of Internet technology in meeting *today's* corporate data communication needs is a more specific statement than it might appear at first glance. Although the current TCP/IP standards are flexible and offer substantial performance, the ceiling on that performance is approximately equal to that of third-generation LANs. Moreover, high-performance data communication network standards substantially exceed current TCP/IP standards as illustrated in Table 3.3.

Table 3.3 illustrates that while TCP/IP offers substantial advantages over the traditional packet-switched networks, a factor that helps explain the Internet's growing dominance, it is substantially slower than the upper limits of either Frame Relay or ATM technologies. This need not be a very severe problem so long as the costs of IP networks remain relatively inexpensive and LANs are operating at the top speed of 10 Mbps. However, it can become a much more serious consideration as LANs are upgraded and competition reduces the costs of services based upon Frame Relay or

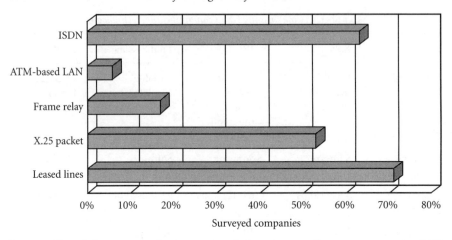

FIG. 3.7. Use of data communication services in large western European companies, 1997

Source: Adapted from International Data Corporation (1997); Passamonti, Sisti, and Cattaneo (1997).

ATM technologies. As can be seen in the last row of Table 3.3, Internet technology does not dominate on the basis of cost.

The urgency of Internet upgrading in Europe depends upon how rapidly companies are developing demand for high-speed networking services. Figure 3.7 indicates that as of 1997, the demand for the higher-performance Frame Relay and ATM services was affecting a relatively small number of companies. Figure 3.7 suggests as well that a certain amount of delay is possible. It is important, however, to keep in mind that, as companies do move towards the use of ATM and Frame Relay services, they will be investing in equipment that will create future legacy problems of integration when the TCP/IP standards are upgraded.

The second and third issues with respect to the Internet involve interactions between Internet usage and public switched telecommunication networks. The ability to provide dial-up services for the Internet is becoming an enormous management task for service providers. Support for registered addresses, multi-protocol environments, and higher-speed infrastructures is encouraging service providers to look for alternative methods of supporting the explosive growth of the dial-up Internet community. New classes of virtual dial-up solutions that allow multiple protocols and the use of unregistered addresses over a public infrastructure are being examined.[39]

The goal of a virtual dial-up service is to allow many separate and autonomous protocol domains to share a common access infrastructure including modems, access servers, and ISDN routers. By providing virtual dial-up solutions, service providers can offer a full range of services closer to the remote user. A key component of the virtual dial-up service is tunnelling, a vehicle for encapsulating packets inside a proto-

---

[39] Examples including IPX, SLIP, and PPP are responses to growing demand in this area.

col that is understood at the entry and exit points of a given network. These entry and exit points are defined as tunnel interfaces. The tunnel interface itself is similar to a hardware interface, but it is configured in software.[40] This is a key component for defining and using Virtual Private Networks (VPNs) mainly for business use.

As data traffic becomes an increasingly large part of the public telecommunication network operator's business, the makers of inter-networking products are challenging the traditional suppliers of telecommunication infrastructure equipment. At stake is the very nature of the telephone switch, the heart of the voice network. This 'rewriting' of the network is rooted in the unprecedented attempt to bring reliable levels of business computing to a public network designed and built for voice services. That goal will change the public networks markedly, and it is testing the mettle of switching and router companies that must re-engineer their products to withstand high levels of reliability within an Internet that is itself in danger of overloading.

Over the years, telecommunication engineers have constructed statistical models of how much traffic the telephone network can expect to receive and they have built and deployed telephone equipment to handle that expected volume of traffic.[41] It is known, for example, how likely it is on average that a call will last a certain amount of time and how much capacity will be used in a given span of time. The assumptions underlying the models change when a modem is used to dial into an ISP. In the United States, the average call to an ISP is estimated at 20 minutes or almost seven times the average duration of a voice call.[42] This increase in the average length of the call significantly alters the traffic that can be safely carried on a telecommunication network without risking service interruptions.

Without increasing the overall traffic on the network, long Internet calls result in a higher overall probability of an individual receiving a busy signal when making a voice telephone call. Internet usage could jeopardize the traditional guarantees of access to the telephone network for basic voice service. Ideally, equipment vendors would like the ISPs to buy high-bandwidth data connections to receive the packetized output of the calls terminated on the switches. In this way, the data call is removed from the voice network all the way to the ISP's premises. The public telecommunication operators would take over from the ISPs the task of managing modem banks. But the ISPs are not rushing to throw out their modems since this is what they are currently in business to provide. Over time, ISPs may relinquish the handling of modems to focus on higher-

---

[40] Tunnelling involves the three types of protocols: (1) The passenger protocol is the protocol being encapsulated; in a dial-up scenario, this protocol could be any PPP, SLIP or text dialogue; (2) the encapsulating protocol is used to create, maintain, and tear down the tunnel; and (3) the carrier protocol is used to carry the encapsulated protocol. IP will be the first carrier protocol used because of its robust routing capabilities, ubiquitous support across different media, and deployment within the Internet, see Bernard (1998).

[41] The main portion of switching costs is comprised of port costs which are driven by BHEs, a measure of the throughput of calls in the network in the busiest hour of the day. The Erlang is a dimensionless measure of call density defined by the number of call seconds per second on a circuit or group of circuits. In a single circuit, the Erlang is the share of time that the circuit is occupied, typically 0.6 on a junction circuit and 0.05 for a residential circuit, see Mazda and Mazda (1999). There are also processing costs with respect to the number of busy hour call attempts and other unattributable costs, see Cave (1997: 276).

[42] In the USA, without metered calling, a portion of Internet calls will be 24 hours or more in duration.

level services such as e-mail and web home pages. The network operators may also move to own the ISPs, in which case, they could resolve traffic congestion and related problems in a variety of different ways.

The issues of Internet performance and interactions with the public switched telecommunication network are serious. They will require mitigation through performance improvements in the TCP/IP standards. As the Internet is called upon to deliver video and audio material, technological alternatives will be tested in real-time network environments. Many protocols and architectures are likely to emerge to support better performance or new services. If Internet-related technologies and applications are to meet expectations, the separation between the new assortment of web servers and clients and the well-established infrastructure of client/server and host-based applications in terms of performance, scaleability, and reliability, will have to be overcome. Connections between the two worlds of computing are difficult to create. For example, a Common Gateway Interface link from a web server to a relational database consumes excessive system overhead. And the web server itself provides no support for the multithreading and load balancing that enable an application server or database server to support heavy loads of transactions. Web servers provide a rather cumbersome intermediary for these kinds of applications.

This discussion indicates that barriers may lie ahead for the spread of Internet technology. It seems unlikely, however, that these problems will create a critical short-term bottleneck for the continuing development of TCP/IP standards. IP data networks have enormous momentum to become the common infrastructure for communication and information services. Those who adopt a wait-and-see attitude will do so at some risk. The extent of this risk has much to do with whether the explosion in recent years of the use of the Internet to distribute information resources will continue to accelerate, confirming the use of the Internet as the platform of choice for distributing business information. This is the subject of the next section. It also is related to rates of growth in the use of the Internet for entertainment and electronic commerce, the subjects of the next two chapters.

3.4.1 *The Soft Driver of Diffusion: The Internet as Information Resource and Software Change Agent*

A commonly mentioned feature of the information society is that new information and communication technologies will form the basis for the creation of major new repositories of information. Often, these developments are believed to be taking place in the context of markets for information content and the distribution of copyrighted information that are examined in Ch. 7. This section reviews the development of Internet-related software technologies as a dynamic source of demand for the use of the LANs and telecommunication services discussed in the previous sections. Understanding this issue requires shifting the perspective from the hardware-oriented discussion of the previous analysis to a discussion of the role of software and information resources as accelerators of the Internet's diffusion.

From the diffusion perspective, software can be regarded as a component within information and communication systems. Some software, such as the operating system, is deeply embedded in the system and is necessary for its operation to perform any useful function. This type of software is called 'system software'. Other software is essentially an add-on, extending the functionality of the basic system in the acquisition, processing, or output of information and is called 'application software'. In the case of personal computers, a specific category of application software has emerged called 'multimedia software'. Multimedia software employs the display and audio capabilities of a personal computer to display content and, usually, to elicit interaction with the user under the control of a 'script'. Although multimedia software may be used to implement educational or recreational applications, for example, game scripts, user interfaces increasingly incorporate elements of multimedia design and the personal computer may be viewed by the software designer as a 'multimedia platform' or 'information appliance'. Important compatibility problems exist in the development of multimedia software for computer applications.[43]

A large and growing network of inter-computer connections and a suite of software standards and applications are the fundamental features of the Internet. The software defining the Internet can be divided into categories similar to those for software in general. The operating system of the Internet is the set of inter-computer communication software standards that are implemented in hundreds of machine-specific software products to create the basic functionality of data communication systems. This basic functionality is extended through the definition of software applications (services) for the transfer of files and e-mail. Other basic applications include the ability to access files stored on a remote computer and to operate a remote computer locally using a terminal emulation interface (if the user has appropriate user privileges on a given computer). These services are exciting and useful for the computer literate and basically boring or useless for the rest of the population.

The transformation of the Internet's software that is responsible for its explosive growth is the development of the World Wide Web based upon a March 1989 proposal of Tim Berners-Lee of CERN.[44] The World Wide Web is based upon a set of standards for the creation of linked information files called documents and the development of an application programme, the browser, to read this information.[45] Browsers require a graphic user interface (a computer capable of displaying information in 'windows'

---

[43] This view of the PC has until recently confronted major compatibility problems. Substantial variety existed in the display formats of PCs using Microsoft operating systems and the Intel iAPX family of microprocessors (e.g. the 8088, 286, 386, and Pentium), the dominant PC platform. In addition, the precise type of graphic display interface card installed determines the capabilities of the video display to support animation and television-like content. Similar problems exist with regard to sound capabilities where, fortunately, an early *de facto* (market-led) standard from Creative Labs has served as a platform for achieving compatible audio development.

[44] CERN, the Conseil Européen pour la Recherche Nucléaire, was established following UNESCO-sponsored meetings in 1952. In 1954 it was dissolved, although the acronym was retained with the establishment of Le Laboratoire Européen pour la Physique des Particules or The European Laboratory for Particle Physics by twelve EU Member States. By 1999, membership had grown to twenty European countries.   [45] Initially HTML, which is now evolving towards XML.

that can be manipulated using a pointing and selection device such as a 'mouse').[46] The scheme for linking documents, 'hypertext', allowed the document creator to create a link to any other document on the web that could be selected with the pointing device.[47] Because the web was devised to be an Internet service, a principal aim in its development was to ensure a consistent user interface for data files (documents) across all devices that could support a pointing device and the graphic display of information.[48] A final initial design feature of the web was Berners-Lee's interest in an expansive definition of the term 'document' to encompass a wide range of information types. This design feature has proved to be particularly important in supporting the extension of the web as an application platform for software development.

From these simple and basic elements, a global information network began to spread on the Internet after the invention of the Mosaic browser in 1993.[49] Vocabulary such as a web 'page' (the document), 'site' (location of a collection of web pages), 'link' (hypertext link), and 'home page' (the welcoming page of a site which should provide a guide to navigating its information content) emerged and provided a more popular flavour for the World Wide Web. The technical origins of the system are retained by the prefix to addresses http:// (HyperText Transfer Protocol) which, although mysterious to many users, has now become a well-identified signifier for the availability of web information.[50] The development of browsers available from commercial suppliers (for example, Netscape and Microsoft) in 1994 was particularly important for the rapid expansion of the Internet. Commercial browsers provided the ability to add 'plug-in' software allowing the display of information not supported by the browser directly. The commercialization of the Internet allowed the development of companies offering various types of access as a service via ISPs.

The flexibility of the Internet allows users to be simultaneously information collectors and providers. Any user can set up a Home Page on the web and a very wide range of organizations have developed a 'web presence' with home pages offering information and services. The World Wide Web's ability to support both the generation and supply of information in a multimedia format offers an enormously flexible medium for creating information resources either for public access or specialized for a par-

[46] The mouse was invented by Douglas Engelbart (with William English) in the 1950s and 1960s at SRI in Menlo Park, California, and publicly demonstrated at the Joint Computer Conference in 1968 in San Francisco. Engelbart now leads the Bootstrap Institute, http://www.bootstrap.org accessed 6 April 2000. The Xerox PARC 'Star Computer' was given a live demonstration in 1981.

[47] The idea of hypertext had already been devised and implemented on a variety of computers including the Apple Macintosh where it was the basis of the HyperCard application.

[48] The World Wide Web was developed by Tim Berners-Lee at CERN based on a 1989 proposal and the W3C (World Wide Web Consortium) based at the MIT Laboratory for Computer Science, the National Institute for Research in Computing Science and Control in France, and Keio University in Japan. See www.w3.org/History/1989/proposal-msw.html accessed 6 April 2000, for the original CERN proposal for the Internet written by Berners-Lee.

[49] Berners-Lee devised the components defining the World Wide Web which include a HTML, a service protocol definition for transferring files across the net HTTP, and an addressing method for identifying files, URL. Mosaic was developed by students working at the National Center for Supercomputing Applications (NCSA) at the University of Illinois in 1993, see Cusumano and Yoffie (1998: 3).

[50] The term HTTP (Hypertext Transfer Protocol) corresponds to the File Transfer Protocol (FTP), an earlier Internet service devised for file transfer which, along with other Internet services, is accessible from most browsers.

ticular interest or organization. The rapid diffusion of the web has created problems for both web and other Internet users. Speed of access to information, reliability, and congestion problems occur as more users come on-line. These problems are exacerbated by the transfer of large documents, some of which are designed for access at connection speeds unattainable by dial-up users, potentially decreasing the performance and value of the Internet to its existing set of users.[51]

World Wide Web information uses the information transfer standards of the Internet which involve the use of packets containing information defining their destination. Users share networks, not only by sharing a common transport layer with users from their location, but also through access to intermediate connection points in the network serving distant users. The sharing of network facilities and resources has been a key feature of the economic model within which the Internet is expected to operate. This model is based upon users of a particular network undertaking its funding and maintenance regardless of its usage by other networks under the mutual understanding that other networks will provide the same open access. Thus, the costs of setting up the Internet have been distributed widely among ISPs, and the costs to users of accessing information through a myriad of networks extending across the world have been the same as accessing the local ISP.[52]

The very rapid diffusion of the World Wide Web has been facilitated by the distribution of software for Internet access through the network itself, the existence of relatively straightforward tools for content creation, and the novelty of the system as a new application for the networked personal computer. Any of these features, alone, might prove ephemeral as new systems and content access methods are introduced. However, the impact of the growth of the web suggests, collectively, that the generation of substantial network externalities will play a major role in the future development of this global information infrastructure. The value of producing information content using web standards for information transfer is increasing at an enormous pace as the number of users expands. Correspondingly, as the number of users expands, the value (measured not only directly in monetary terms from potential electronic commerce services, but also in terms of publicity, customer support, advertising, and public service) of producing content according to this standard is increasing at a very rapid pace. The interaction between these two trends is the kind of virtuous or self-reinforcing circle that is often responsible for the creation of *de facto* or proprietary-led standards. In the case of the World Wide Web, developments are all the more rapid because the software standards themselves are freely available. The extremely rapid pace of development in the web is now being reinforced by the creation of labour skills for creating information content and managing web-based services. Increasingly, business users are turning to web-related standards and tools as a means to distribute information internally within companies, further reinforcing the use of this technology.

At present, two of the largest markets created by the World Wide Web are the market for user access and the market for distributing information content. Both these

---

[51] For a full discussion of this see Bailey (1997) and McKnight and Bailey (1997).
[52] For a discussion of these issues, see Huston (1999).

markets stimulate demand for telecommunication services with the latter market providing demand for higher-speed access to serve increasingly congested network paths as the number of users seeking access increases. Similarly, users are experiencing delays, particularly in trans-Atlantic links and the existence of such delays has led to the widespread creation of 'mirror' sites in which information from Europe (and elsewhere) is available on North American computers and vice versa.

The development of the web has had a number of important implications for the software industry. For over two decades there has been widespread speculation in the software community about the possibilities of a new 'paradigm' of software creation based upon 'objects', i.e. reusable program code modules with clearly defined interfaces. For the most part, these developments were confined to computer science research departments and specialized computer languages such as 'Small Talk'. It now seems possible that the Internet-based software distribution methods that are being used by America Online-owned Netscape and other Internet software companies to achieve broad penetration of their products offer a model for the distribution of 'objects' and the creation of operating systems that will co-ordinate the use of local computer system resources by objects. This development could result in a dramatic reconfiguration of the market for personal computer operating systems and have major implications for the use of the telecommunication network for the distribution of software.[53]

There are, however, many unanswered questions in projecting major changes in this area. It is unclear, for example, whether standardized interfaces among objects will emerge creating the network externalities necessary for their broad adoption. There are also likely to be substantial problems in locating the sources of faults or 'bugs' created by objects that do not conform to these interface standards, or are themselves faulty. Finally, it is unclear what the business model is for the development of this market. How will users select and pay for the objects that they use? Which objects will be freely distributed and which will be distributed on a commercial basis? Answering these questions will require considerably greater development of network-based payment systems than is currently available and it remains to be seen whether the performance and quality of traditional stand-alone applications such as word processors or spreadsheets can be improved through network distribution.

3.4.2   Intranets as Demand Drivers for Business Communication Services

An Intranet can be defined as 'a data communication network that uses the TCP/IP protocol to implement the distributed hypermedia system referred to as the World Wide Web to a group of users internal to a specific organization'.[54] This definition

---

[53] The most visible development is the Open Source Movement developments and the emergence of the Linux operating system developed by Linus Torvald which, in fact, is based on 30-year-old technology. Although some envisage that Linux will be able to take on Microsoft Windows (2000) in the form of Windows NT 5.0, others are much more sceptical, see Metcalfe (1999).

[54] When used in an Intranet, the web is not world wide except in the sense that the standard is also employed on the Internet. The spill-over from global public use to private use is a key issue explored in this section.

conveys little of the economic and social potential arising from this particular technology. Intranets are rapidly becoming a major method for distributing information within organizations such as business enterprises, government administrations, and educational institutions.[55] The growth of the web on the Internet is broadening the constituency for high-speed data communication access as a growing number of dial-up users encounter the World Wide Web as the World Wide 'Wait'. For 'users internal to a specific organization', access to web-type information stored on the LAN server can occur at the data transmission speed supported by the LAN, frequently as high as 10 Mbps or between 350 to 1,250 times faster than the speed experienced by dial-up users. This difference in speed creates a qualitatively different environment for the use of web technology. Applications that would be tediously slow to utilize in a dial-up environment become indistinguishable from applications that are resident to the personal computer used to operate the web browser. The result is that Intranet applications have the potential to be used to pioneer the leading edge of technological development.

The potential of Intranet applications has been reinforced by the spill-overs that organizations receive from the rapid expansion of software tools developed for creating web applications. These tools are transforming the process of applications software development. Web browsers can be regarded as extensions of the computer's operating system, defining a 'virtual machine' that is relatively standardized across different models and vintages of computers. Applications that would previously have been developed for operation under the control of the computer operating system are now being designed to employ the services provided by 'browser' software. At first glance, browsers are application programs similar to word-processor or spreadsheet programs; their real significance begins with their use as an intermediary between other application programs and the operating system. This, by itself, would not be noteworthy. What makes this revolutionary is the capability rapidly to add and reconfigure the resources available to the browser by downloading extensions from the web and the enormous installed base of browser software. Thus, the browser is not only an intermediate operating system, it is one that is extensible and for which the resources may be made available wherever web access is possible, that is, essentially wherever computers are located.

These two capabilities of Intranets, their use as a publication medium and their ability to have their capacities rapidly upgraded and easily extended, make them a very attractive platform for the development of all types of information resources including multimedia applications and the use of the multimedia technique in other applications programs. In addition, however, two further developments have occurred that strengthen the Intranet even further.

The significance of the first, extensions to the browser, is that the computer's oper-

[55] Zona Research, an American market research company specializing in Internet and Intranet developments, estimated that businesses worldwide spent US$ 6b. in 1996 in direct costs for the construction of Intranets and forecast that this would grow to US$ 28b. by 1999 (http://www.zonaresearch.comnfo/press/IntraOpp.htm accessed 12 September 1999). Their 1996 annual report indicated that the installed base of Intranet exceeded Internet servers in that year and forecast Intranet server shipments would outpace those for the Internet at a four to one ratio for the remainder of the 1990s (Zona Research, 1996: 45).

ating system can be viewed as open and extensible. A number of products have emerged to exploit this opportunity including JAVA and ShockWave. JAVA is the most far-ranging extension to emerge so far, providing the emulation of a complete general-purpose computer with a rich virtual operating system that controls the real resources of the computer (display, sound, printing, etc.). In principle, JAVA can implement any computer applications program on its virtual computer.[56] The gap between principle and reality, however, is significant. Virtual computers, like emulation programs, must work through several layers of automated interpretation and may therefore suffer from reduced performance compared to software that is designed for a particular computer environment. Thus, there is a trade-off between generality and performance. The performance penalty seen by the user, however, is being reduced by continuing rapid improvements in microprocessor operating speeds, the borrowing of Reduced Instruction Set Computer (RISC) concepts in the design of virtual computers, and the use of the capacities of specific computer systems for performance of critical functions. Only the last of these is likely to introduce further complications into the design of applications.[57]

The second development was the announcement of the decision on 22 January 1998 of Netscape Inc., the leading browser producer, to provide the source code for its product (Cusumano and Yoffie, 1998: 36). This decision allows other companies to incorporate browser resources into their application programs. Netscape's decision to distribute this asset free of charge to the software community remains controversial and the company posted net financial losses in its final income statement before being acquired by America Online Inc. (AOL). It has, however, confirmed the likelihood that the tools for *utilizing* World Wide Web resources will remain inexpensive and that the platform represented by web software technology will continue to be an active area of development for the foreseeable future. The specific ways in which this technology is being exploited are the subjects of the next sections.

3.4.2.1   *Local Development of Advanced Information and Communication Services*

The consequence of rapid data transfer excess capacity is that LAN-based Intranets are a promising area for the development of 'frontier' services such as video conferencing, video messaging, and other audiovisual services. Defining and implementing these services are more likely to depend upon organizational issues, such as conservatism about their value, than on technological capability or upgrade cost.[58] One opportunity provided by advanced services involves the system integration and software develop-

---

[56] The approach of JAVA advocates is to extend the cross-platform use of JAVA so that virtually all microprocessor environments, including dedicated control or embedded systems can be programmed using the same language. These developments may create further advantages for some companies where software development is often highly differentiated by the 'target machine' for which software is being developed.

[57] These complications are similar to 'system resource' extensions to operating system software. New extensions may not be fully compatible with earlier versions so that two different application programs may demand incompatible operating system resources. When a single company controls the operating system, the responsibility for these problems can be clearly attributed and resolved. When multiple companies are responsible for extensions, co-ordination of offerings and resolution of problems may become much more difficult.

[58] See Hills (1997) and Ch. 9 for a discussion of these issues.

ment possibilities for creating user-friendly interfaces. The other opportunity is created by the likelihood that, as these services are implemented in the LANs of research laboratories or central administrations, there is a need to extend them more broadly throughout the organization. For example, the opportunity to distribute audiovisual training materials throughout an organization may be developed in a 'pilot' through LAN deployment. If the value of such a service is confirmed, there will be interest in extending it throughout the organization. Such extensions involve additional demand for WAN services. Initially, some of this demand may be met by lower priority scheduling of the WAN for the transfer of non-real-time applications. As real-time applications such as videoconferencing become more popular, demand for capacity of the WAN is likely to increase, driving expansion in the demand for telecommunication services.

3.4.2.2 *Platforms for Vertical Applications*

As a platform technology, Intranets are well positioned to address one of the central problems in the software industry, vertical market applications.[59] These are sector-specific software applications that also offer substantial capabilities for user customization. They address the recurring and persistent shortcoming of generic or packaged software solutions by developing applications that are intended to be responsive to needs within specific business sectors. For example, while general-purpose accounting software applications exist, they rarely take into account the specific costing and billing methods that are used in particular sectors. Information generated by the packaged software application is frequently re-entered into other application programmes for the purpose of cost accounting or invoicing. These additional links and interfaces create significant software design challenges and often involve inelegant and difficult to manage procedures. This opens an opportunity for more specialized applications. More specialized applications, however, suffer from a lack of standardization which limits their extension. They also tend to be based on bespoke or customized solutions that create an ongoing dependency on computer consulting services or on in-house information systems departments. While users are familiar with these trade-offs, their choices are often shaped by the unavailability of suitable alternatives.

There is no guarantee that the emerging Intranet platform will be able to remedy the historical problems of vertical software applications. The Intranet platform does, however, provide a new basis for reconsidering how these problems can be addressed effectively in the light of experience over the past twenty years. The prospects for better outcomes will depend upon how two issues are resolved. The first issue is the problem of database formats and interfaces. Substantial progress has been made over the past twenty years in the theory of database data structure theory and practice so that it is now possible to specify the most relevant design choices in creating a database structure (Date, 1995). There has also been considerable progress in understanding the design of query and reporting functions so that a number of broadly similar, but still competing, approaches can be described as 'best practice'.

---

[59] For a more complete discussion of the vertical market application issue see Steinmueller (1996).

There is ample room for the design of proprietary products that are difficult to translate across applications but that offer advantages in particular technical applications. This problem is closely related to the general problem of vertical market applications. An incentive exists to differentiate software products in order to lessen direct competition. Users are willing to adopt these solutions because no general solution exists and because the specific application offers particular advantages. The result is the proliferation of competing and non-compatible standards vying for the position of *de facto* commercial standard. For many users, the emergence of a single *de facto* standard would be attractive, even if it had initial disadvantages relative to competitive alternatives. The reason is that the larger stream of revenue available from a *de facto* standard could well lead to a faster rate of technical improvement than would occur in a more fragmented market. The problem is that there is no co-ordinating mechanism across users other than the market and, in the market, each user may choose a different candidate *de facto* standard as the solution to his or her needs.

A second possibility is that, even with the proliferation of proprietary standards, methods for integrating databases using gateway or converter technologies may emerge. It is too early to assess whether such a solution will emerge in the case of the Intranet platform. A favourable environment for such technologies has been created by European and American decisions to permit the reverse engineering of software interfaces for the purposes of achieving interoperability between software application programs.[60]

3.4.2.3   Content Delivery Standards

From the beginning of discussions about the 'paperless office', a central problem has been the non-existence of a common format for information exchange.[61] This problem was accompanied by the related conversion problem of storing and retrieving information that was received in paper form. Twenty years later, it is clear that paper use is on the increase rather than in decline as a medium for distributing information and that the amount of information to be distributed seems to be increasing due to the declining cost of information storage and distribution. The absence of a common standard for information transfer is only one of the contributing factors to preserving paper as the medium of office exchange. Paper is easier to annotate and, perhaps most importantly, offers a greater variety of methods for archiving, filing, and rearranging documents. These advantages, however, come at a cost. Updating information that is recurrently used, for example, procedure reference manuals, requires systematic procedures for replacing out-of-date information. Cross-referencing paper-based information is complex and requires an *ex ante* design that must be maintained at an overhead cost that is often substantial relative to its use. Recombining data from multiple paper sources often requires re-entry.

---

[60]   The European decision was made in 1991 in European Council (1991: Art. 6), while the United States decision occurred in 1998 in United States Congress (1998: S 1201f).

[61]   For early discussions see Muter and Maurutto (1991). Today paperless office concepts are mainly associated with various software systems for workflow and document management.

In the areas of updating, cross-referencing, and recombining, electronic document storage and retrieval offers substantial advantages. These advantages can be further enhanced in the case of multimedia information where stacks of audio and video cassettes entomb information of potential value for reference or recombination. The principal advantage of Intranet-based tools is to centralize the storage of paper and multimedia information in ways that may facilitate their functionality for the organization and for the individual user.

While the basic tools for storing and accessing information are now available, substantial further developments will be required at the level of both tools and custom applications to improve this functionality for users. Intranets provide an advantage over other distributed computer systems in providing a platform for the user-side of information access. The entry opportunity provided by these applications is on the server side of the system. Interactive software for updating information, for example, by automated recomposition of web pages, for updating cross-references to information, and for recombining information through both hyperlinks and automated recompilation of information, are all ways to take advantage of a large data archive. When 'data-mining' techniques for analysis and pattern finding are added, some of the promises of the paperless office for ease and utility of document recovery and analysis appear once again to be attainable.

Intranets alone, however, do not create the solution to the conversion and reconversion problems. Advances will also be needed in organizational schemes for efficiently employing scanners, printers, and other adjunct technologies to build advanced data libraries. The key problem to be solved, however, is one in which Intranets will be of value. To be useful, information must be stored in an accessible format, facilitating access as well as the functional attributes. Intranets offer effective foundations for creating and distributing content and it will be easier to build other capabilities upon these foundations. Telecommunication traffic will be increased through the extension of intensive use of LAN-based Intranets to WAN telecommunication services. The more difficult problems will involve the reshaping of the organization's culture to empower users to access and transform information for productive and useful purposes.

3.4.2.4 *Inter-Organization Use*

Intranets that span organizational boundaries are called Extranets. Extranets are distinguished from the Internet because of their closed membership to specific groups of users who are not part of the same organization. Extranets are often implemented over the Internet by the creation of a security layer that authenticates user access.

Extranets provide a means to improve linkages between customers and suppliers and between organizations that are engaged in a variety of co-operative relationships.[62] The appeal of the Extranet is similar to that of the Intranet. By providing a common format for access to data and a platform to build interactive applications,

---

[62] The same organizations may also be engaged in competition which creates a need to establish boundaries between Extranets and Intranets to prevent the flow of proprietary information across the boundaries of the firm.

Extranets overcome a number of compatibility problems between software systems. In the inter-organizational context, these incompatibilities are particularly important because firms have rarely made similar choices with regard to either packaged or semi-customized application software. Engineering information bridges between organizations can be a substantial and costly activity for which Intranets provide some useful tools.

The Japanese approach to reorganizing manufacturing is a topic that has attracted enormous attention over the past two decades.[63] While many of the innovations are now broadly diffused, most were not developed and few have been implemented, using sophisticated information and communication technologies. A key element in their success, however, was informational, and involved tightening information feedback between parts suppliers and manufacturers, between different stages of the production process, and between customers and manufacturers. In practice, feedback is an extremely complex communication process that involves problem-solving at many different levels. The extension and improvement of these techniques in computer-mediated communication environments offers new opportunities for improvement, particularly in the service sectors. A key feature of Extranets is their ability to create an 'object' for mutual discussion and improvement, similar to the tangible qualities of manufactured products. The features of Extranets that work and those that do not can be readily identified, discussed, and resolved. The differences in perspectives across organizations and the mutual dependence on effective designs create opportunities to realize the goal of continuous improvement.[64]

3.4.2.5 *Accelerating the Client-Server Revolution*

A fundamental change in the computer industry during the 1990s was the growth of client-server architectures for information systems. Centralized data and computational resources, increasingly, are being re-engineered to offer users more directly useful tools in augmenting their work activities. These tools extend beyond the desktop in that they bring organizational databases and enterprise-critical applications to the client. While there are many problems to be overcome in the administration and security of client-server architectures, the Intranet offers a means to accelerate these developments. Regardless of whether cross-platform applications such as JAVA are widely diffused, a principal value of client-server networks is that they allow employees direct access to information needed to improve productivity. Advanced industrial countries (and increasingly newly industrializing countries) with substantial accumulated histories in the use of information systems share a common set of problems in the development of legacy applications and data resources. Within the organization, these information resources have often become central to routines and to the division of labour.

The opportunity offered by Intranets is the possibility of building new 'front ends'

---

[63] See Abegglen and Stalk (1985); Freeman (1987); Hobday (1995); Kaplinsky (1994).

[64] There are, of course, some potential problems as well. Collaboration does not necessarily mean closure and the possibility of multiple contributions does not necessarily create synergistic effects. As with other collective activities, there is a role for managing Extranet resource development.

to these legacy applications that can be used to access and enter information. The flexibility of Intranet development tools for this purpose is one of their highly desirable features. These advantages are the same as those supporting the development of vertical applications using Intranets. In addition, however, the architecture of client-server networks involves the rapid improvement of server technology. The costs of servers are amortized or distributed over a network of less costly client machines that, nevertheless, offer significant value added in application design. This combination is strengthened when the design of client applications can be accelerated so that user feedback becomes an active part of the development process. Such a development cycle for information systems offers major improvements over the longer traditional development cycle in which new applications are developed off-line and then implemented. This process requires retraining at the time of the new software's implementation and inevitably reveals flaws in conception and implementation that must be reworked to achieve an acceptable improvement in the system. Intranets are therefore likely to accelerate the growth of client-server computer architectures. Since such networks are often geographically dispersed, the result will be further increases in the demand for telecommunication services.

The availability of a software technology that offers a universal and extensible operating system and standardized user interface would be an important advance in the information and communication infrastructure. That the same technology allows document formats ranging from typeset quality manuals to video recordings to be universally distributed is an extra bonus. The same technology preserves much of the computational and other functionality of the machines it operates upon. This allows the development of any conceivable application and the provision of access to it through a universally understood interface. The collective impact of these features of web-based Intranet technology offers a unique platform for developing information resources within the organization. While the same principles apply to the Internet's web the unique advantage of the Intranet is that it often operates in an environment in which data transfer speeds are much faster than those available on the Internet. Making this performance available to other portions of a company provides an important driver for data telecommunication demand, reinforcement of LAN development, and, therefore, the whole chain of development that has been the theme of this chapter.

3.4.3 Intranet and World Wide Web Developments in Europe

The potential offered by Intranet technologies is substantial, but their full exploitation requires the accumulation of substantial experience. A primary source of this experience is Internet use. As noted in Ch. 2, the use of the Internet in Europe is increasing rapidly, although the rate of increase may be slowing as it is in the United States which maintains a substantial lead in the number of hosts, the best available internationally comparable approximation of the number of users.

In early 1997, Europe was lagging significantly behind the United States in Intranet adoption. According to International Data Corporation data, only 6 per cent of

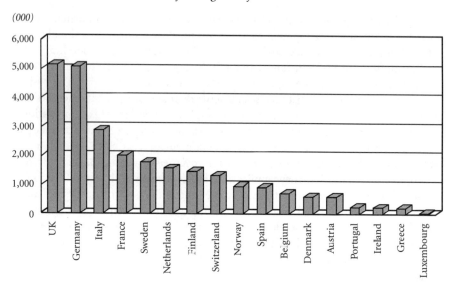

(000)

FIG. 3.8. Web pages in the European Union, July 1997

Source: Adapted from Databank Consulting (1997).

European business sites had access to an Intranet compared to 23 per cent of American business (International Data Corporation, 1997). Intranet servers were, nevertheless, expected to grow steadily in terms of units and revenues over the next five years. The United Kingdom was the largest country market for Internet/Intranet server software in Europe, closely followed by Germany. France and Italy were lagging considerably behind. The market growth of Internet/Intranet servers in Europe and the gap with the United States in terms of Intranet adoption do not tell the full story. In Ch. 2 we considered the evidence concerning the uneven development of Internet diffusion in Europe in general, and the accessibility of the network for public organizations such as schools and museums. In this chapter we focus more directly on World Wide Web content.

Using the Altavista Search Engine, one study analysed the growth of web pages in the European Union finding that they increased from 3,419 million in January 1996 to 23,484 million in July 1997.[65] The total number of pages is shown in Fig. 3.8. The rank of countries by total number of web pages is similar to their rank in terms of number of hosts and the extent of use measures we reported in Ch. 2. An important measure was developed to examine the intensity of web development by dividing the number of web pages by the number of hosts. This new measure suggests that there are distinct differences in the pattern of web site development between northern and southern Europe. In northern Europe there is a relatively low ratio of web pages to host penetration (the extreme example being Finland). In southern Europe, however, the lower

[65] The following is from Databank Consulting (1997).

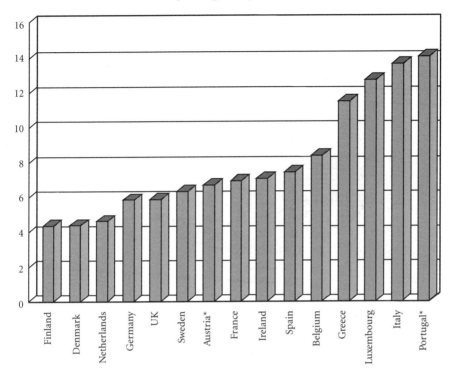

FIG. 3.9. Number of web pages per host in the European Union, July 1997

* In Austria and Portugal the Network Wizards Survey reported for July 1997 a lower number of hosts than in Jan. 1997, causing the ratio of web pages to hosts to increase more rapidly than in other countries.

Source: Adapted from Databank Consulting (1997).

number of hosts, combined in cases such as Italy with a relatively high number of web pages leads to a very different ranking of the intensity of web development. Figure 3.9 illustrates the situation in the middle of 1997.

Although Internet access and telecommunication usage tariff levels were closely associated with the patterns of host diffusion by country (lower tariffs correspond to higher host penetration), this relationship did not appear to hold for web page development. Web use and development instead appeared to be influenced more strongly by the structure of a country's economy and the social characteristics of the use of the Internet and the World Wide Web. Where national economies are characterized by the prevalence of small and medium-sized enterprises, there was greater vitality in the growth of web pages.

Finally, it is often claimed that the web is an English-dominated communication medium. A strictly proportional view of the European population of web sites shows that there was an excess of English-only and bilingual sites (with English as the second language), see Fig. 3.10.

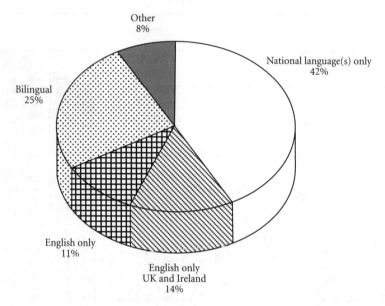

Fɪɢ. 3.10. Distribution of languages on World Wide Web sites in the European Union

Note: Based on a sample of 1% of visited commercial web sites.

Source: Adapted from Databank Consulting (1997).

English was not the dominant language in the sense that a non-English-speaker would encounter a majority of sites where a language other than English was available. Native language only sites accounted for 42 per cent of total sites surveyed while bilingual sites accounted for another 25 per cent in 1997 suggesting that, for non-English-speaking Europeans, a dominant share of European sites offered languages other than English. Of course this does not mean that the second largest language category that is represented will be able to vie with English for dominance. The distribution of sites among German, Italian, French, Dutch/Flemish, and Nordic languages was such that users would find fewer sites in their languages than in English, particularly when bilingual sites in a language other than their own and English are considered. However, for German speakers, there was no major disparity (if North America is ignored) and Italian speakers were relatively well represented.

3.5   Conclusion

The purpose of this chapter has been to initiate our discussion of the role of technological and market developments in shaping the physical networks underlying the development of the information and communication infrastructure. These developments began with the hope that the potential of technological convergence, that is, the unification of the digital technology responsible for both modern communication and computing, might be realized through the development of a universal medium in the form of the progressive development of an ISDN-based infrastructure. These changes were expected to stimulate new markets at the intersections of the information technology, communication, and content industries. They were also expected to produce a blurring of the boundaries between these industries and thus to initiate a process of industrial convergence. The major deficiency in this vision has proven to be that it failed to encompass the uneven nature of the developments that would bring these possibilities to life.

The unevenness in the technological development of the information and communication infrastructure is not an accident. It is the result of the effectiveness of the competitive process in generating variety in technologies and services, and the ability, indeed the preference, of users to find the best solutions to their own needs from what is on offer and according to their abilities and willingness to pay. Rather than an orderly advance towards the universal standards of the broadband ISDN network, these choices have promoted the emergence of the Internet and its protocols for connecting a heterogeneous array of computing and communication equipment. Instead of the 'death of distance' as a major consideration in whether users are able to obtain access to the highest quality networks, *where* the user is exchanging information continues to make a great difference to his or her experience and engagement with the information society. If these exchanges occur within a LAN it is already possible for them to occur at the speeds promised by broadband ISDN. At the other extreme, the typical small business and home Internet user continues to wait for an affordable way to upgrade the voice-line modem. Virtually every service level between these extremes for inter-organizational and interpersonal electronic information interchange is to be found somewhere in Europe.

The most important message of this chapter concerns the meaning of 'choices' between alternative technologies that emerges from a consideration of how the diffusion of new technologies proceeds. European users did not elect to reject ISDN as a common platform for the development of the information and communication infrastructure. They chose instead to adopt the technologies that became available to meet their needs as these appeared in the market-place. The timing of ISDN availability did not support mass adoption while the timing of voice-line modems coincided with other developments that encouraged the relatively more rapid diffusion of IP networks. Companies did not choose to reject primary rate ISDN. Rather they opted to engineer their internal LANs using the technologies that were available when they found that there were advantages in connecting personal computers into local networks. The fact that these LANs provided higher performance than primary rate ISDN was the consequence of the competition between LAN suppliers. Their insurgent strategies succeeded in pushing the pace of technological advance at a faster rate than the planners of the ISDN had anticipated. Telecommunication network operators sought to meet the evolving needs of customers by offering a diverse collection of configurations of leased-line and packet-data networks to the larger customers. Due to liberalization, these customers experienced a growing range of choice. Smaller organizations and individuals were left with few alternatives and, in fact, they had very little choice.

The choices that were available and were taken made it even more unlikely that ISDN could serve as the unifying technology by which the infrastructure could be implemented. Instead of a common revenue base, the market became fragmented according to ability to pay. Rather than having to make the investment to extend a common service infrastructure, the telecommunication network operators could extend the capabilities selectively, incrementally extending access. At the same time, however, the telecommunication network operators have been upgrading their own networks to meet the competitive challenges of liberalization. The public switched telecommunication network is now an advanced digital network where technological convergence has been, or is about to be, realized.

In retrospect, the ISDN vision appears to be an idealistic conception arising from the belief that the expansion of the quality and scope of telecommunication access should proceed according to the technological capacity to supply, rather than the economic ability to pay for advanced information and communication technologies and services. The capacity of network operators to adopt an incumbent strategy of rationing high-speed network access has been much reduced because the larger businesses and other organizations now have a choice in the selection of network access arrangements. In these markets, the incumbent strategy of the public telecommunication operators may be transformed into an insurgent strategy of vying for market share to the extent that effective competition emerges from alternative network operators.

The second important message of this chapter is that the process of demand growth can be greatly accelerated by the development of features of the information and communication infrastructure that lie outside the technical aspects of the physical network. The information resources provided by the Internet are an important influence on the demand for *using* the information and communication infrastructure. Even more important, however, is the role of the Internet in supporting the growth of a new class of software tools and organizational innovations for the creation and management of information. The investments that companies are making in their LAN-based information resources are expanding rapidly, greatly accelerating the volume of information that they will seek to make available to other sites of their own organizations, their business partners, and, ultimately, to their customers. The diffusion of the Internet, itself a beneficiary of network externalities, has stimulated a cascade of new network externalities that will greatly accelerate the rate at which demand for data communication services expands.

The process of technological convergence has, so far, been piecemeal. Within the telecommunication network operator's network and at the level of the LAN, the capacities for convergence exist. Within the LAN environment it is increasingly feasible to pioneer and develop the new services that were imagined by the advocates of integrated broadband communication. Due to liberalization these capacities seem certain to be linked. The alternative is the displacement of the telecommunication network operators by companies with insurgent strategies based upon extending their success in selling the Internet-related tools being used to develop new information services on the Internet and in LAN environments. The main question for tele-communication network operators appears to be how they can take an active role in these developments rather than being consigned to the role of bit transport service providers.

The larger question is whether, and if so how, the collective demand for these technologies and services will be extended to the broader market. Chapter 4 examines the issues surrounding the development of particular consumer markets as a basis for exploring how the local access to high-capacity networks may develop. This is followed by an examination of the role of electronic commerce in supporting the extension and improvement of network access of all types.

Finally, it should be noted that the developments discussed in this chapter are largely adverse for many of the social interests that we examined in Ch. 2. Virtual communities are beneficiaries of the spill-over of the Internet-related technologies that are being used to develop new services. Since higher-speed networks are mainly available to larger organizations, the current virtual community developments must be based upon more modest technologies, that is, those that can be supported using voice-line data communication networks. Virtual community developments also can occur using higher bandwidth networks in those places where they can be embedded in larger organizations. Users based in universities are likely to continue to play a major role in the evolution of virtual communities because, as we have shown in Ch. 2, universities are the main social or cultural institutions in Europe with effective access to higher-speed network capacities. However, participants in information society developments within university communities are a small fraction of the population that needs to be included in these developments.

4

Chaos in Service Innovations and Applications

4.1 Introduction

In the preceding chapter, we considered the business-led, local area network-based demand that is contributing to the construction of the information and communication infrastructure which is part of the piecemeal process of technological convergence. In this chapter we examine how the development of markets for equipment and services for the mobile communication service user and for people in their homes is creating a second set of processes from which the infrastructure of the information society is emerging. The mobile market is particularly important because European companies have considerable strengths throughout the vertical chain of production from equipment to services. The delivery of an effective infrastructure for home access to advanced information and communication services represents an even larger potential market for European companies. The timing of the development of this market will influence the opportunities for European participation in the production of equipment as well as services.

The extension of telephony to mobile applications and the creation of 'augmented' mobile telecommunication networks and services are increasing the ubiquity of telecommunication activities.[1] Providing the opportunity to communicate 'on the move' and 'on demand' is proving to be a service that European citizens and especially business users welcome. The broad acceptance of mobile telephony is creating an opening for the development of additional information services and for the use of the wireless communication network for the distribution of new types of information. These developments are based upon more intensive use of the terminals through which individuals access the mobile telecommunication infrastructure. The principle of more intensive use also applies to the mobile communication network itself. New types of communication devices and systems based upon inter-machine communication are being devised, which utilize the existing capability of mobile networks. Examples include the creation of intelligent logistical networks for monitoring goods in

This chapter draws in substantial part on research undertaken by Gert van de Paal, MERIT, University of Maastricht, see van de Paal (1997); van de Paal and Steinmueller (1998). Section 4.5 draws substantially on research undertaken by Emma Jansen, former SPRU Master's student, see Jansen and Mansell (1998).

[1] There are two reasons for applying the term 'augmented' to these services. The first is that 'wireless' is associated with radio, while the networks that we have in mind may also use infra-red or other segments of the extended radio frequency spectrum to achieve communication. The second is that, while the systems themselves may include components that operate without wires, they may also utilize other communication network infrastructures such as the switched telecommunication network or LANs.

transit, security monitoring systems that can be installed quickly and modified easily, and remote instrumentation and control for equipment or machinery. Augmented mobile communication services are providing a stimulus for market growth and leading to new employment opportunities, many of which are only beginning to be explored. Inter-machine communication makes it possible for artefacts to 'locate themselves' in space, for messages to 'find' their destinations through arrays of fixed and mobile telecommunication networks, and for people to receive assistance when they need it. Assisting people in meeting their needs by using new services and applications is gaining in importance over helping people to use technology. The development of services that are more responsive to people's needs is becoming a high priority for information system designers and such approaches are supplementing more conventional concepts of telecommunication services as the means of interpersonal communication.

The opportunities available to people who are able to access the information and communication infrastructure in their homes are changing as multimedia applications based upon entertainment, education, and other services become increasingly available. The technological processes of convergence make it possible to package multimedia content for delivery to home users over a growing array of distribution paths, or channels. In Ch. 3, the construction of the infrastructure was portrayed as a relatively organized system in which networked PCs, LANs, and the telecommunication infrastructure are being brought into technological and economic alignment by the rapid diffusion of Internet applications and technology. Major questions were raised about the sustainability of this diffusion process as the 'demand driver', that is, business data telecommunication services, pushes at the limitations of the current Internet standards. Questions in this area concern network congestion and service quality issues and these are relatively straightforward because the resolution of this set of issues is related to the upgrading of TCP/IP standards.

In the case of augmented mobile communication services and multimedia applications, there is greater uncertainty about the emerging structure and significance of the markets in Europe. Our assessment of trends in these markets is complicated further by the variety of rival technological solutions and the thicket of regulatory issues in these two areas. A consequence of the pervasive uncertainty in connection with market evolution and regulatory change is that 'road maps' of the likely paths of service and technology deployment can be misleading. Our main emphasis is on identifying the processes through which augmented mobile communication services and multimedia applications may come into broader use.

In the case of augmented mobile communication services, there are four key issues. First, the appropriate terminal technologies must become widely diffused in the market. This issue is complicated by the contest between upgraded Global System for Mobile Communication (GSM) terminals and the new, third-generation, mobile communication devices based upon the Universal Mobile Telecommunication System (UMTS). Second, technological and business standards supporting more intensive use of the existing infrastructure and favouring the new infrastructure must be developed. Third, and closely tied to the issue of standards, a 'critical mass' in applications that will support network externalities and hence accelerate the diffusion process, must be achieved.

Improving home access to the information and communication infrastructure involves competition for end-user acceptance between various platforms, between the infrastructures supporting these platforms, and, ultimately, between the variety and appeal of services, such as multimedia applications. In the markets for home access to the infrastructure, data communication applications are potentially less significant than advances in the distribution of digital television and the possible convergence of television and data service provision.

This is a problematic situation for several reasons. First, the focus on the 'passive' consumer of information that is characteristic of broadcast television and related services, such as video-on-demand, may foreclose on broader utilization of the infrastructure for cultural, educational, and social applications. Second, the construction of a broadcast-oriented information and communication infrastructure for the European home market would accentuate divisions between those who have access to a rich computer-mediated communication environment and other resources in their workplaces, and those who do not. Those who are likely to be excluded are people who are not part of the workforce, such as children and the elderly, those who are self-employed or employed in small and medium-sized enterprises, and those who are excluded by rules of access and use in the workplace from significant use of the information and communication infrastructure. Third, the existence of strong media and broadcasting producers within national markets is likely to prevail because of differences in culture and language, but the development of rich intercultural exchanges and dialogues is more likely to be promoted by the transfer of substantial amounts of multimedia content across national boundaries. This is less likely to occur if the information and communication infrastructure is developed principally as a broadcast medium.

The two areas that are the focus of this chapter—augmented mobile communication services and multimedia applications—are linked by the similarities that are also features of the information and communication infrastructure considered in the previous chapter, that is, the platform, infrastructure, and content features. The processes by which these are organized or co-ordinated in the two areas discussed in this chapter are considerably more chaotic because of the uncertainties noted above. It is, therefore, even more appropriate to regard the trajectories of evolution as unsettled and emergent. The absence of clear trajectories has important implications for the willingness of actors to make large-scale commitments to new offerings and for the stability of the commitments that are made. In the absence of an understanding of the sources of this instability, it is likely that serious mistakes in the reasoning about the nature and direction of causation will occur. For instance, uncertainties about the platforms for accessing information, the emergence of attractive content, platforms competing to deliver this content, and improvements in competing 'broadband' access technologies, all make it difficult for companies to commit to a 'unified' information and communication infrastructure for home access. These uncertainties also affect the timing of the growth of specific service markets.

The telecommunication infrastructure is supporting a growing number of innovative service applications. In this chapter we look at estimates of demand for new on-line entertainment and teleshopping services and at the strategic positioning by firms as they seek to develop web-based electronic commerce in areas such as the on-line music market. The latter instance demonstrates clearly that flexibility and entrepreneurial momentum, that is, the virtual community strategy, are not necessarily sustainable in the medium- to long-term once major incumbent players begin to implement their strategies in a forceful way. The case study of the on-line music industry highlights the importance of a systematic empirical examination of the alternative business strategies for electronic commerce that are emerging which highlights the implications of developments in this area. This is a theme that we develop further in Ch. 5.

4.2 Platforms for Augmented Mobile Services and for Home Access

The availability of augmented mobile communication services, and services that are based upon home access to the information and communication infrastructure, depends upon the diffusion of new electronic devices and their integration into the infrastructure. These devices themselves are only a means of facilitating the delivery of particular types of services. The rate and direction of their diffusion will be shaped by the alternative means of delivering services. For example, the existing GSM infrastructure and existing types of GSM terminal equipment (hand-held devices) may become the favoured platforms for delivering augmented communication services if available alternatives are ineffective. Alternatively, the rate at which new services and devices are introduced will influence the opportunity for partially upgrading existing GSM standards for data communication, a step that could provide a bridge to the deployment of more advanced technologies.[2]

Correspondingly, the vast infrastructure for broadcast communication with its millions of terminal devices, that is, television sets and radios, is already facing competition from the distribution of content through the medium of pre-recorded videotapes and discs. This market is also being influenced by the possibility of bridging existing technology with the new networks and equipment for digital transmission that will eventually support higher performance audiovisual reproduction. The market importance of multimedia content, especially the traditional medium of broadcast television and services for delivering broadcast content such as video-on-demand, is creating substantial pressure to devise channels for tapping into existing platforms.

The following sections examine the changing nature of the platforms available for

[2] The latter viewpoint is expressed in an Analysys Ltd. report commissioned by the UMTS Forum (1999: 61) which states, 'a clear strategy for the migration from current network technology to third-generation network technology is essential in order to create a stable and predictable environment for operators to invest. Furthermore, the early development and implementation of services based on the [General Packet Radio Service] GPRS standard is seen as an ideal opportunity to create a test bed for future mobile multimedia services . . .'

delivering augmented mobile communication services and home access to the information and communication infrastructure with a focus on multimedia applications. As noted earlier, our assessment of the prospects for platforms that are already broadly diffused or that are being widely marketed at present, is complicated by the uncertainties of technological competition, market development, and regulatory change as well as the changing dispositions of users towards the new services.[3] Major changes are possible, not only in the variety of new electronic devices but also in the uses of existing devices to construct service platforms. Existing patterns of competition, however, do suggest some of the possibilities and provide a perspective on how the potential development of new platforms and services may be analysed.

4.2.1 *Platforms for Augmented Mobile Communication Services*

Augmented mobile communication service markets require the diffusion of system components supporting the wireless functioning of the systems supporting these services. At the same time, the diffusion of such system components requires the existence of services to support them. These bottlenecks in the construction of a large-scale technical system are not unusual and are overcome (or widened) by the effects of spillovers from related technologies. The widespread diffusion of Internet technology and the growing acceptance by a fraction of the population of electronic mail as part of everyday life, is a spill-over that is very likely to support demand for mobile data communication services.

One examination of European demand for mobile multimedia services classifies the potential applications according to whether they are basic, horizontal, or vertical. Basic services are available now and are familiar to users (Hjelm, 1998). They include voice service, electronic mail, fax, web browser, and Short Message Service (SMS). The last of these would be considered basic only for those who already use this service on their mobile phones. Horizontal services are new and have a potentially broad appeal in the general area of 'infotainment' (information and entertainment) with travel-related applications holding a leading position in terms of user interest. Vertical services, as defined by Hjelm, include professional services such as administrative and secretarial support, database access, group-working, and services ranging from shared data access to high-quality videoconferencing (ibid. 31).

The paradigm of augmented mobile communication services suggested by these examples may be associated with augmented *interpersonal* communication. This paradigm represents a straightforward extension of mobile telephony into the data communication arena. It is commonly believed to be the most important source of demand for existing mobile data communication applications involving second-generation GSM devices and it is expected to remain the leading application for third-generation UMTS devices. The growing ubiquity of mobile terminals as platforms for

---

[3] Optimistically, it would appear that new mobile standards have a development cycle of a decade. On the other hand, Ericsson reports that it replaces its complete product line about every two years, see Bengtsson and Wihdén (1997).

the delivery of services suggests numerous other applications that presently lie outside the traditional paradigm. For example, coupling information about the location of a mobile terminal to service directories would allow mobile users to locate the services they need near their current locations. Use of 'common channels' specific to an event, for instance, could support interactive communication between a speaker and an audience or the spontaneous assembly of shared-interest groups within a conference setting. Common features of these examples are the automated assemblage of user-specific information and the retransmission of this information to interested parties. The creation of applications and the equipment supporting them is an interactive process. It is important to recognize that many potential applications involve abandoning the traditional paradigm of establishing a communication channel for continuous communication in favour of 'messaging' models that have radically different requirements for both terminal devices and the networks supporting them.

The paradigm of continuous interpersonal communication continues to be influential in how we think about the relationships between mobile platforms and service applications. As the density of inter-machine communication increases, however, this approach may become increasingly misleading for applications design. People do not need to have an interest in establishing direct communication with the growing variety of communicating devices.[4] The role of the new types of inter-machine communication is to implement information gathering, processing, and distribution functions that are designed to provide the human user with information that otherwise would be tedious or demanding to assemble and analyse. This class of applications, which falls into the vertical applications domain of Hjelm's classification scheme, involves a more complex system architecture in which the mobile or wireless features are an important component, but not the sole defining attribute, of the network.

For example, modern parcel-tracking services are based upon networks of checkpoints that record the passage of each parcel through semi-automated data entry or automated monitoring systems. Some of the checkpoints—for example, that of 'pick-up'—may make use of mobile communication devices. The significance of the systemic nature of the application is apparent when the use of such systems by customers is compared with their use within the parcel-shipping service. A shipper may be interested in the location of a particular parcel within the system, while the person assigned the task of scheduling the use of transportation resources will be interested in the larger patterns of flow and congestion within the network. With the thousands of items involved, it is possible for the latter function to be performed only if the system is able to aggregate the details about each parcel. These aggregations of information must be meaningful for scheduling transportation resources, for example, portraying the weight and volume of hundreds of parcels in terms of 'loads' compatible with transportation equipment.

The same principles may be employed to monitor and control flows of items

---

[4] The individuals responsible for maintenance and fault monitoring will, of course, need to have such communication capabilities.

ranging from automobiles on motorways to breakfast cereal boxes in retail distribution chains. Whether communication links will be extended from checkpoints to individual artefacts depends upon the value that can be achieved by tightening control and the costs (in time as well as direct labour inputs) of data entry at checkpoints. When it is people rather than artefacts that are being tracked, additional issues are raised about the privacy and security of systems that can determine the location of people from minute to minute. We return to this issue in Ch. 8 in the discussion of the privacy implications of mobile telephone cell networks.

The two paradigms of voice telephony augmented by data communication and complex wireless system applications coexist in the European vision for the future of augmented communication services.[5] While the extent of demand is uncertain, the approaches being taken by European companies and their expectations for desirable outcomes are based upon earlier experiences with the diffusion of GSM. The deployment history of GSM has been interpreted as demonstrating the value of 'open' standards for the rapid diffusion of technology. European companies have been attempting to reach a collective view on the set of standards that should be adopted for third-generation mobile telecommunication services that focus on the technical content of UMTS/IMT-2000 services.[6] This approach can be termed a 'standards-led' solution to the problem of market development. In a similar fashion, attempts are being made to limit the extent of standards diversification of bridging technologies for both older second-generation GSM devices and new 'low-end' devices that provide mobile data communication capabilities.

A standards-led solution has a number of potential advantages in promoting the rapid diffusion of new technology. The advantages of a common UMTS/IMT-2000 standard include the possibility of defining services and developing devices utilizing the standard with the assurance that there is a reasonable possibility that they will be interoperable throughout Europe and in many other parts of the world that may follow the European lead. This supports market growth and price reductions for equipment as well as investment in the software and content needed for services. At the time of writing, the European Telecommunication Standards Institute (ETSI) had established only the terms of reference for the UMTS standardization process.[7] The specification of the UMTS standard, which many believe will lead to the third generation of European mobile telecommunication services, is unlikely to emerge by the target date of mid-2000 despite efforts to reach a consensus.

---

[5] It is interesting to note that a spokesperson for Ericsson argues that voice will continue to be the most important service despite the expected growth in data-related services, see Henningsson (1999*b*).

[6] IMT-2000 is a radio interface standards framework established by the International Telecommunication Union for high-capacity, high data rate mobile telecommunication systems incorporating both terrestrial radio and satellite components, see Universal Mobile Telecommunication Forum (UMTS) Forum, (1998). IMT-2000 plays an important role in defining the global radio spectrum allocation for third-generation mobile services. It is important to note, however, that in the USA the frequency defined for such services by IMT-2000 is unavailable and this means that third-generation systems may be global, except in the USA. UMTS is the European label for the use of this standard and is the responsibility of ETSI, see http://www.umts-forum.org/ or http://www.etsi.org/ accessed 6 April 2000. FPLMTS was the former label for UMTS.

[7] See http://www.umts-forum.org/ accessed 6 April 2000 for the latest developments.

The potential benefits of a standards-led approach can be dissipated if the timing of the diffusion of the standards for equipment and services is sufficiently delayed. A delicate balance exists between the value of adopting standards that are sufficiently comprehensive to meet potential needs, needs that continue to evolve throughout the standards definition process, and the value of partial or complete closure in the standardization process to facilitate technological development. Under these conditions, the principal threats to achieving the goals of the standards-led process are that partial solutions, such as those that disrupted the diffusion of ISDN, will be deployed earlier and will fragment the available market for the comprehensive solution. One such threat would be the development of telecommunication satellite-based solutions in some of the markets for which UMTS is being devised.

In the United States, no national standard is being sought for third-generation mobile telephony.[8] As a consequence, mobile service providers and network operators that are seeking to upgrade their technology can apply for service licences for use of the available radio frequency spectrum using technology of their own choosing. This may allow segments of the market in the United States to develop rapidly and it may encourage considerable experimentation with new technology and services. This situation could lead to problems with interoperability and shortfalls in achieving the scales of adoption that would be consistent with price reduction and service deployment. At the same time, however, the competition between the different technologies that are implemented can yield substantially more information about the robustness of a technology and the sustainability of a service than field trials or other marketing approaches. At a minimum, this approach may give American-owned companies important patent positions in the development of the technologies.

The prospect of a 'mobile Internet' is likely to stimulate demand for new mobile terminals. It is unclear at the time of writing whether this market will integrate mobile communication with the personal digital assistant or palmtop computers offered by Psion, 3COM-PALM, or Hewlett Packard, among other companies. Palmtop computer functions may be integrated into new mobile devices from companies such as Nokia and Ericsson. Or, some hybrid strategy may be employed, such as the improvement of the mobile-laptop telecommunication link for data display using technologies such as Bluetooth which offers 1 Mbps data transfer rates in a localized wireless environment.[9]

The standards-led approach towards the development of the European mobile communication services market may succeed in enhancing the technological competition between alternative equipment solutions by delivering a common telecommunication standard. If new standards are delayed, however, the more *ad hoc* approach that is being used in the United States for the development of advanced mobile

---

[8] One reason for this is that in the USA, the IMT-2000-specified frequency for mobile–satellite telecommunication is not available.

[9] Named after the Viking king, Harald Bluetooth, this concept is supporting the development of inexpensive radio communication between mobile phones and accessories and participating companies include Nokia, Intel, Toshiba, and IBM, together with Ericsson. The partners agree to share competing patents in exchange for the right to manufacture products based on Bluetooth, see Henningsson (1999a).

applications may create important spill-overs for the design and delivery of particular configurations of equipment. Even though the transceivers used in Europe will differ from those used in the United States, spill-overs from the United States' market may influence the development of the European market. Companies in the United States and Europe have yet to adopt a strong proactive position with regard to inter-machine mobile communication in a way that would provide them with a lead in the development of services and applications based upon systems with mobile components.

4.2.2   Multimedia Distribution Platforms for Home Access

The term 'multimedia' has spawned a bewildering array of definitions. One reason for this is that the term was created to differentiate the new capacities of 'convergent' networks from those already in existence. Thus, 'multimedia' was meant to refer to content other than that which was available in broadcast applications distributed using television or data communication (including the World Wide Web) platforms, or using access platforms such as the personal computer, to run an application programme. This is not very helpful because each of the platforms is adaptable for carrying a variety of content. For example, web pages may be used to access broadcast video, televisions may be used to access these web pages, and personal computers may be used to access similar content from discs and from telecommunication channels. A second, somewhat diffuse use of the term is meant to convey the idea that digital technology will allow new types of content to be developed. New types of content would appear to be a possibility using digital technology. For example, virtual reality is arguably one such new type of content.[10] Attempts by those seeking more precise definitions usually begin with the creation of a list of types of content, for example, sound, static picture, or motion picture, associated with particular media, for instance, radio or television, photographs, and television or cinema, and the pronouncement that multimedia is some combination of these types of content. Finally, many definitions of multimedia call attention to the role of the user as an active agent in controlling or influencing the presentation of content, through the principle of 'interactivity'.[11]

Since our purpose is to investigate the platform, network, and content issues surrounding the emergence of multimedia, we take a relatively broad view of the meaning of 'multimedia'. We identify multimedia content as digital information for multi-

---

[10]   One type of virtual reality aims to achieve the illusion of 'being there' or, more technically, kinesthetic presence. This requires fooling the very basic elements of human perception into responding as if the sensory inputs they are receiving originated in a reality distinct from that of its actual receipt, that is, from the human–computer interface. For example, a successful virtual reality of skiing down a mountain slope might induce perceptions of exhilaration or vertigo. A second type of virtual reality is simply to model a real or imagined world in so much detail that the user's curiosity and exploratory impulses are stimulated by the environment.

[11]   In our view, the term 'non-interactive multimedia' is an oxymoron since content that has this characteristic is essentially indistinguishable from a single medium definition. Hence, personal computers playing segments of full motion and sound video are serving as video playback devices. The fact that the user may be able to pause, rewind, or set the starting position of such segments is of little inherent interest.

sensory display, typically visual and audio, that is digitally encoded and that includes a significant element of interactivity, that is, substantial user control or influence on the presentation of display. This definition excludes digital broadcast television, which has no element of user control of presentation.[12] It includes digital recorded television programming because the platforms used to access this content may, in fact, provide a basis for interactive education or entertainment applications. Multimedia platforms are electronic devices capable of utilizing multimedia content.

This definition has shortcomings, however, for discussing the new forms of digital media that are likely to emerge from innovative technological capabilities. An example of such a development is the MP3 phenomenon.[13] MP3 is a digital compression format that permits a dramatic reduction in the number of digital bits to encode sound and reproduce the listening quality of audio recordings. MP3 is much more than a method for the compression and digital encoding of audio recordings; it is also establishing a new and controversial method for the distribution of audio recordings.[14] The MP3 controversy stems from the use of the compression standard to distribute copyrighted material, a development that is reviewed below in s. 4.5.2 and more extensively in Ch. 7. Our discussion of multimedia will include innovative digital media even if, like MP3, they do not meet other characteristics of multimedia, that is, MP3 is a single sensory (audio) media.

Our major concern is with the contributions of multimedia and other innovative digital media as sources of demand for network infrastructure utilization. The use of these types of content, however, has important complementary relationships with the growth of the various non-networked multimedia 'appliances' including personal computers that are not connected to networks, videogame players, and audio equipment such as CD players. Multimedia content and innovative digital media can be made available on an off-line basis using pre-recorded or recording media on optical discs. There is a growing array of equipment, other than the traditional multimedia personal computers, for accessing the content of such information.

It is also possible that the development of networked services could change the personal computer in a fundamental way. There has been considerable speculation about

---

[12] The only options generally available are the ability to change channels or turn off the television. Even broadcast television may move towards our view of multimedia with provisions for multilingual selections of language. European television already incorporates elements of multimedia in videotext programming accompanying television broadcasts (which can also be used to provide subtitles in languages other than the broadcast or in the language of the broadcast for the hearing-impaired).

[13] MP3 is a shortening of the name of a formal standard ISO-MPEG Audio Layer-3 (IS 11172-3 and IS 13818-3), which was devised through the work initiated by the EUREKA project EU147, Digital Audio Broadcasting (DAB). See Fraunhofer-Gesellschaft (1999) for a short history of MP3 developments. MP3 is sometimes believed to represent MPEG − 3, one of the standards developed directly by the MPEG standards group. This is not the case. Instead, the standards MP − 1 and MP − 2 each has a layer 3 audio standard which references the ISO-MPEG standards cited above, i.e., IS 11172 is MP − 1 while IS 13818 is MP − 2. See Chiariglione's (1996) discussion of the MPEG family of standards. This source also has trenchant observations about convergence and takes the view that the meaningful distinctions to analyse the multimedia phenomenon are 'transport, equipment, and content', essentially the same as those we have employed.

[14] See http://www.wired.com/news/news/mpthree/ or http://www.mp3.com accessed 6 April 2000 for reviews of recent developments and controversies.

the emergence of a 'net computer', a type of multimedia appliance that relies upon interaction with the World Wide Web and other Internet services to achieve most of its functionality. Such a device could dramatically simplify the design of the personal computer, which remains a general-purpose device. At the same time, it is less than clear why computer users would wish to rely upon a network connection, particularly at currently available speeds, to access application programs and essential data. For the time being, the latter issue appears to dominate. Although in 1997 there was considerable speculation about the possible growth of a market for such products, the initial product offerings faded out as the price of multimedia personal computers fell during 1998 and 1999 and industry news stories touting the potential of such devices vanished.[15]

Multimedia content and innovative digital media are increasingly provided as on-line services. The World Wide Web has proven to be a platform that facilitates both types of content. Web browsers have been constructed as open-ended platforms with regard to the use of add-on 'readers' that can be installed by users with a modest level of technical skills.[16] These readers enable the display of sound, video, still images, and other types of information and they are widely available and numerous.[17] Once installed, the user is able to display, to listen to, or to experience a new *type* of innovative media or multimedia content. Companies are actively engaged in promoting their market positions by the free or low-cost distribution of implementations of these systems. Many versions with enhanced capabilities are being sold commercially. Off-line/on-line hybrids are also emerging as various technological alternatives are used in ways that complement each other. For example, an optical disc may provide web links that activate a personal computer's web browser and fetch information from a remote site or, less commonly, a web link may fetch information from an optical disc in the user's system. Such systems provide yet further opportunities for devising innovative digital media and multimedia content.

The growth of multimedia and innovative digital media has significant implications for the emergence of new types of equipment and local infrastructure in the home and office. The major appliance for accessing these types of content continues to be the personal computer and dial-up or LAN-based access to the Internet. The use of personal computers to access this content for entertainment, education, or other purposes presents several problems, however. For example, the use of the home computer as a home office workstation is not entirely compatible with its use as a home entertainment centre. Moreover, televisions and stereo systems are designed to provide more satisfying renditions of the content than the typical personal computer. The

---

[15] Oracle, one of the companies that announced its intention to enter the market with a £500 net computer, was providing no information on net computers in the summer of 1999. An interesting feature of the World Wide Web is that companies are able to rewrite history by deleting web pages.

[16] That is, about the same level of skill as is required to install a packaged software application program from pre-recorded media.

[17] e.g. on 12 Aug. 1999, Netscape offered 176 software plug-ins, most of which facilitate access to multimedia content or innovative digital media, classified in the categories: 3D and Animation, Audio/Video, Business and Utilities, Image Viewers, and Presentations. Netscape's offerings are only a fraction of the 'reader' software programs available on the Internet.

development of home 'networks' connecting all these information appliances is one possibility, but one that has not yet created a significant market.[18] Although some new types of equipment have emerged that do make use of the personal computer as the 'base station', such as portable MP3 players and digital still image cameras, establishing the interface for these devices requires more than a modest level of user skill and experience.

4.3   Network Implications of Augmented Communication and Multimedia

The new platforms discussed in the previous section create a foundation for the expansion of demand on existing networks and for the construction of new networks. It is unclear whether these developments will significantly accelerate the construction of the information and communication infrastructure envisaged for the European information society. The addition of new infrastructures could fragment demand for telecommunication network-based access to the Internet, reducing the pressure to upgrade telecommunication networks to high bit rates. Alternatively, the new infrastructures, including some components that are not immediately obvious, such as the role of the newsagent in distributing optical discs, may become complementary and reinforcing developments that will accelerate the demand for public telecommunication network operators to upgrade and improve their services. These are the central issues addressed in this section.

4.3.1   *Network Implications of Augmented Communication Services*

The network implications of augmented communication services involve the same 'chicken and egg' problem that is influencing the diffusion of terminal equipment for such services. Without the devices and content, the upgrading of the existing cellular radio infrastructure must proceed at a relatively modest pace. As noted above, the Internet provides a major impetus to overcome the terminal and equipment bottlenecks. The relatively cautious pace in defining standards that would advance mobile data communication services beyond the use of mobile devices for dial-up data access suggests one of two possibilities. The first may be that the major European players are unwilling to cannibalize demand for current GSM-based data communication applications. The second may be that they are unsure about how to reproduce the standards-led path to third-generation mobile communication. Either of these possibilities suggests a moderate or relatively slow pace of development and a modest incremental growth in demand for telecommunication network support.

A wild card in the development of mobile communication is the possibility of

---

[18] One possibility is the extension of wireless technologies, such as the Bluetooth standard (which operates in the unregulated 2.4 GHz radio spectrum) to create such networks. Although Bluetooth offers a strong platform for many applications, its 1 Mbps speed would require digital compression to be used as a home multimedia network.

accelerated development of the satellite infrastructure. The satellite communication industry is competing with media and terrestrial telecommunication operators not only for the mass entertainment market, but also for communication and multimedia services. At the beginning of 1997, the market was dominated by geostationary technology, but the first launches of non-geostationary satellites for civil use occurred during that year.

Several consortia are candidates to offer mobile services on a global basis. These include Iridium, Globalstar, ICO Global Communications, and Ellipso using Low Earth Orbit (LEO) constellations of satellites to support two-way voice and data communication using hand-held terminals (Margaris and Mansell, 1998; Nourouzi and May, 1996). Geostationary Earth Orbit (GEO) satellite operators intend to offer Global Mobile Personal Communication by Satellite (GMPCS) using even smaller palmtop terminals.[19] By September 1999, only Iridium was operational.

Existing non-interoperable cellular services create a window of opportunity for the provision of these new services. Two of the six digital cellular systems, GSM and Digital Communication Service (DCS) 1800, have captured about 22 per cent of total mobile subscriptions while Code Division Multiple Access (CDMA) and Digital Advanced Mobile Phone Service (D-AMPS), mainly used in the United States, together account for approximately 13 per cent. Some forecasts indicate that GSM (and DCS) technology could reach a share of 45 per cent by 2002 and that eventually GSM will become a world standard. In this case, there would be no need for a satellite system that bridges different standards.

Another stimulus for GMPCS diffusion is the partial coverage of cellular terrestrial networks. However, it is expected that terrestrial coverage will be enhanced in the near future, thus reducing the demand for GMPCS. In addition, the use of satellite systems for the local loop represents a temporary solution until it becomes cost-effective to install terrestrial wireless local loops.[20] Table 4.1 shows some of the key features of GMPCS projects.

Very Small Aperture Terminals (VSAT) applications in western European countries represent a relatively small market. In eastern Europe where the terrestrial infrastructure is less developed, the opportunity for VSAT applications is considerably larger. This segment of the satellite market grew substantially in 1997. The number of installed VSATs in the first quarter of the year in Europe reached 14,000 terminals with a forecast installed base of 38,000 units at the end of the year as compared to the United

---

[19] GMPCS uses the acronym originally coined by the International Telecommunication Union in 1994, to designate Global Mobile Personal Communication Systems, that is, LEO systems offering voice communication. In 1995, the acronym was changed to designate Global Mobile Personal Communication by Satellite to encompass a range of innovative satellite systems and services, see MacLean (1996).

[20] In addition to competition from the spread of mobile terrestrial networks and wireless local loops, GMPCS operators face significant technical and regulatory challenges. At the time of writing, both Iridium and ICO had filed a voluntary petition for reorganization under ch. 11 of the United States Bankruptcy Code in the US Bankruptcy Court. In July 1999, Iridium faced several action suits filed in US courts on behalf of investors who felt they had been misled about subscriber levels and technical problems, see Foley (1999a); ICO (1999); Walz (1999). See also Arroio (1999) for a detailed analysis of the evolution of this industry segment with special reference to Brazil.

TABLE 4.1. *Global Mobile Personal Communication Systems (GMPCS) Project features*

Features	Iridium	Globalstar	ICO	Ellipso	CCI
No. of satellites	66 LEO	48 LEO	10 MEO	14 Elliptical	46 LEO
Cost of project (becu)	3.0	2.1	2.1	1.4	0.9
Leading investors	Motorola	Space System Loral	Hughes Elec. National Telecom Operators	Mobile Com. Holding	Constellation Com.
Start of service	1998	1999	2000	2001	2001
Services					
Voice	Yes	Yes	Yes	Yes	Yes
Fax	Yes	Yes	Yes	Yes	Yes
Data transmission	Yes	Yes	Yes	Yes	Yes
Positioning	No	Yes	Yes	Yes	Yes
Data transmission rate	2.4 kbps	9.6 kbps	9.6 kbps (64 kbps CUG)	9.6 kbps	9.6 kbps
No. of earth ground stations	13	150–200	12	20–40	n.a.
Number of gateways*	Many	150–200	Many	20–40	n.a.
On-board processing	Yes	No	No	No	No
Intersatellite links	Yes	No	No	No	No

Notes: n.a. = not available; LEO = Low Earth Orbiting satellite; MEO = Medium Earth Orbiting satellite; CUG = Closed User Groups.

* No. of gateways depends upon service providers and local regulations.

Sources: Adapted from Evans (1998); Nourouzi and May (1996).

States market with an installed base of 125,000 terminals (Passamonti, Sisti, and Cattaneo, 1997).

Growth of the market in Europe is attributable, in part, to the liberalization of the satellite services market as a result of a European Commission directive (European Council, 1992c). Price decreases due to lower maintenance costs and to the introduction of shared hub stations have also contributed to the growth of the market. Increased transponder supply is also a factor. VSATs are being used to support Internet access, the development of Intranets, and to provide higher bandwidth for delivery of multimedia services, digital video, and high-capacity data relays. The arrival of Ultra Small Aperture Terminals (USATs) may endanger further diffusion of VSATs although this is unlikely to occur much before 2002 or 2003.

The modest rate of expansion of both terrestrial and satellite-based mobile data communication services suggests that they will offer a relatively small contribution to accelerating the development of the information and communication infrastructure.

Instead, the demand for these services is likely to follow from the further development of the Internet and to hinge on the growing appeal of portable Internet terminals that are integrated in novel ways with mobile telephony applications.[21] Over the long term, however, the development of augmented communication services raises two important issues for the future of the telecommunication network. The first is the problem of introducing a pricing structure for inter-machine communication needed further to advance systems in which there is a mobility component. Many of the existing applications in transport and distribution are relatively low bit transmission rate applications and the growth of these is easily discouraged by prices based upon connection times. Such pricing may be necessary in some areas to ration available switching capacities. Over the longer term, however, these considerations should become less pressing and new models for encouraging the use of mobile inter-machine communication may make a substantial contribution to the data communication traffic that flows through public telecommunication networks.

The second network issue raised by augmented communication services is the demand that is likely to emerge for higher performance in Internet linkages. This will affect mobile telecommunication operators before the other telecommunication operators. The practical use of TCP/IP networks in mobile applications requires a more rapid rate of response and a faster data throughput rate upstream from the user terminal to the station connection than would be acceptable in other dial-up applications. This is because of the inherent difficulties in establishing and maintaining communication linkages with mobile as compared to fixed locations.[22] Unless these difficulties are overcome, this issue is likely to represent an important barrier to the diffusion of many Internet-based augmented communication services. If the technical difficulties are resolved, this will magnify the growth of what would otherwise be a small contribution to the flood of fixed network Internet traffic.[23]

4.3.2 Network Capabilities for Home Access to Multimedia

A major issue influencing the future development of the Internet continues to be the development of more rapid access speeds than are available through dial-up modem access. Several different strategies have been developed for improving access speeds

[21] e.g. Ka band satellite systems operators such as SkyBridge (Alcatel and Loral); Astrolink (Lockheed Martin), Spaceway (Hughes), and Teledesic, plan to offer high-speed broadband connectivity to the Internet using satellites in geostationary and/or low earth orbits. Most of the planned broadband satellite operators aim to start service in 2002, see Foley (1999b).

[22] While many mobile users are stationary at the time of placing their calls, it is often the case that the communication process is the primary activity with few attractive alternatives. For every user who can leisurely sip a cup of coffee while waiting for an information request to be processed, there will be two or more users who are staring impatiently at the screen or listening to the earphone in less appealing surroundings.

[23] Satellite links are being used intensively by ISPs in developing regions. In the Middle East and North Africa, for example, 30.8% of ISP connections travel thorough satellites, for Latin America and Asia the figures are 23.9% and 10.3%, respectively. In contrast, only 3.7% of western Europe ISPs are connected by satellite, and in the United States only 2.1% of Internet-related service traffic is carried over satellites, see Foley (1999b).

including cable modems, direct broadcast satellite World Wide Web services, and an upgrading of local telephone services using a family of technologies generically represented by the term x-type Digital Subscriber Line (xDSL). These areas, which are examined in the following sections, are under simultaneous development in the United States and Europe.[24]

4.3.2.1 Cable Modem Developments

Cable modems involve the upgrading of the cable television networks to allow high-speed data access on frequencies that are employed for television broadcasting. In the United States, the penetration of cable television is higher than many (but not all) European countries. This has provided a first-mover advantage in developing cable access for multimedia and innovative digital media. Until 1995, European cable companies, who perceived a very different market for interactive services, had largely written off the Internet (*The Economist*, 1995a). Continuing interest in breaking the 'local-loop' bottleneck to high-speed Internet access and some initial successes by American companies have suggested that, in offering Internet services, the cable operators may have advantages. The extent of these advantages is also being tested in many joint ventures with European companies. The availability of new-generation modems with very high digital processing capability opens the door to the development of intelligent multifunctional products that go far beyond the modulation and demodulation of analogue voice signals. The new processing capabilities supported the first commercial introductions of cable modem services in 1996 and 1997.

Cable operators believe they can offer high-speed access to the Internet and on-line services through upgraded cable systems and new modems. By dedicating an entire television channel to a service, cable companies can pump through data at a rate of 30 megabits (30,000 kilobits) per second, although the industry seems to be heading towards a standardized speed of 10 Mbps. This, of course, is much faster than the 14.4 or 28.8 kbps used to access the Internet over most telephone lines. In practice, however, cable may deliver little more than 200 or 300 kbps at peak times.

Internet users represent a ready potential market for cable operators because cable modems have, in fact, the potential to prise open bandwidth bottlenecks, enabling new services for residential users. The total available market for early adoption of cable modems is the share of households owning a personal computer (that is, the proportion of households that would currently be able to take advantage of high-speed data services, if they were available) who can also be connected by cable. The share of households that have both capabilities cannot be estimated accurately. There are four different situations in Europe, as shown in Fig. 4.1. In Italy, Portugal, and Spain, low personal computer and cable penetration create an unattractive market for national cable modem development. In the United Kingdom, France, and Norway, less than one half of the households are passed by cable, but cable modem services may still be attractive for particular communities. A similar situation is present in the five countries clustered around the 60 per cent cable penetration level with Germany and

---

[24] Developments are also occurring in Japan, but these are not discussed here.

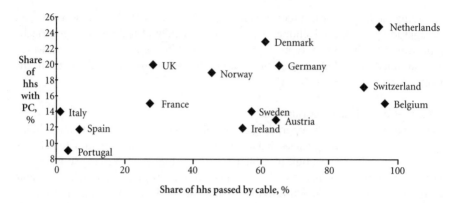

FIG. 4.1. Personal computer penetration rates and households passed by cable in European countries, 1996

Source: Passamonti, Sisti, and Cattaneo (1997) adapted from Ovum Consulting (1997).

Denmark offering greater opportunities due to their higher personal computer penetration. The Netherlands, Switzerland, and Belgium represent the most attractive cable modem markets. In these countries, it may be assumed that virtually all homes with personal computers also have cable access.

Cable modem services will be delivered over a Hybrid-Fibre Coaxial (HFC) or Fibre-to-the-Curb (FTTC) network. Older coaxial-only networks, which make up much of the installed plant in the United States and some European countries, such as Belgium, The Netherlands and Denmark, are in the process of being upgraded to HFC. Cable modem solutions are mainly aimed at residential users. Technical constraints render them less suitable for businesses.[25] Cable modem services seem particularly suitable for residential casual users to support Internet browsing, e-mail, and information services in the short run, and video and real-time entertainment, such as advanced interactive multi-user games, in the long run.

4.3.2.2 *Direct Broadcast Satellite Potential*

Europe has had a reasonably strong position in the development of Direct Broadcast Satellite (DBS) services. As yet this infrastructure has been employed largely for broadcast and pay-TV services. However, a number of innovative applications are possible using this network infrastructure. Thus, there is a variety of channels through which multimedia and innovative digital media may be distributed in Europe. In many cases, these channels are being constructed with new equipment and, therefore, with technological capabilities that are more advanced than those embedded in the older infrastructures in many areas in the United States.

---

[25] The limitations include the inability to guarantee bandwidth to individual users for the duration of the application's use, a narrow upstream data path imposed by spectrum allocation, and the perceived lack of network security.

European digital television has been characterized by major consolidations, such as the mergers of Canal Plus and Nethold, and Première and DF1, the German digital television service. It has been estimated that the pay-back period of the costs to acquire a new digital television customer is, on average, two years, including the costs of commercial service, the promotional material, the cost of free promotion campaigns, such as free monthly subscription, free dish, etc. (Passamonti, Sisti, and Cattaneo, 1997). Broadcasters are searching for new sources of revenues including Near-Video-on-Demand (NVoD) and Pay-per-View (PPV). The European market for digital television is still very small when compared to the market for analogue and cable television services and to new terrestrial digital transmission systems (see Table 4.2).

Access to the final customer is crucial for the media, telecommunication, and multimedia suppliers that are competing to provide pay-TV, interactive services, and advanced telephony services to the mass market. The characteristics of digital conditional access platforms for customers have important consequences because they may lock customers in to proprietary systems or discriminate at other levels.[26]

The Directive on the use of standards for the transmission of television has addressed the need for standardization of digital transmission systems (European Commission, 1997a). It also establishes the principle that conditional access services platforms must allow all broadcasters to offer technical services on a fair, reasonable, and non-discriminatory basis. However, the Directive does not address new issues arising from the convergence of the broadcasting, telecommunication, computing, and publishing industries such as the rights of non-broadcaster interactive service providers. The technical characteristics of the digital conditional access system may discriminate against third-party access even when they respect the basic principles of openness and interoperability for certain classes of services. The high production costs associated with the enhanced functionality of planned new-generation set-top-boxes are leading some consortia to consider subsidizing the price of customer equipment. Some of the advanced functionality of next-generation set-top-boxes is an area where the development of standards, or the implementation and deployment of standards, is immature. This situation may result in proprietary systems discriminating against third-party access.[27]

4.3.2.3 xDSL Developments

After considerable delay, xDSL markets are beginning to open in both Europe and the United States.[28] The xDSL technology allows the local loop of telecommunication carriers to carry a much greater volume of digital information and the significant diffusion of xDSL capabilities could have a major effect in widening the bottleneck of local access speeds to the Internet. This technology is also likely to have a major effect on the demand for telecommunication network-based data transmission services. A com-

---

[26] For a discussion of this aspect see D. A. L. Levy (1997); Mansell (1997).

[27] See e.g. Cave and Cowie (1998).

[28] France has announced the availability of the ADSL services in the first six *arrondissements* of Paris and three villages in the Paris vicinity (in the Hauts-de-Seine), http://www.finances.gouv.fr/presse/communiques/ accessed 15 September 1999.

TABLE 4.2. *Digital satellite television market in major European countries*

Country	Operators	Shareholders	Subscribers digital satellite TV	Operating system	Conditional access platform	Subscribers pay-TV end 1996
UK	BSkyB	News Corp. (40%), BSB Hold. (14%), Pathé (13%), Granada (6.5%)	Start mid-1998	Open TV[1]	NDS[2]	BSkyB 5.5 m.
Germany	Première/DF1[3]	CLT/Ufa (50%), Kirch group (50%)	30,000 (Première) DF1 58,000	D-box[4] —	Irdeto —	Première 1.4 m. —
France	Canal Satellite	Canal Plus (70%), Pathé (20%), Générale des Eaux (10%)	500,000	MediaGuard[5]	Mediahighway	Canal Plus, Canal Satellite 4.9 m.
France	TPS	TF1(25%), France Télévision (25%), M6 (20%), Lyonnaise des Eaux, CLT-Ufa[6] (20%)	210,000	Open TV	Viaccess	—
France	ABSat	Groupe AB	12,000	—	Viaccess	—
Italy	Telepiù	Telecom Italia (40%), Canal Plus (30%), Fininvest (10%), RAI (10%), Cecchi Gori (10%)[7]	160,000	Irdeto[8]/ MediaGuard	D-box/ Mediahighway	Telepiù 826,000
Spain	Canal Satellite España	Sogecable (85%), Antena 3 (15%)	140,000	MediaGuard	Mediahighway	Canal Plus 1.5 m.
Spain	Distribudora de Television	Retevision, Telefonica	75,000	Nagravision Digital	—	—
Netherlands	Canal Plus Nederland	Canal Plus	90,000	—	—	FilmNet: 343,000
Nordic	Canal Digital	Telenor (50%), Canal Plus (50%)	Start Dec. 97	—	—	FilmNet/ TV100 544,000

[1] Open TV is the operating system of Thomson, Sun, and Multichoice International.

[2] NDS (News Digital System) is a company owned by News Corp. Murdoch owns 39.9% of BSkyB Holdings (Nethold).

[3] DF 1 was to merge with Première in 1998, but the merger was not approved by the European Commission.

[4] D-box is produced by Beta Research.

[5] Mediaguard and Mediahighway respectively use SECA OS and CA systems. SECA is owned by Bertelsmann (50%) and Canal Plus (50%).

[6] CLT-Ufa is 49% owned by Bertelsmann and 49% by Audiofina.

[7] The agreement was pending ratification.

[8] Irdeto (CA) is 100% owned by Multichoice International Holdings (Nethold).

Source: Based on *ScreenDigest* biweekly newsletter, London, and IDATE, Montpellier, 3rd quarter figures 1997, cited in Passamonti, Sisti, and Cattaneo (1997).

munity of Internet users (whom the French have dubbed 'Internauts') with xDSL access is likely to generate a considerable volume of broadband or near-broadband data traffic in its use of audiovisual services for viewing, communicating, and interactive gaming.

Telecommunication operators, including France Telecom, are experimenting with ADSL technology that may be able to deliver 8 Mbps or more. Local loops have not previously been the target of substantial investment because they have been used for the job for which they were designed, that is, carrying analogue telephone calls. In recent years, however, network operators have been considering the use of the copper local-loop network as a medium for high-speed transport of data. There are several alternatives for creating digital subscriber lines that use copper cabling to move data between the home and high-speed fibre networks. These rely on powerful banks of digital signal processors at the 'edge switch' and transceivers at both ends of the line to process digital data and send them down the line to the home or office. The various alternatives differ in the stage of their development, their performance characteristics, and costs as shown in Table 4.3.

Furthest along the development curve is High-bit-rate Digital Subscriber Line (HDSL), a technology that was developed to provide a less expensive way to implement T1/E1 circuits (1.5 or 2 Mbps) on twisted pair copper wires. This loop architecture uses two full-duplex pairs to provide repeaterless leased-line service in both directions up to 12,000 feet. It is being used in private networks for universities, hospitals, and certain commercial companies where the space between buildings is within the distance limitation.

ADSL implementation can provide a downstream path of 6.1 Mbps with a return path of up to 640 kbps over a single twisted pair. It is 100 times faster on the down path than ISDN. This architecture uses frequency modulation algorithms to force

TABLE 4.3. *The Digital Subscriber Line family*

Acronym	Speed	Duplex transmission	Distance
HDSL	1.5–2 Mbps	Symmetric	12,000 ft.
SDSL	1.5–3 Mbps	Symmetric	5–10,000 ft.
ADSL	1.5–8 Mbps (downstream)	Asymmetric	18,000 ft. @ 1.5 Mbps
	16–640 kbps (upstream)		12,000 ft. @ 6.1 Mbps
VDSL	13–52 Mbps (downstream)	Asymmetric	4,500 ft. @ 13 Mbps
	1.5–2.3 Mbps (upstream)		1,000 ft. @ 52 Mbps

Source: Bernard (1997) by Technology Investment Partners, Paris.

additional bits into the 1-MHz bandwidth of the local loop. Lower-cost processors are beginning to make xDSL look like a cost-effective technology. The assumption is that Internet users will be more concerned with how fast data moves to their computers than with how long it takes for prompts and commands to return to the network. Downloading a web page requires far greater bandwidth than requesting the page. The average Internet user receives many, many more times the quantity of data for every bit he or she sends. In addition to the downstream and upstream channels, xDSL also accommodates an analogue telephone channel making it possible for people to talk on the telephone while they are downloading files from the Internet over a single copper line. All of the xDSL technologies require sensitive signal-detection chips and other gadgetry in order to perform reliably and this tends to inflate the costs per connection.

The xDSL technology also offers an alternative to HFC delivery systems, which have been found to be more costly to implement than initially expected. When telecommunication network operators are confronted with significant dial-up problems resulting from the explosive growth of Internet access requests, DSL technology can alleviate the circuit-blocking problem because it maintains separate channels for packet data and digital voice. Switches can pre-emptively separate data calls from voice circuits with simple line splitters.[29]

The existence of multiple networks for the delivery of multimedia content considerably increases the uncertainty about when and how high-speed access to the information and communication infrastructure, and the Internet in particular, will be achieved. The potential for competing networks may, in fact, serve as a mutually reinforcing mechanism for slowing the rate of investment in upgrading any one of the networks for high-speed access. Even though the price of the enabling technology is falling, the investment costs required to deliver a broadly accessible multi-megabyte-per-second service to the home are high. No operator can commit to such an investment with the certainty that the technology will not be followed by other network upgrades. When viewed from the perspective of equipment producers or network operators, and in the light of the uncertain rate at which broader utilization of the Internet will evolve, the construction of Europe's information and communication infrastructure is a risky proposition. It is possible to take the lead in these markets and the technology is available. The question, however, is whether enough users will follow to make the investment pay.

The most likely solution to this conundrum is offered by growing use of the Internet and more intensive demand for high-speed Internet services. These are likely to be the sources of demand that will promote further investment in equipment and network services. It is important to recognize, however, that users' interests in, and demand for, information services are complex. In some cases, they may be served effectively by technologies that do not rely upon telecommunication network access in

---

[29] However, as with many of these technological advances, there are problems in implementation. e.g. one 1998 market forecast observes that DSL problems in handling crosstalk will need to be worked out and that this technology is labour intensive to install, see http://www.data.com/issue/981207/forecast2.html accessed 7 Aug. 1999.

any way. The following section examines the role of pre-recorded optical discs for the distribution of information. It is a cautionary tale. For some users, connection to the information and communication infrastructure is achieved by a trip to the newsagent to purchase an optical disc rather than through a connection to the telecommunication network.

4.4 Finding the Information Society at the Newsagent: The Role of Optical Discs

The continuous stream of technological improvements in optoelectronics and integrated circuits has opened an enormous frontier for information and communication technology-based products and services. This frontier is poorly understood and it cannot be mapped by broad generalizations about the convergence between telecommunication and information technologies. Nor does the nostrum that 'what has been wired will become wireless while what has been wireless will become wired' provide a complete catalogue of the strategies that actors involved in the process of building the European information society may adopt to utilize new technologies.

The issue of which technologies and services will generate adequate revenue to fund the costs of upgrading the telecommunication network is a major contributor to uncertainty in this area. New technologies often have evolutionary, as well as revolutionary, implications for their users as they serve to revitalize and stimulate processes of adaptation and adjustment between the new and the older technologies. The most important uses of new technologies are almost never those that are imagined during the early diffusion process.[30] From this perspective, it is possible to recognize that the distribution of some forms of multimedia content may be achieved without telecommunication transmission. The post office and the newsagent's van are also part of the information and communication infrastructure and they are becoming integrated with the electronic infrastructure as well.

The development of a very high-capacity European information and communication infrastructure faces significant competition from more specialized technologies for delivering information that may be developed and diffused more rapidly than the corresponding telecommunication networks.[31] For example, the development of some on-demand services, such as interactive games, is stimulating and shaping demand for set-top-boxes for cable television systems. This section examines the development of an alternative infrastructure for the distribution of multimedia content, that is, the storage capacity of the optical disc. The optical disc is a physical artefact that must be distributed using the variety and complexity of existing distribution systems such as newsagents, urban kiosks, or the postal service. Distribution of information through the optical disc medium, however, would be meaningless

---

[30] See e.g. Dervin and Shields (1990); Mosco (1982).
[31] There are, of course, many applications that are meaningful only in a network context, including extensions of voice telephony and facsimile communication to video-telephony and multimedia messaging.

without the prior diffusion of the personal computer as an information appliance capable of reading this medium.

Historically the diffusion of personal computers in Europe has lagged behind that of the United States while exceeding the level of penetration in Japan. As a result of this later widespread diffusion, the stock of the computers in Europe is of a more recent vintage and, therefore, is more powerful than the average in the United States.[32] The share of CD-ROM drives installed as part of personal computer systems in some European countries is approaching the levels achieved in the United States with significant implications for the multimedia content market.[33] User familiarity with the performance of CD-ROMs in displaying multimedia and interacting with software shapes expectations about network performance and features. Multimedia content that is available on the network faces competition from content distribution using CD-ROMs. CD-ROM distribution engages a wide array of existing retail outlets ranging from newsagents or kiosks to computer stores, whose experience in selling information packages to users is being further developed as network-based distribution of multimedia becomes more pervasive.

Information distribution using optical discs is of particular interest because it is both a potential substitute for, and a potential complement to, telecommunication network distribution of information.[34] The extent to which the optical disc medium is a complement or a substitute to telecommunication services depends upon the development of markets for content and the specific implementations of network services. For example, it is a common practice in on-line service markets to transmit graphic images for local storage on the user's personal computer thereby permitting a richer display and faster user interface than would be possible if these images had to be transmitted over the telecommunication links for every viewing. In a similar fashion, other images are distributed to the user on the discs that are used to enable on-line service subscription. As a result, there are numerous possibilities for creating 'hybrid' optical disc resources based on simultaneous use of the very rapid processing power available within the computer, that is, in excess of 2 Mbps, combined with slower telecommunication network access.

It is often suggested that problems created by the currently limited capacity of networks at important junctures will disappear with the availability of a high-capacity information and communication or broadband infrastructure. There is reason to argue instead, however, that choices about how to distribute information will change simply in response to the relative prices of different modes of information transmission. For example, CD-ROMs capable of holding around 650 megabytes of informa-

---

[32] The practice of 'retirement' of older computers in industry statistics is usually accomplished by assumptions about the decay of previous years' shipments data. To our knowledge there is no accurate source for determining the true rate of replacement of newer for older models.

[33] e.g. in Sweden the share of surveyed individuals reporting access to a personal computer with CD-ROM in their homes was 49.5% while in Denmark it was 44.8% (INRA, 1999). This figure is substantially lower for the larger markets of Germany (22.9%), the United Kingdom (19.7%), Spain (17.9%), France (17.1%) and Italy (16.8%).

[34] For additional sources on the history of multimedia in Europe and the United States see Ayre, Callaghan, and Hoffos (1994); European Commission Information Market Observatory (IMO) (1994); Inteco (1994); Ovum Consulting (1995; 1997); Roth (1988).

tion can be produced very economically in relatively small quantities and distributed by retail or mail-order networks. The promotion of these products follows in the tradition of book and magazine distribution with availability now widespread throughout Europe in urban newsagents or kiosks and other retail outlets.

CD-ROMs provide an important economic substitute for a variety of information distribution activities that might otherwise occur over telecommunication networks. The importance of the CD-ROM lies not in its technological capacity *per se*, but in the possibility that it will become well-entrenched long before a network means of distributing similar information content can match the performance and cost of this medium. CD-ROMs are capable of being major complements to the use of telecommunication networks since they can serve as a guide to information available via the telecommunication network. They can serve as a local store of data that can be exploited by telecommunication services operating at slower bit rates, and as a high-performance source of data and programs that can complement on-line delivery of interactive services and media.

A significant number of homes and businesses in Europe are equipped with the means to access both on-line and CD-ROM information services. Given the slower development of higher-speed data links for home and small business users, a *mixed* system of information content delivery is a reasonable scenario for Europe. The CD-ROM can play a major role in complementing, or substituting for, on-line distribution of information content. This development suggests a very broad diffusion of a network access method or platform that is flexible with regard to future developments in telecommunication networks, information services, and content provision. It also suggests that the development of information service access will be shaped by the interaction between CD-ROM and telecommunication technologies.

4.4.1   *CD-ROM Technology and Market Development*

The CD-ROM was first introduced on the commercial market in 1985. The technology it is based upon is similar to that of CD-audio (CD-AD) which was brought to the market in the late 1970s by Philips and Sony. These same companies led the initiative for the development and the introduction of the CD-ROM and, additionally, for the functional specifications of CD-ROM. The High Sierra Group, consisting of manufacturers such as Hewlett-Packard, DEC, Apple, Philips, and Sony as well as the National Information Standards Organization (NISO) in the United States, contributed significantly to CD-ROM development by proposing a CD-ROM standard to the International Organization for Standardization (ISO). The ISO adopted this standard as the ISO 9660 CD-ROM standard.

CD-ROM is an optical disc storage medium with a theoretical capacity of 650 megabytes that can store text, data, sound, and photographic or video images.[35] It was not until the late 1980s, however, that the CD-ROM became associated with

---

[35] Techniques exist to extend the storage capacity of CD-ROMs but they require specific disc drives for their operation. Compression technology also provides a means for extending the storage capacity of such discs.

multimedia. Until that time, CD-ROM technology mainly was used for storing large quantities of text and data for archival and distribution purposes. Many CD formats and variants have been introduced in spite of the existence of the ISO standard; virtually all these standards were, however, developed for proprietary game consoles that are designed to be connected to televisions.[36] In 1993, recordable formats of the CD-ROM began to be distributed to the mass market and, most recently, the Digital Video Disc (DVD) format with a much larger storage capacity (4.7 Gb and higher) has been introduced. DVD was designed to use advanced compression techniques for the encoding of full-length feature films, a feature that makes this storage medium particularly well suited to the further development of multimedia markets as discussed below.

CD-ROM technology can be used in combination with a television or a personal computer as the delivery platform. The personal computer is the main delivery platform for CD-ROM at present although television-based platforms continue to be important. The existence of a common personal computer platform standard as compared with the proprietary television CD-ROM standards has reduced the uncertainty for publishers and content providers in the personal computer CD-ROM market. This has resulted in an increase in the number of personal computer CD-ROM titles 'in print' and has stimulated sales of personal computer CD-ROM drives. Backward compatibility has also contributed some stability to the market and led to a reduction of uncertainty for publishers.

4.4.2 Changing CD-ROM Usage Patterns

The two main uses of CD-ROM are professional or business, and consumer. At the outset the CD-ROM was used by such professional organizations as libraries, businesses, and government departments as a convenient and cost-effective way of storing and retrieving information. In the field of professional CD-ROM titles, there are those that are sold for professional purposes on the commercial market and in-house produced titles that are manufactured by organizations for their own use. Consumers are now the most important user group for CD-ROMs and, for many people, CD-ROM technology has become synonymous with multimedia.

The extent of penetration of CD-ROM technology in Europe can be gauged roughly by referring to the figures in Table 4.4. The two columns, unfortunately, are commensurable only when assumptions are made about translating individual to household use. For example, if it is assumed that every household includes two or more adults, that is, persons of 18 years of age or more, who share the personal computer with a CD-ROM, the individual use figure must be substantially reduced to reflect household availability. There is, however, no strong basis for making an adjustment. What can be

---

[36] An exception is the CD-ROM XA which is an enhanced version of the CD-ROM and was introduced in 1988; it is better suited to multimedia than its predecessor. This format uses interleaving, a method of storing different types of data on the disc (enhanced sound, photographic images, text) that enables smooth handling of data. The XA format uses better audio (Adaptive Differential Pulse Code Modulation) which improves the sound quality.

TABLE 4.4. *Installed base of CD-ROMs, December 1995 and 4th quarter 1998*

	Households with PCs, Dec. 95 %	Individuals reporting home access to PC, 4Q98 %	Households with PCs and CD-ROMs, Dec. 95 %	Individuals with home access to PCs with CD-ROMs, 4Q98 %	Share of computers with CD-ROMs, Dec. 95 %	Share of computers with CD-ROMs, 4Q98 %	Growth in share of computers with CD-ROMs, 1995-8 %
Belgium	15	33	7	19	47	58	24
Denmark	24	57	9	45	38	79	111
France	15	23	6	17	40	75	88
Germany	19	31	11	23	58	75	30
Greece	10	12	3	7	30	57	91
Italy	14	27	6	17	43	63	47
Netherlands	25	59	10	40	40	67	68
Spain	21	28	7	18	33	63	89
Sweden	27	60	9	50	33	83	148
UK	20	35	7	19	35	55	56

Note: German figures are for West Germany in 1995 and for all of Germany in 1998.

Source: The 1995 figures are from Inteco (1996) as cited in van de Paal (1997) and the 1998 figures are from INRA (1999).

TABLE 4.5. *Commercial CD-ROM and multimedia CD titles by subject*

| | Year end 1995 |
Subject	No. of titles
General interest, leisure	5,635
Arts, humanities	2,859
Advertising, design, marketing	2,820
Education, training, careers	2,339
Computers and computer programs	1,863
Biomedicine, health, and nursing	1,590
Science and technology	1,315
Earth sciences	1,282
Language and linguistics	1,144
Business and company information	1,047
TOTAL	21,895

Source: Derived from TFPL Publishing Ltd. (1996).

said is that the entire personal computer base in Europe is rapidly becoming CD-ROM-compatible as indicated by the last two columns in Table 4.4.

The conclusion to be drawn from these figures is that the installed base of CD-ROM drives seems substantial enough to support a further uptake of the CD-ROM medium in the home. The reduction of uncertainty about acceptance of CD-ROM technology has sparked the interest, and, correspondingly, the entrepreneurial initiative of publishers and content providers.

In 1989, it was estimated that the number of commercial CD-ROM titles available worldwide was 817. At the end of 1995, the number of titles was 21,895 while other estimates for 1995 and 1998 were 25,000 and 29,000 respectively.[37] Table 4.5 gives a breakdown of CD-ROM titles by subject as of 1995, the most recent date for which statistics were readily accessible. The most important category is labelled 'general interest and leisure'. These titles are for entertainment and include games. Although the number of professional titles represents only a small portion of all commercial titles published, their role in revenue generation should be more than proportionate since these titles are usually more expensive than consumer titles and have higher margins. The share of United States companies in the total sales of CD-ROMs exceeds that of European companies but the number of companies in Europe has outnumbered those in the United States since 1993. The reasons for this include language differences and the important role of CD-ROM-producing companies in the training sector

[37] The 1995 estimate is from TFPL Publishing Ltd. (1996) while the other 1995 and 1998 estimates are from Smart Storage (1999: 3).

which also involves substantial local content (Policy Studies Institute and PIRA International, 1996).

Only a small portion of consumer CD-ROM titles is believed to be profitable. This is due to the limited number of successful titles published and to the practice of bundling which involves the selling of CD-ROM titles together with CD-ROM drives. Bundling is a common practice in the CD-ROM industry. More intense competition due to the large number of new publishers, has reduced the selling price of CD-ROM titles. Industry observers expect a consolidation in the number of publishers, followed by mergers, acquisitions, and an accompanying shake-out, especially in the United States publishing industry where a greater concentration of publishers is likely than in Europe.

Europe lacks the advantage of a homogeneous market; the market is fragmented due to language and cultural barriers (SCIENTER, 1998). Nevertheless, this offers niche opportunities to European publishers. Several factors favour further growth in the number of European publishers. These include the rapid growth in the number of readers installed and, therefore, increased opportunities to sell discs in Europe and opportunities for producing titles that more closely serve European cultural and language needs. Europe also has export opportunities especially for English titles.

To exploit this potential several conditions will have to be met. There is a need for local content to create niche opportunities for publishers and for localization initiatives.[38] Furthermore, there is a need for quality titles and greater marketing and distribution efforts.

4.4.3   Warding Off Obsolescence

Industry analysts have predicted that the Internet and other on-line services will make CD-ROMs obsolete. Some years ago most discussion centred on whether CD-ROM would replace on-line services. With important exceptions, such as the growth of use of the Encyclopaedia Britannica on-line service, this has not occurred. Usage patterns suggest that a major portion of consumer on-line service use was dominated by 'concurrent' or 'time-delayed' electronic communication, for example, chatboxes and e-mail. This was followed by the use of information services for current financial, news, and related services. Access to multimedia services continues to occupy a growing, but less important, source of use.

What has prevented obsolescence? One salient factor is that on-line services do not provide the optimal content carrier; on-line connections may be interrupted, and access is often congested and therefore slow. These are factors that hinder the distribution of video images. In many locations, high-quality on-line connections are simply not available or affordable compared to the alternatives even for those who can (with effort) afford the equipment. Until this situation changes and on-line

---

[38] See Williams and Slack (1999) which reports the results of the European Commission's Social Learning in Multimedia (SLIM) project, an 8-country study, funded under the TSER Programme, that looked particularly at the incentives and opportunities for the localization of multimedia products.

services achieve their potential, there is a substantial motivation to develop optical disc storage.

Many supposedly 'obsolete' technologies have had prolonged lives due to the introduction of improvements to meet the challenge of competitive alternatives. Developments in CD-Recordable (CD-R) and CD-Rewritable (CD-RW) are further enhancing and revitalizing the position of the CD. The developments in CD-R and CD-RW are important because these formats increase the possibilities for small publishers and individual work groups to produce in small batches adding many CD-ROM titles and offering opportunities to create specialized product niches that collectively strengthen the CD-ROM medium. These developments offer unique advantages in Europe where local markets are not always large enough to make small batch production feasible. Although these developments suggest that the future of optical storage will brighten rather than dim, the current CD-ROM format may be supplanted over the next five to ten years by the DVD which was introduced commercially in 1997.

4.4.4 Continuing Developments in Optical Disc Storage

The CD-ROM has not been a faultless medium for the mass distribution of multimedia content. There have been a number of changes in the speed of drives and these have led software developers to develop ways of utilizing the more rapid CD-ROM speed. While software designed for the faster drives often degrades performance rather than producing outright failures when used on slower drives, the problems are significant enough to raise customer uncertainty. In addition, the development of market outlets for CD-ROM distribution has been uneven, particularly for titles that are based upon a 'packaged software' business model that requires a significant purchase price.

The industry practice of bundling numerous 'free' CD-ROMs with the purchase of drives has resulted in intense price competition. Like other 'first-copy' industries, such as books, recordings, film, and periodicals, the costs of CD-ROM multimedia production are amortized according to the number of copies sold. Intense competition to create attractive content increases first-copy costs and increases the number of discs that must be sold to achieve profits at prevailing prices.[39] These features of the industry are persistent and it is commonly claimed that publishers have, on balance, failed to achieve a profit although many individual publishers have claimed profits in this segment of their business.[40]

A major problem facing CD publishers is distribution and the apparent shortage of shelf space in retail outlets. Stocking titles that have a low turnover represents an

---

[39] In some specialized CD-ROM markets, such as those related to legal and medical information, the content commands substantially higher prices, which reduces the break-even point required for profitability. A major segment of the CD-ROM multimedia market, however, resembles the film industry where new products often fail to recoup production costs and incur heavy promotion costs. For analysis of the characteristics of this type of industry see Samarajiva (1985) from an institutional economics perspective and Besen and Raskind (1991) from an economics perspective.

[40] According to Infotech Research (1998).

inventory cost for retailers as well as a cost in terms of physical space utilization. Some of these problems are reduced in areas that are populous enough to support large computer software outlets. In these stores, larger areas are employed to offer more selection and to attract more customers relative to smaller city centre or shopping centre outlets. In many cases, publishers grant some form of exclusive contract to distributors. Promotional services offered by distributors range from the use of catalogues and direct mail, sales forces, and advertising, to the use of web sites and telemarketing. Some distributors take an even more active role in the distribution of CD-ROM titles. In order to reduce the chance of disappointment for the consumer, the French CD-ROM retailer, FNAC, for example, which holds a very large market share, introduced a label for certain selected titles that were believed to deliver the greatest value for buyers. Although stores may also carry titles that do not have FNAC's seal of approval, the ones that do are more actively promoted.

All these developments are associated with the business model of recovering the costs of multimedia production by setting a price which, multiplied by the number of purchasers, will recover the cost of producing and distributing the CD-ROM. This model may work for titles that are heavily promoted and represent very large development costs. At the same time, however, a significant market has developed in the distribution of multimedia content through the 'free' distribution of the discs as supplements to magazines devoted to personal computers, the Internet, or interactive gaming. Products distributed in this way may generate revenue through sales to the media companies responsible for the magazines. They may also represent a collection of incomplete products for which registration, typically using the Internet, is required to receive the complete product. Users have begun to accept this shareware model that was originally developed to distribute software titles. There is very little difference between this mode of distribution and the growth of Internet electronic commerce in the downloading of software titles. The shortcoming of the CD-ROM is that only a limited number of titles per month can be distributed by the larger circulation magazines. The advantage is that users may experience installation times that are much faster than downloading and installing the relevant software from the Internet.

Despite the mixed results, the technological development of optical discs has continued. The product life of the CD-ROM format cycle has been extended through the introduction of systems that enable the user not only to read a CD, but also to record and write a CD.[41] Philips and Sony took the lead in the development of new products, but the diffusion of inexpensive recording devices did not occur until the mid-1990s.[42] As new products have been brought to market there have been several layers of 'orphaned' devices. The technology for recording and writing has become affordable

---

[41] The distinction is between media technologies that allow for a one-time recording of information, recordable, and those that allow multiple recordings, writable. A variant we do not discuss is CD-Erasable, or CD-E, which involves a more elaborate and time-consuming procedure to prepare the disc to receive a second recording. CD-E is being supplanted by CD-Rewritable.

[42] The initial lack of compatibility of CD-RW has now been solved through the use of MultiRead, a development for which the Optical Storage Technical Association (OSTA) was responsible. However, a significant portion of the installed base of CD-RW disc drives is not equipped with this feature and, therefore, cannot read rewritable discs.

to the home user and has now reached the rapid growth phase of the diffusion process. At the same time, the new formats seem to mark the end of the CD life-cycle. The CD successor, DVD, was brought to the market in mid-1997. Although DVD has the same physical characteristics as the CD, it plays in another league.

4.4.5 DVD: The Next Generation

The Digital Versatile Disc standard was defined in 1995, ten years after the introduction of CD-ROM. It was the result of joint development efforts by a larger consortium, known initially as the DVD Consortium and later as the DVD Forum, than was responsible for the CD-ROM.[43] The film industry has had a considerable interest in the development of the DVD as an improved means of distributing films through a digital medium and Time-Warner is a member of the DVD Forum. Not surprisingly, the abbreviation DVD initially stood for Digital Video Disc. At first, it seemed that there would be another technical standards battle headed by Sony and Philips on the one side working on the MultiMedia-CD (MMCD), and the Super Density Digital Video Disc (SD-DVD) alliance headed by Toshiba and Time Warner, on the other. After American computer manufacturers rejected the idea of having multiple DVD standards, the developers found it possible to agree upon a single standard.

DVD is better suited for multimedia than CDs for several reasons. First, it has a greatly enhanced storage capacity compared to the 'meagre' 650 megabytes that the CD-ROM has to offer. The twenty-five-fold increase in the storage capacity of the DVD-ROM allows a high-definition film to be stored on the disc along with up to 32 different subtitles and 8 different soundtracks.[44] DVD further offers Dolby Digital (AC-3) sound compression using 6 audio channels that can create a stereo-surround effect.

From the user's viewpoint, it would be desirable to have a single inter-operable format for all optical discs. The problem is that the standards for the new technologies as well as the capabilities of existing drives are limited by the state of technical development. It is reasonable to expect that new, more versatile, and higher-capacity disc drives will come into existence after a particular drive has been purchased. Nevertheless, it would be desirable for more advanced devices, at a minimum, to be able to access information from earlier formats.

Unfortunately, upgrade paths involve trade-offs. It may prove costly to incorporate backward compatibility as the technology evolves. Producers are not eager to become champions of 'commodity' systems that face intense price competition early in the product life-cycle and before the costs of development have been recovered. Producers are also keen to provide strong incentives to media producers to provide a software library for their new devices by upgrading the standard of existing titles. These market

---

[43] The DVD Forum consists of Sony, Philips, Hitachi, Toshiba, Time Warner, Matsushita, Mitsubishi, JVC, Pioneer, and Thomson.

[44] The actual number of films depends on the amount of compression used. The file structure on the DVD, the logical format, is called Universal Disc Format and was developed by OSTA. It is the follow-up of the ISO 9660, the standard for CD-ROM.

features provide incentives for producers to differentiate their products with respect to competitors and to create proprietary versions of the next-generation technology in the hope that their product will become the *de facto* standard that others must imitate.[45]

The result of these incentives is that manufacturers often choose not to implement backward compatibility and seem to prefer their proprietary standards to a consensus standard for the next-generation systems. There is a price for this strategy, however. Customers can become confused as a result of incompatibility problems and a wide variety of standards may lead them to postpone buying the new systems. At the beginning of the product cycle, considerable attention is paid to those users who are willing to gamble along with producers on the viability of proprietary standards or, in the case of recordable formats, who have a real need for higher performance for particular applications.

DVD comes in two versions, one of which is meant to be used in a personal computer environment. It is basically an extension of the CD-ROM and is referred to as DVD-ROM. DVD drives are sold either integrated into some of the high-end personal computers and notebooks or separately as upgrade kits. The other version of DVD, which is called DVD-video, uses a DVD-video player and is a candidate to replace analogue VHS cassettes and Laserdisc. It is also a competitor for on-line delivery of video-on-demand and may bring the personal computer and television platform competitors closer together. There are upgrade kits on the market that connect PC-DVD players to the television.

Industry experts suggest that DVD will develop most rapidly in the personal computer environment for several reasons. First, the users in the television environment are less accustomed to radical change and continuous improvement in technologies than are those in the personal computer environment, and this may impede the diffusion of DVD in the television environment. Second, despite the higher quality of their signal output, DVD video drives are expensive compared to the alternatives, that is, VHS recorders and players in combination with tape.[46] Acceptance of DVD is also likely to be limited as long as it does not offer a recording capability.

Over the long term, DVD could provide significant competition to the on-line distribution of multimedia information. Its ability to store very high quality audiovisual material and to provide enormous capacity for data, including software programs, will provide developers with the ability to create 'immersive' entertainment, education, and experiential environments in direct competition with such efforts on the web. The likelihood of continuing shortfalls in the capacity of the web to display similar programming, even with digital compression technology, indicates that many people are likely to continue to associate CD-ROM with multimedia rather than with the web.

These potential developments illustrate the contest between alternative

---

[45] Preferably imitation also requires the payment of royalties for patented technology embedded in proprietary systems.

[46] To take advantage of the quality difference, a high-quality television receiver must be used. This may involve an even greater cost of upgrading the television receiver and purchasing the DVD player.

technologies to become the major home information appliance. Convergence, that is, the merging of information exchange into common digital bitstreams and the progressive achievement of higher bandwidth communication paths for distributing these bitstreams, does not erase the distinct historical developments of existing systems. The enormous installed base of television sets serves as the 'electronic hearth' around which families gather. This is an attractive platform for the distribution of audiovisual material but it has very real and substantial limitations as a data display device. The home personal computer, increasingly, has the capacity for multimedia material, but it is primarily used by one person (at least in the industrialized countries). The potential for change does exist. Personal computers can be seen as originating devices for home entertainment in the same way that video cassette recorders or videogame players have become accepted. Similarly, set-top-boxes can be seen as sources of inputs for the individual or family personal computer, much as some people use telephone lines to connect their personal computers to the Internet and its information services. In either case, for most residential users, there are still major problems associated with the need for cabling and installation expertise.

Regardless of whether DVD or CD-ROM drives are used, for off-line multimedia to prosper, disc drives must be sold. The principal problem is the proliferation of model speeds. This variety is creating substantial problems for media producers. New multimedia products can be designed for higher-speed players if the publisher is willing to forgo the substantial installed base of slower-speed players,[47] but markets for the higher-speed drives will be more restricted. Publishers are being forced to make strategic choices between the levels of product quality that are drive-speed dependent and the installed base of platforms capable of playing discs designed for higher speeds.

Some optimism may be expressed about the future development of the DVD market. While it took about ten years for the CD to reach a mass scale of diffusion, it is reasonable to assume that PC-DVD will achieve mass acceptance much faster. There are several factors that support this observation. First, DVD-ROM is a continuation of CD-ROM and consumers are now familiar with optical storage and the CD-like format. Further, the backward compatibility of DVD helps to overcome resistance to the new technology that may arise because of earlier investments in CD-ROM titles. Third, the technology is notably superior to that of CD-ROM and introductory prices are reasonable. It is quite likely that DVD market development will achieve the milestone of being incorporated in the majority of new multimedia computers early in the 2000s.

4.4.6   *Optical/On-Line Hybrids*

The choice between optical and on-line multimedia publishing is not necessarily an either/or proposition. There is also an evolving symbiosis of CD access and its main

---

[47] Although the 8X segment has achieved a substantial market penetration its growth is being curtailed by faster drives.

competitor, some form of on-line access (Reisman, 1995). Delivering broadband via glass fibre cable, satellite, or ISDN to the home on a mass scale will take time in most European Member States. In the absence of adequate delivery capacity using on-line networks, especially the Internet, optical discs offer an attractive alternative for fast delivery of bandwidth at a reasonable price. The information on optical discs, however, is often not up to date and they cannot provide interpersonal interactivity, both of which can be offered on-line. For example, retail catalogues on disc may offer the possibility of on-line ordering, such as is offered by the German mail order company, Otto. Other opportunities include the possibility of playing games on the Net, interacting with other users in an on-line computer-mediated communication or virtual community environment, and obtaining additional information on-line through a hypertext link.

There are many opportunities for publishers as long as they make creative use of the strengths that the two forms of electronic publishing offer. Instead of CD-ROM being swept away by on-line services, publishers and software developers have recognized the potential for cross-fertilization between on-line and CD access. Off-line and on-line access can be complementary and may be consumed together. This often results in very rapid growth in the number of hybrid CD-ROM titles; titles with some kind of embedded on-line accessibility, providing fast local access to multimedia content, which supplement and extend information transmitted over the network.

As noted earlier, a major problem facing CD publishers is access to distribution outlets and the apparent shortage of shelf space in retail outlets. One means of mitigating the distribution bottleneck is to introduce some form of direct selling, such as mail-order purchase or subscription services. Other solutions include Internet sales. In addition to the publication of hybrid CD-ROMs, where CD-ROM and on-line access can coexist as content deliverers, the Internet can be used as a promotional and distribution tool for the sale of CD-ROMs. For example, some game producers use the Internet as a marketing instrument by offering free demonstrations or free access to the first few levels of a game. In this area, marketing creativity is likely to be as important as creativity in content creation.

4.4.7 Summary

Several important developments have characterized the optical disc market in recent years and the CD format has been pulled into the maturity phase of its life-cycle. A new life-cycle has begun through the introduction of DVD in the market-place. The technologies are affordable to the general public or are well on their way to becoming so, with dramatic declines in the prices of CD-ROM and recording CD-ROM format drives. The multimedia personal computer has become the standard system offered on computers sold for home and many small office and home office users. This means that a broad platform for the sale of multimedia titles has been established. In theory, there is a large enough installed base for publishers to achieve title sales sufficient to recoup the high development costs.

There are, however, significant problems associated with fragmentation of the market by drive speed and distribution channels. So far, the acquisition of new, unbundled CD-ROM titles has been a barrier. There are also serious problems relating to quality and value in the market although the few titles that overcome these problems appear to be able to garner relatively large sales. The margins available through the alternative shareware distribution channel appear to be thin and it is unclear whether this model is sustainable for higher-quality multimedia products.

The backward compatibility of DVD combined with the reasonable price of DVD-drives should lead to widespread DVD-drive diffusion. This diffusion is likely to occur much faster than it did for CD-ROM. The first shake-out of electronic publishers has taken place and is likely be followed by another round. Electronic publishers that have managed to stay in the business have rationalized their title development efforts or are in the process of doing so. Better knowledge of the market and the peculiarities of electronic publishing as well as in-depth understanding of consumer demand are factors that are contributing to the improved quality of titles brought to the market.

At present, the Internet and the optical disc appear to be highly complementary. Numerous examples exist of combinations where the strengths of both delivery modes are being used in a complementary way. There is potential for on-line distribution of content but, in the absence of widespread high-capacity network access, hybrid publishing is an alternative for delivering information services to the final user. Not only can the Internet enhance the value of the CD-ROM by creating the possibility to update information frequently and to introduce two-way interactivity, the combination of the two approaches also allows publishers to use a variety of business models to achieve higher revenues. The Internet provides publishers with an inexpensive distribution channel and promotional tool. These developments suggest that optical discs will remain a key means of distributing information and persist in a symbiotic and co-evolutionary relationship with on-line services.

4.5   Electronic Services for the Information Society: A First Look

Regardless of which network structure evolves to serve the needs of the information and communication infrastructure, the structure will ultimately be determined by the availability of information services. The premise of Ch. 3 was that the 'informatization' of the modern businesses was sufficiently developed to generate not only a large and growing demand for information services, but also for the terminal equipment and network usage to support these services. There are clearly spill-overs from the business use of information and communication technologies into other parts of people's lives which link the development of business and home information services. The extent of home demand is also being influenced by the extension of the business communication environment to facilitate teleworking and the extension of the office into the home. After these substantial spill-overs are taken into account, there are questions about the extent and nature of home use of information services and the implications of this market for equipment and network development. The remainder of this chapter is devoted to providing a first look at these information services, first by providing an overview of teleshopping and tele-entertainment applications, and then by taking a detailed look at the development of the on-line music industry. This discussion provides the context for the broader discussion of electronic commerce in Ch. 5, a development that involves both business and household demand.

4.5.1 On-Line Entertainment and Shopping

Assessments of the demand for new interactive services delivered using web technology must rely upon a number of assumptions to assess the likely future evolution of the market in Europe. One such study was undertaken by Databank Consulting of Milan in 1997 (EURORIM Project, 1997a). The authors employed several assumptions to estimate how much European consumers might be willing to pay for real-time interactive web services by the year 2007. First, they assumed the availability of a network infrastructure to carry on-line services and that services, such as networked games and teleshopping, would be available.[48] Second, they assumed that user costs included charges for specific services and excluded tariffs for telecommunication services and equipment costs at the subscriber's premises, for example, set-top-boxes, satellite antennae, cable-modems, etc. Based on these assumptions they estimated that European Union household spending on tele-entertainment services would reach 2.5 becu in 2007 expressed in real terms and in constant 1996 exchange rates as shown in Fig. 4.2.

The level of spending was expected to vary considerably across the Member States by the middle of the coming decade, as shown in Table 4.6. Teleshopping was defined as networked-enabled shopping activities from homes and the analysis focused on the purchase of consumer products (retailing) excluding transactions such as financial, insurance, travel, etc. The number of expected teleshoppers and the penetration rates are also shown.

The success in Europe of the Internet, and particularly the World Wide Web, compared with other home-oriented information services highlights the importance of content. Content providers are attempting to expand their customer base by experimenting with new ways of selecting, packaging, and delivering available content. The outcome of the battle for sales will depend on the content that competing suppliers are able to offer. Despite strong evidence that the Internet is acting as a catalyst for the convergence of markets, convergence is progressing on a 'case-by-case' basis rather than uniformly in all markets. The business models for the new services focus alternately on personal computer owners, on television consumers, on cable television subscribers, and on satellite television viewers.

The immaturity of electronic commerce in Europe in 1997 was associated in another study by Databank Consulting (1997) with several distinctive characteristics. Users were found to evaluate the Internet/World Wide Web positively as an outlet for advertising and communication but not necessarily for completing transactions. Although it is commonly believed that implementation of electronic commerce is

---

[48] Video-on-demand services were assumed to be deployed from 1998.

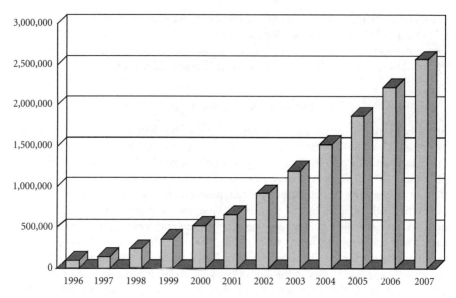

Fig. 4.2. Household spending on tele-entertainment services in the European Union

Note: Includes video-on-demand, audio-on-demand and networked games. Expressed in thousands ecu, 1996 constant prices and exchange rates for 15 EU Member States.

Source: Based on EURORIM Project (1997*a*).

Table 4.6. *Number of teleshopping subscribers and household penetration*

	No. of teleshopping subscribers (000)			Penetration rate %		
	1996	2002	2007	1996	2002	2007
France	43	1,140	2,793	0.2	4.9	11.7
Germany	150	3,132	7,687	0.4	8.1	19.3
Italy	2	88	219	0.0	0.4	1.0
UK	22	1,226	3,062	0.1	5.3	13.3
Nordic[1]	17	701	1,703	0.2	8.1	19.5
Southern[2]	1	59	140	0.0	0.3	0.7
Rest of EU	13	568	1,443	0.1	3.7	9.3
TOTAL EU15	248	6,914	17,048	0.2	4.6	11.1

[1] Denmark, Finland, and Sweden.
[2] Greece, Portugal, and Spain.
Source: Adapted from EURORIM Project (1997*a*).

concentrated in on-line ordering activity, and while most users were planning to invest in the improvement and growth of their web sites, only a minority expected to invest in electronic commerce applications. This diffidence was attributed to low levels of awareness and the continuing inadequacy of networks and services.[49]

The uneven development of demand for Internet services by users in Europe indicates that a greater understanding of the factors shaping the patterns of development of specific services is essential if the diffusion process is to be examined effectively. The following section examines the emerging characteristics of one such market, the demand for on-line music, with a focus on the United Kingdom.

4.5.2   The On-Line Music Industry—Electronic Commerce Take-off?

Content, its packaging, and the way it is sold, are essential features of the European information society. In this connection, the sound recording industry is one of Europe's key assets.[50] Three of the world's six largest music groups are European. Bertelsmann Music Group (Germany), Polygram (The Netherlands), and Thorn-EMI (United Kingdom) together with Time Warner (United States), Universal (formerly MCA) (Canada), and Sony (Japan) account for about 75 per cent of the world market for pre-recorded music, a market that was worth 31.5 becu in 1995 (Information Society Trends, 1997). The music business in Europe also has many small companies. About 60 per cent of recordings sold in the European Union are produced locally and it is widely held that local audiences are likely to continue to demand 'local' products despite the globalization of the music industry.[51]

Technical change has been affecting the music industry in many ways. For example, digital audio broadcasting employing MP3, the music compression standard, is enabling consumers to listen to music on demand. The on-line retailing of music could make products available on a global basis but the accessibility and the build-up of new markets depends on the diffusion of personal computers and Internet access and on the development of other equipment such as portable players and stereo system components. To examine the development of markets for music more closely we focus on developments in the United Kingdom.

In the United Kingdom, three major chains dominate the retail music business, two of British origin (HMV and Virgin) and one from the United States (Tower Records). What is the likelihood that these large players will adapt successfully to the new opportunities for on-line sales? Will the opportunities created by the development of an

---

[49] The survey was carried out in France, Germany, Italy, The Netherlands, Spain, and Finland based on 317 telephone interviews with professionals, small and medium-sized enterprises, educational and cultural organizations (schools, universities, libraries, and museums), and public administrations with an active web site and a home page, see Databank Consulting (1997).

[50] This section is based in part on research undertaken by Emma Jansen who conducted interviews with representatives of major players and start-up companies in the music industry in July and Aug. 1997.

[51] The European Union music industry provided more than 300,000 full-time jobs and had a turnover of 18.8 becu in 1995. There were over 3,000 record companies issuing over 25,000 albums and singles. The record companies employed about 45,000 people. There are also some 85 CD manufacturing plants and some 80,000 people involved in retailing music (European Music Office, 1996).

advanced information and communication infrastructure provide a new stimulus to the European smaller producer market? Will larger companies be overtaken by new entrepreneurial companies who can take advantage of low entry costs to Internet-based selling?

Many artists would argue that the modern music business has very little to do with music. It consists essentially of fast-moving, unit-led production, marketing, licensing, and distribution functions, and the ability to promote and distribute music, rather than to perform it. The primary business issues in the industry concern how much product will sell in which territories, how quickly the product can be shipped, and how fast products can be restocked. On first examination, the World Wide Web appears to offer a high-speed digital distribution channel that could disrupt the record companies' control of the distribution chain. When music is distributed over the Internet, only one master copy is required. New artists who can create their own product will potentially be able to produce, market, and distribute their works without the involvement of the major record companies. This scenario is an example of disintermediation (cutting out the middle layers of certain distribution channels) in the extreme and would result in the collapse of the existing record business. It is an ideal, however, that is very unlikely to be realized. The potential for disintermediation is providing an impetus for the major players in the record business to reposition themselves in order to retain their competitive edge in the changing conditions of the new Internet-based economy.

Many of the implications of the Internet for the music business are related to changes in the paradigm of distribution of the artefacts of pre-recorded media rather than in the direct distribution of the content as digital information. For example, the retailing of pre-recorded music on the Internet is likely to grow as technologies become more affordable and reliable. The potential benefits for organizations using the Internet as a retail outlet include the widening of their markets, new opportunities to meet customer needs, faster introduction of innovative products and services, improved customer–supplier interactivity, and enhanced market intelligence, together with lower costs and faster turnover. However, for the realization of these benefits, a number of fundamental changes would be needed.

In 1997, according to a survey for *The Economist*, it was confirmed that most on-line music stores were losing money (Anderson, 1997). Like other service industries, the music industry is undergoing structural changes that are being influenced by technological innovation. The possible entrants to the on-line music market are both large and small firms and they include store-front retailers, mail-order retailers, record companies, and start-up enterprises with no previous experience in the music business.

4.5.3   The Music Business in the United Kingdom

The United Kingdom has a large international music industry. The retail value of sales amounts to over £1b. per year and employment associated with the industry exceeded 48,000 in the mid-1990s (Monopolies and Mergers Commission, 1994). In addition, the industry earns considerable income from licensing its recordings overseas. Records are sold both through shops that specialize in music and outlets that sell a much wider range of products. The specialists include chains, such as HMV and Virgin/Our Price, and many small independent retailers. The non-specialists include multiples, such as W. H. Smith and Woolworths, as well as an increasing number of non-traditional outlets such as supermarkets and petrol stations. In addition, mail order and record clubs account for some 12 per cent of the market. British consumers are the world's greatest spenders on music. In 1996, on average, they bought four albums per person compared to the European average of 2.3 albums, the United States average of 3.9 albums, and the global average of 0.8 albums (International Record Industry Association, 1996).

The core activity of a record company is creating and exploiting copyrights in sound recordings. Most record companies achieve this by signing contracts with artists under which the artist usually agrees to record exclusively with that company for a set period of time. In exchange for this commitment, the artist will receive an advance of royalties at the start of work on each record album and, by virtue of copyright legislation, the record company will own the copyright in the recordings (Klaes, 1997). An artist also typically receives technical assistance with studio recording from one or more record producers who, in turn, mobilize engineering and often additional artistic resources to create a master recording. When a satisfactory master recording has been made, the record company sends it to the manufacturing plant where it is reproduced on CDs, cassettes, or vinyl. The most important activities for the record company, then, are marketing and promotion of the new release and its distribution to retailers. Promotion may take the form of videos and television interviews, advertisements in the musical press and other media, and personal appearances by the artist. Some promotion may be carried out jointly with particular retailers. In the case of a pop music record, the aim is to ensure that the record is played on the radio and to secure a place in the record charts, which will then lead to further exposure and increased sales.

There are five large multinational record companies operating in the United Kingdom and these are known as 'the majors'. Table 4.7 shows market shares by volume of albums sold in 1995 by the companies and their subsidiaries. Together, these five companies have nearly a 77 per cent share of the market in the United Kingdom.

The remaining 23 per cent of the market is supplied by some 600 independent record companies. Thorn-EMI, PolyGram, Sony, Warner, and BMG all own and operate national distribution systems, distributing their own and third-party sound recordings to retailers, wholesalers, and smaller distributors. Several of the majors also own and operate their own CD, cassette, and vinyl record manufacturing facilities. As well as supplying records in the United Kingdom, the record companies exploit their recordings in overseas markets. The United Kingdom is second only to the United States as a supplier of recorded music to the rest of the world. The largest retailers and their 1995 market shares are shown in Table 4.8. Together, these companies make up almost 63 per cent of total retail sales.

Records reach the retailers from the record companies by a variety of routes. Some 60 per cent go directly from the record company's nominated distributor to the

TABLE 4.7. *UK market share of major record companies, 1995*

Company	%
Thorn-EMI	22.3
PolyGram	21.8
Sony	13.1
Warner	10.9
BMG	8.7
Others	23.2
TOTAL	100.0

Note: The figure for Thorn-EMI includes a 50% share in Virgin Records.
Source: Adapted from Miller Freeman Entertainment Ltd. (1997).

TABLE 4.8. *UK music retail market shares, 1995*

Company	% by volume
Virgin/OurPrice	23.7
HMV (part of Thorn-EMI)	13.5
Woolworths	13.0
Britannia	6.7
W. H. Smith	6.0
Others	37.1
TOTAL	100.0

Note: Virgin/Our Price is owned by W. H. Smith (75%) and the Virgin Group (25%).
Source: Adapted from Miller Freeman Entertainment Ltd. (1997).

retailer, 28 per cent go through a wholesaler and the remaining 12 per cent reach consumers through mail order suppliers (Monopolies and Mergers Commission, 1994). Almost all deliveries to retailers go directly to individual shops rather than to retailers' central warehouses.

The relatively low cost of setting up a retail outlet on the Internet presents record companies with the possibility of selling directly to the consumer. This may allow them to undercut the retailers' prices at some risk of endangering the co-investment by retailers in promotion and sales effort, or to increase their profit margins. However, consumers may prefer the wider selection retailers are able to offer since retailers have the advantage of being able to sell stock from a variety of different record labels. The

Internet, as a new retail outlet, provides the means for retailers to widen their markets without building new stores. It also allows artists to sell directly to the consumer, although they may lack the influence and funding to promote their works.

In 1997 web-based services were offering limited downloads of audiovisual material, and John Richardson, company secretary at Cerberus Central, was forecasting that digital distribution would be on a par with CD sales by 1999.[52] However, sceptics argued at the time that this prediction ignored consumer requirements, that is, the very nature of downloading music to a personal computer restricts its mobility and many music enthusiasts like to own a material product complete with cover art, lyrics, and notes on the artist.

There were four distinct groups of on-line retailers in 1997 (Kalakota and Whinston, 1997). These included retailers operating off-line stores, 'getting their feet wet' with on-line storefronts and which were concerned mainly with the new web-based methods of catalogue retailing. 'New age' retailers were not operating retail businesses, but instead were seeking to understand how the new medium might revolutionize shopping. Manufacturers were exploring the potential to go directly to consumers. On-line music retailers, the first group, encompassed retailers such as the American-owned Tower Records and HMV in the United Kingdom. The second group comprised mail-order catalogue retailers, such as Britannia Music. The third was made up of start-up companies such as CDNow, based in the United States, and the fourth included record companies and the artists themselves, rather than the manufacturers of the tangible products.

The possibilities for the Internet to affect music retailing are not limited, however, to record companies and existing retailers, or even to specialized Internet music retailers. Music titles are only one of the many media that have become the basis for the sales of larger Internet retailers such as Amazon.com or large retailers such as Borders which entered the market in the United Kingdom in 1999 offering both music and books as well as a World Wide Web presence. Broadcasters are also active in promoting and retailing music with increasing activity in the British radio market, often tied to Internet sites offering the latest releases or best-selling albums. The Internet appears to be a fruitful source of new entry in music retailing.

4.5.4   Innovation and Competitive Advantage in the On-Line Music Industry

Any casual surfer of the Internet will know that the medium is swamped with music and that few music sites are truly commercial. Most are used for 'relationship marketing' purposes and the commercial benefits are captured elsewhere in the value chain. These promotional sites aim to advertise a company's brands, goods, and services. Transactional sites may promote new products or special offers, but are also capable of

---

[52] The Cerberus Digital Jukebox allows users to purchase CD-quality audio on-line. When a customer logs on, snippets of songs can be obtained for no charge. A full song requires registration and costs around 60 pence (0.4 ecu) (Morrell, 1997).

processing payment transactions (usually via secure transmission routes) and delivering—via a database—real-time pricing and information to the user. They also generally have a customer service dimension and a back-end fulfilment mechanism.

The transactional music sites differ widely in terms of the services offered. One of the largest on-line music stores, and a leading entrepreneur, is CDNow, an Internet company based in the United States. It has been described as 'one of the most successful retail sites on the net', although this measure of success is rather misleading because in the same paragraph CDNow was reported to be making only 'an operational profit' (Waldman, 1997). A review of the site's features provides a benchmark for the appraisal of the British on-line music shops.

CDNow offers a broad selection of titles on CD and cassette, and music videos. There is a search facility that, for example, supports searching for a classical recording using numerous parameters such as the composer's name, the title, the performer or soloist, the conductor, the record label, the primary instrument, the genre, etc. Information about payment methods, credit card security, shipping costs, delivery times, refunds, etc., is well organized and easily accessible. The CDNow site is fully transactional and purchases can be made using secure on-line credit card transactions or by electronic cash.

The closest British equivalent to CDNow is the Internet Music Shop. The Internet Music Shop describes itself as 'The Largest On-line Multimedia Store in Europe' and the site was launched in November 1995. This company's Managing and Marketing Director had identified two key advantages to early entry into the on-line music market. First, the company had already created strong customer loyalty (40 per cent of customers were returning to the site) and many customers were from international locations where the major British record retailers were scarcely known. Second, the Internet Music Shop had a head start in the learning process. It was able to focus on future strategy, for example, by analysing accumulated information on consumer buying habits and targeting promotions accordingly. The major British retailers were noticeably absent from the early on-line music market, unlike the American company, Tower Records, which had developed an impressive transactional site.

The majors arrived in 1998, and both HMV and Virgin Megastores now have Internet retail outlets. The potential for the Internet as a sales medium for music had been investigated by EMI International in the mid-1990s. According to a representative of EMI, there were no significant advantages in early entry to the on-line music market for the majors because the market was insufficiently developed to yield significant profits (Jansen and Mansell, 1998). Another problem for the company was the potential for conflict between record companies and record retailers in the on-line marketplace. For example, EMI owns a record company and is a record retailer and this would be in competition with the on-line site if a move were made into the new market. For this company, one scenario would result in the removal of the intermediary chains in the music industry as a result of disintermediation, but another, more attractive, scenario would enable value to be transferred via alternative delivery mechanisms resulting in a process of 're-intermediation'. The control of various elements in the production value chain would simply move to different players.

Virgin Entertainment Direct (VED) is the mail order division of Virgin/Our Price. The potential for an Internet retail outlet was first discussed by the group's parent company, W. H. Smith, in March 1996 (ibid.). Although VED lacked the technical know-how to set up an on-line store at this time, the company had the advantage of preferential rates for services supplied by Virgin Net, such as graphic design capabilities and technical consultancy. Early retail outlets on the Internet in Britain included the Music Stop, a small independent music company with two stores in Bristol. The site was set up for less than £1,000 and offered a catalogue of 200 albums. The Britannia Music Club entered the on-line market in early 1998 although its Marketing Director believed that there would be few advantages in being an early entrant to this market. Britannia was considered to be in an advantageous position relative to the record retailers and record producing companies because the order fulfilment operations were already in place.

The decision as to whether to adopt a technological leadership or 'followership' strategy is a difficult one for incumbent firms. Leadership means building on reputation and first-mover advantages may accrue as a result of early learning experiences and the opportunity to define standards. However, there are also disadvantages in the shape of the costs associated with pioneering, including the need to build infrastructure and awareness and the chance that initial systems and services will be superseded and that later entrants will build on the first mover's success.[53]

The pioneers or leaders in the on-line music in the United Kingdom were mainly start-up companies with considerable technological expertise. The early entrepreneurs were unable to sustain a competitive position in the market when the major players arrived although they have been able to exploit niche markets. The first-mover advantages for Internet start-up companies included the ability to establish customer relationships, study consumer habits, and define market trends. The early entrants were flexible and had the ability to react quickly to changes in the market. Nevertheless, in spite of the relatively minimal costs required to set up a web site compared to a physical store, both large and small companies experienced problems when they went on-line. The smaller companies needed capital to invest in advertising, web site design, search facilities, and links to other sites. The larger companies experienced organizational problems relating to order fulfilment and the need to establish an up-to-date database of products. Strategic decisions with respect to pricing also had to be taken. The prices of CDs in the United Kingdom on-line market are not much lower than in the stores. Although value can be added to the products in the virtual store by providing improved information for customers in the form of other customers' views, sound bites, information about the artists, etc., this has not necessarily provided a basis for building a profitable market segment.

The barriers to the electronic distribution of music experienced so far are only partly technological. Even as the on-line music business takes off, it is unlikely that music will be promoted entirely through the Internet. Radio broadcasting, television

---

[53] See Porter (1985: 180–8) for a discussion of the advantages and disadvantages and von Hippel and Urban (1988) for a consideration of the characteristics of lead user firms.

advertising, and other media are expected to remain important in attracting listeners. Some artists are likely to continue to turn to the support of a record producer for production, access to recording studios, video construction, and promotion. It is also possible that the functions of the players in the industry will change. For example, the record companies may abandon manufacturing and distribution functions in order to specialize in production and promotion. Alternatively, the major retailers may acquire entrepreneurs to take advantage of their specialist knowledge. Whatever the outcome, in order to defend their market shares from increasing global competition, the major players in the United Kingdom music business and other companies in Europe are in the process of adapting their business strategies to the changes in the Internet-based economy.

Although there were first-mover advantages for the start-up companies who entered the on-line music market early, at least in the United Kingdom, these proved to be relatively short-lived. This case study of the nascent on-line music industry illustrates how quickly the large retailer firms can move into a position that challenges the early efforts of entrepreneurs. The large retailers have the resources to invest in the promotion of on-line retail outlets as a result of their dominant position in the high street market.

4.6   Conclusion

The emergence of augmented mobile communication services and home access to the European information and communication infrastructure are chaotic processes. One reason for the chaos is uncertainty about the extent and nature of user demand due to the lack of experience with the use of new services. A second is the enormous variety of possible network configurations for delivering these services. A third, and perhaps the most important, reason is that substantial inertia is present in both markets in the form of existing network capacity and terminal equipment. There is considerable tension and drama in this process. Upgrading existing GSM capacity to provide a test bed for advanced services may provide the most appropriate path forward rather than the full-scale leap into new infrastructure and services represented by UMTS. Hesitating at the brink of the deployment of the new technology may open the way for an entirely new approach to emerge and dominate, perhaps originating in the United States where an even more chaotic process of third-generation mobile communication is emerging. Cable broadcasters face growing competition from satellite services. They are moving rapidly to upgrade their broadcast signals to digital format even though the digital signals, in the vast majority of homes, must be downgraded, using additional equipment, in order to connect to existing television receivers. Satellite broadcasters face the threat that cable companies may provide Internet services beyond the current technological capacities of their networks. It is an unsettled landscape and one that is not likely to achieve coherence until well into the first decade of this century.

We have argued that understanding these markets requires a simultaneous consideration of platforms, infrastructure, and content. These issues must be considered together because the absence of, or uncertainty about, any one element is the most common barrier to forward progress. The relative absence of services, for example, blocks the construction of infrastructure (and even the resolution of standards) as well as the purchase of platforms for augmented mobile communication. Yet the absence of a clear standard and commitment to provide the infrastructure is also likely to block the construction of service and hardware platforms for building this market. The dominant strategy of devising a method to help the passive user migrate from broadcast television to a richer array of digital services nudges the development of the information and communication infrastructure for the home towards a 'broadcast' model. This model, in which clear and simple choices are made for users, avoids confronting them with the complexity of Internet access alternatives. At the same time this strategy offers little assurance of success as the number of competing channels for delivering such services to the home user proliferates.

The implications of these developments for competition between incumbent, insurgent, and virtual community strategies are relatively clear. Incumbents are facing threats in maintaining their exclusive access to customers as other infrastructure suppliers move into the market. So far the new entrants have attempted to adopt incumbent strategies of their own based on differentiated product offerings that might win an exclusive customer base as has occurred in the digital satellite broadcasting market. In other markets, such as satellite-based mobile telecommunication, however, expensive infrastructure projects have not been able to generate the customer base to support an incumbent strategy. The role of insurgent strategies and players has so far been limited to exploring linkages through joint ventures with incumbent infrastructure suppliers. This is an increasingly frustrating position for insurgent suppliers. Fragmentation of the infrastructure market increases their negotiating strength. However, mounting an insurgent strategy, with its requirement of large network externalities in the mass adoption of new services and use of content, seems to be a fading possibility. Instead of a single family of platforms and a well-defined infrastructure, insurgents face the more difficult problem of creating a multi-platform and multi-infrastructure strategy in order to build the markets that they favour. Virtual community strategies have largely been pushed to the sidelines in this process, sacrificing numerous opportunities to begin delivering social, cultural, and education content.

Although the absence of a clear path towards augmented mobile communication services and home access to the information and communication infrastructure makes for a chaotic process, it is not necessarily one that will become simplified over time. A major reason for this is that competing infrastructures are gaining in strength in the wake of technological progress. The efforts of one group of incumbent strategy players to advance in a particular direction are likely to provoke others to follow and, in addition, will bring the risk of stimulating still further entry by infrastructure providers with novel technologies.

The absence of a clear resolution for delivery of home multimedia using telecommunication networks is supporting the continuing growth of the optical disc for multimedia distribution. While unable to offer many of the real-time features or as many possibilities for interaction with other users, CD-ROM and DVD-based multimedia are increasingly identified with 'multimedia' by many users. As systems incorporating this fast and increasingly capable medium for local storage of images and sound improve, possibilities for bridging between users or updating information from 'slow' telecommunication channels will become increasingly attractive as a means of building insurgent strategies. These strategies are already apparent in the games market and are likely to continue to emerge as users can find the multimedia information infrastructure at their newsagents or kiosks rather than having to navigate the telecommunication network.

These developments will be seen by many as indicative of an unacceptable delay in the implementation of the convergent information and communication infrastructure. They offer important opportunities for exploration and readjustment to change. For example, our discussion about the music industry in the United Kingdom indicates that the Internet is creating substantial pressure to rearrange existing patterns of marketing and distribution. The process of change, however, is relatively gradual compared to what it might be if users were able to 'dial up' an evening of musical entertainment on a pay-by-play basis.

There are two, more significant, concerns, however, about the gradual pace of development of augmented mobile communication and home access to the information and communication infrastructure. The first is that the relatively gradual pace of change may be preventing the development of services that would support economic and employment growth in mobile or home services markets. The size of the markets that will eventually develop for these services is a matter for speculation. It is difficult, therefore, to assess what the opportunity costs of delay are, as compared to the costs that would be incurred in moving to develop an advanced information and communication infrastructure more rapidly. The second concern is relevant mainly to home access to the infrastructure. The absence of improved access forecloses on the opportunities for children and the elderly, many caregivers, and a range of other Europeans to participate in the use of new services. They risk being excluded from important resources and their absence shapes the development of content on World Wide Web and related services towards those that are presently able to access the infrastructure. One possible force for helping to resolve these roadblocks is the more vigorous development of electronic commerce, and this is the subject of the next chapter.

5

Controlling Electronic Commerce Transactions

R. Hawkins, R. Mansell, and W. E. Steinmueller

5.1 Introduction

This chapter examines electronic commerce—or e-commerce—which, for many observers, represents the beginnings, not just of a new commercial paradigm, but of a new general paradigm for interactions between technology and service suppliers and users. In this chapter we suggest that implementing e-commerce to enhance European competitiveness presents issues that go well beyond the provision of technical and policy infrastructures. Addressing these issues offers one means of developing an alternative to the 'passive' user, broadcast media model for the development of home access to the information and communication infrastructure.[1] It is important to be realistic about this alternative. As we observe, e-commerce is principally about business-to-business interactions. Most of the opportunities and challenges in the e-commerce area relate in one way or another to changes in the structures and processes of transactions between trading partners, and this, in turn, is related directly to the evolution of business models and organizational forms within individual trading communities.

In Ch. 3 we investigated the role of business information and communication services as a source of demand for the upgrading of telecommunication networks and the diffusion of new equipment and services supporting movement towards the development of the European information society. That discussion deferred examination of e-commerce. In effect, we grouped the demand for services without differentiating between demand generated mainly by internal organizational requirements for communication and information access, and demand generated mainly by demand for external communication and information services. In practice, it is very difficult to

Sections 5.2–5 are based in major part on research by Dr Richard Hawkins, SPRU; see Hawkins (1998*a*) for the original presentation of the arguments. The authors of this book bear full responsibility for any modifications to the original presentation. The basis for this chapter is an extensive monitoring of trade, professional, and policy literature supplemented by a limited number of interviews with experts in commercial networking and with managers of firms implementing various kinds of e-commerce solutions.

[1] We use the term 'passive' to draw a simple distinction between media and services involving a one-way flow to the user which is subject only very indirectly to user control and those media and information and communication services that involve some kind of control and/or interactive participation by the user. We acknowledge that the so-called 'passive' user is engaged in an active process of consumption within the traditional media environment but we do not explore these processes in this book. For a discussion of this issue see e.g. Silverstone (1999).

separate the two types of demand. In Ch. 4, we examined how in some situations, such as home use of multimedia, the demand for communication services may be separated partially from the demand for multimedia information content. We noted that demand by European home users for on-line services is evolving at a relatively modest pace and that a broadcast model may be emerging as a means of simplifying inter-actions with digital services for users. However, a leading application supporting utilization of the Internet within the home is e-commerce, that is, various forms of structured interactions and communication with businesses. This chapter brings the two discussions together by assessing the emerging pattern of economic activity that is referred to as e-commerce.

E-commerce is one of many classes of applications for the use of the information and communication infrastructure.[2] It is a particularly significant application for several reasons. First, it provides a basis for business interest in establishing a presence on the World Wide Web and, through this experience, enabling contact with many opportunities to extend access to customers and to build stronger supplier–customer relationships. Second, it provides an important motivation for citizens to consider obtaining a connection to the Internet. Even if people have little idea about how they might actually buy something using the Internet, the knowledge that companies are offering information about goods and services in a way that is readily accessible to their friends or neighbours is likely to stimulate their curiosity. Third, the Internet appears to provide a means for small and medium-sized businesses to participate in procurement or supplier networks which larger enterprises have developed through EDI (Electronic Data Interchange) and other forms of electronic trading networks. Fourth, from a policy perspective, many countries have been persuaded that e-commerce facilitates globalization and provides a competitive advantage to those countries that are able to develop a leadership position in the use of advanced infor-mation and communication infrastructure. Although there are important critical points to be made about several of these reasons, collectively they provide a major impetus to the expansion of interest and participation in e-commerce activity.

We examine three common myths about the dynamics of e-commerce in this chapter: (1) cyber-trading, (2) virtual, non-hierarchical business structures, and (3) disintermediation, in order to identify how and why firms actually choose to partici-pate in e-commerce, and what new dynamics they encounter in this environment. We suggest that the business-to-business interface is far more highly developed than the customer–business interface, and that gains in process efficiency may not provide a sufficient basis for investing in e-commerce business solutions. For most organiza-tions, the reasons to migrate to e-commerce must be based upon strategic con-siderations rather than on any immediate pay-off they may receive from adopting e-commerce approaches. We also suggest that most start-up and insurgent business models are likely to remain at the fringes of e-commerce in terms of economic significance for some time. Start-up firms will be important as explorers and trend-setters, attracting and cultivating new trading communities. A few of these firms may

---

[2] From this perspective, virtual communities, on-line libraries or museums, distance-learning institu-tions, and government services are similar classes of applications.

be able to translate this type of leadership into new brand and organizational images that have lasting appeal. These firms are helping to develop consumer interest in trading on the Net and they are developing new methods of organization that, in many instances, are being emulated by larger established firms when they move to establish their own e-commerce systems. Large established traders are frequently in commanding positions to lead e-commerce developments that target consumers because of their visible market presence and high levels of confidence in their brands. They often have substantial advantages at the enterprise level as well, because of their capacity for economic and/or technological leadership, as we saw in the preceding chapter in the case of the music business.

Progress towards a more ubiquitous e-commerce trading environment is evolutionary in most instances. It involves the development of activities that are complementary to e-commerce as well as the replacement of traditional activities. We argue that the predominant focus on e-commerce solutions as a *substitute* for existing forms of business intermediation both overemphasizes and mis-specifies the development trajectory of new forms of virtual trading. As we will discuss in greater detail, the view that business intermediaries, such as distributors or retailers, are unproductive and can, or will, be easily displaced through direct connection with suppliers is simply wrong. E-commerce *will* have implications for existing intermediaries and it will form the basis for the growth of new intermediary services, developments that we refer to as reintermediation. The relationship between intermediation and disintermediation is complex and it can be paradoxical. Disintermediation can create efficiencies but, at the same time, it can increase risks. E-commerce offers greater opportunities for disintermediation, but at the same time, reintermediation is one of the business areas with the highest growth potential.

For small and medium-sized enterprises, many of what are seen as current options to develop e-commerce quickly may become imperatives imposed through conditions of contract. It is also possible that virtual industry structures may create more, rather than fewer, barriers to entry and exit, as technological and organizational compatibility factors rival price and competency in partner selection. First-mover advantages, if and when they exist, do not appear necessarily to be related to the specific type or size of the enterprises involved or to the development of particular technologies, many of which are generic and broadly available. Nevertheless, it appears that the costs of some forms of e-commerce may create a substantial barrier to entry into certain business value chains for smaller enterprises.

E-commerce is now high on the policy agendas of governments and businesses around the world. In the past six years major e-commerce initiatives have been launched by national governments, as well as at intergovernmental level through the Group of Seven (G7) countries, the European Commission, and the Organization for Economic Co-operation and Development (OECD). Developments in e-commerce are also of considerable interest, and concern, to the public and private sectors of many developing countries and regions. The issues involved in building an e-commerce environment bring public and private policy agendas very close together. An electronic market-place entails much more than the construction of an appropriate technological infrastructure. Ensuring stability and prosperity in this new environment requires a commercial governance framework that is transparently in the interests of all trading parties. This framework must take into account the evolutionary nature of e-commerce and its requirements for diversity, experimentation, and learning. Policies that would prematurely curtail diversity and experimentation or erect barriers to learning are inconsistent with the healthy development of e-commerce. Governments also have a role in ensuring that the benefits of e-commerce are non-exclusionary and widely distributed, that the barriers to entry into electronic markets are minimized, and that the public interest is understood and protected as the electronic market-place evolves. For governments, a complementary concern is how to reap the same perceived benefits of e-commerce in public administrations as may be available to private industry. Electronic administration or e-government is the public-sector twin of e-commerce.

The interests of industrial players in government policies for e-commerce are tempered by their concerns about the timing and focus of the implementation of these policies. First, many firms are concerned that the potential of e-commerce might be stifled if laws and regulations, whose implications are not fully understood, are applied too hastily. Undoubtedly, the highest profile example of this fear is evident in debates about the use of encryption. Second, industrial players are concerned that in other cases governments might elect *not* to act quickly enough. These players often lobby for the further liberalization of telecommunication and physical transport infrastructures, for example, or for the improved co-ordination of government procurement and administrative processes with the emerging commercial rhythms of e-commerce. Third, there is concern that overemphasis on the electronic side of e-commerce will divert the attention of policy-makers from other equally, or even more, important aspects of governing commercial activity. Even the most effective governance of the information and communication infrastructure will not, in itself, ensure that legal and regulatory frameworks support the healthy development of e-commerce.

For European policy-makers, many of the concerns about the development of e-commerce stem from historical asymmetries between Europe and other regions in production capabilities for information and communication technologies. European production capabilities tend to be concentrated heavily in the telecommunication sector. Europe also has a lower general level of penetration of information and communication technologies in the business sector and for household use than the United States, but a higher level than Japan. Both the United States and Japan are welcoming e-commerce developments because these are reinforcing their existing respective strengths in mass production and distribution. While welcoming the opportunities offered by e-commerce, European policy-makers are concerned about whether asymmetries in the production of information and communication technologies and in the diffusion of the information and communication infrastructure will disadvantage European firms in the evolving e-commerce environment. These concerns are often expressed by such questions as: Is Europe behind in e-commerce? If so, how can Europe catch up? What alternative pathways exist? What policies are needed at the European level?

Our argument is that historical asymmetries of information and communication technology supply and information and communication infrastructure development and use need not disadvantage European firms in the development of e-commerce. The e-commerce environment is still largely inchoate. Most buyers and sellers remain at the base of steep technological and social learning curves. Moreover, it is not clear how many of the often highly publicized pioneer traders in this medium are acquiring sustainable first-mover advantages in markets, or capabilities for technological innovation and commercialization, that will be significant in the longer term. The window of opportunity for European firms to take action, however, is likely to be limited. Significant capability gaps are certain to develop unless action is taken. The character of the necessary action depends upon the specific characteristics of traded products and on the requirements and behaviour of buyers and sellers in enormously heterogeneous markets. E-commerce will succeed where trading communities experience benefits in exploiting it and are prepared and able to co-ordinate their actions to make electronic markets work. Realizing the potential of e-commerce in Europe is likely to be dependent less upon the ability to source all the technological elements from within the region, and more upon proactive product and marketing strategies by firms that employ e-commerce.

In developing both business and policy strategies for e-commerce, it is especially important to examine carefully the many kinds of commercial transaction structures that operate in the conventional, as well as in the electronic, market-place. Most business strategies involve the management of key transactions related to the choice of product designs and configurations, the provision of advertising and technical information, the arrangement of supply logistics, and the specification of ordering and payment systems. E-commerce portends many new transaction forms, some of them revolutionary. But e-commerce also is part of an evolutionary trajectory that is driven largely by commercial rather than technological criteria.

The principal aim of this chapter is to clarify the structure and dynamics of e-commerce with respect to how European firms and policy institutions can best co-operate in facilitating productive migration into this environment. There are four basic objectives. First, to examine the origins of e-commerce and describe its emerging dynamics, particularly the role of the Internet. Second, to assess how and why firms adopt and develop e-commerce by examining critically the commercial logic of some of the current mythology surrounding e-commerce. Third, to examine the evolving transaction structure in e-commerce in terms of its implications for developing business and policy strategies. And, finally, to suggest approaches and priorities for e-commerce policy in Europe that would best enhance the efforts of European traders.

5.2 Electronic Commerce Origins and Dynamics

In the examination of the genesis and evolution of e-commerce as a new form of trading environment, we focus particularly on the crucial role of the members of the trading communities themselves in developing e-commerce in Europe. We use terms such as 'trade', 'trader', and 'trading' to refer to commercial interactions between buyers and sellers in the market, whether on an individual or corporate basis.[3] Our use of the 'trader' terminology is intended to maintain a distinction between traders of products and services of all kinds, that is, the potential users of e-commerce, and the suppliers of technologies and services, that is, the providers of e-commerce equipment, systems, and trading services.

The early development of the most economically significant e-commerce applications has been led by major traders who know specific markets well, are powerful in them, and are able to mould information and communication technology systems to reflect market dynamics. Existing e-commerce applications are based in distinct trading sectors, typically led by key firms and/or industry organizations, and they are usually associated with above-normal levels of capabilities for developing or using software and information systems. Now that the concept of e-commerce is spreading rapidly and widely, major tensions are building up between these established trader communities and the technology and service suppliers who are attempting to build up business for their often-proprietary e-commerce platforms, systems, and services. Both established and new traders alike will face new forms of technological lock-in if the development and operation of technologies that define important transaction points in the electronic trading environment drift out of user control. This tension is significant in that one of the most important aspects of e-commerce is the change it portends for transaction structures, that is, who can transact with whom, where, and how in an electronic market-place.

Clearly, if e-commerce is to be market-led, then it must be user-led in the sense of being primarily oriented to the needs of traders in the market-place, including firms and individuals, and only secondarily to the research and development and marketing objectives of the suppliers. Achieving the primary goal calls for the enabling development of a wide spectrum of e-commerce applications targeted at the diverse requirements of users. The pace of movement towards e-commerce as a pervasive virtual environment for business transactions is creating threats and opportunities for existing firms and their networks. One such threat is that the rapid diffusion of new Internet-based e-commerce platforms may overwhelm the systems that have evolved over many years to provide reliable and efficient service. Internet-based e-commerce platforms have distinct advantages in extending network connections and standardizing some of the more basic elements of trading networks. They may appear to offer cost advantages relative to current trading solutions, particularly for the costs of acquiring the platform technologies. At the same time, the need for, and costs of, customization as well as the ownership costs of the new technologies, may offset the advantages of flexibility and lower acquisition cost. In many cases, businesses will need to find ways to integrate Internet-based e-commerce solutions into their existing trading networks and technologies. For some, the wholesale replacement of these existing technologies will make sense, even after taking into account the costs of own-

---

[3] The terms do not refer necessarily to trade in the sense of imports and exports.

ership and customization. For others, Internet solutions will be grafted or bolted on to existing systems so that they operate in parallel. The mix between these strategies will change over time as e-commerce software evolves and as the character of trading networks changes.

In the following sections we examine the origins of e-commerce as a business concept or philosophy and offer a precise definition of the term for our purposes. The specific role of the Internet and life-cycle costs to the enterprise are also considered.

5.2.1   The Genealogy of Electronic Commerce

For the better part of thirty years, businesses throughout the European Union and their major trading partners have been increasing their exploitation of advanced information and communication technologies and for some time many aspects of commerce have been conducted by electronic means. The vast majority of financial transactions currently undertaken in the industrialized countries involve information and communication technology-based services at some point. So what *is* new?

Part of the answer to this question lies in the genealogy of the term 'electronic commerce' which began to enter the business vocabulary, primarily in the United States, in the mid-1980s. Initially, it was unclear what scope and range of activities would be encompassed by the term. The first e-commerce applications that were envisaged were close in form and idea to Electronic Data Interchange (EDI) and Value Added Network (VAN) concepts. EDI services provided the means for businesses to establish transaction-oriented databases and transfer methods that would support purchasing, invoicing, and logistical operations. VANs provided the infrastructure to bridge differences between company data-processing systems so that exchanges, such as those enabled by EDI, could occur in volume. Indeed, the earliest corporate promoters of e-commerce were firms already involved with EDI and VAN implementations.

The use of the term was further coloured by early linkages with government procurement, and with various production management concepts that began to acquire high profiles in business and policy circles in the late 1980s, such as Business Process Re-engineering (BPR), Quick Response (QR), and Just-in-Time (JIT). All these concepts were underpinned to a large degree by developments in electronic communication, at least in their implementations in North America and Europe, and they were promoted to varying extents by the procurement and industrial policies of many governments. The concept of e-commerce gathered much of its early momentum through its close association with the restructuring of government procurement practices, particularly defence procurement, that began to occur in the early 1980s in the United States. In the United States, the Departments of Commerce and Defense initiated the first major e-commerce awareness and implementation programmes. The first putative general framework linking e-commerce ideas to production management and logistics processes was Computer-Aided Life-Cycle Support (CALS), originally a programme in the Department of Defense (Hawkins, Molas, and Walker, 1996). Governments in many European countries have taken similarly proactive roles in promoting the use of EDI in government procurement. Before 1990, e-commerce had primarily an accounting orientation, centred on firm-to-firm and firm-to-government transactions in supply chain and logistics contexts.

By the end of the 1990s, the vision of e-commerce was that of a universal and ubiquitous electronic market-place relevant to all commercial activities and trading partners. One of the chief catalysts of this vision was the spectacular growth of the Internet, particularly following the commercialization of World Wide Web browsers that began in 1993. The Internet radically changed the thinking about what was possible in an electronic market-place and about who might participate in such markets. Significantly, the business community quickly began to adopt Internet standards for content and to support network connections, initially in closed user configurations, but, increasingly, in interactive environments as well.

However, in many ways the proliferation of the Internet and the expansion of the e-commerce vision have made the problem of defining e-commerce more difficult. The assumption that it is possible to bring virtually any commercial activity into the electronic environment generates many questions about how appropriate and productive this might be and under what circumstances. It also raises questions about the relative risks of e-commerce developments for different kinds of commercial enterprises that may be associated with embracing, or failing to embrace, this new environment. There are far-reaching issues concerning the social dynamics of emerging markets and we take these up in subsequent chapters.

5.2.2   Defining Electronic Commerce

E-commerce is the application of information and communication technologies to one or more of three basic activities related to commercial transactions: (1) *production and support*, that is, sustaining production, distribution, and maintenance chains for traded goods and services; (2) *transaction preparation*, that is, getting product information into the market-place and bringing buyers and sellers into contact with each other; and (3) *transaction completion*, that is, concluding transactions, transferring payments, and securing financial services. E-commerce differs in concept from its networking precursors primarily in terms of its envisaged scope and scale, and its nominally open philosophy regarding network architecture.[4]

E-commerce encompasses existing and new forms of commercial networking but it is actually a business philosophy more than an aggregation of technologies. The philosophy is not simply that commerce *can* be conducted electronically, but that it *ought* to be. That is, the organizational efficiencies and economic gains that are possible in an electronic environment are believed by many proponents to be superior to those available in the conventional market-place.

The scope of e-commerce can be described in terms of four specific features: (1) *Technology*; it can employ text, sound, and image formats in interactive and/or non-interactive modes, purpose-made hardware platforms, or existing platforms such as

---

[4] For a recent discussion of the potential for closure of the network openness that characterizes the Internet and the regulatory issues specifically in the US context, see Bar *et al.* (1999).

telephony and television. (2) *Product characteristics*; it can be used to facilitate links to the physical logistical and distribution infrastructure for material products as well as for the direct distribution of non-material or information-based products and services. (3) *Participant group*; it can encompass transactions between firms, organizations, governments, and individuals at all levels of market participation including the enterprise, organizational, business–customer, and person-to-person levels, as in the case of e-Bay's electronic auction house. (4) *Organizational objective*; e-commerce is often linked explicitly to the management of change in business processes and organizational behaviour.

Given this scope of potential activity, the scale of e-commerce is potentially very large. However, the scale is also impossible to measure reliably because, as yet, there is no systematic statistical approach for comparing levels of activity across the e-commerce spectrum.[5] In fact, both the scale and growth potential of e-commerce are consistently misrepresented in the trade and policy literature. The misrepresentation is caused by failures to differentiate between the various arenas in which e-commerce is being applied, which is necessary to bring the relative size and growth of different elements into perspective. Growth projections for one kind of e-commerce trajectory are routinely and erroneously transposed to provide estimates of other trajectories that have very different dynamics.

Typically, the attention given to consumer-oriented Internet transactions is excessive since, by any available measure, it was still the least economically significant e-commerce activity at the time of writing. Figure 5.1 illustrates a typical market projection derived from rudimentary data on growth in the quantity and revenues of Internet-based businesses, coupled with inferences about the relationship between the growth of Internet penetration and the propensity of consumers to use Internet retailing services.

Even if projections of the growth of interactive retail sales, such as those in Fig. 5.1, are correct, they still represent a relatively small portion of total retail sales. For that matter, it is not clear that increased levels of electronic sales can be equated with increased sales levels overall (much less with increased production), or provide a basis for inferences about how the profits on these sales compare with those from other selling methods. For e-commerce to yield real productivity effects, it must reduce the costs of promoting, selling, and distributing goods and services, or support higher levels of sales without increasing costs. Neither replacement, nor productivity effects, have been demonstrated convincingly by publicly available research by the end of the 1990s although it is not unusual for business consulting companies to make claims of large cost savings.[6]

---

[5] One representative of a major market research firm in the USA commented that various figures used as estimates of the growth of e-commerce are 'spun out of a variety of sources into what might be kindly called a happy approximation (ladle on the Fairy Dust)'. The anonymity of the contributor of this comment is protected by the authors.

[6] Giga Information Group Inc., a marketing research company founded by Gideon I. Gartner, claimed that worldwide e-commerce-driven cost savings amounted to US$ 17.6b. in 1998 (of which $15.2b. were realized in the USA) and projected that these savings would amount to US$ 1.25 trillion by 2002. The company provided no public information on the methodology that it employed to make these estimates, see Giga Information Group (1999).

Billions of dollars

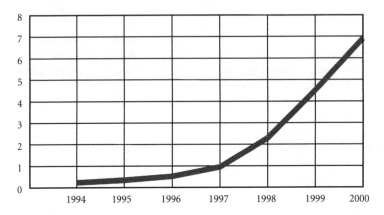

FIG. 5.1. Typical interactive retailing projection

Source: Hawkins (1998*a*) based on Forrester Research.

To put the matter further into perspective, most e-commerce transactions of any economic significance do not occur at the retail level at all, but at the enterprise level. A substantial and growing number of large firms now engage in electronic trade with suppliers and corporate customers in volumes that exceed US$ 1b. per year. Based on a synthesis of miscellaneous industry statistics for all types of electronic transaction media, including EDI and VANs as well as web-based applications, Fig. 5.2 indicates the relative volumes and growth rates for e-commerce among the various participant groups.[7]

A rough approximation of the orders of magnitude in terms of money for the transaction types involving firms that are represented in Fig. 5.2 would be: firm-to-firm, hundreds of billions;[8] firm-to-government, tens of billions; and firm-to-individual, hundreds of millions of euro.

In terms of identifying new business opportunities, the rates of growth for interpersonal and consumer-oriented e-commerce are significant despite their currently marginal economic significance. Nevertheless, growth in these areas is not indicative of the potential scale or development dynamics of e-commerce as a whole. The vast majority of e-commerce transactions, the fastest rates of growth, and the most exten-

[7] EDI involves the ability to exchange electronic documents and other information automatically, for example, orders and invoices, between organizations. VANs are networks that support services in addition to those defined, generally for regulatory purposes, as basic services. Basic services include telephony but are not limited to this functionality. In the North American region, VANs are broadly comparable to Enhanced Service networks.

[8] Zona Research estimates the overall figure for 1998–9 business-to-business e-commerce in the United States at about US$ 50–60b. and projects that the figure will exceed US$ 100b. in 1999–2000. These figures represent about half the value that some other major research and analysis firms are projecting (personal communication, 10 Nov. 1999).

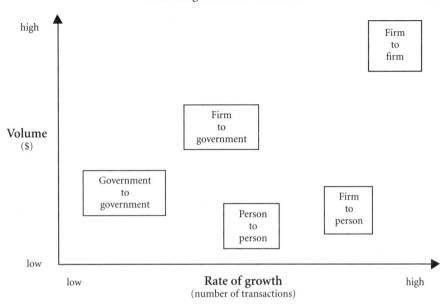

FIG. 5.2. Relative volumes and growth rates for participant groups

Source: Prepared by Richard Hawkins (1998*a*).

sive implementations of leading-edge technologies, are occurring at the enterprise and organizational levels.

Keeping the scale, scope, and dynamics of various kinds of e-commerce in perspective is very important for policy as well as for corporate strategies. This is because business opportunities exist at all levels, and the relationship between these levels in terms of the overall development of e-commerce is very likely to be symbiotic. Marketing and sales opportunities at the transaction preparation and completion levels can be highly contingent upon developments at the production and support levels. Similarly, new business opportunities at the production and support levels are likely to arise in response to signals from the other two levels.

5.2.3   *Electronic Commerce and the Internet*

If the Internet does not yet embody the promised contribution of the information and communication infrastructure to growth and employment, certainly it has come to symbolize it. Although the Internet is only one of many possible vehicles for e-commerce, it is the most visible and its implications are the most far-reaching. A survey undertaken in October 1997 indicated that by 1996 just under 45 per cent of the technologies used for e-commerce were based on the Internet protocols

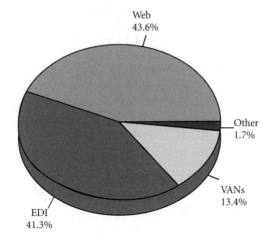

FIG. 5.3. Electronic commerce technology profile, 1996

Source: Hawkins (1998*a*) based on Datamation (1997).

(Datamation, 1997). Just fewer than 55 per cent were EDI and VAN applications as shown in Fig. 5.3.

Business interest in the Internet is indicated also by the steeply rising domain name count in the commercial *.com* category. By the middle of 1999, there were 18.7 million *.com* registrations on the Internet. The number of *.com* registrations has paralleled the total growth in Internet hosts, which doubled annually between 1993 and 1996 and increased by approximately 50, 90, and 50 per cent on an annual basis in 1997, 1998, and 1999 respectively.[9]

However, statistics like these can be misleading as we also saw in Ch. 2 in the analysis of the scale of European user involvement with the Internet. A *.com* registration is not a reliable indication that trades in goods and services are occurring at a *.com* address. Also, the economic significance of transactions using the various available technologies is not necessarily related to the number of firms deploying these technologies. For example, during the 1995 to 1996 period, the majority of EDI use was in very large companies, involving, in many cases, hundreds of millions of EDI transactions per firm per year (Forrester Research, 1996). Thus, the amount of economic activity involving EDI is proportionally much higher than the number of firms using EDI. We do not yet know whether a similar pattern will apply to web-based applications.

Historically, small and medium-sized enterprise engagement with most aspects of

---

[9] See Network Wizards (1999*a*; 1999*b*). These statistics are constructed by Network Wizards, http://www.nw.com, and are distributed by the Internet Software Consortium, http://www.isc.org both accessed 6 April 2000. Both organizations play a vital role in supporting public and academic research on the Internet.

e-commerce, as in the case of EDI, has come about, not by choice, but as a result of contractual requirements as and when firms have become suppliers to larger firms that had already implemented e-commerce.[10] In the EDI context, these arrangements are often difficult for smaller firms as they may involve disproportionate implementation costs, and they can create technological lock-in with specific trading partners (Ferné, Hawkins, and Foray, 1996). Applications such as EDI are designed to support highly structured routine exchanges within closed user groups. The Internet offers a radical alternative that comes closest to meeting the technological requirements of the e-commerce vision. In principle, the Internet trading environment is technologically 'open', allowing different configurations of buyers and sellers to form and re-form according to product and market dynamics, rather than according to proprietary technological criteria. It is also universally scalable to the requirements of any transaction type and volume. Nevertheless, many difficulties lie in the path of implementing this alternative, most of which stem from the fact that the Internet was not originally intended for commercial applications. As a result, it presents many security and network management problems.

There are at least three types of Internet space, each with its own profile of users and uses. First, there is the public Internet space that generally is available to anyone with a personal computer and modem, normally on a dial-up basis. Second, there is the group Internet or Extranet space supporting various forms of inter-organizational applications that may or may not include provisions for access by other user groups (sometimes including public access) under controlled conditions. Finally, there is the private Internet or Intranet space providing intra-organizational and intra-corporate applications of the Internet protocols for computer networking.

The dynamics of this emerging typology are illustrated to some extent in the few available implementation statistics on the private Internet space. These tend to indicate that commercial development of the Internet is as much about creating essentially 'closed' spaces in an 'open' environment as it is about creating a universally open trading space. The deployment of Intranets is a significant growth industry.

Migration to Intranets and Extranets does not imply immediate radical change in commercial networking practices. Most of these implementations are designed for internal communication, or communication with existing commercial partners as was discussed in Ch. 3. One of the most significant emerging trends is the transfer of structured closed user group applications such as EDI to an Internet environment (Forrester Research, 1996). Group Internet space allows firms to define private spaces for dealing with suppliers and customers. In terms of developing e-commerce skills and inculcating an e-commerce culture throughout a wide population, the public Internet space is perhaps the most commercially valuable space of all. The configuration of Internet spaces that is becoming common in firms is illustrated in Fig. 5.4. Gateways, usually involving security firewalls, are used to segment parts

[10] See David and Foray (1994); and Graham *et al.* (1993) for discussions of the processes of EDI development theoretically and empirically. See Rejane-Legey and Maculan (1999) for a detailed study of the factors influencing EDI implementation in Brazil.

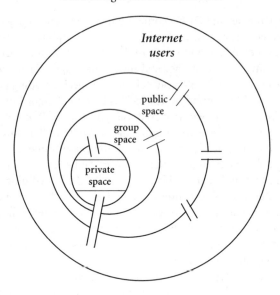

FIG. 5.4. Internet spaces

Source: Prepared by Richard Hawkins (1998*a*).

of the private and group space, and then to link them either together and/or to the public space.

The commercial value of all three Internet spaces depends on how effectively they can be managed to achieve specific commercial ends. There are several basic management requirements for traders in Internet space. These include: network management, that is, guaranteeing that the required bandwidth is available at a cost that is appropriate to the type of commercial activity being undertaken, and information management, including control over content in terms of ownership and distribution rights. Security management involves control over access to, and use of, network facilities, as well as over transaction-oriented information and the content of information-based products and services, together with transaction management to ensure that transactions flow through to order fulfilment, logistics, and accounting functions. The actual management requirements in each domain will differ depending upon whether they apply in public, private, or group space. In all cases, connections between the various domains require access to reliable, customizable, and interoperable technologies.

The Internet is unlikely to be the end-point in network evolution for e-commerce even though the e-commerce vision is, at present, largely identified with the Internet. Changes in the Internet's architecture and features will be made as it is upgraded to serve a growing range of uses. As a principle, open inter-networking is the cornerstone of efforts to develop e-commerce applications and this concept is likely to be robust in the face of technological change for some time.

5.2.4 *Assessing the Costs of Implementing Electronic Commerce*

Although security concerns and technological issues present impediments to e-commerce implementation, costs are probably the single most important obstacle for most firms. In a survey of firms in the United States in 1997, nearly 47 per cent of respondents cited costs as primary obstacles, slightly outweighing security and technology concerns combined. Only about 26 per cent cited security concerns, and less than 20 per cent cited technology problems (Datamation, 1997). The Gartner Group has estimated that the cost of developing a fully fledged Internet e-commerce site for retail trade amounts to approximately US$ 1m., the dominant share of which is employee costs.[11]

Furthermore, in many ways, security and technology concerns are in fact cost issues. The total cost of information and communication technology applications extends well beyond the initial capital cost of platforms and software acquisition and the recurring costs of network access and use. All these costs can decline in real or relative terms over time. As more firms gain experience with new systems, and acquire greater independent evaluation capabilities for them, they become aware that most information and communication technology investments are long term. They also come to understand that the life-cycle system costs of maintenance, upgrading, and staff training are larger than the initial capital outlay or network costs. Typically, these costs *do not* decline over the life-cycle of a system, and they may even increase. Furthermore, during the implementation period, and often for a significant period afterwards, declines can (and usually do) occur in overall productivity and work quality. All this is especially significant for smaller organizations whose investment costs in information and communication technology-based systems are typically greater as a proportion of revenue than for large firms. Experienced managers compensate for life-cycle costs and productivity fluctuations in their implementation strategies and business plans, but such experience typically is not as available to smaller firms as it is to larger firms.

Technology obstacles are partly generated by the infrastructure, particularly the public telecommunication infrastructure, that is needed to support e-commerce. These problems are the same for all market participants, but solutions to them are not available to all participants at the same relative cost. Especially for small and medium-sized enterprises, lack of stability in terminal equipment and/or public network technology increases the probability of lock-in effects, and raises significant reinvestment issues.

Some of these problems can be addressed by technical standards, but the organizational and business dynamics of the standards development process are undergoing profound change (Hawkins, 1997*b*). Typical business solutions using information and

---

[11] See Gartner Group on their ephemeral 'hot content' page. The statistic is within the range reported by Amusao and Fluss (1999). This research note indicates that the lowest levels of e-commerce site development offering little integration with the rest of the company's service infrastructure or enterprise computing requires US$ 500,000 to $1m. of investment. It also defines three higher levels of functionality with price tags of US$ 1–3m., $3–35m. and $35m., the last for a fully integrated site. The article suggests that even these high investments can be justified, when the costs of servicing customers by telephone and for physical site visits are properly accounted for, if the volume of business is sufficient.

communication technologies involve rather fragile formal standards, the so-called 'publicly available specifications', and proprietary technologies. This can lead to questions about the openness of nominally standardized environments. Internet banking is a good example. Several leading banks in the United States are collaborating with Microsoft to develop Open Financial Exchange (OFX), a publicly available specification that, in principle, will prevent the standards for financial transactions from becoming proprietary. By contrast, Microsoft is entering into alliances with major manufacturers of point-of-sale devices, a move that could lead to proprietary dominance of financial server software. OFX will not guarantee a non-proprietary environment for e-commerce if there is proprietary control over the tools and server software needed to implement it.

5.2.5   Summary

E-commerce has become a pervasive philosophy with a strong 'normative' content reflected in the view that companies that fail to participate in these developments are doomed. Exactly what participation means, however, is complicated by the variety of opportunities available for business activities using electronic communications. In terms of the Internet, such participation can range from providing product information and company publicity to offering supplier linkages and direct sales support. The costs of increasing functionality rise substantially as a company moves towards the latter model of e-commerce. The extent of these costs raises significant issues about whether small and medium-sized organizations that do not have strong in-house technological capabilities will be able to sustain the costs of participation. To examine the desirability of moving towards fuller implementations of e-commerce, a more complete analysis is needed of the rhetoric and reality of e-commerce, and this is the subject of the next section.

5.3   Exploring the Myths and Realities of Electronic Commerce

Led largely by enthusiasm about its possibilities, but also by uncertainty about how these can be realized, e-commerce is generating its own mythology about the sources of benefits and the kinds of structural changes that will be required to realize them. Most myths fall into one or more of three categories: (1) firm characteristics and strategies, (2) organizational and inter-organizational dynamics, and (3) sources of wealth creation in the electronic market-place. Myths are rooted in reality and examples can be found of enterprises that operate in many of the ways described in the mythology. If mythologies take root in the corporate and policy communities during the development of the e-commerce environment, which is still open to dramatic changes in direction, inferences may be drawn from isolated and unrepresentative cases. We must be careful not to infer too much from the early experiences of these new traders or from cases that only appear to indicate significant trends. For user firms, and especially for small firms, acting on the basis of mythology can establish dubious preconditions and goals that can lead to ill-judged decisions about whether or not to participate in e-commerce.

5.3.1   Three Pervasive Myths about E-Commerce

We examine three of the most high profile myths about e-commerce in the discussion that follows and then consider some of the actual influences on the evolution of the new electronic markets. Our purpose is to clarify the factors that are motivating firms to embrace e-commerce and to suggest some of the more probable requirements for success in the electronic market-place.

5.3.1.1   The Myth of the Cyber-Trader Advantage

The first very popular myth holds that e-commerce is primarily about minimizing links with physical infrastructures. As a result, it offers special advantages to smaller innovative firms in entering new and existing markets. A cyber-trader is generally defined as a firm or individual trader that deals with its suppliers and customers entirely in cyberspace, that is, on the Internet or in some similar environment. This concept has an anarchist or libertarian and anti-establishment flavour, and was born of the hacker culture and nurtured in the burgeoning on-line communities of the mid-1990s.

There is little question that cyber-traders exist, although many simply sell material products using the Internet. The cyber-trader market began with an enormous entry wave. In 1996, it was estimated that about 250,000 such endeavours were operating in the United States alone, the vast majority being niche market retailers (*Business Week*, 1996*b*). Nevertheless, the economic significance of this type of enterprise in e-commerce also began at a very modest level. The combined sales for the cyber-traders at this time amounted to a rather paltry US$ 0.5b., on average only US$ 2,000 per firm per year and a tiny portion of total retail sales. The rate of growth of this activity has, however, proved to be spectacular. In a report cited by the American Booksellers Association, Boston Consulting Group estimated that 1999 on-line retail sales would amount to US$ 108b., two-and-a-half times the 1998 level (Hoynes, 1999). It is important to stress, however, that the cyber-trader portion of this total is expected to be no more than US$ 41b. Comparisons between different types of cyber-trader prototypes provide a perspective on the likely developments.

Amazon.com is now probably the best known cyber-commerce address in the world. In much of the popular and business press, the company exemplifies and embodies many of the virtues of Internet-based e-commerce, especially individualized customer information and service as a means of mediating between producers and consumers. The company began with the aim of creating the largest virtual bookstore in the world and has added a continuing range of products and services to this basic position, including pre-recorded music and video, toys and games, electronic products, and electronic mail greeting cards. Amazon uses mainly postal and courier services for delivery and the credit card for payment. As yet, no one can say whether the company will make profits. Amazon is a niche-market catalogue sales company that is highly entrepreneurial, but it is more opportunistic than innovative. Two of its main innovations have been to provide content reviews, with the opportunity for readers to contribute reviews, and the ability for a user to request notification of new publications by a particular author. Amazon is clearly pursuing an insurgent strategy, but one based on the rather weak network externality provided by its brand name identification with electronic book and media selling. The relatively low barriers to imitating this model must raise questions about its sustainability over time.

On-line book purchasing has been able to capture a share of the United States book market, at least 3 per cent and perhaps as high as 6 per cent of sales according to the American Booksellers Association (ibid.). The implications of this for Amazon.com are both good and bad. On the one hand, its early position and investments in brand image have made it well known. On the other hand, its success has attracted an enormous number of entrants, some 650 in the United States with many of these advertising that they can fill orders for more than a million different titles. These entrants will certainly take some custom away from Amazon while further legitimizing on-line book purchasing, thereby bringing more customers to Amazon due to brand association. Amazon conforms most closely to the cyber-trader model, since it maintains virtually all its contact with suppliers and customers electronically. The longer-term implications of the 'virtue' that Amazon owns and controls very little of the physical production and supply chain on which its business depends is questionable. Lack of control of these assets may make it vulnerable to competition from bookstores or book distributors with more substantial physical assets or simply from the profusion of new entrants, each attempting to take part of the market.

It is instructive to compare Amazon.com with Cisco, the company that controls about 85 per cent of the global Internet router technology market. Cisco does over US$ 1b. of business per year on the web, sells leading-edge technology, the very product that makes the Internet work, and is very profitable although the contribution of Internet sales to its profitability is not publicly known. Cisco is one of the ten largest suppliers of communication network products in the world with sales revenue growth routinely better than 100 per cent per year. A similar example is Dell Computers, which booked US$ 18m. per day in customer orders from its web site in the first quarter of 1999.

Cisco and Dell are both manufacturers with extensive physical plant in addition to their web presence. Both companies began trading on the web only after each had built up substantial market share in the conventional transaction environment over several years. Amazon provides a convenient service, but does it demonstrate sufficient value-added characteristics to define a new commercial paradigm? In our view, probably not. Has it acquired first-mover experience and brand advantages that will sustain its market position? This will only become clearer as the market evolves.

Cisco and Amazon.com are alike in so far as both are niche players, that is, each vends goods or services in a concentrated market segment. The difference between them is that Amazon 'occupies' its niche, being dependent upon other firms for the physical production, supply, and distribution of its merchandise. In this sense, it is the more traditional niche player because its continued operation is largely dependent on the degree to which it is perceived to enhance the profitability of the firms that supply and deliver the products it sells. In contrast, Cisco 'owns' its niche, as it is in control of the design, production, and distribution, at least on the web, of its whole product line, and because it is in a commanding position to define the future technological parameters of its niche environment. The contrast between occupancy and ownership is not meant to be a statement about the relative value of the two models for a niche strategy. For example, many successful insurance companies occupy specific niches and rely upon independent broker networks to sell and deliver their products. The occupancy strategy does, however, dictate that the firm must develop a specialized position or seek an insurgent strategy, such as the one that Amazon.com is pursuing, of attempting to associate on-line book and other sales with its corporate image.

The future of niche players in e-commerce is even more intriguing when we look at the growing presence on the web of large diversified firms. Most current estimates are that only between 3 and 4 per cent of corporate web sites could accommodate business-to-business transactions by the end of the 1990s, but this is certain to change. In the United States, General Electric does business with its suppliers on the web in the amount of about US$ 1b. per year. Again, in the United States, independent Internet-based dealers are beginning to capture a discernible share of automobile sales, but they are facing head-to-head competition from major automobile manufacturers that are using the same medium. In this case, the manufacturers have an advantage. They can link the Internet capabilities with their existing dealer networks and to their increasingly demand-responsive production and specification routines.

The key point is that the scalability and flexibility of the Internet yields many of the same kinds of advantages for large diversified firms as it does for small niche players in terms of expanding the range of e-commerce customers and transactions. Through divisions, joint ventures, and acquisitions, diversified firms can decide to pursue niche strategies and/or to assume the functions of existing niche players. Perhaps the most straightforward explanation for the early prevalence of niche players in the e-commerce environment is that niche markets are good places for firms to experiment with innovative technologies using new business models. Very often, a customer base can be built up relatively quickly, especially if the dynamics of an existing trading community, and/or community of interest, can be exploited. Although cyber-trading systems are scalable, there is little evidence that smaller or more specialized firms can reap disproportionately large cost savings from the e-commerce approach relative to their larger rivals. As the scale of their businesses grows, the costs of maintaining and integrating their e-commerce sites scale upwards as well. Amazon.com largely exploited demographic relationships between higher education and book acquisition habits that grew up with the first generation of Internet users. Cisco exploited its existing high level of externalities in the global router market. Other enterprises are exploiting individual professional, trade, and interest communities as markets for targeted goods and services. Firms that remain niche occupiers can become highly vulnerable, however, because of their dependence on production and distribution facilities over which they have little or no control. Niche owners generally control the production and distribution facilities for their niche, but may also be vulnerable when the nature of the niche market changes, usually, due to the emergence of a significant competitor.

In questioning the myth of the 'cyber-trader' advantage, we are not claiming that there are no opportunities for entrepreneurial firms in cyber-space. On the contrary, opportunities like these are abundant and we have chosen Amazon.com as a company illustrative of many of the features that may lead to eventual success. The problems arise when these opportunities are taken to be evidence of fundamental structural changes in the relationships between market actors, established and new, large and small. At this point, we do not know whether these niche opportunities create a temporary or long-term advantage, or whether one type or size of firm is necessarily in a better position than another to exploit them. In the longer term, first-mover advantages may be overcome by firms who can learn to exploit existing brand images in new ways and that already have control, or can acquire control quickly, over crucial transaction points in a given market segment.

5.3.1.2   *The Myth of the Virtual Organization*

The second major myth concerns the implications of the increasing automation of transactions. This myth is that the application of information and communication technologies will produce more open and dynamic business and market structures and lower barriers to market entry. A virtual organizational structure at the enterprise level can be defined as commercial collaboration among firms, carried out in an electronic environment, in which entry to, and exit from, the structure is flexible and determined on an 'as required' basis. This model is the apogee of much current management thinking about computer-integrated business and logistics processes. As noted above, early initiatives to re-engineer these processes played a substantial part in the genesis of the e-commerce concept and the links have remained especially close.

E-commerce is undoubtedly associated with substantial organizational adjustment and this can be used in creative ways to re-engineer redundant or inefficient business processes. However, as all re-engineering initiatives involve risks and costs, this aspect of e-commerce is also one of the chief obstacles to its implementation. The main problem with the myth of the virtual organization is uncertainty about the pay-off. There is no prima facie logical connection between virtual organizational structures and open structures. Firms can re-engineer processes, but it could be that basic structural relationships between firms in business enterprises do not change, or that they change in ways that create new barriers to participation.

Chesbrough and Teece (1996) suggest that fully integrated hierarchical and virtual structures are essentially theoretical states at opposite ends of a continuum. The implication is that no contemporary business structure is likely to be fully hierarchical or fully virtual. In this framework, decisions about whether a given structure is optimal for an enterprise are based largely on the degree of risk that the collaborating firms can absorb. These risks increase as the virtual pole is approached. Movement towards the virtual pole is offset by the degree of control over information and communication that is necessary for the enterprise as a whole to function, control that is likely to require a hierarchical structure (ibid.).

This view encourages consideration of all of the possible outcomes of computer-mediated business relationships. For firms in supply and production chains, the logical end point could well be smaller, less open structures, perhaps with very inten-sive internal integration, rather than expansive open structures. Indeed, the accumu-lated evidence from most past experience with commercial networking, EDI for instance, is that closed clusters of activity can form for commercial reasons, and not only as a result of technological and organizational incompatibilities (Mansell and Jenkins, 1992*b*). As noted above, even the nominally open Internet is experiencing a segmentation phenomenon as its commercial potential is developed.

Furthermore, as a concept, the virtual business structure is predicated largely on the assumption that business partnering in an electronic environment will be driven by lower costs of forming dynamic, temporary business structures. This assumption ignores the principal sources of costs in forming business relationships, the problems of establishing trust, reconciling different operational routines, and establishing inter-personal relationships that can bridge or remedy misunderstandings and mistakes that are an inevitable part of human interaction. For these and other reasons, firms place value also on cultivating stable supplier communities (Garcia, 1995). As firms employ electronic means to mediate more business processes and organizational structures, historical experience with partners and their technological capabilities becomes an important factor in partner selection and collaboration management (Hawkins, Molas, and Walker, 1996). Moreover, information pools that develop through commercial exchanges and collaboration can become commercially sensitive. There can be strong incentives to share this information fully *only* with trusted partners.

As in the case of cyber-trader advantages, the purpose of examining the myth of the virtual organization is not to question whether organizational structures of this type are possible or might, in some cases, lead to significant advantages. The issue is the extent of the opportunity they provide for firms in an electronic market-place, and whether e-commerce must necessarily be linked to the radical, as opposed to incremental, reorganization of business processes and structures as a prerequisite for successful implementation. Net benefits are likely if the volume of business is sufficient to support the costs of organizational adjustment.

5.3.1.3 *The Myth of Disintermediation*
E-commerce will eliminate intermediaries through automation, thereby creating more direct links between producers and final customers. This is the third myth that we address here. The disintermediation argument is that e-commerce will facilitate the removal of many, or even most, of the processes that now intervene between buyers and sellers in the conventional market-place. The assumption is that intermediaries make the transfer of goods and services inefficient, and that they are primarily a busi-ness cost. Disintermediation through e-commerce is seen as a way of making the transaction structure more efficient by centralizing and automating routine business processes and eliminating the proverbial 'middle-man'.

The mythical element creeps in because of a failure to separate the commercial reasons for disintermediation, along with its processes and effects, from the role of information and communication technologies in facilitating and stimulating disintermediation. From the observation that information and communication technologies can be applied to many commercial functions, the leap is made to accepting the truncation and centralization of these functions as necessarily desirable or valuable. But disintermediation is nothing new and it has a somewhat dubious reputation. In some circumstances, disintermediation is little more than a euphemism for 'market concentration' or 'discount outlets' and it embodies many of the same implications for competition policy and the difficulties of sustaining adequate relations with the customer.

In its most extreme form, disintermediation implies the virtual elimination of the distribution and retail trade service sectors as we understand them, presumably along with most of the jobs these sectors provide. In its less extreme form, the argument is merely for the elimination of those intermediate services that do not add value to the process of commercial exchange. As an objective, this seems reasonable and desirable. The problem rests with the assumption that a new intermediation dynamic comes into play in the electronic market-place that does not exist already in the conventional market-place (Gristock and Mansell, 1997). It is possible to imagine the potential for such innovation to occur. For example, Paul Allen, Microsoft's co-founder, and Marc Andreeson, the founder of Netscape, have transferred the idea of the buyer's co-operative to the Internet. This, itself, is not innovative, but what they have done with their web-based Mercata venture is to specify a time-delimited subscription for a group purchase. A potential purchaser may make a bid for one of the items on offer by committing irrevocably to paying a maximum price. As the number of commitments grows, the actual price that committed purchasers must pay for the item falls, reflecting the buying power of group purchase. What is innovative about this scheme is not the auction element but rather the 'bundling' of group demand into a single package allowing for economies in the dispatch of a lot and reducing or eliminating costs of inventory.[12] The Mercata product is, of course, an example of reintermediation at work.

The idea that simply advertising a product and selling it on the Internet creates a large gain in efficiency through disintermediation is, in most cases, simply mistaken. This results in much confusion as to the nature of the value that is added by e-commerce itself and about its trade and competition implications. Enormous diversity in intermediaries already exists in the conventional market-place and not all of the value they may add is quantifiable directly. Particularly in the consumer market, 'rational' choice-making is coloured by all manner of social pressures and cultural conventions, both positive and negative (Leiss, 1976; Scitovsky, 1986). For the consumer, the market-place is also a social and cultural experience, and many intermediary functions are aimed at adding value to the experience rather than necessarily to the utility of the transaction (Lane, 1991). Retailers such as Harrods or Les Galeries Lafayette, for example, are in a position to attract customers solely on the basis of reputation and image, and many producers are keen to compete for visibility in these premium retail-

---

[12] In the United States, distribution by 'drop shipment' of 'lots' of merchandise is a common practice that has been refined over the years so that individual items can be despatched at virtually the same costs as a bulk shipment. This is partly due to the aggressive competition between parcel service firms.

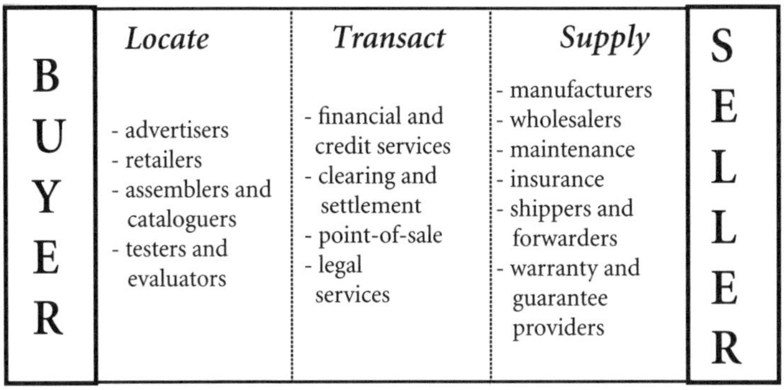

	Locate	*Transact*	*Supply*	S
B			- manufacturers	**E**
U	- advertisers	- financial and credit services	- wholesalers	
Y	- retailers - assemblers and cataloguers	- clearing and settlement	- maintenance - insurance	**L**
E	- testers and evaluators	- point-of-sale - legal services	- shippers and forwarders	**L**
R			- warranty and guarantee providers	**E** **R**

FIG. 5.5. Intermediary roles

Source: Prepared by Richard Hawkins (1998*a*).

ing environments. Indeed, emulating a quality shopping experience in cyber-space is one of the most difficult challenges for designers of consumer interfaces for e-commerce.

Furthermore, it is difficult to determine what can be disintermediated without destabilizing a market structure entirely. There is no reason to assume that intermediaries will exist for long in the conventional market-place if they do not add some degree of value, that is, unless they are preserved through special circumstances or intervention. There is considerable controversy about this issue in Europe due to the existence of numerous fair-trade pricing arrangements within the retail sector. Some argue that these arrangements reinforce the market power of distributors and retailers by providing gross profit margins that can be invested in discouraging competitive entry. Others argue that these investments are made in improvements in service and produce a greater variety than would otherwise be available given the structure of European retailing. Some intermediary functions are sustained only by statutory and regulatory circumstances. The costs of national transport infrastructures or state-run postal services that are shielded from competitive entry are called into question frequently in this regard.

Most intermediaries, however, are specialists in some aspect of connecting and/or supporting buyers and sellers. It is not certain that their disappearance is either required or desirable in the electronic market-place. Figure 5.5 illustrates some of the main intermediary roles arrayed according to their principal function: (1) locating products, (2) facilitating transactions and payments, and (3) supplying goods and services. They are positioned in the diagram according to whether their primary interface is with the buyer, seller, or both, in the case of transaction intermediation.

In principle, the seller can encompass many of the supply and some of the transaction functions, that is, manufacturers who sell direct, and many sellers, are also intermediaries. Firms might maintain all these functional capabilities in-house for

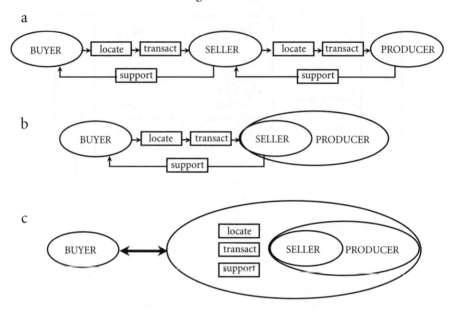

FIG. 5.6. Intermediated and disintermediated configurations

Source: Prepared by Richard Hawkins (1998*a*).

efficiency reasons, or as part of a strategy to control transaction points for competitive, and sometimes anti-competitive, purposes. Relatively few sellers encompass
product location functions and, in some cases, it may be unethical or illegal to do so.[13]
  Figure 5.6 illustrates a range of possible intermediated and disintermediated
configurations. Section (a) shows a typical retailing or wholesaling configuration. The
seller, in this case, sells goods obtained from producers either to other sellers or directly
to final customers. Own brand goods may also be sold, but many, and probably most,
of these will be procured rather than produced directly by the seller. To sustain the
supply chain, a full range of locate, transact, and support functions is required between
seller, buyer, and supplier. Provided that the seller is also the producer, the seller–
producer axis can be disintermediated to a large extent (see Fig. 5.6 (b)). Some of the
functions, such as wholesaling, become redundant. However, many intermediaries can
remain between the source and ultimate destination of the goods or services, such as
advertising, financial, and delivery services. Figure 5.6 (c) depicts what advocates of
disintermediation see as the ideal state, that is, direct interaction between buyers and
sellers. Here, the seller has assumed all the intermediary functions. Ideally, the seller is

---

[13] A well-known example is American Airlines which once fell foul of American competition law by
offering an advanced electronic reservation system to travel agents (basically an interactive catalogue),
configured such that it listed American Airline flights in preference to those of its competitors, see
Guerin-Calvert (1989).

also the producer, or is otherwise in control of the supply and production chain. In a fully disintermediated e-commerce scenario, as many of these functions as possible would be centralized and automated, allowing the final customer to interact directly with the producer.

Examples of disintermediation can be found that approach the model in Fig. 5.6 (c), although they are much more likely to arise in non-material product environments. Cisco, for example, conforms to most of the characteristics depicted in Fig. 5.6 (c), at least for its non-material products. It is much more difficult to envisage examples involving material products. Amazon.com maintains most of the characteristics of the fully intermediated model (see Fig. 5.6 (a)) as only the location function between buyer and seller is disintermediated to any significant extent. Furthermore, in the case of both Cisco and Amazon.com, numerous intermediaries are required to give them and their customers access to the Internet and to payment services.

The disintermediation argument maintains that location, exchange, and supply functions can be combined through automation, thus lowering transaction costs. But intermediation is also a way of spreading investment risks and partially distributing products through geographically extensive networks. Risks to single actors may increase as disintermediation occurs, and transaction and transport costs are often not so much saved as transferred up the supply chain. An example in a material product environment is the food retailing business in the United Kingdom. The four main supermarket chains, and some of the smaller chains, now own or control most of their supply and distribution systems. This does not necessarily mean that the costs of these supply chains go down, but that the retailer now assumes direct responsibility for the losses or gains of each intermediary function. Food retailing margins in the United Kingdom are typically between 4 and 6 per cent, whereas elsewhere they are typically less than 2 per cent. This is largely the result of the uniquely high degrees of supply chain control that characterize the British food sector, that is, more of the total cost of the supply chain is reflected in the retail margin (Hall, 1999).

For non-material products and services that exist in digital form, distribution can be by electronic means. In this case, the logic of full disintermediation seems inescapable on superficial examination. However, many examples can be found of non-material products and services that have migrated from an originally disintermediated environment to intermediated ones such as the distribution of download-able software from sites specializing in managing this process. Furthermore, not all service providers see advantages in dealing directly with final customers. Financial and insurance services are routinely wholesaled and retailed even though, in principle, the actual lenders or underwriters could deal directly with clients through e-commerce. Intermediary buffers are useful in industries like these in which there is a strong element of the seller choosing to do business with the buyer, instead of the other way around. Suppliers must decide also whether or not to accept the customer's risk.

Ultimately, however, the weakness of the disintermediation argument in an e-commerce context is that if automation through information and communication technology applications can lower transaction costs for producers and customers, then it can lower these costs for intermediaries as well. Many major firms that are

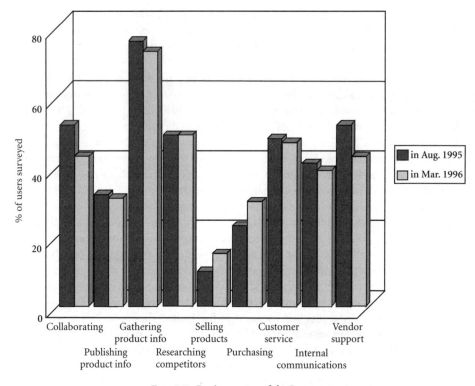

Fɪɢ. 5.7. Business uses of the Internet

Source: Hawkins (1998*a*) based on CommerceNet–Nielson Market Research, 1997.

active already in e-commerce have exploited these reduced costs for some time. This is the core of the majority of outsourcing strategies, and it confirms that most firms make intermediation-disintermediation decisions on the basis of a commercial, rather than technological, efficiency criterion. Clearly, there are many reasons for firms and customers to see intermediation in a positive light. Many of the characteristics of the electronic market-place create new intermediation opportunities related to overcoming problems ranging from product visibility in electronic space to transaction management and security (Kokuryo and Takeda, 1995).

Most recent surveys of Internet use convey at least one common message about business users. In general, they use electronic media more extensively to gather and disseminate information about products, producers, competitors, and customers, than to engage in transactions. As shown in Fig. 5.7, Internet use for sales is increasing, but the most common use of new information media is to communicate with customers, suppliers, and intermediaries. These use patterns suggest that in both the short- and long-term, there are enormous opportunities to develop markets for specialized intermediation services in a virtual environment. These could more than compensate for any reduction of intermediation in the material environment.

Our questioning of the myth of disintermediation is not to argue that in some situations, and subject to legal restrictions, disintermediation cannot be an effective business strategy. Neither is it to deny that information and communication technologies can be used to facilitate disintermediation where this makes commercial sense. The main danger arises when the myth of disintermediation is used as a rationale, particularly by corporate strategists and public decision-makers, for promoting the wide-scale migration of firms to e-commerce. For the immediate future, and into the long-term, intermediation is probably the single largest source of new business opportunity in e-commerce for many new and existing firms. This is especially so for smaller firms, since as Dyson (1997) argues, many of these, and probably most, are already structured around intermediate goods and services.

5.3.2   Three Pervasive Realities about E-Commerce

For the most part, the mythology of e-commerce revolves around abstract visions of how it might radically alter the commercial environment. Eventually, some aspects of this vision may become reality, but in the meantime real firms have much more pragmatic agendas, and e-commerce is being embraced to varying degrees by real firms in increasing numbers. If the mythology does not explain the dynamics of e-commerce, then what are the principal motivations and rationales of participants in this new medium? Why and how does e-commerce evolve in firms and sectors? Answers to these questions are to be found in three closely related areas.

5.3.2.1   Increased Visibility and Opportunity

A greatly increased scope for interactive media has become available in more sectors of the economy and at lower costs than ever before. For the originators of the e-commerce concept in the 1980s, the idea of engaging directly with consumers was, to a large extent, technologically inaccessible. It became feasible when relatively cheap Internet connections became available to large numbers of firms and individuals. The opportunities for a greater variety of market participants to become involved with e-commerce have increased dramatically. Although debates continue about the characteristics, scale, and pace of market liberalization and technology investment, a significant range of telecommunication costs in many industrialized economies has been declining in real terms, accompanied by substantial increases in technical capabilities and network reliability. Presumably, as costs decline further and facilities improve in more areas, even more commercial possibilities will become feasible.

The proliferation of interactive media in businesses and households over the past decade is, in most cases, still only indicative of trends, but these trends are significant enough to push many firms actively to explore commercial opportunities in this environment. This is particularly so for firms with close affinities to non-material products and services. Interpretation of the trends may have been intensified by the high public profile accorded to information and communication technologies, much of it created by the equipment vendors and service providers, and reinforced by government-sponsored awareness programmes and industrial policies.

Increased opportunity has some negative as well as positive implications, not least being the problem of bandwagon effects that are sometimes generated when technological enthusiasm or the fear of being left behind obscures commercial realities.[14] More problematic are asymmetries in the abilities of firms to control the terms of entry and exit into the electronic market-place. It was noted above that as more large firms embrace e-commerce, more small firms are being compelled to follow suit in order to be able to do business with these larger firms. This increases the risks for small firms more than for larger firms.

5.3.2.2 *Evolutionary Advantage*
For most firms, the path to e-commerce is evolutionary rather than revolutionary, and involves the enhancement of existing market positions and commercial structures. As outlined above, the e-commerce environment is becoming populated by two types of firms: start-up firms that are built from the ground up to operate in an electronic market-place, and established firms that migrate to e-commerce. The economic significance of firms in the first category is still very small even if the growth rate is relatively high. Most of the economically significant migration to e-commerce occurs along evolutionary paths that are numerous, complex, and may vary from industry to industry. As a consequence of migration, radical changes, intended and unintended, can and do occur in trading structures and practices. Several general stimuli for evolutionary developments are beginning to emerge. Four of the most common are as follows.

First, there are increasing requirements and expectations among trading partners. These are a major stimulus as many supply-chain contracts become dependent upon possessing, acquiring, or expanding an e-commerce capability. Increasing requirements and expectations also fuel the development of user cultures that accommodate e-commerce at the enterprise and customer levels. The more e-commerce users grow in sophistication and experience, the more likely they are to embrace new service offerings. Second, alliance-building seems to be encouraging, or to be encouraged by, the adoption of e-commerce. However, the links that are evolving are likely to be structured within closed groups of traders as well as within open virtual structures. One advantage of electronic transaction environments is that firms may be able better to monitor the qualities of suppliers and customers, such as their reliability and flexibility, their collaborative problem-solving capabilities, and their capacity for organizational innovation. This can result in the application of even more rigorous

---

[14] For an explanation of bandwagon effects see Farrell and Saloner (1987). Bandwagon effects refer to the processes of accelerated adoption that occur because the adopter takes others' adoption as either a positive signal of the value of adoption or as a signal of the potential risk of not adopting. Both types of expectations have the potential to incur costs for firms before there is a clear benefit. Many economists question whether such effects can occur because they are 'irrational' from a profit standpoint. In rapidly evolving markets, however, not acting upon surmise may also be irrational if rivals are able to achieve an advantage by doing so.

alliance-formation criteria than might otherwise be the case, especially with regard to technological capabilities. In other words, there is less incentive than is usually supposed for firms to want their alliance structures to be more flexible or inclusive of more actors. Often the situation is quite the opposite.

Third, at the enterprise level, logistics have been and remain a major evolutionary factor. E-commerce can expand the scope of integration between the transaction and logistics structures. The evolution of most e-commerce applications in enterprises begins with routine accounting, including ordering and invoicing, and inventory processes, and moves on to encompass supply and production-chain management. In some cases, it incorporates design and engineering processes and it can open up interfaces directly with customers. All these developments can occur in intermediated as well as disintermediated structures. Finally, the precursors of the contemporary e-commerce concept have demonstrated the importance of leading actors in establishing the viability of alternative evolutionary patterns. Key firms and industry organizations that champion e-commerce in sector, national, and regional contexts play decisive roles in the evolution and diffusion of e-commerce. Dominant market actors can often impose e-commerce elements quickly across a range of principal, and even subsidiary, value chains, thus exerting top-down co-ordination pressures, particularly on suppliers.

5.3.2.3 Pursuit of New Business Objectives

Ultimately, firms become proactive in e-commerce because they see in it opportunities to develop new business models for innovative kinds of products and services. It is seldom productive for firms to become involved in e-commerce because it is possible or because they fall into line with an evolutionary trajectory controlled largely by other firms. For most firms, there are two main ways of proactively using e-commerce to generate business opportunities. One is by gaining tactical advantages through improved transaction management and the other is by pursuing strategic objectives for new business development. These objectives are closely related and most e-commerce scenarios involve both.

Firms realize tactical efficiency gains primarily from learning to use transaction-generated information in more creative ways, and from speeding up routine, especially high-volume, transaction processes. One of the most unique features of e-commerce as a trading environment is that it provides unparalleled opportunities for the capture, manipulation, and management of all the information that is generated with each transaction, an aspect that we consider in greater detail in Ch. 7. This can assist in business planning and facilitate more efficient production and distribution processes. It can also enhance vendor and customer support.

However, tactical efficiency gains can become very abstract if pursued for their own sake and their benefits can be ephemeral. In the first place, even the most efficient e-commerce systems remain subject to 'natural' fluctuations in supply and demand. In the second place, efficiency innovations effected in one firm can easily spread to competitors. In an electronic environment, this diffusion can be rapid, and network externalities can create greater incentives to share these innovations up and down the supply chains. For example, many business process re-engineering and quality control systems that were exotic and exclusive to a few firms in the mid-1990s are already fodder for all manner of off-the-shelf consultancy products that incorporate information and communication technologies.

If they are not tied to strategic objectives to create new product and business forms, the pursuit of tactical efficiency goals can produce a dead end. New business opportunities arise in several ways depending upon the types of products and services involved and upon already established evolutionary trajectories. They often occur when the pursuit of tactical objectives yields outcomes that can be turned into products in their own right. An example is the commercializable data-mining products and services developed from management routines for analysing transaction-generated customer or logistics information.

For non-material products, such as entertainment, information services, and financial services, e-commerce immediately suggests new wholesaling and retailing forms based upon the direct digital transfer of non-material content in both archival and on-demand contexts. For material products also, e-commerce can result in new ways of matching products to customers. For many firms, at least in the short- to medium-term, these are likely to result in complements to conventional marketing outlets rather than in outright alternatives. Internet-based automobile trading is an example of this type of complementarity. The physical showroom is both a transaction arena in its own right, and a physical annexe to the electronic transaction arena. Customers can survey product and price information on the Internet and then use dealerships for access to demonstrator vehicles. For many material commodities, e-commerce could progressively replace more substantial amounts of face-to-face trade as in the case of electronic standing orders for staple foodstuffs or office consumables.

In both material and non-material product environments, the source of most strategic opportunities is business substitution. Business models oriented to material goods are substituted in whole or in part by models developed from non-material service environments that evolved originally around the production and delivery of material goods. In other words, the substitution process is driven by the relative strength of complementary capabilities or resources. Thus, although firms such as Federal Express or United Parcel Service have substituted a sophisticated logistics information business model for part of their original model, that is, a fast and efficient 'mover of parcels', they continue to own and operate a physical forwarding and delivery infrastructure. It is conceivable that these firms might eliminate the material side altogether and merely exploit their logistics sophistication in order to provide intermediate services to senders, shippers, and receivers of material goods.

In the already non-material market-place of information services, the business substitution process is subtle but just as real. Reuters, for example, has substituted a high value-added, real-time, on-line corporate information services business model for much of its more traditional news agency model. In the process, it has become a major investor in research and development for information and communication technology-based products and services. In 1997, the firm was estimated to have the ninth largest overall research and development budget in the United Kingdom, larger than that of British Aerospace or British Petroleum (Department of Trade and Industry, 1997*b*).

The role of complementary capabilities and resources in driving business substitution provides a guide to the evolution of e-commerce activities. E-commerce applications, originally designed to service one particular transaction element, become capable of encompassing other elements as well. There are historically strong structural links, for example, between electronic financial and trading systems and the manufacturing and retail sectors. Systems designed originally to handle financial settlements can evolve such that they encompass other business functions such as orders and inventories.[15] The global reservations systems of airlines and hotels have been linked for some time, due largely to the complementary benefit of being able simultaneously to book travel and accommodation. In many cases, the existence of complementary capabilities and resources generates shifts in focus between the production and support, transaction preparation, and transaction completion elements of e-commerce.

5.4   Changing Transaction Structures and Firm Strategies

Several key points emerge from our discussion which have important implications for the ways in which firms can position themselves strategically to capture the potential benefits from e-commerce. Business-to-business e-commerce is much more developed than the business-to-consumer relationship. Prospective gains in process efficiency are not sufficient reasons to invest in e-commerce business solutions. Companies should choose to migrate to e-commerce for strategic reasons rather than seeing it as an opportunity for short-term gain. Correspondingly, business models in which e-commerce is the central part of a start-up strategy are likely to remain at the fringes of e-commerce. However, start-up firms are important as explorers and trend-setters, attracting and cultivating new trading communities. Large established traders are often in strong positions to lead e-commerce developments at the consumer level because of market presence and brand confidence, and, at the enterprise level, because of economic and/or technological leadership.

Given these contextual features, most of the strategic choices available to a firm concerning e-commerce are related in some way to the evolution of transaction characteristics and structures. The value chain of a given product or service contains key points at which commercial decisions must be made. Certain decisions have traditionally been undertaken by either the customer or the supplier without direct consultation with the other party to the eventual consummation of a sale. The fact that many, and perhaps all, of these decisions can involve a process of mutual

---

[15] For early case studies of these processes of migration in the electronic trading network environment see Mansell and Jenkins (1992*a*; 1992*b*).

determination and commercial exchange make them potential sources of transactions and, therefore, worth including in the definition of a market's transaction characteristics and structure. Thus, even if a decision in a particular context is taken unilaterally by either the supplier or the customer, the decision may be thought of as a 'transaction' in which the other party is silent.

For example, traditionally, product specification was, in many industries, a decision taken exclusively by the supplier. Customers were offered a choice between available product types and their only 'voice' was whether they chose to purchase or decline a particular offering. In some industries, customers also made product specifications, and the process of matching or reaching a compromise between producer and customer specifications was a task delegated to manufacturers' representatives and purchasing agents. Many factors were responsible for gaps between supplier and customer requirements, including different product planning cycles, technological capabilities, and differences in market power. In yet other industries, efforts were made to cater to customer product specifications, even if they created costly modifications of process engineering. In all these cases there are opportunities for commercial exchanges to arise as a means of bridging the producer and customer product specification process. Supply contract negotiations, one example of such commercial exchanges, reveal some portion of the flexibility of both the supplier and customer to modifications of the initial specification and, depending on the skill of the negotiating parties, a slight or major improvement might be made in the final commercial transaction.

Product specifications are only one of many specifications that involve choices by suppliers and customers that might be bridged by co-determined transactions. Other examples include the logistical arrangements for product supply, reorder procedures, credit clearing arrangements, and the ordering and invoicing processes. While institutional mechanisms, such as commercial codes as well as industry practices and customs, make it unnecessary to reinvent these transactions for every commercial exchange, these same institutional mechanisms may create barriers to organizational innovation or efficiency gains. Existing transactions are often not neutral with respect to the relative market power of the participants. It is not surprising, for example, that government procurement involves strong customer influence in the product specification process.[16] Correspondingly, producer dominance of an industry may lead to transactions that impose additional costs on customers, particularly when these costs otherwise would be borne by the dominant producer.

The way that transactions are defined can be utilized as a means of perpetuating and extending market power. One of the most common transactions in which market power is extended and reinforced is the practice of bundling a package of goods and services together and of requiring the customers to purchase the entire package even in situations where they might prefer to purchase a single component. Thus, a convenience store with local market power over its customers might only sell plastic cups in units of two dozen even though few customers require this number. This kind of

---

[16] It should be noted, however, that this might substantially raise the costs of procurement when the government buys items from a firm with substantial market power.

strategy can be, and is, extended to very large transactions when alternative supply options (competition) are unavailable to the customer.

Transaction structures can also be used as a means of overcoming existing patterns of market power or creating new ones. For example, a local restaurant may offer picnic baskets with plastic cups and cutlery included in appropriate numbers for the typical customer as a means of contesting the market power of the local convenience store. In creating a different bundle, the restaurant may create its own source of market power, through product differentiation, relative to the convenience store.

Even in these relatively simple examples, the definition of transactions quickly becomes a complex matter involving considerable understanding of customer preferences and buying patterns as well as creative approaches to defining what is supplied and is offering value in the commercial transaction. These same principles are at work in more complex market contexts. In the e-commerce situation, relationships between buyers and sellers are likely to evolve over time as experience is gained in e-commerce relationships. How transactions are defined and who defines them will influence the nature of customer and supplier relationships. The specific role of technology is only a tool in the process of transaction definition although in certain circumstances it may constrain the opportunities for developing such relationships.

The production and acquisition of a typical product or service presents a complex series of decisions and possible points of transaction that can be negotiated by many configurations of actors. Referring to our definition of e-commerce, transactions apply to production and support activities, to preparation for commercial exchange, and to commercial exchange and completion activities. Transactions may also be defined in ways that span these activities. The structure of transactions refers to all the processes that might, in principle, involve commercial exchange and co-determination. In defining the structure of transactions, both buyers and sellers take decisions about how to organize and implement specific business processes that are intended to culminate in the exchange of the suppliers' goods and services for the customers' money.

Among the decisions that are taken, some may not lead to commercial exchange. For example, a supplier may define and offer a product that finds no takers. Some decisions involve product and service delivery as a commercial exchange, but many others are exploratory, involving the acquisition of market information such as advertising and personal enquiries. The transactions that contribute to commercial exchange are very relevant to the 'transaction structure' of any particular market. For example, a telephone enquiry about the price or availability of a product, or an Internet search for a *.com* web site are both transactions, as is the supply, acquisition, and perusal of a mail order catalogue. The transaction of accessing information can be just as vital to the eventual commercial exchange as physical access to the goods and/or services being traded.

The transaction structure is a kind of 'activity tree' that should, in principle, lead to a commercial exchange from both supplier and customer perspectives. Commonly the number of possible transactions is greatest in production and support activities; substantial in activities related to preparation for commercial exchange, and fewer and more straightforward in activities related to completion of the commercial exchange. Transactions in which the final customer participates are generally less of a factor in production activities than in preparation and completion activities.

The role of e-commerce is that it provides new opportunities for defining the transaction structure and new methods for achieving commercial exchange and co-determination of specific transactions. For example, suppliers can provide customers with information about their production capacities and capabilities that allow the customer to locate more desirable alternatives than might be available through an exclusively producer-defined series of offerings. Suppliers offering these capabilities bear the risk that customers will, in the end, generate commercial exchanges that are less profitable than traditional supplier-directed processes. It is also possible, however, that offering the customer this opportunity will lead to larger purchases than would otherwise have occurred. Learning how to shape this outcome is a key feature of the process of achieving evolutionary advantage in the use of e-commerce methods.

In general, a common assumption in e-commerce is that more information is desirable for both suppliers and customers. This need not be true, and, in particular, suppliers that have substantial market power are unlikely to provide customers with access to 'upstream' transactions precisely because it might reduce their market power. In addition, it is also necessary that the additional information should be meaningful and that it should not compromise the company's competitive position. Providing detailed information about the state of a supplier's inventory of raw materials may offer little meaningful information to most customers, but it might allow rivals to interfere with the company's production operations by pre-empting raw material supplier capacities.

In activities related to preparation for consumption, provision of more information is more likely to be of value to both suppliers and customers. The range of products that a supplier is prepared to supply to any taker, their costs and specifications, the information necessary to anticipate the qualities of the good or service in use, and so forth, are all means of attracting additional customers to the supplier. Correspondingly, larger customers can attract product offerings and competitive pricing information by disseminating information about their needs more broadly. It is also the case, however, that customers may find it in their interest to work closely with a more limited group of suppliers with the aim of developing product and service offerings that best meet the customers' needs. In this respect, a key feature of the transaction structure is the definition of who is allowed to participate in particular transactions. A mix of uses of the Internet and Extranets appears to offer some advantage over existing electronic trading networks for the exchange preparation process. This is largely due to the relative ease of formatting and communicating information utilizing Hypertext Markup Language (HTML) or eXtensible Markup Language (XML) documentation, which allows the smooth integration of graphical information, and the use of Extranets, which allow the definition of 'private' spaces for favoured partners to gain access to information resources.

Finally, in the area of completion of commercial exchanges, it is likely that both suppliers and customers will seek to simplify the information necessary for transactions.

Issues of commercial exchange completion increasingly involve electronic payment systems, a topic which we deal with in Ch. 8. The primary issues involved in transactions related to commercial exchange completion concern an assurance that both parties are committed to the transaction and that the incentives are established in such a way that both parties will perform in the completion process. Information available within the e-commerce process can facilitate these objectives but the set-up process for its use can be costly and is only justified when there are substantial numbers of commercial exchanges between parties. In business-to-business transactions existing methods of accomplishing these aims may continue for some time to be superior to Internet alternatives.

The analysis of the activities of a firm in terms of transaction structures illustrates the range of issues that tacticians and strategists in different firms and sectors face when they are planning e-commerce applications. Each industry is likely to have a different mix of transaction structures in production and support, exchange preparation, and exchange completion. Careful thought must be given to what information should be disclosed and to whom. Most e-commerce opportunities are created either by targeting deficiencies in existing transaction structures, or by developing wholly new structures oriented to new product characteristics and the stimulation of new business expectations. The range of possible strategies that could be adopted by a firm for exploiting these opportunities will be influenced strongly by the characteristics of its present transaction structure and by those of the companies with which it conducts commercial exchanges.

Characterization of businesses in terms of their basic transaction structures provides a framework for analysing the historical and current implications of the opportunistic, strategic, and evolutionary factors that are influencing the emergence of e-commerce. The transaction structures of some businesses will be found to be less flexible than others. Some trading environments will prove to be more transaction-rich than others. Traders will not embrace e-commerce with the intention of giving up advantages in the market that they enjoy already. This is as true for individual buyers and sellers as it is for firms and organizations in complex supply chains. Traders become proactive in implementing e-commerce because they perceive that it will confer advantages that might be unavailable, or not available to the same extent, in the conventional market-place. However, other traders implement e-commerce for reactive reasons. These can relate to conditions in individual contracts or to the growing intensity of information and communication technology use in new and established transaction structures. In some cases, greater intensity of use makes market participation all but impossible except via electronic media. In all cases, strategies revolve around minimizing loss of control over some transactions, while acquiring control and perhaps compensating for loss of control over others. Analysis of the transactions profile of a firm is significant in choosing whether to engage in e-commerce because it helps to define the range of complementarities and substitution possibilities that might be exploited strategically.

Having control, or at least degrees of control, over crucial transactions is one of the principal ways that buyers or sellers gain advantages in the marketplace (Mansell and

Jenkins, 1992*b*). Usually, customers have non-discriminatory access to common currencies or systems of weights and measures that are used to regulate specific aspects of the transaction process. These confer relatively symmetrical advantages on all market participants. Other advantages can be highly asymmetrical, however. These usually involve high entry barriers sustained by factors like market concentration, technological dominance, or skill concentration. Most commercial situations fall somewhere between these extremes, but each transaction can present opportunities for both positive and negative control.

Control does not necessarily mean outright capture of the transaction via some kind of monopolistic/oligopolistic structure, although in some cases it can and does mean this. Control may also mean that suppliers and customers are able to co-determine the transaction, and to initiate, complete, or terminate the decision processes underlying the transaction on terms that are mutually favourable to them. Control can also include the option of establishing proxy arrangements whereby either the supplier or the customer agrees voluntarily to transfer control over the transaction point to a proxy who the customer or supplier believes will exercise control in the respective party's interest. These sorts of proxy arrangements provide a means for reintermediation to occur in ways that might benefit both suppliers and customers.

Before committing their firms to e-commerce, business strategists need to examine the existing and potential control implications of the technological change for each type of transaction. They need to consider the new symmetries or asymmetries e-commerce might encourage if its implementation widens the access to, or alters the process of, the transaction. They must determine where, and to what extent, e-commerce strategies fit into the transaction structures for both suppliers and customers and assess carefully the size and growth rate of the technology user-base for each type of transaction. Some transactions will be technologically stable and others will be unstable. Some points in the transaction structure will be locked in to proprietary technologies while others will involve closed user configurations. All of these factors are important for the viability of specific strategies in the use of e-commerce.

Above all, traders must assess the control profiles for managing the key transactions of those firms that provide e-commerce platforms, network facilities, software, and support services. Information and communication technology suppliers that begin involvement in product or service value chains as providers of enabling technology and network facilities can acquire degrees of control over various transactions. This might become prejudicial to the interests of traders at large for whom the ability to shape the access conditions and operational characteristics of certain transaction points is a vital business requirement.

The analysis in this chapter suggests strongly that no single form of e-commerce could, or should, be applied within every commercial environment. In particular, it suggests that e-commerce can never be defined as a monolithic entity in terms of transaction characteristics and technological features. Rather, e-commerce is a *process* involving mainly incremental changes in the ways organizations apply information and communication technologies in support of commerce. Within this process there is much variety and very different rates of development. Two policy implications flow from this analysis. First, certain technological and commercial principles must be established for ensuring that traders can maintain levels of control over transaction structures that are reasonable and commensurate with consumer and citizen interests. Second, the scope for technical and policy harmonization in this environment may be more constrained than is often supposed.

5.5 E-Commerce in Europe: The Policy Challenge

The current policy problems in e-commerce are diverse and highly complex. Most of our understanding of the role of information and communication technologies in commerce has been gained from observing closed user groups. As the spectrum of users becomes wider and the network environment more open, the need for appropriate policies is increasing. The policy challenge in Europe is to create a synthesis between governance of the electronic networking environment, which includes stimulation of technological development and deployment, and governance of the commercial environment. The two are joined in e-commerce, but they are not necessarily the same.

Most policy discussions are articulated in terms of the challenge of ensuring that European firms do not lose out in the e-commerce revolution and in terms of how to co-ordinate the various public and private institutions of political, market, and technological governance to this end. The belief is that, in order to prevent domestic industry from being severely disadvantaged in home and foreign markets, governments must enter a race to build an e-commerce infrastructure comprising technological and policy elements. Most of these 'losing out' arguments are based on assumptions that e-commerce will generate many, predominantly positive, micro and macro economic outcomes. In fact, on the basis of current knowledge, the implications of e-commerce for employment, market restructuring, pricing, consumer behaviour, industrial organization and development, and sociocultural dynamics are very difficult to demonstrate qualitatively or quantitatively at either the micro or macro levels (Hawkins, Mansell, and Steinmueller, 1997).

The European Commission's efforts to find an appropriate scale and focus for policy action for e-commerce were presented in its 1997 initiative for e-commerce (European Commission, 1997d). This called for an extensive effort to co-ordinate measures to ensure that Europe is not left behind in the race to introduce e-commerce in a wide variety of business sectors. This agenda portrayed e-commerce in rather monolithic terms, that is, as a definable state to be achieved or as an existing state that required a co-ordinated reaction. But to what is this a reaction? The Ministerial declaration following an OECD meeting in October 1998 emphasized the necessity of 'supporting and encouraging the development of effective market-driven self-regulatory mechanisms that include input from consumer representatives, and contain specific, substantive rules for dispute resolution and compliance mechanisms . . . [and] encouraging the development of technology also as a tool to protect consumers' (OECD, 1998*b*: 2). It is difficult to separate aims such as these from the general objective of extending ordinary rules of commerce to the e-commerce environment.

By November 1998, the European Commission had presented its draft proposal for a new directive on the legal aspects of e-commerce (European Commission, 1998*l*), noting that there was already divergent legislation either in place or being discussed within the Member States of the Union. A major consideration of the legislation is the role of e-commerce as a substantial asset for the internal market. The potential benefits of rapid expansion of e-commerce are seen as being the ability to 'bring together the peoples of Europe, promote trade between them and increase knowledge of their cultural diversity' (ibid. 6). These objectives are rather close to the general aim of promoting the European information society vision and it may simply be that e-commerce is seen as a necessary facet of a complete vision. The deployment of the new services is expected to bring benefits for consumers and citizens in the form of increased access to better quality goods and services and to encourage investment and the growth of European enterprises. A major benefit is also expected in terms of employment.

Even if it is not possible to estimate the total number of people currently employed in e-commerce activities, these activities offer a true employment potential. For example, according to recent estimations more than 400,000 information society related jobs were created within the Community between 1995 and 1997. It is estimated that one in four new jobs is derived from these activities; that there are 500,000 unfilled vacancies requiring information society skills and that 60 per cent of these are in SMEs seeking to develop their electronic commerce activities (ibid.).

Like the 1993 White Paper on growth, competitiveness, and employment (European Commission, 1993*b*) that provided the starting-point for our investigation of the European visions and pathways towards the information society, the proposed e-commerce directive is strongly motivated by the challenge to create improved conditions for the economic and social development of Europe. In the intervening years, the vision continues to be articulated in terms of the potential benefits of information and communication technologies.

The relatively modest scale of serious research on the changing nature of e-commerce is a basis for concern about whether its promises can be delivered. It is even more difficult to develop e-commerce as a part of the European information society vision that is 'designed for all' than it is to ensure that the World Wide Web serves as a social, cultural, and education resource for all. Some countries in Europe appear to be reaping considerable benefits from the application of information and communication technologies while others are falling behind. In addition, European firms and citizens have not (yet) expressed the same levels of enthusiasm for using the Internet and related information and communication technology applications as their counterparts in the United States.

Internet-based e-commerce in the European Union is occurring at lower volumes than in the United States. This may begin to change, however, as European regulatory reforms provide a basis for the introduction of the same kinds of network access as exist in the United States. One lesson to be learned from experience with the Internet so far is that it can spread very quickly if network access conditions and tariffs are favourable (Paltridge, 1996). In addition, the current level of Internet penetration and usage in Europe is not necessarily a long-term disadvantage. It may even be an advantage. Throughout the history of e-commerce, users have played an important role in its technical as well as its organizational configuration. Given the asymmetries between the information and communication technology production profiles of Europe, the United States, and Japan, ensuring that e-commerce develops through user-led initiatives could be a source of advantage for European technology producers as well as for European traders. These developments are less likely to result from an exclusive focus on 'generic' policies favouring the growth of e-commerce.

Relative to the United States and Japan, the European position is least asymmetrical when it comes to the configuration and application of computing products and networks. We do not suggest that areas, such as component design and manufacture, are unimportant for Europe. A more effective way forward for European suppliers and users of e-commerce facilities, however, may be in developing superior customer solutions and services for citizens that are geared to the dynamics of specific European markets and social orders. While the American model suggests that the 'virtualization' of industrial markets is a matter of individual company initiative, a European strategy may involve supporting the role of industrial associations in ways that lead to broader participation of smaller organizations in e-commerce initiatives. Achieving these objectives may require very substantial efforts to encourage developments in e-commerce based upon targeted policies. For example, the appellation system that has proved to be a major benefit in creating differentiated markets in the food and beverage industry can achieve a place in the e-commerce world, but this creates the need to solve important supplier co-ordination problems. Not only is the European environment diverse in terms of industrial and agricultural activity, but it is diverse culturally and linguistically as well. The development of effective marketing arrangements for cultural and entertainment products, for example, may require policies that encourage investment in promoting and distributing materials with European content.

E-commerce is not a state but a process. The process is unfolding at different rates and in different ways within a variety of commercial structures. Many of the 'new' obstacles for policy may not be obstacles at all, or they may not be unique to e-commerce. One benefit of the detailed examination of the implications of e-commerce is to draw attention to problems that exist in more traditional market environments. In practice, rather fewer of the issues in the economic, political, and social governance of networks or commerce are tied uniquely to e-commerce, although e-commerce provides many examples of the possible consequences of different policy choices. In many cases, e-commerce may expedite policy actions that would have been beneficial in non-electronic contexts. Issues such as consumer protection, taxation, and privacy of personal data fall into these categories, as do issues of access to network facilities.

Most of the governance problems apply across the board to all information and communication systems. Electronic traders are only one of the many interest groups that will benefit from a general regulatory framework that ensures a reasonably open network environment in Europe. The responsibility of policy-makers should be to ensure that the public interest in these developments is clarified. There is no reason to expect that a workable interpretation of the public interest will coincide with that favoured by the promoters of e-commerce to any greater degree in the electronic market-place than would be expected in a conventional physical market. There is a risk that by concentrating on the technology and network dynamics of e-commerce, the fact that this is essentially an evolving commercial environment, which must be treated accordingly, will be lost from view. The focus for e-commerce policy should be on commercial governance issues and on encouraging existing and emerging trading communities to develop applications that support their specific tactical and strategic objectives. The policy environment should also encourage experimentation with new commercial models in an electronic market-place, as well as learning such that transferable e-commerce competencies develop in as many areas as possible.

Most commercial governance is related in some way to establishing and maintaining trust and confidence in the market system. Markets are approached by traders according to the degree of trust and confidence that is invested in them. If e-commerce is to expand, its participants will need to have at least the same level of trust and confidence in the electronic marketplace as they have in the conventional marketplace. They must have assurances that electronically-traded products are fit for their intended use, that market facilities are open, flexible, secure, and reliable, and that the public and private institutions of commercial governance that underpin public trust in the market system will not be compromised.

Some trust and confidence problems are essentially technological. They centre on such questions as, 'Will the system function?' No e-commerce system will be acceptable that does not employ reliable network technologies and standards, provide adequate network management capabilities, and guarantee acceptable levels of security. However, most trust and confidence problems are social, political, and economic in origin. They focus on such questions as, 'Who can access and use the system under what conditions?' or 'What happens when a transaction goes wrong?' Providing assurances in this context requires a high degree of socialization for e-commerce, built up in buyer and seller constituencies over time through familiarity and skills-building, and supported by procedures or legislation that define and limit risk and liability.

5.6   Conclusion

This chapter has focused on the potential of e-commerce to support the development of the information and communication infrastructure of the information society. A central concern expressed throughout our analysis is that the enthusiasm about e-commerce developments is being transformed into a set of expectations that may prove difficult to meet. In particular, e-commerce does not appear to be a panacea for developing consumer interest in the information and communication infrastructure. The idea that e-commerce will lead to a rapid and large-scale transformation of industrial markets in favour of more open purchasing arrangements and a higher degree of effective competition is equally troublesome. The new possibilities opened through the use of the Internet for commercially related purposes are potentially revolution-ary. However, this revolution is likely to have its greatest influence for some time to come on areas of the transactions structure related to advertising and other means of identifying the qualities of goods and services. Long before e-commerce brings sub-stantial benefits to the processes of selling and distributing goods and services, it will influence how businesses conduct their exchanges with one another within established trading communities in important ways. Many of these influences will not follow the model of increasing openness and transparency in commercial relationships. Instead, they will involve strategic efforts to further differentiate product and service markets and to gain control of key interactions in ways that will justify the costs of investing in e-commerce by already established and strong market players.

The process of building trust and confidence among a critical mass of potential e-commerce users calls for careful assessment and review of commercial policy. Policy actions will be required to encourage the openness of the electronic market-place. It is very unlikely that this openness will evolve smoothly through market competition. Even though large-scale applications of e-commerce are becoming less expensive to implement, the costs of maintaining and servicing the trading networks created by these applications are substantial. Buyers and sellers must perceive that they can retain a degree of choice, and in this case, choice refers to more than a profusion of goods and services. It refers to the choice of price, vendor, and conditions of sale and delivery. Most consumer protection issues fall into this arena. Policy in this area requires ongoing assessment of potentially new barriers to market entry due to the increasingly closed character of many electronic business structures.

The central proposition that we have advanced in support of these observations is that the process of developing e-commerce markets is an evolutionary one involving the accumulation of learning and experience in the construction of trading commu-nities. The fact that a revolutionary technology is available to conduct commercial transactions is far less important than are the problems of reshaping organizational customs and practices and institutional rules and norms to take advantage of these possibilities. We have argued that the spread of e-commerce is an incremental process subject to many of the same problems that face any new market development. E-commerce is not a 'state' that a society can achieve in a single step but rather a process that involves substantial adjustment and transformation. This process is subject to the same problems that any other market faces, including the difficulties of achieving trust and reliability, and the potential detours arising from efforts to capture market control and power.

Monitoring technical and commercial standards that have a bearing on the build-up of trust and confidence in electronic transactions is a major issue where the pro-active involvement of government will be necessary. Market participants must be able to access and negotiate the electronic marketplace without becoming locked into pro-prietary trading environments or being subject to discriminatory commercial prac-tices. The nominal openness of a networking environment such as the Internet does not translate automatically into an open environment for e-commerce. Internet trans-actions take place within specialized environments that employ interfaces, platforms, applications, and services that often are neither compatible nor inter-operable. This is complicated by a large and growing array of proprietary and non-proprietary networking products and standards of various descriptions. If the Internet marketplace fragments into clusters of closed markets, each bounded by incompatible technologies, the overall diffusion of this new form of trading will be slowed.

Efforts to make e-commerce a central process in information society developments have been centred so far on the need for generic commercial rules and standards to encourage entrepreneurial initiative. There is nothing wrong, *per se*, with these efforts, as they are, indeed, prerequisites for the effective development of e-commerce. It is, however, questionable whether efforts that are completely general will suffice to produce an e-commerce structure that reflects the diversity and variety that are features of the non-virtual European commercial environment. Specific promotion of industrial, commercial, regional, and other aspects of economic and social life are likely to be necessary if the high expectations with regard to e-commerce developments are to be realized in Europe.

The technology base in this field is extremely dynamic and it is particularly difficult for public research to achieve results that will have a significant influence over commercial technological developments. A considerable role for publicly funded research does exist, however, as a means of establishing networks of knowledge creation and transfer. Substantial experience in trading networks already exists in larger organizations and there are numerous reasons to adapt and upgrade this knowledge for use in the Internet environment. The need to do so in large organizations is considerable, but it is likely to be particularly acute in smaller organizations, including industrial and regional associations. In order to allow room for experimentation with new kinds of e-commerce applications, especially in areas where Europe is at an advantage, policy action should concentrate on defining the key commercial transaction interfaces and promoting their openness, rather than relying on the outcomes of industry standardization to accomplish this. Policy should concentrate on defining rules for ensuring that essential interfaces between e-commerce platforms, both hardware and software, are open to all, rather than seeking to reduce the number of platforms as such, or defining their technical and operational features.

Neither the 'electronic buyer' nor the 'electronic customer' is the typical buyer or customer at present. For them to become typical, much social learning and adjustment will be required within a larger cross-section of consumers. E-commerce skills are both technical and social. Some apply to the training of workers for the e-commerce workplace. It is very important, however, for buyers and sellers to accumulate the skills for negotiating e-commerce environments. This will involve new understandings of the processes of gathering and applying market information and carrying out transactions. A role for policy in this area is to address access deficits not only to facilities, but also to appropriate skills and training.

Promoting a more rapid rate of consumer participation in e-commerce raises a number of problems with regard to exclusion and access. It is certainly the case that many affluent individuals who are currently deriving benefits will derive even more benefits in the future from the extension of business-to-consumer commerce.

Whether these benefits can be extended more broadly, however, will depend upon the issues of access and inclusion that were examined in Ch. 2. As access is broadened and extended, a range of institutional and policy issues will become increasingly pertinent. In particular, issues related to intellectual property, which will be examined in Ch. 7, and issues of privacy and security, in Ch. 8, will be of critical importance.

Our principal conclusion is negative with respect to the near-term role of e-commerce as a primary force for supporting the extension of the information and communication infrastructure. Nevertheless, e-commerce will be a major influence on commercial activities throughout Europe. These influences will be greatest in business-to-business interactions for some time to come. During the period of experimentation and development needed to create a larger role for business-to-consumer e-commerce and to extend and articulate commercial trading networks more fully, government policy and company practices will have a major role in shaping the character of e-commerce in Europe. If present 'generic' policies are pursued, it is likely that patterns of market dominance that exist in current market structures will be reproduced in the e-commerce environment. If, on the other hand, more attention is devoted to opportunities to alter and extend the transaction structures and to open these structures to a greater range of the commercial exchanges, we may expect a richer and more competitively healthy environment to emerge.

6

Liberalization and the Process and Implications of Standardization

R. Hawkins, R. Mansell, and W. E. Steinmueller

6.1 Introduction

An information society that encourages broad participation and the effective use of information and communication technologies requires an appropriate set of regulations, legislation, and agreements. These comprise one component of the institutional framework. Other components of the institutional framework include the policy-making bodies that craft the regulations and laws and the industrial and social associations that establish the agreements underlying the construction of markets and organizations. In the next three chapters we examine these components of the institutional framework as they influence a series of issues including the governance of market liberalization, universal access, and technical standards (this chapter), intellectual property rights (Ch. 7), and privacy and security (Ch. 8). Our analysis is based upon a simplified account of institutionalized action in which we do not attempt to capture processes such as representation, negotiation, and closure that have been used by other authors to examine the outcomes of government and inter-organizational decision-making processes.[1] Instead, we are interested in the extent of alignment or misalignment of current institutional arrangements as they bear upon the issues that we analyse. Our assumption is that fundamental misalignment will provoke change, but our purpose is limited to outlining the direction of the changes needed rather than speculating upon specifically how such changes may be brought about.[2]

The institutional framework governing the construction and operation of the information and communication infrastructure is as important as the market and technological dynamics discussed in the previous three chapters. The issues that we highlight are, however, all ones where economic and technological as well as institutional considerations are important. What differentiates the issues dealt with in these three chapters from those raised in the previous three chapters is the latitude of insti-

---

Section 4 of this chapter is based on original research on standardization by Richard Hawkins, see Hawkins (1997*b*; 1998*b*) and modified to complement the argument of the authors of this book. The other sections of this chapter are the responsibility of the authors.

[1] See Schmidt and Werle (1998) for an example of this approach in the standards field, and more generally Bijker and Law (1992); Jasanoff (1987); and MacKenzie (1992) for other areas.

[2] The concept of misalignment is central to detailed and systematic research on the specific processes through which these kinds of changes do come about, see e.g. Molina (1995). This methodology was not employed in our work.

tutionalized action in relation to the actions of individuals and enterprises. While many of the developments described in the previous three chapters can be traced to the first issue that is discussed in this chapter, market liberalization, the decision to liberalize was sufficient to set in motion most of these developments. Liberalization provided a basis for the insurgent strategy to emerge as a rival to the incumbent strategy. Liberalization is also responsible for the outcome that virtual community interests cannot readily negotiate their agenda with a fixed group of incumbent players who are required to take social aspirations and interests into account. The implication is that the European information society would be simpler and offer a more straightforward basis for the negotiation of social interests without liberalization. While this may be true, the consequences of failing to liberalize would have been, in our view, disastrous for Europe's competitive standing in global markets and for the realization of many of the other potential benefits of technological progress in information and communication technologies.

Once the decision to liberalize is taken, however, many more developments than those discussed in the previous three chapters are set in motion. Liberalization involves the transformation, rather than the elimination, of regulation if its original intentions are to be realized. The specific regulatory issues that come to the fore in a liberalized communication industry are those of interconnection, interoperability, and the necessary new arrangements to reconcile a liberalized market structure with the social goal of achieving widespread access to information and communication services. These issues require a new regulatory framework that we will examine in this chapter, beginning with a recapitulation of some of the main goals and purposes of liberalization.

Two themes have been central to the European efforts to achieve the construction of an information and communication infrastructure. The first is the principle of market liberalization for communication services, which is expected to bring new players and a greater impetus to innovation within the information and communication sector. The second theme is the implementation of the 'vision' of social solidarity as a key component of the European information society. The first provides the basis for the governance of interconnection and interoperability while the second is the foundation for considering new arrangements for reconciling a liberalized market structure with the social objective of widespread access to the information and communication infrastructure.

Market liberalization in the telecommunication sector is, in the first instance, an extension of the principle of the single market to the telecommunication field. By abolishing special and exclusive rights for public telecommunication operators in national markets, the liberalization process opens possibilities for competitive entry in the supply of infrastructure and services. The prospects for entry are being influenced, however, by the nature and conduct of the regulatory process that replaces the former systems of administrative oversight of the public telecommunication operators. Without a regulatory process that supports equitable access by entrants to interconnection with the existing telecommunication infrastructure and that discourages the potential abuse of existing market positions, liberalization measures will not achieve the aims of encouraging innovation and competition, at least not to the extent envisaged by many policy-makers. More broadly, the liberalization of markets has been extended to the cable television industry and the audiovisual sector. The twin goals of liberalization in these sectors have been to stimulate competition between alternative service delivery networks and encourage content production, especially in the area of interactive multimedia products, in ways that are responsive to Europe's cultural and social aspirations and that will be competitive in world markets.

The second theme in the European movement to construct a common information and communication infrastructure is the implementation of the 'vision' of social solidarity as a key component of the European information society. Social solidarity implies that applications of the new technologies should take into account, and respond to, the aim of inclusion, and resist trends or outcomes that would result in exclusion. There are of course alternative views. One is that any effort to support social solidarity risks substantially reducing the pace of change that it is believed is bringing benefits to all, albeit more directly and quickly to some than to others. A second is that the active competition resulting from liberalization will allow everyone to take part in the information society. In Europe, there is very little regulation of sales of commodities, such as potatoes, and few individuals are excluded from this market.[3] Why should we be concerned about regulating the market for the commodity information and communication infrastructure services? In other words, some believe that social solidarity is a basic principle, others view it as having costs as well as benefits, and still others believe that it is an incidental issue. These views are reflected in discussions about the appropriate source of any initiative to build the information and communication infrastructure.

There is a strong commitment to the view that 'liberalisation of telecommunications markets, within the agreed timetable, *will stimulate [the] private and public investment* necessary for the development of the information society in Europe' (European Commission, 1996*f*: 1, emphasis added), and to ensuring that regulation does not slow the innovation process or the diffusion of new information and communication technologies and services. The European Commission, however, does suggest that the role of market leadership should adhere to a particular performance standard: 'For Europe to meet the challenges presented by this information society it is vital to ensure that business, industry and Europe's citizen's can *access* modern, affordable and efficient communications infrastructures over which a rich and diverse range of traditional and new multimedia services will be offered. This revolution has been recognized at the highest political level' (European Commission, 1995*g*: 2–3). Behind this commitment to a market-led approach is a range of views with respect to how market liberalization will produce this outcome. Reflecting their disparate interests in the diffusion of new services, suppliers and users give different emphasis to market-led versus public-policy-led initiatives. For example, those who promote the 'private goods' interpretation of the market for information and communication tech-

---

[3] There are, of course, substantial regulatory issues regarding the *production* of potatoes and the sale of foods, including potatoes, is regulated by standards with regard to health and safety.

nologies and services stress the voluntary actions of private network operators and information service suppliers. Others adhere to a 'public goods' interpretation emphasizing the geographical and demographic extension of the information and communication infrastructure, voice telephony, and a small number of additional services. A third group of suppliers and users promote what might be termed a 'merit goods' approach. This approach is promoted by those who seek to encourage broader access to new information and communication services for public institutions such as schools, libraries, hospitals, government agencies, and museums.

These different views are expressed when specific issues, such as the timing, nature, and costs of access are discussed, and the extent to which infrastructure development is associated with goals such as universal or open access. Differences in these views arise from the emphasis that is given to ensuring that market liberalization produces gains in terms of European competitiveness in the supply of infrastructure and services and to social concerns. Advocates of an exclusive focus on the market tend to assume that competition will reduce the price of access to advanced information and communication services to levels where the gaps between information 'haves' and 'have-nots' can be addressed by public actions targeted specifically at the excluded groups. However, substantial gaps in the accessibility of new services already exist and are likely to continue due to the increasingly widespread access to advanced services by professional people in their business, academic, and government settings. Such groups are building the European information society in ways that are responsive to their interests and preferences. It would not be surprising if other segments of society expressed indifference or resistance when they are later admitted to the information society having had little, if any, opportunity to play a role in developing the systems and services that support it.

Parallel to debates about the need for a greater or lesser emphasis on market-led approaches there has been ongoing discussion about the need for a European Union-wide regulatory agency or agencies covering telecommunication matters and developments in the audiovisual sphere.[4] Apart from the legal form of such an agency, the benefits and disadvantages of embracing carriage and content issues within a single regulatory organization, and issues of subsidiarity, there is debate about the need for sector-specific regulation versus 'regulation' by reference to competition policy.

The diversity of markets within the European Union and the continuing market dominance by some of the larger firms in the telecommunication and audiovisual sectors suggest that competition policy is likely to be an important policy instrument. How it should be applied is, however, controversial. Some would argue that the larger companies are best positioned to resist the insurgent strategies of US-owned companies and preserve a strong European presence in this field. Others argue that this path leads to a strengthening of the incumbent strategy that will reduce the diversity and variety, and ultimately the competitiveness, of the telecommunication and audiovisual sectors. We are among those who argue for the second viewpoint, not because

---

[4] NERA and Denton Hall (1997) provided a comprehensive analysis of the options and this theme is present in the review of telecommunication markets that was initiated in 1999.

of a blind faith in competition, but for two other reasons. First, our concern is that a policy of strengthening the incumbent position will have deleterious implications for the virtual community interests and initiatives. Second, we believe it is likely that firms in the telecommunication and audiovisual sectors with incumbent strategies would fail to invest the gains from a stronger position in innovation.

In this chapter we briefly summarize some of the features of the evolving policy and regulatory framework for information and communication services and networks. The measures aimed at achieving universal access in support of the social solidarity component of the European information society receive particular attention. In addition, the implications of regulatory measures and legislation aimed at strengthening the role of competition in both the telecommunication and audiovisual markets of Europe are considered. In the latter case, we focus on the importance of standards in establishing a basis for the interoperability of services, the interconnection of networks, and widespread diffusion of new technologies and services. This discussion provides the foundation for the detailed case study of how standardization processes are contributing to the emergence of new technology clusters. In some cases, these emergent clusters are in line with the interests of European firms and give rise to systems and services that favour interoperability and interconnection. In others, however, they are inconsistent with efforts to ensure that virtual community strategies are represented within the decision-making processes that lead to the design and implementation of the network infrastructure and content that Europeans will access in the information society.

6.2   The Two Faces of Market Liberalization

The liberalization of the telecommunication market was initiated formally with the 1987 Green Paper on Telecommunications.[5] The European Commission's initial move preserved the public telecommunication operators' monopoly on infrastructure and basic service provision and addressed the requirements of large business users by introducing competition into the markets for value-added services and terminal equipment. The liberalization of the equipment and services markets and public procurement was followed by measures culminating in the full-scale opening of the telecommunication market in most Member States in January 1998.[6]

Thus, one of the faces of the liberalization era is a new regime of regulation aimed at ensuring that competitive entry occurs in all segments of the market (European Commission, 1998c). By early 1998, most of the necessary legislative framework for the new regime was in place. The Commission took the view that it was being applied in a way that would stimulate the development of a market for telecommunication

---

[5] See European Commission (1987). Earlier recognition of the importance of the sector was reflected in European Commission (1983), see also European Commission (1988a).

[6] See European Commission (1988a; 1990a); European Council (1992c; 1993c). The Green Paper (Part 1) (European Commission, 1994b) led to the liberalization of the cable industry (European Commission, 1995a).

services valued at about 141,000 mecu and growing at about 8.2 per cent per year (European Commission, 1998*n*).

A key step in establishing effective competition in the telecommunication market is related to ensuring open access to public networks and to abolishing discriminatory and unfair restrictions on network access and usage. The Framework Directive on Open Network Provision (ONP) provided the regulatory means to allow competitive and fair use of the network infrastructure for competing operators. It also sought to harmonize the conditions for open and efficient access to, and use of, public telecommunication networks and certain public telecommunication services (European Council, 1990). This legislation was aimed at establishing a transparent regulatory environment by ensuring the harmonization of the conditions under which technical interfaces between networks, interconnection of networks, interoperability of services, and pricing schemes are introduced in Europe.[7]

The second face of market liberalization is revealed in efforts to ensure that the social and cultural potential of the information society is realized. Thoughts about meeting this goal are entangled with the widespread consensus, in some countries reached only relatively recently, that there are major social benefits in the universality of voice telephony services. Whether universal service definitions should be extended to other services such as Internet access or universal 'access' to certain types of information are problematic issues that have yet to be resolved.

Even with regard to telephony, there are still concerns that 'universal' service provision is not as inclusive as the term would suggest. In all the Member States of Europe there are people who are excluded from accessing and using basic telephone services. Their exclusion is due to factors including poverty and the rise in the larger cities of an underclass comprised of some lone parents, immigrants, manual workers, young people, or drop-outs (Murroni, 1996; Office of Telecommunications, 1994). Thus, even for basic telephony services, the problem of eliminating the gap between those who are included and those who are excluded from this community of users is difficult to address. The liberalization of telecommunication markets has been accompanied by adoption of formal definitions of universal service provision for those operators that are charged with this responsibility as a condition of their licences.[8] The Council resolution on universal service, for example, calls for 'access to a defined minimum service of specified quality to all users everywhere, and in the light of specific national conditions, at an affordable price' (European Commission, 1994*d*: 1–2).[9]

---

[7] For details of the Open Network Provision rules see European Commission (1995*j*; 1996*p*; 1997*b*; 1997*i*; 1998*b*) and European Council (1990; 1992*a*).

[8] See European Commission (1993*a*; 1994*a*; 1994*d*); and European Council (1994).

[9] Where universal service obligations have been defined explicitly, the definitions generally include some or all of the following elements: general principles, such as access to information/communication as a basic right, universal geographical availability, non-discriminatory access, reasonable costs/affordability, universal service quality. The services included in a universal service obligation are generally voice telephony, public phone booths, directory enquiries, free emergency calls, touch-tone telephones, special facilities for the handicapped; with an enforcement mechanism setting out the organization and financing of universal service (general taxation, levies on users or contributions from operators) (OECD, 1995).

In the liberalized environment in which incumbent telecommunication operators face competitive entry by infrastructure and service providers, they will have incentives to seek definitions of universal service that minimize the costs that must be borne by them to upgrade network facilities in markets where they face effective competition.[10] In those markets where they retain substantial market power there will be incentives unevenly to assign more of the costs attributed to network modernization to users and to seek new definitions of universal service that include new service features in order to strengthen their incumbency position. New entrants face the prospect of costly universal service obligations that, in themselves, do not improve the viability of business plans. They will generally seek to minimize the costs associated with any specification of universal service objectives and, in some cases, such as the introduction of Internet telephony or the entry of Internet Service Providers (ISPs), the claim will be made that new entrants are not providing a 'telecommunication' service.[11]

Although in Europe it is recognized that changes in technology and in demand characteristics may result in a redefinition of universal service over time,[12] most policy discussions stress the geographical dimension of universal service or access and the physical access problems of the disabled. They pay little attention to income, class, and other status factors that are associated with whether individuals have access to telecommunication networks. Market liberalization is creating stresses and strains in the mechanisms that historically have governed public telecommunication operator strategies. National regulators, such as the Office of Telecommunication in the United Kingdom, have recognized the value of an extended concept of universal access: 'It may be that the overall public interest, in economic and social terms, is best served by ensuring a higher level of service available and affordable to educational establishments, such as schools, and maybe also other "public service" customers' (Office of Telecommunications, 1995a: 22).

The benefits of *new* kinds of universal service provision through the active promotion of the delivery of certain higher-capacity services at public access points

[10] In Europe there have been efforts to investigate the costs and revenues associated with the categories of services offered by public telecommunication operators. Special attention has focused on the costs of the local access network and use of the local and long distance portions of networks (Analysys Ltd., 1995a; 1995b; European Commission, 1995j; Office of Telecommunications, 1995a).

[11] In Europe and the United States the provision of Internet Telephony service has been deemed for the purpose of regulation not to be a telecommunication service. In addition, where universal service funding has been sought by levying a charge against service providers licensed to provide public telecommunication service with a universal service obligation, new entrants offering value added services have been excluded from this obligation. This is also the case with new market entrants offering telecommunication services until they achieve a specified market share (European Commission, 1996j). In the United States, enhanced service providers including Internet Service and Access Providers have argued that they should not be subject to any levy to contribute to universal service funds, see e.g. Federal Communications Commission (1999a; 1999d; 1999f) and Oxman (1999).

[12] The main elements of universal service provision in the European Union currently include: the provision of basic service and improved quality of service; cost-oriented tariff principles and pricing flexibility; dispute resolution mechanisms; and special public service features (operator assistance and emergency services) (European Commission, 1993a).

such as schools and libraries, are also under consideration (European Commission, 1994*e*). Under the existing definition of universal service, the costs of provision for operators have not been particularly burdensome. Although there is substantial discussion about the need for a broad political commitment to social cohesion, safeguarding the rights of citizens to communicate, and protecting consumers via legislation and other actions, there is little evidence of the sustained investment that would be necessary to achieve this goal (Graham *et al.*, 1996). Unless a new definition is provided that incorporates more broadly based access to advanced networks and services, it is unlikely that new measures will be taken to extend access to those who are unable to afford the costs of equipment, training, or network use in the information society.[13]

Until recently in the United States, policy initiatives focused on increasing telephone penetration levels in economically depressed areas using a variety of policies designed to offer discounted service packages.[14] With the passage of the Telecommunications Act of 1996,[15] the universal service goal was extended to provide support for eligible schools and libraries by facilitating the deployment of advanced technologies. The contributions to a fund for this purpose are based on carrier end-user telecommunication revenues and administered by the Universal Service Administrative Company (USAC).[16]

The 1996 Act also required that progress towards the availability of advanced telecommunication capability be monitored.[17] In early 1999, the Federal Communications Commission (FCC) (1999*e*: 5) reported that 'we are encouraged that deploy-

---

[13] There are several options for financing a newly defined universal access/service definition. They include: general taxation-supported access; the levying of access charges by incumbents on the interconnection of new entrants; a universal service fund using levies on customers and/or payments by the operators; virtual funds that rely on direct payments between the public telecommunication operator and universal service providers instead of transfers organized by a dedicated institution; government-supported voucher-based systems for certain groups of targeted users, e.g. low-income groups such as the elderly and the disabled; and competitive tendering for the obligation to provide universal service.

[14] The interpretation of universal service in the United States evolved from Theodore Vail's early vision for AT&T, which sought to maximize connectivity, into an interpretation that is more closely related to the maximization of the penetration of the potential market for particular telecommunication services for all customers (Mueller, 1997).

[15] United States Congress (1996) amended the Communications Act of 1934.

[16] The maximum that can be collected by the USAC for the 12-month period beginning July 1999 in support of schools and libraries was set at US$ 2.25b. and for rural health care the maximum was US$ 12m. In May 1998 it was estimated that US$ 2.02b. in discounts had been requested by applicants filing for school and library discounts for the first funding year for priority services (telecommunication service and Internet access). Assistance may be available for the most disadvantaged institutions (those eligible for 90% discounts on establishing connections) to make provisions for internal connection (Federal Communications Commission, 1999*c*). See also Federal Communications Commission (1998*a*; 1999*b*) and Oxman (1999). By 1998, it was estimated that 51% of American public school instructional rooms had Internet access based on a National Center for Education Statistics survey, see Oxman (ibid. 4).

[17] Advanced telecommunication capability was defined 'without regard to any transmission media or technology, as high-speed, switched, broadband telecommunications capability that enables users to originate and receive high-quality voice, data, graphics and video telecommunications using any technology' (Federal Communications Commission, 1999*e*: 3).

ment of advanced telecommunications generally appears, at present, reasonable and timely'. This view was based on the fact that some 375,000 residential consumers were purchasing broadband services and that many more had access to the capability. However, it was noted that this conclusion concerning the speed of diffusion was based on assumptions and predictions as well as on the assertions of companies which 'may not ultimately prove accurate' (ibid.).

The FCC has been pursuing what is described as an 'unregulation' policy with respect to the diffusion of advanced communication infrastructure and services. This means that Enhanced Service Providers (ESPs), including ISPs, are exempt from access charges or contributions to universal service funds.[18] In addition, users who dial up an ISP over the telecommunication network do not incur usage charges for the time they spend on-line, a factor that renders comparisons between the speed of diffusion of advanced information and communication services in Europe and the United States extremely difficult. In Europe, at least at the time of writing, all Internet users incurred usage costs for their use of the communication infrastructure either directly or indirectly.[19] By mid-1998, in the United States there were estimated to be some 6,000 ISPs offering dial-up service to the Internet and over 95 per cent of Americans had access to at least four local ISPs. At the same time, surveys indicated that no more than 25 per cent of households had adopted Internet access despite its availability, and that personal computer adoption did not exceed 45 per cent of households (Downes and Greenstein, 1998). This compares with the estimate of 30.8 per cent of adult Europeans in 1998 reporting that a personal computer was available in their home, which would suggest about 18 per cent of all European households have personal computers, assuming that there are 1.7 adults per household on average in Europe.[20] The smaller share of personal computer households is amplified by the lower tendency to connect the home personal computers to the Internet in Europe. In 1998, 8.3 per cent of all adult Europeans reported a connection of their home personal computer to the Internet and this would suggest that about 5 per cent

[18] Access charges are per-minute charges that interexchange carriers, i.e., the long-distance companies, pay to originate and terminate calls with local telephone companies. This view is consistent with decisions in the 1980s that found that there should be no regulation of enhanced services. In an order adopted in Feb. 1999, the FCC addressed issues of how local operating companies should be compensated for their role in delivering traffic to ISPs but made no changes in the decision that ISPs are engaged in providing enhanced services, see Federal Communications Commission (1999a; 1999d).

[19] At the time of writing it was expected that the first ISP to offer subscription-free and telecommunication usage-free access to the Internet would be launched in the UK before the end of 1999.

[20] The basis for this estimate is that in 1991, 29% of households in fifteen European Union Member States (excluding Spain and Italy for which no single-person household enumeration was available) were one person (assumed to be an adult) (Eurostat, 1995: 42). Of the remaining 71%, it is necessary to make a conjecture about the number of adults since there will be both single-parent households with children (but only one adult) and households with more than one adult. In addition, since 1991, the more recent year with a widespread population census, the number of single-person and single-parent households is very likely to have increased significantly. We estimate the average number of adults per household at 1.7 (which is $0.29 + 2 \times 0.71$) by assuming that the factors that would increase and decrease the estimate of the number of adults per household are equal in effect. The result, including the unfortunate exclusion of Spain and Italy (countries that are likely to have a higher than average number of adults per household), is likely to be an underestimate.

of European households were connected to the Internet. As stressed in Ch. 2, the penetration of personal computers and Internet connections varies considerably across Europe.[21]

Issues of universal service or access are not restricted to the telecommunication infrastructure and services market. Facilitating access to services and content is equally important in view of the expectations for the European information society. Given the emphasis on stimulating innovation and competition in the audiovisual markets (and future interactive multimedia services and electronic commerce), measures in this area are concerned with ensuring that customers are able to access and communicate with service suppliers of their choice. In addition, there is the intent that conditional access systems offering gateways to new information and audiovisual services should not inhibit competition.[22] This issue is becoming especially important as the number of channels and services multiplies with the deployment of digital broadcasting systems. Although principles for third party access to conditional access systems have been established by the Commission,[23] as Pauwels (1998) argues, the definition of what will be regarded as an anti-competitive restriction on access is subject to interpretation. In addition, the Commission has been slow to act to address the problems created by an increasingly concentrated audiovisual and content industry in Europe.

A regulatory regime is likely to be needed for some time to prevent the interactive services that are controlled by conditional access systems, the proprietary use of navigation systems such as Electronic Programme Guides (EPGs), or the proprietary implementation of software operating systems and their interfaces, for example, proprietary Application Programme Interfaces (APIs), from becoming a basis for anti-competitive strategies by vertically integrated content and information service suppliers. Cave and Cowie (1998) argue that the chain of supply for digital information includes content, packaging into channels, bundling of channels into packages, delivery, conditional access, reception, and revenue collection. By controlling multiple segments of this chain, there is potential for firms to act in ways that foreclose markets to competitive entry and to bias or restrict the choices available to consumers and citizens. On balance, however, Cave and Cowie suggest that competition law, rather than sector-specific regulation, will offer a more effective method of alleviating anti-competitive behaviour. Finally, Collins and Murroni's (1996) overview of the media policy arena in Europe, and Venturelli's (1998) more recent analysis, highlight in their different ways the ambiguity of policy and regulation in the audiovisual sphere. Policy-makers face a continuing dilemma about how best to ensure that firms in this sector contribute to the cultural and social aspects of the information society in

---

[21] See Table 2.4.

[22] Conditional access systems allow an operator to restrict which homes receive television channels or programmes and they are incorporated within Integrated-Receiver-Decoders (IRDs) providing a gateway to a range of new services that enable information delivery and various transactions, see Levy (1997) for a very useful discussion of the issues.

[23] See European Commission (1994c; 1995h; 1997a). The main legislation for the broadcasting sector is European Commission (1996g). For detailed analyses of the issues raised for the regulation of digital conditional access systems, see Cave and Cowie (1996; 1998); Levy (1997).

Europe and, at the same time, adopt strategies that will produce competitive enterprises on the world market.[24] A 1995 amendment to proposals for the use of standards for the transmission of digital television signals recognized the need for unbundling the prices for components of the new service platforms (European Commission, 1995*h*). Although this applies to conditional access for digital television services there is no detailed level of regulation such as that which is characteristic of the ONP directive in the telecommunication sector.

The paradox is that the advanced information and communication infrastructure and services give customers and citizens potentially greater control over the information being delivered in terms of timing, format, destination, and billing. However, the customer or citizen runs the risk of paying high access costs and being locked into packages of electronic services through conditional access systems (European Commission, 1995*d*). Lock-in strategies, regardless of whether they are adopted by incumbents or insurgent firms, create the potential for the exercise of market power in ways that could contravene the goal of open and competitive markets for advanced information and communication services. Some market power is inevitable in the emerging communication markets because of the costs of infrastructure construction and delays in customer movement between competing services and service providers. But the purchase of advanced information and communication services is not the same as purchasing potatoes. The extent of lock-in will depend upon the evolution of market structure and decisions taken with respect to the extent of access by regulatory authorities.

It is unclear whether the existing legislative framework for the telecommunication and audiovisual sectors is sufficiently comprehensive to enable it to address issues of market power under conditions where there is convergence of the broadcasting, telecommunication, computing, and publishing industries (Collins and Murroni, 1996). Some degree of market power in new markets is likely in the coming years as a result of dramatic consolidations in the ownership of content and distribution companies. Mergers and acquisitions, joint ventures, and strategic alliances are growing in number. Consolidations that limit entry in content provision have the potential to create market power in distribution markets where exclusive arrangements may prevail. The fact that concentrated content providers can squeeze distributors' profits will be of little solace if consumers must pay high costs for access to a limited range of service alternatives. Similarly, concentration in distribution achieved through consolidations has the potential to create barriers to distribution for the content providers.

Ultimately, all forms of information and communication services will be delivered using a mix of cable television, terrestrial and satellite broadcasting, and fixed and wireless technologies. As technologies converge and the boundaries between industry segments change, the potential for the exercise of market power will also change. Bottlenecks in the chain of relationships between information producer, network

---

[24] For a comprehensive analysis of some of these issues comparing the UK, the USA, and Sweden, see Lips, Frissen, and Prins (1998).

operator, and service application user can occur at any point in the production–consumption chain (Cave, 1994). Monitoring these bottlenecks through independent agencies responsible for each of the possible network technologies presents, at the very least, severe co-ordination problems.

If the official view of the European Commission were to be fully accepted, it might be imagined that the new regulatory regime, at least for telecommunication, would prove fully adequate to the challenges presented by the new market environments and by social policy concerns. As the then Commissioner Martin Bangemann put it in early 1998,

The signal going out to market players, consumers and the EU's trading partners under the WTO (World Trade Organization) agreement on telecoms, which came into force on 5 February, is first that a regulatory framework is in place which will ensure that markets develop to their full potential; second, that the system is working, with licences being issued and players entering the market; and third, that the national regulatory authorities provided for in the package are established and are taking steps at national level to ensure compliance. (European Commission, 1998*n*: 1)

There has been considerable debate in the political realm about the impact of the efforts directed at the liberalization of the telecommunication infrastructure itself, but as technical innovation and convergence have progressed, the contours of the information and communication infrastructure and services landscape have changed. The sites of actions on the part of suppliers that are likely to suppress competition in ways that run counter to the economic and social aspirations of policy for the information society have changed. They are now much more centrally focused on issues of interoperability, the need for open standards and interfaces, and the extent to which negotiated arrangements for the interconnection of network infrastructure will lead to the upgrading of the infrastructure in a way that supports access for all. Promoting competitiveness and the social or public interest goals for the European information society will require creative approaches to alleviate the new bottlenecks to full participation within the information society.

The debate in Europe sparked by the 'Convergence Green Paper' addressed many of these issues (European Commission, 1997*f*) and the overall results of the consultation process which was completed with the publication of the results in March 1999 are indicative of the very difficult issues that the European Commission will need to tackle (European Commission, 1999*c*). For example, on the issue of access to networks and gateway facilities, the Commission reported that:

New on-line service providers wanted regulated access to networks, whereas incumbent operators thought that such regulation would discourage investment in infrastructure. Traditional broadcasters called for open access to networks and gateways for the provision of digital television and other services. Many commentators feared that vertically-integrated operators might abuse their market power and control of access to one or more elements of the value chain in order to foreclose market entry by others. The divergence of views was illustrated by calls from some parties for detailed regulation of certain bottlenecks and from others for a lighter touch and a more flexible regulatory environment. . . . most commentators saw a continued, albeit transitional role for regulation as the convergence of technologies and markets leads to increased competition.   (ibid. 2)

At the time of writing, the Commission was planning to address reforms in the regulation of infrastructure and services as part of the overall 1999–2000 review of European Community telecommunication legislation and to address those relating to the regulation of content services through adjustments to existing legislation or the introduction of new measures. Overall, with regard to the access question, the Commission's summary of the views of commentators indicated that:

a balance would have to be struck to avoid the pitfalls of over-regulation while at the same time meeting legitimate public interest requirements and encouraging sustainable competition in the market-place; gateways, bottlenecks and essential facilities would need to be clearly defined, and decisions would need to be made as to which such bottlenecks or essential facilities will require sector specific regulation in addition to the standard application of competition law in order to realise stated policy objectives.   (ibid. 9)

The European Parliament's position calls for 'ONP-type open provision rules' and the application of the concept to 'network inter-connection in the audiovisual sector, service interoperability, conditional access and decoders, subscription management and network navigation systems' (ibid. 12). It is thus very likely that the Commission will move towards a more horizontal approach to regulation 'with a homogeneous treatment of all transport network infrastructure and associated services, irrespective of the nature of the services carried' (European Commission, 1999*f*: 1). With these issues at the forefront of European policy-making, it is crucial that alternative weightings of issues affecting the public interest, that is, the consumer and citizen interest, and those that affect the different interests of the stakeholders on the supply side of the industry be considered. Much has been, and will continue to be, written in this regard. Our approach in the following section is to consider the implications of a major shift in the definition of 'access' from the end-user's perspective. This is followed in the final section of this chapter by an analysis of why it is increasingly difficult to attain consensus and action at the European level for promoting the implementation of common interface standards between new services in the development of multimedia.

6.3   Promoting Open Access for Competitiveness and Social Inclusion

The implications of a European policy commitment to extend electronic mail and World Wide Web access on a universal basis would be substantial. A policy measure of this kind would signal that the information society is to include all citizens and would focus commitments aimed at the development of advanced information and communication services. It would place the issue of how widespread access to these services is to be achieved at the forefront of public consideration. It would focus attention on the economic costs and political challenges of implementing a policy that puts the social considerations of access to the information society on an equal footing with the economic considerations of competitiveness and the interests of technology and service producers in proprietary versus open networks.

A policy commitment to a universal electronic mail or e-mail service might be implemented initially by using existing institutions to enable access to terminals at libraries and other public facilities. Access could also be enhanced through the franchising of local delivery operators and use of the postal system to deliver incoming messages addressed to those without access to information terminals.[25] This form of universal access would involve large investments in infrastructure, but it would provide incentives for the extension of access.

Thinking through the implications of universal e-mail access helps to illustrate the range of issues that must be considered if early universal access to advanced information and communication services is to be pursued. First, it involves *assessing* access and, therefore, more intensive efforts to measure how and where access can be delivered. Second, it requires conventions or 'standards' to be established for identifying recipients that would be compatible with both electronic delivery and fallback systems.[26] Third, there would be a need for a delivery system of last resort that communicates messages to addressees.[27] Fourth, a business model for covering the costs of such a system would need to be devised, a process that might itself strengthen the foundations of electronic commerce. Implementing such a system could create incentives for small and medium-sized businesses such as cafés and news stands, to offer local residents a way of accessing and originating messages. This would expand the market for the sale, installation, and maintenance of publicly available information terminals that could be used to deliver additional services. The current approach to universal access defers the participation by many citizens in the advanced information and communication services environment until a common infrastructure is constructed and there has been very widespread adoption of the means of accessing these services. There are many ways, however, of accelerating the diffusion process so that broad participation is possible long before every home has a personal computer or other information appliance.

Many of the benefits of such an infrastructure will only be realized if the means to transfer information and interconnect its parts are effective and reliable. Providing these means involves addressing issues of both network interconnectivity and service interoperability. Interconnectivity is achieved when it is possible to transfer information between systems, although such transfers may involve the transformation of the content or format of the information. Interoperability indicates that information that

---

[25] It may be observed that writing and posting a letter is a far less cumbersome procedure than going to the post office to use a terminal to write the letter. This issue is heightened further if the only way that the recipient receives the message is on a print-out that would be as private as current practice for telegraphic services or photographic processing laboratories. The point is that using universal access as a means of co-ordinating incentives can lead to considerably richer and less cumbersome methods of access, both in sending and receiving messages, for the vast majority of users.

[26] No country has established such a standard despite the interesting possibilities it offers for postal authorities and others to deliver new types of services.

[27] It would be desirable at the outset to allow a broad array of message types, perhaps all those conforming to Multipurpose Internet Mail Extensions (MIME) standards, to be sent through the system but it would clearly be inappropriate to provide for delivery of all such messages.

may reside in one part of the telecommunication infrastructure can be transferred directly, without further complication, to another.[28] The achievement of some combination of interconnectivity and interoperability permits the construction of a common infrastructure rather than a piecemeal network and set of services in which specific communities of users are isolated from one another. The principal advantage of attaining a well-connected infrastructure and interoperable services is to maximize the possibilities for network externalities.[29]

A principal means of achieving network externalities in the information and communication infrastructure is the adoption of 'technical compatibility standards' (hereafter simply referred to as standards) that provide rules for interconnecting parts of the infrastructure (David and Greenstein, 1990). Producers of information and communication technologies face important strategic choices in determining the level of interconnectivity and interoperability of their products. A very high degree of interoperability may be a more suitable strategy for a firm with a relatively small market share that is seeking to make inroads against an incumbent. The incumbent, however, may have an incentive to differentiate its product from that of its competitors, preserving its market position against challengers. Users have an incentive, other things being equal, to prefer the highest available standard of interoperability to increase their freedom of choice and the range of potential suppliers. The result of these conflicting incentives is that the process of standards formation is complex. Similar conditions apply in the case of interconnectivity, although interconnectivity offers suppliers greater latitude for product differentiation and, depending upon market conditions, may not be viewed as a major problem for users.

Standards may be established through the creation of large market shares for particular implementations of a technology and this method of standard formation is said to result in *de facto* standards. Standards that are achieved through a process of deliberation are referred to as *de jure* standards (David, 1987; Schmidt and Werle, 1998; Sirbu, 1989). There are a large number of international standards-making organizations that enact *de jure* standards in the interests, and with the support, of producers and users.

Since the Green Paper on Telecommunication in 1987 (European Commission, 1987), European Union policy for standardization in the information and communication technology sector has assumed two main dimensions. The first is support for single market objectives with the goal of achieving an open market in the European Union Member States. This has required the harmonization and rationalization of technical regulations and standards, often by *de jure* processes. For telecommunication, the development of common European standards has been linked explicitly to

---

[28] These definitions are simplified for the purposes of the present discussion. In particular, interoperability has broader implications for the seamless quality of interconnection than is suggested here. See Putnam (1995) for a discussion on interconnection issues and see European Commission (1995j) for a discussion on issues raised by interoperability.

[29] See Ch. 3 for a definition and discussion of increase in the value of the network stemming from more users being connected and the effects this has on accelerating the diffusion of technology.

the liberalization of markets for telecommunication-related goods and services as we saw in the foregoing section.[30] Standards have been sought that will support an open network environment to enable all kinds of voice and data messages to flow unhindered throughout the Member States and there has been a strong emphasis on *de jure* standards that would support competitive entry.

The second is co-ordination of European Research, Technology, Development and Demonstration (RTD&D) in advanced information and communication technologies and related applications and services. Recognizing the need to encourage technical upgrading of the European information and communication infrastructure, the Commission has initiated collaborative industry programmes to develop new technologies and service applications. The results of these programmes have been fed into *de jure* standardization process and standards bodies, such as the European Telecommunication Standards Institute (ETSI) which has engaged in standardization projects that are RTD&D projects in all but name. The Global System for Mobile Communications (GSM) and Digital Enhanced Cordless Telephony (DECT) are two examples. Standards have functioned as vehicles for the co-ordination of RTD&D, the definition of a European technology base, and the marketing of European information and communication technology products and services.

In the case of the GSM standard for digital cellular telephony, the standard has been adopted widely beyond Europe. In the next section, we consider whether GSM was a special case that may not occur again. This involves assessing the significance of the imbalance between the relative strength of the European-owned telecommunication equipment sector, which is mostly oriented to public network equipment, and the relative weakness of the European-owned computer and data-networking sector.[31] The major competitive edge that European firms have on their United States and Japanese competitors is the creative use of the radio interface. This must be weighed against the relatively low profile of European firms in providing the video and computer platforms upon which interactive or multimedia applications depend.

Regulatory efforts to ensure interconnection and interoperability within an ONP framework, even when extended from telecommunication into the audiovisual sphere, will continue to be implemented at the Member State level. And because of the concern to emphasize a market-led approach, it is very likely that implementation will rest largely on negotiated agreements and settlements between commercial entities. Some of these firms will be adopting incumbent strategies while others seek to strengthen their competitiveness by adopting insurgent strategies. Ultimately, the decisions about when to move towards compatible standards in various components of the network infrastructure and associated services will reflect the manufacturers' and network operators' judgements about whether proprietary or open standards are in their respective interests. It is instructive, therefore, to form an understanding of not only how, but also by whom, such judgements are forged. In the next

---

[30] For a review of the changing modes of institutionalizing the standards-making process, see David and Shurmer (1996).

[31] See European Commission (1996*a*; 1996*c*; 1996*q*) and European Commission High Level Group of Experts (1997).

section, we illustrate the implications of alternative strategies by looking at the performance of the corporate stakeholders in Europe and the United States with respect to standards-making in key technology areas that will affect the convergent landscape in the future.

6.4 Emerging Technology Clusters for New Electronic Services

The information and communication technologies necessary for constructing a common information and communication infrastructure are, without exception, product or service components in some larger system. Technological change in these components requires the integration of new products and services into existing systems. The systemic interdependencies that require this integration are complex and it is often necessary to implement many changes in order to make progress towards the implementation of new technological possibilities.[32]

The enormous variety and substantial complexity of information and communication technologies ensure that there will almost always be more than one solution to a problem or approach to a new opportunity.[33] The need to integrate the implementation of new components with existing systems reduces, but does not eliminate, the variety of solutions that is generated by investment in the RTD&D process by private and public actors. To achieve market acceptance, substantial investment must be made in ensuring that new technologies and services will offer a complete and well-integrated solution to a problem or exploitation of an opportunity. This further reduces the number of technological solutions that are vying for acceptance. Even after these reductions, however, there are likely to be competing groups of technological solutions that we refer to as 'clusters'. Specific clusters will be supported by different firms according to their strategic objectives for the market and their commitment to incumbent, insurgent, and virtual community strategies. An analysis of new or 'emergent' clusters, provides a means of simplifying and organizing the vast amount of detailed observation about individual technologies. It also offers a way of assessing the likelihood that Europe will retain technological leadership in areas such as mobile technologies and services, or acquire leadership in emergent multimedia technologies. It is important to consider both the technical and institutional factors that create the conditions that will support, or impede, the formation of emergent clusters. In some cases, technologies that are complementary never cohere into a cluster, either because the co-ordination costs of cluster formation outweigh the economic potential of new service environments, or because there are disagreements between firms about how the service market should be exploited.

As part of the process of simplifying the technological variety associated with clusters it is useful to define three architectural levels within networks in which clusters

---

[32] The complex system features of these technologies have been examined by Davies (1996); Hughes (1987); Rosenberg (1976; 1994); Summerton (1994).

[33] It might be suggested facetiously that the number of solutions is likely to correspond closely to the number of engineers tasked with finding the solution or exploiting the opportunity.

may form. The lowest level is the *substructure* of networks, which defines how hardware devices establish, maintain, and correct errors in their use of the communication media. Standards at this level allow interoperability of hardware devices or other artefacts such as optical disks across networks or between different platforms. At the middle level of the information and communication technology architectures are arrangements for *access* to the substructure of the network. Access arrangements can be as simple as a user interface that allows the user to establish communication, such as the touchpad of a telephone, or as complex as the choices that must be made to configure an e-mail service application to access e-mail from multiple server locations and types. The highest level of the architecture is the *service* level, which defines what the user can 'do' with the information or communication technology device. For example, a common telephony service is 'call waiting' which provides users with a signal during a telephone call that another caller is seeking connection and a procedure for temporarily interrupting the call in progress to answer the incoming call. More advanced services include software application programmes that allow multimedia messages to be composed, transmitted, or received.

The incumbent, insurgent, and virtual community strategies of firms are similarly stratified. For example, companies that favour incumbent strategies tend to concentrate on the access and substructure levels, while those that are following an insurgent strategy tend to concentrate on the service and access levels. Those following virtual community strategies are likely to focus their technological resources on services. The Internet is a good example of how the strategic interests of firms are beginning to cross traditional market boundaries. Internet-related activities are often associated with services and the strategies of insurgent and virtual community firms. The underlying capability for the Internet is provided by the Transport Control Protocol/Internet Protocol (TCP/IP), a set of internetworking standards that is implemented at the access and substructure levels and in which companies following incumbent strategies are more involved. As a result, the future of the Internet is as much bound up with the technology investment strategies of companies following incumbent strategies as it is with insurgent or virtual community strategies. This is so despite the heightened visibility of the new Web-based service suppliers and the multitude of ISPs offering access to the Internet.

The co-ordination of new service capabilities with emerging demand is one of the key factors necessary to encourage innovation at all three network levels. Co-ordination activity at the services level is particularly dynamic and involves a greater degree of direct interaction between companies following incumbent, insurgent, and virtual community strategies than normally occurs at the access and substructure architectural levels. It is at the services level that many industry observers expect the greatest opportunities for the ascendance of new firms. We focus on the participation of firms within technical, trade, and commercial associations, including standards organizations, to examine emergent patterns in the relationships between these organizations and their implications for the emergence and growth of particular clusters. Special attention is given to the positioning of key European firms and their profiles in Europe and to global institutional arrangements that influence the direction of investment for the establishment of common information and communication infrastructures.

6.4.1   Institutional Frameworks for the Co-ordination of Technology Clusters

Developers of advanced information and communication technologies employ several mechanisms or processes in the co-ordination of their RTD&D activities.[34] The first is intra-enterprise co-ordination in the form of outright collaboration. In the advanced information and communication technology field, collaborations are becoming the rule rather than the exception. As products and markets become more complex, and as the investment risks in new technologies intensify, fewer firms are able to maintain a broad range of in-house design, production, and marketing competencies. Collaboration may occur in the form of joint ventures, technology sharing agreements, and strategic alliances that may or may not involve acquisition by one firm of substantial holdings in another (Hagedoorn and Schakenraad, 1992). Collaborations indicate that firms have commitments to particular products and suggest that complementarities may exist between the respective technology and business profiles of those firms. They do not necessarily indicate that an industry-wide momentum to co-ordinate technological development is underway.

When technological innovation is co-ordinated it will usually involve extensive inter-enterprise arrangements for collaboration, that is, collaboration across an industry or product sector. Industry consortia, trade organizations, professional societies, and standardization bodies can all be mobilized to play roles in such endeavours. Inter-enterprise arrangements need not, however, be deeply committed to the formation of a standard. These arrangements often exist to promote exploratory, often called 'pre-competitive', RTD&D, and their memberships typically cross firm, sector, and national boundaries. Many enterprises and organizations tend to acquire a participation portfolio that encompasses several co-ordination efforts and it may be difficult to discern which of these represents the strategic emphasis of the enterprise.

The third kind of co-ordination occurs on an extra-enterprise basis. Organizations can elect to participate in associations that do not engage directly in technology development, but instead, seek to influence commercial and/or regulatory environments. Examples are user groups, industry lobbies, promotional organizations, and interest groups. It is not uncommon for intra- and inter-enterprise co-ordination initiatives to maintain an extra-enterprise dimension to increase their voice in *de jure* standards-making processes.

Our focus in this section is on *inter-enterprise* co-ordination mechanisms and, particularly, on the activities of two types of inter-enterprise organizations, one referred to collectively hereafter as consortia, and the other as the Standards Development Organizations (SDO). A consortium can be defined as an alliance of firms and organizations, financed by membership fees, formed for the purpose of co-ordinating

---

[34] The organizational concept used here—'enterprise'—is closely related to the technological concept of the 'enterprise network', an influential approach to matching the configuration of distributed networks with user configurations that increasingly involve crossing intra-firm and inter-firm boundaries (Mercer, 1996).

technology development and/or implementation activities, within discrete technological and/or product and services boundaries. Standards that emerge directly
from consortia are generally *de facto* standards although it is common for a consortium to seek formal ratification of these standards by *de jure* standards bodies. The
SDOs define a process for achieving a *de jure* standard that is generally portrayed
as representative and inclusive of industry interests. The standards formed by SDOs
may be further supported or validated by legal or regulatory provisions requiring the
use of such standards for public procurement or in systems subject to regulatory
control.

Consortia in the information and communication technologies field have most of
the general organizational characteristics of trade and industry associations. Consortia can be singled out as a distinctive *class* of industry grouping because of the very
similar circumstances and timing of their origins, their focus on developing and/or
supporting the implementation of technical specifications, and the relative congruence with SDOs of their internal structures and procedures. The main distinction
between consortia and SDOs lies in the definition of the SDO as having a central
responsibility for the 'public interest' and the enactment of governance structures
designed to assure this outcome. While consortia may see themselves as acting in the
public interest, they are accountable ultimately to their members and it is less certain
that conflicts between the members and the public interest will be resolved in favour
of the latter.

Most consortia are oriented to the publication of technical specifications. Some
consortia operate virtually as 'companies' that distribute specifications developed by
their members, usually on some kind of cost-plus or not-for-profit basis. Although
some consortia concentrate more on market research, information sharing, or the co-
ordination of RTD&D results between their members, all consortia focus on the development and/or implementation of technical specifications. The technical focus of
most consortia is narrowly defined, that is, they work individually on specific technological subjects such as object-oriented programming, teleconferencing, operating
systems, transmission technologies, video compression, or digital broadcasting rather
than on a broad range of public and/or private network technologies.

Several consortia in Europe have wider remits such as the European Workshop for
Open Systems (EWOS) and the European Computer Manufacturers Association
(ECMA), the largest European-based consortia. These cover a diverse range of computer networking subjects. Most commonly, consortia outputs appear as 'publicly
available specifications', that is, they are available free or at a nominal cost to non-
members. In preparing these specifications, consortia employ informal working
methods based on voluntary inputs from their members.

The official position of most organizations in which inter-enterprise technology co-
ordination occurs is that the activities concerned are either pre-competitive or extra-
competitive. 'Pre-competitive' means that they prepare a new playing-field on which
competition can take place. 'Extra-competitive' means that they create conditions con-
ducive to the more efficient exploitation of an existing technology that are non-
prejudicial to the interests of any particular enterprise. In both cases, collective action

is employed in order to remove what are deemed to be obstacles to the economic performance of all firms. Not all enterprise groups in a collaborative technology initiative start from the same position with respect to the technology or the market. In addition, the costs and benefits of developing and adopting a pre-competitive or extra-competitive specification typically are not distributed evenly. Especially in the case of firms adopting incumbent or insurgent strategies, it is often difficult to separate their standards-related actions from their overtly competitive objectives. Furthermore, as most technological developments tend to be rapid, incremental, and interrelated, it is usually impossible to separate pre-competitive and extra-competitive actions.

The motives for participation in either consortia or SDO activity need not be limited to the issue of setting standards. Market position, design principles, and intelligence about allies and rivals all involve possible spill-over from the activities of discussing standards-making. Of course it is true that when either the SDO or consortium process agrees standards, the result is harmonization and variety reduction which may yield efficiency advantages. The information exchanged in the process of achieving the efficiency benefits of standardization, however, may extend considerably upstream in the firm's technology planning from the actual standards process and it may engage and stimulate the strategic planning of the firm. The strategic and technological design influences on the standards process have grown in importance within the standards-making process over time, partly as the consequence of more actors being involved in the process.[35]

The formation of industry consortia is largely a phenomenon of the late 1980s and early 1990s. Of approximately fifty significant consortia that are the focus of our analysis, only ECMA predates 1985.[36] Of the new consortia involved in our investigation, over 90 per cent were based in the United States and their activities were encouraged under the steady liberalization of the anti-trust regime with respect to inter-firm collaboration in high-technology industries that began in the mid-1980s (Jorde and Teece, 1989). In the late 1980s, with reference mainly to the 1988 Omnibus Trade and Competitiveness Act, the legal regime in the United States was liberalized with respect to collaborative research and development (R&D) arrangements involving American-owned firms. At the time ECMA was formed in Europe, the law in the United States actively discouraged industry-wide groupings from developing common technical specifications except through officially acknowledged formal standardization processes. Even these could become the subject of anti-trust investigations in some circumstances. Standardization committees had to ensure that their activities were as open to public participation and scrutiny as possible lest these activities be interpreted as illegal attempts to use technology in order to concentrate and control markets (Swankin, 1990). Changes in legislation in the United States from 1988 encouraged closer R&D collaboration between American firms.

---

[35] This has been observed by Cargill (1989); Hawkins (1996; 1997a); J. S. Metcalfe and Miles (1994); Schmidt and Werle (1992) among others.

[36] When ECMA was founded in 1963 its members were primarily European subsidiaries of US computer companies. The primary mandate of ECMA was to engineer interoperability between different manufacturers' platforms.

The increasing significance of consortia is related to changing industry perceptions about the form and function of standards. The basic networking paradigm has changed decisively over the years from connecting to centralized facilities provided by a single vendor, to distributed networking in a multi-vendor environment. Although firms continue to employ various technical and non-technical means to tie customers into their proprietary orbits, they no longer seriously consider making products that are obviously intended to be non-interoperable with other products (O'Connor, 1994). This new philosophy does not prevent conflicts between the agendas of participant companies. In fact, in many ways it intensifies them. Groups of companies following similar strategies, or with other allied interests, seek ways to control key transaction points, that is, points along the value chain where market power can be garnered.[37]

The reason offered by participating firms for the decision to pursue a consortium-based initiative is often that SDOs take too long to produce the required specifications. This may be so to an extent, but it is not the complete story. Generalist SDOs tend to be bound by trajectories to which many incumbent firms have already made considerable investments and, historically, the members tend to be dominated by organizations pursuing incumbent strategies.[38] Most consortia assert that, although they develop technical specifications on an industry-wide basis, they are not SDOs. As we will demonstrate, this is a simplification. Consortia may not have all the procedures of SDOs, but their products can achieve at least as much status as standards in the market as do the products of SDOs. Furthermore, it is a common practice for consortia to develop specifications that are tabled for fast-track approval into SDO processes.[39] Many consortia refer to their products as pre-standards with the implication that they will eventually find their way into the SDO arena. The activities of consortia and SDOs are most likely to overlap when there is significant convergence of technologies.[40] In the next section, we turn to the specific character of several emerging technology clusters for advanced digital applications.

6.4.2 Emerging Technology Clusters for Advanced Digital Applications

An advanced digital application is a networked electronic service or service environment, developed for a specific user requirement, and enabled by a configuration of computer and telecommunication technologies that spans the service, access, and substructure levels of the network architecture. By this definition, computer-integrated

---

[37] For a detailed consideration of transaction points, see Ch. 5.

[38] Most SDOs have open membership criteria, but participation in a standards initiative can extend over many months, even years, and become very costly, especially for smaller firms. This tends to marginalize participation by all but the most directly interested stakeholders who have the resources to sustain activities over long periods.

[39] ECMA and IEEE have had a relationship of this kind with ISO since the 1960s, a relationship that was reinforced by the formation in the 1980s of JTC1 on information technology by ISO and IEC.

[40] A Japanese study demonstrated that most consortia have technological profiles that act to bridge long-standing technical and institutional gaps between the telecommunication focus of the ITU and the computer network focus of ISO/IEC (Telecommunication Technology Committee, 1995).

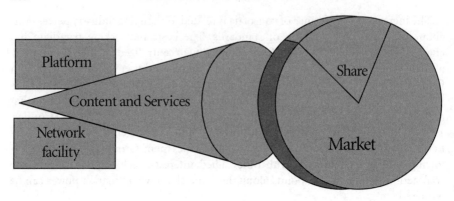

FIG. 6.1. Multimedia industry constituencies

Source: Elaborated from Hawkins (1997).

telephony, Internet telephony, and any form of inter-networking between computer systems would be called an advanced digital application. Nearly all advanced digital applications involve combinations of media. The terminal interfaces for the delivery of services to the user include enhanced digital fixed and mobile telephone terminals, personal computers, workstations, and enhanced televisions, for example, digital televisions with conditional access equipment.

The concept of converging information and communication technology media is not new and previous attempts to create market environments around this concept have met with very mixed receptions. For example, attempts to sell video-telephony began in the 1950s and there are no signs that a viable mass market for this service will develop.[41] It is easy to envisage a service environment based on the potential of new technologies, but it is difficult to package it in products for which demand can be identified or readily created. For multimedia service markets to develop, significant co-ordination is required between three industry constituencies with different institutional structures and product types, and with different ways of acquiring customers and capturing revenues. This relationship is shown in Fig. 6.1. In the creation of multimedia markets, providers of network facilities, concentrated mostly at the access and substructure levels of the network architecture, and producers of hardware platforms, for example, mainframes, personal computers, and workstations, are linked and projected into the market-place by software-oriented content producers and service providers.

Multimedia is a powerful concept for describing the evolving service environment for advanced digital applications and for specifying the capabilities that will be

---

[41] The Internet and LAN services are providing a platform for familiarizing users with video-telephony. From a diffusion perspective, the principal deficiency of video-telephony has been the difficulty of trying out the technology.

required of future network technologies.[42] It also is the object of considerable market hype as to when services will appear, what they will look like, what their benefits will be and for whom, how reliably they will perform, and what they will cost. By emphasizing the mass-market potential of multimedia, content and network service providers can construct arguments that seem to justify the wide distribution of the very considerable costs of network integration and upgrading.

The range and complexity of the technologies that could be integrated within advanced digital application scenarios are reflected in the diversity of industry consortia and standards bodies involved in the industry-wide co-ordination activities in this area.[43] In this section, we look at a sample of organizations across service environments, technological areas, and strategic orientations (see Annexe for a list of twelve SDOs and twenty-two industry consortia that provide the basis for the detailed analysis).[44] The sample contains organizations that represent five technical areas that require co-ordination to support an advanced digital application environment: (1) telecommunication and computer network management; (2) terminal equipment and peripheral hardware; (3) software; (4) transmission media; and (5) content production. The application of the sampling criteria produced a sample in which only seven of twenty-two consortia were based, or co-based, in Europe, and only four of these were European in focus.[45] American organizations also predominated in the SDO category and most of these organizations had an international membership with many European firms as active participants.[46]

6.4.2.1 *The Institutional Topography for Advanced Digital Applications*
The network of connections or alliances that links these organizations illustrates the blurring of distinctions between SDOs and consortia. We defined an alliance in terms of the presence of one or more of three conditions: (1) official agreements that bind organizations; (2) organizations that formally recognize each other's outputs and/or co-direct specific initiatives with respect to these outputs; and (3) organizations that acknowledge that their output is dependent upon the output of another

---

[42] For a detailed consideration of the definitions of multimedia, see Ch. 4.

[43] The institutional landscape is changing and the analysis in this chapter is based upon the institutional relationships that prevailed in 1996. However, we are reasonably confident that the observations from our analysis would apply to an updated data set.

[44] The sample was chosen from a larger group of over fifty organizations, and then stratified to reflect a cross-section of the characteristics of the group as a whole. The selection criteria were: (1) that all organizations had a significant presence in one or more major technological areas of direct or supporting importance to the development of a range of advanced digital applications, and (2) that each organization demonstrated substantial international membership and/or influence.

[45] DVB, EWOS, ECMA, and EURESCOM, the public telecommunication operator organization.

[46] The method was to trace liaisons, linkages, and movements of firms, consortia and SDOs, and technologies. For each organization in the sample, the major technology focus of the organization; specific applications of the organization's products and links to complementary technologies; the principal instruments of technical co-ordination; the main external institutional linkages; and memberships were examined. The analysis is based on information available from the organizations between Oct. 1996 and Jan. 1997.

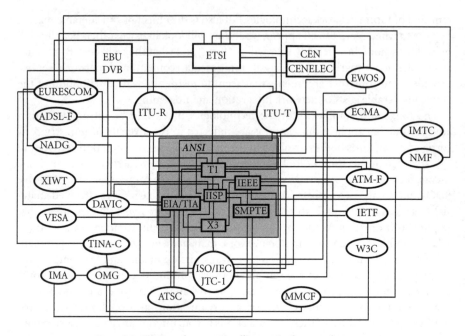

FIG. 6.2. SDO and consortia alliances in the sample group

Source: Adapted from Hawkins (1997).

organization.[47] Using this definition, direct and significant alliances were identified between all but four organizations and the 'outsiders' had a single issue or dominant firm focus.[48] The alliances linking the other organizations are shown in Fig. 6.2. The most striking feature is the centrality of the American National Standards Institute's (ANSI) accredited standards committees clustered around the Information Infrastructure Standards Panel (IISP). Any SDO or consortium that is not linked into this cluster can be assumed to be risking marginalization or to be pursuing a discrete agenda for strategic or tactical reasons.

The IISP is not a standards-making body as such, but a committee set up in 1995 to co-ordinate activities in response to the United States Government's National Infor-

---

[47] There is no necessary correspondence between the dominant criteria on which the alliance was maintained and its overall significance in the alliance structure as a whole. Nor was there a necessary correspondence between the number of alliances formed by an SDO or consortium and the overall significance of its work. Types and quantities of alliances were given significance only on the basis of all the information about the link that was available.

[48] AIW was a consortium formed solely around IBM's proprietary APPN technology. The Forum (APPI-F) was led by Cisco to check the growth of IBM proprietary 'peer-to-peer' solutions. MSAF was largely an AT&T-led initiative to provide globally networked multimedia services. Stardust Winsock Labs was exclusively focused on developing Microsoft Windows-based networking applications.

mation Infrastructure Initiative and to promote collaboration between American and foreign SDOs and consortia. The IISP had about 100 members including all the major SDOs in Canada and the United States working in the areas of computing and telecommunication, several Canadian and American government agencies, a group of about thirty multinational firms based in the United States, some industry associations and consortia, and a very small contingent of foreign SDOs and industry bodies. European participation consisted only of Ericsson, Siemens, and the members of EWOS.

The IISP consisted overwhelmingly of companies identified with incumbent strategies and those, such as Microsoft, Apple, and Hewlett-Packard, associated with insurgent strategies. The only potential leaders of virtual community strategies in the IISP were government agencies in the United States by virtue of their interest as very large users of advanced services in promoting a competitive procurement environment.[49] The significance of the IISP lies in its potential for agenda-setting, and in the scope and global influence of its collaborating organizations in the United States. Its work covered virtually the entire scope of advanced digital applications. IISP also maintained a unique relationship with the Internet Engineering Task Force (IETF) which had been involved in the identification of the IISP standards needs.

Most of the mainstream standards requirements of the computer and data networking industry in the United States are addressed by the Institute of Electrical and Electronics Engineers (IEEE), and X3, the umbrella group for open systems activities and the primary interface for American companies with the Joint Technical Committee 1 (JTC1).[50] Taken together, the mandates of the American National Standards Institute (ANSI T1) and the Telecommunications Industry Association (TIA), covered most of the standards areas for fixed and mobile telecommunication. The Electronics Industry Association (EIA), of which TIA is a subsidiary, is the focal point for the standards requirements of the American computer hardware and consumer electronics industry, and the Society of Motion Picture and Television Engineers (SMPTE), as one of the most influential technical organizations in the international entertainment industry, was strategically well placed to carry digital audiovisual production solutions developed by American companies into an international market-place. SMPTE is a member of the Interactive Multimedia Association (IMA). With over 800 members, IMA was the world's largest on-line services development consortium. SMPTE was also linked into the advanced digital high-resolution video community in the United States, and was the publisher of the Advanced Television Systems Committee (ATSC) specifications.

The three most pivotal ANSI groups in advanced digital applications were the IEEE, the EIA, and ANSI T1. Together, these SDOs maintained extensive contact with the International Telecommunication Union (ITU) and JTC1, and they had established alliances with most of the important consortia. Although every firm with an interest in advanced digital applications had a stake in the Internet at the time this analysis was

---

[49] These interests could be diluted by strategies of trade promotion that tend to favour larger companies, few of which are sufficiently diversified to follow the virtual community strategy.

[50] In the 1980s JTC1 on information technology was formed by ISO and IEC.

undertaken in late 1996, the IEEE was the only standards body to have established an official joint committee with the Internet Society, the parent body of the IETF.

The Digital Audio Visual Council (DAVIC), the Asynchronous Transfer Mode Forum (ATM-F), and the Object Management Group (OMG) were becoming pivotal consortia at this time. Reflecting the origins of Asynchronous Transfer Mode (ATM) as a compromise solution for delivering a wide range of electronic services, ATM-F was linked firmly into the telecommunication and computing arenas. It was also entering into arrangements with a specific multimedia services focus. OMG is the world's largest software development consortia, and many of its links with other organizations involved the use in different settings of OMG products. OMG was also a member of the World Wide Web Consortium (W3C). The other interesting cluster of organizations was the ATSC-SMPTE-EIA-T1, a configuration based around advanced video display and production technologies. Other consortia were primarily outcroppings of national and/or international SDO activity, such as the International Multimedia Teleconferencing Consortium (IMTC) which existed to develop applications for the ITU in the video-teleconferencing field.

Major European firms were participants throughout the spectrum of SDO and consortia activities and alliances. Europe is the only region to have developed institutions for technological co-ordination that have competed successfully, albeit on a limited basis, with the American institutions. At the end of 1996, the European position in the institutional alliance structure was delicately balanced and centred in a very few key organizations.

There was no European counterweight to the global influence of the combined forces of the United States telecommunication and computer industry SDOs and consortia clustered around the IISP. Although officially the focus of computer-related standardization in the European Union, the European Committee for Standardization (CEN) appeared to have been pushed to the margins. The European Committee for Electrotechnical Standardization (CENELEC) also appeared to be a peripheral organization, although many of its technical subject areas, for example, electrical components, were close to those of the EIA in the United States. The processes whereby CEN and CENELEC had been pushed to the margins of global standards-making processes were a reflection of their orientation primarily to European regional co-ordination. In the information and communication technology field generally, however, the activities of European firms and organizations have migrated their activities very quickly to the international arena as most services are intended to be international in scope and to use enabling technologies for which global standards have been established.

Of the three significant European consortia, EWOS was providing the only major institutional link that might connect European firms into JTC1 and the IISP cluster. EWOS counted major multinational telecommunication and computer firms among its members, but most were small and specialized European-based firms and organizations. The most significant consortium was ECMA which was dominated overwhelmingly by European subsidiaries of American and Japanese firms. The European Telecommunication Standards Institute (ETSI) was the only hub in terms of international promotion of distinctly European co-ordination initiatives that are broadly based in the European industries. ECMA and ETSI were collaborating closely in several areas focusing on the interface between public and private networks, but the relationship between them had experienced a troubled history as a result of frequent boundary disputes between the computer and telecommunication communities.

6.4.2.2 The Dynamics of the Institutional Topography

There is a core group of companies worldwide that are involved in nearly all the consortia and standards organizations. In this analysis, for instance, there was a group of very large generalist firms, mostly incumbent equipment and service providers. Table 6.1 presents this group classified according to each firm's primary revenue areas.

At least half the top twenty telecommunication and computer vendors were represented in each of the sixty significant consortia, and in each of the most important SDO committees at national, regional, and international levels. In our sample, they had an overwhelming presence. There is also a much larger group of firms that specialize in a selected range of products and many of these are companies associated with insurgent strategies. Some of these firms were very dominant actors in their respective sectors, Microsoft, Apple, Oracle, Sun, Ciscom, and Compaq, for example. Others were specialist subsidiaries of larger companies such as Corning, Lockheed-Martin, Hughes, Mitsubishi, and Samsung. These firms were prominent and participated in a broad range of SDOs and consortia. Individually, none supported the kind

TABLE 6.1. *Core group of generalist participants*

Equipment vendors

Telecommunication	Information technology	Public telecommunication operator
Alcatel	Digital Equipment Corp.	AT&T
Bosch	Fujitsu[2]	British Telecom
Ericsson	Hewlett-Packard	Deutsche Telekom
Lucent	Hitachi[2]	France Telecom
Motorola[1]	IBM	GTE
NEC[1]	Intel	MCI
Nokia	Matsushita	NTT
Nortel	Texas Instruments	PTT Nederland
Philips[1]	Toshiba	Sprint
Siemens[1]	Unisys	Telecom Italia
		Telia
		Telstra
		US Regional Bell Operating Co.

[1] Also a significant supplier of computer and/or computer networking equipment.
[2] Also a significant supplier of telecommunication network equipment.

Source: Adapted from Hawkins (1997*b*).

TABLE 6.2. *Prominent specialist participants*

Telecommunication	Information technology	Consumer electronics
Corning	3Com	Dolby
General Instrument	Apple	Hyundai
Lockheed-Martin	Bay Networks	JVC
Matra	Cascade	Mitsubishi
Newbridge	Cisco	Panasonic
Racal	Compaq	Pioneer
Ricoh	Hughes	Sharp
Scientific Atlanta	National Semiconductors	Sony
	Novell	Thomson
	Microsoft	
	OKI	
	Oracle	
	Samsung	
	Sun	
	Tandem	

Source: Adapted from Hawkins (1997*b*).

of blanket coverage observed in the case of large incumbents. Table 6.2 lists some of the more prominent firms in this group classified according to their primary product areas.

Relative to the incumbents, most of the companies in this group tended to be of moderate size in terms of revenues, between US$ 1b. and 2b., as compared to over US$ 6b. for most of the incumbents. However, the growth in the revenues of firms in this group has often been spectacular. Since 1993, for example, such firms as Scientific Atlanta for satellites and cable systems, General Instrument for cables, and 3Com and Cisco for data networking products, have been reporting revenue growth averaging more than 40 per cent annually, compared to an average of about 15 per cent annually for the top ten suppliers of public telecommunication network equipment.

In most consortia and SDOs, firms with the potential to become leading proponents of virtual community strategies were a minority. No case was found in the sample of a firm with a virtual community strategy that was represented in a significant cross-section of organizations. The participation of organizations that might represent virtual community interests was concentrated in a small number of specialist bodies.

Although companies associated with incumbent strategies have the disadvantage of being less familiar than some specialists with specific new technology and market areas, they retain the advantage of being able to link new developments into a larger arena of global network components, many elements of which they already control. Several major firms were difficult to classify. These firms were specialists in the sense that their range of products was relatively concentrated, but generalists in the sense that their products had achieved market penetration in enough key areas that they were influencing the overall development of networks and services. These firms employed both insurgent and incumbent strategies and were generating virtual community-type relationships with their customers. The most obvious example of this type of strategy is Microsoft, but firms such as Oracle, Sun, Apple, Novell, and Cisco displayed similar characteristics.

As in the case of firms following incumbent strategies, some of the multi-strategy firms are capable of promoting and sustaining their own consortia structures. Thus, Microsoft had spawned the Winsock and New Technology communities, Oracle was leading the Object Definition Alliance oriented to World Wide Web applications, and Sun was mustering an interest group around its Java programming language. In some cases, relatively small firms with highly successful products had promoted new consortia in strategic opposition to the actions of much larger incumbents. In 1992, for example, Cisco formed the Advanced Peer-to-Peer Internetworking Forum (APPI-F) to stake a claim on an open systems approach to peer-to-peer inter-networking in the face of IBM's Advanced Peer-to-Peer Networking Implementers Workshop (AIW Forum), formed to promote proprietary IBM solutions in this environment. The Cisco initiative attracted the support of AT&T, Sprint, Digital, Unisys, Alcatel, and British Telecom. In other cases, smaller specialist firms had teamed up with incumbents to establish consortia. The four charter members of the ATM-F, for example, were specialists, Adaptec and Cisco, and generalists, Nortel and Sprint.

Organizations based in the United Sates were acquiring a higher profile in international technological co-ordination initiatives. With a few significant exceptions, most of the interfaces between the American structure and the 'rest of the world' were provided through international bodies, such as the ITU and ISO. The consortium system has changed this by providing a much greater number of direct, specialized relationships between firms owned by American interests based in the United States and non-US-owned firms. Nevertheless, the system is largely America oriented and all but a handful of consortia are based in the United States.

The distribution of subject areas between different types of co-ordinating institutions has become increasingly complex. The consortia phenomenon has been affecting the structure of the technical co-ordination hierarchy that was formerly centred in the international SDOs and a select group of national SDOs. The SDO hierarchy (see Fig. 6.3 (a)) can be viewed as a step configuration where a progression occurs from firm-level initiatives to industry-wide, national, and possibly international, acceptance of a common specification or process.

However, most co-ordination activities involve simultaneous actions undertaken in a variety of institutions at many levels. In practice, a wheel configuration (see Fig. 6.3 (b)) is more appropriate for describing the international processes for developing common technical specifications. However, there are a number of institutional frameworks in which standards continue to be developed in a tree configuration under an initiative by an international SDO (see Fig. 6.3 (c)).

The consortium structure has both positive and negative implications for marginal

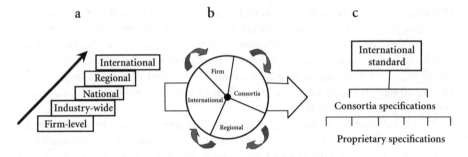

FIG. 6.3. Institutional configurations

Source: Adapted from Hawkins (1997).

or specialist participants. On the positive side, consortia can operate a more manageable structure in which firms might build power bases to countervail those of incumbents. On the negative side, a proliferation of organizations has implications for the distribution of the limited resources available to participating firms. The primary concern for all participants is the degree to which the work in an initiative is allocated and monitored in a co-ordinated way. As work becomes spread out among different organizations, often working to different rules, the risks increase of redundancy, duplication, and the emergence of irreconcilable approaches. Incumbent generalists are better placed to absorb this risk, or even to use the fragmentation of initiatives in strategic ways, that is, to control the emergence of insurgent and virtual community influences over key technological developments.

Although there are similarities, there also are differences between the consortia and SDO committees. Consortia tend to have more limited and explicit technological agendas than SDOs. As shown in Fig. 6.4, incumbent firms were dominant in SDO committees for both telecommunication and computing. This is partly due to the historical position of companies identified with incumbent strategies in these bodies, but it is also attributable to the relatively heavier concentration in SDOs of technical subject areas that are of more immediate concern to generalist companies than to the other industry players. Companies following insurgent strategies were an increasingly significant factor in SDOs, but they were especially active in the consortia. The interests of firms and organizations in the virtual community area were under-represented in both consortia and SDOs, but they were better represented in the former than in the latter. For example, consortia such as DAVIC and the Digital Video Broadcast (DVB) had a strong television media orientation and attracted major information and entertainment providers such as Time-Warner, Bertelsman, the American Public Broadcasting System, and British-Sky-Broadcasting. These are firms that would be expected to play only peripheral roles in telecommunication-oriented committees. Our analysis of the membership lists and work programmes of consortia and SDOs suggests that, in general, users of network technologies were gravitating towards the technical organizations that were software rather than hardware oriented.

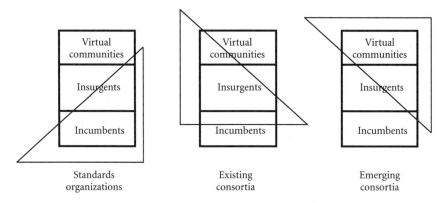

FIG. 6.4. Incumbent, insurgent, and virtual communities in SDOs and consortia

Source: Adapted from Hawkins (1997).

6.4.3 *Institutional Criteria for Cluster Formation in Advanced Digital Applications*

This discussion has illustrated some of the features of the milieu of inter-enterprise co-ordination through which technological clusters may form or fail to form. Four criteria need to be met to consolidate the support that is necessary for the success of embryonic technology clusters in the advanced digital applications area. First, complementarities are necessary. Second, inter-organizational distribution is essential. Third, there needs to be a critical mass of dominant companies. Finally, support from firms based in the United States seems essential given the centrality of such organizations in the SDO and consortium structure for advanced digital applications.

Evidence of clustering for advanced digital applications must be tempered by uncertainty regarding the kinds of service environments they may eventually support. In the work programmes of the SDOs and consortia in the sample, three generic frameworks stood out that are relevant to advanced networked applications in both desktop (PC and workstation audiovisual interaction and data exchange) and set-top environments (video terminal via set-top encoding/decoding devices and digital video terminals): (1) *Multimedia Application Structure*, the framework that enables the portability of applications, messages, and documents between different systems; (2) *Image Processing*, the framework of encoding and decoding technologies for maximizing bandwidth efficiency in the provision of digital audiovisual services; and (3) *Digital Audiovisual Services*, the framework for provision of specific services utilizing digital audiovisual technologies.

In this section, we map the relationships between consortia and SDOs and the technologies within these frameworks with the aim of detecting where clusters are most likely to form.[51] The nucleus in each of the following figures is comprised of the core

[51] The consortia and SDOs in the sample were located in an orbit around groups of standards each of which is indicative of significant lines of co-ordination activity. The organizations appear on the diagrams based upon a comparison of the information collected with respect to each one.

standards and lead organizations and the remaining organizations are arrayed according to their relative degrees of direct interaction with this framework. The organizations closest to the nucleus are the most likely supporters of clustering initiatives.

6.4.3.1 Multimedia Application Structure

The key international standards for multimedia applications include:

- Multimedia/Hypermedia Expert Group (MHEG) developed by the Joint Technical Committee (JTC) in collaboration with the ITU. MHEG is an object-oriented standards framework supporting multimedia and hypermedia document representation that is independent of file structure.
- Open Document Architecture (ODA), is a standardized format for the exchange of documents between open systems, developed jointly by JTC and the ITU.
- Standard Generalized Markup Language (SGML) is a JTC-developed mark-up language for text and an ISO standard.
- Presentation Environment for Multimedia Objects (PREMO) is an initiative to provide a standardized development environment for multimedia objects that was under development in JTC.
- Hypermedia/Time-based Structuring Language (HyTime) is a JTC application of SGML for the representation of open hypermedia documents and an ISO standard; Image Interchange Facility (IIF) is the first part of the International Image Processing and Interchange (IPI) standard developed by JTC.

These core standards define most of the technical subject areas that make up the multimedia application structure. Although the interests of individual firms and organizations typically do not encompass every standard in this group, firms with a stake in any one of these standards are also likely to become involved with some of the others. Figure 6.5 illustrates the orbit configuration of the SDOs and consortia in the sample.

This area of standards activity shows signs that it could support a technology cluster. First, the primary technological orientations of the organizations in the first orbit are to MHEG, SGML, and ODA. SGML receives the most cross-references in the products of SDOs and consortia in the sample, with ODA receiving the least.[52] Significantly, SGML had developed a very different and more diverse support community than ODA. Although incumbent telecommunication firms and insurgent computer firms were very much involved with SGML, most producers of SGML products were specialized computer graphics software houses that had little association with the Open Systems Interconnection (OSI) framework. ODA, in contrast, was centred in the incumbent OSI community.

ODA had substantial input from European firms, especially through EWOS. The EWOS ODA Expert Group and SGML/ODA convergence team had made substantial

---

[52] When this snapshot was produced, there was no interface between ODA and MHEG, although SGML and ODA were related as they were part of a large group of JTC1 and ITU standards dealing with the exchange of documents between systems. Most of these refer in some way to the OSI initiatives in JTC1.

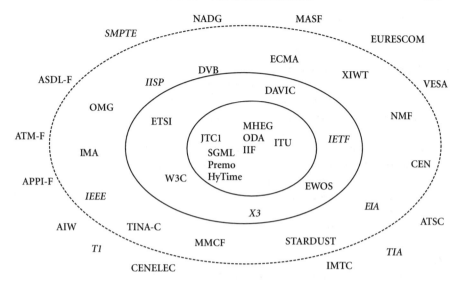

FIG. 6.5. Multimedia application structure

Source: Adapted from Hawkins (1997).

contributions to the Joint Technical Committee (JTC1) on ODA subjects. This effort had been backed up by the formation of the ODA-C, a consortium not included in the sample because of its small membership and narrow field of influence. ODA-C was made up primarily of European firms and subsidiaries of American-owned firms that had already developed ODA products.[53]

X3, an American National Standards Institute SDO, maintained a Working Group mirroring JTC1 work on hypermedia/multimedia applications which acted as a channel for JTC1 inputs by American firms.[54] For example, HyTime was developed mostly by an X3 committee and then fed into the JTC1 process. The IEEE, the other major American organization involved with computer networking standards, had explored the outputs of MHEG in specific applications but withdrew from this area.

On the consortium side, the World Wide Web Consortium (W3C) involvement was centred on the generic aspects of SGML, but it was also evaluating aspects of MHEG and HyTime. Significantly, however, W3C had no commitment to any of these standards, all of which it regarded as too complex for the web applications environment. The Internet Engineering Task Force (IETF) had issued design principles for eXtensible Markup Language (XML), permitting more efficient use of SGML in

---

[53] ODA-C members were Bull, Siemens-Nixdorf, ICL, IBM Denmark, DEC Ireland, Unysis Austria, and WordPerfect, United States. Other firms associating themselves with ODA products included Olivetti, Rank Xerox, and British Telecom.

[54] X3 was the official American interface with JTC1.

Internet applications.[55] In Europe, the European Telecommunication Standards Institute (ETSI) had listed several standards dealing with aspects of information retrieval in an MHEG multimedia environment and had published a European standard for ODA communication in an ISDN environment.

The uncertain status of many of these standards reflects one of the criticisms of SDO-led frameworks particularly by those following insurgent or virtual community strategies. They often claim that too much effort is focused on the effort to standardize, creating over-complex solutions and increasing the attractiveness of proprietary solutions. Consortia-led and proprietary standards were strong competitors for defining aspects of the multimedia application structure. An example is Acrobat, a system developed by Adobe that allows for document portability based on its widely used Postscript technology. In the case of multimedia document standards, the W3C consortium-led effort to promote XML has become increasingly dominant since this case study was constructed.

6.4.3.2 Image Processing

There are two international standards for image processing. One is the Motion Picture Experts Group (MPEG), a family of standards covering various stages in the evolution of digital video and audio storage and retrieval technologies enabling efficient, compact coding of digital signals. The second is the Joint Photographic Experts Group (JPEG), a standard for compressing digital still images. The configuration of the SDOs and consortia in this area is shown in Figure 6.6. MPEG and JPEG are two of a large group of proprietary and non-proprietary, software and hardware, image coding technologies. In early 1997, among the software-based proprietary solutions were Microsoft's MS-Video and IBM's Ultimotion, both capable only of low resolution. The leading proprietary hardware and software systems were Cinepak by SuperMac and Indeo by Intel, again, both supporting low-resolution images. Intel owned the Digital Video Interactive (DVI) technology, a hardware-based solution that became widely available in the personal computer multimedia market, but Intel later abandoned this approach. Image compression is at the heart of most of these technologies, and MPEG, JPEG, and their proprietary competitors offer solutions for the compression problem.

As shown in Fig. 6.6, MPEG and JPEG had attracted a much wider and more diverse configuration of firms than other contenders. MPEG brought together most of the prominent SDOs and consortia in the sample, covering telecommunication, computing, broadcasting, motion picture production, and consumer electronics. Nearly all of the principal owners of proprietary image technologies were involved to some extent in MPEG. MPEG and JPEG had two advantages. First, there was uncertainty concern-

---

[55] XML gathered considerable momentum in 1998 and 1999 with its adoption by companies such as GMC, DaimlerChrysler and First Union Corporation in the United States and appears to be positioned to dominate future developments, see Orzech (1999), and Pender (1999). XML is represented by its proponents as a subset of SGML with the exception of a very limited number of changes. This means that an XML document can be converted into a standard SGML document using an automated syntax checker.

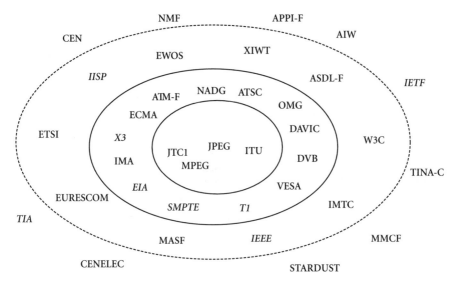

FIG. 6.6. Image processing

Source: Adapted from Hawkins (1997).

ing the development of proprietary solutions because of diversity in the approaches and capabilities. Second, the firms had become wary of device-based solutions as a result of the *de facto* standards wars that occurred with VHS/Betamax, High Definition Television (HDTV), and AM stereo. MPEG generated an early bandwagon effect by producing its initial specifications very quickly. The standard achieved wide acceptance as the basis for the HDTV community in the United States, the European Digital Video Broadcasting group, and the high density compact disc community. MPEG is also one of the major factors linking the generic aspects of image processing to the specific aspects of digital audiovisual services.

6.4.3.3 Digital Audiovisual Services

The audiovisual services area encompasses a very wide range of related applications such as audiovisual terminal technology, both set-top and desktop, video-telephony, teleconferencing, digital television, and video-on-demand. In this area, one of the interesting developments has been videoconferencing. The principal standards frameworks in this area in early 1997 were:

- ITU-T G.700 series, digital audio encoding standards for videoconferencing applications in the general switched telephone network.
- ITU-T H.200 and H.300 series, standards for digital audio-visual teleservices in an ISDN framework and including the Internet.
- ITU-T T.80 and T.120 series, for image compression and transmission control for multimedia data conferencing.

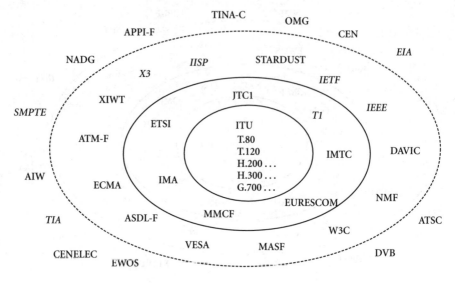

FIG. 6.7. Videoconferencing

Source: Adapted from Hawkins (1997).

Figure 6.7 shows the configuration of the SDOs and consortia in the sample with respect to the ITU's standards.

The primary contributors to the videoconferencing initiatives were the main telecommunication SDOs with historical commitments to ISDN, for example, the European Telecommunication Standards Institute, the American National Standards Institute, plus the Joint Technical Committee and a handful of consortia. EURESCOM was a public telecommunication operator consortium with commitments to the development of broadband videoconferencing services. The International Multi-media Teleconferencing Consortium (IMTC) was a product champion for certain standards with links to the interests of public telecommunication operators and computer hardware and software firms developed by encouraging multimedia videoconferencing applications in Local Area Network (LAN) and Wide Area Network (WAN) environments. The Multimedia Communications Forum (MMCF) had an interest in videoconferencing for desk-top applications.

Microsoft, Intel, and over a hundred additional companies, had announced that they would develop an open platform for Internet telephony that would encompass video, voice, and data services in the Internet and Intranet environments. This platform was to be built upon the International ITU and Internet Engineering Task Force (IETF) specifications. At the time, IETF and the World Wide Web Consortium (W3C) were not directly involved in the ITU videoconferencing series. The promotion of Internet telephony, in contrast, was undertaken by those pursuing a virtual community strategy in every sense. There were only a few service providers and the user

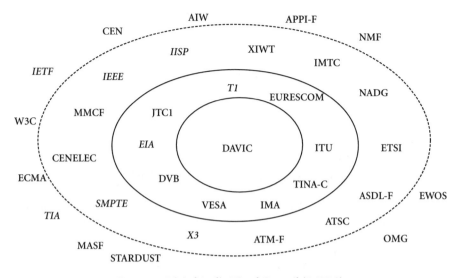

FIG. 6.8. Digital Audio Visual Council (DAVIC)

Source: Adapted from Hawkins (1997).

community primarily was made up of enthusiasts, many of whom had the technical acumen to contribute to the development of the service. However, firms such as IBM, Microsoft, Netscape, an assortment of cable television companies, and even some public telecommunication operators, were poised to take active roles in developing this market.

Figure 6.8 displays another configuration, this time around the specifications developed by DAVIC, a consortium with widespread significance in terms of digital audiovisual services.

The purpose of DAVIC, which grew out of MPEG,[56] was to develop a common basis for integrated audiovisual applications that would be interoperable between platforms and available over a variety of transmission media. Its rapid rise to prominence illustrates the advantages of maintaining institutional continuity between SDO and consortia activity. In the first and second DAVIC orbits there was a relatively even mix of SDOs and consortia encompassing telecommunication, computing, content, consumer electronics, software, and networking technologies. The initial goal of DAVIC was to produce a set of internationally agreed specifications for video-on-demand (VoD), but this agenda evolved into a more segmented range of technological issues. For example, the Internet was featuring more prominently in the DAVIC agenda, and graphics capabilities for web applications were to be included in the DAVIC tool kit.

---

[56] The leader of the MPEG initiative, Leonardo Chiariglione of CSELT, the R&D company in Italy's STET group, was also the founder of DAVIC.

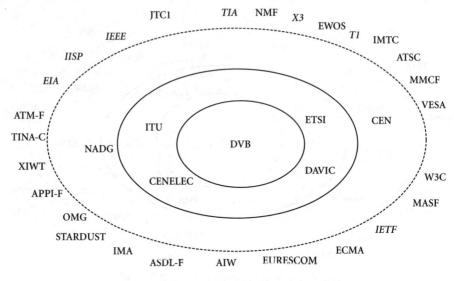

F IG . 6.9. Digital Video Broadcast (DVB)

Source: Adapted from Hawkins (1997).

Integration of audiovisual services into the mobile telephony environment was also being considered.

Finally, Digital Video Broadcast (DVB) was a European initiative that was very closely tied to MPEG and DAVIC. Through its association with the European Telecommunication Standards Institute (ETSI), the DVB consortium provided a vehicle to link the telecommunication interests of ETSI members more strongly into the arena of services. The DVB objectives were similar to those of DAVIC, but they focused more specifically on digital broadcasting. The goal of DVB was to support open platforms for a range of broadcasting services on a pan-European basis.[57] Although the DVB framework enabled MPEG audiovisual coding to be applied across the range of transmission media and represented a technical achievement that could support the formation of an international cluster, clustering was localized in the European Union.

As shown in Fig. 6.9, DVB was isolated in terms of alliances with the rest of the SDOs and consortia in the sample. The low degree to which the DVB was being referenced within the overall SDO and consortia milieu was a problem, especially considering the scope and extent of the DVB initiative and the potential size of the European market for digital television services. There was a substantial degree of international participation in DVB by dominant firms, but there were only two primary links between

---

[57] DVB was an application of MPEG-2 to digital broadcasting.

DVB and activities in the rest of the standards community. An objective of DVB was to offer its specifications to the ITU, but there was little indication that the specifications would be accepted as international standards.[58]

6.4.4   The Potential for Clustering

Overall, the multimedia application structure had only modest potential for cluster formation at the time of our analysis. In terms of complementarities, SGML had achieved the most widely distributed following, but a document mark-up language, in itself, is insufficient to catalyse the formation of a technology cluster in the multimedia application structure. Of all the international standards related to advanced digital applications, MPEG was the framework most commonly cross-referenced in the specifications of other organizations, and no SDO or consortium in the sample was seriously promoting an alternative to MPEG. However, MPEG encompasses a range of standards with different capabilities and the extent of cross-industry commitment to future versions of the standard for interactive audiovisual services was unclear.[59]

The ITU series for videoconferencing had the potential to become central to several clusters but developments in Internet applications were expected to influence this outcome at the time this analysis was undertaken. In the case of DAVIC, a cluster had already formed. DAVIC was the only framework that not only linked other coordination activities within the audiovisual services framework, but also served as a link between this and the multimedia application and image processing frameworks. Finally, DVB had strong institutional support in Europe, including political support, but was isolated in terms of non-European institutional support.

This analysis provides the basis for several insights into the ways that European interests are represented in the global structure for technology co-ordination in the area of advanced digital applications. First, structurally, organizations based in the United States are increasingly central to the global co-ordination system. Much of the co-ordination activity of European firms at the services level is now centred in these organizations. European regional organizations offer the only viable countervailing force to this dominance, but the European organizations are focused and few in number with a greater emphasis on telecommunication standards than other elements of advanced digital applications.

The consortium phenomenon enlarges the number of access points to the coordination structure, but it also concentrates the power to influence the selection of alternative technical standards within firms and consortia that can monitor and inter-

---

[58] By 1999, DVB-S, the DVB standard for digital satellite broadcasting, had been globally accepted as the *de facto* standard and DVB-C (the digital standard) was dominant. DVB-T, the DVB standard for digital terrestrial broadcasting, had been rejected by the US in favour of ATSC-TV. DVB and DAVIC had formed an alliance to develop a new initiative, the MHP (Multimedia Home Platform).

[59] In addition, the refusal of American companies to adopt DVB-T for digital terrestrial broadcasting involved a rejection of the MPEG audio standards in favour of a Dolby Labs standard.

vene in a comprehensive range of activities. Participation by firms following insurgent strategies is growing in the SDOs, but they are very active in the consortia, reflecting the tendency for consortia agendas to focus on subjects related to the convergence of information and communication technologies and services. Virtual community participation in the co-ordination structure is more prevalent in consortia than in SDOs, but it remains a marginal factor. The technical community that has grown up around the Internet is becoming closely integrated into the wider technology co-ordination structure for advanced digital applications.

A substantial amount of activity in Europe focuses on advanced digital applications for migration to mobile access. The digital mobile network environment is almost exclusively under development by telecommunication companies, many of which are following incumbent strategies, and in international or regional SDOs. Among these firms, Europe has counterweights to Lucent and Motorola, but not to IBM, DEC, and Intel. Among the firms pursuing insurgent strategies, Europe has no counterweights to Cisco, Sun, and Microsoft. In terms of the inter-enterprise technological co-ordination structure, European firms are best placed to influence developments at the access and substructure levels of network architectures. At the services level, which is characterized by more dynamic interaction with companies following insurgent and virtual community strategies, European companies are less influential. The lower levels of insurgent and virtual community activity in Europe, relative to the United States, will prompt European firms to seek greater collaboration with non-European partners. There are opportunities for European firms to lead in the construction of technology clusters as in the example of the DVB area.

6.4.5   *Strategic Implications for European Firms and Policy*

The implications of this analysis for European firms are that the consortium phenomenon greatly increases the diversity of standardization activities, and, for logistical reasons, is fully accessible only to multinational companies. In the previous section, we have considered consortia in terms of their roles in supplementing or providing alternatives to formal standardization processes carried out in national and international SDOs. In practice, most consortia explicitly disassociate themselves from 'standards' as such. Most issue disclaimers to the effect that they are not standards organizations and that the specifications they issue have no 'official' status as standards. Most consortia describe their specification-drafting activities as being only one part of a more general aim of creating holistic environments for implementing new generations of products and services. The differences between SDOs and consortia are subtle, but crucial in determining why firms decide to pursue co-ordination initiatives primarily in SDOs or in consortia. Most SDOs have a responsibility built into their constitutions to ensure that all identification of standards requirements is bottom-up, that is, that standards projects are defined and initiated by the stakeholders themselves. On the one hand, this reduces the numbers of idiosyncratic and redundant standards but, on the other, it tends to introduce greater uncertainty into the process.

A major stimulus to the formation of consortia was the appearance of disturbances in the bottom-up SDO model. In the International Organization for Standardization (ISO), for example, the computer standardization programme grew from being a minor item on the agenda to being a major sustaining initiative.[60] The Open Systems Interconnection (OSI) work was meeting neither its delivery targets nor its technical objectives and a more top-down or managed standardization process emerged in ISO (International Organization for Standardization/International Electrotechnical Commission, 1990). In the ITU, the problem was different. In this case, the steady broadening of the base of its participants that occurred between 1989 and 1995 extended the base of technical subjects and commercial perspectives from which bottom-up identification of standards priorities could emerge. This encouraged a more managed approach to achieving industry consensus. Initially, poor communication and a lack of co-ordination of overlapping work between the ISO and the ITU reinforced the view that the formal SDO process was becoming too complex and remote from industry and user needs.

The consortium phenomenon was also influenced by the diffusion of the Internet which reoriented thinking about the implications of open network environments. Consortia agenda often focused on technological possibilities in open network product and services environments that had never been considered within the mainstream of SDO activity and the SDO system retained technological and institutional legacies that were regarded as impeding rapid exploitation of commercial possibilities in the new network environments. Firms join consortia because they have stakes in the work of the consortia and they tend to support initiatives with technical contributions, absorbing the costs this entails over and above the membership fees if they perceive that substantial benefits are to be realized. In this sense, consortia are very similar to SDOs and their voluntary committee structures. Given the concerns of firms about the SDO procedures, why do they join consortia?

6.4.5.1 *The Consortium Model Advantages*

The basis for membership in most consortia is payment of a membership fee and the signing of a membership agreement committing the member to the objectives, rules, and procedures of the consortium. The typical range of yearly membership fees for commercial businesses is between US$ 5,000 (about the minimum) and US$ 60,000.[61] The fee schedules are most commonly linked to company revenues.[62]

For a large European company, fees in the range of US$ 20,000 to US$ 60,000 per consortium are not very significant, but the scope of the typical consortium is small and most large companies belong to several consortia. A comparison of the membership lists of the major consortia reveals that roughly forty to fifty large multinational vendors of computer and telecommunication equipment and services blanket the whole consortium spectrum. If large firms such as Alcatel, Siemens, IBM, Intel, or

---

[60] This occurred as the ISO/IEC JTC1 evolved in 1997–8.

[61] Survey of fees undertaken for this analysis.

[62] Special dispensations are made in some instances for non-commercial members (e.g. academic and professional organizations), and some consortia allow observer status.

Ericsson each cover thirty consortia, this means an average yearly budget item for membership dues approaching US$ 1.5m. per firm. This is in addition to the costs of participating in the traditional SDOs. On the basis of miscellaneous estimates by standards programme managers in several multinational equipment manufacturers, costs directly attributable to standards-making may be in the range of US$ 5–8m. per firm per year and rising.[63] These estimates are indicative of only the directly attributable administrative costs, that is, maintaining standards/consortia departments in firms and the travel and subsistence costs of sending participants to meetings, and the full costs are likely to be much higher. Thus, the rise in consortia activity appears to represent a shift in the locus of standardization costs from intra-organizational procedures to inter-organizational co-ordination costs.

One of the advantages usually cited for participation in consortia is the reduced 'time-to-market' for a new technology but no comprehensive, independent time-to-market study has been undertaken. In addition, early standards are not always an advantage.[64] The time-to-market argument is based upon the premise that all members of consortia are positively engaged in the work of the consortia to which they belong. This may be so in some instances, but it is unlikely always to be so. Consortium membership may be entered into for flagwaving and place-holding reasons or in order to gather intelligence on general developments in these various fields.

If multinational firms are supporting the consortium system they must be able to see clear advantages and particularly so for those that appear prominently as founder members of consortia. The dynamics of technology and market co-ordination change as network environments become more open and the supporting technology base becomes more modular and convergent. In closed networks, defined by technology that was either proprietary or controlled by a select group of network operators and equipment suppliers, revenues were generated through rents protected by hierarchical ownership of the basic enabling technologies and systems. This is the essence of the incumbent strategy. In an open network, additional options for revenue generation are open to all the players in the form of value-added services. However, generating revenues in an open network environment is not straightforward (Mansell, 1996b). The key is to establish a standard in the market so that it can attract a network of users large enough to reduce incentives for them to seek alternatives (Arthur, 1996), and this is a defining feature of the insurgent strategy. Once a user network is established around a standard, there is the potential to earn revenues through the sale of operational and support services. These dynamics supported the rise of Microsoft and they were at the heart of the strategies of such firms as Netscape.

An increasingly common commercial strategy in electronic networking is to give

---

[63] Based on informal estimates by individuals interviewed by Richard Hawkins between 1995 and 1997. Managers acknowledge that separating the costs of standardization from total R&D and marketing expenditures is practically impossible.

[64] In the mid-1990s, for example the ATM Forum had to slow production of specifications for a time as the rate at which they were being released and revised was overwhelming potential users and confusing the market.

away the means of access to network environments in order to build critical mass. When this strategy is predominant, the incentive to reach agreement on standards in certain areas is strong and this is the link between consortia and SDOs. Consortia offer a counterbalance to the possibility that a key new technology will fall under the control of one firm or a group of firms. At the same time, consortia provide venues for firms to co-ordinate their market and technology strategies. The consortium structure also allows groups of firms to exploit the complementarities that exist between their respective proprietary technologies in a milieu that encourages other firms to acquire a stake in the outcome of such co-operation. This objective is reflected in the active knowledge dissemination and training focus adopted by many leading consortia. Much of this is directed at potential users of the specifications rather than at potential developers.

6.4.5.2 Developing a European Consortium Strategy

The standardization philosophy in the European Union has changed significantly from the policies leading up to 1992 and the Single European Market. The quota-style production targets for new standards aimed at the European Committee for Standardization (CEN), the European Committee for Electrotechnical Standardization (CENELEC), and the European Telecommunication Standards Institute (ETSI) in the Green Paper on Standardization (European Commission, 1990b), have been replaced by market-sensitive criteria and encouragement for European regional SDOs to co-operate with consortia.[65] The SDOs now eschew the comprehensive standards framework approach that was common from the 1970s and are committed to acting only in response to bottom-up industry initiatives.

Structural and procedural adjustments in ETSI have yielded procedures that resemble a collection of virtual consortia. ETSI Technical Committees are close to having the autonomy in setting agendas that are common in consortia, and ETSI voting and approval structures are now reasonably streamlined. Initiatives, such as that for the DVB group, suggest that in-house consortia could populate ETSI. Besides the European Computer Manufacturers Association (ECMA), the only consortia based in Europe that are, or could become, comparable in membership and international influence to the major consortia based in the United States are the Universal Mobile Telecommunication System (UMTS) Forum and the DVB consortium.[66] Other European-based consortia, such as DAVIC and the World Wide Web Consortium (W3C), which is co-located in Europe and in the United States, have no particular European focus.

The DVB consortium is potentially significant, but the major European and non-European firms that participate in it also participate in consortia based in the United States with similar interests in digital video and conditional access technologies. The

[65] See also European Commission (1990b; 1991; 1995b; 1996r). Levy (1997) provides an interesting commentary on changing perceptions in Europe concerning the process of standards-making in the context of conditional access systems for digital media.

[66] The only other European consortium with breadth of membership and subject-matter to rival the larger US-based consortia was EWOS, but this was dissolved in 1997.

UMTS Forum is potentially a very significant European-based consortium, given its head start in co-ordinating digital cellular service markets in Europe. Founded in 1996 by the major suppliers of mobile equipment and services in Europe, this consortium represents an opportunity for European firms to establish a distinctive presence in the global consortia structure and it is attracting interest from outside Europe, although mainly from the subsidiaries of non-European multinational companies.

European firms are, nevertheless, significant players in the consortium structure. The European multinational companies that supply public telecommunication network equipment, for example Alcatel, Siemens, Ericsson, Philips, and Nokia, and the major European public telecommunication operators, including Deutsche Telekom, British Telecom, France Telecom, Telecom Italia, PTT Nederland, and Telia, are visible across the consortium spectrum. Part of the reason for the heavy involvement of European firms in what are essentially American trade associations is that these firms are seeking to develop market positions in the United States and, like American firms, they have a global perspective.

The strategic parameters for European multinational companies are reasonably clear, but the options are much less clear for nationally or regionally based firms, many of which are small and medium-sized enterprises that provide specialized or complementary products and services. Growing numbers of firms in this category are joining consortia on a selective basis. The difficulty is that consortia are not stand-alone organizations, but are part of an international structure of inter-firm activities in which communication and co-ordination are achieved primarily through cross-membership of firms large enough to have the resources, technological scope, and logistical acumen to participate in the entire structure. Smaller firms generally participate by monitoring and contributing to the work of one or two consortia. Since the focus of consortia is on constructing communities of suppliers and users around technical specifications, technologies that could promote smaller firms and support virtual community strategies are likely to be blocked in favour of outcomes that offer larger and more homogenous market development potential.

There are two ways in which the procedural mechanisms and the latent 'authority' of SDOs may continue to be useful. First, they can provide an arbitration mechanism when proprietary and/or consortia activities fail to achieve outcomes that are deemed to be equitable by the stakeholders including suppliers, users, and policy-makers. Second, information about the scope and direction of technical co-ordination activities is of growing value to firms. SDOs are in a unique position to supply services by exploiting their positions as facilitators of industry-wide technical agreements. Such services are especially valuable to smaller, specialist firms that have a greater stake in the implementation of standards than in their development. From the perspective of ensuring that policy objectives for a co-ordinated information infrastructure in Europe are met, the availability of information about standards and related activities worldwide is a major factor in mobilizing European investors in infrastructure and services to co-ordinate their efforts for an interoperable network and a common information infrastructure and services.

6.5   Conclusion

The centrepiece of the European strategy for developing a common information and communication infrastructure is the liberalization of European telecommunication markets. Liberalization has been undertaken with the intention of creating the private investment incentives necessary for upgrading and expanding the capabilities of communication networks to offer advanced technologies and services. Liberalization is expected to deliver effective competitive pressure in basic as well as advanced service markets as the result of the opportunity it offers for competitive entry. Similar developments have occurred in the audiovisual market, particularly in the area of cable television broadcasting. In both telecommunication and audiovisual markets the capacity of firms to sustain incumbent strategies remains to be tested by market developments. Persistent control of key features of the communication infrastructure seems a likely outcome of the historical position that large companies have achieved in particular markets. Our identification of the risks associated with liberalization should not be taken as scepticism about the need for it. What we oppose is the conclusion that liberalization is sufficient to deliver the effective competition which is its primary stated purpose.

Instead of eliminating the need for regulation, liberalization brings about a transformation of the regulatory agenda. The 'new regulation' involves the issues of interconnection and interoperability, which become more complicated as the result of liberalization, as well as sustained attention to the issues of extending access to the new technological and service capabilities that liberalization fosters. The procedures that have been established for arbitrating disputes about interconnection have not yet been extensively tested. We remain sceptical that any simple procedure of arbitration will effectively resolve the variety of interconnection disputes that is likely to develop in coming years. However, it is premature to speculate on what institutional mechanisms will be necessary to resolve these conflicts before substantial experience has been accumulated in the European context and under the changing market and technological conditions shaping interconnection issues. What can be said is that the process of technological convergence makes it increasingly necessary to address the regulatory issues of interconnection in a coherent fashion. The division of regulatory authority and the absence of a capability for a unified review of audiovisual and telecommunication issues are a serious deficiency in the institutional framework for the European information society.

The issue of interoperability has a particularly high priority due to the nature of the growth processes for information and communication technologies. The presence of network externalities and the capacities that they yield, not only for rapid growth, but also for technological lock-in to specific technologies and services, make addressing interoperability at the beginning of various growth processes an urgent matter. These issues are particularly important in the area of conditional access devices for access to audiovisual materials and these have begun to be addressed by regulatory policy. We should expect similar issues to develop in the use of the Internet as insurgent companies vie for market share in the markets arising from the Internet's growth.

Many of the regulatory issues in the area of interoperability that arise from the Internet and other advanced information and communication services are not subject to traditional regulatory processes or institutions. Our extended examination of the changing institutional framework governing the creation of interoperability standards indicates that institutional change combined with the strategic behaviour of specific actors has a major potential to reduce the role of European organizations and companies in the standards-making process. Under ideal conditions, interoperability or technical compatibility standards provide a co-ordinating mechanism that fosters innovation and competitive entry in new and growing markets. Standards can also be the basis for anti-competitive outcomes and sub-optimal performance in innovation and technological progress (David and Steinmueller, 1996; Mansell, 1995). Remedying these outcomes is not a straightforward matter as it may involve substantial changes in the private strategies of firms that are largely outside the remit of government review. Nevertheless, governments do have a responsibility for representing the common public interest in preserving the conditions for successful entry of new business organizations and for the social uses of the evolving information and communication infrastructure. Thus, governments may choose to act as large users or as the representatives of a broad constituency of user interests. Governments may also help to encourage the rethinking of the strategic issues involved in standardization processes by providing more extensive and detailed assessments of how these often arcane processes operate and what their consequences are for the public interest.

There is no simple or once-and-for-all solution to the problem of extending the definition of universal access or the services that should be supported by the evolving infrastructure. As noted in Ch. 2, the common perception of what constitutes a socially appropriate level in the distribution of services is an evolutionary process, subject to the development of citizens' perceptions about their entitlements and rights within democratic societies. We maintain that addressing the issue of extending public access to advanced communication capabilities such as the Internet by substantial efforts to connect schools, libraries, hospitals, and other public institutions is an important priority. Our view is that the connection of these institutions has a substantial capacity to demonstrate the value of advanced information and communication services and to support the acquisition of skills that are increasingly needed in business and other organizations. This conclusion, however, is a temporary measure since the growing utilization of advanced information and communication services will eventually increase the pressure to broaden the definition of universal service in the telecommunication field and to bring into focus the appropriate means of ensuring universal access to the advanced information and communication infrastructure.

The issues of the interconnection, interoperability, and universal access are the most basic elements of the 'new regulation'. In the next chapter we turn to the issue of intellectual property rights where the direct conflicts in the interests of incumbent, insurgent, and virtual community strategies are even more apparent. This is followed by an examination of the issues of privacy and electronic payment systems in Ch. 8 which completes our survey of key institutional framework issues underlying the building of the European information society.

Annexe: Consortia and SDOs Relevant to Advanced Digital Applications

Name	Type
ITU-T and ITU-R International Telecommunication Union Telecommunication Sector and Radiocommunication Sector	International SDO
ISO/IEC JTC1 International Organization for Standardization/ International Electrotechnical Commission, Joint Technical Committee 1	International SDO
IETF Internet Engineering Task Force	Technical development body of the Internet Society
ETSI European Telecommunications Standards Institute	Regional SDO
CEN European Committee for Standardization	Regional SDO
CENELEC European Committee for Electrotechnical Standardization	Regional SDO
ANSI-IISP American National Standards Institute— Information Infrastructure Standards Panel	ANSI information infrastructure co- ordinating body
EIA/TIA Electronics Industry Association/Telecommunications Industry Association	Trade Association/ANSI SDO (TIA is part of EIA)
IEEE Institute of Electrical and Electronics Engineers	Professional Association/ ANSI SDO
SMPTE Society of Motion Picture and Television Engineers	Professional Association/ ANSI SDO
X3	ANSI SDO
T1	ANSI SDO
ADSL-F Asymmetric Digital Subscriber Line Forum	US-based international consortium
AIW Advanced Peer-to-Peer Networking Implementers Workshop	US-based international consortium (specific to IBM products)
APPI-F Advanced Peer-to-Peer Internetworking Forum	US-based international consortium
ATM-F Asynchronous Transfer Mode Forum	US-based international consortium

Cont.

Name	Type
ATSC Advanced Television Systems Committee	US consortium
DAVIC Digital Audio Visual Council	Swiss-based international consortium
DVB Digital Video Broadcasting Project	European consortium (based in the European Broadcasting Union)
ECMA European Computer Manufacturers Association	European consortium
EURESCOM European Institute for Research and Strategic Studies in Telecommunications	European consortium
EWOS European Workshop for Open Systems	European consortium
IMA Interactive Multimedia Association	US-based international consortium
IMTC International Multimedia Teleconferencing Consortium	US-based international consortium
MMCF Multimedia Communications Forum	US-based international consortium
MSAF Multimedia Services Affiliate Forum	International consortium led by AT&T
NADG North American Digital Group	US consortium
NMF Network Management Forum	US-based international consortium
OMG Object Management Group	US-based international consortium
TINA-C Telecommunications Information Networking Forum	US-based international consortium
VESA Video Electronics Standards Association	US-based international consortium
Stardust Winsock Labs	US-based international consortium
W3C World Wide Web Consortium	Consortium—co-located in the US and Europe
XIWT Cross-Industry Working Team	US consortium

Source: Compiled by R. Hawkins (1998*b*).

7

Electronic Intellectual Property and Creative Knowledge Production

7.1 Introduction

In this chapter we continue our examination of how legal and institutional infrastructures are being adjusted to promote the development of the information infrastructure and the move towards the information society. The theme of this chapter is intellectual property rights and our focus is on the copyright of software and content. In many areas of information society development, businesses either want government to leave them alone or hope that it will promote specific standards and regulations. They are concerned that government will prematurely or inappropriately take decisions in areas that are unsettled and subject to important new developments. Such views were a highlight of the discussion in Ch. 5 on electronic commerce. These contrasting views do not, however, seem to apply to the copyright of content and software. Indeed, a common view is that existing protection is either insufficient or that stronger measures are needed to ensure uniform penalties for infringements. In the face of technological convergence and the networking of information, the need for a parallel convergence in the legal and institutional apparatus governing the management of rights in electronic information is being actively promoted. Concerns about rights management for electronic information have become attached to the issue of counterfeiting and piracy, which includes violation of trademarks and other protected intellectual property, as well as copyrights. As observed in the European Commission's Green Paper on combating counterfeiting and piracy,

Counterfeiting and piracy have grown into an international phenomenon accounting for between 5% and 7% of world trade. The phenomenon is affecting the proper functioning of the Single Market as, in addition to the deflections of trade and distortions of competition to which it gives rise, it is leading to a loss of confidence among business circles in the Single Market and to a reduction in investments. It has major repercussions not only at an economic and social level (100,000 jobs lost each year in the Community) but also in terms of consumer protection, especially as regards public health and safety. [. . .] Under the circumstances, action by the

This chapter draws upon research undertaken by Dr Puay Tang, Research Fellow, Dr Willem Hulsink, former Research Fellow, Ingrid Standen, former Research Officer, and Emma Jansen, former Master's student, all of SPRU, and by Gert van de Paal, MERIT. Section 7.3 is adapted from our report (Mansell and Steinmueller, 1995) commissioned by STOA (Scientific and Technological Options Assessment Programme of the European Parliament), and the European Parliament's support for this research is gratefully acknowledged. See also Mansell and Steinmueller (1995; 1996a).

community may prove necessary in order to deal comprehensively with the phenomenon in the Single Market. (European Commission, 1998f: 2)

The force of this denunciation reflects European producers' concerns about the importation of low-price imitative products, many of which have a lower quality than branded goods in the style and fashion industry. The industries said to be hardest hit by piracy and counterfeiting, on a world basis in terms of the percentage of illegal activity as a proportion of total turnover, are the data-processing industry (35%), the audiovisual industry (25%), and the toy industry (12%) (ibid. 4). Public health and safety issues arise from the counterfeiting of pharmaceutical products and other goods where the brand name is intended to create a quality assurance upon which consumers can rely. Violations of copyright in information products are, however, an integral part of the campaign against counterfeiting and piracy.

The suppression of counterfeiting and piracy is aimed at a particular economic activity, that is, the derivation of profit through the misappropriation of trademarks, copyrights, and other intellectual or industrial property from their owners. The problem is that the boundary between these activities and other more 'casual' violations of copyright interests are blurred. For example, it is a violation of copyright when a business consultant reproduces a copy of a print or electronic magazine article and sends it to his or her client as part of the consulting relationship. Here, too, economic gain or profit is being realized through the theft of copyrighted information. Proceeding from this example, it may be argued as a more general principle that copyright owners are always entitled to compensation for the reproduction of their work. Someone who reproduces and distributes copyrighted materials among his or her friends, or pupils, is, therefore, also engaged in an act of theft. Although such activities may be completely disconnected from any profit-making motive, they do not yield any financial compensation to the copyright owner.

In practice, remedies for any illegal act are limited to the ability to detect and prove that an offence has been committed. In civil litigation it is also common to consider the issue of threshold value involved in the illegal action. This mitigates, but does not eliminate, the problem. Teachers who copy articles for their classes of 25 students or the consultant who distributes an article to 25 clients may well cross a threshold of commercial significance, particularly if the copyright owner believes that prosecution may serve as a deterrent to others. Rules that render everyone a criminal lose their legitimacy and are likely to encourage fatalistic, rather than compliant, behaviour.

Because of the problems of setting boundaries for illegal behaviour, the complexities of harmonizing international rules protecting the interests of rights holders, and the range of activities that is necessary to increase effectiveness in the collection of payments for the use of copyrighted material, the extension of copyright protection has become controversial. Unfortunately, and in our view not accidentally, much of this controversy involves portraying opposition to stronger intellectual property protection, its global extension, and strengthened collection procedures as irresponsible. Proponents of the rights to exclusive ownership and control of invention and expression often take the statutory provisions for copyright or patents as the embodiment of 'natural law' rather than as an instance of the legal resolution of conflicting interests.[1] Extending and reinforcing historical decisions without reopening a discussion of the social trade-offs of such changes is inappropriate. Although open debates about the problems of extending copyright are often missing from European policy discussion, there is, nevertheless, practical opposition to the implementation of specific rules.

In this chapter, we review technological and institutional developments that are influencing new directions in copyright regulation and enforcement. Our analysis of the implications of changes in intellectual property rights legislation in recent years is framed by a consideration of the social and economic interests of groups of actors with different interests in the nature of copyright protection. Our viewpoint is that there are communities of interest who are ill-served by the predominant rationale for copyright protection that has contributed to recent extensions and strengthening of the rights of rights holders.

The predominant rationale influencing current actions is that networked information is a commodity that can, and should, be transferred between 'owners' through an explicit contract, or what might be called a 'commodity transaction model'. Because of the desire to simplify the definition of rights in support of this model, copyright is now a universal feature of information creation. This makes it increasingly difficult for individuals to identify their obligations and to limit their potential liability resulting from their use of information that they receive from the Internet or other parts of the information and communication infrastructure. The salience of what might otherwise be regarded as an interesting academic debate is heightened by the recent and extensive effort to achieve global harmonization in intellectual property rights definition and enforcement through new international treaties and the elaboration of existing agreements on reciprocal enforcement of national laws.

The effort to create a global framework supporting copyright is aimed at improving the conditions of trade in copyrighted information and enhancing the incentives to create such information. The history of international agreements in the area of copyright has been influenced by a 'regulatory trajectory'. This trajectory involves extension of the framework to embrace more types of works, the automatic and implicit attainment of rights through 'publication', and the extension of the meaning of publication to embrace virtually all public disclosures. International agreements extend the definition of copyright to encompass new technologies that can be used to express creative works and that provide a means of suppressing pirating behaviour. A relatively simple framework for extending and strengthening intellectual property rights pro-

---

[1] See Hadfield (1988: 1–2) who says, 'debates over how copyright law is to be interpreted, developed and applied essentially are debates over the nature of copyright itself. If the copyright is a natural property right for authors and other creators, then copyright law must focus on identifying the dimensions of the property and the threats to an individual's ownership. If, on the other hand, copyright is an instrument of public policy, designed with the objective of promoting the wise and efficient production of creative work so as to serve social rather than individual welfare, then the law must be addressed to the economics of creative work. The objective one sees in copyright fundamentally affects what one sees as the proper scope and application of copyright law.'

tection is a requirement for the successful conclusion of international negotiations. The need for simplicity, combined with the historical regulatory trajectory of forging international agreements and defining the remits of institutions, reinforces the commodity transaction model of information.

Regardless of the definition of intellectual property rights, the practical enforcement of these rights depends upon technological and institutional capabilities. Our examination would be incomplete without consideration of these issues. Technological capabilities for the protection of intellectual property rights are evolving rapidly. Technologies exist that can enforce the rights holders' interests effectively without the active co-operation of the user. So far, however, these restrict the user's choice of readers or other devices for accessing copyrighted information. Technologies for copyright protection that do not restrict the means of access rely upon the identification of infringing copies and, because of the ever-improving methods for altering digital information, must be relatively sophisticated to provide legally enforceable evidence of infringement. As there are conflicting interests in the enforcement of intellectual property rights, it is particularly useful to examine the co-evolution of rights holders' and access device approaches to technological issues. The issues raised by this co-evolutionary process have been highlighted by Intel's decision to implement individual identification for its most advanced personal computer microprocessors. We consider these issues in more detail in s. 7.5.[2] While a definitive technological resolution of copyright and other intellectual property enforcement issues that can be widely accepted by users should not be ruled out, it has yet to emerge.

There has been considerable progress over the past decade in the creation of automated systems for metering use of copyrighted information and in levying charges, in cases where users are willing to co-operate actively in protecting the security of rights holders' information. With user co-operation, the commodity transaction model is being made to work for certain types of information. If relatively transparent mechanisms of identifying the price for receiving particular information can be devised, a means of addressing the significant issues of reducing the costs of making transactions and defining the contractual terms for information transfers, will have been found. However, important issues will remain to be addressed, including the rights of users to modify and retransmit copyrighted information and the determination of rights subsequent to initial sale, such as the rental and 'borrowing' of copyrighted information. Even when markets for copyrighted information are in place, these markets will con-

---

[2] Intel provided a means of disabling this function temporarily or permanently. Nevertheless, in explaining why they implemented the feature, Intel reports 'increased use of the Internet for communications and electronic commerce is raising personal computer users' concerns about the confidentiality and integrity of transaction-oriented data. Since computers are the primary connections to the Internet, they are a logical place for companies to add security features. Over the next several years, Intel is adding security building blocks in order to move the industry forward in developing secure solutions for our customers', http://www.intel.it/support/processors/pentiumiii/psqa.htm accessed 6 April 2000. In effect, Intel is providing a technological capability that could, in principle, become a condition for the use of particular software as a means for ensuring copyright compliance. Software companies now have the option to adopt a fairly strong copy protection method by linking licences to individual personal computers.

tinue to be vulnerable to 'pirates' who can be expected to use any, or all, parts of the information and communication infrastructure to further their ends. As in the case of the history of the suppression of piracy on the high seas, decisions will need to be taken regarding the culpability of those whose intentional or inadvertent actions facilitate pirating activities. Should the 'safe harbours' of pirates be attacked and the businesses of their agents confiscated? Should those who benefit from the pirate activities be prosecuted? The extent of desirable action and of the action that is feasible will depend, in large measure, on the amount of popular support and sympathy for copyright owners.

In the absence of a definitive technological solution to copyright infringement issues and the growing predominance of a 'commodity transaction model' for the exchange of information, the institutions responsible for the collection of copyright fees and licensing procedures for gaining access to material with copyright protection are of central importance. Collecting societies, such as Reproduction Rights Organizations (RROs); publishers', authors', and composers' associations; and enforcement organizations are seeking to stem piracy and to increase public awareness of copyright issues as a means of fostering co-operative behaviour with regard to stakeholder interests.[3] The dual role of pursuing piracy and facilitating trade in intellectual property is an uneasy one for the organizations involved in this area since they have markedly different histories, purposes, and methods of operation (Bainbridge, 1994). Some organizations, especially those representing the software industry, have focused their attention on relatively large-scale copyright infringement or piracy, while others are principally concerned with the use of copyrighted material in compilations or performances and focus their attention on the outlets for information. Yet other organizations are concerned with the ease of infringement using new technologies and are devising methods for pursuing infringement activities within user organizations by securing agreements with organizations on how to pursue self-enforcement activities. As enforcement and monitoring activities increase, other constituencies with an interest in less cumbersome and costly information access are beginning to come to the fore bringing new pressures to extend the personal use, public interest, and public domain concepts associated with information use. Thus, we consider the future evolution of these institutions, their responsibilities, and how to reconcile the competing interests of different social groups in the access to, and use of, information.

In the next section we begin this task by reconstructing the foundation of the debate about the extension and strengthening of intellectual property rights focusing on the issue of copyright. This is followed by a critical analysis of the recent history of policy discussions aimed at achieving a greater degree of global harmonization in the definition and enforcement of intellectual property rights. The technological alternatives to legal enforcement and the specific issues raised by new technologies are exam-

---

[3] Some members of the legal profession argue: 'the answer must lie in treating copyright piracy as a crime as serious as robbery of tangible possessions. Stiff piracy laws plus active police forces have, indeed, succeeded in virtually stamping out analogue video cassette piracy in many countries' (Common Law Institute of Intellectual Property Rights, 1994: 3).

ined to highlight the fact that the conflicting interests of digital technology developers and the resistance of users can frequently thwart the application of a technological 'fix' for copyright infringement. The chapter concludes with an examination of the roles of the institutions that are responsible for the collection of copyright fees and the negotiation of copyright licences.

Finding appropriate balances between the interests of the constituencies for information use and the private interests that seek greater protection continues to be a difficult challenge. The balance that emerges in the coming years will have significant implications for the degree of experimentation with innovative technologies and services in the Internet and on-line services markets. Greater emphasis on copyright enforcement and implementation could dampen the growth of markets for applications targeted at small users who lack the economic resources to verify whether their use of information falls within, or outside, the scope of allowed uses. Important issues also include the exceptions that are permitted in the use of electronic information for public and education purposes. Different approaches to site licensing and the costs associated with implementing new administrative systems may become factors that differentiate between markets for products and services in the European Union Member States that are regarded by suppliers of services as being attractive for the start-up of new commercial ventures.[4]

7.2   The Social and Economic Interests in Copyright

Intellectual property laws extend the right of property protection under law to creations such as inventions, literary or artistic works, and trade marks. After a particular creation is granted protection under one of the several systems of intellectual property law it may be sold, licensed, or mortgaged (ibid. 3–22). The goals that may be served by extending and strengthening property right protection include: (1) promoting invention and the authorship of new work by enhancing the revenue-earning capacity in the sale of that work; (2) safeguarding the right of creators from others simply copying their ideas or works; (3) encouraging the dissemination of ideas and the disclosure of inventions to foster the creative activities of others; and (4) protecting the rights of authors to be recognized and to receive income from their work. Intellectual property rights protection attempts to balance the exclusive right to control and profit from invention and authorship with a broadly defined social interest in the disclosure and dissemination of ideas. It is possible to have either too little protection, which will reduce the incentives for invention and authorship, or to have too much protection, which will discourage the adaptation and improvement of ideas.

The intellectual property right most pertinent to the creation of multimedia and

---

[4] This possibility was raised by the European Commission with the publication of its Green Paper on combating counterfeiting and piracy. 'The question is whether the mechanisms already in place are adequate to ensure uniform application of the legislation, or whether counterfeiting activities have moved location in order to take advantage of differences in the level of penalties' (European Commission, 1998a: 2–3).

much of the other content that is distributed through the information and communication infrastructure is copyright. A copyright is an exclusive right granted to the owner and/or author of information content for its reproduction and distribution. As with other intellectual property, the exclusivity of the copyright supports establishment of a price for information content above the (potentially) very low costs of information reproduction. The costs of reproduction may be further reduced by the use of modern information and communication technologies. The pricing of content above its costs of reproduction provides an incentive to individuals and groups to seek less expensive means of accessing the information that has received a copyright. Some individuals will be deterred from making copies of protected works by civil or criminal penalties and others will refuse to make or use such copies because of sympathies with the efforts of the author or publisher in making the content available. It is possible for illicit copying to become a socially inappropriate behaviour, much as plagiarism is shunned and reviled. After taking account of these sources of resistance to infringement, the major factor influencing the extent of infringement of copyright is likely to be the ease with which illicit copies can be made.

The transformation of information content into digital form greatly increases the ease with which copies can be made. The principal purposes of information and communication technologies include acquiring, storing, processing, and displaying information. Each of these functions involves making identical copies of information in different parts of the same information processing system or between different information processing systems. These capabilities are intrinsic to the operation of personal computers and other information technologies and they form the technological basis for data communication. The technological performance of these systems is, indeed, judged by the speed and reliability with which they copy and move information. The argument that digital technologies facilitate the infringement of copyright, therefore, is correct.

The facility with which digital information can be copied has a number of specific implications. Within organizations, the ease of transferring digital content creates challenges for managing the use of electronic information in ways that will avoid civil and criminal liabilities. Within the community of users, compliance becomes more complex as digital technologies also allow the transformation of specific types of content.[5] For the international community, the ease and scale of trans-border transmission of digitized information raises issues about the harmonization of different national legal systems. At a global level, even more dramatic developments are conceivable, such as the possible emergence of safe havens from which 'pirates' can operate outside the reach of whatever rules are adopted. Responding to such activities when they occur within a globally interconnected data communication network is clearly a major problem.

The difficulties of maintaining copyright protection in digital information are similar to those that were encountered for print information with the advent of new

---

[5] This point was a central theme in the US Office of Technology Assessment's review of issues in this area with the advent of widespread access to electronic sources of information, see Office of Technology Assessment (1986).

technology. For example, the problem of enforcing book copyrights traditionally involved detecting the creation of infringing copies and interdicting their distribution. The fact that a book is a physical artefact with a relatively low economic value per unit of volume or weight greatly aided efforts to curtail infringement activities in earlier decades and created a major barrier for smaller-scale activities. The diffusion of inexpensive plain-paper copying greatly increased the problems of copyright protection for printed material. Plain-paper copying provides a technology that the information user can readily employ to infringe copyrights, and its advent also raised the issue of who should be liable for copyright infringement, the person infringing or the owner of the tools that allowed the infringement to occur. In the case of the publication of copyright-infringing books, where the use of printing presses and binding, warehousing, and distribution facilities were needed to make infringement worthwhile, legal authority supported the practice of laying claim to these assets in recompense for the economic damage to the copyright owner. This tradition of pursuing the 'tool owner' has been carried forward to the owners of copying machines and is being applied to organizations that own or control any part of the information and communication infrastructure, including providers of services such as electronic bulletin boards and electronic mail servers.

The provision of copyright protection supports the creation of new business models for enterprises that base all, or some part, of their business on the Internet. It also provides a basis for markets in the sale and distribution of information over a medium that is designed to facilitate copying. The means by which this protection is enforced are particularly important in determining the economic viability of copyright protection. The existence of copyright is influencing the types of information that are becoming available to citizens and consumers in the European information society. The legal rules and policies underlying the definition, grant, and enforcement of intellectual property rights are, therefore, among the most important of Europe's interests in the construction of the information and communication infrastructure.

7.2.1   Social Purposes and Intellectual Property Rights

Intellectual property rights protection interacts, and sometimes conflicts, with competition and social policies. The exclusivity of intellectual property rights may create the basis for the accumulation of market power, which would be a concern if this were achieved through the exclusive control of some other asset such as the only site for a shipping dock. In the case of copyright, a principal concern is that the owner of a copyright in computer software may be able to accumulate market power by virtue of the network externalities created by the common use of a particular program. This, of course, is the essence of the insurgent strategy. Network externalities arise through the widespread investment in the skills for using a software program and this makes it desirable to adopt the software as a *de facto* standard. The investment by people in acquiring these skills becomes complementary to the value of the software. The software producers benefit from this investment as well as their own investment in creating the software.[6] In a similar fashion, network externalities also may be generated if the software enables the creation of data files. The ease with which data files may be exchanged will encourage either the common adoption of software, or the use of software that is able to access the same data files.[7] The ability to translate data files created by other software applications limits the extent of the market power of a successful software program producer. However, it does not eliminate the potential for the accumulation of market power because the successful software producing company can alter the formats of its data files over time. This may make it more difficult for companies to assure their customers that they will be able to access files created by the software of competing companies. In both Europe and the United States, exceptions have been granted to copyright rules to permit the modification of software in order to achieve interoperability between competing products.[8]

Social interests provide a key rationale for many of the exceptions granted to copyrights. In the United Kingdom, for example, the principle of 'fair dealing' permits the reproduction of portions of copyrighted material for the purposes of criticism, review, and reporting of current events as well as for research and private study. A central issue in the 'fair dealing' exception to copyright is the financial motivation for making a copy of all, or part, of a copyrighted work. Even when there is no profit motive associated with making copies, however, the exception is limited (ibid. 136–42).

The limitations on copying for social purposes, other than making a profit, raise difficult questions about the trade-offs between the public's interest in offering an incentive for the creation and distribution of information and the value for all purposes of accessing information. By no means are all the motivations for accessing information commercial in nature. Yet copyright is principally motivated by the creation of a property right in information, that is, transforming information into a commodity. Even if the original author of the information freely discloses the information, recompensing the distributor of the information for the expense and risk-taking will often require the enforcement of copyright. There may be substantial costs to society arising from this practice. For example, medical information distributed in scholarly journals may be of substantial social value. Paying the costs arising from copyright protection, however, may put health authorities in the position of restricting the budgets for the direct provision of healthcare in order to provide better information to physicians about treatment options.[9]

---

[6] The existence of network externalities in the supply of specialized labour skills raises the effective price of competing products (which require similar levels of investment in specialized skills). This allows the software producer to set a price higher than would be feasible in the absence of such externalities. The companies that provide employment are more likely to benefit from this skills investment than are the employees themselves, particularly in situations where the mastery of these skills is widespread.

[7] The strategic implications of this type of network externality have been examined for the case of personal computer spreadsheet software in which the 'import' capability of particular products was an important source of their competitive advantage, see Shurmer and Swann (1995).

[8] See Art. 6 of the 1991 Council Directive on the legal protection of computer programs (European Council, 1991) and the Digital Millennium Copyright Act of 1998, Section 1201(f) (United States Congress, 1998).

[9] It is implausible to argue that it is possible to make a precise decision between purchasing an additional unit of direct healthcare provision or a unit of professional information.

Information may be created for a wide variety of purposes other than making it into a commodity for market exchange. As we observed in the introduction to this chapter, the view that information *is* created for the purpose of sales can be called a 'commodity transaction model' of information creation. Other models, such as a cultural exchange model, where the purpose is to preserve and exemplify the language, history, and view of human life in a culture, can also be articulated. Alternatives to the commodity transaction model suggest that different principles should govern the creation of property rights in information. It is our view that the commodity transaction model limits the space for other models of exchange to be developed.

Social policies are intended to promote education and lifelong learning, improved healthcare, better environmental protection, and a host of other objectives. The implementation of social policies often involves the use of information that may be subject to intellectual property protection. With some important exceptions, the right of the information creator to legal protection is absolute, without regard to who infringes upon the copyrights, or for what purpose. A copyright adheres to the creation of almost any form of information regardless of authorial intention or purpose. Whether desirable or not, the commodity transaction model has become the predominant principle for the exchange of intellectual creations. Alternative views about the extension and enforcement of intellectual property rights not only have implications for the balance between incentives and costs, they also involve issues that influence matters such as the distribution of power and control in the social and economic system. The assignment of copyright is a specific means by which power relationships are established and maintained through the increasing primacy of the commodity transaction model of information creation and distribution.

7.2.2   Intellectual Property Rights Systems

Systems for granting rights in intellectual property embody and reflect legal doctrines and principles that are particular to the development of legal systems. For example, French law focuses on the protection of the authors' right to control the copying and potential modification of their work. By contrast, copyright law in England emerged from a desire to regulate the nature of competition in the commodity exchange of literary and artistic works and was endorsed in the United States constitution as a means to 'promote the progress of science and the useful arts' (David, 1993). The British and American motives for protecting the commercial interests of publishers have been emphasized in economic analyses of copyright law. The French tradition of *droit d'auteur*, including *droit moral* (the moral rights of authors to be identified and to forbid alteration of their work without permission) and *droit de suite* (the right of authors to benefit from the subsequent sales of their work), continue to influence efforts to harmonize European copyright protection systems.

Copyright law grants the creator of particular types of works an exclusive right to control the making of copies, and the broadcasting, or other forms of distribution of that work to the public (Bainbridge, 1994: 25). A broadly accepted definition of what constitutes a work is that it includes 'every production in the literary, scientific and artistic domain, whatever may be the mode or form of its expression' (World Intellectual Property Organization, 1979: Art. 2(1)). This definition encompasses much of the information that might be created for distribution in the information society. Indeed, the belief that existing law does not, in principle, protect new digital forms of information is generally misplaced (D'Amico, 1997). Instead, the aim of passing new legislation specifically mentioning digital technologies appears to be an effort to capture the attention of law enforcement agencies and to enhance the enforcement of penalties against specific forms of infringement. Increasing the publicity about legal protection for intellectual property rights has become a much more central concern with the widespread availability of effective copying techniques. Raising the willingness of individuals and organizations to self-enforce copyright protection is both less expensive and more effective than other types of enforcement programmes. Without such co-operation, the frequency of small-scale and individual infringements may collectively amount to a far larger source of revenue loss to copyright owners than organized pirating, which is easier to detect and to prosecute.

It is important to understand that copyright 'protection' is not synonymous with the possession of copyright. Although copyright in many countries has traditionally required a registration procedure, one implication of efforts to achieve global harmonization of copyright protection is that a creator of original content has a copyright on his or her work from the moment that the work is created. This does not mean, however, that the creator will be able to enforce exclusive ownership. Works must meet certain standards, including originality and a certain level of effort or amount of skill must have been expended in their creation to qualify for protection. This limits the ability of information creators to enforce their exclusive ownership and it makes it somewhat uncertain as to whether any particular work will receive protection. In general, the courts have been willing to enforce copyrights where a relatively low level of originality, skill, and effort has been involved in their creation.

This willingness to enforce copyrights meeting rather modest standards of originality, skill, and effort has heightened the importance of the issue of 'originality'. In the copyright law in the United States there is a clear doctrine that protects how ideas are 'expressed' rather than the ideas themselves, but the line between expression and ideas is often not clear-cut (Bainbridge, 1994: 36–7). In the United Kingdom, although this principle is not explicit, legal judgements have produced a similar standard (ibid. 37). For example, no one owns the copyright to the idea of a detective novel. It is possible to produce a detective novel that so closely copies the plot and other elements of, for example, a Simenon detective novel, that it will be deemed to violate copyright, even if no sentence is exactly the same. The demarcation line between an idea and its expression is important for software and multimedia creators because the innovative character of these works may reside in their 'look and feel' to users. It is also important because of the relative ease with which a particular 'expression' may be modified through the use of software authoring techniques. These possibilities heighten the concerns of copyright owners who fear that they will not be able to capture economic returns on their efforts, and encourages arguments in favour of a broader definition of 'expression'.

The same set of issues, however, raises concerns for potential suppliers of new information. How will such suppliers document the originality of their creations and defend themselves from claims that they have made use of copyrighted material illegitimately? Alternatively, how will they be able to defend the originality of their works so that they may enforce their exclusive ownership? The history of the resolution of disputes over copyright does not offer reassuring responses to these questions. This is particularly so in the light of popular accounts that there need be only a tenuous link between existing copyrighted material and 'new' material in order to support litigation and even awards for copyright infringement. Extending and strengthening intellectual property rights may further encourage such claims. These are active areas of litigation in spite of efforts to update national legislation.[10]

In practice, the legal enforcement of copyright is complicated because an exact definition of what constitutes a 'derivative' work requires judgement in all but the most transparent cases of direct copying of copyrighted work. Since this judgement is exercised within national legal domains, inevitably there is divergence between national legal practices. A practising solicitor in one jurisdiction may reason that a particular use of a copyrighted source is legal while a practising lawyer in another jurisdiction may view the same use as unsafe. There is risk for the information supplier in following either judgement because, ultimately, a claim of infringement will have to be adjudicated with its attendant uncertainties. International efforts to harmonize different national systems of copyright protection are aimed at creating a common framework within which similar decisions are made with regard to what is protected and how it should be protected and enforced. This process is unlikely, however, to result in identical practice.

In addition, efforts to create a common framework are sometimes overridden by other more specific concerns. For example, in Europe, concerns about the interoperability of software were taken into account in the drafting of the 1991 directive on the legal protection of computer programs (European Council, 1991). This directive instructed that Member State implementation of copyright protection for software should grant the owners of a software program (or their agents) an exception for the express purpose of revising the program to make it interoperable with other software.[11] A similar provision was included in the Digital Millennium Copyright Act of 1998 in the United States, which, in effect, harmonized practice between the United States and Europe (United States Congress, 1998). Legal precedents to resolve poten-

---

[10] IP Worldwide (http://www.ipww.com/index.html) and Stanford University's site on copyright and fair use (http://fairuse.stanford.edu/articles) are two sources for information in the United States with some international coverage (both accessed 10 April 2000). In Europe, the European Legal Advisory Board (LAB) at http://www2.echo.lu/legal/en/labhome.html accessed 18 September 1999 offers access to LAB documents and news on LAB-related issues for the European Union information market.

[11] 'The authorization of the rightholder shall not be required where reproduction of the code and translation of its form within the meaning of Article 4(a) and (b) are indispensable to obtain the information necessary to achieve the interoperability of an independently created computer program with other programs' and several conditions apply (European Council, 1991: Art. 6).

tial conflicts between this exception and copyright owner interests have yet to be established.

Similarly, the 1996 'Directive on the Legal Protection of Databases' provides *sui generis* protection for the compilation of databases (European Council, 1996*b*). To whit, 'In accordance with this Directive, databases which, by reason of the selection or arrangement of their contents, constitute the author's own intellectual creation shall be protected as such by copyright. No other criteria shall be applied to determine their eligibility for that protection' (ibid. Art. 3.1). This is a very broad protection indeed. It does not set a threshold with regard to the originality of the arrangement, the amount of effort required to create it, or any other consideration. It is unclear how conflicting claims as to the provenance of particular databases will be resolved as there is little basis for deciding what the phrase 'selection or arrangement of their contents' implies for the purpose of resolving conflicting claims of authorship. Whatever desirable features may arise from the incentive to create new databases which, by reason of the selection or arrangement of their contents, constitute the author's own intellectual creation, the costs of enforcing and establishing contracts for improvements in databases are likely to be substantially elevated by the enforcement of this Directive.

The point of these examples is a simple one. Although the effort to create a common global system of governance for copyright protection might provide a useful framework for conducting trade in copyrighted material, the practice of implementing legislation is likely to create divergent systems of copyright protection. The level of the costs that will arise as a result is not yet known, but it is clear that considerable diversity is inevitable in enforcement practice. In the context of efforts to strengthen such protection, there is likely to be more, rather than less, uncertainty governing trade in copyrighted material. The potential liability of the producer of copyrighted information to other parties holding copyright interests is likely to be amplified in this environment of uncertainty. This suggests the need to re-examine the nature of markets for copyrighted material with a view to assessing how such uncertainties and liabilities may affect social well-being.

7.3   Social Constituencies in the Information Society

The nature of the property right conveyed by copyright raises the costs of accessing information and, as a result, provides an incentive to develop and distribute information. As previously noted, provisions for copyright involve drawing a balance between the interests of copyright holders and other members of society. The incentives provided by property rights in information are not the only motivations for the creation or distribution of information as we suggested in the preceding section. Efforts to extend and simplify the process of obtaining copyright ensure that virtually all information that is new is, in fact, copyrighted.

Ideas about the purposes and methods for exchanging digital information, including markets for copyright licences, are not nearly as well developed as the new technologies for facilitating the exchange of that information. This creates a paradoxical situation. Although a considerable amount of information available from on-line service providers is owned and protected by copyright, the providers of such information may have little or no intention of enforcing their rights. Indeed, many individuals are not aware that the information that they provide in electronic mail messages, on-line postings of discussion comments, or essays on their hobbies or interests contained in their web sites are all, in principle, copyright protected.

Some guidance as to the motivations for the supply of different types of information and for the interest in accessing this information is available from examination of the collection of publicly accessible information services. These services include, for example, the Minitel system in France, Internet-based commercial services such as CompuServe, and research- or university-oriented computer networks, such as Janet, the academic network in the United Kingdom, as well as support services provided by hardware or software companies. The goals for developing these networks and for supplying information to them include, for example, contributing to publicly available information, promoting activities such as research and education, and generating commercial revenues.

Users or subscribers to these networks also have a diverse collection of reasons for accessing this information. They are suppliers of information themselves when they communicate political, cultural, and social views, share practical information, 'post' research results, and offer goods and services for sale. What is striking about almost all these information and communication systems is the amount of material that is available without specific payment or assertion of exclusive ownership. Nevertheless, a user cannot be assured that the particular information that he or she uses is not owned by an individual or organization who will assert copyright and demand payment for subsequent use of this information. This situation points to the growing importance of providing clear distinctions between different motivations for information distribution. It also creates the need for explicit provisions for reducing the potential liability in the use of information that, although copyrighted, is not intended to be part of the commodity transaction model for information creation.

7.3.1   Three Constituencies

In this section we describe the uses of copyright by three different constituencies of individuals and organizations. The first constituency makes either no use, or only limited use, of copyright protection. The second constituency uses copyright protection to maintain control over the content of works, but benefits from the wide dissemination of copies. The third constituency seeks direct control over who may make copies in order to be able to sell the copied information. The defining characteristic of these constituencies lies in how their members tend to regard the use of information that they *own* by virtue of the nearly universal copyright on new expression. A given organization or individual may be a member of one, two, or all three of the constituencies because the information that is contributed may have many different purposes. By examining these constituencies it is possible to identify potential conflicts in economic or social interests between these constituencies with respect to copyright protection. When the same individual or organization has multiple allegiances to different constituencies, there may be divided or mixed opinions about how conflicts about copyright protection should be resolved.

7.3.1.1 The Public Domain Constituency

The first constituency of producers of information includes those who receive a benefit from the dissemination of their works unrelated to their receipt of revenue or income, as well as those people who simply want their contributions to be freely available to others. Associated with this constituency are users who are interested in information for both personal and commercial reasons. An example of the latter is the monitoring of publicly disclosed research results to identify commercial opportunities. A very substantial amount of information now provided on the Internet and commercial bulletin-board services is non-commercial in nature. The authors of much of this information seek the broadest possible dissemination of their contributions without charging receivers. Examples of members of this constituency include researchers who want to share scientific data, individuals wanting to exchange political viewpoints, and teachers who want to share their insights about education. Both the producer and user portions of this constituency support the inexpensive distribution of public domain information using information and communication infrastructures. Producers within this group often have an interest in copyright protection in accord with *droit moral* so that the content of their contributions remains unaltered and they continue to be recognized as the author of the material they contribute. Their motives, however, do not include an interest in payment for contributing specific information.

Even though the contributors of public domain information may have no interest in receiving payment for their contributions, this type of information distribution generates commercial opportunities. The most direct commercial return available from public domain information is the revenue that information service providers receive for access. Information service providers include the larger commercial providers as well as those offering networks of bulletin-board services that can be organized using a telephone connection and a modest investment in equipment. The values of these service providers' businesses are higher due to the existence of freely available information than they would be if suppliers had to pay for the information itself. In addition, the desire of producers to improve the value of their public domain contributions partially supports the creation of books, magazines, and software devoted to tools for improving the display qualities and usability of public domain information. Users have an interest in discovering useful public domain material and this interest is partially supported by a market for guides to information services and the creation of electronic databases to such resources.

It is possible that such information providers can achieve their ambitions by explicitly stating the terms of use for the information that they provide. A disclaimer such as 'The right to reproduce the information contained herein is freely given provided that the following notice of authorship is retained' may or may not be meaningful. To our knowledge, there has not yet been a legal case in Europe or North America testing whether such a disclaimer constitutes an effective and non-rescindable transfer of rights to the user. Moreover, to our knowledge, there is no effective means of limiting liability stemming from third parties. Thus, even if a producer claims that information provided to a user is original, the user (as well as the producer) is still liable, in principle, to third-party claims of copyright infringement. In short, the means to ascertain and assign liabilities in the exchange of information are very inadequately provided for under existing law.

7.3.1.2   *The Related Revenue Constituency*

A second constituency of information producers shares an interest in distributing information without direct payment for the receipt of that information but expects the distribution of the information to increase their future revenue or income. Examples of the members of this group, which we call the 'related revenue constituency', are businesses that hope the information will improve their positions with investors, with the public, and with customers, in particular. Such information, which often falls into the categories of public relations and advertising, is normally costly for businesses to deliver to their existing or potential customers. Similar advertising and promotional activities are conducted by charitable and non-profit organizations that rely on voluntary contributions.

At present, there are important differences between the practice of advertising and public relations in the electronic environment and the use of more traditional media. The use of media such as newspapers, magazines, and, particularly, direct mail, involves the study of the demographic characteristics of target audiences which leads to highly selective and focused strategies for achieving exposure. All these techniques can be markedly improved as the information and communication infrastructure is extended, ultimately providing the means to address specific advertising and promotion messages to individuals. Uses of the information and communication infrastructure for these purposes are emerging quickly, which is bringing with it concerns within the user community about the unsolicited nature of such information.[12] In addition, since an attractive technique is to monitor and analyse information service requests and other information about the individuals using the service, concerns about privacy are likely to become more important for the information users in the related revenue constituency.

Innovative uses of the information and communication infrastructures, including physical exchange of information on discs between individuals, the distribution of CD-ROMs with printed magazines, and the availability of downloadable files on the Internet, are being made by the producers of shareware computer programs and other

---

[12] The issue is viewed by some as one of freedom of choice with regard to the receipt of information that may or may not be desired and by others as a more fundamental invasion of privacy that should be subject to social control. The latter view is similar to the views of those opponents to the use of 'subliminal' advertising messages, see van Warrebey (1998). There are also substantial differences in the types of concerns about these issues between countries and cultural traditions.

variants of 'free' information products. These producers promote the copying of their products and exhort users to make a financial contribution if they use the product for more than investigation and trial. At an early stage in its evolution there was mixed evidence that this strategy would, in fact, lead to commercial returns for producers (Takeyama, 1994). The further technological advance of this means of software distribution development has included 'limited functionality' trial versions (and trial versions software that may be used indefinitely but offers only a subset of the features available in the purchased version) that stop functioning after a pre-determined trial period or number of accesses. With these advances, the method has become widespread and is a major medium for the distribution of computer software.[13] In effect, this technology allows a 'locked' product to be given away and the 'keys' to make the product useful to be sold.

Other innovative uses of the information and communication infrastructure by the related revenue constituency include the offer of post-sales support to customers, such as fixes or upgrades to software products. Distribution of this information is complementary to the sale of products and services in which the primary copyright or other contractual protections are established outside the infrastructure. In rapidly moving product and service markets, this form of relationship with customers provides information supporting product improvement and helps to retain customer loyalty, thus contributing to future sales. These examples by no means exhaust the types of activities that commercial enterprises and individuals are employing in seeking related revenues. These uses of the information and communication infrastructure are distinct from those that occur within the framework of the commodity transaction model of information creation and distribution. In general, the members of the related revenue constituency identify a link between the information distribution capabilities of the infrastructure and their business activities. Virtually all the conventional methods of promoting products or customer interests have digital equivalents including new product announcements, hints and tips for product uses, and customer support phone lines.

The related revenue approach requires the selective application of copyright enforcement. Companies using this strategy have no interest in and presumably no claim to revenue from users who copy their products for the intended use, for example, for trial of the software. However, they will assert their copyright when the user modifies the software to allow its indefinite use or alters advertising information to divert revenue from the producer of the information to some other party. Whether such claims will eventually be accepted by the courts under the provisions of copyright protection like the *droit moral* stricture on the 'mutilation' of products, that is, alteration of a work, or some other argument, remains to be seen.

---

[13] The related revenue implication of this kind of distribution involves the recognition that there is no direct exchange of money for a product or service. In this respect, the distribution of a trial version, even one that only requires the entry of a password to make it fully functional, can be regarded as a form of advertising. The sales transaction occurs only with the distribution of a full version or the password 'key' to unlock the program. In the latter case, some type of legal liability stems from the user's distribution of the key to others rather than from a further distribution of the locked programme.

The law of copyright provides a large and rather blunt instrument for enforcing such claims.

Users of information provided by the producers in the related revenue constituency face problems of searching and filtering information of value to them that are similar to those which they experience when they participate in the public domain constituency. This generates a demand for guides and directories, and related revenue information producers are often identified in guides to public domain information. It is unclear, therefore, whether users in this group are distinct at this time from the members of the constituency that are using public domain information. In the future, however, these two user constituencies may develop more distinct identities corresponding to differences between those individuals who avoid advertising messages and those who seek them out.[14]

7.3.1.3   The Direct Revenue Constituency

A third constituency of producers and users has an interest in selling and buying information goods and services using the information and communication infrastructure. This constituency is built around the commodity transaction model of information creation and distribution. Producers in this direct revenue group need a means of protecting the value of their goods and services from those who would like to receive them without paying. The members of this group are strongly interested in direct copyright protection and, at least in principle, will attempt to recover damages from the possessor of any unlicensed copy of their copyrighted information. The markets created for these goods and services are based upon: (1) winning a share of the existing markets for information distribution using other media with information and communication infrastructures eventually being able to deliver audio, audiovisual, and multimedia products; (2) creating new products and services involving information that may be subject to copyright protection but that is, either by choice or by technical limitation, not distributed using other media; and (3) creating new services that may employ the telecommunication features of networks, for example, videophone services. Intellectual property protection is particularly relevant in the first two of these markets.

The sale of information products and services that may be distributed using other media is reliant upon a number of developments outside the intellectual property rights domain. It is often assumed that the costs of reproducing and distributing information products will fall dramatically when such information is distributed via communication networks. This view is in line with the argument in Ch. 5 in which disintermediation is regarded as an efficiency-improving quality of e-commerce. What is often not appreciated is that the manufacturing costs of creating copies of information embedded in other media are already quite low. For example, in book publishing, the costs of manufacturing a copy are a small fraction of the price paid for a book. The remaining larger fraction of the price covers the costs of retailers and distributors who promote, stock, and deliver the books; the costs of the publisher in promoting the

---

[14] It is already common practice for some web sites to distinguish between software referred to as 'crippleware' (limited in functionality) from 'full release' software.

work; absorbing losses on copies of books that are not sold; and the payments to the author. While distribution and unsold inventory costs may be reduced by electronic distribution, some or all of the costs that distributors and retailers now incur in promoting copyrighted works must be covered by publishers or must be received by electronic distributors. Similar considerations apply to compact discs, packaged software (where the author and publisher are usually the same), and pre-recorded audio- and videotapes.

Thus, digital products and services will continue to compete with other media for distributing copyrighted works, such as books and pre-recorded audio or video recordings. Competition between media for the distribution of information is important because it explains why a very high level of intellectual protection may be sought by publishers as a prerequisite for choosing to distribute works using the information and communication infrastructure. Electronic distribution does not create business opportunities that are identical to existing markets. For example, the publishers of academic journals have long sought effective methods of price discrimination that would allow them to charge higher prices to libraries and lower prices to individuals. More sophisticated approaches are now available for electronic journals, such as 'site licences'. Electronic distribution also allows for the development of new business strategies that utilize differences between electronic and physical distribution methods. For example, the publication of literary works with attractive bindings and typography is likely to continue even if lower priced copies of the text are made available using information and communication services.

Another important category of information distribution that takes advantage of the information and communication infrastructure is broadcast audio or video programmes. Broadcasts, including those made by public broadcasters, are subject to copyright and the rebroadcast or commercial copying of broadcasts are held to be a violation of copyright. As broadcasting becomes part of a convergent infrastructure, problems of copyright protection such as copying of broadcasts for commercial gain, are transferred to the information and communication infrastructure domain. New problems also emerge, for example, in the wake of the high-performance features of the infrastructure, such as video links that can be used to redirect broadcasts or to distribute copies of them.

Producers and, to a lesser extent, users in the direct revenue constituency have a unique interest in copyright protection and the commodity transaction model of information creation and distribution. Both producers and users have an interest in the development of effective payment mechanisms that afford a secure and reliable means to make payments for products and services distributed using the information and communication infrastructure.

7.4   Shared and Conflicting Interests between the Constituencies

The three constituencies make distinctive uses of copyright protection and rely upon it in different ways. In addition, producers and users have divergent interests in the effectiveness of copyright protection and in the vigour of copyright enforcement. Understanding how the highest value can be derived from these activities requires that we address the shared and conflicting interests between these groups. As previously noted, an individual or organization may participate in one, or in all three, of the constituencies when they become engaged with the features of the information and communication infrastructure.

The primary interest of producers in the public domain sector is in retaining some credit for their works. Although apparently innocuous, assertions of this right amount to a claim of copyright that could provide the basis for claims of damage in civil litigation. The costs of contesting such actions will generate social as well as private costs since all litigation involves the social costs of providing the services of the courts. The courts would be obliged to treat such claims in a fashion similar to any other copyright infringement claim even if they eventually ruled that the information was in the public domain and could be copied, modified, or excerpted by users without any recognition for the producer. The point here is that the existing legal system does not provide an explicit recognition for a modified assertion of copyright. In the United Kingdom, and most other European countries, copyright begins immediately with the expression of a work and continues until fifty years after the death of the author.[15]

The public domain constituency comes into conflict with the other two constituencies in the production and receipt of material that violates copyright. Suppliers who incorporate copyrighted works without authorization in their own distributions, or users who receive unauthorized copies of copyrighted works, are legally liable for the commercial damage that such activities may cause. Similarly, it may be claimed that a particular producer has violated copyright when his or her work is substantially similar in expression to a work that is protected. Legal defences against copyright infringement based on inadvertence or ignorance are unlikely to be successful. Raising the level of intellectual property protection and enforcement, thus increases the liability of both producers and users.[16]

As for other liability issues, the choices include: (1) increasing the level of monitoring and avoidance of risk to reduce liability; (2) insuring against the risk of liability; (3) accepting the risk with the hope of escaping a legal liability judgement; or (4) attempting to transfer the liability risk to another party. Opting for either of the first two choices will directly increase the costs for members of the public domain con-

---

[15] See Bainbridge (1994: 54). For computer software, copyright applies until 50 years after the work has been introduced in the case of organizational or pseudonymous authorship and, for authored works, 50 years after the death of the last surviving author (European Council, 1991: Art. 8).

[16] Note that the May 1999 amended proposal for a Directive on Copyright and Related Rights in the Information Society (European Commission, 1999b), applies to private copying, and photocopying for teaching and scientific research. If agreed, it would oblige Member States to ensure fair compensation for rights holders although the form of such compensation would be up to each Member State to decide. At present, 11 Member States provide for private copying to be exempted from the scope of the exclusive reproduction right, that is, the right of the rights holder to authorize or prevent copying. The United Kingdom, Ireland, Luxembourg, and Denmark do not make a specific provision. The 11 Member States provide for systems of compensation for rights holders through levies on blank audio and audiovisual recording media and in the case of Belgium, Greece, Italy, and Spain, on recording apparatus.

stituency. Selecting either of the latter two choices can lead to higher costs for the members of this constituency at a later time depending upon the level of copyright enforcement. In short, there are conflicts of social and economic interest between the public domain constituency and the other two groups.

The conflict between the related revenue and direct revenue constituencies is less direct. It involves primarily the consequences of the conflicts with the public domain constituency. To the extent that higher levels of protection for copyrighted works either directly or indirectly raise costs in terms of access convenience, the interests of the members of the indirect revenue constituency are damaged. The members of this constituency have a principal interest in easy access to information and cost and convenience are primary determinants of ease of access.

If it becomes possible to resolve these conflicts by developing a widely accepted and secure means of transferring copyrighted information between producers and customers or citizens, then the extent of conflict between the constituencies could be markedly reduced. Security issues involve two aspects: (1) the security of particular types of information from unauthorized reproduction; and (2) the security of the information and communication infrastructure from being used to transmit unauthorized copies. The first aspect takes precedence since a reliable means of securing individual works would ensure that those who benefit pay the costs of security. A reliable means of addressing the first aspect *could* also encourage simplification of the standards for enforcing copyright. For example, a rule could be established whereby transmission of 'unsecured' information by its legitimate owner creates presumptive rights to use and reproduce that information. This, however, would require changes in copyright legislation. The second aspect may impose costs on all users of the information and communication infrastructure and, therefore, may lead to sustained conflicts between the interests of the three constituencies. As we discuss later in this chapter, neither type of security is widely accepted or effective. In this case, public policy, including policy on copyright protection, must weigh the balance of interests between members of different constituencies and devise solutions.

In recent years, the exclusive focus of changes in copyright protection has been to increase its scope. The European Directive on the Protection of Databases, which we noted earlier, is instructive in this regard. This Directive defines a database as follows: ' "database" shall mean a collection of independent works, data or other materials arranged in a systematic or methodical way and individually accessible by electronic or other means' (European Council, 1996b: Art. 1.2). A literal reading of this definition makes a shopping list subject to *sui generis* protection as a database.[17] Inevitably, there will be substantial social and private litigation costs before the scope and applicability of the legislation created by this Directive are worked out in Member State jurisdictions. In our view, it would be appropriate to take proactive action on behalf of the public domain and related revenue constituencies. This could be achieved by defining

---

[17] The significance of the term *sui generis* is that 'No other criteria shall be applied to determine their eligibility for that protection' (European Council, 1996b: Art. 3). The Directive does not instruct that Member State legislation protect the contents of the database, which may consist of information that is in the public domain or for which alternative sources may be available.

alternative models of copyright protection that, for example, would permit authors to make lasting grants or deeds of the property right conveyed by copyright to the public domain; and that would create a contractual model whereby limited and specified obligations could be required of information users.

The foregoing argument demonstrates that copyright protection involves costs as well as benefits. The exclusivity of the copyright grant and the economic benefits derived from owning information provide incentives to strengthen and extend control of the distribution of information to prevent 'pirating' or other breaches of copyright. There are, however, other incentives for information creation, distribution, and use than the market exchange of copyrighted information. Encouraging widespread use and public support for investments in the information and communication infrastructure requires that all parties' interests be taken into account. There are trade-offs between extending the framework of copyright protection and maximizing the value of that infrastructure for users.

7.5   The Global Framework for Digital Information Protection

There are two main reasons that the issues discussed in the previous section have not yet become central in the process of intellectual property rights reform that is being conducted on a global scale. The first is that there is a historical regulatory trajectory with regard to the enforcement of copyright that has been dominated by the emergence of new technologies of expression and copying. In this respect, computers are a new means for displaying information content and they present a challenge similar to the emergence of plain-paper copiers. There was some basis for comparison when personal computers were stand-alone devices rather than access devices in a global information and communication infrastructure whose value and growth depends upon the ready availability of content.

The business models for generating revenue from content are now often only tangentially related to the historical models of selling a tangible item such as a book, a phonograph, or a packaged software product. It is not surprising that the dominant economic interests encouraging the continuation and extension of existing copyright models are centred in the direct revenue community. This constituency is one of the few places in the landscape of the information society where insurgent strategies of capturing mass markets and incumbent strategies of generating revenue from proprietary information assets are completely consistent and aimed at building mass markets for the commodity of information. Although the virtual community strategy firms that are part of the direct revenue constituency may be quite willing to 'free ride' on the efforts of their larger rivals, their interest in strong copyright protection may be more limited. Firms and organizations adopting a virtual community strategy are likely to change their products very rapidly and to have developed a service relationship with their customers that makes the significance of copyright protection far less relevant.

A second reason for the extension and strengthening of copyright protection is that copyright is only one of the bundle of intellectual property rights that comprises a package in global trade negotiations. Strong and simple proposals for rights protection have been characteristic of the international efforts to establish new 'rules of the game' to govern intellectual property rights protection in trade and other contexts. Even though it has been recognized that the enforcement of intellectual property rights agreed via treaty is a complex matter, a globally consistent framework for resolving disputes on these issues has appeared to be much more desirable than the recurrent outbreak of bilateral disputes. In the international forums where intellectual property rights have been discussed to achieve new provisions, the information and communication technology firms have been key players alongside firms from the content-producing industries and those from the pharmaceuticals industry. The potentially divergent interests of these groups of firms could be united around a stronger intellectual property protection agenda.

The international harmonization of copyright laws in a proactive manner is increasingly high on the political agenda. The potential emergence of safe havens for illegal copies of material and the potential for outbreaks of severe bilateral tensions over copyright issues are among the reasons for moving towards harmonization. These concerns have been heightened by the knowledge that computer bulletin boards and other means of distribution provide a means of making illicit copies of new programs globally available, even before the first legal copies are in the shops.

The historical origin of the particular regulatory trajectory that encourages a focus on the tangibility of copyrighted products is deeply rooted in modern European history. National standards for the protection of intellectual property rights were the result of the first efforts by European countries to harmonize their legal systems through international agreement. Signatories to the Berne Convention for the Protection of Literary and Artistic Works of 1886 agreed to enforce the copyright of foreign authors according to their own copyright laws and to enact national laws addressing copyright coverage and other issues (World Intellectual Property Organization, 1979). The Berne Convention is now monitored by the World Intellectual Property Organization (WIPO). This Convention was a major step towards harmonization of copyright enforcement since it allowed legal action in the country in which a violation occurred regardless of the nationality of the author. Successive agreements during this century have extended the minimum rights granted by the Convention, for example, for public performances, and the cinema. The United States becoming a signatory to the Convention in 1989 and the addition of many developing countries as signatories has enhanced its international significance. At present, the Berne Convention provides a workable international framework for copyright enforcement for many of the tangible forms of information that can be made available using the information and communication infrastructure, including those of greatest interest to the direct revenue constituency.

However, the Berne Convention does not determine the level of protection to be applied within any particular signatory country. The existence of relatively weak protection in some non-OECD countries was influential in the establishment of the Trade-Related Aspects of Intellectual Property Rights (TRIPS) agreement. The TRIPS agreement was part of the General Agreement on Tariffs and Trade (GATT) Uruguay Round which was completed in 1994 and came into force on 1 January 1995 (World Trade Organization, 1999). The TRIPS agreement articulates the norms for national law suggested in the Berne Convention and allows for trade sanctions against non-complying nations. For such sanctions to be invoked, however, one of the contracting parties must lodge a complaint with the the World Trade Organization (WTO), the international body that was established following the completion of Uruguay Round. From a developing country viewpoint, the TRIPS agreement provides relief from the uncertainties of bilateral trade disputes that might be resolved against their interests in foreign jurisdictions. On the other hand, the agreement continues to create exposure for developing countries to trade sanctions arising from actions in their countries that they may find difficult to detect or suppress (Correa, 1994; United Nations Conference on Trade and Development, 1996). In effect, the TRIPS agreement obliges developing countries to mount a sophisticated detection and enforcement effort at substantial cost using resources that they may have preferred to devote to other development goals. This could result in the diffusion of information and communication technologies being impeded in some of these countries.

The evolution of intellectual property protection has been co-ordinated over the past three decades by WIPO.[18] The objectives of WIPO are to promote the protection of intellectual property throughout the world through co-operation among states and, where appropriate, in collaboration with any other international organization, and to ensure administrative co-operation among the signatories to the various conventions (World Intellectual Property Organization, 1996a). The regulatory trajectory, which has encouraged the extension of intellectual property rights protection to new technologies, has been reflected in the agenda of WIPO which co-ordinated two extensions to existing arrangements during the 1970s responding to the improvement in audio recording technology and the emergence of satellite broadcasting.[19] In the face of the growth of the Internet and the spread of new ways of exchanging information electronically, further initiatives to develop treaties embodying provisions for copyright protection in the digital environment have been undertaken culminating, in December 1996, with a major diplomatic conference under the auspices of WIPO. Two new treaties emerged from this conference: the WIPO Copyright Treaty and the WIPO Performances and Phonograms Treaty (World Intellectual Property Organization, 1996b; 1996c). As of April 1999, although these Treaties had respectively 51 and 50 country signatories, they were not yet in force.

[18] In 1967 the Convention Establishing the World Intellectual Property Organization was signed and three years later came into force. The WIPO Convention embraced the Paris Convention for the Protection of Industrial Property (1883) and the Berne Convention for the Protection of Literary and Artistic Works (1886). WIPO became a specialized agency of the United Nations in 1974. Both the Berne Convention and the Rome Convention (the International Convention for the Protection of Performers, Producers of Phonograms and Broadcasting Organizations) are administered by WIPO—in the latter case, jointly with the ILO and UNESCO. There is also a Universal Copyright Convention that is administered by UNESCO and the WTO provides the institutional focus for an agreement on TRIPS.

[19] These were the Convention for the Protection of Producers of Phonograms Against Unauthorized Duplication of their Phonograms (Oct. 1971) and a Convention Relating to the Distribution of Programme-Carrying Signals Transmitted by Satellite (May 1974).

The new treaties encompass new rights of distribution and provisions for electronic 'making available', provisions on copy-protection devices and for the unauthorized removal of work identifiers, and a provision obliging parties to provide effective procedures and remedies for infringement of rights. These provisions focus on the technologies related to direct revenue constituency issues, such as the distribution of unsanctioned decoding devices for satellite broadcasts and the continued improvement of recording technology.

The Copyright Treaty recognizes 'the need to maintain a balance between the rights of authors and the wider public interest, particularly education, research and access to information, as reflected in the Berne Convention' and 'the profound impact of the development and convergence of information and communication technologies on the creation and use of literary and artistic works' (ibid. 1996*b*: Preamble). Articles 4 and 5 of the Treaty protect computer programs as literary works whatever the mode or form of their expression and compilations of data 'which by reason of the selection or arrangement of their contents constitute intellectual creations' (a similar provision to that adopted in Europe) (ibid. Art. 5). Like the European Directive on the Protection of Databases (European Council, 1996*b*), protection does not extend to the data in the databases that are subject to ordinary copyright protection. The Treaty creates further obligations with respect to rights management information and other issues related to the physical transport and reproduction of discrete information 'products'.[20]

Delegates to the diplomatic conference were unable to reach agreement on provisions that would have clarified the scope of reproduction rights especially with regard to temporary reproductions, that is, those held in a computer memory or on a network server. This was a contentious issue although a statement did emerge to the effect that the Berne Convention does, in fact, encompass electronic storage of information. In addition, the new Performances and Phonograms Treaty covered only audio performances rather than audiovisual performances and a proposed modification right under this Treaty was deleted in order to reach agreement.

WIPO is not the only institution specifically promoting parallel technological advance between the means of copyright protection and the means of distributing digital information. Another example is the International Federation of the Phonographic Industry (IFPI). Created in 1933, it seeks to protect the interests of the international music industry, including producers of phonograms, that is, records and compact discs, and music videos. It co-operates closely with intergovernmental organizations and has consultative status with WIPO, the International Labour Office, the United Nations Educational, Scientific, and Cultural Organization, and the

[20] Contracting parties must provide legal remedies against any person knowingly removing or altering any electronic rights information without authority; distributing, importing for distribution, broadcast or communication to the public, without authority, works or copies of works, knowing that the electronics rights management information has been removed or altered without authority. Such information refers to that which identifies the work, the author of the work, the owner of any right in the work, or information about the terms and conditions of use of the work, and any numbers or codes that represent such information (World Intellectual Property Organization, 1996*b*).

Council of Europe.[21] IFPI supported an initiative by the United States to develop a Serial Copy Management System (SCMS) that is incorporated into digital recording equipment and prevents the making of copies from copies, although it allows an initial copy to be made. IFPI has also recommended that its member companies use the International Standard Recording Code (ISRC) system developed by the International Organization for Standardization.[22] IFPI and its respective national groupings play a role in copyright law enforcement. Measures include conducting investigations, accompanying local enforcement authorities on raids and seizure of infringing copies, and preparing prosecutions. Although these actions have been effective in the audio equipment industry, music CDs may now be easily produced on personal computers, a development that indicates the difficulty of seeking to match improvements in copyright protection technology with advances in the technological capability to make copies.

The United States has shared leadership in many of the international proposals to extend and strengthen copyrights along the regulatory trajectory of following new technological developments with new provisions for enforcement. Within the United States, however, there has been diverse and sometimes acrimonious debate about the extension of copyright. For example, a 1995 report from the Information Infrastructure Task Force (IITF) Working Group on intellectual property (National Information Infrastructure Task Force, 1995), was perceived by a close observer of these developments to have made proposals that would be detrimental to wider user access to information in a digital network environment.[23] Two of the proposals that received criticism included extending copyright to information that is temporarily stored in computer systems and creating 'first-sale' rights that would not include the right to transfer such works to another individual or company. Continuing the tradition of the tangible 'information product', the report supported the development of new digital copyright management systems and proposals similar to those mooted during the following year's WIPO diplomatic conference with regard to control of unauthorized decoding or protection technology countermeasures.[24]

---

[21] Its main objective is to promote, defend, and develop the rights of its members—producers of phonograms and music videos—both at national and international levels. The organization undertakes several activities including: promoting national legislation; advancing international conventions; negotiating royalty payments; safeguarding performance rights; and proposing technical solutions to minimize copyright infringement, see International Federation of the Phonographic Industry (1994).

[22] An ISRC is assigned by the first owner of the rights to a recording. It identifies the recording throughout its life and is intended for use by producers of musical recordings and videos as well as copyright organizations, collecting societies, broadcasting organizations, anti-piracy organizations, libraries, and others. The ISRC system involves the insertion of a subcode for all digital sound recordings at the time of production of the tape master. Each track on a CD can be given its own unique coded identification number. The ISRC identifies the recording, and not the physical product. The code consists of twelve characters, representing country, first owner, year of recording and designation, and is digitally encoded.

[23] See Samuelson (1995). For an exchange between proponents and opponents of the extension and greater enforcement of copyright protection in the United States, see comments in Stefik *et al.* (1998).

[24] Copyright management information includes 'the name and other identifying information of the author of a work, the name and other identifying information of the copyright owner, terms and conditions for uses of the work, and such other information as the Register of Copyrights may prescribe by regulation', Samuelson (1995: 135–6).

These developments recapitulate the main issues in the copyright discussions that have occurred in the WIPO context. First, there was the question of whether the existing copyright protection framework was adequately addressing information distributed by electronic networks. This subject was dealt with extensively by the European Commission in its 'Green Paper on Copyright and the Challenge of Technology' which enumerated gaps in Member State laws in the late 1980s (European Commission, 1988*b*: 45–53). Second, there were proposals to increase the efficiency of markets for copyrighted information by making technological and institutional changes (such as automated registration) that would allow users who want to comply, to do so with a minimum of difficulty. Many of the solutions were intended to make illicit copying more difficult. Third, there were proposals for technological and institutional changes that would extend enforcement and frustrate the efforts of 'pirates'.

In response to the new WIPO treaties, the United States government introduced the Digital Millennium Copyright Act (DMCA) of 1998 (United States Congress, 1998). This Act implements the provisions of the WIPO treaties and makes clear the exceptions for non-profit libraries, archives, and education institutions to circumvent copyright provisions upon obtaining authorizations. As noted earlier, the Act also makes provisions for reverse engineering of copyrighted software to support interoperability. The Act aims to support encryption research aimed at identifying flaws and vulnerabilities in encryption technologies, to protect minors with access to the Internet, and to protect personal privacy.

From the perspective of liability concerns, the DMCA is both bad and good news. In terms of bad news, the Act provides for further criminal penalties. Failure to comply with the Act carries a criminal penalty for a first offence of up to US\$ 500,000 or five years' imprisonment and \$1m. or ten years' imprisonment for subsequent offences. Non-profit libraries and related institutions are not criminally liable. Some limited good news in reducing liability and encouraging information access was also part of the DCMA. Title II of the Act creates four new limitations on liability for copyright infringement by on-line service providers, that is, for transitory communications, system caching, storage of information on systems or networks at the direction of users, and information location tools. It may also be argued that the high penalties will lead to selective enforcement.

From the early 1990s, the European Commission has been active in the field of copyright legislation. It has focused on challenges to existing governance processes posed by the new distribution technologies and media products, and the harmonization of legislation, and it has been encouraging new arrangements for handling cross-border copyright clearance.[25] Since 1997 a proposal for a 'Directive on Copyright and

---

[25] See e.g., the Directive on the Legal Protection of Computer Programs (European Council, 1991); the Directive on Rental and Lending Rights (European Council, 1992*b*); the Directive on Satellite Broadcasting and Cable Retransmission Rights (European Council, 1993*a*); the Directive on the Harmonization of the Term of Protection of Copyrights (European Council, 1993*b*); the Directive on the Legal Protection of Databases (European Council, 1996*b*). There is also a Council Regulation EC No. 3295/94 of 22 Dec. 1994 for measures to prohibit the release for free circulation, export, re-export, or entry for counterfeit and pirated goods. There is a proposal for a Directive on the harmonization of certain aspects of copyright and related rights in the information society (European Commission, 1999*b*) and a Council Regulation EC

of Related Rights in the Information Society' has been under discussion (European Commission, 1998*j*). By April 1999, these discussions had led to an amended proposal which European Commission officials emphasized aimed to 'safeguard a fair balance between all the rights and interests involved' (European Commission, 1999*b*: 1). The Directive represents a further attempt to harmonize copyright and related rights within the European Union, especially in areas affected by digital technologies. The proposed Directive states that:

whereas a harmonized legal framework on copyright and related rights, through increased legal certainty and while providing for a high level of protection of intellectual property, will foster substantial investment in creativity and innovation, including network infrastructure, and lead in turn to growth and increased competitiveness of European industry, both in the area of content provision and information technology and more generally across a wide range of industrial and cultural sectors; whereas this will safeguard employment and encourage new job creation . . . (ibid. Recital 3)

The Directive explicitly notes that 'especially in the light of the requirements arising out of the digital environment, it is necessary to ensure that collecting societies achieve a higher level of rationalization and transparency with regard to compliance and competition rules' (ibid. 12 *bis*). It also recognizes that

the exclusive right of reproduction should be subject to an exception to allow certain acts of temporary reproduction, such as transient and incidental reproductions, forming an integral part of and essential to a technological process carried out for the sole purpose of enabling the use of a work or other protected subject matter and which have no separate economic value on their own, whereas under these conditions this exception should include acts of caching or browsing. (ibid. para 23)

The proposed Directive is also consistent with the WIPO framework on technological countermeasures to copy protection technologies.

European harmonization is, nevertheless, a difficult agenda given the wide variety of regulatory practices and legal frameworks. The Legal Advisory Board (LAB) of the European Commission lists the following relevant governance regimes: Community law including the treaties of Rome and Maastricht and various directives; national laws on copyright in artistic and literary works; jurisprudence or case law doctrine accumulated in national courts and the European Court of Justice; and usage and custom as manifested in professional practices and routines, standard contracts, and licensing arrangements (Legal Advisory Board, 1995). In practice, adjustments between these institutional layers and different regimes have been regarded as being necessary to promote the development of information society services in Europe. At the time of writing, the Council had not yet adopted the European Commission's amended proposal.

In summary, the development of a global framework for copyright and other intellectual property rights protection does appear to be following a relatively clear trajec-

No. 241/1999 of 25 Jan. 1999 amending Regulation EC No. 3295/94 on counterfeit and pirated goods arising from the Green Paper Combating Counterfeiting and Piracy in the Single Market (European Commission, 1998*f*). See also Marsland (1998).

tory for the new styles of governance of digital information. This trajectory reflects the perspective that, even if 'information goods' are incorporeal, they may nevertheless be regarded as discrete commodities that require protection from counterfeiting or illegal reproduction efforts. As we have suggested, there is nothing intrinsically wrong with this agenda. It is certainly necessary to respond to the needs of the 'direct revenue' constituency by providing a secure market framework for the exchange of information for money. This review of developments also demonstrates how the 'commodity transaction model' simplifies the governance process. Instances of simplification include WIPO's pursuit of countermeasures to defeat available technical means of protecting copyrighted information, the efforts in the United States to enact further criminal penalties for copyright infringement, and the equation in Europe of the need to achieve harmonization with the objective of stemming job losses.

These approaches are addressing only a portion of the issues that need to be considered in establishing a legal framework and a governance process for intellectual property rights protection in the information society. The extension and strengthening of copyright protection may well create markets for the sale of information while raising the costs of developing other means of economically and socially beneficial uses of the information and communication infrastructure. The most disturbing element of these developments is the view that the principal agenda is one of increasing the sanctions against illegal activity. Historically, Europe appears to have had a more complete and balanced perspective within the policy community of the need to encourage market development as well as to provide for rights holders. So far, however, the agenda of strengthening protection is paramount. It is to be hoped that a broader consideration of the problem of encouraging constructive and innovative uses of intellectual property rights protection will encourage the development of a cultural exchange model in the coming years.

As we noted earlier, the possibility of a technological 'fix' would be an intriguing way to resolve the conflicts between the interests of the members of the various constituencies. It would also eliminate the paradox that continuous innovation in information and communication technologies is met with a perceived need on the part of the members of the direct revenue constituency to develop both stronger governance for intellectual property rights protection and new means of using technologies to prevent infringements. The next section is devoted to examining developments in the technological means available for protection.

7.6 Technological Solutions for Securing Copyrighted Information

Information and communication technology systems are designed to transmit and store information and to do so by creating perfect copies of information at the lowest possible cost. Concern about the security of information stored and transmitted over the information and communication infrastructure is a central issue in determining whether copyright protection can realistically be enforced. The development of a secure method for transmitting information and binding that information to a particular grant of rights and obligations would provide a technological solution to the potential conflicts between the public domain, indirect revenue and direct revenue constituencies.

7.6.1   Options for a Technological Fix

There are several routes towards achieving such a technological fix which we will refer to as efforts to increase security, with the understanding that we are referring to the security of the information creators' interests for each of the three constituencies. None of the foreseeable fixes is without cost. Each imposes costs on producers and users that may or may not be necessary depending upon the extent of copyright protection that is deemed to be necessary, being enacted into law, and subsequently enforced. To the extent that these costs fall on producers and users that are not in the direct revenue constituency, the conflict of interest between the constituencies is likely to remain.

7.6.1.1   Black Boxes and Keys

The first route to enhancing security involves the addition of technologies that prevent the unauthorized reproduction of an electronic work that is copyrighted. Several such technologies have been devised throughout the history of the computer industry and especially during the era of the 'stand-alone' personal computer. Computer manufacturers, in most instances, have chosen not to implement such technologies, for example, a mechanism for identifying individual machines that would provide a means for software producers to embed a code in their products linking the copyright licence to a particular machine. For many years, there have been three competing explanations of why this option was not taken up. First, there was the straightforward explanation that software and computers are manufactured by separate profit-seeking organizations. Because computers are more valuable with more software, regardless of the legality of its acquisition, computer manufacturers would have no reason to provide this technology. Second, computer manufacturers who did so would be harming the interests of the computer users who were either non-compliant with copyright protection or who faced substantial costs in maintaining compliance, and their products would be rejected.[26] The third explanation was that technological countermeasures could be devised to defeat such identification.

Recently, Intel began putting electronically accessible serial numbers on their most advanced personal computer microprocessors.[27] There was an initial negative reaction from some segments of the user community and Intel and other parties provided soft-

---

[26] Consider the case of a software product that is linked to a particular computer used to create and access information files of value to the company. The software company goes out of business and the computer fails. What happens to the company's data?

[27] Why Intel did this is subject to competing explanations. One explanation is that Intel has historically had substantial problems with the theft of its microprocessors. A single suitcase of advanced microprocessors may be worth over US$ 1m. and maintaining security at all distribution points is a problem for both Intel and its customers. By providing an internal security number, thefts are traceable and therefore the incentive to steal the microprocessors is dramatically reduced since they must eventually find their way into legitimate channels.

ware for bypassing the identification. Moreover, as of the autumn of 1999, to the best of our knowledge no software company had publicly announced a plan to link copy protection of software with Intel's serial number programme.

For some software products, hardware-based copy protection methods have been devised involving add-on physical keys that are needed for the software to operate. The desirable feature of an add-on physical key is that it may be exchanged between machines allowing back-up copies of the software to be installed if the primary machine fails. This solution also has the desirable feature that it imposes all the costs of copyright protection on those who benefit from it. A variant of the hardware key, the 'master disc' method was attempted for one leading software product (Lotus 1-2-3) and many smaller companies, but this technique proved unpopular with users and was abandoned. Although these methods have been available for over a decade, their use is confined to relatively few high-value software packages and is not part of the distribution of any mass-market software product.

7.6.1.2 Self-Enforcing Software

A second route is to embed copy control schemes in the installation software accompanying software packages. This applies only to executable programs and excludes other mechanisms for distribution of information that might be accessible using alternative readers. Users have been resistant to this technique for a number of reasons including hardware failures that destroy legitimate copies of software or other information.[28] Nevertheless, a version of this scheme has become the dominant means of protection. Users are supplied with a licence code which they must enter during the installation process. Since multiple installations can be made with the same code, this is only a partial solution to the copy protection problem and one that is likely to erode further due to the ease of copying CD-ROM distribution disks.[29]

7.6.1.3 Separating Permission and Distribution

A third route is to link users with copies of information. This technique requires a user to identify him or herself and receive authorization codes from the software manufacturer before any installation. This technique has been used for high-value software, such as that used in mainframe computer installations, but it is costly to administer and may be resisted by users who often suggest other less cumbersome alternatives. The technique requires significant investment in 'authentication' procedures for releasing a code and preventing its reuse. For example, an external reference point (such as a system clock reading) that prevents codes from being reused must be employed. This technique has the potential for resisting all but highly sophisticated efforts in which a fraudulent identity code is discovered that will be accepted as valid.

---

[28] Microsoft implemented a variant of this technique when it distributed software on floppy discs by updating the disc and providing the user with a warning that it had been used previously numerous times for software installation. Even this technique, however, was not absolute as the user could choose to ignore the warning and proceed to install the software.

[29] CD-ROMs cannot be modified by the installation program and thus cannot 'know' how many times they have been used to install the software.

The predominant lesson from this brief history is that only the markets for the highest value software seem to support any strong form of hardware or software protection scheme. Manufacturers of medium-priced packaged software have chosen the second route of copyright enforcement that offers only partial protection, and even this is likely to be eroded. This suggests that emergent markets in multimedia images, software add-ons, and other lower price products, may abandon copy protection schemes.

At present, despite a range of technological innovations, there is no broadly effective mechanism for safeguarding intellectual property rights in software or other data distributed among personal computers. The absence of a broadly accepted standard for strong copy protection in the personal computer world does not foreclose the use of hardware- or software-based protection schemes within the Internet and other electronic environments. In the absence of a highly reliable technological method of copyright protection, attention has focused on methods to discourage, rather than to eliminate, copyright violation and many of these rely upon technological solutions.

A starting-point for discouraging large-scale copyright violation operations is to include methods of labelling individual copies of software and other types of information so that it is possible to discern the provenance of a copy. This technique, accompanied by a registration procedure, offers a method of detecting the legitimate owner of any copy. The inspection of copies for which the user cannot demonstrate authorized use creates a presumption that copyright violation has occurred. This is what the predominant scheme of requiring the user to enter a licence code upon installation achieves. The extent of liability that may be assigned to a user who is unable to demonstrate the provenance of a registered product can be raised through legislation or legal precedent. While the user will be saddled with liability, copyright infringers also might modify identifying marks to obscure the source of the illegal copy. This can be discouraged by encryption techniques and made illegal by further legislation.[30]

Marking techniques and registration procedures require user co-operation, which could be encouraged by various approaches. Efforts to make these procedures as convenient and inexpensive for authorized users as possible further contribute to their acceptance. There are no universal standards for reliable copy protection of software and other information distributed over communication networks. It is often maintained that the extent of and rapidity at which damage can be done to the commercial interests of the owner of information make the greatest possible protection necessary. However, it is also the case that if such a level of protection increases the costs of legitimate transactions or abridges the value of the information to users after receipt, such a standard may not be in the interest of either party. In fact, this may be the primary reason for some of the available techniques not being widely accepted.

If it is accepted that those who benefit should pay the costs of protection, then it

---

[30] This is proposed in the copyright directive for the information society (European Commission, 1999*b*).

follows that members of the public domain and related revenue constituencies should not have to make a financial contribution to these costs. The argument that the present costs of copyright protection should fall on producers and users of copyrighted information is, however, a rather narrow one. This is because there is social value in building the electronic infrastructures for the information society. As much of the expenditure on the infrastructure is a fixed cost, the addition of more users has the potential to reduce the costs to all users. It can be argued, therefore, that the public as a whole should support research to improve protection methods due to their broad applicability in the information society.

Creators and rights holders are putting resources into technologies that combat and prevent copyright infringement. With artistic/creative works increasingly being combined in multimedia format and distributed electronically, these technologies can be used to improve the registration, clearance of copyright, and the combined handling of copyright with the electronic delivery of creative products. Given the concerns of rights holders to protect their works and to obtain a fair return on their intellectual output, the creative and collecting societies are investing in new tracing and tracking, encryption, and watermarking technologies. Representatives from the creative community, and the printing and recording industries, are working on techniques that enable a unique code in the form of a number or a signal to be assigned to a creative product that can be recognized throughout the value chain. These techniques include electronic signatures embedded in text, steganography, which is the term for the inclusion of a digital signature in a picture image, or embedded signalling, or adding a unique signal to a musical work (I*M Europe, 1996).

These techniques are being applied to support a variety of functions associated with the management and protection of copyrights. Copyright information systems are needed for standardized identification of protected works using common identifiers and digital (sub)coding for books, journals, records, compact disks, and audiovisual works.[31] This approach could then provide a basis for interlinked copyright information systems between the various nationally based collection societies.

The availability of digital technologies offers opportunities for advanced tracing and monitoring of usage which would support copyright clearance systems. New technologies can be used for accessing licensing terms and conditions and for handling the transfer of licence fees and royalties. In the United States an operational system for electronic copyright clearance and information metering on electronic network transaction-based systems in the domain of on-line scientific publishing has been developed. For example, the Reed-Elsevier, Folio Infobase Technology, and LEXIS-NEXIS database,[32] supplied in collaboration with the Copyright Clearance Center in the United States, have implemented a technical and contractual system that allows for electronic access to books, journals, newsletters, and newspapers, while at the same

---

[31] e.g. books—International Standard Book Number (ISBN); periodicals—International Standard Serial Number (ISSN); records—International Standard Recording Number (ISRC); CDs—Source Identification (SID).

[32] The LEXIS-NEXIS database is one of the word's largest legal, government, and business information databases owned by Reed-Elsevier Inc.

time protecting the copyrights of, and enabling royalty payments to, rights holders (Folio and Copyright Clearance Center, 1995).

Electronic multimedia rights clearance systems are also under development. These are integrated systems within a large digital storage delivery centre that enables the transfer of copyright information, handling of the licensing of copyrighted works, and the delivery of digital copies (PIRA International, n.d.). Within the framework of the European Commission's INFO2000 Programme considerable attention was given to the development of such systems. These were defined as 'the process whereby multimedia producers search for relevant components, assess the legal status of those components and seek to obtain from the rights holders (or their representatives) the required rights for the intended use of components in a multimedia product' (ibid. 1). In Europe, the question of whether there should be a centralized or decentralized system for clearance has continued to be contentious. The two principal issues appear to be the cost of rights and the cost of clearing rights in relation to the income that can be achieved from the exploitation of rights. The need for a system is recognized in the light of the cross-media nature of multimedia products and the importance of the application of technologies to support copyright management is reflected in the European Commission's research and development programmes.[33] There are, however, few signs that the fragmentation of the existing systems will be resolved in the near term.

Given the variety of possible means of protecting rights in intellectual property it is helpful to examine closely the concerns of the members of the different copyright constituencies in the case of a specific segment of the information industry. In the next section, we consider the views of the stakeholders involved in the development of optical disc technology and the Internet music business.

7.6.2 *Optical Discs and Internet Music Copyright Protection*

Violation of copyrights is a persistent problem for all digitized information.[34] The purpose of mass storage peripherals is to provide precise copies of digital information. As the costs of individual and 'pirate' violations of copyright fall, it is reasonable to suppose that these behaviours will become more widespread. For example, the CD recorder has made it easier to (illegally) copy software at only a fraction of its normal retail price. Such copying is done not only by consumers, but also by 'pirates'. Film producers and Digital Video Disc (DVD) developers share a concern about how to reduce the potential for increasing the incidence of copyright violation and the costs of enforcing copyright. Technical solutions have been sought and these have produced an enlightening case study of the problems associated with 'black box' measures for the protection of intellectual property rights.

A DVD-based technology was developed to provide films in an encrypted form on disc. The system was known as Digital Video Express or Divx and was introduced in

---

[33] See European Council (1996*a*) for a framing declaration and the ESPRIT Project AMIDE (http://amide.ip.lu accessed 6 April 2000) for an RTD&D project promoting these objectives.

[34] The protection of optical disks is considered in van de Paal and Steinmueller (1998) while a portion of the Internet music case is drawn from Jansen and Mansell (1998).

the United States in 1998. The system was developed by Digital Video Express and is backed by some of the largest film studios, including Universal, Paramount, and Disney, and disc drive producers such as JVC, Matsushita, Zenith, and Thomson. The idea behind the system was that consumers would purchase, at a low cost, a Divx film title allowing 48 hours of viewing after the first use. After this period the consumer would pay for additional viewing by using a code that could be obtained using a credit card in combination with a built-in modem that would come with the playing device. This, of course, is a version of the third technical method of copy protection discussed above, that is, one of the two strong methods. There was also an option to buy the disc and acquire unlimited numbers of viewing sessions. The system was designed so that Divx drives were able to read DVD discs but that DVD drives could not play Divx discs. After demonstration at the January 1998 Consumer Electronics Show in Las Vegas, Nevada, Divx was trial launched in the San Francisco Bay area in California and in Richmond, Virginia, later in the year (Academy, 1998).

By the end of 1998, Divx appeared to be headed toward success with as many as 200,000 players sold in the American market during the Christmas season in 1998. Despite this, however, a number of consumer interest groups emerged opposing the technology and consumer resistance began to mount (Fost, 1998; 1999). In addition, an advertising campaign by DVD manufacturers was launched disparaging Divx as a 'closed' system (despite the fact that Divx machines could read DVD media). Many arguments, both technical and economic, were offered against the technology and considerable negative publicity appeared both on the web and in the conventional news media.

On 16 June 1999, Digital Video Express announced that they would cease marketing the system and discontinue operations, with existing customers able to view discs over a two-year phase-out period. Customers who purchased the machine were offered a US$ 100 rebate for the players, which would continue to be useful for playing DVD discs. The company noted in the press release announcing this discontinuation that 'the majority of customers purchasing DVD players in Circuit City [a major electronics retailer which was majority owner of Digital Video Systems] stores had selected players that include the Divx option. Unfortunately, we have been unable to obtain adequate support from studios and other retailers. Despite the significant consumer enthusiasm, we cannot create a viable business without support in these essential areas' (Digital Video Express, 1999). One reason for this lack of support was the rapid increase in the number of DVD disc titles which dramatically exceeded those that Divx was able to license, despite a pre-committed royalty payment schedule amounting to US$ 112 m. (ibid.). Companies such as Warner, Sony, and Toshiba suggested that the results of focus groups had convinced them that consumers wanted to 'buy and collect' their discs rather than to 'borrow and pay as you go' as the Divx system permitted. Many retailers failed to support the technology because it was backed by one of their competitors in the retail market.

Other forms of DVD-based copy protection include the prevention of analogue and digital copying. 'Videotape (analogue) copying is prevented with a special dedicated circuit in every player. Composite video output will have pulses in the vertical blanking signal to confuse the automatic-recording level circuitry of VCRs' (European

Information Technology Observatory (EITO), 1997: 106). Similarly, for music CDs 'digital copying is controlled by information on each disc specifying how many times (if any) the data can be copied. This is a "serial" copy management scheme designed to prevent copies of copies' (ibid.).

These methods work as long as the generally available technologies support the copy protection methods. The advent of inexpensive recorders for CDs is allowing the technical fixes to be defeated. A significant breach is in the area of CD audio material where the contents of any CD can be captured on a computer hard disc as a file that subsequently can be recorded to a second CD. Similar developments may be expected for DVDs as recording capability emerges. The significance of these developments has been highlighted by the burgeoning of the on-line distribution of audio files of content copied from major music publishers.

The following FAQ (Frequently Asked Question) exchange illustrates the ambiguity of the legal issues surrounding the use of such software. It is from one of the leading bulletin boards providing information on the use of MP3 (one variety of compression and encoding which is based on Motion Picture Experts Group (MPEG) standards) to capture, exchange, and record audio material.[35]

Q: I would like to know if MP3s are legal?
A: Yes and no, its legal if you encode MP3s from your own CDs and keep them to yourself. But its (*sic*) illegal to encode and trade them with others unless you have the permission of the copyright holder of the music. To put it another way, MP3 is simply a file format that can be used either legally or illegally.

This, of course, is the same response that might be offered by a plain-paper copier company with regard to the use of this technology to make infringing copies of a printed source. The particular significance of the MP3 development is that the marginal cost of an additional copy of an MP3 file is very low. An individual who converts a portion of a copyrighted CD into an MP3 file has utilized a technology specifically designed by the Fraunhofer Institute, the developer of MP3, to provide a psycho-acoustic equivalent quality recording to the original. The fact that the new file can be transferred quickly to any other computer user throughout the world means that there is the potential to create an alternative mass market in the musical recording which might be called the 'MP3 infringement community'. Note that we use the term 'MP3 infringement community' to distinguish infringing acts from legitimate uses of the MP3 technology, such as the rapid growth of copyright royalty-free music distribution.

The principle of operation of the MP3 infringement community is a gift exchange economy in which individuals distribute illegal copies and exchange those that they have made for those that others have made.[36] Like many other network technologies, the MP3 infringement community is subject to network externalities with growth in

---

[35] See http://www.mp3.com/ accessed 18 Aug. 1999.
[36] The notion of a 'gift' economy was developed formally by Marcel Mauss in 1935 where a gift was understood as '(1) the obligatory transfer, (2) of inalienable objects or services, (3) between related and mutually obligated transactors' (Kollock, 1999: 221).

the number of participants increasing the value of membership. Unlike licit communities, however, this community is subject to interdiction by civil and criminal law enforcement activity. It is not possible, therefore, to openly advertise the availability of bootleg MP3 music files within open communication networks. While legal enforcement limits the size of the community and affects the operation of the MP3 infringement community, it has not suppressed the behaviour. Exchanges within the community proceed based upon direct personal communication through various networks such as password-protected ftp (file transfer protocol) sites which contain the infringing material. Passwords to these sites are exchanged through IRC (Internet Relay Chat) on-line 'private' communication between users. These sites have some protection from enforcement actions based upon their status as private or personal communication.

The controversy over the operation and spread of this community has alternately waxed and waned. In the United States, the Recording Industry Association of America (RIAA) took active steps through civil litigation and legal injunction to suppress the most blatant of the sites offering infringing MP3 files.[37] A widespread enforcement action against the underground of the MP3 infringement community has not been launched, as yet. The existence of a legitimate MP3 music community is also growing rapidly. The business, MP3.com,[38] offered over 100,000 such recordings for downloading in the summer of 1999. At this time, the market capitalization of the company was US$ 2.25b.[39] A variety of other companies is joining in this alternative business model and record companies themselves are distributing demonstration and advertising recordings using the MP3 system.

This account highlights the rapid emergence of new technologies supporting the development of intentional copyright infringement activities. It offers three lessons. First, the technological means to improve upon 'pirating' activities as well as smaller scale infringement, which can amount to significant revenue effects for rights holders, continue to develop and to incorporate technologies that initially were designed for legitimate purposes.[40] It is not appropriate to regard the problem of technological improvement in infringement methods as transitory or ephemeral. Second, while aggressive response can curtail the network externality-led growth of illicit communities, the privacy of personal communication on the Internet provides a means for illicit activities to occur. A direct conflict potentially exists between rights holders and all users. Aggressive suppression of the remaining illicit MP3 community or other communities of interest devoted to copyright infringement is likely to violate the personal privacy of Internet users in ways that would provoke substantial resistance. Third, the creation of the MP3 technology that can be employed illicitly is also the basis of a

---

[37] See http://www.eff.org.pub/Legal/Cases/RIAA_v_Diamond accessed 6 April 2000 at the Electronic Frontier Foundation's web site for one such case.

[38] See http://www.mp3.com accessed 6 April 2000.

[39] See http://biz.yahoo.com/p/m/mppp.html accessed 6 April 2000.

[40] Fraunhofer-Institut für Systemtechnik und Innovationsforschung (FhG-ISI), the developers of the MP3 method of digitally encoding audio information owns copyrights on the MP3 encoding technology and offers software licences for this technology, see http://www.iis.fhg.de/amm/legal/index.html accessed 6 April 2000.

significant new and legal industry in 'royalty free' music which appears to be sustainable. Thus, in this instance, the virtual community strategy has led to the formation of both illicit and licit communities.

7.7   Institutional Change: The Role of Collecting Societies and Related Institutions

Copyright legislation seeks to protect creators and rights holders by stipulating a number of specific exploitation rights. These include the right to reproduce any kind of work; distribute or communicate copies of the work to the public; rent copies of certain categories of works; perform for the public; translate literary works; and the right to adapt any kind of work or to include it in a new audiovisual work. The administration of these exclusive exploitation rights of creators or rights holders has often been delegated to specialized collecting societies that issue licences, collect royalties, and monitor the actual use of works.

Collecting societies have evolved in tandem with the development of intellectual property rights legislation. The availability of software-embedded multimedia technologies (for example, graphical formats or hypertext mark-up languages, and business software relying upon proprietary hardware equipment and/or standards, including some implementations of Motion Picture Experts Group (MPEG) standards) in the emerging information society cuts across and blurs the distinction between copyright, industrial property, and patent systems (Greguras and Wong, 1995). This widens the scope of collection society activities and makes for a more complex programme of work for these organizations.

Collecting societies attempt to represent the interests of publishers, authors, and composers in promoting the availability of information that is subject to copyright and to ensure that the respective copyright holders receive financial compensation for the use of their works. As Leer (1996: 106–7) has argued, 'The evolution of copyright organizations illustrates how technology has been allowed to directly influence the organizational structure. Every time a new media has emerged the response has been to establish a new collecting society, rather than to build on existing structures.' For example, Reproduction Rights Organizations (RROs) have been set up at the national level in Europe to license the photocopying of protected information.[41] With the widespread diffusion of electronic works, questions are being raised as to the future role of collection societies in the digital age. For example, should existing collection societies also license electronic rights and how should they administer such rights?

Technical systems that facilitate the rapid and unambiguous clearance of rights, for example, Electronic Copyright Management Systems (ECMS), are being developed with the aim of alleviating the administrative difficulties and high costs associated with clearing multiple rights from multiple sources. Software packages are

---

[41] The various national RROs comprise the International Federation of Reproduction Rights Organization (IFRRO).

available to manage rights administration, and systems are under development that will complement existing rights clearance services with the aim of providing 'one-stop shopping' for the licensing of rights. For example, at the World Congress of the International Organization for Standardization (ISO) in November 1994, French collection societies achieved agreement with the international community that the digital compression standards for the transmission of fixed images (Joint Photographic Experts Group, JPEG) and moving images (MPEG) should contain the space necessary for inscribing codes to identify works. A special committee of the International Confederation of Societies of Authors and Composers (ICSAC) was established to define international codes for identifying dissemination of such works (Tournier, 1995). But, as Leer (ibid. 120) observed, the implications of new mechanisms for protecting intellectual property rights would go far beyond the potential benefits to rights holders.

Mechanisms for encoding and identifying information assets will be of vital importance to the development of the global information market for the purpose of protecting IPR [intellectual property rights] and preserving original assets, as well as securing the integrity and reliability of trade. However, it is important to realise that technology is now making it possible to mark, monitor and control the use of information on a scale never known before. The implications for privacy, data-protection and consumer rights need to be considered very carefully.

By 1999, the need for standards for the development of ECMS was still a pressing issue. Technology developers were calling for standards to provide a 'generic tattooing definition' to encompass identification, copyright information, and possible usage conditions. It was recognized that these technologies would need to be indelible, non-modifiable, and traceable if they were to have a chance of widespread use. In addition, it was the view of many developers that a 'black box' should be embedded in any hardware that processed digital information, thereby identifying the protected information, preventing unauthorized use, and enabling a clearance fee to be collected by means of a smart card. The similarities of such proposals with the experience of the computer software industry are notable and there is every reason to suppose that the same outcome, that is, very limited use, will prevail. It is not surprising, then, that no agreed standards have emerged to provide these functions, although a wide range of standards has been developed.

As we noted above, these problems have largely been ignored in the effort to strengthen and harmonize copyright protection through the 'Directive on Copyright and of Related Rights in the Information Society'. Among those objecting to the initial draft of the new legislation presented in 1997 were the library community, represented by the European Bureau of Library, Information, and Documentation Associations (EBLIDA) (European Commission, 1998*h*), an organization whose members would be comprised largely of our public domain constituency. They sought a broader interpretation of rights of access to information for education and scientific uses. Such proposals are consistent with a cultural exchange model of intellectual property rights protection, but are strongly rejected in the draft legislation under consideration by the European Council at the end of 1999.

To assess the extent to which the combined forces of technological and institutional change may alter the balance between stronger enforcement of copyrights in digital information and the interest of users in accessing and using such information, we look more closely at the case of developments in the United Kingdom.

7.7.1 The United Kingdom's Approaches to Enforcement and Access

In the United Kingdom, the Copyright, Designs and Patents Act 1988 provides the framework for the monitoring and enforcement of rights in intellectual property.[42] Under this Act, infringement of copyright is a criminal offence and carries a maximum of a two-year jail sentence. The implicit threat of criminal penalties is a central component in the rationale and operation of the collection societies that undertake their work within the existing legislative framework. For example, according to Peter Shepherd, the Copyright Licensing Agency's (CLA) Chief Executive,

Illegal copying is the most common crime in the UK today. As a consequence authors and publishers are being deprived of millions of pounds in royalties and lost sales. This cannot be tolerated. Our Copywatch campaign will use all the latest investigative techniques to expose copyright theft in local and national government, universities, schools and colleges, as well as business.[43]

This effort is focused not only on the actions of pirates who directly profit from the wholesale violation of copyrights, but also on individual employees. For example, according to the CLA's research 'nearly eight out of ten employees photocopy illegally at work'.[44]

According to copyright law in the United Kingdom, nationals or residents of almost all countries are entitled to copyright protection, and this includes first publications outside the United Kingdom. The first owner of copyright is usually the author or creator, except in the case of an employee whose creation has been made during the person's employment, unless otherwise stipulated or agreed. Copyright, however, may be assigned (as in the case of journal articles or books where the author signs over the copyright to the publisher), bought, sold, and licensed.

Primary infringement of copyright might include, for example, copying, including 'storing' the work in electronic form and making 'transient' (temporary) copies; and issuing and/or disseminating to the public copies of the work not previously in circulation in the United Kingdom or elsewhere. In addition, performing, showing, or playing the work in public in any mode or form (there are exceptions for education establishments for which clearance has to be received from the rights holder(s)), or

---

[42] See the Copyright, Designs and Patents Act 1988 in the United Kingdom. In addition to the Broadcasting Act 1990 and 1996; the Copyright (Computer Programs) Regulations 1992 SI 1992 No. 3233; the Duration of Copyright and Rights in Performances Regulations 1995 SI 1995 No. 3297; the Copyright and Related Rights Regulations 1996 SI 1996 No. 2967; the Copyright and Rights in Databases Regulations 1997 SI 1997 No. 3032 are also part of the legislative framework, see http://www.patent.gov.uk/index.html accessed 6 April 2000.

[43] The CLA is a non-profit making organization that looks after the interests of rights holders in respect of copying from books, journals, and periodicals. It was established in 1982 and is a member of IFRRO. See CLA site at http://clans.cla.co.uk/www/copywatch.htm accessed on 26 Aug. 1999.

[44] See CLA site at http://clans.cla.co.uk/www/sectors.htm accessed on 26 Aug. 1999.

broadcasting, or incorporating the work into a cable programme service, are included. Cable programme service is widely defined and could include works found in databases, for instance, those provided by an Internet service provider.

Secondary infringement requires that there be knowledge, or reason to believe, that copies are infringing the Copyright Act. For example, importing for purposes other than for private use; possessing in the course of business; exhibiting in public in the course of business to such an extent that the interests of the copyright holder/owner are prejudicially affected, are defined as infringing acts. In addition, selling or offering for sale, and electronically transmitting through a telecommunication system with the full knowledge, or having reason to believe, that the infringing copies will be received in the United Kingdom or elsewhere, are infringing acts.

The numerous possible 'offences' in the misuse of copyrighted information present a challenge for any governance process. A first response is to extend the range and intensity of activities devoted to enforcement, that is, the detection, documentation, and prosecution of offenders. While this response seems appropriate to curb the growth of commercial infringement activity, there are likely to be diminishing returns in extending it very broadly. No industry derives more than a small fraction of its revenue from penalties imposed through civil litigation and the costs of collection of revenues through this method are likely to be relatively high from both social and business viewpoints. From a business viewpoint, widespread enforcement actions must be directed at information users who are also the customers of the publishing industry.

A second response is to pursue the strategy of enforcement as a deterrent. A sufficiently high level of enforcement activity will create the perception that the misuse of copyrighted information is a risky behaviour. Experience has demonstrated, however, that this is also a problematic strategy. In order to recover the high costs of enforcement, a principal target must be institutions that retain significant concentrations of copyrighted material, such as libraries or large business organizations. Increasing the liabilities of these institutions is, in effect, attacking some of the larger customers for information. Moreover, these institutions are likely to seek methods for reducing the extent of their liability. Reductions in the convenience of plain-paper copying and lack of interest in even more effective copying technologies, such as high-speed image scanners, are two of the possible consequences. To impose these costs on major customers, publishers have to be convinced that they control information that will continue to be in demand regardless of the evolution of technology. The evolution of the World Wide Web as an alternative medium of information distribution is challenging this assumption.[45]

Both these enforcement responses are reflected in the recent evolution of the

---

[45] Many communities, including academia, are concerned about the decline in the quality of information resulting from a universal ability to publish on the web. Without intermediation and review, the meaning of 'reliable knowledge' is likely to be devalued. In one sense, this is a simple matter of economic competition. If information must be expensive to be reliable, the marginal information user, for example, the student, will choose the substitute, unreliable, but cheap, information. The exit of marginal users from systems that acquire expensive information raise the costs to the remaining users, generating new marginal users who also defect. There may be no limit to this process. There are, however, likely to be permutations in this outcome that are attributable to evolving codes and norms of social exchange and behaviour, see e.g. Boczkowski (1999) which also provides an extensive bibliography.

copyright industries in the United Kingdom. Although national authorities in Britain have amended legislation, legislators often find themselves lagging behind technological developments and the ingenuity of those who seek to infringe upon copyright restrictions, fostering the view that more needs to be done. Trade associations, industry organizations, and collecting societies, in concert with the police and other law enforcement agencies, have been strengthening their monitoring and enforcement operations in an effort to reduce sales of counterfeit products produced by pirates *and* to extend enforcement to other institutions. The information producing industry, and especially the publishing industry, appears to favour the tightening of intellectual property rights in electronic information products and services and it is conventionally assumed that publishers are concerned with maintaining revenue and, therefore, will oppose any move that might threaten their income (Tuck, 1996). The two enforcement options create an important paradox in the role of collecting societies. On the one hand, these societies are agents of the copyright owners who are interested in increasing the sales of their product. On the other hand, by pursuing enforcement actions, the collection societies are engaged in a policing activity. Being a merchant and a police person simultaneously is an uneasy social role.

A third, less commonly articulated response is based upon dramatically reducing the costs of copyright compliance while extending the services offered by rights holders to their customers in the use of information. Although this approach would initially reduce the economic returns to rights holders, it offers the prospect of extending the intensity of use of copyrighted information and provides an effective response to the growth of the relatively low-quality, but cheap, information available through electronic distribution networks, such as the web. There is some evidence that this strategy is gaining in popularity among information producers. Examples include the use of 'site licences' that permit unlimited numbers of copies of copyrighted information for specified classes of users, and the use of copyright management systems to define and establish the price for mass reproduction of specific information. In the United Kingdom, the collection agencies have been attempting to move towards this strategy for some types of information.

The CLA has the responsibility for licensing digital products for use in the higher education system. In February 1999, a licensing system was announced that permits the exact representation of originally printed pages of text. The goal is to ensure that the interests of authors and publishers are respected at the same time as their materials are widely used in support of teaching and learning (Copyright Licensing Agency, 1998). The scheme is a voluntary one covering only existing printed material and does not apply to electronically published information, such as CD-ROM, multimedia, or on-line publications. The CLA operates a clearance system called the Copyright Licensing Agency's Rapid Clearance Service (CLARCS) which made £1,026,094 worth of photocopying clearances for the financial year 1999.[46]

---

[46] See Copyright Clearance Agency (1999), revenue generated on over 10 million pages cleared at the publisher set rate of 5p per page of extract from a book, journal, or magazine. The actual fees are set by the copyright holder of each work.

There continues to be considerable uncertainty about how these collection agencies will evolve in the United Kingdom. The CLA, which has adopted the third response to copyright enforcement in the case of some forms of academic use, is the same organization that has pronounced that eight out of ten business information users are copyright violators. The relationship between being an agency of enforcement and an information merchant is an uneasy one. In the next section, we examine developments in this area across Europe to discern the extent to which there are any emerging alternative processes of governance that have the potential to resolve the 'enforcer-merchant paradox'.

7.7.2   Institutional Alternatives to the Enforcer-Merchant Paradox

Within the broad array of legal institutions and traditions within the European Union, there are many more approaches to the issue of copyright enforcement than the model illustrated by the experience in the United Kingdom.[47] An issue that has only briefly been considered is the trade-off created by this diversity.[48] On the one hand, diversity has the potential to significantly raise the costs of transactions in intellectual property across Europe. This is viewed as undesirable from the single market perspective, which holds that the commercial rules operating in different Member States should be harmonized to prevent opportunistic exploitation of national differences and to promote unfettered trade. On the other hand, harmonization precludes the opportunity to experiment with, and learn from, different mechanisms for defining and enforcing intellectual property rights, including copyright. This is a small issue if it is accepted that the standard of copyright enforcement should be uniform and high. It is a big issue if the present system serves to suppress the emergence of alternative contractual or legal standards for the exchange of information. In this case, promoters of alternative models must strive for change at the European level which, practically speaking, requires consensus among the Member States. This is a much higher hurdle to clear than convincing a single Member State's government that the governance process should be designed to encourage experiments to test the viability or sustainability of new business models and the legal arrangements for copyright protection.

Several institutional alternatives to the management and distribution of copyrights have been discussed in Europe (Hoeren, 1995; Legal Advisory Board, 1995). The first is compulsory or statutory licensing where rights holders would no longer be able to prohibit the reutilization of copyrighted works in multimedia products. Instead, they would benefit from a right to equitable remuneration. According to the Berne Convention, compulsory licensing is permitted only in special circumstances, that is, when other, less drastic measures fail. Also registration in a multimedia environment would not be obligatory. The multimedia producer or creator could not be sure, therefore, whether all the necessary licences to create a multimedia product had been obtained

---

[47]   This section draws substantially on research by Dr Willem Hulsink, see Hulsink (1996).

[48]   See Foray (1995) who argues that the variety in international systems of intellectual property rights protection is inevitable and healthy because: (1) of differences in national/cultural conditions; and (2) it creates value by providing a larger stock of possible models from which to select for more 'global' solutions.

or all the terms set by the different collecting societies had been met. The second model employed in Europe is individual licensing or management whereby all the terms and parameters of granting authorization for the use of the artistic work are negotiable between the individual rights holders and producers, publishers, or end users.

The third model is collective management or licensing where the author entrusts the management of his or her copyright to a collecting society. Membership of a collecting society is based on the composition of a particular group of authors or holders of copyrights and the organization is specifically directed towards accomplishment of the following three goals: (1) monitoring the use of works in cases of large-scale exploitation; (2) promoting the negotiation of optimum financial terms; and (3) facilitating the respect of copyright by the user. The society seeks to represent all the holders of rights within a particular domain, thus securing a monopoly over their products and all aspects of enforcement. Organizations strive for a 'representational monopoly' on copyrights. In broad outline, the third model is the predominant means for enforcing copyright throughout Europe.

The implementation of this third model, however, has been more diverse. Leer distinguishes between four different regimes in Europe for organizing reproduction rights (Leer, 1995). The first regime is the Anglo-American approach, which relies upon voluntary contracts where RROs enter into agreements with individual rights holders and organizations representing rights holders in collective agreements. Collection and distribution of remuneration in the form of fees and royalties are based on statistical surveys and title-specific information provides a basis for estimates of the intensity of use, which, in turn, determines remuneration of individual rights holders. A second regime is employed in Germany and Spain where there is a statutory provision for a levy on the sale of photocopying machines and for licensing fees charged for volume copying which are determined by regulation.

The Dutch have implemented a third regime in which the Dutch RRO operates under a statutory licensing system and the Copyright Act authorizes users to copy as long as remuneration is made to the respective rights holders. The size of remuneration is set by regulation except for copying of educational course material, which is negotiable. Finally, the Nordic countries operate a fourth regime in which RROs will enter into agreements only with organizations representing a substantial proportion of rights holders. Individual rights holders enter into agreements with publishers only indirectly through their respective trade organization. The Nordic system presupposes that most individual rights holders and other stakeholders, such as publishers, are represented through collective organizations such as unions and trade associations. There is no individual tracking or identification of protected works and individual rights holders can obtain a return only through a process of application for grants provided by the rights holders' organizations.

Similar agreements on limitations to exclusive exploitation rights, for example, personal use, scientific and educational use, and archival copying, exist in the countries in western Europe. There is, however, divergence in the approaches to electronic document delivery and associated rights and, as Hugenholtz (1995: 57) argues, 'national copyright laws are extremely heterogeneous, both as to the scope of the protected (restricted) acts and to the scope and content of the limitations'. For example, in 1997 some countries had detailed media-specific definitions incorporated in their copyright legislation (the United Kingdom and Germany), while others were using general notions such as 'communication to the public' or reproduction (France, The Netherlands, and the Nordic countries). On-line services distribution is considered as 'communication to the public' (telediffusion or public access) in France and Spain, as cable programming in the United Kingdom, or is not legally covered at all (Germany). Greece has a copyright tax, which is levied on the sale of computers and discs. The supervision of collecting societies also varies across Europe. In Germany and The Netherlands, collecting societies are rigorously regulated and subject to regular state supervision. In other countries, oversight of collecting societies is almost absent (Hoeren, 1995).

The European Commission has argued that the management of multimedia products by collecting societies should be voluntary and that the possibility of individual rights management should remain open. The main reason for advocating individual contracting and licensing is 'that the parties' freedom of contract must be respected' (European Commission, 1995e: 77). The same logic argues against the development of a compulsory licence regime, under any terms.

This legal patchwork is being put to the test by the emergence of new distribution technologies and multimedia applications and by new subculture practices that promote information sharing and public domain solutions.[49] Service providers active in a digital environment and who are involved with experimentation and commercial development of multimedia products are experiencing a number of problems. First, as it is difficult to identify the individual rights holders of protected works in a multimedia product, licensing and remuneration are difficult. The administration of copyright in the newly emerging multimedia market will be a highly complex activity, with an array of pre-existing works, a large number of copyright owners, and a patchwork of overlapping rights. Second, the ownership and the licensing of electronic rights were unclear in the mid-1990s. RROs were not mandated and publishers were reluctant to grant electronic licences because of the fear of losing control over the primary market. Some of the experiences of the Dutch rights holder's societies are instructive of the difficulties that are encountered in attempting to devise a new methodology or practice in the copyright field.

In the spring of 1996, the Dutch authors' rights societies, BUMA/STEMRA, initiated an awareness campaign to educate people about the legal implications of copyright protected digitized musical works. Their campaign focused on the use of music on the Internet. The campaign coincided with a temporary arrangement regarding the recording, multiplication, and publication on the Internet of musical works (or fragments of music longer than 30 seconds).[50] This involved music files that were presented on the Internet by site holders, advertising companies, or service providers

---

[49] See Dibona, Stone, and Ockman (1999) and Jeong (1999) for overviews of the emerging cultures of exchange specifically in the field.

[50] See Hill (1995) who has examined the question of what the smallest copyrightable element in a multimedia work may be.

using servers in The Netherlands.[51] Using advanced scanning techniques,[52] it was possible to trace people who infringed on copyright protection and to inform them about the legal implications of their actions. People 'caught' in this experiment tended to fall into three categories. First, there were householders treating their home site as a 'living' room and decorating it with things such as their favourite music and quotations from books. These people were angered by the detection and expressed this on bulletin boards about the invasion of privacy. Second, there were advertising companies that were using music to add value to their products, and third, there were the record companies that were using fragments from their forthcoming records as exposure on their Internet site.[53]

By May 1996, BUMA/STEMRA had negotiated the first temporary agreement with a Dutch Internet service provider, Veronica Internet, for the use of musical works and fragments on the Internet. This move was regarded as a strategic effort to pre-empt proposed amendments to copyright legislation in the United States. At the time of implementation it was believed that on-line service and Internet access providers might become liable for copyright infringement even when the provider had no knowledge of, or participation in, copyright infringement and exercised no control over content.[54]

BUMA/STEMRA sought collaboration with software and multimedia developers and urged them to link up with the existing statutory framework for the Dutch copyright sector.[55] An organization called CEDAR was established as a turnkey operator that would provide administrative and bookkeeping facilities and information to new creative and administrative societies in the copyright field that would be dealing with the management of reproduction rights (such as photocopying), levies on cassettes, and videotapes. In this case, a means of strengthening the capacity of collection societies to manage intellectual property rights protection systems has been found in organizational convergence.

As well as simplifying rights management, joint institutions or close alliances of collecting societies offer a meeting place for producers and editors who seek multiple authorizations for the re-creation and reproduction of multimedia products. The regrouping or quasi-integration of collecting societies to provide multimedia artists and producers with a one-stop shop where all the necessary rights can be acquired is likely to prove to be problematic, however, in the field of reproduction. Some concerns were expressed about any moves to establish a pan-European copyright clearing-house.[56] This was partly because it would create another dedicated European institu-

---

[51] Musical Instruments Digital Interface (MIDI) files were excluded from this temporary arrangement.

[52] These scanning techniques search for matches between tunes or musical patterns stored in a database and the ones that are distributed (or downloaded) via digital or terrestrial networks.

[53] Interview by W. Hulsink with Mr Willem Wanrooij, Director of Strategy and Development, BUMA STEMRA-Cedar, 9 July 1996, Amstelveen, The Netherlands.

[54] This was suggested by some readings of Information Infrastructure Task Force (1995: 114–24).

[55] Interview by W. Hulsink with Mr Willem Wanrooij, Director of Strategy and Development, BUMA STEMRA-Cedar, Amstelveen, The Netherlands, 9 July 1996. The same trend towards inter-organizational convergence is taking place in Germany, see Kreile and Becker (1996).

[56] Interview by W. Hulsink with Mr Ronald Mooij, Secretary General of Bureau Internationale des Sociétés Gérant les Droits d'Enregistrement et Reproduction Mécanique (BIEM), 14 Aug. 1996, Paris.

tion, but, perhaps of greater importance, it was expected that support from large publishers and record companies would be weak.

Major publishers such as Bertelsmann, for example, were unwilling to externalize their rights management systems to any collective clearance centre because the large, integrated content producers prefer to manage their rights systems internally. Others argue, however, that collective administration of rights management is the way of the future. Gervais (1996: 26) argues, for instance, that 'it will be impossible for individual rights holders, except perhaps very large entities, to monitor, license and collect royalties around the world'. The large publishers and software companies seek to control the information and communication value chain including creation and rights-ownership, packaging and repackaging of multimedia products, selective distribution to retailers and customers, billing, and monitoring and acting on copyright infringements. Publishers such as Bertelsmann have developed competencies in the safe, secure, and effective delivery of content on demand. In most instances, they are seeking to reduce the transaction costs involved in the collection of revenues and their dependency on collecting societies. The in-house alternative allows publishers to maintain exclusive control over corporate digital storage and delivery centres.

The challenges to this established copyright community or direct revenue constituency come from the public domain constituents who seek a relaxation of the rights protecting creative works, which they see as restricting dissemination. Individual users of the Internet, and organizations such as the Electronic Frontier Foundation, are promoting the free distribution of products and the use of alternative payment systems.

In summary, there are considerable co-ordination problems in the management of copyrights in an electronic environment. There is a need for legal and institutional harmonization, for closer collaboration and integration between creative and collecting societies, for promotion of common standards and new electronic copyright management systems, and for new ways of respecting the social interests of those members of the public domain constituency who seek access to digital information. With growing exposure to problems of copyright infringement, pressures to limit broad public access to extensive public networks may grow. Alternatively, these networks may be subject to increasing user monitoring and security procedures, increasing costs, and the compromise of individual privacy in a bid to strengthen the commodity transaction model for the exchange of digital information products and services.

7.8 Conclusion

The process of technical convergence involves the creation of a common digital bit-stream representing all forms of digital media. The legal system asserts that those who arrange digital bits in a particular order own the arrangement. Technical capabilities provide a limited ability to establish the provenance of any particular collection of bits. The technologies for reading these bits can embed protection methods that restrict access to authorized users. Both the technologies for identifying the provenance of material and requiring authorization can be defeated, although the means required for the more complex and costly protection schemes require organized 'pirate' activity to be effective. There is no shortage of 'pirates' and efforts to make such activities criminal offences with increasing penalties have had limited success.

Despite these developments, national governments and the European Commission have been keen to strengthen copyright protection. The public interest justification for both enacted and proposed measures to strengthen copyright protection is that they will increase the incentives to create copyrighted material, thereby providing a source of competitiveness, growth, and employment. The exceptions to stronger enforcement of copyright protection are becoming more narrowly defined over time. Social and educational uses for copyrighted information are generally not granted significant exceptions to the principle of 'just recompense' to the owners of copyrighted information.

Changes in regulation are accompanying efforts to strengthen copyright protection. This involves extending coverage of the works that are subject to copyright protection together with the implicit granting of copyrights through 'publication' so that it is rapidly coming to embrace virtually *all* public information disclosure. In effect, a universal model is being adopted such that all information should be regarded as a commodity with a legitimate owner, or owners, and which promotes the establishment of formal mechanisms of exchange in order to transfer information to others. This commodity transaction model of information is one solution to the problem of information as an economic commodity, the increasingly low cost of its reproduction. It is not, however, the only solution, nor is it necessarily one that is in the public interest.

Producers and users of information may be identified with several different constituencies. Many information producers have no intention or desire to participate in the commodity transaction model for information transfer. Instead, they seek to provide information to the public domain and to encourage its dissemination. Some of these producers would also like to be recognized as the original authors of their contributions. Many information users participate in this public domain constituency and have no expectations of paying for information that they receive, either at the time of receipt, or retrospectively. In practice, however, the strengthening of copyright protection makes it impossible for producers or users in the public domain constituency to meet their goals. The commodity transaction model which is embedded in legislation and which is encouraging the harmonization of global standards of copyright protection, is rapidly becoming the universal standard for the exchange of information. This model makes no provision for the public domain constituency, nor does it adequately represent the interests of the related revenue constituency. The related revenue constituency has little or no interest in raising the uncertainty and cost of acquiring particular types of information, such as 'shareware', advertising messages, product support information, and so forth.

The 'direct revenue constituency' represents the convergent interests of companies engaged in incumbent and insurgent strategies. Their intense interest in copyright protection is based upon legitimate concerns that the information and communication infrastructure will make it increasingly possible to duplicate and distribute infringing copies of copyrighted information. Faced with this prospect, they have lobbied for the extension of criminal and civil enforcement to prevent pirating and other infringing activities. The focus on enforcement has been accompanied by efforts to raise voluntary compliance through the encouragement of societal norms and standards with regard to the illegitimacy of copying activities. Strategies that would reduce the costs to the user of acquiring information in recognition of the ease of copying and the technical difficulties of protection are generally receiving a lower priority in the efforts of producers in the direct revenue constituency.

The process of implementing the commodity transaction model as a universal legal and institutional standard is complex and it is not assured of success. Nevertheless, major steps have been taken to harmonize copyright protection arrangements within the European Union and on a global basis. These efforts have been accompanied by further articulation of the role of collection societies in the United Kingdom and other countries. Harmonization on a universal and strong copyright protection agenda presents the real hazard of setting a standard that will make experimenting with new business models for information distribution more costly and difficulty. The use of criminal penalties against copyright infringement is creating a substantial Internet underground community that is likely to provide a home for other objectionable activities, such as those considered in Ch. 8.

Efforts to create a cultural exchange model embodying commercial activities in parallel with commercial information transfer have not yet received substantial legislative attention or political debate. This is unfortunate. Commercial information providers and their customers are not the only constituents of the information society. The unlimited extension of the commercial motive in connection with the Internet or the information and communication infrastructure, more generally, reduces its social and educational value and, ultimately, endangers the political support for both infrastructure, and information society, initiatives.

8

Building Trust for Virtual Communities

8.1 Introduction

In this chapter we continue our examination of how legal and institutional infra-structures or regimes are being adjusted to promote the development of the infor-mation and communication infrastructure and the move towards the information society in Europe. Our themes in this chapter are security and privacy as they bear upon the cases of electronic payment systems, data identifying individuals, and the privacy of personal communication between individuals in electronic environments. Security and privacy involve social exchanges that are embedded within legal and institutional regimes. As in the case of copyright protection, which we considered in the previous chapter, these regimes must be arranged so that a balance is achieved between the conflicting interests of the parties involved.

The definition of privacy refers to the state of being undisturbed, the freedom from intrusion or public attention, and the avoidance of publicity.[1] The literal translation of 'privacy' from the Latin *privatus* is 'apart from the public life'. The definition generally involves a consensus about where a boundary can be maintained between what is public and what is private. Establishing and enforcing this boundary may be addressed through social conventions or legal sanctions. Although there is growing emphasis on technological methods to support a boundary between the private and public lives of citizens and consumers, most social science research on issues of privacy and security in electronic environments recognizes that technological means cannot take respon-sibility for social and legal policy choices.[2]

It is important to understand that privacy cannot be absolute for a number of reasons that we explore below. The extent of privacy must be socially negotiated for various purposes. The messages communicated within an electronic infrastructure involve volitional and non-volitional elements that have implications for privacy. While people may choose some of the content of the messages that they communi-cate, in other instances the content of messages arises from the automated or semi-automated processes involved in distributing them over networks that are linked by

This chapter draws upon research undertaken by Dr Andreas Credé, former D.Phil. student and Research Fellow; Lara Srivastava, former SPRU Master's student; Uta Wehn de Montalvo, SPRU DPhil student; David Sayers, Independent Consultant, Brighton; and Ingrid Standen, former SPRU Research Officer.

[1] See Pearsall and Trumble (1996).
[2] See e.g. Agre and Rotenberg (1997); Raab and Bennett (1995); Samarajiva (1994; 1996b; 1997); Viswanath, Samarajiva, and Park (1994).

human as well as machine nodes. The disposition of messages is a useful starting-point for an analysis of security and privacy issues, but we must extend our investigation to encompass issues raised by aggregations of data that are generated or collected by electronic means. Developments in this second area have considerable significance for those engaged in electronically mediated communication. The security and privacy of particular messages, and information about these messages, including aggregations of the messages themselves, define the scope of our enquiry in this chapter.

Technological advances in the capabilities to store and process messages are creating an unprecedented potential for the use of aggregated data for purposes ranging from the protection of national security to securing commercial competitive advantage. In some cases, the capabilities of state and commercial actors to regulate these uses are falling behind the pace of advance in technological capability. In others, it is necessary to enlist or conscript the co-operation of specific actors in order to obtain compliance with evolving norms of behaviour with respect to privacy and security. It cannot be presumed that regulation will be effective in protecting personal privacy, commercial confidentiality, or national security, but it is feasible to limit the extent of risk involved in using the information and communication infrastructure and to identify the potential for adverse outcomes. We draw examples from developments in electronic payment systems, data identifying individuals, and the treatment of personal communication to illustrate how the processes of social exchange influence the design and application of the technologies for creating, exchanging, and using messages in specific contexts.

In the case of electronic payments systems, message creators, and a variety of other actors, have interests in the content of messages that are created in connection with these systems. For example, the message creator's interest encompasses both the security and the privacy of the message exchange process. It would be meaningless, however, for an individual to have exclusive control of such messages because the purpose of messages in this context arises from the need to realize an economic exchange between the message creator and a second party, whether an individual or an organization. Third parties may become involved to complete the execution of an electronic payment. Although all these parties, including the message creator, have interests in security and privacy, their interests are not identical and may be conflicting. For example, a retail business will be interested in retaining information about a customer's history of purchases, and retail businesses, as a group, will be interested in capturing information about the creditworthiness of individual customers. Regulations that limit the retention and utilization of electronic payment messages in order to ensure greater privacy for the originator of a message raise the costs of transactions for the message receiver. If electronic payment systems are to achieve more broadly based acceptance and fully support visions of the development of electronic commerce—or e-commerce—the systems must be designed in such a way that a balance is struck between these potentially conflicting interests.

The accumulation of aggregations of data that are linked to individuals, either directly or indirectly, and information about messages or about the processes of exchanging messages, may be put to socially beneficial purposes. For example, the ability to determine the location of a person carrying an operating cellular telephone by monitoring the signal strength at several cellular receiving stations may be of enormous benefit in the case of an accident or emergency. However, this same capability to identify a person's location using mobile telephone data may be regarded as creating a threat to individual welfare in other circumstances.

Similar arguments may apply to the identification of individuals from aggregations of data. Some, although relatively few, consumers who understand that it is feasible to use aggregate market research data in this way may prefer the complete abolition of market research in order to protect their privacy. Other consumers may recognize that improved market research can lead to products and services that are more closely tailored to their preferences. However, even these consumers might be concerned if they became aware that information about every one of their purchases was subject to inspection by one or more unknown parties. The potential for achieving unprecedented levels of detail in the analysis of the vast range of behaviours that directly or indirectly generate messages is a concern for social policy. This is because, while such analyses may be anonymous in so far as individuals are not identified as such, their behaviour can be examined at a level of detail that would be discomfiting if they were cognizant that the capabilities exist to conduct this type of analysis. How the balance should be struck between the individual's interest and the interests of actors within firms or the institutions of the state is a social decision, and this presents difficult issues for policy and for industry self-regulation. The water in this area is much murkier than in the case of electronic payment systems. The capabilities for identifying or analysing data about messages are subject to very rapid technological advance, for example, in the field of intelligent 'agent' technologies, and considerable specialized knowledge is needed to assess the social consequences of the application of these technologies.

Collective interests in abridging the privacy of personal communication between individuals are often accorded less legitimacy than is given to the treatment of privacy in the context of either electronic payment systems or aggregations of data. However, it is a widely accepted principle of civil society that the communication of threatening or harmful messages should be discouraged. In some cases, it is obligatory for law enforcement agents, or those responsible for maintaining national security, to concern themselves with the personal or private messages communicated between individuals. The use of electronic services for the genesis of conspiracies or for the co-ordination of harmful acts suggests that there is a need to breach the privacy of personal communication in some circumstances. When the circumstances do not compel intervention, it is possible that some actors will gain access to the personal messages of others and that they will use this information to the detriment of the message creators.[3]

The issues that we deal with in this chapter feature prominently in discussions about the social and economic dimensions of the information society. A frequent starting-point for such discussions is articulated in terms of a 'soft' form of technological determinism that is presented using constructions, such as the 'impact' of technology 'on'

---

[3] The communication of messages of affection and sexual interest from one person to another may evoke a different response if delivered to a third person and the sanctity of the messages of a mistress may be viewed rather differently from messages of ardour expressed to a child.

privacy. Our view is that, for the most part, it is people who make the choices to use the technological tools, rather than a case of the tools 'choosing' which people to use. However, the issues in this area are becoming more complex as machine-to-machine communication increases within the information and communication infrastructure. In many instances, people now have little or no means of knowing how their behaviour is being monitored, or the uses to which such information is being put by the human controllers of the machines.[4]

The use of the new computer and software tools interacts with legal and regulatory frameworks and procedures creating expectations of a series of presumed outcomes unless proactive preventive measures are taken. This feature of the information society has become a priority for policy-makers and privacy and security issues are the subjects of active policy discussion and action. Indeed, as Branscomb (1993) has suggested, global networks are facilitating the production of new forms of information property and new types of communities and forms of behaviour that fall outside consensual social norms. A high-profile illustration of these developments is the promotion by policy-makers of e-commerce as being a high priority. Substantial consideration is being given to issues of electronic security and to self-regulatory and legal measures for the protection of personal privacy, the security of payment systems, and the uses of data identifying individuals. For example, the OECD has observed that 'direct business-to-consumer electronic commerce will not reach its full potential of a trillion US dollars by 2003–2005 until consumers are assured that the online environment is a safe and predictable place for them to do business' (OECD, 1998a: 4).

Building trust requires accurate information, clarification of electronic contracts, possibilities for consumer redress, measures to combat on-line fraud, and adherence to privacy protection guidelines. It also requires security and authentication mechanisms as well as consumer education in their use.[5] Although establishing a basis for forging trusting relationships in support of economic transactions has been a traditional role of government, the availability of technological solutions for achieving security and authentication means that the private sector is playing an increasingly important role. In 1998, an OECD Ministerial Declaration called for self-regulatory measures to protect consumer interests and emphasized the need for input from consumer representatives and specific and substantive rules for dispute resolution and

---

[4] These developments raise issues concerning the social features of control over the behaviour of actors within different kinds of spatial environments. For example, Samarajiva (1996b: 132) suggests that a complex form of proximate space is produced when actors have asymmetric knowledge of each other. The space constituted by a voyeur utilizing the communicative properties of a one-way mirror is an example. Control-oriented surveillance techniques employ the concept of the panopticon developed by Bentham, that is, an architecturally spatial device that allows a guard to observe prisoners while being invisible to them. The prisoners cannot be certain when they are being observed and they behave as expected by the controlling guards (Gandy, 1993). Although this view of behavioural control has been questioned it suggests lines of research into the potential differences between behaviour within physical and electronically mediated spaces.

[5] Authentication is the process of establishing with reasonable certainty that a message is from the person whom it purports to be from. The OECD definition of authentication is 'a function for establishing the validity of a claimed identity of a user, device or another entity in an information or communication system' (OECD, 1997a: 1).

compliance. It also called for the further development of technology as a tool to protect consumers (OECD, 1998*b*).

In 1997 the European Commission set out an agenda for the development of e-commerce (European Commission, 1997*d*). This was followed by a proposal for a new directive on the legal aspects of electronic commerce within the European Union market in November 1998 (European Commission, 1998*l*). The proposed directive defined 'information society services' as 'any service normally provided for remuneration, at a distance, by electronic means and at the individual request of a recipient of services' (ibid. Art. 2). In explaining this definition of a service, the Commission noted that the remuneration need not be made by the recipient and that it was not concerned with the way in which the provision of a service was financed. This definition, therefore, covers advertising or sponsorship-supported services, including on-line newspapers, databases, financial and professional services, on-line entertainment services and direct marketing, and services provided using the World Wide Web. It also covers both business-to-business and business-to-consumer services.

The proposed directive established an exemption from liability regarding acts of transmission of information in communication networks when the service provider plays a passive role as a conduit of information to third parties. The liability exemption covers both those cases when a service provider could be held directly liable for an infringement and cases where a service provider could be considered secondarily liable for someone else's infringement. To be granted an exemption, three conditions must hold: (1) that the provider has not initiated the transmission; (2) that the provider has not selected the receivers of the transmission; and (3) that the provider has neither selected nor modified the information contained in the transmission. The Directive covers issues of storage, caching, and hosting, and it limits liability for these intermediary functions. The place of establishment of a service provider is defined as the place where an operator actually pursues an economic activity through a fixed establishment, irrespective of where web sites or services are situated or where the operator may have a mailbox. With respect to direct marketing and advertising, the proposal requires that commercial communication by e-mail is clearly identifiable. Furthermore, service providers would be subject to supervision in the Member State in which they are established.[6]

In the United Kingdom in the spring of 1999 the Government released a consultation document on 'Building Confidence in Electronic Commerce'. In this case, e-commerce was extended to include 'using an electronic network to simplify and speed up all stages of the business process, from design and making to buying, selling and delivering' (Department of Trade and Industry and Home Office, 1999*a*: 4). The government's goal is to provide a positive framework that will encourage all forms of electronic service activity. In the autumn of 1999, at the time of writing, it appeared that the government would move to introduce legislation in advance of the framework

---

[6] In Sept. 1999 the proposed directive was revised to incorporate changes suggested by the European Parliament and to provide greater consumer protection from unwanted electronic mail advertising (European Commission, 1999*a*). See also the proposed directive on electronic signatures, which is designed to ensure minimum levels of security in the use of electronic commerce (European Commission, 1998*k*).

to be provided by European Union legislation. The perception of the need for urgent action stems from a concern to stimulate commercial activity and to ensure lawful access to e-commerce transactions in the interests of law enforcement. As the 1998 'Competitiveness' White Paper put it, 'digital technologies are a key enabler of a modern, knowledge-driven economy. Electronic business—and in particular electronic commerce—is radically changing the nature of individual businesses, of markets and of entire economies' (Department of Trade and Industry, 1998b: i). One of the key features of the British government's intentions to legislate is to put in place a system of rules and institutions that will enhance competitiveness and enable those using the information and communication infrastructure to forge trusting relationships. Measures to protect personal privacy and to secure electronic transactions for business are to be introduced in order to achieve these conditions. Intense discussion has focused both on the benefits of the use of encryption technologies for promoting e-commerce and to protect privacy, and on the need for lawful access to encryption keys by law enforcement agencies in order to protect citizens from crime and terrorism.[7]

Following a brief consultation process, a consensus appeared to be emerging on the preferred characteristics of any new legislative framework for e-commerce. A light regulatory approach, combined with the decoupling of legal access to messages from the measures necessary to build confidence in e-commerce, appeared to provide a basis for initiating a new institutional regime. Many of those commenting on the proposed measures supported the principle of properly authorized lawful access as long as this did not hinder business processes. Those representing law enforcement interests were unanimous in their view that the actual or potential use of encryption by criminals represents a serious threat to society and most said that an effective solution was needed (Department of Trade and Industry and Home Office, 1999b).

In this chapter, we examine issues of governance that are raised by the development of e-commerce and alternative models of social interaction that appear to be shaping the contours of the new electronic public and private spaces. We also consider the interactions of developments in social and economic processes with the deployment of new applications of information and communication technologies. Regulatory and legislative means are being employed with the aim of encouraging the formation of trusting relationships in the new electronic environments. A key feature of our argument in this chapter is that institutional processes and social considerations are very important for the successful application of any legal or regulatory measures aimed at building trust in the use of electronic services. Notwithstanding the emergence of technological solutions, security and privacy are as much matters of management and social ethics as they are matters of the application of technologies within network systems. The way that boundaries are being negotiated and established by a variety of interested parties between individuals and collective actors in the information society has major implications for privacy and security.

Legislative measures or recommendations and self-regulatory codes of practice

---

[7] This is in line with the Justice and Home Affairs Council of the European Union conclusions on encryption and law enforcement. See Justice and Home Affairs Council of the European Union (1998).

offer broad safeguards for privacy protection, but they cannot prevent the processing of data that have been rendered non-personal by the removal of the information that would identify individuals. Moreover, the practice of rating individual contributions to public electronic forums, or similar public disclosures of personal information, and the compilation of dossiers for national security or law enforcement purposes, indicate a new set of problems with the use of information that is publicly available but is otherwise widely dispersed or disorganized. Existing provisions for the protection of privacy are based on models and conventions that may not be applicable to the move towards the information society. There is a potential for a divisive polarization to occur that would undermine public confidence in the safety and privacy of personal communication in the information society. If public confidence in privacy and security is endangered, those privacy guarantees that are provided may come to be perceived as available for use as shields by those who engage in activities for which there is broad social disapproval or outright condemnation. Mapping these tensions, and the measures taken to lessen their force, is a principal theme of this chapter. It is useful, however, to begin with a summary of the largely implicit habits of thought that influence attitudes towards privacy.

8.2   Theories of Information and Privacy

The moves to introduce legislation and regulation for e-commerce, and the concerns about the need to build trusting relationships in such interactions, are strongly, but largely implicitly, influenced by how we think about 'information' and 'privacy'. Exposing the implicit habits of thought underlying different approaches to issues of privacy is important for understanding the significance of proposals to regulate privacy. In this section, we articulate three distinct views that are characteristic of these different approaches: a commodity model, an organizational design model, and an integrated cognitive and social exchange model. The first two models are associated with economics, but they are also prevalent in other social science and legal approaches to the issue of privacy. The third is associated with sociology and political economy. The views embedded in these models are cumulative in the sense that the second and third recognize and extend the first, but they are also in conflict with each other as the second and third contest the assumptions, scope of relevance, and conclusions of the first.

The commodity theory of privacy encompasses two different perspectives derived from economic theory, both of which consider information and privacy as commodities subject to economic exchange. The first perspective is the theory of asymmetric information, which is developed within the field of information economics, and the second is the analysis of consumer preferences for privacy as a 'commodity'. The theory of asymmetric information is derived from the observation that economic actors *know* different things, and that, under some circumstances, this knowledge may create a *private* benefit. For example, the seller of a used car may know more about the qualities of this car than a potential buyer. This may allow the seller to ask for a higher price than the car would be 'worth' if the information were available to the potential buyer.[8]

Since buyers must assume that there is a risk that the car on offer is of lower quality than is claimed by the seller, they will only be willing to pay a price that reflects their ideas about the average quality of used cars available in the market. This will be a lower price for some used cars and a higher price for others than would be offered by buyers if the actual characteristics of each used car were known. Following this line of argument, we can consider the effect of the average market price on a potential seller of a used car that is of high quality. The seller will be offered less than the car would be worth if its quality were known, but because the seller has no means of convincing potential buyers that the quality of the car has been accurately portrayed, the seller cannot receive what he or she believes is its appropriate value. Again, following this line of argument, the seller will choose not to sell. The withdrawal of the car from the market will further reduce the average quality and price of used cars in the market.

There is no obvious limit to the decline in the average quality and price in a market for used cars if people behave according to these rules, since the above average cars will always be withdrawn from the market. In this case, information that is private results in the potential loss of social welfare, that is, individuals making appropriate trades in the market in which both gain from the transaction. Numerous regulatory responses are possible to attempt to avert this problem, such as making it illegal to reset the odometer of the automobile or making the seller responsible for stating known defects. In each case, the regulatory response is an effort to reduce the asymmetry of information between the buyer and the seller.

The possible gains from asymmetric information create incentives for specific types of behaviour. For example, the inability of a contractor to monitor the activities of a worker creates an incentive for the worker to engage in 'opportunistic behaviour' resulting in a lower quality of effort than was initially agreed.[9] The insurance company that is unable to ascertain behaviours, such as tobacco use or proclivities to drink and drive, faces a 'moral hazard' from undisclosed private behaviour.[10] These distortions arise from the problem of asymmetric information, that is, the fact that one party in a transaction knows more than the other. From a social viewpoint, it would be more efficient (more gains from trade could be realized) if the supplier and purchaser were equally well informed. This argument supports regulatory initiatives that attempt to reduce the uncertainty created by information asymmetries. Within the framework of this model, from a *social* viewpoint full disclosure is more efficient although it is recognized that individual social actors may fail to co-operate with full disclosure because it is in their *private* interest to gain from knowing things that their trading partners or rivals do not. It is sometimes recognized that certain things that are privately known

---

[8] The original statement of this problem was by Akerlof (1970). Our discussion draws upon Molho (1997: 19–59) who presents subsequent theoretical and empirical work. It should be noted that the empirical work summarized by Molho has provided only weak confirmation of the model as formulated by Akerlof.

[9] This problem and the problem of 'moral hazard' are grouped together under the heading of principal–agent problems in the economics literature.

[10] These issues are considered in greater detail in Molho (1997).

require investment and that encouraging this investment by promoting various kinds of commercial privacy may ultimately increase efficiency.

As we discussed in Ch. 7, however, the usual solution to this divergence between public and private incentives in the case of information that requires investment is to create an intellectual property right that promotes disclosure, ensures exclusive control of a limited claim of ownership, and which eventually dissolves. The principal exception to this is the law of commercial secrecy, which allows companies to retain knowledge indefinitely. This exception can be explained as a recognition of the inevitability that companies will attempt to conceal certain information from rivals. Granting a property right in commercial secrets serves to 'keep the peace' by allowing companies to take direct legal action against their employees or business partners who violate commercial secrets, rather than seeking alternative means of retribution. The granting of a property right in commercial secrets is also explained as a means to encourage companies to exchange knowledge. For example, due to property rights in commercial secrets, it is possible to write non-disclosure contracts that allow potential buyers to investigate information while being barred from using it.[11] Thus, for producers and merchants, the commodity approach to privacy provides a very limited rationale for privacy. It encourages the explicit or implicit limitation of privacy in commercial contexts while calling attention to the numerous social or collective and private costs of 'privacy'.[12]

When individuals are acting on their own behalf, economic analysis is more cautious with regard to the issue of privacy. Individuals may have a preference for privacy that they choose to exercise in substitution for other behaviours. In this circumstance, the cost of the individual's preference may be analysed, but the argument would be resisted that it is in the social interest to limit the exercise of this preference, for at least as long as that individual's behaviour does not involve others. To argue against privacy in this context would violate the canon of voluntary exchange that is a core assumption used to justify the exchange economy. Thus, privacy may be commodified in the sense that individuals may demand, or be willing to accept, a price for reducing their level of privacy. An example of this is when individuals complete disclosure forms in the process of seeking to qualify for credit or insurance. The price they pay is the reduction in privacy in return for access to the opportunity to trade, an opportunity that is likely to be denied if individuals refuse to compromise their privacy.

Individuals release private information in specific transactions. It is, therefore, a natural extension of the law to grant the individual presumptive rights to the subsequent use of information that has been released for a specific transaction. This is the principle underlying legislation protecting the use of name-linked data that businesses possess as a by-product of their grant of access to trading opportunities. A variety of other laws governing individual privacy can be explained in terms of the goal of rendering privacy-reducing choices taken by individuals 'transaction-specific'. In each

---

[11] Such non-disclosure agreements are limited in effectiveness if the commercial secret can be used surreptitiously by those to whom it is disclosed.

[12] The social losses arise from the loss of potential uses of the secret information by others that are not possible to realize because the information is unavailable.

case, the principle is that the individual should remain in control of private information even if it is disclosed for a specific reason in a particular transaction.

The commodity theory of privacy, encompassing the issues both of asymmetric information and of individual preferences regarding privacy, is a useful analytical technique for examining the incentives of economic actors. This theory influences how policy-makers think about information and privacy, although few would explicitly acknowledge that their views are derived from this theory. Instead, there is a general belief in the policy community that improvements in the amount and quality of information will lead to improvements in the competitiveness of firms, and indeed, of national economies. This belief provides a basis for policy actions aimed at improving the amount and quality of information.[13] The commodity theory of privacy does not offer a comprehensive framework for examining the use of private information or the social meanings of privacy. The main limitation of the commodity theory of information with respect to the *use* of information is its presumption that the qualities or characteristics of information can, in principle, be observed and that information is sufficient to transfer knowledge between two individuals or organizations.[14]

A second approach in the economics literature has been developed to explain the existence and design of organizations. This approach focuses upon the consequences of information (including private information) use rather than on the precise mechanisms of how information is used. We label this approach as the economics of 'organizational design', and we include in this category 'transaction cost' theories as well as other theories in which the consequences of information processing are considered, such as the 'new' institutional economics.[15] From this perspective, the very existence of the firm is understood as the result of the collective ability of actors to acquire and manage information more efficiently than would be possible using markets, given the costs of specifying, monitoring, and enforcing market exchange contracts. The complexity of the precise mechanisms by which firms do this does not lend itself to comprehensive analysis. It is possible, however, to examine some of the effects of specific changes in rules concerning the way organizations are structured and how they behave. This perspective is more realistic with regard to the difficulties in reproducing and transferring knowledge by exchanging information than the commodity theory approach. It does not deny that information can be commodified and

---

[13] From a social viewpoint, economic analysis does not necessarily support this view. It is possible to establish that, if an economy is 'perfectly' competitive, it will produce and allocate through trade in goods and services as efficiently as any alternative means of organization (Arrow and Debreu, 1954). However, many economists would agree that real world economies are not perfectly competitive. Making an imperfectly competitive economy more competitive does not necessarily improve efficiency, a principle that economists call 'the theory of the second best' (Lipsey and Lancaster, 1956).

[14] Using a commodity theory of information, it may be concluded that the organization is a 'nexus of contracts', each of which is subject to the problems of asymmetric information. It is possible to extend the economic theory of information to incorporate many, if not all, the features suggested by other theories. In doing so, however, the theoretical and mathematical complexities of the models become daunting and their predictive value diminishes.

[15] This theoretical work began with Coase (1937). Recent perspectives as well as a reproduction and exegesis of Coase's original contribution are provided in Williamson and Winter (1991). Williamson's own contributions include Williamson (1975; 1985). A useful starting-point for examination of these approaches is Williamson (1995).

exchanged, but it does assume that the processes involved are relatively inefficient compared to simply using the information as an integral part of economic activity.

Within the framework of this approach, it is useful to examine the forces that influence the relative efficiency of internal versus external co-ordination of information and knowledge production and exchange. Full disclosure of information is not a meaningful goal within this theoretical approach regardless of the intentions or incentives of actors. This is because a considerable amount of information and knowledge relevant to economic activity cannot be articulated effectively or economically for the purposes of either disclosure or exchange. The complexity implicit in this perspective makes it very unlikely that anyone, policy-maker, economist, or business leader, will be able fully to comprehend *all* the potential implications of changes in institutional structures and processes within which information is produced, distributed, and utilized in modern economies. In this context, it is appropriate to regard policies towards privacy and information as being experimental and subject to improvement through experience. This approach can be helpful in identifying situations in which incentives are misplaced or where market failures are at work which is a more realistic goal for policy analysis than the commodity theory perspective where the aim is to discover how to optimize the operation of markets.

Both the commodity theory and the organizational design models that are rooted in economic analysis tend to ignore the social or relational characteristics that influence whether individuals and organizations will or will not choose to participate in the new public and private electronic spaces. When e-commerce and information are treated as social processes (Zuboff, 1988), it becomes important to understand how the new technologies and services mediate social and economic processes that lead to the production and exchange of information.[16] A focus on social dynamics also brings changes in the power relationships within organizations and between individuals and groups within society to the fore.

A third model for examining information and privacy is an integrated cognitive and social exchange model that takes into account the construction and enforcement of social norms and opinion. In certain circumstances, including transactions involving others, some social groups regard privacy as an absolute right of the individual that should be preserved automatically, even if the conclusion of economic analysis would suggest otherwise. It cannot be assumed reliably that people will process information in the same way or have the same degree of trust in the warranties offered concerning the maintenance of privacy. In an integrated cognitive and social model there is room for rational and irrational fears about the potential misuse of information. There is also room to consider how social processes evolve to render electronic information useful in certain contexts and useless in others. For example, the difficulties of achieving a common understanding of the meaning of a collection of information signals may create insurmountable problems for the use of electronic systems. Many of the delays in implementing electronic information systems are attributable to the time needed to work out how to avoid designing-in procedures that would violate strongly

---

[16] This discussion is based in part on research by Dr Andreas Credé (1997*b*).

held beliefs, to assess the capabilities of individuals to process information, to overcome fears about information misuse, and to establish a common understanding of the meaning and interpretation of information.

An interest in how individuals create information that, in turn, is the product of codification, abstraction, and diffusion of otherwise undifferentiated sensory data, is shared by proponents of both economic and social theory.[17] The production and exchange of information are particularly important when the limitations that apply to the ability of human beings to process raw data are considered. Individuals economize to overcome these constraints but this means that data are reduced to abstract codes, that is, information that can be diffused only when there is a shared context that will permit their interpretation.[18] This latter aspect is a fundamentally social process and is central to the extent to which efforts to govern e-commerce will be successful in building trusting relationships. Within this perspective, knowledge represents a disposition to act on the basis of data made intelligible through information production and exchange processes.[19] The uses of electronic networks and services, therefore, are likely to be a reflection of, and mediated by, the characteristics of the institutions and governance processes that interact with information production and exchange.

When the focus is on these kinds of interactions, as Boisot (1995) suggests, it is important to examine whether and how information and communication networks enable the 'repersonalization' of information-exchange relationships. Information and communication infrastructures and services may permit smaller or larger degrees of richness in the preservation of social cues within network environments containing interleaved sequences of voice interactions, electronic mail, shared documents, and recorded audio or video messages (Rice, 1993; 1999). Some communication media may, in fact, retain substantial implicit components of information that are revised through interaction rather than being interpreted on the basis of definitive understandings about the meaning of data (Boisot, 1995). The evolving characteristics of information production and exchange processes are important for understanding each of the features of the information society. The roles of implicit understandings and social interactions are clearly important, but they are difficult to take into account when analysis focuses exclusively on the amount and quality of information. Heuristic, experiential, and internalized knowledge is difficult to communicate and is best learned through practical example.[20] Within any commercial institution or social organization, many processes play a role in establishing the way that usable information can be derived from unverified, privileged, or confidential data.

Trusting relationships are important in establishing the boundaries between public

---

[17] See Cowan, David, and Foray (1999) and MacKenzie (1996: ch. 10).

[18] Information refers here to the result of a complex production process whereby undifferentiated data are codified, abstracted, and diffused so that meanings, interpretations, and significance emerge. The relevance and significance of data have to be established and confirmed by the social actors, see Boisot (1998) and Macdonald (1998).

[19] Boisot (1995; 1998) points out that there is confusion in the economics literature where the three terms—data, information, and knowledge—are often used interchangeably, he cites Machlup (1962) as an example.

[20] Polanyi's starting-point was 'we know more than we can tell' (Polanyi, 1966). Simon (1955) argued that what is learned is profoundly connected with the conditions within which it is learned.

and private within organizations and the ways that organizations establish interfaces for their transactions with the external world. Boisot (1995) draws attention to the fact that highly uncertain and complex transactions bring the problem of trust into focus in such a way that the greater the uncertainty, the greater the amount of trust that may be needed between the parties to reduce the uncertainty. Procedures for authenticating information are essential for users to establish trust in data. The implications of the authentication process, which is a key component of the integrated cognitive and social exchange model, for privacy can be illustrated by a case study of the use of the information and communication infrastructure and services within the banking industry. This case study also offers an example that illustrates the other two models of information and privacy outlined above.

A principal role of banks is to 'add trust to data', that is, by managing a process of authentication alongside the application of information and communication technologies to achieve gains in the efficiency of information processing.[21] Credé (1997a) has argued that the need for authentication has influenced the banking industry's organizational processes, its selection and deployment of advanced electronic services, and the design of digital network architectures. Commercial banks depend heavily on confidential, proprietary data that are made available to them by their clients. These data are provided within trusting relationships between bank personnel and clients, but the data themselves undergo an internal process of authentication before they become usable information for the banks. The authentication process can be mediated by electronic information and communication services only to the extent that such services preserve or create a rich context for human interaction, one that preserves the heuristic, experiential, and internalized knowledge gained through social interaction.

A detailed examination of the credit review process within the banking community in London shows that these banking institutions engage primarily in producing information from confidential customer data rather than in processing information that is available from public and other sources (ibid.). For the information to be accepted by bank personnel an authentication process is necessary and this is an integral element of the credit review process. For example, credit applications are prepared and then reviewed and analysed by individuals within an approval hierarchy. Key elements of the credit application are filtered through the review process and different values are attributed to the data. The credibility of an application is established through a series of personal contacts and interactions involving varying degrees of personal trust. The credit review process is not primarily an exercise in information processing; rather it is a complex process of giving meaning, significance, and relevance to data.[22]

Key bank processes, and particularly those associated with credit assessment, involve complex processes of authentication that depend upon privileged access to

[21] Research undertaken by Dr Andreas Credé (1997a). The empirical analysis for this case study was based on twelve major world-class commercial banks selected by size, global presence, and ability to provide representation from all the major industrial regions.

[22] Further empirical evidence of the importance of institutional factors and the complex process involved in acquiring the necessary authentication skills is revealed by variations in development paths experienced by each of the major commercial banks, see D. Rogers (1993).

customers. Relatively little automation supports the credit evaluation process. In spite of substantial investment in information and communication technologies by the banking industry to support activities in other areas, credit evaluation continues to be conducted largely on a face-to-face basis or with the use of those technologies that are believed to offer the maximum capabilities to preserve a social context for interpretation, for example, voice telephony, fax messages, and videoconferencing services.

The internal data that commercial banks hold within automated information systems or traditional paper-based files that play a role in the credit review process are not widely distributed and are controlled through a process of negotiated access. Data in customer files are strictly controlled and become the responsibility of accounts managers. This may explain why commercial banks have put relatively little emphasis on the digitization of their internal data and prefer to retain extensive paper-based systems rather than introducing information systems for manipulating data in electronic form to support the credit review process. Extensive investments have been made by banks in electronic networks, but these are used largely to improve communication between employees and to support routine office automation rather than to enable access to data supporting credit decisions.

While the banks are preserving their paper record systems as an adjunct to the operation of the personalized authentication process, they are also among the largest investors in information and communication technologies and in the use of telecommunication services. The information, largely concerned with transactions, that is processed using these technological capabilities is subject to standardized procedures and, therefore, it is possible to automate the authentication process and to depersonalize the network. These systems can incur significant costs due to their lack of personalization, as, for example, when a person loses a purse or wallet containing an Automatic Teller Machine (ATM) card and a Personal Identification Number (PIN). They are, nevertheless, widely deployed because their use yields efficiency advantages in transactions. While such systems attempt to ensure the privacy of users from third parties, both the banks and their customers share information about customer accounts. The customers completely relinquish privacy as to the identity of payees and the amount of payment in order to facilitate the accurate payment of obligations, but this release is only to their bank, and only for the purpose of facilitating transactions. Reuse of this information by the bank in another context would raise a number of privacy concerns.

In effect, this creates a potential information asymmetry within the bank. Should the bank be able to analyse a customer's banking records for evidence of creditworthiness? Analysis derived from the economics commodity model would suggest that this is not only in the bank's interest, but also in the interests of those customers for whom such an investigation would provide 'above average' indications of their creditworthiness, for example, regular payments on recurrent obligations. Despite this, banks employ other means to collect such information, such as asking for references from creditors. It could be argued that this is because the banks' records are unreliable or too difficult to analyse. Alternatively, banks may wish to preserve their customers' trust that information deriving from their primary financial transactions remains private.

We suggest the cognitive and social exchange model provides the best understanding of the banks' practice in this case.

Banks are also engaged in the process of co-ordinating a growing collection of financial services. In performing these activities, it is less important to analyse the behaviour of specific individuals than it is to understand more general patterns of behaviour. Determining whether bank customers might wish to enrol in a savings programme for 'back-to-school' or Christmas expenses can be achieved by analysing spending patterns without identifying specific individuals.[23] Information about spending or saving patterns by age group can be derived in so far as the banks collect and use this information. These examples illustrate the value of the organizational advantages that banks may have over other institutions that might seek to compete in the financial services market. The outcomes are consistent with the 'organizational design' perspective on information and privacy. Regulatory provisions that seek to bar these kinds of analyses are likely to affect the banks' abilities to offer valued services and to alter the relative attractiveness of other financial institutions for customers. For example, if policy-makers become convinced that banks are misusing their market power, they could encourage competitive entry and the growth of rivals to the banks by extending the reach of privacy protection rules, thereby reducing the market power of the banks.

Features of all three theoretical models are useful both for understanding industry and consumer practice and for crafting policies. The second and third models suggest that information-related relationships are very complex. As a result the reliability of the application of these perspectives to predict specific outcomes from privacy protection policies is relatively low. Policies devised with regard to information and privacy issues cannot be regarded as precise instruments that can be applied to achieve specific purposes. However, it is appropriate to consider the potential influences that changes in policy and regulation with respect to privacy may have on the choices that such organizations as banks are likely to make, as well as the way such changes will affect evolving market structures and competition. Other businesses that make intensive use of information, and which are predicated on specific social norms regarding privacy as in the case of e-commerce, are likely to be affected by changes in policy and regulation in ways similar to the banking industry.

The processes involved in building trust in e-commerce are more amenable to analysis when attention focuses on the way that the processes of authentication, data reuse, and contractual commitment operate, and on the extent to which these processes can be facilitated by the application of information and communication technologies. These processes are closely linked to the specific skills, abilities, and routines that organizations develop for particular forms of information production and exchange and these aspects are crucial to the way e-commerce develops. Firm-based organizational processes, practices, and procedures for e-commerce are evolving alongside governance institutions and processes that are being put in place by the state. With an emphasis on *both* the information processing and the relationship issues

---

[23] Clearly, it would be useful to know whether a customer has school-aged children or is likely to celebrate Christmas, but the point here is that it is not necessary to know this.

involved in the social processes of mediated communication and tacit authentication, we have a basis for examining the perspectives on information and privacy, as well as security, of the stakeholders involved in e-commerce.

The stakeholders involved in the governance of e-commerce with interests in privacy and security are numerous at the international, regional, and national levels. They are not confined to governments and they embrace a large number of individuals and institutions. The instruments available for the governance of e-commerce manifest themselves as laws, regulations, treaties, conventions, codes of practice, and standards. These instruments may be employed in the exercise of governance aimed at enabling the use of a technological system or they may be aimed at preventing the abuse of a system. Different communities of social actors with interests in the outcomes of evolving governance regimes are likely to be 'reunited in rejecting some alternative vision of the world. . . . There is substantial latitude among members of the community about the precise right answer, but there are strong common aversions' (Cowhey, 1990: 173). Research on 'communities of knowledge' by Cowhey and by Haas (1992) has stressed the importance of common sets of beliefs and principles shared by members of communities. [24]

We examine cases in the following section that focus upon two specific issues related to e-commerce policy and one issue concerning regulation designed to protect social interests. In the e-commerce area we examine electronic payment systems, the application of cryptography, and the incidental use of data gathered in transactions or as the result of interconnection to electronic networks. We examine 'unwanted intrusions' that encompass concerns about pornography as an illustration of the issues of concern to social policy and regulation. Electronic payment systems provide a means of conducting e-commerce on the Internet. They also raise the possibility that present regulation governing the creation of money, the recording of incomes, and the payment of taxes may be bypassed by the application of new technologies. In a similar fashion, cryptography is being used to ensure the privacy and confidentiality of some types of exchange, but it also provides a means for illegal activities. The nuances of the individual's 'right' to privacy are illustrated by the complexities of the incidental use of data gathered through electronic transactions or, as a consequence, the ability to monitor an individual's connection to an electronic network. In many ways, information that is thus disclosed is the joint property of individuals and service providers who use and produce e-commerce or other services supported by information and communication infrastructures.

Finally, with respect to pornography, although we have considerable sympathy with the opposition to pornography represented by MacKinnon (1987) and other feminist perspectives, we do *not* take pornography *itself* as intrusive in our analysis. Instead, our approach is based upon the principle that community standards should govern the regulation of pornography on the Internet. This makes paramount the issues of establishing community boundaries and providing the means of enforcing these

---

[24] Haas (1992: 2) uses the concept of epistemic community within the international policy-making context and calls members of such communities 'knowledge-based experts'. Cowhey (1990: 173) refers to such communities as 'communities of knowledge'.

boundaries. Some readers may regard this viewpoint as a morally compromised position; others may see it as an effort to extend the police powers of the state. Our view is that the most that community standards permit the governance apparatus to achieve with respect to pornography in most industrialized societies is to provide the means for individuals to protect themselves and their families from the unwanted intrusion of pornographic messages. Collectively, the issues we address in the subsequent sections of this chapter indicate that privacy considerations are, and are likely to remain, among the more difficult issues for governance in the Internet environment.

8.3   Electronic Payment Systems and Strategic Positioning

The development of electronic payment systems can be used to illustrate the interplay between the commodity theory of information and privacy, and the organizational and cognitive and social exchange approaches to the analysis of information use. A key issue is whether these payment systems will be perceived by various stakeholders, including citizens and consumers, as preserving privacy and rendering commercial data secure. The physical representation of money has become more abstract over time, moving from commodity 'standards of value', such as metal coins, to the use of legal-tender paper currency, to bank deposits, and other credit balances. One explanation for the replacement of bartering by coinage lies in the difficulty of retaining and negotiating 'stores of value' for a diverse set of goods and services. The eventual shift from precious metals to the legal-tender standard with ordinary metals for coinage and with paper currency was possible when people were willing to trust a symbolic store of value.[25] Money became an institution for transparent exchange of goods and services based upon a convenient unit of transaction that was universally accepted within a given societal group. Money is still in part a material commodity, that is, physical notes and coins are exchanged for various goods and services. However, increasingly, information about money is becoming more important than material money itself.

Electronic payment systems, like their physical forebears, are being designed with payment amount size and frequency as key parameters. New applications and versions of what are now based upon rather 'old' information and communication technologies are adding electronic cash and on-line banking functions to the range of financial instruments available throughout most of Europe. The two most promising new technologies are smart, or chip, cards,[26] and secure Internet transactions. Our

[25] Lycurgus, the head of the Spartan State, grasped the idea of 'symbolic currency' well before the modern age. Concerned that money competed with deeper virtues, he decreed that money should be struck in iron. The purpose seems to have been to dissuade people from amassing wealth, as moving large amounts of metal from one place to another was cumbersome and inconvenient, see Plutarch (edn. published in 1928: 229).

[26] The chip or smart card became available for use in 1974 but the costs of portable processing power and memory functionality initially prevented its widespread use. By the end of the 1990s, the technologies of chip encapsulation and contacts with the receiving terminal had become the main cost factors, but the absence of compatible standards and the difficulty of refreshing data continue to limit widespread use. Almost all magnetic stripe reading devices must be upgraded if smart cards are to become widely diffused.

examination of the institutional and historical development of earlier electronic payment systems provides a context for assessing the potential of the new technological applications.

Electronic payment systems have a wide variety of applications and functions. Differences exist in the typical amounts paid using the system; in the frequency of payments; in the incidence of fraud and other losses and in the costs to the major users; in the legal frameworks and safeguards; and in the sophistication of the user communities that the systems serve.[27] The costs of these payment systems are also substantial (Brown and Capelli, 1996). There is considerable variability in the starting-points from which European countries have begun their transitions to the widespread use of electronic payment systems. There are differences in people's payment attitudes, habits, and culture, and in the capacity of the information and communication infrastructure to support these systems across the European Union Member States (ibid.). The diffusion of electronic payment systems for consumers has been uneven and these systems are likely to continue to coexist with traditional payment systems for some time.[28]

8.3.1   The Development Trajectory for Electronic Payments

The early development of electronic payment systems in the 1960s involved Electronic Funds Transfer (EFT) between banks.[29] EFT systems are governed by contractual relationships between banks that are established by organizations, such as the Clearing House Automated Payments System (CHAPS) in the United Kingdom and the Society for Worldwide Interbank Financial Transactions (SWIFT), which handles the major portion of payments between banks internationally. SWIFT was introduced in 1974/5 to curb the growing volumes of paper that international transaction growth created. The system has a near-military level of security, for example, heat sensors to detect how many staff enter a given maintenance area, which is then checked against a pre-filed plan. The input devices are subsystems of the member banks' computers and these subsystems incorporate particular security features that are precertified for use. Commercial, often called 'wholesale', payments are made by cheque or a similar banking instrument, that is, direct debit and credit transfer. These payments are usually large

---

[27] These systems involve an input device, for example, a cash till, or a transducer reading the passage of an identifiable car in a road pricing scheme. For consumer transactions, there is a process of identification and payment authorization. A transport mechanism, typically a telecommunication network, moves the initiating command to a gateway system that checks the security of the initiation and the satisfactory completion of the transaction. The settlement system conducts a form of electronic dialogue with the initiating party and a counterpart gateway system representing the other party in the payment. Processes of recourse and redress usually exist, ranging from retry functions, letters accompanying bounced cheques, and major precedent-setting law suits (Worthington, 1996).

[28] Within Europe, the applications of electronic payment systems are diverse and this is confirmed by the variety of cards in use which serve as a proxy for this activity. The numbers of international payment systems—i.e. Visa, MasterCard, American Express, and Diners Club—outlets exceeded the numbers of national systems in only Denmark and France in 1995. Substantial differences exist between European countries in the extent to which credit or debit cards are held, the value of transactions per card, and the availability of EFTPOS terminals (Retail Banking Research Ltd., 1995).

[29] Background research for this section was undertaken by David Sayers, Independent Consultant (Sayers, 1997a).

in value, for example, representing about 33 per cent of the value of transactions in the United Kingdom, but represent less than 2 per cent by number of transactions. The cost of servicing these is not a pressing issue for the banks, though interest on the 'float' or money effectively in transit and thus not in an account earning interest, is significant. Despite the importance of EFT in the banking system, it is unlikely to offer strong competition to Internet payment systems. This is because, for retail purposes, SWIFT and other means of international clearances are costly and cumbersome as they were designed to co-ordinate banking practice rather than to provide an efficient system for electronic payments.

A transaction-oriented system, Electronic Funds Transfer at Point-of-Sale (EFTPOS), has developed from the EFT structure. EFTPOS brings together the banks' EFT systems and the retail distribution industry's Point-of-Sales (POS) systems. The cost of goods and services purchased by the buyer is entered into a POS terminal using a plastic card. The data relating to this purchase are sent to the appropriate bank using a telecommunication link. The bank then deducts the funds from the buyer's account and effects a transfer to the seller's account. In other words, the buyer's bank credits the seller's account and, in so doing, undertakes a debt to the seller. Generally, EFTPOS systems immediately change the information concerning indebtedness. This is termed a 'direct debit', reflecting the fact that the presentation of the plastic card, along with the bearer's ability to reproduce the signature inscribed upon it, constitute an immediate claim on the account. EFTPOS systems are used in connection with what are known as debit cards.[30] These systems effect payment by substituting a third party's obligation, that is, that of a bank, to pay for the debtor's obligation, that is, the buyer of a service, for the debtor's own ability to establish creditworthiness.[31]

One means of translating the EFTPOS system to the Internet is by a service provider who acts as the customer's agent. An example is provided by First Virtual Holdings Inc., which operates an Internet Payment System. First Virtual issues clients with a Virtual Personal Identification Number, an alias for individual credit card information. Funds can then be debited from that card in favour of First Virtual. When making a purchase, potential buyers send properly authenticated Internet payment messages to First Virtual, which then immediately debits their credit cards. The company keeps an account of sums received from buyers and periodically deposits these amounts (less charges) in the seller's bank account. Merchants sign up with First Virtual on the basis that all transactions will result in collection from the customer and payment to the vendor. The effect of a First Virtual transaction is that the buyer's debt to the seller is transformed into a debt to his or her credit card provider as well as a debt of First Virtual to the seller. First Virtual, therefore, acts as a third party repository for sensitive information, replacing the buyer's obligation to pay the merchant with its own obligation to pay (Centre for the Study of Financial Innovation, 1997). Essentially, it

[30] Systems in some countries allow the use of credit instead of direct debits, and some POS systems offer deferred payments.

[31] Some electronic cash systems function in a similar manner, i.e. they create an equivalent of cash by substituting either their own debt or that of a third party and they work essentially in the same way as credit or EFTPOS direct debit payments.

plays the same role as the buyer's bank in a traditional EFTPOS transaction and this system is built upon the earlier model. The example of First Virtual indicates that EFTPOS systems have the potential to become viable Internet payment systems.

Most electronic payment services exhibit two trends. First, there is a merging of services 'towards' the customer, offering to arrange payment options according to customer needs. Second, there is a proliferation of services into specialities that are combined, priced, and packaged in original ways under strong brand names. The corporate stakeholders include not only the banks, but also other organizations that believe that they have a strong 'franchise' within their chosen market segment regardless of their present line(s) of business. Banking and financial service players are forming alliances with others to move closer to their customers. The offerings of these organizations cover a wide spectrum of financial and other services, branded in ways deemed to appeal most powerfully to the target customer segments. Companies from outside the banking sector that plan to offer lower costs, greater flexibility, or higher service levels are potential entrants into the payment services market. These include Visa and MasterCard, who show every sign of being able to stay in the lead. Their franchise style of operation makes their presence highly visible to consumers/users and, although their organizational form may produce slow decisions, their achievement in covering the world in their chosen markets, defined by payment frequencies and amounts, makes their incumbent strategy reasonably robust. The wide availability of credit cards, such as Visa and MasterCard, makes them strong candidates for Internet payment systems.

Optimistic forecasts during the 1990s provided a basis for visions of a rapid growth in on-line cashless transactions with on-line shopping and branchless banking (Worthington, 1995). Much of the optimism about the future of such systems was based upon the presumption that transactions in an electronic environment would be automatically authenticated and credited instantaneously to the credit or demand deposit accounts of customers. These forecasts took little account of how the strategic behaviour of the financial services sector might influence the diffusion of payment systems, or of the viewpoints of merchants, accountants, and users. The growth of electronic payment systems has been slower than initially forecast, largely because of the difficulties in working out the details of the implicit credit guarantees, and recourse for errors, omissions, and disputes that must accompany their deployment. The growth of e-commerce is widely seen as contributing new vitality to these developments. If the new technologies for electronic payment systems initially presented a threat to the status quo in the financial services sector, there are now many signs that banks and other stakeholders are forming partnerships with some non-traditional partners drawn from the retail sector and new entrants from other sectors.

Insurgent strategies by the new entrants in chip cards and Internet payment systems are likely to succeed only in so far as they do not generate a strong competitive response from the established players. Such a response is inevitable, however, in our view. The realization of an insurgent strategy of developing new sources of network externality in their offerings is likely to hinge upon the capacity of new entrants to displace existing systems. It seems likely that businesses and consumers will continue to maintain their primary trusting relationships with the banks as the issuers of EFTPOS-capable debit and credit cards, and through use of credit cards such as Visa and MasterCard. Neither technical nor commercial advantages appear to favour the new players in Internet payment systems. Similarly, virtual community types of strategies are less likely to emerge in this area because of the costs entailed in managing all the components of the monetary exchange process for payments and because of the strong position of the incumbent players. The development of electronic payment systems provides an illustration of the delicate balance between entrepreneurial initiative and the maintenance of market dominance in this area. It also reveals the relatively slender advantages that appear to be offered by innovative Internet payment systems. A variant of electronic payment systems, electronic cash, has been introduced in an attempt to overcome the incumbency advantages held by the providers of existing systems. The prospects for electronic cash are considered in the next section.

8.3.2   *Electronic Cash and the Innovation Process*

Electronic cash—or e-cash—is an emerging electronic payment system that provides an example of the operation of the insurgent strategy for targeting the micro and small payments end of the market.[32] The market for e-cash is defined by the potential value of an electronic payment system that does not require a telecommunication link to verify the creditworthiness of the person offering to pay with electronic cash. Although this is not a universal feature of all systems identifying themselves with e-cash, it is a feature of the three systems that we consider in this section, Mondex, DigiCash, and Visa Cash. It is also, arguably, the feature that most clearly differentiates e-cash from debit and credit cards.

Not having to establish a telecommunication connection to a verification service for e-cash systems offers cost and time savings for the user and the receiver of e-cash. These potential advantages need to be tested in the market for an extended time interval before it will be possible to ascertain how successful this option is likely to be. Our purpose is not to offer opinions about the relative merits of competing systems. Indeed, since the material underlying this section was researched, the sponsor of one of the systems examined, DigiCash, has filed for bankruptcy and the underlying technology has been transferred to a new entity, e-cash Technologies Inc.[33] Instead, our purpose is to illustrate how the insurgent strategy operates in two recent attempts to create a viable e-cash system.

E-cash is a relatively new application of information and communication technologies but there are many pilot schemes operating throughout the world. About 63 per cent of all consumer payments are made in cash and the systems that are emerging attempt to target the cash payments market (Brown and Capelli, 1996: 20). E-cash can be used for physical transactions but it is also expected to play a major role in facili-

---

[32] This section is based on research by Lara Srivastava, former SPRU Master's student, see Srivastava and Mansell (1998). The major players in the electronic cash market were interviewed in 1997, including banks in the UK, as well as the major credit card schemes.

[33] See T. Clark (1998) and e-cash Technologies Inc. (1999).

tating commerce over the Internet. The functions include storing the value as digital information independent of a bank account, and enabling that value to be transferred to another. There are two main types of e-cash, 'prepaid' and 'true'. The former is float-based and the latter token-based.[34] Both systems ultimately depend upon a transfer of liability from the debtor to the company maintaining the system. However, unlike EFT and EFTPOS, liability is not based upon recording and approving individual transactions. Instead, it is based upon the integrity or security of the system and its capacity to reflect accurately the creditworthiness of the customer and the likelihood of the eventual receipt of funds by the creditor.

The first example we consider is Mondex. The initial concept of Mondex was developed in 1990 by Tim Jones and Graham Higgins of the National Westminster Bank (NatWest) in the United Kingdom and was joined by Midland Bank in 1993.[35] It is controlled by Mondex International (MI). Many banks are shareholders, and in 1996 MasterCard acquired a 51 per cent controlling interest. This diversification of MasterCard into e-cash may represent a learning effort with respect to the new technology or an effort to hedge MasterCard's market position as a dominant player in electronic payment systems.

The first pilot trial of Mondex was conducted in Swindon in the United Kingdom in July 1995,[36] and international trials have also been conducted. Mondex claims that its system is not a replacement for cash or demand accounts, but a complement to these other forms of money. Smart card technology forms the basis of the Mondex system. Value is stored on smart cards until it is used as payment for goods or services.[37] Alternatively, value can be transferred to another consumer's card. Transactions are not centrally recorded, as in the case of traditional non-cash payment systems. Data relating to the last ten transactions are stored on the chip of each individual card. The configuration of the Mondex system is summarized in Fig. 8.1.

---

[34] In float-based systems, the claim to value is held elsewhere, for instance, in a bank account. The issuer of e-cash receives payment from the consumer (debtor) and deposits it into a float account. For this payment, the consumer receives a store of value that can be spent by those equipped to receive such payments (creditor). A third party, for example, a bank, undertakes a contract to cover the debtors' obligations to the creditor and make a claim against the issuer to cover the payments to the creditor from the float account. In effect, the third party may maintain its own float accounts from the deposits of creditors. Float-based systems are similar to Electronic Funds Transfer in that they create a symmetrical pattern of credit obligations. Although every transaction does not have to be cleared by the issuer, it could be. Token-based systems are closer to physical cash than their float-based counterparts. The transfer of possession of the e-cash transfers its ownership, and transfer of possession (accepted by the transferee) discharges the debt owed by the transferor to the transferee. In contrast to 'prepaid' systems, the liability of the issuer of token-based electronic cash arises only when a token is presented to it for payment. Tokens may be exchanged or transferred an infinite number of times before the issuer's liability for payment arises and, thus, come closer to fulfilling the role of money as an intermediate medium of exchange.

[35] See Mondex web site at http://www.mondex.com accessed 6 April 2000. The first patents were applied for in Apr. 1990.

[36] The Swindon trial involved 700 retailers and a target consumer market of 40,000 (Swindon's total population being 190,000).

[37] The transfer of units of value between chips takes place as follows: (1) the chips identify themselves to each other, (2) the value of the transfer is deducted from the sending chip, encrypted together with the receiving chip's identifier, and transmitted to the receiving chip, (3) the receiving chip decrypts the transmission, adds value to its store and acknowledges the transfer. If the transfer fails, the value is recredited to the sending chip, see Fancher (1996: 25).

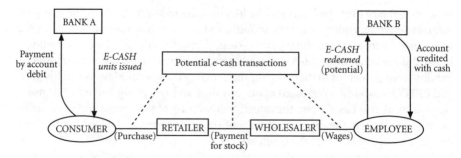

FIG. 8.1. The Mondex system

Source: Adapted from G. J. H. Smith (1996: 117).

In this example, the customer of Bank A makes a purchase from a retailer by transferring the necessary electronic value (acquired from Bank A) to the retailer's Mondex terminal. The retailer does not need to redeem the electronic cash immediately at the originating Bank A. For example, the e-cash can be used by the retailer to pay its wholesaler for stock. The wholesaler may be able to pay the wages of its employees in e-cash, and in this example, he or she *would* redeem the e-cash for a cash balance in an account. Technically, this chain could continue indefinitely, with the employee consuming goods and services from retailers who transfer the e-cash to various parties.

Mondex differentiates itself from EFT systems by its claim that it has no requirement for clearing, that is, it does not need a third party to settle and clear transactions between its users. This has the advantage of increasing the speed and adding to the simplicity of transactions. The feature of Mondex that makes it attractive to banks is the possibility of maintaining 'float' accounts in Mondex 'currency' that can be uploaded to a user's Mondex card. It is necessary to involve issuers only when the user wishes to transfer Mondex currency to cash or a conventional demand account balance. In the example given here, Bank B is willing to redeem the e-cash for a conventional cash balance. The extent to which Bank B is, in turn, then able to reissue e-cash balances in exchange for cash will determine whether it is content to hold these floating e-cash balances or, instead, to correspond with another bank who has a demand for greater e-cash balances.

Thus, Mondex is an attempt to implement an insurgent strategy by providing an incentive scheme for banks to adopt this cash format. The greater the number of Mondex accounts and users, the more valuable this incentive will be to banks, providing them with further incentives jointly to publicize and promote the new medium of exchange. Since banks may institute service delays and costs for the exchange of Mondex e-cash for cash or demand account balances, the term 'float account' is apt. It seems likely that banks and regulators would credit Mondex float accounts as deposits in a conventional sense since the issuer undertakes to monetize these upon demand.

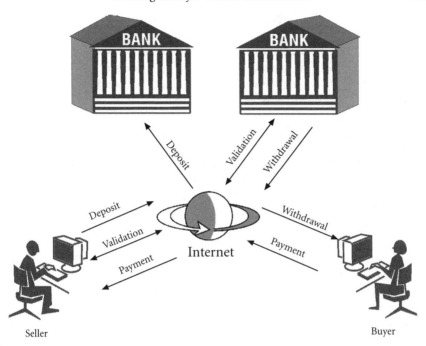

FIG. 8.2. The DigiCash system

Source: Adapted from Reed (1996).

Correspondingly, Mondex and AT&T announced in February of 1997 that they planned to launch a system to make micro-payments commercially viable on the Internet using the Mondex electronic cash platform (AT&T, 1997).

Our second example is DigiCash, which was launched by a private company founded in 1989 by Dr David Chaum based in Amsterdam. DigiCash created an Internet money product patented as 'ecash' and had experience in the development of smart card technology. DigiCash's ecash system was designed to effect secure payments from any personal computer to another workstation via e-mail or the Internet. It was intended to operate in the same manner as physical cash and had the configuration indicated in Fig. 8.2. Customers would connect to their bank to withdraw ecash tokens or coins, differing in denominational value as dictated by software and user requirements. The value of the coins was then stored digitally on the hard disk of the customer's personal computer. Each coin was encrypted with the identity of the issuing bank, a unique serial number, and its value. The customer selected the amount of payment for a good or service. This payment value was transmitted across a network to the payee merchant's workstation. The payee then checked the validity of the coins used for payment with the issuing bank and deposited them at his or her bank. The bank receiving the ecash value validated each coin deposited against its own digital signature. Once validated, the bank stored the serial numbers in a database containing the numbers of the coins already spent and used the database to verify whether coins were being used fraudulently. In this system there was a requirement for some clearing of funds. Although the issuing bank would be aware of the value of each coin issued to the payee, the coins were issued using a 'blind signature process' (Chaum, 1992). This meant that the issuing bank could not connect the customer with the serial number of the deposited coins and, in this respect, the customer's transactions remained private.

DigiCash developed a technological system to run its ecash on the Internet, including terminals, PIN pads, host computers, and the related software. It configured its system for compatibility, not only with the Internet but also with off-line commerce. The main concept trial started in October 1994. It was based on an artificial currency called the 'cyberbuck'. The company made the cyberbuck available over the Internet to 30,000 individuals and 150 retailers. Consumers participating in the trial were given a certain number of cyberbuck tokens that were deposited in the First Digital Bank (a mock bank run by DigiCash for the purposes of the trial). The tokens could be withdrawn and deposited into these accounts. In the cyberbuck trial, and in live pilot projects, DigiCash's ecash was used for many different types of transaction, such as the purchase of mail order goods and information, stock quotations, and on-line versions of magazines (Brown and Capelli, 1996).

The method that DigiCash used to promote its insurgent strategy was based upon the 'freeing' of the exchange process within the community of its users. Clearly, the goal was to create a large stock of stored value that could circulate among a growing number of users. Compared to the Mondex system, the extent to which value would be exchanged independent of reference to the issuer and also to any intermediary, was expected to be large. Therefore, if DigiCash had achieved its strategy of creating a large enough base, the technical incompatibility of the system with others would have provided the opportunity to translate an insurgent into an incumbent competitive advantage. Unlike Mondex, with its double-pronged strategy for creating an incentive for financial intermediary co-investment (service fees and value from float accounts), the principal incentives that DigiCash provided to financial intermediaries were the service fees in issuing tokens or redeeming them for cash, or demand deposit accounts. In the end, this insurgent strategy failed with DigiCash filing for bankruptcy protection in the United States. The ecash technology was transferred to e-cash Technologies Inc. under the ownership of its venture-capital backers.[38]

A major competitor to the preceding two e-cash systems was run by Visa International and known as Visa Cash.[39] Visa Cash also uses chip card technology and is aimed at small-value payments. It is a financial institution that is a member of Visa and issues Visa Cash cards, which are preloaded with value for consumers who may then make low-value purchases at registered merchants. To make a purchase, the consumer inserts the Visa Cash card into the merchant's terminal. The terminal reads the infor-

---

[38] See http://www.cnet.com/news/o-1003-200-334992.htm accessed 25 Oct. 1999. Capital, Applied Technology and Gilde IT-Fund, who were shareholders of DigiCash, have carried their interest over to e-cash Technologies Inc.

[39] See Visa's home page at http://www.visa.com accessed 6 April 2000.

mation stored on the chip and effects the transaction. The transactions are collected and sent to Visa, which then clears them and performs the necessary settlement among the participants. This is similar to the way Visa operates its credit and debit cards. The main difference is the increased speed of transaction and the use of chip technology that allows for disposable or reloadable cards. This involves a similar principle to the offerings of Mondex and the former DigiCash, that is, the creation of network externalities in the availability of networks of merchants or automated payment devices accepting this form of payment. However, this payment system is different in that it involves a centralized settlement and clearing procedure and is based upon credit and debit card operations.

Although banks have the authority, as a result of government support and legal jurisdiction, to issue stores of monetary value, opportunities for supplying e-cash services are available to new entrants. The new payment systems do not necessarily require the involvement of a bank for the issue or transfer of value. The players in the electronic money market include independent issuers of e-cash, banks, and credit card companies, telecommunication operators, and Internet Service Providers. Most of these firms can play the roles of suppliers of the service, or of users. Development of a novel and sophisticated technology for payments in the financial services sector has several implications for legal and regulatory authorities. Assurance must be established that contractual payment obligations will be discharged, confidentiality must be maintained, data protection regulations must be respected, and controls over illegal money flows, that is, tax evasion and money laundering, must be in place (Reed, 1996; Reed and Davies, 1995). If any of these new services is to achieve widespread diffusion, one of them will have to prevail by the building of a significant user community that supports substantial network externalities. If this occurs, the outstanding regulatory issues will need to be resolved very rapidly.

The process of implementing an insurgent strategy in this area involves more than the simple recognition that network externalities can have a major impact on the outcome of competitive battles. It also requires effectively harnessing the process of new technology adoption to achieve those network externalities. This process entails the complexities of the adoption process and the 'alignment' of incentives of participating firms, as well as those created by the system of public governance.[40] For the end-user, the main benefits of e-cash systems are presumed to be convenience, simplicity, and checkout speed. However, there have been few signs of any clearly articulated need or demand on the part of the consumer for these products.

In the case of Mondex, NatWest was in the position of being both the innovator and user of 'ecash' technology, a distinct proprietary technology. It addressed the complete supply chain from user to producer to supplier. Similarly, the British banks that have become shareholders of Mondex International are playing the role of suppliers as well as users. Banks supply new service products to their customers but they are intermediate users of the technology. The innovation process is said to be user-led

---

[40] Our use of the concept of alignment in this case corresponds closely to Molina's analysis of factors that produce misalignment in the numerous economic, social, and technological factors that influence the selection of a new technology, see Molina (1995).

when the user perceives the need for the product, actively conceives a solution, builds a prototype, and demonstrates the value of the prototype by its use (von Hippel, 1978). NatWest perceived a need for an electronic payment system and, having invented a new payment product, it acted in an entrepreneurial manner to derive maximum benefit from its diffusion into the economy by selling the design concept to a consortium of banks and creating an independent company.

Converting physical cash to an electronic form has potential as a significant cost-saving measure. E-cash also gives banks the opportunity to offer new services. NatWest first developed Mondex in the early 1990s when there were few players interested in the concept and the product was not well defined. The principal problem was the need to secure the customer base and to thwart disintermediation whereby the central clearing functions of the banks could be bypassed by firms such as DigiCash following insurgent strategies. By developing e-cash systems, the bank was able to address this priority while benefiting in other areas such as cash handling, fraud, and security management, and the potential to enter new markets. The banks have the ability to tie in their banking services with smart cards and with specific brands of service, thus fostering customer allegiance and even lock-in, which may prove to be a highly profitable strategy.

The banks have much to gain from the development of e-cash systems and the industry has paved the way for their deployment, although some banks have been cautious.[41] With increased competition in financial services, banks are offering enhanced services to customers to generate new business and to protect their customer base. The main contenders in the e-cash market are the credit card companies. Visa International has the Visa Cash platform and MasterCard is a major shareholder in Mondex International. The construction of both user and supplier networks is likely to play a major role in the relative success of these systems. Mondex International has been involved with players other than banks including Sun Microsystems, British Telecom, and AT&T. Mondex International was also instrumental in creating the Multi-Application Operating System (MAOSCO) consortium, which involved a group of players from the smart card industry in a bid to develop an industry standard.[42] In contrast to Mondex, DigiCash was not as active in collaborative ventures. DigiCash had no bank involvement in its early development phase, it focused on Internet payment systems and it sought integration of its product with smart card technology.

Comparison of the strategies of companies vying for leadership in the e-cash market indicates that the implementation of these strategies can be very different with regard to the nature of the network they construct, and from which they derive the benefits of network externalities. In addition, there are significant differences between the companies in the extent to which they attracted other suppliers as co-investors in their systems, in the sequencing of the 'rolling out' services, and in the perceived value

---

[41] There was one exception to this general rule. A representative from one of the British banks (not a shareholder in Mondex) stated that banks wanted to slow the diffusion process because of the fear that e-cash would erode currently profitable lines of business.

[42] MULTOS is the multi-application operating system for smart cards with the potential to allow many different operating systems on one smart card. The consortium included companies such as Hitachi, MasterCard International, and Motorola.

of the systems that rendered them attractive for adoption. These differences are the essence of the competitive process promoted by those following incumbent and insurgent strategies since it is from the diversity of competing strategies that successful new services emerge.

Each of the e-cash systems that we have considered involves the implementation of a cryptographic system for encoding messages about the nature and amount of stored value on a chip card or a computer file. Messages about e-cash are, of course, only one type of message that needs to be secured in order to facilitate e-commerce. In the next section, we review some of the issues involving the application of cryptography that are relevant to the development of e-commerce. We also consider the privacy and security issues raised by the increasing capability of networks to generate data about individual behaviours and to provide a means of intervening in personal or private communications.

8.4 The Place of Cryptography in Building E-Commerce Markets

Cryptography is the art and science of keeping messages secure.[43] Encryption describes the process of disguising the true meaning of a message and replacing the original message with a disguised message. The legitimate inversion of this process is called decryption. Other forms of recovering the original message, that is, illegitimate ways, are part of the art and science of crypt analysis.[44] Together, cryptography and crypt analysis define the field of cryptology which many regard as a branch of mathematics. Cryptographic techniques are developed either to protect messages or to protect stored data and they are intended to prevent penetration from the outside. The secure transmission of messages also aims to ensure their integrity and genuineness and to protect privacy by enabling only authorized participants to comprehend the messages (Association for Computing Machinery US Public Policy Committee, 1994; Schneier, 1996).

8.4.1 The Emergence of Cryptography

Cryptology has advanced significantly during the twentieth century. Specialized intelligence agencies played a central role during the Second World War (Association for Computing Machinery US Public Policy Committee, 1994; Kahn, 1983; Schneier, 1996), but it was not until the 1970s that there was a spectacular increase in effort, both commercial and academic. In 1972, the National Bureau of Standards (now the National Institute of Standards and Technology) in the United States initiated a programme to protect computer and communication data that led to the development of a standard cryptographic algorithm. The standard, Data Encryption Standard (DES),

---

[43] This section draws substantially upon research by Uta Wehn de Montalvo, SPRU doctoral student, see Wehn (1996), and to a lesser extent on research by David Sayers, see Sayers (1997b).

[44] The original message is also referred to as plaintext, while the encrypted message may be called the cyphertext.

a modified design of an algorithm proposed by IBM, was issued formally in 1976. During the period leading to the confirmation of this standard, progress was made in the academic cryptography field with the discovery of a family of techniques known as public-key cryptography in 1975 (Schneier, 1996).

Once the details of the DES were published, the algorithm of the standard could be studied in the public domain,[45] setting the stage for the dual use of cryptography for civilian and military purposes. Those responsible for national security generally want to maintain a monopoly on the most effective means of cryptography and the evolution of cryptography from a military tool to a corporate product has often involved government agencies in seeking to limit the practice of cryptography in the commercial environment. This has produced the paradoxical situation where very effective means of cryptography are available in the public domain, but their implementation in commercial products and services is resisted by government agencies.

In the civilian domain, business applications of cryptography include both confidentiality and authentication. The application of cryptography for civilian and military purposes may be the result of a direct product conversion, a 'pull' from the defence sector, concurrent development of civil and military applications, or newly emerging commercial initiatives that are transferred to the defence sector. Walker, Graham, and Harbor (1988) argue that the term 'dual-use' technology refers to more than mere technical artefacts and, as Molas-Gallart and Walker (1992) have shown, there is rarely a distinct line between military and civil technologies. While it may be feasible to limit the diffusion of a particular encryption product to some degree, it is more difficult to control people's technological capabilities. Creativity, experience, and knowledge contribute to a variety of spin-off or spin-back processes between developments aimed at the defence and civilian markets (Watkins, 1988: 19).

Cryptography can be implemented by using software or by employing dedicated hardware devices. Specialized hardware devices for cryptographic methods have been the dominant products until recently. These are usually encryption/decryption boxes that are plugged into a communication network, consisting of a dedicated microprocessor with built-in software. The security aspects of hardware implementation are influential in the military preference for hardware devices, despite advances in the software implementation of cryptography.[46] Ease of modification allows for continuous upgrading of the software, but this leaves these systems open to a variety of attacks, for example, an attacker may render the algorithm ineffective, steal the key(s) from memory, or modify the program to leak the keys during each session. The major disadvantage of hardware implementations is their cost as compared to software cryptography.

---

[45] According to Schneier (1996), the National Security Agency (NSA) had not forecast that the details of the standard would be made public.

[46] The encryption process is protected from physical or other means of tampering and cannot be bypassed. Advances in this area consist of encapsulation of the chip in a tamperproof box and special purpose Very Large Scale Integration (VLSI) chips. A classified algorithm may be protected from disclosure, thus increasing the degree of difficulty of crypt analysis. Keys are provided with a high degree of protection since they never appear unencrypted outside the device. For a secret private system, a hardware device ensures that the verification operations are performed (Schneier, 1996).

Examples of hardware devices include self-contained encryption modules for password verification and key management for banks, or dedicated encryption boxes for communication links and personal computer boards to encrypt everything written to the hard drive. Trends in encryption boxes are towards higher bit rates and more versatility (Datapro, 1994). More generally, manufacturers of communication equipment are building dedicated hardware cryptography devices into their equipment, for example, secure telephones, facsimile, and modems (Schneier, 1996). Software implementations of cryptographic algorithms are application programmes that run on computer systems. These implementations benefit from cheap reproduction, ease of modification, and their potential for integration into a wide variety of applications. Security concerns, however, have slowed their application for military and commercial use (ibid.).

The application of encryption in the commercial sector has achieved prominence as interest in secure e-commerce has grown. Although encryption involves the coding or scrambling of messages it also embraces issues of authentication, message integrity, proof of delivery, non-modification of content, digital signatures, and other security issues, all of which engage a variety of social processes. Those systems that have been seen historically to require security have had security technologies implemented as part of their initial design specification. Examples include Automatic Teller Machine networks, the SWIFT network, and government and security environments. In many other areas, for instance, Electronic Data Interchange, bank clearing, foreign currency interchange and settlement, and telecommunication networks, encryption has not been implemented in the initial design phase. Encryption is simply one of several means of securing a system as illustrated in Table 8.1.

Data that remain within an organization's private computer system can be protected by internal systems, passwords, and in-house monitoring, and supervised using monitoring and audit tools. Access can be restricted to specific groups, single sign-on systems can be mandated and, should an attack or loss of data occur, it should be possible very swiftly either to tighten the controls and identify the culprit or to increase the audit trails. The moment that data leave an organization, the protection offered by in-house security, however incomplete, disappears. The term 'firewall' gives an immediate feeling of protective security to a network or service applications manager who is charged with protecting in-house systems from external attack.

In the era of closed financial networks, the suppliers were able to specify all aspects of the system including hardware, software, and communication protocols. This gave them end-to-end control over the system design and operation and enabled users to feel secure. End-to-end control is eroding with the distribution of publicly available encryption methods, such as Pretty Good Privacy (PGP), throughout the Internet.[47] PGP is the cryptographic method of choice in many applications and costs only about US$ 35 per station to implement.[48]

---

[47] Developed by Phil Zimmerman in the USA, PGP uses the patented Rivest Shamir Adleman (RSA) Public Key Algorithm without paying a licence or royalty fee (Hoffman, 1994).

[48] The original plaintext message is enciphered using a randomly generated key that is generated for 'one' session. The recipient's public key is used to encipher this random session key. The public key enciphered

TABLE 8.1. *Security techniques and systems security*

Technology	Purpose
Top secret data	
Strong authentication	Verifies that a user is who he/she claims, creates audit trail to security server
Access control lists and authorization	Sets tight privileges for actions taken on servers
Encryption	Protects data in transit from sniffers or from being copied
Single use passwords	Generates on-time password, especially useful for remote access security
Audit tools	Discovers security holes in systems
Internal data	
Virus scan	Protects against viruses being transmitted through floppy disks and the Internet
Automated password management	Implements mandatory 60- to 90-day changes for password protection
External data	
Firewalls	Shields Internet servers from outside attack. Isolates secured subnets internally
Secured applications	Allows business transactions to be carried out on the Internet

Source: Mansell and Steinmueller (1996*b*).

Other methods are available for performing some or all of the functions sought from the message encryption approaches or complementing their implementation. For example, neural network techniques are being used to spot departures from normal usage patterns as early warnings of security lapses in some systems. There are other contenders but they have not been acclaimed by the security industry and have not achieved a sufficient period of satisfactory use to assess their market viability. Biometrics techniques attempt to identify the human body seeking access unambiguously from a set of measures obtained from some known behaviour, and may be measured by soft tissue, for example, a retina pattern, or hard tissue, for example, hand geometry. Most biometrics measures that are used on their own suffer from variable readings and have a margin of error that may be unacceptable.

With the growth of e-commerce based on the Internet there is an increasing need for a means of securing messages in a way that is both non-proprietary and accepted by the majority of service suppliers, information providers, card companies, and

session key is sent to the recipient along with the ciphertext. The recipient uses his/her private key to decipher the session key which uses that key to run the conventional fast single-key algorithm to recreate the original plaintext. PGP also uses digital signatures. The recipient, or anyone else, can verify the signature of the sender by using the public key to decrypt the signature.

financial institutions.[49] In the following section we look at the companies who play a role in the growing security systems market and at the respective interests of the various groups of suppliers and users of cryptographic techniques.

8.4.2   *Cryptographic Competencies and Interests*

While telecommunication equipment and network operators are unprepared to admit publicly to security breaches, confidential interviews with suppliers and users often reveal these concerns (Sayers, 1997*b*). The public debate on encryption has been augmented by the fascination and involvement of both the press and the public in stories about hackers, government eavesdropping on private communication, and issues of national security.

Government enforced key recovery through trusted third-party procedures—or key escrow as it is referred to in the United States—occurs when part or all of the cryptographic keys are kept in escrow by a third party.[50] The keys are released only upon proper authority to allow someone other than the original sender or receiver to read the message. The United States government has recognized that when encryption is applied to modern communication systems there are benefits to both public and private organizations, but there has been a longstanding concern that the use of strong encryption may threaten national security. Commercial key escrow systems have been discussed as an alternative to government-managed escrow agencies. Similarly, there have been proposals for software-based systems that could handle an exchange of key management within a public key framework (Froomkin, 1995).

During the last twenty years and, to some extent at the present time as well, the United States government has treated cryptography as munitions. General purpose cryptographic tools and development tool kits could be exported from the United States while controls were put in place covering exports embracing a range of cryptographic devices and encoding/decoding systems. Amendments have removed certain categories of technology from the prohibited list—including message authentication devices, television descramblers, automatic teller machines, virus protection software and smart cards—and certain types of mass-market software have also been removed from the restricted list.[51] In September 1999, the White House announced partial

---

[49] In the Internet context, web transactions can be secured at three different levels: above Hypertext Transfer Protocol (HTTP), at the HTTP level, or below. In the first, HTTP is used as a transport mechanism for data that will be decoded by external applications. In the second, the protocol can be enhanced to deal with encryption and authentication in an *ad hoc* way or by adding security to the protocol. In the third, a number of protocols can be used to secure a session on top of which transactions take place (Skouby, 1998).

[50] When implemented in hardware, each escrowed device has a unique identification number and secret key. While messages are encrypted with a randomly generated session key, the session key itself is encrypted using the secret key. Any Trusted Third Party that has knowledge of the secret key specific to the device can decrypt any messages enciphered by this device. Software implementations of key recovery algorithms are also possible but may be rendered redundant if the software is tampered with so that the key recovery is circumvented.

[51] See Koops (1999) for a review of recent developments. In the USA, cryptography export was controlled by the International Traffic in Arms Regulation and at the end of 1996 it was transferred to the Export Administration Regulations of the Department of Commerce. The export policy was relaxed to favour export of data-recovery cryptography and in 1998 there was further relaxation with the exception of exports

liberalization of regulatory barriers to the export, but not the publication, of mass market encryption software, which effectively means that individuals or companies cannot publish their software on the Internet without obtaining permission from the government (Electronic Frontier Foundation, 1999*b*).

The adequacy of controls is a significant issue in so far as encryption algorithms are available on the Internet. In the United States, the Software Publishers Association identified 340 non-US-owned suppliers of hardware, software, and encryption devices operating in twenty-two countries in 1993. Of these, 155 employed the DES and further investigation revealed over 462 companies in thirty-three countries and in the United States that were marketing and distributing cryptographic products, and the Association was able to obtain copies of these programs within the United States without any difficulty (Sayers, 1997*b*).

Suppliers of cryptographic systems in the United States have argued consistently that the prohibition on export limits their ability to tender and trade in the global market-place. They claim that other governments do not impose such controls on the export of strong encryption and that this imbalance puts unfair restrictions on American companies. The need to develop a set of weaker products for export complicates the product line, reduces flexibility and makes it difficult to market and support software (Electronic Frontier Foundation, 1999*a*). The converse is argued by suppliers of encryption systems outside the United States who see the American market as the largest potential market for encryption and security devices, but are obliged to meet import controls.

The Wassenaar Arrangement was established in 1996 by thirty-three signatory countries to maintain controls over the export of certain dual-use technologies. It revised restrictions on the export of cryptographic products in 1998 such that all products of up to 56 bits would be free for export; mass-market crypto software and hardware of up to 64 bits would be free for export; and the restrictions on products using encryption to protect intellectual property, such as Digital Video Discs, were relaxed.[52] All other forms of cryptography continue to require a licence for export. The revised position made no reference to public-domain cryptographic products nor to electronic exports via the Internet. Within Europe, each Member State is obliged to implement the Wassenaar provisions according to national legislation, which creates scope for variation (European Commission, 1998*i*).[53]

---

to certain countries. In 1999, several legislative initiatives addressed the export of specialized cryptographic products to some forty-five countries where a similar product is available on the international market without export restrictions.

[52] This arrangement was the first global multilateral arrangement on export controls for conventional weapons and sensitive dual-use goods and technologies. It was approved by thirty-three co-founding countries in July 1996 and began operating in Sept. 1996 with a secretariat based in Vienna. The arrangement was put into place as a follow-up to the Co-ordinating Committee for Multilateral Export Controls (COCOM) which was an international organization for the mutual control of exports of strategic products and technical data from country members to proscribed destinations (Koops, 1999). COCOM decided to allow export of mass-market cryptographic software (including public domain software) in 1991, but the USA maintained separate regulations. COCOM was dissolved in 1994.

[53] e.g. the DTI maintains a list of export controls related to telecommunication and information security. In this case, the length of 'keys' for goods sold outside the country should not exceed 64 bits, but there are further restrictions related to different types of products with specific uses and profiles, which leads to

European approaches to the issue of cryptography as a dual-use technology have focused on regulating the length of the 'keys' that may be offered in exported products. Although the Wassenaar Arrangement provides for free export of products with keys up to 56 bits, several signatories, including France and the United Kingdom, have allowed certain types of products to include longer keys which provide stronger protection from decryption. Thus, the solution to disputes between the representatives of commercial and military communities seems to lie in the development of a regulated market with periodic review and revision of technical specifications.

Encryption is an integral part of many electronic information and communication systems and, as private networks merge into the larger worldwide public networks, there is an increasing need for encryption systems that can be trusted and easily implemented. If this is not achieved, there is a risk of a reaction against the use of certain advanced information and communication networks and services, and this may slow their diffusion in unpredictable ways. Where encryption techniques are implemented, there are concerns about their reliability and the completeness of their implementation. Encryption is important because of the realization that the proliferation and availability of information and communication technologies and services provide the opportunity to speed up the flow of international commerce and trade. If technical innovations fail to create and maintain the security of the messages flowing through the world's trading arteries then user trust and confidence are likely to decrease rapidly. In addition, network traffic projections are unlikely to be achieved and the incentives for increased investment needed to build innovative architectures for the information and communication infrastructure will decline.

Software designed specifically to provide encryption capabilities represents a competitive market segment with a significant share held by United Kingdom firms.[54] In contrast, major players in the network equipment market that incorporate cryptographic algorithms into their software packages are predominantly American companies, such as Microsoft, Netscape—now owned by America Online—and Lotus.

The combined European market is similar in size to the market in the United States but companies in Europe rely more heavily on export sales. The scale of activity has increased over the past twenty years with a shift from the military to the commercial sector and from the commercial market in the United States to other mainly European markets. The market for cryptography products was estimated at US$ 1b. (Department of Commerce and National Security Agency, 1996) in 1995, and in June 1996 there were over 1,262 products worldwide employing cryptography. Of these, 730 were produced in the United States (Balenson, 1996). As of December 1997, the number of products had increased to 1,619, and of these 656 were produced outside

restrictions beyond the use of a key of 56 bits (Department of Trade and Industry, 1999a; 1999b; 1999c). See also Department of Trade and Industry (1998c) which addresses issues concerning electronic mail transfers. In France, in Mar. 1999, 'Décret No. 99-1999' freed the use, import, export of encryption with keys up to, and equal to, 128 bits. At the time of writing in late 1999, the legislation was still undergoing modification (Government of France, 1999; Jospin, 1999).

[54] Based on a British expert estimate, the UK share was estimated at 80% and the US share of the world market at 15%. France, Germany, and Israel were also named as strong competitors (Department of Commerce and the National Security Agency, 1996: ss. 3–10).

the United States. These products were distributed by 949 companies worldwide, of which 475 were American companies. Some 46 per cent of all cryptography products used DES implemented in software by manufacturers outside the United States.[55]

There is a growing number of companies active in the commercial market, and growing attention on the part of governments and the media is being given to the implications of the widespread use of cryptographic techniques. The interests of vendors and users can be characterized by the views espoused by the members of various communities who have coalesced around the alternative governance roles of the state and the private sector, as well as the rights of individual citizens. For example, the 'crypto anarchists' (Denning, 1996) or 'cypherpunks', as we will refer to them, represent one of the communities that has an interest in security and encryption technologies. Cypherpunks tend to promote the universal availability of cryptography without key recovery mechanisms for law enforcement purposes. Justifying their position by fears of the potential for a 'cyberspace police state' (S. Levy, 1994), they are opposed to government access to private communication and unconvinced by measures aimed at ensuring only legitimate access to keys held by third parties. Cypherpunks attempt to obstruct government control of the technology by distributing cryptographic tools. They tend to regard cryptography as a liberating tool that guarantees absolute privacy and anonymous transactions. They generally envisage a civil society with a libertarian free market and no government control (Denning, 1996).

A second community, defined by its opposition to the cypherpunks, might be termed the 'state democrats'. They support the role of government in the provision of law and order, accepting that absolute privacy for the individual and untraceable anonymity in all transactions is not compatible with an effective governance role for the state.[56] They are inclined to favour law enforcement capabilities being built into technology systems, and they tend to condemn crypto anarchists for encouraging an environment in which criminal and terrorist activities may thrive. These two groups can be regarded as polar opposites. Other groups and institutions cluster around the views expressed by the members of these communities.

Closer to the cypherpunks are liberal interest groups, such as the Electronic Privacy Information Centre (EPIC), the Electronic Frontier Foundation (EFF), and users of free encryption software. EPIC suggests that '[Law enforcement agencies] are going to have access to very personal, private information . . . they will be able to read your messages, find out who you talk to, even what your fetishes might be. And right now, very little of that information is being protected' (Galasyn, 1996: 3). These groups tend to share a common aversion to infringements of individual privacy. They often transcend national boundaries by operating their campaigns mainly over the Internet. Their influence is generally achieved through public debate rather than integration

---

[55] Of 656 non-American products from twenty-nine countries covered in the survey, 43% were DES based, see http://www.nai.com/nai_Labs/asp_set/crpto/crypt_surv.as accessed 9 Aug. 1999. Of a total of 963 domestic products, 466 used DES.

[56] This group may be placed in the sphere of liberal-democratic theory, which is concerned with the sovereign power of the state while at the same time justifying limits on that power, and is not synonymous with the Liberal Democrats political party in the UK.

within formally institutionalized decision-making processes. This community also includes organizations such as Privacy International, which describes itself as a human rights group formed in 1990 as a watchdog on surveillance by governments and corporations.[57]

Industry and business members of a broad array of organizations occupy the middle ground between cypherpunks and state democrats. They tend to support limitations on state interference in the market for cryptographic products and in the interception of communication but eschew the confrontation tactics and policies of the members of the libertarian communities. The vendor firms' interests are in the commercialization of cryptographic products, while business users in this community often demand strong cryptography for the conduct of business internationally. For example, a representative of British Telecom, who was interviewed during the research on which this chapter is based, believed that encryption technologies should be subject to some government control in the public interest. Similarly, an IBM representative expressed concerns about potential threats posed to both law enforcement agencies and businesses by the wide diffusion of cryptography. A representative of the Racal Data Group also regarded decision-making with regard to the civilian use of cryptography as a government role. Similarly, a Zergo interviewee, whose principal activity was consultancy and the design, development, and manufacture of computer-related hardware and software for information security, thought the government should play a role.[58]

The security industry constitutes a relatively distinct community in its own right. Most of the leading players are government security specialists or are under contract to government specialists and this contributes to the ethos of the members of this community, which leads to alignment with state democrat organizations. In the United Kingdom, for example, this group includes Zergo, the specialist British security consultancy and solution supplier, as an acknowledged leader, as well as Racal and the General Electric Corporation (GEC). These companies work extensively on advanced information and communication technologies and services for the Ministry of Defence, mainly through the Government Communications Head Quarters (GCHQ) in the United Kingdom. GCHQ works closely with its American counterpart, the National Security Agency (NSA).

Even more explicitly in the state democrat camp are the members of communities involving representatives of government. Within this community, a pro-control group tends to have an interest in maintaining regulatory controls on the use of encryption and information security. In the United Kingdom, the Department of Trade and Industry falls broadly into this category although the Government's position on issues relating to key recovery and the relationship between the use of encryption and the growth of e-commerce markets has been changing since discussions of policy

---

[57] See http://www.privacy.org accessed 6 April 2000. Privacy International's web site claims that it is administered by EPIC in Washington, DC, while the EPIC web site claims that it works in association with Privacy International, see http://www.epic.org, accessed 6 April 2000.

[58] See Wehn (1996) based on interviews with companies and representatives of the Federation of the Electronics Industry and the European Security Forum, a non-profit user organization with approximately 120 members from the user, regulatory, and supplier environments in Europe.

measures in the mid-1990s. Early proposals called for the licensing of trusted third parties to encourage the establishment of a certification authority infrastructure to authenticate messages in the e-commerce environment, and to enable law enforcement by providing for government access under some circumstances to the keys for decryption. By 1999, prior to the introduction of planned legislation, the position of the government had shifted towards a voluntary licensing scheme and the issue of key recovery had been separated from the legislation in support of the growth of e-commerce markets (Department of Trade and Industry and Home Office, 1999a). The difficulties for legislators in this area are considerable as suggested by the following extract from a report on the ethical issues raised by the Internet.

It is possible to encrypt data to give an appearance of unencrypted data, for example, pornography appearing when encrypted, as an innocent image. This will make censorship totally impossible because of the cost effort and intrusiveness of checking every image and message to see if it has been encrypted. Encryption is crucial to on-line commerce, and must not be outlawed, or it will weaken the UK's economic position. With encryption there can be no control over the flow of data; without it there can be no authentication or commercial transaction. (Collaborative Open Group on Ethics, 1995: 2)

Within the wider European context, the European Commission created a framework in 1992 to facilitate consideration of the security of information systems. Position papers were developed by 1996 with the objective of developing a robust regulatory and legislative framework at the regional level (European Commission, 1996l). The Commission's Green Paper provided several justifications for the use of encryption to safeguard commercial interests and privacy. Discussion continued until the end of the decade through several iterations of a proposed directive on the legal aspects pertaining to electronic commerce (European Commission, 1998l; 1999a).

For the OECD countries, guidelines were developed on the security of information systems as early as 1992, with the objective of 'the protection of the interests of those relying on information systems from harm resulting from failures of availability, confidentiality, and integrity' (OECD, 1992b: 4). The guidelines drew attention to the fact that 'users must have confidence that information systems will operate as intended without unanticipated failures or problems. Otherwise, the systems and their underlying technologies may not be exploited to the extent possible and further growth and innovation may be inhibited' (ibid. 10). By 1996, the OECD had developed draft Guidelines on Cryptographic Policy. They took account of the growing recognition that increasing amounts of personal data can be stored electronically and that requirements may be needed to ensure that these data are encrypted (Kamata, 1996). These guidelines were adopted by OECD members in March 1997 (OECD, 1997a). The Guidelines emphasize that cryptographic methods should be trustworthy, that users should have the right to choose any method subject to applicable law, and that the rights of individuals to privacy should be respected although national policies may allow lawful access to plaintext or cryptographic keys. At the time of writing, further consideration was being given to issues of authentication (OECD, 1999c) with a clear focus on how a 'web of trust' can be developed to support e-commerce activities.[59]

A system built upon pre-existing relationships can also work to create an informal 'web of trust' arrangement for developing trust among previously unknown communicating and transacting parties. Such a web of trust operates when identification information is validated from person to person or from organization to organization in the context of established relationships. In this way, confidence in electronic representations extends from parties who have a direct relationship with each other to those who do not; by relying on a third party with whom each person has a pre-existing direct relationship to 'make the introduction', the communicating parties can create a reasonable assurance that they are who they say they are (at least to the extent that they each trust the third party). (ibid. 3)

The challenge from a technological perspective is how to ensure the safe exchange and storage of symmetric cryptographic keys and certified public keys. From a public policy perspective, however, the requirements encompass whether the availability of cryptographic techniques and algorithms is subject to control because of the dual-use implications and restrictions. As one observer of developments in this area has commented:

The drive towards the vision of an Integrated Information Systems Infrastructure has captured the imagination of the public and now of industry and commerce. The Internet provides a manifestation of this vision, and represents a major source of innovation through the development of novel computing and communication technologies. The World Wide Web has provided an information rich environment, and has itself created a drive towards the development of corporate Intranets reusing the range of information search and retrieval technologies being developed on the Internet. This openness and interconnectivity carries a caution and a penalty, namely that dependency can arise, and with that dependency on technology: vulnerability. (Ferbrache, 1996: 3)

The openness and interconnectivity of network environments such as the Internet create a new incentive to develop strong encryption. The different communities display incompatible views regarding the involvement of government in the control of cryptography. Implementation of a key management infrastructure raises questions about whether key recovery facilities are a means of extending, or merely maintaining, current communication interception capabilities. While the pro-control group considers the use of cryptography to be a threat to its law enforcement capabilities, the middle group, and, more particularly, the civil libertarians, perceive what they consider weak cryptography to be a threat to privacy, both corporate and private. Nevertheless, having matured into a dual-use technology and outgrown the control regime applicable to a military technology, the civilian use of cryptography is becoming well established.

To the extent that cryptographic technology has, in fact, escaped from effective

---

[59] Electronic authentication can be defined to encompass any method of verifying a piece of information in an electronic environment, whether it is the identity of the author of a text or sender of a message, the authority of a person to enter into a particular kind of transaction, the security attributes of a hardware or software device, or any one of countless other pieces of information that someone might want to confirm.

government control, the efforts to regulate the use of cryptography, as such, may become a moot point. It does not follow, however, that this is the end of the story. Regulatory efforts are likely to shift from a focus on how cryptography may be used in electronic networks and, in particular, to the legal liabilities that users of cryptography may face. A general prohibition on the use of cryptography in electronic data networks would impose very high costs upon legitimate cryptography users, such as businesses wishing to maintain confidentiality or individuals wishing to maintain privacy. In either case, it may not be cost-effective or socially appropriate to monitor the use of cryptography or attempt to decrypt substantial numbers of messages to monitor them for illegal content. This does not mean, however, that governments are helpless with respect to encrypted communication. For encrypted information to have value for illegal purposes it must be decrypted, and, in many cases, the message will generate action that can be monitored. Alternatively, activities that are monitored may be associated with the exchange of encrypted messages. A presumption that further violations will occur in the exchange of encrypted information can raise the legal liability of those accused or convicted of crimes. Thus, for example, if individuals are convicted of the crime of fraud, they may face additional penalties for the use of encrypted information unless they can prove to the court that the encrypted information in question was innocuous.[60]

Further regulation of the use of encrypted information would raise the liability for its use and this is one means of providing an incentive to users to employ 'trusted third parties' that receive 'key' deposits. As recounted in the next section, however, the same communities that support the public availability of strong encryption resist the creation of trusted third party institutions. The outcome is likely to hinge upon the determination of regulatory, military, and police authorities to have some instrument for deterring and punishing those who may use cryptography in support of criminal acts or military aggression. The arguments for unlimited free use of cryptography are similar to those for the possession of guns in the United States, where it is argued that it is the use of the weapon, rather than its possession, that constitutes the crime. Since the use of cryptography in the commission of a crime may become impossible to prove, it may be necessary to shift the burden of proof to those accused of crimes to demonstrate that their use of cryptography has been innocuous. This would be a major shift in the 'burden of proof' requirements favouring the prosecution or state authority. The following section examines intentional efforts to breach privacy for commercial gain and the gradations in privacy reduction that can occur using information and communication technologies.

8.5   Breaching Privacy

Although individuals have a considerable interest in the privacy and security of the messages that they initiate with regard to financial transactions, they must assent to

---

[60] This raises the unfortunate possibility that forgetting a password may become a crime if a person is convicted of another criminal act.

sharing this information with the institutions that mediate these transactions. In order to achieve security and privacy in the commercial domain, cryptographic technologies have been converted from military to civilian use, as we have shown in the preceding section. The issues that are raised by this development for national security and law enforcement involve compromises that are not acceptable to all the members of the communities with an interest in the use of cryptography. Indeed, issues of cryptography are fundamentally about the nature of control of the Internet as a medium for communication and commerce. The Internet is not the only element of the information and communication infrastructure that is facilitated by innovations in technologies. We examine two important kinds of information resources that are being created using these technologies and both of these may involve the Internet in various ways.

The first involves the reuse of information gathered for the purpose of making financial transactions or some other interaction between organizations and individuals that allows the amassing of name-linked data, such as healthcare records. Name-linked data are data about an individual or an individual's behaviour that are clearly identifiable with that individual. There may be a public interest in the use of these data for the design and marketing of products and services that, in principle, might benefit the individual and impose no costs upon her or him.[61] At the same time, the means by which such data are collected and made available for these purposes are not under the direct control of the individual and there are many possible abuses of the availability of such data. The conflict between the individual's and other social interests is examined in the next section to illustrate how such conflicts are being resolved. This case study illustrates how European Union legislation and regulatory enforcement are being put into place in order to severely limit the uses of name-linked data.

The use of telecommunication networks gives rise to enormous volumes of data relating to the transmission of messages as well as to the messages themselves. The second of our case studies examines issues surrounding the reuse of this kind of information. Some types of reuse raise issues similar to those that arise in the case of name-linked data, while others bring broader social concerns to the fore concerning the appropriate uses of technological capabilities by particular social actors.

8.5.1   *Name-Linked Data and Personal Privacy*

There are two, somewhat grey, areas of concern about name-linked data. The first is that such data may be collected voluntarily or involuntarily as a result of a lack of awareness on the part of the person who these data concern. The second is that the data

---

[61] In such applications, a major use of the specific link to an individual is not to identify the individual *per se*, but to provide a means of combining disparate data accumulated at different times, or from different sources. It is this capability, also, that provides the potential for abuse because of the retention, after combination, of the link to the individual. The name-link may be retained for seemingly innocuous purposes, such as allowing further data to be added, for purposes that are objectionable to some and acceptable to others, for instance, the addressing of advertising or other 'helpful' messages, or for purposes that are objectionable to most, for example, the revision of an individual's credit history based upon behaviour not otherwise observable by their creditor.

may be held perfectly legally in the context in which they are collected initially. Data protection legislation notwithstanding, as information and communication infrastructures are extended there are likely to be continuing concerns about the extent of what is legally knowable about individuals. The capabilities of social actors, ranging from the state to commercial firms, to integrate previously separate data files on citizens may represent a psychological, if not a legal, diminution of privacy. This potential encourages views that are articulated in the form, 'soon we will know more about citizens than they will know themselves'. If people come to regard their use of the information and communication infrastructure as contributing to the ability of others to monitor their actions and to devise strategies that affect their behaviour, the trusting relationships that are necessary to build an inclusive information society that is widely perceived to be for 'all of us' may be eroded.

What is legally knowable that is of commercial significance about an individual is generally greater than is realized by most citizens. The most important instances of such data collection are the result of credit referencing, the production of mail order lists, and the use of detailed profiles that are not officially designated as name-linked. Credit reference databases are concerned with risk reduction and, specifically, with the risks associated with an individual. This is an instance where individuals relinquish some of their privacy in order to receive something that is desired, for example, an extension of credit. There is great potential, however, for errors or misuses of data that individuals provide for this purpose. Experience with credit-rating systems suggests that considerable attention must be given to consumer education so that individuals are in a position to know their legal rights. Once they are informed about their rights they may insist on a review of the information that is retained about them in order to ascertain its accuracy and to contest errors and omissions. Once established, data protection guidelines can set out relatively straightforward ways of checking the data that are held about an individual, but perseverance and skill are needed to compile written evidence about changes that may need to be made in order to have errors corrected. Redress is relatively difficult to achieve and most complainants appear to be happy to be relieved of the barriers to continuing their lives that can result from incorrect name-linked data that may be held, for example, by the commercial sector for credit-rating purposes (Sayers, 1997*b*). While this is a significant problem, it seems to be a necessary social cost of improving the quantity and quality of credit services available to the individual.

The treatment of data accumulated in the construction of mailing lists involves a more difficult set of problems. A direct mail shot, or e-mail multicast to a selected list of potential respondents in order to sell a service or product may yield a 1 per cent response rate. The mailing list database will be of economic value if it contains information that is typical for a particular class of goods or services, that is, it will be competitive with other such databases. If the response rate could be significantly increased, this would influence the value of the database dramatically. Such a database would attract customers from competing mailing lists and allow the seller of the database to select customers with the greatest willingness or ability to pay. Mailing list construction and maintenance is a major industry. Some lists are constructed by taking a basic list of potential candidates and adding new names and details about existing names. Other lists are constructed without the use of 'names' as the means of linking observations. For example, postal codes allow data from several sources to be matched with great accuracy to create neighbourhood profiles. These detailed profiles can be built up from a wide variety of sources that are used in a legitimate way. The value of such profiling lies in the fact that the data do not need to be complete and the personal identifiers, such as names, are unnecessary. The size of such data resources that are commercially available can be measured in several ways including the numbers of people covered, the extent of neighbourhood detail available, or the precision of targeting of specific groups in society.[62]

For example, the former CCN Marketing, a member of the CCN Group, which merged with TRW Information Systems & Services of the United States in June 1997 to become Experian, is the largest direct marketing agency in the United Kingdom.[63] Its database contains details of over 44 million adult consumers in Britain. It offers computer bureau services to the direct marketing industry and specializes in all aspects of address management, database marketing, and direct mail production for the consumer and business sectors. The other two major players are CACI Information Services, which was founded in the United States in 1962 and moved into the United Kingdom in 1975 to specialize in consultancy, software, and data for marketing, and Equifax Europe (UK) Ltd., a subsidiary of Equifax Inc., one of the largest credit reporting agencies in the United States, which was founded in 1899, and which provides credit card processing services, database marketing advice, and credit risk consulting for consumer business transactions.

Data for name-linked data lists are gathered from sources such as the electoral roll and census data; references from subscribing financial institutions and mail-order houses; purchases and matching of other lists; court judgements; and telephone directories, retail data, questionnaires, interviews, and focus groups. Some of these sources contain public domain data, while others are subject to copyright protection, but are very difficult to protect. Yet others may represent problematic reuses of name-linked databases. While none of the companies mentioned above may, in fact, employ practices that are questionable, the incentive to do so is potentially very great. Will other, perhaps smaller and less successful, companies respond to the potential opportunities to improve the value of their databases through the illicit use of name-linked data? The answer to this question will depend upon the additional value that such data can provide and the strength of enforcement of regulatory sanctions against their use.

---

[62] See Direct Marketing Association Directory and Fact Sheets 1 and 2, London, http://www.adassoc.org.uk/members/dma.html accessed 15 Nov. 1999.

[63] CCN Group merged with TRW Information Systems & Services to become the leading supplier of information on consumers, businesses, and property. With sales of £169.9m. in the UK and a total of £600.5m. in North America in 1999 the company offers 'Canvasse Lifestyle', which comprises information on over 12 million individuals in the UK, selectable by more than 5,000 lifestyle and purchasing intent characteristics, as well as lifestyle contacts for all 44 million adults classified by one or more of 380 lifestyle profiles, see Experian (1999*a*; 1999*b*).

8.5.2   *Telemetadata and the Potential for Surveillance*

In addition to data about individuals, data are also generated by the patterns of individual interaction with electronic networks and services. The combination of information technologies with network transmission of detailed information about transactions for both economic and social purposes is enabling an unprecedented level of analysis of buying patterns and other personal transactions, regardless of whether the individuals conducting these transactions are identified or identifiable. The issue in this case is not whether the content of individual messages can be captured, as this issue is dealt with largely through the architectural design of telecommunication network technologies and the array of legal measures designed to preserve the confidentiality of individual messages.[64] It is that, in addition to the use of methods for preventing, or substantially raising the costs of, interception of the content of messages, privacy and security issues are associated with issues of authentication, that is, the inability to repudiate a message, and the legal validity of messages. At a minimum, linkages between personal data files are necessary to assess creditworthiness and to authenticate access to various types of on-line services in the e-commerce environment. There are pressures to permit access to these files for commercial purposes and to compel users to release substantial amounts of personal information so that they can participate in e-commerce.

Telemetadata, or 'call pattern data', are constituted by data transmitted as part of the set-up, progress, clear down, billing, and network management of a message through a public telecommunication network and these data exclude the content of call itself.[65] Elements such as billing data, call routing data, origin and destination station identity, time of call initiation and cessation, whether a call invokes special services in addition to simple transmission, and information about where such extra services are charged, are all examples of telemetadata.[66] The information that can be derived from telemetadata includes the names and addresses of the sending and receiving station subscribers; the choices of television viewing; the identity of the service provider(s); or the cells in which a call begins and is completed in the case of mobile telephony. Data on mobile telecommunication cell transfers, for example, can provide location information that is accurate within a few kilometres. With micro- or even pico-cells, the fineness of this location data will improve. Analysis of the telemetadata generated by an individual can reveal a great deal about behaviour patterns. In the face of the growing adoption of strong encryption for publicly transmitted messages, the use of

---

[64] In general, modern telecommunication networks are highly multiplexed. Although tapping single communication paths, even with multiplexing, is technologically feasible, the costs of doing so are unattractive relative to alternatives and it is generally more effective to intercept communication after de-multiplexing. Access points involving network control points are generally physically secure although the growing use of general purpose computers, typically running commercially available operating systems for various telecommunication services, raises new concerns.

[65] For a review of issues raised by telemetadata that are termed telecommunication transaction generated information (TTGI) in the USA, see Agre and Rotenberg (1997) and Samarajiva (1994; 1996a; 1996b).

[66] The International Telecommunication Union signalling protocol, known as Signalling System No. 7 for ISDN, defined signalling data in a 16 Mbit/s channel. The content of this channel is telemetadata, as are data about the call. Other network protocols support additional means of gathering similar content.

TABLE 8.2. *Intelligent agent attributes*

Attribute	Description
Autonomy	Initiates actions not part of the specific task(s) at hand, such as, preparation, education, investigation, etc.
Personalization	Remembers different user preferences, behaviours, voice patterns, etc.
Discourse	Task is carried out to a verbal specification often requiring interaction to clarify ambiguity, hidden assumptions, inexact orders, etc.
Risk and trust	Delegation to an agent must be a low-risk action for the use of an agent to be worthwhile but this implies trust in the agent and/or very limited scope for the agent's actions
Domain specificity	There is a clearly defined domain of activity in which the agent acts
Graceful degradation	In cases of misunderstanding or discovery of an awkward counter-fact, the agent reduces functionality only to the point where some part of a task can be achieved
Co-operation	The task-specifying, personalization and discourse elements take the form of collaborative 'pseudo-human' formats
Anthropomorphism	There is debate as to the extent to which an agent must offer a human-like user interface and in the case of telemetadata this is not a high priority
Expectations	An agent should conform to expectations about its behaviour

Source: Sayers (1997*b*).

telemetadata is one means open to law enforcement agencies to exercise control over the messages of those involved in illegal acts, or to obtain insights into their actions and plans.[67] For law enforcement agencies, telemetadata are regarded as 'the last toe-hold on illegal communications' now that strong encryption makes it difficult for the state to decypher message content, notwithstanding the legislative right it may have to do so.

Intelligent agent technologies play an important role in the generation of data about individuals and their uses of networks. An intelligent agent is a computer program that can carry out tasks automatically from a brief, objective-specified task. Intelligent agents are often characterized as having attributes, such as those shown in Table 8.2.

Discussion about the roles that these agents are likely to play in the information society have been on-going since the early 1970s (Martin, 1973). Much of this discussion is concerned with whether agents' responses can be made indistinguishable from those of humans.[68] For example, in the context of telemetadata, an agent

---

[67] This section is based on a telephone and mail questionnaire survey of those believed to have a potential interest in the generation of telemetadata in the UK in 1997 conducted by David Sayers on behalf of SPRU.

[68] That is, the development of agents that attempt to pass the 'Turing Test' (Turing, 1950).

program might be set to discover details about a target user, to enter unauthorized databases, and to translate data patterns generated by transactions into meaningful observations for those with access to such information. Progress in agent research depends upon further breakthroughs in semantics and problem-solving but other software developments are also influencing the potential role of telemetadata. For example, JAVA applets have implications for privacy because these down-loadable executable programs, or program components, can run in standard environments and raise the spectre of invading software. For example, an unsolicited applet could serve an eavesdropping function, capturing and retransmitting details of messages.

The volume of telemetadata that is being held by telecommunication network operators is increasing rapidly for several reasons. Telecommunication market liberalization has led to new entry and, as a consequence, there are many new players with the capacity to access and store such data and they are often operating in multiple countries. New transmission technologies tend to be more data-intensive than their predecessors. For example, Asynchronous Transfer Mode implementations require networks to measure and act upon the varying bandwidths being used by each message on a channel shared between many messages. This provides a source of data that is not available from a fixed bandwidth service. Services such as language translation, call-back, conference calls, and call line identification, all generate and rely upon telemetadata. In addition, techniques for improved data storage, for example, data warehousing and advances in disc capacity, performance, and decreasing costs are encouraging the development of techniques for analysing these vast volumes of data to extract meaningful patterns. The pattern of a user's calls, and the possible use of cryptographic techniques will be discoverable easily with digitally controlled exchanges; and the usage pattern itself constitutes data about a user. The increasing capacity of conventional computer processors can be used in a data mining mode to extract call patterns that are presently used for network planning and optimization (Bicknell, 1995).

As in the other cases we have examined, the spectrum of interests in protection against the collection of name-linked data and telemetadata and their analysis tends to be polarized. This is equally so for the range of interests in the wider use of these data to promote effective marketing and, in some cases, beneficial social outcomes. For example, telecommunication network operators have a considerable interest in developing techniques for the analysis of telemetadata. Analysis of such data offers a guide to managing network service provision and efficiency as a result of the capability to assess traffic patterns to determine when particular elements of the network will need upgrading. Telemetadata also are the basis of basic billing processes and, for these processes, the data may typically be kept for only a few months.[69] Some network operators have the capability to use telemetadata to track cases of fraud by monitoring overseas telephone calls while the calls are in progress to detect whether the call, in

---

[69] Although it has been suggested by some operators in confidential interviews that legal record-keeping requirements may require such data to be held for up to seven years in the UK.

fact, originates from a given billing address.[70] In addition to the technical features of networks, it must also be borne in mind that human and organizational factors are significant contributors to how telemetadata are used. Members of the cypherpunk community end of the spectrum would argue that any such use of telemetadata represents an invasion of personal privacy.

Public telecommunication operators have argued that specific issues relating to aspects of telemetadata should be covered by industry codes of practice (ETNO, 1993). They argue that the processing of data generated by networks is the foundation upon which new services are being developed (ETNO, 1994). They also argue that restrictions on the collection and analysis of such data would produce inefficiency in service operation and degradation of the quality of the customer interface. All these developments have been the subject of continuing debate and legislative initiative in recent years.

In the next section we examine these developments within the European Union and draw attention to several specific features of the privacy and security protections that are available in the United Kingdom. Despite attempts to address the potential threats to individual privacy and to the security of commercial operations, there are considerable ambiguities about who can access telemetadata and upon whose authorization.

8.6   Working Towards Governance Solutions

New information and communication technologies and services are adopted first by small groups of users for whom the benefits are perceived to outweigh the costs of introduction. These benefits may be hard to quantify and may take the form of ephemeral values such as image or even self-image. The factors—social, psychological, economic, and cultural—that produce initial acceptance by early adopters may be the very factors that produce resistance on the part of potential users within the wider population. Later adoption phases may involve distinct interactions between the design and architecture of the new technology or service and the characteristics and the perceptions of different communities of users. Such perceptions can be subject to sudden change, particularly where a trusting relationship has been breached or there has been a failure to build such a relationship. A breach of privacy through the manipulation of telemetadata and name-linked data sources arising from information and communication infrastructure implementation could lead to a collapse in user confidence with serious implications for the take-up of services, and even causing existing users to abandon them. Striking what stakeholder communities regard as an acceptable balance between the conflicting interests of technology designers, vendors, and implementers and different types of users following informed public debate is likely to avoid sudden backsliding of user confidence.

---

[70] During a confidential interview, a senior employee of a British public telecommunication operator observed that it would be unwise to draw attention to the role of telemetadata in policing and monitoring civilian activity. A routine practice of passing such data to law enforcement authorities was thought to be the norm, despite the acknowledgement that there may be no specific statutory requirement for this.

Electronic networks offer the potential for monitoring the confidential, secret, and secluded space of an individual, a company, or a national or international organization. This capability for monitoring communicative behaviour as well as the potential for the acquisition and the use of private information has brought concerns about the contravention of civil liberties to the forefront of public debate. This debate is centrally about the boundaries between public and private spheres of activity in the information society. At present, no society maintains that privacy is an absolute value or standard under all circumstances (Ruggles, 1994). Instead, it is accepted that certain types and levels of surveillance will benefit individuals, companies, and national and international organizations. Without such surveillance, privacy would become a shield protecting the transmission of potentially socially detrimental 'information', such as child pornography, fraudulent financial dealings, terrorist activities, and other national security intrusions.

Public opinion with regard to a wide range of privacy concerns in the electronic environment is highly context-dependent. Civil and national security traditions are culturally, and frequently nationally, specific. There is a mismatch between the global reach of current visions of the information society and the bounded nature of national legislation and regulation in the privacy field. There is a fine line in much of the literature devoted to the privacy debate. On the one side there are 'fundamental' rights of freedom of expression and the protection of individual rights. On the other, there is surveillance to ensure that 'illegitimate', threatening, 'socially divisive' material is not disseminated through electronic networks. Considerations of privacy in the context of the information and communication infrastructure invoke a set of contentious social constructs that embrace disparate cultural and social belief systems and values. Reports of e-mail snooping, information monitoring, telecommunication eavesdropping, etc., invoke notions of an Orwellian Big Brother society. Yet reports of banking fraud, child pornography rings, electronic stalking, and terrorist communication networks, all activities facilitated by a more pervasive information and communication infrastructures, provoke calls for regulation and control.

The information and communication infrastructure involves the technical convergence of a large number of hardware and software artefacts that are being designed in ways that offer new means of permeating the boundaries of public and private spaces, including households, workplaces, firms, and public governance organizations. Conventional definitions of privacy are embedded in the formal regulations and codes of conduct that govern the activities of the producers of technologies and services. However, the norms and conventions that are characteristic of the computing, communication, consumer electronics, entertainment, and publishing industries with respect to privacy, differ considerably (Schoechle, 1995).

The norms that influence the protection of privacy within the workplace are also open to question as the Internet becomes increasingly widely available to employees and as e-mail and Intranets support intra- and inter-organizational communication. For example, in the United States there have been court cases concerning employees' uses of electronic services to protest about company practices. Employees have claimed privacy violations as a result of company surveillance of their internal office communications (Sipior and Ward, 1995). Company rights to manage corporate communication systems have so far been upheld by the lower courts in the United States.

Three issues are central to privacy and security considerations in the new electronic environments. First, interests in limiting privacy and enhancing security to guard against activities that are illegal or disapproved of need to be balanced by the social interest in defining fundamental rights to be free from surveillance and the use of private information by others. Specific implementations of the information and communication infrastructure influence the possibilities and procedures for maintaining this balance. Second, whatever policies and practices are established, there is a need for a flexible code of conduct with respect to individual and collective privacy issues and for standards appropriate to locally, nationally, regionally, and globally bounded information environments. Third, there is a need to manage differences between perception and reality with respect to privacy protection and security concerning the use and reuse of electronically generated information.

Privacy and security concerns in the context of national defence differ from those of commercial organizations and private individuals, as we saw in the preceding section. Prevention of espionage and sabotage of electronic networks containing highly sensitive military information requires substantial expenditure and effort. Achieving a similar level of privacy protection for an individual's electronic agenda is not feasible although practices that prevent easy access to such information are often within the responsibility of systems administrators. Even with such efforts, individuals are becoming increasingly aware of the limitations on the privacy of data that are generated by network transactions or stored within networks. Systems administrators and others concerned with maintaining privacy in electronic networks are using an array of tools, many of which extend their surveillance capabilities.

Privacy legislation of various kinds is designed to protect individuals. When existing norms begin to shift, or to be eroded, there are risks that every personal dislike, religious belief, and social prejudice can become a ground for legislative action. Yet social tolerance is based significantly on the ability to ignore the personal lives and choices of the members of social communities. The profusion of database records and e-mail messages, as well as the monitoring and recording of sites visited, open questions about the limits of personal anonymity in the information society. Some argue that the new electronic environments should be treated as public domains in the same way as a postcard. However, much of the monitoring capability of networks is not transparent to the user and the choice in favour of anonymity is considerably reduced in the case of some new electronic services (Galasyn, 1996). In this context, we must recall that the United Nations International Covenant on Civil and Political Rights (ICCPR) states that 'No-one shall be subject to arbitrary or unlawful interference with his privacy, family home or correspondence, nor to unlawful attacks on his honour or reputation' (United Nations, 1976: Art. 17). In the next section we highlight some of the steps that have been taken internationally, within Europe, and at the national level in the United Kingdom, to enhance the protection of privacy and the security of data and to resolve the conflicts between the various stakeholders.

8.6.1   Implementing the Legislation

In the face of growing emphasis on advanced global networks and e-commerce, min-isterial level representatives of OECD member countries reaffirmed in 1998 the OECD Privacy Guidelines that had been agreed in 1980 (OECD, 1981) and the Declaration on Transborder Data Flows of 1985 (OECD, 1985).[71] Guidelines for Cryptography Policy have also been adopted by the OECD Council (OECD, 1997a). The representa-tives of OECD countries have emphasized ways of encouraging the adoption of privacy policies, encouraging the on-line notification of privacy policies to users, ensuring effective enforcement mechanisms, promoting user education about on-line privacy issues, and encouraging the use of 'privacy-enhancing technologies' (OECD, 1998c).[72]

Self-regulatory measures initiated by supplier firms are gaining momentum as, for example, in the case of an agreement by fifty Internet Service Providers from the United States, the United Kingdom, The Netherlands, Japan, Canada, Austria, and Australia, to implement the Freedom Network. The Freedom Network is an interna-tional collection of independent server operators providing technology to support privacy for Web users (OECD, 1999b).[73] Issues such as blocking transfer of auto-matically generated data, reducing or avoiding the number of anonymous payment systems, providing information for users, and creating options for disclosure of personal data, as well as access to personal data, are covered. As the OECD has commented, users leave 'electronic footprints' behind (ibid.).

In the United States, in the mid-1990s, the Privacy Working Group of the Informa-tion Policy Committee of the Information Infrastructure Task Force adopted prin-ciples for providing and using personal information. The need to develop further the technical means to improve user privacy within the spaces created by the use of the Internet was noted at this time. The government administration indicated that privacy, security, and intellectual property rights were the issues of paramount impor-tance for the development of a global information infrastructure (Kalil, 1995: 16). Principles for providing and using information were developed to create a code of fair information practice that would apply to both the public and private sectors.[74] Adher-ence to the code means that organizations that collect personal information about individuals have an obligation to explain why they are gathering it, how they plan to

---

[71] International measures to ensure the protection of privacy gained a profile with the publication of guidelines by the United Nations in 1990 (United Nations, 1990).

[72] In May 1999 a comprehensive inventory of instruments and mechanisms contributing to the imple-mentation and enforcement of the OECD privacy guidelines was published (OECD, 1999b).

[73] The inventory provides an overview of legal and self-regulatory instruments.

[74] A series of publications of the Harvard Information Infrastructure Program has addressed privacy and security issues, either directly or indirectly, since this code was developed (Kahin, 1996; Kahin and Keller, 1996; Kahin and Nesson, 1995; Kahin and Wilson III, 1997). In addition, see Branscomb (1994); Branscomb and Keller (1996). Branscomb notes that 'cultures clash with cultures, and often in the place where minds are meeting there is no consensus, only ferment, argument, and disagreement. Often the technical bound-aries between what can be maintained under personal or professional control and what may freely circulate for others to capture and manipulate is not clear' (Branscomb, 1994: 7).

use it, and how they intend to protect its integrity and confidentiality. They are expected to use technical and managerial controls to protect its confidentiality and integrity and not use it in ways that are incompatible with the individual's original understanding of how it would be used.

Europe's involvement in personal data protection began in the 1970s when Parliamentary initiatives led to moves to introduce legislation. A Council of Europe convention sought to protect individual privacy with respect to the automatic processing of personal data in 1981. The purpose of the convention was 'to secure in the territory of each Party for every individual, whatever his [*sic*] nationality or residence, respect for his rights and fundamental freedoms, and in particular his right to privacy, with regard to automatic processing of personal data relating to him ("data protection")' (European Council, 1981: 1). This convention introduced the concept of the 'controller' of a file. The controller was defined as 'the natural or legal person, public authority, agency or any other body who is competent according to the national law to decide what should be the purpose of the automated data file, which categories of personal data should be stored and which operations should be applied to them' (ibid.).

The convention covered automated personal data files and extended to automatic processing of personal data in the public and private sectors. Derogations from the provisions were permitted in the interests of protecting democratic societies, that is, protecting state security, public safety, the monetary interests of the state, or the suppression of criminal offences; and protecting the data subject, or the rights and freedoms of others.

By 1995 in Europe a directive on the processing of personal data and on the free movement of data had been agreed (European Commission, 1995c). The social responsibility to regulate the collection and use of information about individuals is perceived somewhat differently from the perspectives of the state, the private citizen, and the business enterprise. The premise of the directive is the idea that data-processing systems must be designed and used so as to respect fundamental rights and freedoms, including the right to privacy, and that they should contribute to economic and social progress, trade expansion, and the well-being of individuals. The goal is to ensure that the level of protection in each of the Member States is 'equivalent' and to ensure that protection extends to automatic and manual processing of data that is held in structured filing systems. The collection of data is intended to be as transparent as possible, and individuals are to be given the option of whether or not they provide information. The directive gives data 'subjects' rights, including the right of access to their data, to know where the data originated, to have inaccurate data rectified, to seek recourse in the event of unlawful processing, and to withhold permission to use data in certain circumstances, without providing specific reasons. The directive also calls upon non-European Union countries to ensure an adequate level of protection.

In effect, the directive grants individuals the right to object to the processing of their personal data where those data are being processed exclusively by automated methods to evaluate aspects of their personal life.[75] In creating restrictions on the use of personal data, there remains considerable potential for ambiguity and latitude for those who require data for their business pursuits, for example, direct marketing and profiling businesses. This directive provides broad safeguards regarding the use of 'personal data' defined as 'any information about identified or identifiable individuals' and encompasses not only new information and communication technologies, but also existing non-electronic data collections. The directive serves an important purpose in preventing the transfer and agglomeration of personal data across organizations, thereby avoiding the spectre of mass dossiers on individuals. However, it does not prevent the processing of data that have been rendered non-personal by the removal of information that would serve to identify individual subjects. Moreover, it provides broad exemptions for journalistic purposes that may encompass the question of 'rating' individual contributions to public electronic forums or similar public disclosures of personal information.

The directive aims to reduce differences between national data protection laws in order to remove obstacles to the free movement of personal data within the European Union. The directive makes it the choice of the individual as to whether he or she wishes to provide information for data collectors and this choice must be transparent to the individual. Individuals must be informed of the identity of the organization intending to process data and the main purposes of such processing. There must be a legitimate reason for all data processing and the directive contains broad exemptions for national security and law enforcement purposes.

The rising importance of the Internet for privacy protection was taken up in October 1996 with the formation of an International Working Group on Data Protection in Telecommunications, which began working on data protection and privacy on the Internet.[76] This group agreed a report on data protection on the Internet that highlighted the potentially conflicting interests of the communities that participate in the Internet environment (International Working Group on Data Protection in Telecommunication, 1996). These communities were deemed to include the software, computer, and telecommunication industry representatives who design the networks and services, the telecommunication organizations that provide the basic networks for data transfer, the access providers supplying basic services for storage, transmission, and presentation to the information providers who supply information stored in files and databases to users, and the users who access different services and who use the Internet for various service applications.

By January 1998, a common position was reached on a directive applicable to data

[75] In the directive, the concept of a 'controller' is defined as the natural or legal person, public authority, agency, or any other body, which alone, or jointly with others, determines the purposes and means of the processing of personal data; where the purposes and means of processing are determined by national or Community laws or regulations, the controller or the specific criteria for his nomination may be designated by national or Community law. Certain kinds of processing fall outside the scope of the directive including processing of personal data in the course of an activity that falls outside the scope of Community Law, such as public security, defence, state security and activities of the state in areas of criminal law, and processing of data by a 'natural person' in the course of a purely personal or household activity.

[76] The Secretariat of the Group is based in the Berlin Data Protection Commissioner's Office in Germany.

generated by use of telecommunication equipment and services. It required Member States to prohibit listening, tapping, storage, or other kinds of interception or surveillance of communication, by other than users, without the consent of the users concerned, except when legally authorized. It allowed for certain data, with the permission of subscribers, to be retained and processed under certain conditions for billing, and for marketing of their own services by telecommunication operators and service providers (European Commission, 1998*d*).

The data protection directive called for the establishment of supervisory agencies within the Member States with investigative powers to deal with challenges brought by data subjects relating, for example, to exemptions concerned with national security. During the debate leading to the final legislation, the consumer unit of the European Trade Union Confederation (ETUC) made two proposals. Members suggested the introduction of a European Digital Quality Label and the establishment of a European Data Protection Watchdog that could give special consideration to the ban on the transfer of personal data to a third country. This proposal was not taken forward by the Commission, which responded that its remit did not allow the award of quality labels that could have commercial consequences. ETUC drew an analogy with Eco-labelling schemes claiming that this should be a matter for wider European information society policy.[77]

At the country level, Member States have established data protection registrars, or related offices, under the terms of the directive. These offices have become involved in building a consensus on the ethical practices for the treatment of name-linked data and telemetadata by virtue of the consultative relationships that they build up between practitioners and the experts (United Kingdom Government, 1998).[78] The Data Protection Registrar in the United Kingdom has several means available to enforce compliance.[79] Self-regulatory measures have been taken, as well, by the Internet Service Providers Association (ISPA) in the United Kingdom to establish a voluntary code of practice. The code advises all members to use reasonable endeavours to ensure that services providers involved in the collection of personal information, such as names and addresses, make clear to the relevant party the purpose for which the information is required. Members must also identify the data user (if different from the members or information provider) and give that party the opportunity to prevent such usage (Internet Service Providers Association, 1996). In addition, the Telecommunications (Data Protection and Privacy) Regulations 1999 implement most aspects of the European directive on telecommunication data protection and privacy (United Kingdom Government, 1999). The regulations cover issues relating to traffic and billing data,

---

[77] Correspondence, Emilio Gabaglio, ETUC General Secretary to E. Monino, member of the European Commission, 13 Nov. 1996.

[78] The 1998 Act updated the 1994 Act (United Kingdom Government, 1994). For example, in the UK the Data Protection Registrar issues guidelines, for instance, on credit rating data, the practices of direct marketing companies, and the process of seeking redress.

[79] There is an appeals procedure and the first case to be prosecuted for unlawful procurement and sale of data was decided on 31 July 1996 when a part-time investigator was convicted of procuring the disclosure of personal data and selling the information he acquired. Data Protection Registrar, http://www.dataprotection.gov.uk accessed 6 April 2000.

and its processing for marketing purposes, rules for calling or connected line identification, subscriber entries in directories, and the use of telecommunication services for direct marketing purposes. It applies to voice services and fax transmissions but does not cover e-mail-related issues.

Measures have been taken in both the United States and Europe to forge a governance system that is consistent with the broad consensus in each region on the levels and forms of protection that should be available to the citizen or consumer as the information and communication infrastructure becomes a more pervasive feature of social and economic life. We have illustrated some of the conflicts of interest between different communities of actors and discussed the extent to which there are effective means of constraining socially or economically undesirable behaviour that may be present within the emerging electronic communities. In some cases the legislative or regulatory means are in place to protect the privacy and security of messages to the standards that have achieved common consent. In other instances, however, the unbounded character of the new information and communication infrastructure continues to raise questions, especially when individuals may be recipients of unwanted intrusions into the virtual spaces that they deem private. In the next section, we focus on the discussions about material that is circulated through electronic networks that may be deemed to be defamatory or obscene.

8.6.2   *Privacy and Unwanted Intrusions*

Consumer access to electronic entertainment, business information, educational content, or news content, may involve interaction with material that is defamatory, obscene, or otherwise offensive. Two aspects of modern society make it a virtual certainty that this type of interaction will occur. This is first because the societies within the European Union are pluralistic. There are subcommunities that have very different values from mainstream or majority views. Secondly, the courts that regulate expression are unable to create a clear demarcation between what is permissible and what is not. The existence of markets for information that is perceived as being intrusive is demonstrated by surges in the revenues of the Fleet Street tabloids, and by the seemingly endless supply of pornographic images and services, such as phone sex. The fact that media enterprises regularly approach and transgress the boundary between what is permissible and what is not is indicative of the strength of both supply and demand for such content.

These 'facts of modern life' would be of little significance if electronic information were created and disseminated by only a few business enterprises. If this were the case, content that might prove defamatory, obscene, or offensive would simply not appear, as it would put these enterprises at considerable risk. Large enterprises in the media market often argue that providing them with control over such information is one way of eliminating objectionable material from public access. The markets for consumer electronic access, however, involve information content *production* that comes close to reproducing the diversity of subcommunities within society as a whole. If there is a subcommunity that craves images of bestiality, content producers offering such images will invariably emerge to meet the market demand. The markets for some types of objectionable material, particularly that which is defamatory or libellous, may be small enough to limit growth in the publication of such information. Commercially motivated supply of such material will be supplemented, however, by hate diatribes, amateur pornography, and other potentially offensive material, making it more difficult to restrict the flow of objectionable material. The difficulty of creating a governance system that is responsive to the interests of all those choosing to participate in the information society is illustrated clearly in the case of debates about the distribution of pornography via the Internet, and other electronic means.

'Pornography' is a difficult term to define due to its ambiguous and subjective nature—the English word derives from the Greek 'porno' meaning 'whores' and 'graphos' meaning 'the depiction of'. The term has much broader connotations in contemporary English usage and describes representations of material in literature, drama, the visual arts, etc., intended to stimulate erotic or sexual excitement. It is not clear how far it is technically possible to block access to content that is deemed to be pornographic and unsuitable for distribution (Smith System Engineering Ltd., 1997). Some non-European countries have attempted to block all direct access to the Internet via access providers.

Technical means for introducing voluntary controls on Internet information are being developed to block access to some documents. For example, the World Wide Web Consortium launched the Platform for Internet Content Selection (PICS) in May 1996. However, the role of PICS depends upon how quickly it is taken up by Internet sites. In addition, content providers can develop ratings systems. Manufacturers of consumer electronics view ratings systems and parental control devices somewhat negatively, especially if there is a suggestion that a single technical standard should be adopted. CyberPatrol was introduced in August 1995 and works with Internet access providers and larger on-line service providers. A plethora of such systems has emerged over the past few years.[80]

Discussions about the privacy of electronic environments often draw distinctions between the rights of adults and those of children. Children use electronic networks and applications for entertainment and education purposes, but visions of the electronic learning environment generally do not distinguish between rights and obligations for children and adults. The limits and regulations applicable to children's access to electronic networks are being addressed differently in various national contexts. One of the difficult aspects of issues concerning pornography and electronic networks is the near impossibility of extracting fact from value judgement. Pornography is a social issue which, like privacy, has different meanings and accepted levels for

---

[80] See e.g. the Texas Internet Service Provider Association's (TISPA) web site, http://www.TISPA.Org/filtering.htm accessed 6 April 2000, which is designed to help parents to provide an appropriate environment for their children on the Internet. The material included on the site is a response to the notion that it is parents who are most effective in protecting their children. It includes comparisons of features of blocking and filtering software and information about where to purchase it. Another site is provided by Voters Telecommunications Watch, again in the United States, http://www.vtw.org/ipcfaq, offering extensive commentary on various techniques.

different people, communities, and cultures. Judgements are made on the basis of a framework of social constructs that emerge through personal experiences, and are influenced by family circumstances, gender, age, and other factors.

In the United Kingdom, the Obscene Publications Act (1959; 1964) is the principal legislation with reference to pornography. The test for obscenity is whether an article will tend to deprave and corrupt persons who are likely to encounter the material (Hailsham, 1987). Controversy arises from the ambiguity of the terms 'deprave' and 'corrupt'. The Criminal Justice and Public Order Act (1994) extended the remit of the Obscene Publications Act to include the transmission of electronically stored data which, on resolution into user-viewable form, is defined as obscene. The definition of publication covers any distribution, circulation, sale, giving, lending, or displaying of an obscene article. The Criminal Justice and Public Order Act (1994) also amended The Protection of Children Act (1978) (Home Affairs Committee, 1994), addressing a loophole in the obscenity legislation whereby images of adults are manipulated, using computer techniques, to produce simulated indecent photographs of children. These were not previously covered because they were not, in fact, indecent photographs of children (House of Commons, 1993).

The Telecommunications Act (1984) also contains sections, specifically Section 43, which could be used to legislate against obscene material on the Internet. Under this Act it is an offence to use a public telecommunication system to send offensive, threatening, or obscene material. The penalty for contravening this section of the Act was increased by Clause 91 of The Criminal Justice and Public Order Bill (1994). The maximum penalty now stands at up to six months' imprisonment, or a fine, or both.

In 1994, in its First Report on Computer Pornography, the Home Affairs Select Committee sought an amendment to the Customs Consolidation Act (1876) to include electronic transmissions of pornography from abroad as a form of importation (Home Affairs Committee, 1994). Parliament rejected this stating that,

There are significant practical difficulties in enforcing any tightening of the law in this area which arise largely from the form which importation takes—i.e. the transmission of electronic signals from computers abroad. . . . For instance, the effective investigating of these offences might well require the power to intercept transmissions, although this would only be exercised under careful control and through the normal channels. Such monitoring would inevitably be controversial. There are also serious doubts about our ability to achieve an effective level of control over the generality of such messages. A routine inspection of software would not reveal prohibited content or give rise to suspicion. Even after the discovery of such material on a system, it would be difficult to prove importation by the owner or user of the system. (House of Commons, 1993: 5)

Despite these reservations, criminal convictions have been obtained from computers seized in the course of investigation or sent out for repair. The legislative framework for pornographic material in the United Kingdom has withstood testing and clarification in the lawcourts, but it is controversial. Interest groups, such as the Campaign Against Pornography, believe it to be ambiguous and subjective, whereas free speech campaigners, such as Feminists Against Censorship, consider that it is much too controlling. The polarities of the criticisms of the legislation indicate that the balance is uneasy between the various cultural issues and interest groups. For example, in contrast to the arguments articulated by pornography opposition groups, in 1979 the report of the committee on obscenity and film censorship of the Home Office concluded that the role of pornography in influencing the state of society is a minor one (B. Williams, 1979).

The European Union has taken steps to protect minors and human dignity from harmful and illegal content on the Internet and in audiovisual and information services (European Commission, 1996*d*; 1996*k*). The Commission has been urging co-operation between the Member States to enforce existing legislation and to encourage self-regulation. It is also encouraging the introduction of filtering software and rating systems and recognizing the urgency for international discussion on the need for a convention on harmful and illegal content (European Commission, 1999*e*).

8.7 Conclusion

Managing the issue of privacy in the information society is like trying to keep adding to the number of objects being juggled in the air simultaneously. Eventually, part or the whole collection is likely to fall to the ground with a resounding clatter, or worse. A simplified approach to privacy would be one where there are only two types of issues that need to be juggled. The first would include items that individuals can, and should, have the ability to keep private from others. The second would embrace items that individuals might choose to share with others, such as the information needed to execute an electronic payment. With respect to this latter, there should also be the facility to limit the subsequent reuse of this information that is shared with others. If the social choices could be so neatly divided, issues of privacy and security would not constitute a difficult problem for the information society.

The problems begin when we admit that there is a collective interest in some types of information that specific individuals would choose not to share. There is a collective interest, for example, in individuals' possession and distribution of information related to crime, terrorism, breaches of national security, and some types of pornography. The sharing of information that constitutes libel, or defamation of another individual's character also raises collective issues. If it were technically feasible to restrict surveillance to individuals suspected, or accused, of such activities, and to accomplish this effectively, the problem of privacy would be somewhat limited. The availability of 'strong' encryption is sufficiently widespread that proposals to introduce a trusted third party or key escrow system without direct regulation of the exchange of encrypted information are unlikely to be taken up by users. The resulting proliferation of encrypted messages will give those who would use the information and communication infrastructure for illegal activities adequate 'cover' to prevent effective surveillance.

Although there are countries, such as Syria, that are prepared to simply bar the transmission of encrypted messages, both the structure of the information and communication infrastructure and the political will of governments in most other countries make such a solution either unfeasible or unworkable. There are many legitimate uses of encryption for confidential business and personal information that would make a ban on the exchange of encrypted messages undesirable. The outcome is a stalemate between those who advocate regulation and those who equate civil liberties with the complete absence of the ability to examine a message, whatever its content. The only remaining tool for the control of encryption appears to be the extension of the state's power to compel disclosure of the contents of encrypted material under specific circumstances, such as criminal prosecution.

People may choose to breach their privacy as the 'price' to gain access to information, financial, or other services, and this is the second type of object that must be juggled. The principle governing such exchanges, that individuals should have control over any subsequent reuse of the information that they provide, is easy enough to state. It is not so easy to enforce. Legislation attempting to limit the name-linked data provided by the individual has been enacted throughout Europe. Nevertheless, the incentives to breach these laws are substantial. In addition, the linking of the name of the individual within a database may be an inadequate shield to prevent the reuse of personal data in ways that could have adverse implications. Alternatively, there are uses of personal information without a name-link that can be technologically achieved, but it is likely that people would object if they knew the scope of these technological capabilities. The possibilities for gathering and processing such information are becoming greater over time as information systems become more capable and as people generate larger volumes of personal data as a by-product of their use of the information and communication infrastructure. In particular, telemetadata generated through the use of the infrastructure offer many possibilities for monitoring the behaviours and habits of individuals without their knowledge or consent. Regulating the reuse of data is an idea that makes considerable sense in principle, but is very difficult to translate into effective practice.

In Europe, the views of individuals and stakeholder organizations on these issues vary significantly. Given the differences in legal, social, and cultural norms throughout Europe, there is a reasonable chance that Member States with less stringent compliance procedures will attract a higher proportion of content and service providers seeking the advantages offered by weaker privacy protection regimes. Counterbalancing this potential movement of commercial activity to Member States or countries outside the European Union is the unknown tolerance of citizens for greater intrusions by commerce, or by the state, into their everyday lives. The commercial potential of information and communication services relies upon consumer acceptance and growing demand. If consumers resist the new services provided by commercial entities or by governments in some areas because they fail to encourage the establishment of trusting relationships, then the trajectory of information and communication technology and service diffusion may differ considerably from the projections made at the end of the 1990s.

These conditions amply meet the metaphor of juggling an ever-greater number of objects simultaneously. Eventually, one or more will fall. The most important lesson of

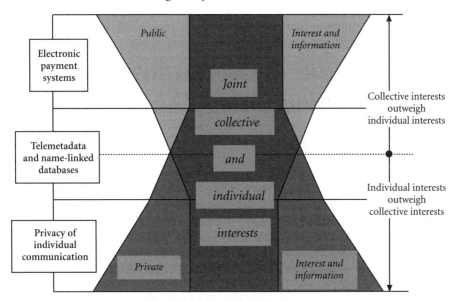

F I G. 8.3. Summarizing the interaction between collective and individual interests

Source: Authors' elaboration.

this chapter is the considerable likelihood that severe problems will emerge. The occurrence of one or more crises will shift the balance of stakeholder interests in ways that are difficult to predict. However, a crisis may be the necessary precursor for creating the foundation for a broad consensus on effective policy, particularly at the intergovernmental level and with respect to corporate practice. We can summarize our discussion in this chapter by referring to Fig. 8.3 which illustrates that the issue of privacy is one in which individual and collective interests are mutually intertwined. The figure indicates that collective or social interests may outweigh individual private interests, even for some types of personal data, while, in some cases, individual interests may outweigh collective interests for certain information that is regarded as public. Whether it is possible to delineate further boundaries between the public and the private and to achieve broad public support for that delineation will be a major challenge in coming years.

9

Locating the Consequences of Information Society Developments

9.1 Introduction

This chapter examines some of the consequences of the movement towards the information society for employment, regional development, and government taxation. Some analysts would refer to this as an investigation of the 'impact' of the technological and socio-economic changes that we have discussed in the preceding chapters.[1] This terminology suggests that a particular course of development is inevitable and that it is 'determined' by some single 'best use' of technological opportunity. It is undeniable, nevertheless, that the accumulation and aggregation of the changes that we have outlined in this book have consequences.

In this chapter we examine the implications of these changes for possible employment growth and skills development, the relationships between the development of the information and communication infrastructure and the development of the 'Third Sector', that is, the non-profit sector, initiatives to develop information and communication technology applications within the regions of Europe, and the potential for the growth of electronic commerce—or e-commerce—to create the need for changes in the collection of tax revenues. Our discussion of developments in each of these areas does not sum to a convenient bottom-line assessment of the consequences of the development of the information society. For example, we do not reach conclusions about the estimated contribution of these developments to the growth of output or changes in the 'competitiveness' of European economies. The studies that purport to make such assessments are predicated upon many strong simplifying assumptions. The results of such studies can offer little more than an indication of whether the consequences of information society developments will be small, medium, or large. It is impossible to develop more accurate assessments because the processes of change are both complex and pervasive.

This chapter draws upon original research undertaken by Databank, Milan under the direction of Gabriella Cattaneo and colleagues Marco Farinelli, Enrico Grazzini, Stefano Kluzer, Guido Lucchi, and Lucia Passamonti at Databank, and Karin Kamp, Huub Meijers, and Luc Soete of MERIT, University of Maastricht. Annaflavia Bianchi (then at Centre for Urban and Regional Development, University of Newcastle) and Peter Hounsome (Welsh Development Agency) also contributed to the original research.

[1] Studies of the impact of techno-economic or socio-political change on society are commonplace, see e.g. Diebold (1959); Freund, König, and Roth (1997); Kiessling and Blondeel (1999); OECD (1997c; 1999a). Although the empirical evidence in studies of this kind reveals factors that are contributing to change, the focus on 'impacts' confines interpretation so that little of the complexity of the processes of change is revealed.

Our expectation is that the consequences of information society developments will be large. The basis for this expectation stems from our recognition of a variety of very significant ways in which the deployment of the advanced information and communication infrastructure can influence how people organize their work and leisure, how they generate and distribute knowledge, and how they undertake the commercial transactions that lie at the centre of market-based economies. There is little doubt that many opportunities will be missed and that others will not be realized to their full potential. Even so, the pattern of economic growth and social development over the past half-century or more indicates the growing centrality of the role of knowledge in generating economic and social development. We continue to live in an age of reason, even if it is no longer an age in which the dream of a single co-ordinated scientific rationality predominates. Indeed, it is precisely because this 'modernist' dream is giving way to a plethora of dialogues that major advances in our means of communicating ideas and information have the potential for making such a profound contribution. The generation of variety in ideas and information, along with their recombination into new patterns, and their rapid distribution and absorption within society, have profound consequences for further enhancing the role of knowledge in economic and social development. These developments alone suggest that the further development of the information society will have large consequences.

The combination of new technologies with changes in social organization and the routines of work suggests an even richer set of contributions from the continuing evolution of the information society. Forty years ago, observers of social change began to be concerned about the consequences that would follow from the continued extension of automation (Diebold, 1959),[2] then seen in terms of the replacement of individual workers by machinery. Bell (1973) later observed that in the industrialized world the expansion of the service industries would eclipse manufacturing, much as the growth of manufacturing in the wealthier industrialized countries had eclipsed agriculture earlier in the twentieth century. As we enter the twenty-first century it is clear that both these predictions were largely correct.

The vast majority of employment in Europe now only incidentally involves the physical transformation of artefacts. Instead, in the manufacturing industries the functions of design, marketing, testing, finance, distribution, improvement, and, in some cases, recycling of artefacts, have become as significant in economic terms as their fabrication. All the functions that have grown in relative importance involve services and they all entail an increasing array of information that must be created, disseminated, and accessed. These developments are accompanied by the growth of industries whose principal outputs are services, such as financial, insurance, and property services, which are among the heaviest investors in information and communication technologies. The information and communication infrastructure provides the only feasible means of supporting continuing growth in the diversity and complexity of both the artefacts and the growing number of service activities. We have observed in the preceding chapters that the consequences of the development of

[2] See also Noble (1986; 1998).

information societies can be negative as well as positive. Progress involves disruption and dislocation as well as growth and development and we return to these issues in the next, and final, chapter.

The potential for employment growth and skill changes in the information society is the subject of the next section of this chapter. We briefly examine present-day echoes of concerns about automation before considering how the diffusion of the information and communication infrastructure is implicated in the recent experiences of the labour markets in the United States and Europe and changes in the level and nature of employment. We review several specific forecasts of possible future levels of employment with the intention of indicating some of the likely structural changes in employment rather than of providing predictions. This section provides the broadest picture of the possible consequences of information society developments. The subsequent sections of this chapter depict several specific themes appearing on the larger canvas of these developments.

In s. 9.3 we consider some of the ways in which non-profit and public initiatives are seeking to take advantage of the deployment of an advanced information and communication infrastructure. We begin with an analysis of the activities of the Third Sector, that is, the non-profit enterprise sector that is based neither in government nor in profit-making enterprise. The activities of the organizations in this sector illustrate several aspects of the virtual community strategy that has been referred to throughout the previous chapters. The Third Sector is an area where virtual community strategies are very clearly under development. This sector is avowedly not dedicated to 'wealth creation' in the sense in which this term has come to be used in recent years, but it is dedicated to the delivery of social and other services that have substantial value to citizens throughout Europe, and it is a contributor to new job creation. We also examine the contribution of 'civic nets' to the European information society landscape. Civic nets are initiatives that public authorities at the regional and municipal level are undertaking to improve public services and information access and they demonstrate the implementation of virtual community strategies through their capacity to build new virtual communities of actors. Finally, in this section, we look briefly at several initiatives at the regional level in Europe to design information and communication technology and service applications that are responsive to the patterns of everyday life within distinct regional (and local) places. To give adequate coverage to this topic would require another book, which would be well worth writing.[3] Just as the Third Sector is delivering a range of valuable services throughout Europe, the initiation of local and regional services involving the use of the Internet has the potential to improve the quality of government services, to strengthen the co-ordination of economic development activities, and to create new opportunities for employment within local labour markets.

In s. 9.4 we return to the theme of governance and regulation, which we also considered in Chs. 6, 7, and 8, by examining the fiscal consequences of continuing growth

---

[3] See Cooke and Morgan (1998) for an analysis of the way firms are building relationships to sustain innovation within regions often supported by the application of information and communication technologies.

in e-commerce. The shift of economic transactions into virtual networks, where taxation becomes both technically more difficult and frequently politically unfeasible, is giving rise to concerns about the social and economic implications of the further development of e-commerce. We consider discussions about whether the Internet and e-commerce activities should be preserved as tax-free zones, as one of the by-products, or unintended consequences, of movement towards the information society. Our aim is to indicate how the growth of the information and communication infrastructure is revealing underlying stresses and tensions in the institutional accommodations that have been laboriously constructed. Further development may unravel some of these accommodations or heighten existing tensions and this is particularly well illustrated by the issues raised by debates around the subject of 'taxing the Internet'.

9.2   Employment and Skills

Opinions about the prospects for economic growth and employment in the information society differ widely.[4] Some economists expect the economy to undergo a prolonged and painful structural transformation that will ultimately bring sustained growth along with innovation (Freeman and Perez, 1988; Perez, 1983). This process is expected to drive prices down and to stimulate greater consumption, opening new markets and creating new employment opportunities particularly in high-technology industries and services. A minority of economists among whom Rifkin (1995) is well known, argue that the information and communication technology revolution will generate wealth, but only for a few, creating growing polarization and permanent exclusion through the 'the end of work' for a large part of the population. Although this view is not widely held, many observers of recent developments worry that the price of the transition to information-intensive economies will be very high. In fact, it may mean that the European Union countries have to abandon their standards of social welfare in order to join the market-led, globally competitive, economic development process. In this section we focus on the opportunities for economic and employment growth that may be associated with the construction of more advanced information and communication infrastructures within the context of macro-economic and labour market trends. We also consider the prospects for job creation and the potential implications for the evolution of skills.

Several recent analyses of the macro-economic consequences of the diffusion of the Internet are based upon the idea of an 'Internet multiplier' effect, that is, that the growing use of Internet, World Wide Web, Intranet and Extranet services has the ability to generate direct and indirect employment growth. We look at the employment forecasts produced by these studies to demonstrate that, in many instances, they do not take the structural constraints attributable to marketing costs, the costs of training, or dynamic changes in technology and service markets into account, or they

---

[4] This section is based on research undertaken by Lucia Passamonti and Guido Lucchi (1998) and Gabriella Cattaneo, Enrico Grazzini, and Stefano Kluzer (1997).

do so very inadequately. By examining the structural characteristics of the 'Internet Industry' and of the 'Internet Value Chain', we highlight some of the sources of uncertainty about employment growth prospects. We also illustrate how the idea of the multiplier effect has been used to produce initial estimates of the employment effects in European countries that may be associated with the growth of e-commerce using the Internet.

9.2.1 Macroeconomic and Employment Growth Perspectives in the United States and Europe

The performance of the United States economy generated 15 million new jobs between 1985 and 1995 and a total of 1.6 million in 1996. The employment creation capacity of the economy has been linked to the resurgence in industrial competitiveness. Some European observers suggest that this has come at the expense of downward pressures on wages resulting from market liberalization. It is the case that during the first half of the period the wages of American workers rose, but did not keep pace with inflation. However, during the second half of the period total wages increased in both nominal and real terms. There is, nevertheless, some concern about the polarization of income levels in the United States.[5] The sectors expected to generate the highest employment growth between 1996 and 2006 include computer and data-processing services and health and residential care services, as well as management and public relations and entertainment and recreation services, as shown in Table 9.1.

Even if substitution effects are taken into account in the information and communication technology sectors, job creation appears to be greater than job losses across all industrialized countries.[6] Most forecasters expect that direct employment within the information and communication technology sectors will be less important than the 'multiplier effects' associated with the adoption of innovative technologies and services by other sectors of the economy. There is also uncertainty about which industries will provide important capabilities for generating and 'absorbing' the technological capabilities that will be needed to take advantage of these multiplier effects. This is a major issue for Europe because of the relatively weak competitiveness of its information and communication technology industry and evidence suggesting that demand related to this rapidly growing industry is weaker than in the United States. In some areas, this may be of relatively little importance and Europe may benefit from foreign production of the hardware or software inputs that are used within the European economies. In other areas, however, the weaker position of the European economies may create problems in realizing the potential offered by the new technologies.

[5] It has also been discussed by Reich (1991: 208) in terms of income divergence, that is, 'the fortunes of routine producers are declining. In-person servers are also becoming poorer, although their fates are less clear-cut. But symbolic analysts—who solve, identify, and broker new problems—are, by and large, succeeding in the world economy.'

[6] Two reports, Department of Commerce (1999) and OECD (1999a) provide syntheses of more recent data on employment in the United States and the OECD countries, respectively, the diffusion of information and communication technologies, and the spread of e-commerce.

TABLE 9.1. *Industries with fastest employment growth, USA, 1996–2006 (estimated)*

Industry Description	Employment		Change 1996–2006	
	1996 (000)	2006 (000)	No. (000)	%
Computer and data-processing services	1,208	2,509	1,301	108
Health services	1,172	1,968	796	68
Management and public relations	873	1,400	527	60
Miscellaneous transportation services	204	327	123	60
Residential care	672	1,070	398	59
Personnel supply services	2,646	4,039	1,393	53
Water and sanitation	231	349	118	51
Individual and miscellaneous social services	846	1,266	420	50
Offices of health practitioners	2,751	4,046	1,295	47
Amusement and recreation services	1,109	1,565	457	41

Source: Adapted from Franklin (1997).

In the United States, employment growth has been accompanied, particularly since 1992, by growing aggregate productivity (output per working hour), despite a significant shift of employment from the goods to the service industries (Passamonti and Lucchi, 1998). By the mid-1990s, manufacturing, excluding mining and construction, occupied less than 15 per cent of the workforce compared to 19 per cent in the early 1980s. Conversely, the service industries have become more important, both in terms of value added, representing about two-thirds of Gross Domestic Product (GDP), and in terms of employment, growing to about 75 per cent of the workforce by the mid-1990s from about 65 per cent in 1982. This is attributable to the growth of traditional industries including business services, wholesale and retail trade, air transport, and telecommunication; the emergence of dynamic new service industries many of which are information and communication technology-based, such as computer software, cellular telephony, and cable television; and the growing contribution of services to the creation of value added in the manufacturing sector. Although some of the jobs created in the United States in the 1980s involved lower-paid employment in the service sector, in recent years new jobs have included highly skilled activities. For example, about 68 per cent of the net growth in full-time employment between 1994 and 1996 was in job categories paying above median wages, while 52 per cent of employment growth was in the top 30 per cent of the wage distribution (ibid.).

In the European Union, 148 million people were in employment in 1995, but unemployment remained stubbornly high at around 10 or 11 per cent in the mid-1990s. Youth unemployment was twice that of adults. Long-term unemployment increased in 1995 from 48 per cent of the unemployed to over 50 per cent. Women have accounted for the growth of the labour force over the past 20 years, but unemployment for women in the mid-1990s was higher than for men in all but two of the Member States (ibid.). Net additions to employment in Europe have been driven by small and medium-sized enterprises. In the period 1988–95, companies with fewer than 100 employees increased employment by an estimated 250,000 per year, while those with more than 100 employees reduced employment by more than 200,000 per year. Between the years 1993 and 1995, a 10 per cent increase in turnover for small and medium-sized enterprises coincided with an increase in employment of more than 5 per cent, while the same rate of turnover growth for large companies contributed to an increase in employment of only 3 per cent. The service sectors, including business, health, education, recreational and personal services, and the environment sector, provided most of the net additions to jobs, and the decline in employment in agriculture and industry, except in instrument engineering, continued.

Differences in the rates of job creation in the United States and Europe are attributable to many factors (European Commission, 1996*i*). In the United States improvements in the competitiveness of industry and strong growth in output have resulted in a much lower rate of job destruction than in Europe. The United States economy also benefited from supportive macroeconomic monetary and fiscal policies until the early 1990s, while in Europe these policies were more restrictive. In addition, although the process of deregulating the air transport, telecommunication, and business services sectors in the United States initially created turmoil in the economy, these sectors are now contributing to the growth of the economy. According to one estimate, the output of the information and communication technology sector in the United States increased by 9.3 per cent annually from 1990 to 1995 compared to a 2.4 per cent annual growth rate in Europe (Passamonti and Lucchi, 1998). The United States achieved a higher rate of net job creation in services, although the growth in output did not differ substantially from that achieved in Europe. Health, social services, education, recreational, and leisure activities contributed nearly 1 per cent annually to employment in the United States, but only 0.5 per cent annually in Europe.

Non-wage-related labour costs, such as social cost contributions, have contributed to labour market developments in Europe and have had a negative impact on low-wage, low-skill groups. However, the greater labour cost flexibility in the United States has been accompanied by greater stratification in access to social services, such as health care, and major strains on the unemployment insurance system. It has been argued that European employers compensate for higher labour costs by achieving greater productivity improvements, but for European employers a major problem continues to be the limited availability of appropriately trained 'knowledge workers' (Booz Allen & Hamilton, 1997). Although European labour markets are becoming more flexible in terms of work organization and working time, the potential for growth associated with this flexibility is not being fully realized, particularly in lower skill-level job categories. In Europe there has been a marked trend towards the up-skilling of the labour. Between 1983 and 1991, the number of people classified as managers and professional and technical workers expanded by over 25 per cent annually.

By comparison, total employment growth during this period was about 1 per cent annually (European Commission, 1997*c*).

A growing polarization of the labour market between high-skilled, highly paid jobs, and low-skilled, lower-paid jobs, combined with a sharp decline in medium-skilled jobs, is common to both the United States and European labour markets.[7] There is evidence that two categories of workers have experienced growth in recent years. The first is the small category of high-level managers, sales managers and shop owners, and knowledge workers, that is, computer and other scientists, lawyers and medical doctors, teachers and professors, consultants, and professionals of various kinds. The second is a larger group of low-qualified workers delivering services that complement the first group's activities, including security staff, home care and health care staff, and transport workers. Employment trends are negative for the white collar, routine, and control types of activities performed by office clerks, secretaries, and middle managers. Computer operators have experienced the highest percentage decrease in numbers in recent years. In the United States jobs in manufacturing, the retail trade, the postal service, and some other service sectors experienced heavy job losses in the 1980s; these sectors began to stabilize in the mid-1990s. In contrast, in Europe further job reductions are likely to occur.

The percentage of employment involved in the service sector in Europe is lower than in the United States (64.5% in 1995 in Europe as compared to 75% in the United States) and the manufacturing industry is likely to continue to decline. As a result, service sector employment is expected to continue to grow for some time. The European Commission's position has been that 'employment-friendly growth must be based on an offensive strategy that promotes increased demand rather than a defensive strategy based on the sharing of existing jobs' (European Commission, 1996*i*: 2).

The liberalization of telecommunication markets and the ongoing convergence of telecommunication, computing, and broadcast media markets are expected to continue to stimulate the creation of employment opportunities. In the United States, for example, Cohen (1996) estimated positive growth in Gross National Product (GNP) and positive employment growth as a result of the introduction of competition in local telecommunication markets and more intense competition in long-distance telecommunication following the implementation of the Telecommunications Act in 1996. However, the magnitude of the projected economic growth effects and the employment effects that may result from these developments are highly uncertain. In the following two sections we review the conclusions of several studies in order to illustrate the problems that are encountered in making such estimates and the strong assumptions that are necessary to make these types of analyses tractable.

---

[7] The analysis is based on interviews by Confidea USA (1996) undertaken with economists in the United States including: Eric Greenberg, American Management Association; Kames Frenkel, Bureau of Labor Statistics; Edward Luttwak, Center for Strategic and International Studies; Dean Baker, Economic Policy Institute; William Wascher, Federal Reserve; Jeremy Rifkin, Foundation on Economic Trends; Martin Baily, McKinsey Global Institute; Lisa Lynch, Office of American Workplace; Gerald Moody, Office of Policy Development; Gary Burtless, The Brookings Institution; Steven Davis, US Bureau of Census; Robert Lerman, Urban Institute; and the interpretation of the results in the light of developments within Europe. This is reported in Passamonti and Lucchi (1998).

9.2.2   A More Detailed European View

A study by BIPE Conseil, IFO Institute, and LENTIC Institute (1997) and a report by Analysys Ltd. (1997*a*) both reach the conclusion that telecommunication market liberalization measures in Europe will yield positive contributions for employment through a net increase in jobs. These estimates are based upon assumptions about the consequences of various speeds in the move towards liberalization implementation in the Member States and the harmonization of market conditions across Europe. In the BIPE Conseil study, a scenario assuming rapid telecommunication liberalization and technology diffusion predicts that up to 1,300,000 jobs are created in Europe by the year 2005, while rapid liberalization combined with slow technology diffusion produces a net increase of 641,800 jobs.[8]

Since the beginning of the 1990s, employment by the public telecommunication operators in Europe has fallen by approximately 2.6 per cent annually. New entry, however, has led to new job opportunities especially in areas such as resale and call-back, value-added, on-line, and Internet access services. While the telecommunication equipment manufacturing industry within Europe employed 361,000 in 1994, this number is expected to fall to 289,000 in 2005. Other telecommunication service suppliers, however, are expected to account for the net creation of 150,700 new jobs by 2005 in the BIPE Conseil scenario predicting the net addition of 1.3 million jobs in all sectors. Indirect employment gains were expected in sectors strongly affected by reductions in telecommunication service prices, such as the retail, electrical and electronics manufacturing, and consumer goods sectors. The study by Analysys Ltd. (1997*a*), produced an estimated net gain of 641,000 new jobs by 2005 under a rapid market liberalization scenario.

Both these studies assume the existence of multiplier effects accompanying structural changes in the European internal markets for telecommunication and related services.[9] The positive outcome for net gains in employment in the Analysys Ltd. study, for example, depends upon strong growth in mobile, multimedia, and value-added services in the liberalized telecommunication services market. The important mechanism for growth in this study comes from ten sectors of the economy,

---

[8] This study employed macroeconomic models and research across the fifteen Member States. The goal was to measure the overall effects on European employment of the liberalization of the telecommunication sector using four scenarios. The study analysed the direct effects of liberalization on the telecommunication sector (including traditional operators and other telecommunication service providers—mobile telephony, Internet access providers, etc., equipment manufacturers and distributors, direct telecommunication suppliers) and the indirect effects for the rest of the economy. The media, computer software and services, and the content industries were included in the analysis of indirect effects.

[9] BIPE Conseil assumed that public telecommunication operators would experience job reductions and that employment growth would be generated by new operators, service providers, and industry suppliers offsetting job losses by 2005 under a rapid liberalization scenario. Analysys Ltd. carried out an analysis of the efficiency levels of the public telecommunication operators and concluded that their relative efficiency, together with increased demand, could produce an increase in employment in the telecommunication sector by 2005 if harmonization of the sector were to be achieved through market liberalization.

which account for about 70 per cent of total business revenues generated by tele-communication services.[10]

The convergence of telecommunication and audiovisual markets within a more flexible regulatory framework is also expected to contribute to economic growth in Europe and to have a positive influence on employment creation prospects. A KPMG (1996) study, for example, forecasts a 173 becu market by 2005 in France, Germany, Italy, The Netherlands, and the United Kingdom for new communication and multi-media services, assuming that widespread technological convergence occurs. Another study by the German Institute for Economic Research (DIW) (1996) focuses on media, consumer electronics, office machines, computer hardware and software, photo-optical equipment, mail and telecommunication services in the German market and estimates that domestic demand will nearly triple by 2010 and that employment will increase by 10 per cent to approximately 2.1 million jobs, represent-ing only about 180,000 new jobs over a ten-year period. This relatively conservative estimate does not include the indirect stimulus to job creation that may be contributed by market liberalization and restructuring.

Many estimates of the employment-creating potential associated with the diffusion of information and communication technologies assume the continuing convergence between public switched telecommunication networks and the newer inter-networking technologies, that is, increasing computer connectivity and the spread of the Internet. Cohen (1996), for instance, has forecast a major shift to the use of Extranet/Intranet systems and that data services will overtake voice services in terms of revenue generation by 2005. Coupled with strong revenue growth from Internet, web-based and Intranet services, Cohen has estimated that new jobs in the United States generated by the direct and indirect contributions will reach 4 to 5 million by the year 2005. This forecast compares with 3 million jobs under a steady state growth scenario for telecommunication services. The growth of the Internet is expected to generate stronger direct and indirect economic growth and employment creation potential as the 'Internet multiplier' takes hold in the economy.[11]

---

[10] The sectors are aerospace, automobile manufacture and engineering, health care, travel and transport services, finance, electrical and electronic industries, retail and distribution, chemicals, pharmaceuticals and petroleum, entertainment, printing and publishing, education, and other government services. The macro-economic model is driven by estimated multiplier effects and its value is to suggest the differential impact of different regulatory and competitive frameworks in Europe.

[11] In one scenario, the GNP effect is calculated using revenues estimated for 2000 and 2005, adding to them the multiplier effect assuming that the fixed terrestrial telecommunication, cable, and the wireless industries have a GNP multiplier of 2. Based on estimates of output per worker in each subsector and assuming limited productivity growth, the resulting employment contribution is 1 million new jobs for fixed terrestrial telecommunication services by the year 2000 and about 3 million by 2005. The wireless tele-phony, cable, and satellite sectors together are estimated to contribute approximately 400,000 new jobs by 2000 and 900,000 by 2005. Internet business growth is estimated by forecasting the size of four possible shifts in demand: (1) telephone calls are used to access the Internet; (2) some long-distance calls shift to the Internet; (3) broadband links are used by consumers and businesses to access the Internet; and (4) leased lines are used by ISPs to provide Internet services to consumers. The size estimate includes the use of facil-ities for Internet services. Services and products sold on the Internet are estimated separately. The size of the intranet sector is estimated assuming that a certain percentage of leased lines used for corporate networks

In Europe the implications of the Internet multiplier are influenced by several factors. First, although most data communication hardware and software come from the United States, the establishment of networks and on-line services is generating new employment in Europe, albeit in relatively small firms.[12] Second, the diffusion of the Internet—and Extranet/Intranets—in Europe has been slower than in the United States. By 1997 the gap was estimated to be 1 to 5 or 6 in favour of the United States and this was forecast to decline to a ratio of about 1 to 2 in 1999 (Bernard, 1997a). In September 1999, the International Data Corporation (1999) forecast that by 2003 Europeans would outnumber Americans as the largest Internet user group. This pattern of growth suggests that there is a risk of a repeat of what happened with the personal computer industry in Europe. Europeans are importing most of their computer systems and data communication equipment, as well as a substantial share of packaged software, from other parts of the world (Bernard, 1997a). The contribution to employment and output growth must, therefore, come from the use of these technologies rather than from their production. In addition, however, European software production remains strong in specific areas. The convergence of media, telecommunication, and computing technologies is encouraging the formation of integrated supply chains to produce and deliver multimedia and information content and services as shown in Table 9.2. The estimates shown in this table suggest that the value-added share of content creation and its distribution and packaging is rising, while the share of distribution, that is, the network operator's share, is decreasing. Content is expected to account for the greatest proportion of the value-added chain for multimedia products, while software is expected to contribute the greatest proportion for business products.

The 'copyright industries', that is, computer software and the motion picture, audio-visual, and publishing industries, are among the greatest employment generators in the United States (Department of Commerce, 1999). They are also expected to have a substantial potential for job creation in Europe. For example, Andersen Consulting (1996) has estimated that these sectors will employ about 5 million people in Europe, of which about 2 million will be in publishing by 2005 with a total of 1 million new jobs created. Additional jobs in the newly emerging electronic media markets will not, however, necessarily produce large net employment growth as job losses may occur in the print media industry. In addition, the digital television market is expected to generate substantial numbers of new jobs in Europe. Estimates, such as those prepared by KPMG (1996), are predicated on dramatic increases in the size of markets for new broadband audiovisual and data services, such as Pay-per-View television, Video-on-demand and Near-video-on-demand, home shopping, home banking, and on-line

---

are used for Intranets. Spending on intranets is adjusted using a demand elasticity estimate to compensate for the lower expenditure by firms on intranet-Virtual Private Networks (VPNs) than on leased lines. In other scenarios, the Internet and intranet-VPNs are given a more prominent role.

[12] e.g. InformConsult specializes in the development and implementation of information technology solutions targeting the Intranet market. Based in Germany, it has approximately 32 employees, more than 20 of whom are professionals. Loud-n-Clear is a 'virtual' company which in 1997 employed about 11 people as well as part-time freelance workers providing Internet services (excluding dial-up access), see Cattaneo, Grazzini, and Kluzer (1997).

√ TABLE 9.2. *The new information value chain*

Source creation	Content development	Packaging	Distribution	End-user access
Actors				
Theatrical performers	Editors	CD-ROM producers	Libraries	Researchers
Programmers	Designers	CD-I producers	Subscription agencies	Small firms
Photographers	Project managers	Print publishers	Museums	Professionals
Authors	Database producers	Multimedia companies	Retail outlets	Training activities
Musicians		Television producers	Cable operators	Public sector
Animators		Database service providers	Broadcasters	Citizens
			Telecom operators	Consumers
			Satellite operators	Education
Objects				
Images and text	Electronic books	Books, newspapers	Magnetic media	Game consoles
Graphics	CD-ROM	Electronic books	Optical media	Personal computers
Music, sound and code	Databases	Magazines	Print media	Set-top boxes
Statistics	Game titles	Interactive television	Cable networks	Televisions
	CD-I	CD-I	Telephone networks	Fax
	Interactive television	CD-ROM	Mobile networks	Mobile terminals
	Content	On-line database services	Satellite networks	
48% share of Value Added and increasing, first three columns			38% and decreasing	14% and constant

Source: Passamonti and Lucchi (1998).

education. Historically, high growth projections in these types of services had to be revised downwards due to slower than expected acceptance by users.

Estimating the multiplier effects associated with the spread of Internet use and Extranet/Intranets for software employment in Europe is very difficult and can be only crudely estimated. For example, at the end of 1996 it was estimated that there were some 150,000 commercial Internet sites in Europe and 50,000 Intranet implementations (Cattaneo, Grazzini, and Kluzer, 1997). The implementation of a simple commercial web site, for example, a few pages for promotion purposes, could require between 3 and 20 person days of work. A more complex Internet and Intranet could require between 0.5 and 20 person years of effort and these are simply the initial costs, rather than the ongoing costs of ownership and operation of the site. Using these estimates, 150,000 commercial web sites multiplied by an average of 10 person days (assuming all sites are simple) produces a conservative estimate of about 6,000 person years of additional work. Part of this additional work will substitute for previous software development and information distribution work, and, therefore, the net result might be estimated at about 3,000 full-time jobs. The analysis for Intranet-related job creation is even less clear-cut, as Intranet implementations tend to rely upon existing staff and, in principle, on cost reductions for business information processes. The extent to which cost reductions will create greater demand for these services rather than being taken as overhead cost reductions remains to be seen.

E-commerce based on the Internet is in an embryonic stage of development, making it very difficult to rely upon current projections. Overall estimates call for growth from a US$ 26b. base in 1996–7 to US$ 1,000b. by 2003–5 and even at that level it would be less than current sales by direct marketing in the United States using mail, telephone, and newspapers (OECD, 1999a).[13] OECD estimates based on a variety of sources are for European revenues of US$ 64,360m. by 2001–2 (ibid.). Forecasts by Forrester Research suggest slow but steady growth in revenues from on-line services in Europe from 395 mecu in 1996 to 5 becu in 2000. The European Information Technology Observatory has estimated that some 56 becu will be generated by 2001 from both on-line and off-line transactions for goods ordered over the Internet and from web advertising revenues, and that European transactions will account for a 20 per cent share of web-generated sales worldwide by 2001. Forecasts produced in late 1999 suggest that seven of the top ten e-commerce countries by 2003 will be in Europe (International Data Corporation, 1999). Germany's e-commerce transaction value is expected to grow at a compound annual rate of 147 per cent between 1998 and 2003 reaching US$ 62.8b., France's value is expected to grow by 197 per cent over the same period, while Sweden, the United Kingdom, The Netherlands, Spain, and Italy are expected to achieve growth of between 140 and 163 per cent. These growth rates compare with an estimated 82 per cent during the same period for the United States.

Table 9.3 summarizes the employment consequences of the studies discussed in this section. The coverage of these studies varies considerably. They may be mutually con-

[13] A Sept. 1999 estimate by International Data Corporation puts total business conducted over the Internet by 2003 at US$ 1.3 trillion, up from US$ 50b. in 1998, see International Data Corporation (1999).

TABLE 9.3. *Summary of estimated European employment changes*

	Net job additions	By which year?	Sector
Aggregate studies			
BIPE Conseil			
Most optimistic	1.3 million	2005	All Europe
Optimistic	642 thousand	2005	All Europe
Analysys Ltd.	641 thousand	2005	All Europe
Sector estimates			
DIW	180 thousand	2010	Germany, ICT-related products and services
Andersen Consulting	1 million	2005	Copyright industries
Databank Cattaneo	3 thousand	1996	Web site development

Source: Compiled by the authors.

sistent, however, if they were each to be made comparable in coverage. Nevertheless, it is clear that the underlying assumptions with regard to the transformation of markets can account for substantial differences in employment forecasts. This is illustrated by the BIPE Conseil study scenarios which differ by a factor of two in their estimation of employment effects.

Despite these growth prospects, substitution effects between the e-commerce mode of retailing and traditional modes may produce strong downward trends in employment in the retail distribution sector. However, some argue that call-centre employment will compensate for these losses. In the next section we look more closely at the dynamic processes and interactions that must be assumed to occur in order for projections of the Internet multiplier effects to be made. We focus specifically on the potential e-commerce multiplier effects in our illustration.

9.2.3   From Internet to E-Commerce: The Multiplier Effects

E-commerce is expected to affect all aspects of the economic environment, the organization of firms, consumer behaviour, and the role of governments as we discussed in earlier chapters (see Ch. 5 especially). There are many qualitative assessments of the implications of the take-up of various forms of network-based transactions for economic growth, productivity, and job-creation in enterprises, but apart from the kinds of market estimates and projections that we have reviewed in the preceding section there have been few attempts to produce models that permit the e-commerce direct and indirect multiplier effects to be estimated in a systematic way. Any attempt to quantify the effects of the e-commerce multiplier in terms of economic growth and employment prospects must make assumptions about the structural changes that will occur within the economy as substantially new ways of conducting business take hold.

This is extremely difficult to do since it is expected that there will be many new roles for firms, and that incumbents in the market-place will shift their business activities, in part, by relying increasingly upon the information and communication infrastructure. As they do so, traditional supply chains encompassing content creation, content packaging, service provision, and final delivery to customers are likely to change. In some cases, consumers may be linked directly to producers without the need for traditional retailers, wholesalers, or distributors. Network access providers, electronic payments systems, and services for authentication and certification of transactions will have to be provided, either by existing firms or by new entrants that provide these intermediary services. We have argued in Ch. 5 that there is likely to be a strong trend towards the *re-intermediation* of many transaction chains.

Preliminary evidence suggests that many of the new services are far less labour-intensive than traditional intermediary services and this suggests that there will be a negative balance for employment direct effects, that is, the number of old jobs destroyed by e-commerce will exceed the number of new jobs directly created through e-commerce activities. However, there are also likely to be second-order effects as a result of changes in inter-industry relationships, and in productivity. For example, reductions in price can be predicted reliably to generate increases in quantities demanded. While some cost reductions will result in the capture of larger profits, other reductions will lead to price reductions. Servicing this greater volume of sales will create demand for additional labour. These indirect effects may result in a positive net impact of the growth of e-commerce on employment. The forecasts of the potential employment effects of e-commerce that are presented in this section are based on an analysis undertaken by Databank Consulting (Milan) in 1998 (Passamonti and Lucchi, 1998).[14] The analysis begins by focusing on the estimated revenue generated by commercial web sites in Europe by country for France, Germany, Italy, and the United Kingdom. Alternative business models for e-commerce were developed and applied to produce forecasts of revenues for several market segments of e-commerce. The business functions relating to the e-commerce market segments, for example, content provider, service provider, network provider, bank, or credit card company, were related to traditional business sectors and the overall economic impact and job-creation potential of e-commerce was measured using an inter-industry input–output model.

Table 9.4 shows the expected sales and advertising revenues generated by commercial web sites in Europe for the four countries and Table 9.5 provides a breakdown of the forecast revenues by product and service market segment for the period 1995–2001. The data are inclusive of several methods of generating sales revenue. For example, a customer may order and pay for an item to be delivered by post or a customer may order, pay for, and receive certain products on-line. These data also include web advertising revenue.

Table 9.6 shows the percentage of revenues by country and by market segment based on adjusted data for 1998. The share of the consumer products segment is increased

---

[14] The study builds upon forecasts for revenues from e-commerce developed by European Information Technology Observatory (EITO) (1997).

TABLE 9.4. *Revenues generated by commercial web sites in Europe by country, 1995–2001 (becu)*

Country	1995	1996	1997	1998	1999	2000	2001
France	0.00	0.01	0.11	0.51	1.89	4.64	8.29
Germany	0.00	0.02	0.18	0.83	3.03	7.42	13.20
Italy	0.00	0.03	0.16	0.53	1.50	3.00	4.52
United Kingdom	0.02	0.15	0.65	1.97	4.90	8.42	10.58
TOTAL	0.02	0.21	1.10	3.84	11.32	23.48	36.59
Europe	**0.05**	**0.39**	**1.93**	**6.53**	**18.63**	**37.34**	**56.36**
4 Countries as % of Europe	40%	54%	57%	59%	61%	63%	65%

Source: Passamonti and Lucchi (1998) based on EITO (1997) data.

TABLE 9.5. *Revenues generated by commercial web sites in Europe by segment, 1995–2001 (becu)*

Segment	1995	1996	1997	1998	1999	2000	2001
Computers and software	0.02	0.12	0.55	1.67	4.16	7.16	9.02
Consumer products	0.01	0.06	0.31	1.01	2.80	5.41	7.89
Finance and insurance	0.00	0.01	0.07	0.23	0.62	1.18	1.69
Manufacturing and industry	0.00	0.02	0.11	0.46	1.55	3.61	6.20
Publications and information	0.01	0.04	0.19	0.65	1.86	3.73	5.64
Travel	0.00	0.02	0.10	0.33	0.87	1.62	2.25
Business and professional	0.01	0.06	0.32	1.21	3.79	8.28	13.53
Advertising	0.01	0.04	0.23	0.78	2.30	4.73	7.33
Other	0.00	0.01	0.05	0.20	0.68	1.62	2.82
TOTAL	0.06	0.38	1.93	6.54	18.63	37.34	56.37

Source: As Table 9.4.

for Germany and France to take account of the strength of their established home-shopping services, for example, mail order and broadcast television shopping. In the case of Italy, the consumer products share is revised downwards to reflect the relatively slow expected diffusion of on-line shopping in that country.

Alternative business models were developed by building upon a very detailed analysis of the interactive multimedia industry with a special focus on teleshopping and teleworking that had been conducted by Databank (EURORIM Project, 1997*b*). These activities were examined using a value chain analysis (Passamonti and Lucchi, 1998) which identified several alternative ways of organizing the teleshopping business. A content provider-centric model, where the content provider organizes the business activities and is directly involved in financial transactions assisted by an external service provider that may or may not be visible to the customer and which is treated as

TABLE 9.6: *Revenues generated by commercial web sites by country and by segment, 1998*

Segment	France %	Germany %	Italy %	United Kingdom %	European average %
Computers and software	25	25	26	25	25
Consumer products	17	20	10	13	15
Finance and insurance	4	4	4	4	4
Manufacturing and industry	7	6	8	8	7
Publications and information	10	10	11	10	10
Travel	5	4	6	5	5
Business and professional	18	18	20	20	19
Advertising	12	11	12	12	12
Other	3	3	4	4	4
TOTAL	100	100	100	100	100

Nos. may not total due to rounding error.

Source: As Table 9.4.

a subcontractor to the content provider, was selected because it was the most common approach at the time the analysis was undertaken in 1998. This model requires only moderate investment to establish and it offers the content provider considerable flexibility with respect to web design. Assumptions also had to be made about the relationship between off-line and on-line transactions and about the relative growth of the business-to-consumer and business-to-business segments of the e-commerce market. These data were supplemented using information about traditional value chains for commerce derived from industry accounts and market surveys.[15] This provided the basis for extrapolations to produce an e-commerce value chain for each revenue segment of the market. The estimated share of revenues for each market segment as a result of the many adjustments is shown in Table 9.7 for traditional forms of commerce and in Table 9.8 for the e-commerce market segments.

The economic activities involved in e-commerce were then mapped onto existing industrial classifications.[16] The value chains were applied to the four countries but the allocation of the content provider's share of the aggregate revenues was based on each country's specific industrial structure. An input–output model was used to produce estimates of the contributions of e-commerce to the economies of the four European countries. Final demand, in this case, revenues generated by commercial web sites, was disaggregated by industrial classification, and effects on activity levels, that is, domestic production, were calculated. The input–output model was used to estimate both direct and indirect effects on production levels for each industry segment and the results provided a basis for estimating both value-added and employment requirements. These estimates of first-order effects were supplemented by estimates of

---

[15] These estimates were based on a large number of sector-specific assumptions.
[16] This was accomplished using the International Standard Industrial Classification Revision 2.

TABLE 9.7. *Value chain for traditional commerce by revenue segment*

Traditional commerce segment	Content provider %	Retail and wholesale %	Transport %	Total %
Computers	93.0	2.5	4.5	100
Software	88.0	9.0	3.0	100
Consumer products	80.0	16.0	4.0	100
Finance and insurance	100.0	—	—	100
Manufacturing and industry	100.0	—	—	100
Publications	80.0	15.0	5.0	100
Information	80.0	15.0	5.0	100
Travel	100.0	—	—	100
Business and professional	100.0	—	—	100
Advertising	100.0	—	—	100
Other	—	—	—	—

Source: Passamonti and Lucchi (1998).

TABLE 9.8. *Value chain for e-commerce by revenue segment*

E-commerce segment	Content provider %	Service provider %	Network provider %	Transport provider %	Payment provider %	Total %
Computers	93.0	1.0	0.2	5.0	0.8	100
Software	88.0	5.8	3.2	—	3.0	100
Consumer products	80.0	5.0	1.0	9.0	5.0	100
Finance and insurance	90.0	5.0	5.0	—	—	100
Manufacturing and industry	90.0	3.0	4.0	—	3.0	100
Publications	80.0	5.0	2.0	8.0	5.0	100
Information	80.0	7.0	8.0	—	5.0	100
Travel	90.0	5.0	2.0	—	3.0	100
Business and professional	90.0	7.0	1.0	—	2.0	100
Advertising	90.0	9.0	1.0	—	—	100
Other	100.0	—	—	—	100.0	

Source: As Table 9.7.

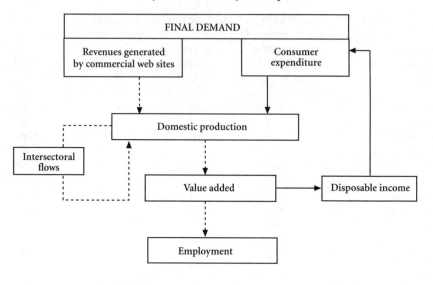

- - - - - - ▶ Input–Output system (Leontief)

──────▶ Consumption–Income linkage (Keynes)

FIG. 9.1. Inter-industry model

Source: Passamonti and Lucchi (1998).

second-order effects attributable to the estimated changes in household disposable income which create new final demand for goods and services. The basic inter-industry model is shown in Figure 9.1.[17]

In order to simulate the economic contributions of e-commerce, 1998 was chosen as the reference year.[18] Table 9.9 shows the results of the simulation.

The e-commerce multiplier effects are most significant for the United Kingdom and France. That is, every ecu spent on e-commerce services generates 3.8 or 3.7 ecu in the respective economies. For Germany and Italy, the multiplier values are 3.2 and 3.4 ecu, respectively. Italy exhibits the lowest multiplier value (1.53) suggesting that the industries directly involved in e-commerce activities are less well integrated with other industries than is the case in the other countries. Second-order effects produced by the analysis of the consumption–income linkage are lowest for Germany, which may be accounted for by the fact that the German economy is characterized by lower average

[17] The model was populated using OECD input–output tables for 1990 for Germany, France, and the UK, and 1985 for Italy. For many industries, market patterns have changed since 1990 or 1985. Adjustments of labour and technical coefficients were made, see Passamonti and Lucchi (1998).

[18] This year was selected because 1998 revenues were estimated to have increased by 200% over 1995 levels; and this year was close to the base year (1996) on which the model was built. According to the original analysis by European Information Technology Observatory (EITO) (1997), 1998 revenue estimates for the four countries were expected to account for 60% of total European e-commerce revenues.

TABLE 9.9. *Economic impact of e-commerce*

	France	Germany	Italy	United Kingdom	Total 4 countries
Production (1998, mecu, 1996 prices)					
Primary: direct (industry direct requirements)[1]	521	860	551	2,053	3,984
Primary: indirect (inter-industry linkages)	352	570	291	1,480	2,693
Secondary (consumption-income linkage)	1,035	1,283	1,005	4,208	7,531
TOTAL	1,908	2,713	1,847	7,741	14,209
Multiplier (direct + inter-industry linkages)	*1.67*	*1.66*	*1.53*	*1.72*	*1.68*
Multiplier (consumption-income linkage)	*1.98*	*1.49*	*1.83*	*2.05*	*1.89*
Total Multiplier	*3.66*	*3.16*	*3.35*	*3.77*	*3.57*
Value Added (1998, mecu, 1996 prices)					
Primary: direct (industry direct requirements)	281	456	328	1,003	2,069
Primary: indirect (inter-industry linkages)	185	300	156	728	1,368
Secondary (consumption-income linkage)	571	688	555	2,022	3,837
TOTAL	1,037	1,444	1,039	3,753	6,234
Employment (1998, units)					
Primary: direct (industry direct requirements)	3,425	4,374	7,205	26,617	41,621
Primary: indirect (inter-industry linkages)	2,733	3,956	4,560	19,681	30,930
Secondary (consumption-income linkage)	9,867	10,339	17,373	62,594	100,173
TOTAL	16,025	18,669	29,138	108,892	172,724

[1] Direct production requirements correspond to revenues generated by commercial Web sites; figures differ slightly from those published in European Information Technology Observatory (EITO) (1997) as they are adjusted for inflation.

Source: As Table 9.7.

consumption than other countries. The employment results shown in Table 9.9 are the estimated employment levels generated by e-commerce revenues in the industries that are: (1) directly involved in the transactions; (2) in all industries in the economy due to inter-industry linkages; and (3) in the whole economy in terms of secondary effects attributable to the consumption–income linkage. These estimates ignore business cycles and labour market changes.[19] It was not feasible to determine how many of these jobs were new ones. For the four countries total primary direct revenue of about 4 becu translates to 173,000 labour units, as shown in Table 9.9, of which 25 per cent is derived from the e-commerce sectors and about 60 per cent is derived from the secondary effects.[20]

In order to address the question of how many new jobs might be created by e-commerce activities, substitution effects must be taken into account. Although assumptions about these effects are subject to criticism, it was assumed that 96 to 97 per cent of e-commerce revenues would substitute for traditional sources of revenues. The remaining 3 to 4 per cent of revenues were allocated to innovative activities, such as web design and consultancy. A comparison of the effects produced by the revenue flows under the traditional and new ways of conducting business indicates that the e-commerce multipliers for production volumes are very similar. The results of this analysis suggested that the movement of labour-intensive activities (such as retail and wholesale activity) to electronic methods has the potential to generate a negative impact on employment. In Germany, for example, this leads to an estimated loss of nearly 500 jobs. Indirect and second-order effects were found to counterbalance direct job losses in all the countries except Germany. Overall, even when the worst case is assumed, that is, that e-commerce merely substitutes for existing commercial activities and that customers pay the same price for goods and services purchased using e-commerce, the number of new jobs created is negligible. Thus, concern about the potential for a severely negative scenario involving substantial job losses does not appear to be warranted.

It is more realistic to assume that substitution effects will be smaller and that a considerable share of e-commerce will involve innovative services that are perceived as such by customers. In this case, the positive effects of e-commerce on economic growth and employment could be substantial. However, because e-commerce revenues are very small compared to traditional retail trade or mail-order shopping revenues, the effects on employment are likely to be very small in both absolute and relative terms. For example, the analysis shows that there are only modest contributions to employment, including first- and second-order effects, in the wholesale and retail trade and transport and storage sectors, sectors that would be expected to be affected by e-commerce activities. The size of these effects is suggested by the result for the United Kingdom where only 0.45 per cent of existing employment in these sectors

---

[19] The basic assumption of input–output analysis is that value-added requirements (and therefore the corresponding employment shifts) are proportional to sector outputs.

[20] Sensitivity tests were conducted indicating that these estimates were relatively robust with respect to changes in revenue segments and the responsiveness (elasticity) of consumption with respect to income.

would be affected, while in France, only 0.11 per cent would be affected (Passamonti and Lucchi, 1998).

The overall results of this analysis suggest that employment growth associated with e-commerce revenues with reference to the year 1998 would be negligible when compared with existing employment levels in the affected industrial sectors. As noted above, for the four countries considered, total revenues of about 4 becu for e-commerce translates into 173,000 jobs. The production multiplier effects associated with e-commerce were largest for France and the United Kingdom, which may be attributable to the structure of their economies and by existing profiles of consumer spending. The translation of activity levels into employment requirements highlighted the relatively good performance of Italy and the United Kingdom in comparison to France and Germany. The different productivity growth rates and mixes of technologies in use in these countries may account for the variations in the results.

9.2.4 Summary

The European Commission provided a consolidated overview in 1998 of its assessment of the relationship between the diffusion and use of advanced information and communication technologies and employment (European Commission, 1998g). At this time it was noted that the industries most closely associated with movement towards the information society are among the largest and fastest growing in Europe and that Europe should be well placed to exploit new opportunities. However, the Commission's report also stated that 'there is worrying evidence that the EU is not making the most of the potential of the information society' (ibid. 1). In the light of the fact that the information and communication technology producing and using sectors of the economy account for more than 5 per cent of GDP, the report called for the development of an enterprise culture, the promotion of organizational change and adaptability, and the boosting of technical skills and levels of technical literacy.[21] The report emphasized especially that 'public access to the tools of the information society, and the skills to use them, need to be prioritized. Everyone should have easy and affordable access to a basic set of information society applications and services' (ibid. 18). At the time of writing, the Member States had prepared national action plans for 1999 to respond to the priorities of improving employability, developing employment opportunities, encouraging adaptability in businesses and employees, and strengthening policies for equal opportunities.[22]

---

[21] The report suggested that the information society industries employed more than 4 million people and that more than 300,000 information society jobs were created between 1995 and 1997 in Europe. It also noted that there were 500,000 unfilled vacancies for information technology professionals in 1998 (European Commission, 1998g).

[22] The European Employment Strategy defined by the Treaty of Amsterdam in June 1997 called upon Member States to co-ordinate their employment policies around four common pillars for priority action with clearly defined targets and objectives. The goals are 'to achieve a high level of employment in the economy and for all groups in the labour market; to move away from a passive fight against unemployment towards promoting sustained employability and job creation; to favour a new approach to work

The issue of employment is closely linked to mobility within the European Union. Information is needed to support the training that is necessary to enhance the mobility of the workforce. In its Green Paper on public sector information (European Commission, 1998*m*: 3), for example, the Commission observed that 'access to public sector information is *essential for the mobility* of both workers and categories like students and retired people within the EU . . . It also has an impact on the way citizens can take advantage of the *internal market*' (emphasis in original). Given that the prospects for small firms to develop new information society services often rely on access to public-sector information, the Green Paper said that these firms 'are *essential for the creation of new jobs in the 21ˢᵗ century*' (ibid. 6, emphasis in original). There are conflicts of interest between those who would like such information to be available in the 'free' market and those who want private-sector firms to benefit from their capacity to add value to such information (see our discussion of this issue in Ch. 7). These conflicts are often discussed in terms of what information may be defined as being 'vital' for citizens and, therefore, available at no charge. In its opinion on this Green Paper, The Information Society Forum called for investigation leading to a clear definition of what might be considered to be vital information and urged that attention be given to the need to ensure access to such information.[23]

The prospects for recombining and adding value to public-sector and other sources of information to provide new information society services offer opportunities to both public- and private-sector organizations. Unfortunately, the aggregate accounts of employment upturns and downturns that we have reviewed in this section, as well as the European position as compared to the United States and other competitors in the global market with respect to e-commerce development, yield little insight into the complicated institutional dynamics through which organizations develop new services for citizens and for consumers. Nevertheless, these institutional dynamics are essential determinants of whether the assumptions upon which the aggregate models are based will have any connection with the actual emergence of the information society in Europe. In the following section we examine the experiences of those organizations that are implementing new services based upon the information and communication infrastructure. The cases we draw upon are emerging at the micro-level, that is, at the local or regional levels, and our purpose is to offer a more detailed picture of the problems and opportunities that are being experienced by organizations that seek access to the infrastructure on behalf of citizens and consumers, and by those who are developing content.

---

organization in such a way that EU firms are able to cope with economic change while reconciling both security and adaptability, and allowing individuals to participate in life-long training; and to provide equal opportunities for everyone in the labour market to participate and have access to work' (European Commission, 1998*e*: 7).

[23] Public-sector information was defined by the Information Society Forum as 'all the information collected, processed and used by the public sector, including the Government, which is "vital" for the citizenship rights achievement and for a healthy and transparent relationships between administration to administration, administration to business and administration to citizen' (European Commission Information Society Forum, 1999: 5).

9.3   Innovation and Learning at the Local and Regional Levels

In this section, we focus on regional initiatives within the European Union that have been undertaken with the goals of building awareness of the potential benefits of the information and communication infrastructure, and of extending its use. The European Commission's attempts to encourage the application of information and communication technologies to support regional development initially involved interesting technical schemes that had little connection with the lives of their intended users. From 1994 to 1998, during the Fourth Framework Programme of Research, Technology, Development, and Demonstration (RTD&D), there was an effort made to rectify this and further efforts are being made under the Fifth Framework Programme.[24] It is now being more widely acknowledged that the information and communication infrastructure and its applications do not, in themselves, ensure positive benefits for economic and social life (Cornford, Gillespie, and Richardson, 1996; Millard and O'Shea, 1996). However, when new applications are embedded within an integrated local or regional development policy, it may be feasible to implement a strategy that increases the accessibility, affordability, and effectiveness of the use of these applications in ways that may enrich and reinforce the positive features of development policies. If positive outcomes for people within the regions of Europe are to emerge from various initiatives, there are complementary factors that need to be in place, including a critical mass of users, skilled human resources, access to information, public administration efficiency, organizational flexibility and adjustment ability, co-operation, quality control, and dynamic intermediaries. We look first at some of the ways in which the Third Sector (non-profit) organizations have been employing the new tools for communication and information exchange. The activities of such organizations illustrate how the application of these tools can encourage the formation of new and productive virtual networks of collaborating citizens and firms.

9.3.1   The Third Sector

The Third Sector, or non-profit sector, lies between the state and the profit-seeking business world.[25] It has attracted much attention in Europe and elsewhere because of its job-creation potential and its role in combating the breakdown of traditional means of maintaining social cohesion. This sector is comprised mainly of non-traded service activities. Although no precise figures are available, it is estimated that this sector accounts for about 4 million employees in the four largest countries in Europe (France, Germany, Italy, and the United Kingdom), or about 10 per cent of total service employment. Its annual employment growth rate is estimated to have been above 10 per cent annually in the 1980s in these countries (Kluzer, 1997). While net job creation is expected to come mainly from new personal care and community services, cultural

[24] See e.g. ASSENT (1999*a*).
[25] The original research on the Third Sector was undertaken by Stefano Kluzer (1997), Databank Consulting, Milan.

production, entertainment, and training activities, the Third Sector is also contributing to improvements in the financial sustainability and social reach of traditional welfare services without expanding the size of the public sector. In addition, organizations in this sector play an important role in assisting socially disadvantaged groups through the revitalization of local communities.

Those who have followed the emergence of the Third Sector in the United States and internationally have commented that the increasing importance of this sector in the latter part of the twentieth century may prove to be as significant as the rise of the nation-state in the latter part of the nineteenth century (Salamon and Anheier, 1994). These organizations have a growing role to play in providing universal access to the information society infrastructures, a role that increasingly complements those played by nation-states and supranational political entities.

Measurement of the scale of activity in this sector is problematic for several reasons. For example, in 1991 the OECD estimated that the non-profit sector in France accounted for 0.26 per cent of GDP while Eurostat claimed that the sector accounted for 49.3 per cent of economic activity in 1993. Estimates prepared within three years of each other which vary by a factor of almost 200 to 1 suggest that this sector eludes available indicators of economic activity or that there are substantial discrepancies in the way the sector is defined and conceptualized as a social phenomenon (ibid.).

Building on Salamon and Anheier's work, a study conducted by Databank, Milan on the emerging features of the Third Sector in Europe took the defining features of non-profit organizations to be the following. The sector would be assumed to include those organizations with some form of institutionalization (formal structure); organizations that are private, that is, institutionally separate from government; organizations operating on a non-profit/non-commercial basis; organizations that are self-governing; and those entities involving some meaningful degree of voluntary participation (even if only at board level). In addition, organizations within the Third Sector were taken to include those that have no religious affiliation and are not formally allied with political parties. Salamon and Anheier's estimate of the size measured in terms of employment and expenditure of the non-profit sector for four European countries, the United States, and Japan in 1990 is given in Table 9.10.

These employment figures can be supplemented by the number of volunteers, which have been estimated for Germany, Italy, France, and the United States as the equivalent of about 4.7 million full-time employees (Kluzer, 1997). Petit and Soete (1996) estimated that the Community, Social and Personal Services (CSPS) sector represented more than one-third of total employment in the European Union in 1993, a share substantially greater than that of the manufacturing industry. This sector is relatively protected from broad macroeconomic swings because it encompasses many non-tradeable activities, that is, activities that depend upon physical contact and presence for delivery.[26] Evidence from a study of the Third Sector in Italy conservatively

---

[26] Freeman and Soete (1994) take a similar view when they argue that strategies for full employment in the older industrialized countries will rely on high-skill, internationally competitive industries and services and a second-tier 'sheltered' non-traded services sector, both of which will be heavily dependent on the use of information and communication technologies.

TABLE 9.10. *Basic non-profit sector, 1990*

Indicator	France	Germany	Italy	United Kingdom	United States	Japan	Average or total
Non-profit employment (000)	800	1,020	420	950	7,120	1,440	1,180
Non-profit as % of total employment	4.2	3.7	1.8	4.0	6.8	2.5	3.4
Non-profit as % of total service employment	10.0	10.4	5.5	9.4	15.4	8.6	8.9
Non-profit % employment growth (1980/90)	15.8	11.0	n.a.	n.a.	12.7	n.a.	n.a.
Non-profit operational expenditure (US$ b.)	39.9	53.7	21.6	46.6	340.9	94.9	597.6
NPS expenditure as % of GDP	3.3	3.6	2.0	4.8	6.3	3.2	3.5

Note: NPS = Non-profit sector; n.a. = not available.

Source: Modified from Salamon and Anheier (1994).

estimate that 200,000 jobs could be created over the period 1996–8 involving some 53,000 non-profit organizations (see Table 9.11) at the cost of an estimated 1.5 becu in additional public spending.

While insulated to some degree from market forces, the Third Sector is involved in providing services that people are able and willing to pay for, in traditional social service areas, and in a range of other domains. Various social and economic trends, such as the growing participation of women in the labour force, the ageing of the population, new demands for medical care, and changing skill requirements in the labour market, are creating a growing demand for services provided by non-profit organizations. In some cases, non-profit organizations are opening up new 'markets', they are becoming increasingly important players in governance processes, and they are contributing to the financial sustainability of the welfare system in various ways including attracting donations that complement the resources provided by the state. They often achieve financial sustainability from the sale of services; frequently producing services at a lower cost than the public or private sectors by mobilizing volunteers or by paying lower salaries (Barbetta, 1996).

TABLE 9.11. *Short-term job creation potential in the Third Sector in Italy, 1996*

Existing activities	Jobs created	Explanation
All areas	40,000	Legislative measures in favour of the non-profit sector
All areas	40,000	New labour legislation
New activities		
Environment	30–35,000	Environmental protection and recovery, recycling, both public and market demand
Welfare	25–30,000	Childcare, home care, and other services for which unmet market demand exists
Culture	25,000	Entertainment and exploitation of cultural heritage, both public and market demand
Training and information services	10,000	Services aimed primarily at the Third Sector itself
Sports	5,000	Services for the general public and special groups (disabled, elderly people, etc.)
National non-military service	15,000	1–2% of all conscientious objectors currently continue their activity as a job
Other areas	5,000	Integration services for non-European Union immigrants
TOTAL	200,000	

Source: Passamonti and Lucchi (1998) adapted from Lunaria (1996).

Such organizations often work with socially disadvantaged groups and they play a variety of intermediary roles. Large numbers of volunteer workers also are being exposed to new applications of technologies and services thereby enhancing the skills base and potentially stimulating the market for hardware and software components, as well as services. A survey of the role of advanced communication and information technologies and services in addressing factors contributing to social exclusion suggests that efforts are concentrated in particular types of organizations (Silverstone and Haddon, 1997). The organizations involved in trial services sponsored by the European Commission's programmes tend to be local and regional governments, universities, and other research institutions, and, to a lesser extent, non-governmental organizations. Small, specialized firms working in new technical areas, such as multimedia software and interface design, often play a more active role. However, Third Sector organizations have been extremely active in developing activities using the Internet. In the United States, FidoNet, for instance, introduced an amateur electronic mail system in 1984, which subsequently spread to Europe and beyond. The community-focused Free-Net initiative also was born in the United States using bulletin-board technologies. In Europe, Free-Nets have been established in Finland, Germany, Italy, the Netherlands, Spain, Sweden, and the United Kingdom. Under different schemes, and often with similar aims and characters, voluntary efforts, donations by private companies, and public support have been responsible for establishing many of these community networks across Europe. In 1996, about 600 non-profit organization web sites located in the European Union Member States were recorded by a major directory containing over 8,000 entries; 44 per cent of these were located in the United Kingdom.[27]

In the further evolution of the European information society, the Third Sector is likely to play an important role in providing a source of new employment and a means of enabling excluded or marginalized groups to experiment with and implement information and communication technology applications that can be provided on a sustainable basis. The Third Sector's contributions in encouraging broad social participation in the information society provide important illustrations of how the virtual community strategy can flourish in an environment that facilitates access to the information and communication infrastructure and which, at the same time, provides for the 'free' exchange of the kinds of information that citizens can use to support their business and leisure-time activities. The public sector is also contributing to a growing number of initiatives that support virtual community formation. In the next section we turn to an investigation of the number of civic web sites, to illustrate the significance of initiatives to use the Internet in Europe to build new forms of social cohesion.

9.3.2 Civic Web Site Developments in Europe

In 1997, another study undertaken by Databank, Milan produced the first evidence of the scale of web-based activity in Europe that is aimed at the construction of innovative 'virtual' towns and cities for European citizens. A survey undertaken at the beginning of 1997 found evidence of about 2,000 web sites for European cities and towns, of which 1,300 had been established by local authorities, which represents about 4 per cent of all the local authorities in Europe.[28] Three types of web sites and networks were investigated:[29] *city web sites*—unofficial sites containing mainly tourist information on

[27] One of the most comprehensive global directories of non-profit organization web sites is provided by the Contact Center Network, which has links to over 8,000 sites in 100 countries. The Network is a New York-based non-profit organization founded in 1994 with the aim of creating a global network of community-based centres, linking individuals and organizations working in the field. The 1996 data were obtained from http://www.contact.org/ in March 1997. The same organization was at http://www.idealist.org in Nov. 1999 and listed many more sites under a variety of subject areas. As is the case for all such Internet directories, full coverage of all non-profit web sites is not guaranteed. For instance, the 266 sites reported for the UK can be compared with over 800 web sites from another list of charities produced in the UK. Based on cross-checking with other lists, some countries appear to be better represented than others.

[28] The original research in this section was undertaken by Stefano Kluzer and Marco Farinelli (1997), Databank Consulting, Milan.

[29] The survey was carried out in Nov. 1996–Jan. 1997. There is duplication of data across directories of European civic/city web sites. The most authoritative and popular listings for each country were identified and the results compared. For civic web sites, where available, the starting-point was the official web site of the public administration, of the association or city, or of a related institution. 'Information-rich' countries (such as Denmark, Finland, Germany, The Netherlands, Sweden) generally provide information in an organized fashion, but there were few references in 'information-poor' countries. Each country has its own characteristics, which are mirrored on the web. For web sites (of non-English speaking countries), electronic project leaders and web-masters of the civic and city web sites were contacted. The absolute numbers of sites

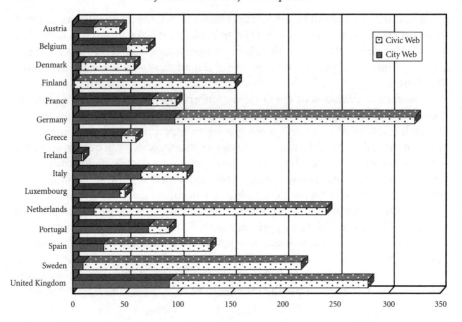

Fɪɢ. 9.2. Virtual towns in Europe, city and civic web sites in European Union Member States,
January 1997

Source: Kluzer and Farinelli (1997).

local attractions, or business information, which are often set up in collaboration with
local tourist boards or economic promotion agencies; *civic web sites*—the official sites
of local authorities normally at municipal level, including all web sites promoted
and/or administered by the local authorities, generally encompassing sites that make
civic information available to the public; and *community networks*—networks created
by education institutions, citizens' groups, and non-profit associations, that operate in
urban or rural areas to stimulate grassroots discussion and citizen participation, and
to assist in the co-ordination of community initiatives.

At the time the survey was undertaken, a common feature of these sites was that they
had a significant component of 'territorial' or 'community' content that was reflected
in the site names. The classification system that was used in the survey was based on
the main actors that appeared to be responsible for designing the sites. The distinctions between the three categories were often difficult to maintain and the breakdown
of the results is presented only for city and civic web sites. The total number of sites by
country is shown in Fig. 9.2 and the civic and city web sites as a proportion of total

should be treated with caution. The classification of all the sites on the basis of local socio-economic development levels and other features is a complex task and it was not possible to resolve all the difficulties in this
study.

TABLE 9.12. *City and civic web sites in the European Union, Jan. 1997*

	Hosts per 100 PCs 1997	City web	Civic web	Total web	Civic webs as % of local authorities	No. of local authorities	
Austria	7.87	20	26	46	1.1	2,301	Gemeinden
Belgium	5.73	52	21	73	3.6	589	Commune
Denmark	12.15	8	51	59	18.5	276	Commune
Finland	31.53	2	153	155	33.2	461	Kaupungit/Kunnat
France	5.28	76	23	99	n.a.	n.a.	n.a.
Germany	6.70	98	227	325	41.8	543	Kreise
Greece	7.03	47	14	61	0.2	5,939	Demoi
Ireland	8.75	9	7	16	0.6	105	Local councils
Italy	5.55	66	43	109	0.5	8,097	Comuni
Luxembourg	n.a.	46	5	51	4.2	118	Commune
Netherlands	11.44	21	220	241	31.3	702	Gemeenten
Portugal	6.60	73	20	93	6.6	305	Concelhos
Spain	6.51	30	101	131	1.3	8,066	Municipios
Sweden	15.54	10	208	218	72.2	288	Kommuner
United Kingdom	9.42	93	188	281	38.8	485	Local councils
EU TOTAL	8.26	651	1,307	1,958	4.6	28,280	

Note: France has more than 36,000 communes and these were not included in order to avoid altering the European Union (EU) total and average figures; n.a. = not available.

Source: Kluzer and Farinelli (1997) and International Telecommunication Union (1999) for Internet hosts 1997.

local authorities are shown in Table 9.12. This table also gives the number of hosts per 100 personal computers for each country in 1997.[30]

The results of the survey of estimated web site activity display a north–south divide. The northern countries, including Denmark, Finland, Sweden, Germany, The Netherlands, and the United Kingdom, had the highest overall presence on the Internet, and a relatively high percentage of their local authorities were on-line. The civic web sites were playing a considerable external promotion role which elsewhere tended to be played by city sites. Conversely, the southern European and Mediterranean countries, including France, Italy, Spain, Greece, and Portugal, had a lower presence of municipalities on the Internet, and more city than civic webs, with the notable exception of Spain. Nevertheless, the opportunity offered by the Internet to publicize local resources and attractions and to establish new contacts with the external world was being

[30] Within the 'city' category, sites were excluded that were citizen initiatives and commercial, as were sites of travel and tourist companies providing information and pictures about guided tours, and accommodation opportunities in a town or area. In order to restrict the scope of the web search for sites, subnational groups and administrative entities, such as regional councils, as well as business associations and education centres, and business or science parks (technopoles) were generally excluded. The data shown in this figure should be treated with caution especially as community networks, initiated and developed at grassroots level, are difficult to identify and they have been added to civic sites.

exploited even by those countries where the Internet was less well-developed. The majority of civic sites and community networks were concentrated in the leading industrial areas, while city web sites tended to predominate in rural and tourist areas.

If a city was a metropolis, it was likely to have a civic and also a prominent city site, studded with satellite web sites. Larger cities had started to promote integration with neighbouring areas. This was the case, for instance, for the Metropolitan Area Network of Digital Metropolis Antwerp, which linked some 30 administrations in its sur-rounding area. Medium-sized cities were characterized by the absence of an on-line presence for local authorities, but they were likely to have city web sites. In the case of smaller towns, rural villages, or tourist locations, there were signs of intermunicipal aggregations often relying on a single Internet Service Provider (ISP) for neighbour-ing areas.

Business-oriented ISPs played a promotional and supporting role, especially for local authorities in smaller towns and tourist areas. Research and educational institu-tions were involved in these initiatives in some countries, such as Germany and Italy. In Sweden, Spain, France, and Italy, local authority associations appeared to be active in stimulating and supporting independent and co-operative initiatives amongst their members. ISPs have been active in providing technical support to local authorities, often on a favourable basis, as they seek to attract a growing critical mass of users. Aside from initiating or facilitating a 'waterfall effect' of attraction to the Internet, once local authorities become aware of the potential of the Internet they are also deemed more likely to be favourable to initiatives to connect local libraries, schools, and health centres, thus creating the potential for new revenues for the ISP.

Although the results of this survey need to be treated with considerable caution because of the problems of measuring the extent of activity, it appears that the range of organizations, including non-profits, public administrations, and private-sector firms, was substantial even at the beginning of 1997 when the number of Internet hosts in Europe was not nearly as great as at the end of the decade. However, the exis-tence of web sites provides little insight into the range of organizational dynamics that underpins the new virtual community strategies. It merely points to the probable exis-tence of such dynamics. The significance of activities that are being developed by local and regional actors to take advantage of the potential of the information and commu-nication infrastructure, is the subject of the two case studies presented in the next section. The case studies highlight the differences in the approaches that are being developed.

9.3.3 Shifts in Regional Powers and Organization

As new forms of global and local relationships in the political, socio-economic, and cultural spheres are being shaped by developments in the global economy as well as at the local and regional levels, many forms of governance are being restructured to enable the devolution of powers to the regional or subregional, and often metropoli-tan, levels.[31] The deployment of information and communication technologies is con-

---

[31] The research for this section was undertaken by Stefano Kluzer, Databank, Milan for Emilia Romagna and Peter Hounsome of the Welsh Development Agency; see Kluzer and Hounsome (1998).

tributing to this process both by reducing the scale at which complex activities can be managed, and by increasing the scale at which the co-ordination of independent actors is feasible. The specific characteristics of the design and implementation of the information and communication infrastructure are putting pressure on established identities and social bonds and, at the local level, the adjustment processes are often very intense.

The European Commission has promoted the co-ordination or 'concertation' of the activities of a large number of public and private actors at the regional and urban levels through the Inter-Regional and Regional Information Society Initiatives (IRISI) and the Regional Information Society Initiatives (RISI). Despite the expansion of the global reach of business transactions, most transactions continue to be localized within national and regional boundaries. In addition, many social interactions within Europe take place exclusively at the local level. Labour mobility in Europe is much more limited compared to the United States, and the new information and communication infrastructures are creating new ways of opening European regions 'to the global'. This opening process is bringing many new opportunities as well as threats to local and regional economies. In response, local and regional initiatives are contributing to a 'refounding' of local communities where traditional boundaries of responsibility are blurring and new social and economic relationships are being forged within the virtual spaces of the Internet as well as other applications of technology.

The experiences of Emilia Romagna in Italy and Wales in the United Kingdom illustrate some of the changes in the relationships within and between the regions of Europe. Emilia Romagna is a wealthy and dynamic region (one of the twenty richest in the European Union), and Italy is not in the lead in Europe with respect to the diffusion of innovative information and communication services or applications. Wales, in contrast, is one of the poorest European regions, but, as part of the United Kingdom, it is located within a leading country in Europe with respect to the transition towards the information society. Both regions are characterized by a strong presence of small and medium-sized enterprises. Emilia Romagna's economy is driven to a considerable extent by the presence of indigenous small and medium-sized entrepreneurial firms. The Welsh economy is also populated mainly by small and medium-sized enterprises, but an important driver of growth during the 1990s has been foreign direct investment. Both regions share the absence of a large metropolis and both have experienced problems as a result of urban and rural imbalances in the regional economy.

9.3.3.1 The Emilia Romagna Region

Emilia Romagna has a predominantly provincial lifestyle and most of its 4 million population live in urban centres of 100,000 to 380,000 inhabitants, or less. Many of its smaller companies operate in high value-added light manufacturing sectors. The region has a thriving food industry, which supports agricultural machinery and food-processing and packaging industries as well as wholesale and retail trade companies. Ceramic tiles and the knitwear industry, and the electro-mechanical and machinery industries, contribute to the health of the regional economy. Service industries are important, including tourism on the Adriatic coast, which accounts for the largest employment share, while manufacturing accounts for almost 30 per cent of employment. The economy is heavily dependent on small and medium-sized enterprises. Of a total of 300,000 firms, 200,000 were actively comprised of only self-employed individuals. In manufacturing, there are about 65,000 firms, of which only about 20 (headquartered in the region) have more than 500 employees, some 1,000 firms have between 50 and 499 employees, and the others are smaller (Micelli, 1997). The region benefits from a good health care and education infrastructure, active municipal governments, and the presence of many small organizations, such as political parties, entrepreneurial associations and co-operatives, and voluntary groups.

The economy is highly export-oriented and acquisitions of local firms by foreign firms have been increasing, which has been paralleled by the expansion of local firms to activities in external markets. The region has a very flexible labour market. Over 50 per cent of all the new jobs created in the first half of 1997 (about 120,000 of 240,000) were temporary jobs, an increase of 27 per cent over the first quarter of 1991. Including part-time, apprenticeship, and work-training contracts, about 75 per cent of all new employment is in the flexible category.

Internet access by the academic and research community in Emilia Romagna began early due to the presence near Bologna of Cineca, a consortium established in 1969 to provide advanced data-processing and communication services to all universities in the north-east of Italy. In July 1994, Cineca opened its Internet service to the public via the Nettuno Network. Cineca played an important role in the first civic network by providing bulk high-capacity Internet access (Foschini, 1997). In terms of the regional distribution patterns, of 380 points of presence in mid-1997, 80 per cent were located in nine provincial capital towns, accounting for about 37 per cent of the regional population, and there was, therefore, a strong urban bias in access. ISPs, especially the smaller ones serving local firms, were playing a crucial role in raising awareness of the Internet's potential and by providing support services from basic training and assistance to web page production and hosting.

To counter the potentially negative effects of such disparities, the regional government initiated a number of projects aimed at establishing Internet services in some of the mountainous and peripheral areas of the region. Nine projects started in 1997 representing 4 mecu. Most of the projects focused on the establishment of a leased-line telecommunication infrastructure and on the development of communication, administrative, and management-oriented services that could be shared by the municipalities (ibid.).

In Italy, local governments provide public relations offices and these organizations have often been the initiators of web-based civic sites and networks. These public relations offices were introduced in 1990 as part of a government reform process. They were able to adopt Internet technology without having to abandon pre-existing networks and equipment. The mandate for reform called for one-stop information access points for citizens, producing pressure to communicate more transparently, and to integrate procedures. In order to promote such integration the regional government initiated a programme to network all the offices in the region. Local governments also introduced civic networks.[32] These networks are characterized by a strong role for the local municipal or provincial governments that initiate them by installing public Internet servers and providing content. These sites aim to move beyond promotion and information provision to on-line administrative services and interaction with the citizens. These developments are providing opportunities to share infrastructure costs and to encourage improved communication and integration between local authorities. Although the most common service in 1998 supported the downloading of pro formas for administrative procedures, in most cases local authorities have looked to the new applications as tools to improve their administrative efficiency and service delivery to citizens, especially in the face of a trend towards the privatization of public services.

Emilia Romagna's experience with electronic government—or e-government— highlights three important issues. First, Internet-based services can be used to create opportunities to reorganize local authorities and administrations to achieve greater inter-institutional integration, to simplify administrative procedures, improve external transparency, and offer greater accessibility, but there is no guarantee that these services will be fully responsive to citizen needs. Second, public-sector employees were often ill-equipped for the new interactive environment and major retraining efforts were necessary. Third, the goals and practices of government with respect to public access to information are often challenged through the introduction of new services. When they are challenged in a co-operative environment, traditional coercive policies may give way to the creation of strong symbolic, identity-building procedures that help to achieve greater co-operation and consensus among community members.

Two factors are contributing to the changes in the way public services are being provided at the local or regional level. One is the move towards bureaucratic simplification and greater efficiency and the other is the growing tradeability of a wide range of business services. In the face of these two factors, some intermediaries are adopting information and communication technology applications to improve efficiency and to achieve cost reductions in the provision of services. These organizations enhance the convenience of service use and encourage considerable opportunities for learning to innovate in the provision of new services. Developments in the e-government area, as in the e-commerce area, suggest that intermediaries will play a continuing and important role despite the potential at least for direct government-to-citizen contact and interaction.

This region has been deeply engaged in managing the institutional (organizational and social) processes of change through a transition from those requiring physical proximity and face-to-face interaction to those that are mediated by the information and communication infrastructure. In the case of the Emilia Romagna region the success of the new forms of interaction appears to depend upon the affinity and complementarity of intentions and interests of the actors, and upon their capacity to communicate effectively regardless of where they are located. The shift to the more

---

[32] The definition of civic networks varies throughout Europe to include digital cities, web cities, civic networks, and community networks and no single definition has emerged as the standard.

intensive provision of e-government services is accompanied by the uneven development of the capacities of citizens to use the new services. This may produce fragmentation and the disarticulation of established local communities at the same time that
new communities are formed.

9.3.3.2 Wales

In contrast to the prosperity of Emilia Romagna, Wales has a GDP per capita that is
only 81 per cent of the European Union average. The region is predominantly rural
with 2.9 million inhabitants. Reindustrialization has led to the introduction of
modern manufacturing techniques within the steel industry, and attracted light engineering, chemicals, plastics, and electronics firms into the region. The attraction
of foreign investment has been central to the redevelopment of the Welsh economy.
A regional development organization for Wales, the Welsh Development Agency
(WDA), was established in 1976 and the region draws considerable strength from a
strong identity founded upon its traditions in education, culture, and co-operative
action, as well as the devolution to a Welsh National Assembly, which was completed
in 1999. The rural areas of Wales are characterized by numerous small, close-knit
communities with strong identities, while the more urbanized areas have a more
ethnically and socially diverse make-up. The rural areas have been under pressure and
a weakening of its communities has been occurring with the emigration of young
people and the immigration of older, often retired, people. There are also high levels
of unemployment in the rural areas as a result of their industrial heritage in mining.

As a result of its peripheral location and relatively low population density, Wales has
seen comparatively low levels of public infrastructure investment. In the 1980s attention began to focus on the contribution that new telecommunication facilities might
make to the economic growth potential of the region. The SWMAN (South Wales
Metropolitan Area Network) was constructed employing switched fibre optics to link
eight universities and colleges in the south and south east of Wales at speeds of 155
bits/s, comprising over 80 miles of fibre optic cable and giving access to some 50,000
students and staff, that is, to 70 per cent of higher education institutions in the region.

However, the extension of this network capacity to other parts of the region has
been difficult because of the comparatively poor economic performance and low
population density. The WDA has sought to bring telecommunication providers
together to consider alternative methods of provision. Where the advanced infrastructure is in place economic benefits are becoming evident. For example, there has
been a rapid growth of call centres for customer service and support. Lloyds TSB telephone banking system's call centre is based in Newport, employing 2,000 people, and
other telebanking and tele-insurance centres are established in south Wales. The
WDA, in association with the Development Board for Rural Wales (DBRW), and
Welsh local authorities, initiated an action to encourage the introduction of a high-
bandwidth telecommunication infrastructure within rural Wales as part of what is
known as the Pathway Project (LlwybrPathway Project, 1998). The LlwybrPathway
Project aims to support local area network access, the development of services, training, and awareness-building among businesses and individuals. The project seeks to

involve all interested parties within rural Wales and has established a number of strategic and operational work groups comprised of experts drawn from public, private, and voluntary bodies operating within the region. One of the main focuses of Pathway to date has been the development of an extensive network of public access points throughout the region.

Another project is the Rural Wales Network, which connects local authority offices and other sites throughout Powys. Built by Powys County Council, the vision behind this initiative was the creation of a network environment that would serve the Council's own internal communication needs, and also serve as a public resource for business and community use throughout the region. At Networks '95, a leading industry show in the United Kingdom, Powys County Council won awards in the public-sector category and for best network project of the year. The network provides county-wide links for public organizations, the primary, secondary, and tertiary education sectors, and the voluntary sector, and has a developing role in support of the development of business and tourism. The network also links into the Internet giving the majority of its 3,000 users, at over 100 sites, full World Wide Web and e-mail access. In 1996, at a cost of almost £0.5m, the network was rebuilt and extended to meet the needs of local government reorganization. European Commission funding was secured to interconnect the networks of local authorities to form an extensive Rural Wales Intranet, with additional access points being developed at schools, telecentres, village shops, and libraries. By the end of 1998, the project had succeeded in funding 124 access points to technology for smaller firms and individuals in public locations to encourage shared access. In 1995 the Welsh Office Education department launched the Welsh Office Multimedia Portables Initiative, which was aimed at equipping all primary and special needs schools in Wales with up-to-date computer equipment including multimedia personal computers and CD-ROM titles. Equipment worth approximately £3m was distributed to schools in the region to be used for teaching literacy, numeracy, and science skills to children, and information technology skills to teachers.

Government services in Wales are delivered either directly or, more commonly, through a network of public, quasi-autonomous or private organizations including local government networks, the Welsh Development Agency and the Training and Enterprise Councils (TECs). The Internet is being used to provide information on local areas through the establishment of area-specific web sites containing details of council services, local businesses, and tourist facilities, and, in certain cases, to provide a means of communication with council members and officers. The Councils are using Intranets to provide communication links between large numbers of remote sites, and between council officers and members who work primarily from home.

Wales is heavily dependent upon small firms: there are over 60,000, and 90 per cent of Welsh businesses employ fewer than ten people. There is little quantitative evidence of the bottom-line benefits from the introduction of new technologies and this is especially so for local services and public-sector applications. The benefits of a web site for a small manufacturer or specialist retailer may be apparent in the form of expansion of the customer base, increased brand awareness, or improved communication.

However, the benefits of a web site for citizen information services are more difficult to demonstrate. The region has the highest concentration of telecottages or telecentres in the United Kingdom with more than 40 centres and some 2,000 associated tele-workers.[33] These are involved in reskilling initiatives that are designed to contribute to the regeneration of economically deprived areas.

9.3.3.3 The Impact of Exclusion

Left unchecked, the spread of information society technologies and services tends to exacerbate ingrained regional inequalities. Without intervention the absence of infra-structure investment will tend to reproduce the status quo or worsen economic dis-parities between the rural and urban areas of regions. The evidence for both Emilia Romagna and Wales suggests that the diffusion of information and communication technologies and services is providing regional authorities and organizations at all levels with opportunities to strengthen the co-ordination of their initiatives. There are expectations that local government services will be offered in a more transparent way and that they will become more accessible to citizens. The use of electronic networks appears to be contributing to measures to achieve greater inter-institutional integra-tion and the simplification of administrative procedures.

At the end of 1998, although there was a wide range of pilot projects underway in the rural areas of both regions, these had not been scaled up and it was unclear whether the new applications and services could be provided on a sustainable basis. The greater accessibility of the information and communication infrastructure in some areas is opening local communities and businesses to the wider European Union (and global) economy, but this has a double-edged effect. The activities of local groups are becom-ing oriented increasingly to managing their participation within global networks rather than within their immediate geographical environment. In the next section we examine some of the tensions between the goals of developing resources within the territorially bounded region and of building new virtual communities by drawing upon and integrating resources that are exogenous to the region itself.

9.3.4 Initiatives for Regional Development

Approaches to economic growth and development at the regional level in Europe tend to be characterized by tensions between the emphasis that is placed on developing exogenous and endogenous resources; between support for traditional sectors and new activities; and the emphasis that is given to supporting large companies and small firms.[34] Some approaches focus primarily on attracting multinational firms into a

---

[33] In Dec. 1998, there were an estimated 1.14 million teleworkers throughout the UK accounting for 4% of the labour force, a proportion exceeded in the European Union only by Ireland and Sweden (European Commission, 1999*d*).

[34] Much of the research in this section draws upon work by Annaflavia Bianchi, then at the Centre for Urban and Regional Development Studies (CURDS), University of Newcastle and Stefano Kluzer, Databank Consulting; see Bianchi and Kluzer (1997). The empirical evidence was drawn from a set of socio-economic studies funded mainly by the European Commission on telematics-related programmes throughout Europe. CURDS and TeleDanmark Consultancy provided sources of data and case studies, supplemented by information from the Local Economic and Employment Development (LEED) programme of the OECD.

region; some seek to increase the competitiveness of existing enterprises; while others focus mainly on avoiding or ameliorating social exclusion.

Most technology-led regional development initiatives are influenced by the view that the application of information and communication technologies will reduce the 'costs of distance' dramatically, thus helping to reduce the gaps between the more advanced and lagging regions. This type of thinking has led to efforts to improve infrastructure before demand has been expressed and the results have been mixed. For example, there is some evidence of success in attracting new service activities in cases where information and communication technologies have been used to render these activities relatively distance independent (Petit and Soete, 1996). Such activities can be located in areas where the workforce has appropriate skills and a willingness to work at wages that are attractive to employers. For the most part, these areas tend to be on the periphery of large metropolitan areas, or in smaller urban areas (Richardson and Gillespie, 1996).[35] In other regions, and especially in southern Europe, the expectations that infrastructure investment would promote regional development have not been fulfilled (Gillespie, 1996). For example, many small and medium-sized enterprises have not been able to operate in distant markets either because they are too small or because they lack the expertise or resources needed to operate outside their local markets. Gillespie (ibid.) has argued that the availability of the information and communication infrastructure may promote market expansion for small firms that are already competitive in the global market, but that there is little evidence that availability as such will guarantee their growth and development.

The European Commission's 'learning region' approach to regional development focuses on the regeneration of the institutional framework, the diffusion of relevant information, and the reinforcement of human capabilities at the local level (Cornford, Gillespie, and Richardson, 1996). This approach favours co-operation between firms to promote specialization, complementarities, and linkages between local clusters of enterprises (see Table 9.13). Where local authorities, trade associations, consultants, and citizen's groups work together with small firms and other citizens it is often possible to foster demand for new information and communication technology applications, as well as to encourage the emergence of diverse regional information societies, each with a different focus and emphasis on various application fields.

Measures to introduce applications that are consistent with active participation in the information society by people within the regions of the European Union require the formulation of strategies in support of virtual community activities.[36] A review of the principal factors in the success of regional development initiatives that have been designed to encourage the use of the information and communication infrastructure throughout Europe suggests that the success of strategies for local and regional development is strongly influenced by a combination of factors including the strength of local authorities in terms of their powers and competencies; the presence

---

[35] An exception to this pattern is the Highlands and Islands of Scotland initiative where the upgrading of the telecommunication network together with fiscal incentives and the presence of a high-quality workforce have drawn new business into this rural region. In the medium term, however, changes in economic conditions could lead to the transfer of these new footloose activities to other locations.

[36] A model for active participation has been developed by Qvortrup and Bianchi (1996).

TABLE 9.13. *The learning region*

View of Information Society (IS)	Information Society as telecommunication society	Information Society as innovation or learning society
Spatial logic	IS → reduction in transaction costs → new locational freedoms → search for lower cost locations → relocation of activities from core to less favoured regions	IS → increased tempo of technological innovation → new market uncertainties and risks → continued clustering of activities in information rich milieux (core regions)
Dominant form of information	Standardized and codified information	Non-standard, ambiguous information
Competitive ground	Cost-based competition	Knowledge-based competition

Source: Cornford, Gillespie, and Richardson (1996).

of key actors that are prepared to take a leading role; the level of enthusiasm for innovative actions and experimentation; the extent to which public and private partnerships have been established; and the willingness to depart from existing routines and practices (Bianchi and Kluzer, 1997).

These institutional factors are important determinants of whether new virtual community strategies can flourish at the regional or local levels. In many cases, local or regional groups must overcome barriers to accessing key components of the information and communication infrastructure. The diffusion of basic components of the infrastructure is generally reported at the aggregate national level. However, disparities between the core regions of the European Union and those defined as Less Favoured Regions, or 'cohesion' areas, are important signifiers of a wider class of constraints that face businesses and citizens who reside in the non-core areas.[37] Table 9.14 shows variations in the availability of the telecommunication infrastructure in the mid-1990s between the two types of region.

A detailed analysis of the costs of infrastructure access in the same time period showed that, on average, the costs of installation of a business telephone line in the cohesion regions was about 40 per cent higher than in the core regions. The costs of a connection for mobile telephony was also about 30 per cent higher in the cohesion regions than in the core areas on average (ibid.).

[37] 'Cohesion' data include four countries, Greece, Ireland, Portugal, and Spain, plus the Italian southern regions, that are eligible for European Commission Structural Funds support under Objective 1. The analysis of 'core' and 'cohesion' region performance was based on empirical evidence drawn from socio-economic studies (funded mostly by the European Commission) of telematics-related programmes and projects during the Fourth Framework Programme. CURDS, University of Newcastle, and Tele Danmark Consult A/S provided the main sources of data and case studies and additional information was provided by the LEED programme at OECD, see Bianchi and Kluzer (1997); NEXUS Europe—Centre for Urban and Regional Development Studies—University of Newcastle (1996).

TABLE 9.14. *Indicators of cohesion and access gaps*

Network or service	Cohesion average	Core average	Cohesion divergence
Public switched telecom network			
Waiting time (years) 1994	0.2	0.0	+0.2
Satisfied demand (%) 1994	96.9	100.0	−3.1
Faults per 100 main lines 1994	32.6	11.3	+188%
Digital lines (%) 1994	60.6	71.2	−10.6
ISDN (primary rate)			
Geographic coverage 1994	32.3%	85%	−52.7
Projected coverage 1996	80.0%	100%	−20.0
Public on-line services			
CompuServe nodes per 1m. people 1995	0.05	0.54	−91%
Dial-up numbers per 1m. people 1995	0.36	1.94	−81%

Source: Data collated from various sources, see Bianchi and Kluzer (1997).

The IRISI (Inter-Regional Information Society Initiative) and RISI (Regional Information Society Initiative), co-funded by the European Commission, were introduced in an effort to establish a common framework, and to provide financial support and co-ordination mechanisms to promote integrated information society strategies especially in the disadvantaged regions of Europe. IRISI was launched at the end of 1994 with the support of several European Commission Directorates with responsibilities for information and communication technology, regional development, and social policy.[38] This initiative involved a bottom-up approach in an attempt to ensure that the European Commission played the role of a catalyst of change and a broker of successful experiences.[39] Based on the experience of this initiative a new generation of actions for the information society, RISI, was launched in 1996 involving twenty-three regions and a budget of 6 mecu. Table 9.15 summarizes the results of a review of the characteristics of regional initiatives to increase

[38] Six regions signed a Memorandum of Understanding on 28 Nov. 1994 in which they committed themselves to promoting the information society in their respective territories through partnerships with the private sector, and between actors in the social and economic sphere. They also committed to co-operating with each other, exchanging experience, and developing applications and services. Financial support was devoted to the definition of a regional strategy and action plan (DG XVI), the creation of a European Network for the six Regions (DG XIII), studies on the information society and employment, human resource and work organization (DG V), and monitoring and evaluating the initiative. The six regions involved were the North-West of England, UK; Saxony, Germany; Nord-Pas-de-Calais, France; Valencia, Spain; Central Macedonia, Greece; and Piedmonte, Italy.

[39] At the beginning of 1995 a consortium was selected to monitor and evaluate the IRISI. The team's main task was to describe the nature, process, and content of the initiative (in each region and in the dynamics between regions and with the EC) and to extract the main lessons from these pilot experiences. The team, co-ordinated by Technopolis Ltd. included CURDS, University of Newcastle, MERIT, University of Maastricht, and regional teams, University of Thessaly and University of Athens, ASTER, Quasar and University of Valencia, Central Management International and Empirica.

TABLE 9.15. *Comparison of northern and southern characteristics in regional telematics initiatives*

Northern Europe regional telematics initiatives	Southern Europe regional telematics initiatives
Often close to urban centres and have narrower geographic coverage	Often remote from urban centres and have wider geographic coverage
More bottom-up involvement in initiatives with exogenous initiation and support	Strong top-down and exogenous initiation and support
Initiatives embedded in competitive and commercially oriented environments	Co-operative and socially oriented approaches
More diversified funding sources and greater flexibility as to use	Reliance on single funding sources which curtails flexibility of usage
Use of fewer staff, many of whom are full-time and/or paid with specialist support (especially in management, marketing, and consultancy)	Relatively large number of staff who are not necessarily full-time or paid
Low staff continuity	High staff continuity
Efficiency and 'best practice' are more important than familiarity with local conditions	Familiarity and integration with local conditions rather than a 'best practice' or efficiency oriented approach
Less reliance on user-friendly telematics technology	Reliance on user-friendly and relatively simple telematics applications

Source: Adapted from Millard (1996: 13) in Bianchi and Kluzer (1997).

opportunities to participate in building the information society. The results suggest that north–south regional differences in terms of project development, top-down versus bottom-up approaches, financial stability, and opportunities for staff development and skills acquisition were characteristic features of the initiatives that were examined (Millard, 1996: 13).

Investment in new information and communication technology applications by the European Commission is intended to strengthen the skills base for using technologies and services in ways that will contribute to the goals of users and to stimulate demand for applications that can be provided on a commercially sustainable basis. In order to achieve this, it is important for potential users to be able to gain experience of new applications through their exposure (or direct involvement) in applications trials and demonstrations. During the Fourth Framework Programme, Bernard *et al.* (1997) reported that within the Advanced Communication Technologies and Services (ACTS) Programme, about sixty trial locations (from a total of 117 trials) for broadband networks, advanced communications services, and multimedia applications were situated in depressed areas, rural areas, industrial reconversion areas, or the Nordic regions. In the Telematics Application Programme, about 25 per cent of validation sites associated with various projects were located in the Less Favoured

TABLE 9.16. *Location of validation sites in the Telematics Applications Programme, European Commission, 1997*

Country	No. of towns	No. of validation sites in the capital	No. of validation sites in the three largest towns	No. of validation sites
Austria	16	9	18	34
		26%	53%	100%
Belgium	22	34	41	66
		52%	62%	100%
Denmark	15	18	29	48
		38%	60%	100%
Finland	17	25	34	64
		39%	53%	100%
France	60	29	49	141
		21%	35%	100%
Germany	59	14	34	140
		10%	24%	100%
Greece	33	45	62	98
		46%	63%	100%
Ireland	14	23	33	55
		42%	60%	100%
Italy	52	33	63	145
		23%	43%	100%
Luxembourg	n.a.	n.a.	3	n.a.
Netherlands	42	18	42	103
		17%	41%	100%
Portugal	n.a.	n.a.	31	n.a.
Spain	36	41	71	116
		35%	61%	100%
Sweden	22	16	28	54
		30%	52%	100%
United Kingdom	56	35	49	147
		24%	33%	100%

Note: n.a. = not available.

Source: Based on data for the Telematics Applications Programme, European Commission, see Bianchi and Kluzer (1997).

Regions. Table 9.16 shows the distribution of these sites between major cities and other areas by country. These data suggest that the geographic concentration of validation sites was rather high on average and this degree of concentration was also reflected in the geographic concentration of the main institutions involved, for example, advanced education and research establishments, local authorities in the larger cities, telecommunication companies, and other large firms.[40] In each of the three cohesion countries, Greece, Ireland, and Spain (data for Portugal were not available), and also in Belgium and Denmark, the capital and the second largest city host over 60 per cent of all validation sites. At the other end of the spectrum in terms of the geographic dispersion of sites, were France, the United Kingdom, and Germany, where the four cities with the largest number of sites hosted less than 40 per cent of the total (29 per cent in Germany) (Bianchi and Kluzer, 1997).

9.3.5 Summary

This section has provided a brief overview of the efforts that have been undertaken through a variety of projects supported by the European Commission and by national, regional, or local authorities to reduce the problems encountered by those in economically disadvantaged, and rural areas, of the European Union. The available evidence indicates that initiatives that have sought to link the application of advanced information and communication technologies and services with regional (and local) development goals have a greater likelihood of success than those that are delivered by technology and service developers without the direct involvement of stakeholders in the region. At least by the mid-1990s, despite a number of initiatives, there was evidence that the reduction of gaps in the accessibility and affordability of the information and communication infrastructure between the advantaged and disadvantaged regions would continue to prove difficult to achieve. Reviews of the experiences of participants in projects financed both by the European Commission and by national, regional, and local authorities indicate that there are very substantial differences in the approaches to supporting information society developments among the regions and countries of Europe. This is both a strength, in the sense that it encourages diversity in the experimentation with new forms of virtual community strategies, but also a potential weakness in so far as it reduces the potential to exploit economies of scale that might help to reduce the investment costs associated with the deployment of infrastructure and services.

The available studies of the progress towards the information society at the regional level in Europe provide few systematic insights into the micro-level at which social transformation, the shift in governance powers to enable greater authority at the local or regional level, and the changes in the competencies and skills base for business enterprises are being experienced by people located in the more disadvantaged regions of Europe. However, the scale and scope of existing efforts to deploy infrastructure and to develop new applications suggests that the process of building new virtual communities is likely to continue to challenge both the public and private sectors, as well as representatives of the non-profit or Third Sector, to achieve increasing co-ordination of their efforts. We argue that this is a prerequisite for sustained action that will support both the economic and social development of the regions of Europe as the

---

[40] See ASSENT (1999c) for an analysis of social and economic factors contributing to the development of telematics applications within the Telematics Applications Programme projects specifically oriented to Urban and Rural Areas.

diffusion of information and communication technologies and services continues to coincide with large transformations in the way business is conducted and civil society is organized. In the next section, we turn to a discussion of the potential of the diffusion and use of the Internet to destabilize the institutional arrangements for taxation by government authorities.

9.4 The Internet and Taxation Issues

The Internet is a breeding ground for new ways of trading goods and services.[41] The possibility of direct access to suppliers is increasing market transparency and some market observers forecast a trend towards declining intermediary costs (Leebaert, 1998). In some cases the intermediary is being bypassed through a process described as 'disintermediation' (see Ch. 5). Although e-commerce is still in its earliest stages, virtually all observers anticipate its rapid growth and maturation as a widely utilized medium for both business-to-business and business-to-consumer transactions. The maturation of e-commerce will raise questions about the relationship between e-commerce institutions and practices, and those associated with traditional modes of business conduct. While e-commerce remains in an experimental stage of development, it is likely that the appropriate nature of this relationship will require a lengthy period of time to emerge and that, for many participants, this period is more likely to involve investments in learning and positioning than in the development of e-commerce as a core business strategy.

The growth of e-commerce is likely to proceed at a pace that allows adjustment and accommodation rather than the displacement and disruption of existing patterns of business. An assumption that e-commerce transactions should bear the same administrative, financial, or regulatory requirements and complexities as existing forms of business transactions is inconsistent with the objective of encouraging the investment and experimentation necessary for its healthy development. Over a longer time period, when e-commerce becomes a serious competitor to other methods of conducting business, concerns will have to be addressed about whether the commercial environment provides a level playing-field for testing the most efficient means of conducting business. The policies that are put in place during the early phase to promote experimentation and growth will come to be viewed as subsidies and their magnitude and effects will have to be quantified.

For the early growth of e-commerce a major, and often misunderstood, policy has been adopted with regard to the 'taxation' of e-commerce transactions (Cigler, Burritt, and Stinnett, 1996). It is important to be precise about the nature of the taxation issues presented by e-commerce because characterizations of the Internet as a tax-free zone for commerce are misleading. The current policy position in the OECD countries is that there should be no taxes that are specific to the conduct of Internet business. Business income taxation, however, is applied by all OECD countries and companies

[41] The material in this section is based substantially upon research by Luc Soete and Karin Kamp (1998).

that derive profits from the business they conduct on the Internet are obliged to pay taxes on these profits. Depending on the jurisdiction under which consumers live they may be required to pay sales or value added taxes on their purchases of physical goods.

Assessments of the implications of e-commerce for the government's capacity to generate revenues must determine the extent to which new business activity is being created by encouraging greater levels of consumption or increasing productivity in carrying out of transactions, or existing business activities are being displaced. In so far as the latter is the case, measuring the implications of e-commerce for taxation requires an understanding of *which* businesses are being displaced. If the displaced business is in areas with relatively low tax obligations, the fact that it is conducted on, or facilitated by, the Internet will have no impact upon the extent of tax revenues that are raised. If, on the other hand, the diverted business presently incurs a relatively high tax obligation, and the Internet makes it possible to reduce that, the result may be a tilt of the competitive playing-field towards further growth of e-commerce over rival means of conducting business, without necessarily establishing that the Internet is the more efficient means of conducting business.

The taxation issues of greatest concern to policy-makers and the private sector are the potential for the Internet to facilitate the arbitrage of international differences in value-added taxation for trade in intangible products (that is, information) and services and the potential the Internet creates for tax evasion. To the extent that consumption activities are becoming globally distributed as a result of the opportunities created by the application of e-commerce, transactions will become more difficult to trace. This is raising fears about the implications of the erosion of national tax bases (Boekhoudt and te Spenke, 1996). The development of e-commerce is enhancing the global accessibility and tradeability of tangible goods as well, and it is raising questions about the country of origin of many traded intangible goods.

The concerns about e-commerce and taxation are expressed somewhat differently in the United States and Europe, in part, because of institutional differences in consumption tax regimes, that is, between the United States sales tax system and the European Value Added Tax (VAT) system. In the United States, the mail order companies' local sales tax exemption means that e-commerce may erode tax revenues from local sales. Mail order sales are not exempt from sales tax in states where a company maintains a place of business (Blum, 1996). However, when these companies sell to out-of-state consumers, no sales tax is levied. Legislatures in the individual states of the United States have attempted to tax mail-order commerce through a 'use' tax. A use tax is a tax on the use of tangible personal property when the user has not paid sales tax; often with the same rate levied as in the case of a sales tax (Washington State Department of Revenue, 1993). However, since the vendor is not obliged to collect such taxes unless there is a physical presence within the state, this rarely occurs. Hence the use tax is only rarely enforced (McWilliams, 1997).

In Europe, retail value added taxes are based on the principle that the value-added generated by sales of goods or services is subject to tax. Value added taxes are synonymous with a final sales tax except for their means of collection. The means of collection makes an important difference in the effectiveness of the tax system (Pearce, 1994:

447). For example, in the United Kingdom the customer pays the full value added tax as a mark-up of the retail price. Retailers, however, do not remit this amount to the government as they are allowed to reclaim the amount of tax paid for all their purchases from their suppliers. This provides a strong incentive for the retailers to disclose their purchases and thus provides a means of monitoring the taxes paid by their suppliers. This incentive structure continues up the supply chain as each seller is allowed to deduct the taxes presumably paid by their suppliers, but this regime is effective only if the retailers record the purchases from their suppliers.

Thus, in Europe, the growth of e-commerce may undermine the VAT policy principle within the European Union by shifting VAT from the destination principle whereby consumption taxes are levied where goods or services are consumed, to the origin principle.[42] In addition, the issue of how to levy VAT on services, such as those offered by banks, insurance, telephone, or content-provider companies that are located outside the European Union is of concern to policy-makers. In practice, differences exist among European countries in the extent to which these services are currently taxed and in the rates at which they are taxed.

The intangibles sold via the Internet are typical information goods in so far as the marginal cost of producing an extra unit is close to zero. If the price of an intangible good is also close to zero then there is little opportunity or justification for raising tax revenues from the sale of such a good. However, if the price of the intangible good is significant, the vast majority of the revenue is, in effect, 'value added' and should be subject to taxation. The problem arises from the concentration of value addition at the point of delivery of the intangible product. The intangible goods supplier will recoup the value added tax from its suppliers for items, such as computers and office supplies, used in producing and delivering the immaterial good, on a proportion of its revenues. After this amount has been received, however, additional revenue will incur tax obligations at the full value added tax rate and the intangible goods provider has a strong incentive not to report this income. This will lead, however, to further problems if the company must account for its profits to tax authorities and shareholders.

Efforts to reduce the incentives to omit revenue would require improvements to the means of auditing revenue receipts. At present, 90 per cent of all financial transactions linked to consumption take place using cash, cheques, and credit cards. These systems involve intermediaries such as banks, credit card companies, or other financial institutions that leave an audit trail of payment. Electronic cash systems do not create such a trail. E-cash systems use 'tokens of value' expressed in digital form (see Ch. 8). E-cash transactions rely on deposit accounts allowing person-to-person transfers of e-cash. If e-commerce results in the widespread removal of these intermediary institutions from the transaction chain, an important source of information for tax authorities would no longer be available. In addition, the Internet might increase the possibility for citizens to access off-shore financial centres. The increasing convergence of technologies supporting information transmission and those enabling information provision also means that clear distinctions for taxation purposes will become difficult to maintain.

---

[42] The destination principle requires the monitoring of cross-border goods and services flows, which it is desirable to avoid in an integrated economic area.

If the role of retailer as tax collector becomes less appropriate as a result of the growth of e-commerce, it is unclear which institutions should play the role of tax intermediary. To preserve an audit trail, it has been suggested that tax registration numbers could be used to establish national boundaries for transactions. For example, in the case of the European Union VAT, suppliers of electronic goods and services located outside the European Union could be required to register for VAT and would be given a unique tax registration number. This information could be held in a central database that financial institutions would have to check before a payment could be made outside the European Union. If the validation process were unsuccessful, the financial institution could levy a withholding tax. Another approach might be to attach taxes to the process of issuing e-cash tokens such that when an individual buys the tokens, taxes would be collected immediately. In this case, financial institutions would play the role of intermediary *ex ante*. Other agents, such as telecommunication operators or ISPs, could collect taxes on the goods and services ordered via the Internet. Software producers could provide solutions to the problem of tax collection by building collection systems into browsers or e-commerce software.[43] These approaches represent efforts to plug the potential leak from sellers of intangible goods and services who choose not to report their sales. The costs imposed by their implementation would be substantial.

Yet another measure that has been proposed in response to concerns about the potential for the erosion of tax revenues is a bit tax (or transmission tax) which is basically a tax on electronic information transmission (Cordell *et al.*, 1997; Soete and Kamp, 1996; 1997). A bit tax would not be related in any direct way to the value of a transaction and, instead, would focus on the transmission of information. A bit tax would involve the introduction of bit measuring equipment within the information and communication infrastructure, enabling consumers to monitor the volume of bits transmitted via networks. ISPs could perform the function of tax collectors (Soete and Kamp, 1996; ter Weel, 1997). This measure is subject to criticism in so far as it would attribute a uniform value to information because 'value' would be related to the number of message bits that are required to transmit the information. There is no basis at present to believe that the size of a transmission is related to its added value. A bit tax would also levy taxes on transmissions that do not involve commercial transactions, such as the distribution of public-domain information that we discussed in Ch. 7.

The extent of the erosion of the tax base that will result from the loss of sales or value added tax revenue as a result of growth in the use of the Internet to support e-commerce is unknown. It is clear that the Internet provides significant new opportunities for choosing to locate business activities in jurisdictions that impose low rates

---

[43] Software systems exist that calculate the taxes on goods sold around the world. One software company is researching whether a VAT compliance system can be developed which would manage the VAT collection and remittance process. Such a program could provide Internet suppliers with a facility to register for VAT compliance worldwide in conjunction with an automated service bureau that could collect and remit local VAT taxes to the appropriate authority. Or, alternatively, assuming support from tax authorities, Internet suppliers of goods and services would establish a clearing facility where local taxes are collected and remitted by the software system without the need to register for tax purposes in all countries.

of taxation on either sales or profits. However, ultimately, sales must be made to, and paid by, individuals who are located in particular jurisdictions. From the experience with use taxes in the United States it seems unlikely that individuals will remit to their local authorities the value added, or sales, tax on their purchases. For merchants that are located within the European Union, it is likely that the combination of reporting requirements for business income taxation and accountability will make the collection of value added taxes feasible. When merchants are located outside the European Union, the conduct of e-commerce in immaterial goods suggests that value added taxes will be difficult to collect without additional, burdensome, withholding procedures for international payments. Proposals for the introduction of new forms of indirect taxation in the form, for example, of a bit tax, raise a new set of problems because of the lack of a correspondence between the quantity of information and its value. In the United States the taxation issues arising from the growth of e-commerce are an exacerbation of their existing problems with the interstate administration of sales taxes. In Europe, the taxation problems arising from e-commerce largely stem from the difficulties of imposing value added taxes on immaterial imports, accompanied, perhaps, by additional problems created by non-reporting of income. It is instructive to examine how policy is evolving to deal with these issues.

9.4.1   Emerging E-Commerce Policy Positions

In the United States in 1998, the Clinton administration declared the Internet a duty-free zone for all electronic goods and services delivered across it for at least three years (Borland, 1998; Moltzen, 1998; Scannell, 1998). Under this duty-free system, a customer who orders software, or procures professional services, using the Internet is free of paying customs duties. This is consistent with the law in the United States where, for example, in the case of computer software, tariffs are imposed on the value of the medium, that is, on the computer disc or tape, and not on the value of the software. If the medium is eliminated by virtue of an electronic transaction, there is no transaction to which a tariff can be applied. However, when physical goods are ordered using the Internet and delivered by conventional means, such as in the case of a mail-order sale of clothing, then the transaction is subject to any generally applicable duties as if the goods had been ordered using the telephone or by mail.[44]

The argument in favour of a duty-free Internet trading system is intended to promote the use of e-commerce and the total amount of transactions that are conducted within the domestic economy (Dunahoo and Carlisle, 1997).[45] At the same time, however, there has been discussion within the United States about the viability of the current position. A plan that minimizes the government's role in the development of e-commerce has been introduced by President Clinton (De Bony, 1997;

[44] In practice, many imports into the United States and European countries, including mail-order purchases, are charged duties and/or value added tax. This is a problem for domestic trade in the United States where taxes often are not levied on mail-order goods transferred between states.

[45] See also coverage in *The Economist* (1995b; 1996a; 1996b; 1996c; 1997a; 1997b) and *Business Week* (1996a; 1996c).

Schneideran, 1999). In October 1998, the United States Senate approved a three-year moratorium on any new Internet taxes,[46] and by August 1999, the National Tax Association, which includes both government and private-sector representatives, had prepared a report on alternative options for future e-commerce taxation policy. The report reached no firm conclusions about the most appropriate future taxation regime because of the inability of the members of the association to reach agreement (Hardesty, 1999b).[47] A detailed study by Goolsbee (1999) of on-line consumers in the United States had suggested that the application of sales taxes to e-commerce could reduce the number of on-line buyers potentially by up to 24 per cent and reduce spending by more than 30 per cent.[48] These estimates clearly suggest that any move to introduce new forms of taxation on e-commerce transactions would be regarded as running counter to the government's objectives of stimulating the growth of e-commerce. The National Tax Association report was submitted to the Electronic Commerce Advisory Commission (ECAC), which was established to consider the need for future policy initiatives.[49] At the time of writing in December 1999, no further action had been taken at the federal level of government. The state level authorities in the United States have adopted varying approaches to the issue of Internet taxation. Some have taken no action, or are applying taxes based on existing laws (Frieden and Porter, 1996). Others have altered their interpretation of existing laws in order to include or exclude Internet activity for taxation purposes. Yet others have created new legislation to confront the issue and the majority of these new measures have been geared towards exempting the Internet from taxation.[50]

The OECD's response to the controversies over taxation as e-commerce expands throughout its member states was to propose a moratorium to 'avoid a proliferating patchwork of tax laws that could stifle e-commerce while this review is being conducted . . . such a moratorium would allow the authorities to participate actively in

---

[46] The Internet Tax Freedom Act (S.442/HR.1054) affects all taxes except those imposed and enforced prior to Oct. 1998 and prohibits multiple or discriminatory taxes on e-commerce, see Communications Media Center at New York Law School (1998a). During debates before the passage of the Bill, President Clinton stated that 'We cannot allow state and local jurisdictions to stifle the Internet, but neither can we allow the erosion of the revenue that governments need to fight crime and invest in education' (Communications Media Center at New York Law School, 1998b: 1).

[47] The report states, 'The inability to reach a comprehensive agreement may be traced not only to specific substantive disagreements, but also to the more profound policy differences—including the clash between state and local governments' concern for their authority, their need to preserve their tax base, diverse fiscal requirements, on the one hand, and the business community's concern for a simple, uniform, and administrable tax regime in which it can operate at a reasonable cost', cited in Hardesty (1999b: 2). Hardesty notes that 'the business models of many remote sellers, and especially e-commerce start-ups, depend on the fact that sales tax is not collected by sellers (or paid by buyers) on remote sales. For consumers, this amounts to a price reduction, which offsets both shipping costs, and the disadvantages inherent in purchasing from remote vendors' (ibid. 6).

[48] See also Hardesty (1999a).

[49] The Commission includes representatives from the California Board of Equalization (Chair), AT&T, the US Trade Representative, the Dept. of Commerce, Virginia, Oregon, Utah, Washington, Dallas, the National Conference of Commissioners on Uniform State Law, Americans for Tax Reform, Time Warner, America Online, Charles Schwab and Co. Dept. of the Treasury, MCI Worldcom, Association of Interactive Media, and Gateway.

[50] For further details, see 'Internet Taxation, Questions & Answers', Vertex Tax Cybrary at http://www.vertexinc.com, accessed 17 Nov. 1999.

devising internationally consistent policy recommendations' (OECD, 1997*b*: 1). In June 1998, the OECD Committee on Fiscal Affairs adopted new 'Framework Conditions' stating that the taxation principles that guide governments in relation to conventional commerce should also guide them in relation to e-commerce.[51]

The European Commission, like the United States administration, agreed to impose no new duties on Internet commerce in December 1997 (European Commission, 1997*d*). The Commission has addressed other taxation problems associated with the diffusion of information and communication technologies. For example, for telecommunication and Internet services, the 'supply of services' rules within the European Union have been amended such that, from 1998, non-European Union suppliers of telecommunication and Internet services must charge VAT to their European customers.[52] Foreign-owned companies must register and account for VAT in the country where the telecommunication services are supplied. In this case, tax is levied at the point of consumption rather than of supply.

The Commission rejected the proposal for a bit tax on the grounds that VAT already applies to electronic trade in goods and services transactions (European Commission, 1997*h*). The Commission also argued that a bit tax would trigger double taxation because communication on the Internet is taxed in the same way as communication services and equipment. The bit tax would not solve the issues raised by electronic transactions with respect to auditing, but this issue has been resolved for payment for the use of on-line databases, premium telecommunication services, and financial transactions. Companies engaging in electronic business transactions are required to levy the relevant VAT, or report why it has not been levied (Hutchison, 1996). The Commission also observed that a tax on physical transactions would be extremely difficult to implement in the e-commerce environment. The Commission's rejection of the bit tax proposal was also motivated by a concern that incentives for tax avoidance could be created and that techniques such as data compression or maintaining information in analogue form might be adopted. It was also argued that a bit tax could produce distortions in the economy that would be difficult to predict and that, as Europe was lagging behind the United States in 1997 in terms of Internet development, the prospect of taxation could slow take-up in Europe even more.

At a conference in Bonn in 1997 industry leaders and ministers from twenty-nine European countries, the United States, and Japan agreed that no additional tax or tariff should be imposed on transactions using global electronic networks. The Declaration called for a technology-neutral tax regime on information distributed electronically such that there is no discrimination for or against information distributed by other means. A future role for the OECD and the World Trade Organization in coordinating an international, uniform system for taxation and excise tax on information and communication technologies was also highlighted (Global Information

---

[51] See also Inland Revenue and HM Customs and Excise (1998) for the UK position which stresses the principles of neutrality with respect to technology, certainty and transparency, effectiveness, and efficiency.

[52] The VAT rules for taxation of services (or 'supply of services') are covered by a European Commission Directive and the general rule is based on the location of the supplier's business establishment, or other fixed establishment from which the supply is made or the place of residence. There are, however, exceptions.

Networks Conference, 1997*a*). In spite of the evident reluctance to consider any new forms of taxation for e-commerce transactions, the potential for revenue loss was acknowledged:

The potential speed, untraceability and anonymity of electronic transactions may also create new possibilities for tax avoidance and tax evasion. These need to be addressed in order to safeguard the revenue interests of governments and to prevent market distortions. Thorough analysis is therefore needed to evaluate the possible impact of electronic commerce on legislation (on issues such as definition, control and enforceability) and to judge if, and to what extent, present legislation needs to be adapted. (Global Information Networks Conference, 1997*b*: 2)

In the next section, we examine a preliminary effort to estimate the potential implications of the growth of e-commerce in Europe for the tax base. Given the complexities of this type of modelling exercise and the limitations of available data, the analysis is restricted to a single country case study.

9.4.2   Estimating the Revenue Implications

Value added tax, or VAT, is one of the main sources of government income in the Member States of the European Union and it is based on the nominal value of the transfer of goods and services from sellers to buyers.[53] For intra-country and intra-community transfers, it seems likely that few problems will be created by e-commerce since taxes are based on the country of origin and the selling firms will transfer the appropriate amount of taxes to their governments.[54] However, for extra-community transfers, the present system is based on the traceability of the goods that pass across the border of the buying party's country. Existing audit systems are not well-developed to trace extra-community business-to-consumer intangible imports. With the growth of e-commerce it is expected that the extra-community trade in intangible goods will increase as markets become more transparent. The transfers of intangibles will be invisible to tax officers and there is little doubt that e-commerce will have implications for the tax base.

The potential scale of e-commerce and the possible effects on taxation, especially in the business-to-consumer segment of the market where auditing systems for the payment of VAT (or sales tax in the United States) are relatively undeveloped, are enormously difficult to assess. It is useful, nevertheless, to provide some benchmarks for analysis. We briefly consider a study that was undertaken by the Maastricht Economic Research Institute on Innovation and Technology (MERIT), which employed a macroeconomic model to assess the potential impact of e-commerce on tax income.[55]

---

[53] This section draws in substantial part on research undertaken by Huub Meijers (1998), MERIT, University of Maastricht.

[54] The tax revenue estimates are subject to the reliability of auditing systems, but this is also the case for traditional commerce. One main difference is the relatively low reproduction costs of information products and services, which can complicate auditing methods.

[55] See Meijers (1998). Initially, the intention was to use an aggregate model of the European Union economy (the mini-Quest II model), but data problems and the fact that taxes were not implemented in this model made it inappropriate for use in the present context.

As intra-community trade has a less direct influence on taxation, the analysis of the effects on tax income attributable directly or indirectly to e-commerce in this study concentrated on trade in on-line goods and services with the United States.

To investigate the size and nature of e-commerce, two issues must be addressed. The first is to estimate how many people or households will have access to the Internet and/or other on-line services, on the basis of the best available independent evidence. The second is to forecast the purchasing behaviour of those who have access to the Internet in terms of size and country of origin of the goods and services purchased on-line. In this study, conservative growth estimates of total sales using the Internet were used, that is, for about US$ 300b. in 2001 or about 1 per cent of worldwide gross domestic product, two-thirds of which would be generated in the United States.[56] The implications of the growth of e-commerce for the taxation system are difficult to forecast because of the uncertainty surrounding the actual diffusion of Internet access and subsequent changes in consumers' purchasing behaviour and patterns. Nevertheless, despite the inadequacies of existing data and the uncertain evolution of new electronic services markets, it is possible to envisage alternative scenarios for purchases using the Internet and the possible consequences for government tax income.

It can be assumed, for example, that current tax policy within the European Union does not change and that all consumer purchases via e-commerce within a Member State are taxed according to local VAT rates. For trade in consumer goods within the European Union, it can be assumed that the VAT rate of the country of origin applies, and that, for imports from extra-European Union countries, the appropriate VAT rate is levied at the border of the country of the consumer. Using these and other assumptions, the effects of e-commerce on tax revenues can be modelled using a macroeconomic model.[57] In order to simulate the effects of trade using the Internet, the model must be modified to take into account estimates of future purchases using the Internet as a percentage of total consumption expenditure and the country of origin of these purchases.[58]

When this exercise was undertaken for the Dutch economy, the results suggested that the estimated reduction of tax income would amount to fl. 1.4b. in 2020 due to e-commerce. When compared to the nominal value of GDP in 1997 relative to 2020, this amount would be equivalent to about fl. 0.5b. in 1997, approximately the same amount as the total budget of the Dutch Ministry of Finance in 1997 (excluding the interest on government debt) or the Ministry of Agriculture. This amount is also equivalent to about one-third of the total budget of the Ministry of Defence and one-seventh of the budget of the Ministry of Education, the largest Dutch Ministry in

[56] Data from Activmedia and Ministerie van Economische Zaken (Dutch Ministry of Economic Affairs).

[57] The FKSec model used by The Netherlands Bureau for Economic Policy Analysis was used in this analysis. This is a quarterly sector model used, for example, in the evaluation of economic policy and for budgetary forecasts. The supply-side of the model is disaggregated into several sectors including an exposed sector, a sheltered sector, building, mining and quarrying, and non-market services.

[58] See Meijers (1998) for a detailed explanation of the procedure which followed Armington (1969). In the analysis reported here, it was assumed that the on-line imports from other countries within the European Union to The Netherlands can be treated as domestic demand. On-line intra-community trade was treated as originating from The Netherlands whereas American firms were assumed to sell all on-line imports. Adjustments were made to the FKSec model's treatment of taxes and time horizons.

terms of budget. At least according to this study, the estimated effects of e-commerce on national tax revenue are significant, but they are small enough that it is conceivable that other developments, such as growth in the Dutch national income from the use of the Internet, might offset the revenue losses attributable to e-commerce.

9.5   Conclusion

Assessing the consequence of the movement towards the information society is an inherently difficult task because the transformations that are occurring in the use of the information and communication infrastructure are so pervasive. If this were not the case, then it might be feasible to localize the effect of a change in one part of the economy or society and examine the spill-over effects in other parts of the economy. However, the use of the new technologies and services is influencing not only the costs of inputs and the nature of outputs in the economy, but also the way that work is organized and skills are articulated. If we want to assess the potential effects of a specific feature of information society developments, such as the growth of e-commerce, it is necessary to take account of the possible implications that e-commerce will have for existing ways of doing business, the organization of work, and the use of leisure time. A little more than a decade ago, Strassmann (1990) commented that the preceding decade of research on the implications of the development and diffusion of information and communication technologies indicated that very little could reliably be predicted by examining either the rate of investment or the types of technologies that are being acquired. On the basis of our assessment of research undertaken during the decade of the 1990s, the same observation must be made. In addition, the same problems confront analysts when efforts are made to measure productivity effects associated with the growing use of information and communication technologies (David and Steinmueller, 2000).

In the first part of this chapter we addressed the question of whether it is possible to associate structural transformations in the labour force with the spread of the information and communication infrastructure. There certainly are reasons to believe that certain associations *might* exist. With the growth of the service economy as a share of total output, and service employment as a share of total employment, there is a growing need for technological advance that will contribute to improvements in the productivity of service activities in the economy. The problem is that service outputs are extremely malleable. The services produced today are very different from those produced a decade ago and the way that labour is organized to deliver them includes the use of call centres, user-support hot-lines, direct marketing automation, and a host of 'process' innovations. In many cases, what is being delivered is not only different and often of higher quality but, in some important senses, it is greater in quantity. These changes in quality and quantity cannot be accurately tracked using available statistical techniques because of both their diversity and the inadequacy of reference points from which to assess the process of change. The same issues are present in the assessment of the transformation of manufacturing where, in many cases, ancillary service activities play a more important role in generating revenue than the physical fabrication of manufactured products.

The changes in the economy cannot be attributed exclusively to the development of the information and communication infrastructure and the diffusion of new services. The ever-increasing level of education of the labour force and the expansion in the variety of specialized labour make it possible to engage in a growing variety of activities that are directly connected with, or ancillary to, the production of goods and services. These changes are allowing new patterns to emerge in the division of labour. Many former managerial functions can now be conducted on the shop floor and individual workers or teams can take responsibility for regulating the flow of production, assuring quality control, and responding to a growing diversity of opportunities to apply knowledge and problem-solving skills to their work. These changes are evident in the continual upgrading of job descriptions, a process that is also connected with changes in the division of labour across organizational boundaries. In the face of these and many other changes that parallel the changes in the specific feature of the development and use of the information and communication infrastructure, it is not surprising that we have reservations about the empirical foundation for assessing the consequences of any one set of effects associated with changes in the technological infrastructure, let alone the systemic effects of these changes.

There are, nevertheless, important issues that can and must be addressed. One of the most important of these is the changing requirements for skills that are accompanying the processes of organizational and technological change. The need to understand more precisely what skills are required and how these are gained presents a measurement issue of profound importance for all economies. The broad categories that are used to examine the relationships between the diffusion of information and communication technologies and employment growth and reduction are simply unsatisfactory. Such oversimplifications are unavoidable because of our inheritance of industrial-age habits of mind with regard to labour and labour skills. Many individuals do fall into well-defined categories, such as assembly worker, miner, maintenance operator, and the like, but there is a growing number of individuals who fall into ill-defined categories, such as technician, salesperson, or manager. The lack of clarity of existing classifications of employment and, perhaps, even the whole idea of categorizing labour in terms of job descriptions, means that assessing job losses and gains associated with changes in technology and organization is, at best, an exercise in crude approximation. Since organizational and technical changes often involve alterations in the division of labour across organizational boundaries, the task of accounting for job gains and losses becomes even more difficult. Instead, we have very little choice but to examine broad macroeconomic shifts in the composition of the labour force. This type of analysis indicates that employment is not disappearing from the economy and that a growing number of jobs appear to involve higher skill levels than in the past. This observation raises further important issues. The figures for unemployment in the European Union suggest that once an individual becomes unemployed the process of re-employment may be arduous. This can be explained partly by the costs of employment which may make companies reluctant to create new positions, but it is also a consequence of the obsolescence of particular skills and the difficulties, especially when a person is not in the labour force, in gaining new skills. On the basis of the evidence that we have considered in this chapter, there is a very strong case for more research on the processes of skill acquisition in relation to organizational and technical change.

Retreating from issues raised by the macroeconomic consequences of technical and organizational change, we devoted the second main section of this chapter to an examination of more localized consequences of movement towards the information society. The Third Sector appears to be a dynamic arena for the creation of new jobs and it also offers opportunities for individuals to invest in new skills. Many of the services being delivered by this sector are making a positive contribution to the social well-being of Europeans even if they are not directly connected with the processes of wealth creation that often receive the greatest attention in policy debates. Similarly, development of new government services and regional and municipal initiatives is contributing in important ways to the social and economic infrastructure of European societies. The achievement of transparency and easing of the costs of business-to-government and government-to-citizen relationships through the application of innovative information and communication technologies and services has considerable potential to increase the value of taxpayer investments in government services. Regional and municipal governments also appear to be taking a proactive role in fostering new types of businesses including those involved with the Internet and information content production. Both Third Sector and civic government efforts are key components of virtual community strategies that may be effective in ensuring that the movement towards the information society is beneficial 'for all'.

In the final main section of this chapter, we considered the potential for the erosion of the tax base stemming from the growing use of the Internet for e-commerce. We have sought to avoid the exaggerated speculations that are so prevalent in this area, but we do not dispute that the potential for a decline in revenues from taxation is significant. Many of the problems in this area arise because of the reliance of European countries on indirect taxation through the levy of value-added taxes, and the possibility that the Internet provides a means for avoiding these taxes. Within the European Union jurisdiction, this possibility is significantly diminished by the multiplicity of ways in which companies can be audited and held responsible for their revenues. The growth of e-commerce based on the Internet on an international scale, however, raises an important new set of issues. This is because of the potential to make foreign remittances in order to purchase intangible services that can be delivered using the Internet without clearing customs in the way that other extra-European tangible imports must do. As the size of this trade in intangibles increases, there will be a need to devise a means to compensate for the erosion of the tax base.

Unfortunately, the solutions that have been devised thus far are unsatisfactory for several reasons. Proposals for taxing the transmission or receipt of information using a bit tax or similar measure attribute value to information that is not in any conventional sense 'sold', and are likely to discourage the expansion of the virtual communities whose use of the Internet to support information exchanges in the public domain is likely to generate substantial collective benefits. Proposals for levying a withholding tax on international payment transfers could be cumbersome. In addition, selectively applying restrictions to payments for 'intangible' goods and services would probably require a vast increase in costly regulation. European trading partners would undoubtedly view such action as an unfair barrier to trade. However, in failing to address this issue, the competitive playing-field will be tilted towards non-European companies unless all e-commerce transactions on the Internet are exempted from value added taxes. This brings us full circle to the problem of tax erosion as the share of intangible purchases increases with the growth of e-commerce. Although instituting a remedy is not a matter of pressing urgency, we believe that deeper consideration of the consequences of the Internet for arbitraging existing taxation systems is a high research priority.

The use of the Internet and other components of the information and communication infrastructure is likely to continue to increase rapidly during the coming decade. In some instances it will become easier to investigate the organizational, economic, and social consequences of this growth using existing indicators and measures. However, in many other instances, significant effort will be needed to develop appropriate indicators and measures in order to track these consequences. As we have noted above, improved means of assessing changes in labour-force skills and in patterns of skill acquisition are needed, and there is an urgent need for measures of the volume of particular types of transactions, the size of intangible investments in creating content, the value of new patterns of marketing and product support using the Internet, and the implications of improvements in the information and communication infrastructure for mobile and remote workers. Without such indicators, we will be hard pressed to say more than that 'profound changes are underway' in our future assessments of the opportunities and risks of moving towards the information society.

10
Recapitulating the Themes and Facing the Future

Like its predecessor, the Atomic Age, the information and communication technology revolution, or the Information Age, has captivated the public imagination. During the past thirty years, it has raised both hopes and fears. Like the hoped-for energy abundance of the Atomic Age, there has been the expectation that the flow of information would become 'too cheap to meter'. Reductions in cost, and increases in availability of information exchange and communication capacity have made this more of a possibility than was the case with atomic energy. Information Age fears have centred on the dislocations and disruptions in existing patterns of work and knowledge that accompany the introduction of the new technologies and services. As the significance of information society developments becomes more apparent, attention is shifting towards the consequences of exclusion and uncertainties about how best to take advantage of the new technologies and services to improve both economic competitiveness and the quality of human life.

Unlike many of the technologies of the Atomic Age, information and communication technologies have proved to be suitable for domestication.[1] The introduction of the telephone at the beginning of the twentieth century demonstrated the value of 'virtual' connections. After some initial hesitance, it rapidly became one of the first domestic electrical appliances. Like many Atomic Age technologies, the computers of the Information Age were born into sealed, remote, and controlled operating environments tended by a technological priesthood and their acolytes. The advent of the personal computer liberated computer technology and transformed it into an information appliance that could join the telephone on the desktop or travel with its user alongside the cellular telephone. In the process of their domestication, vast numbers of people have acquired the complex new range of skills needed for integrating these intricate technologies into their daily lives. The use of these technologies or 'tools' began to become widespread throughout the industrialized nations in the 1980s and has supported fundamental changes in the organization and conduct of both work and play.

This book has focused on the current era and the next steps in the evolution of the Information Age in which networked information appliances, and the networks supporting them, have become the pivotal artefacts. This era encompasses the late 1980s and the 1990s. During this period new applications of information and communication technologies and services began to exhibit some of the features of the long-

---

[1] See Silverstone and Haddon (1996a) for a discussion of the 'domestication' of information and communication technologies.

heralded 'convergence' between computing and telecommunication. While many of the expectations for the convergence process have not been realized, the Internet and the World Wide Web have become the paradigm around which the processes of 'convergence' are organized and it is this paradigm that has provided an organizing framework for our history of this era. This paradigm involves the use of networked information appliances and related new technologies as broadcast and receiving engines for a growing array of information and communication functions. Even more significantly, these technologies serve as instruments that are supporting new forms of social exchange within and between organizations, as well as throughout society. A central purpose of our examination of these technologies has been to demonstrate that their productive *use* involves a complex series of social and economic developments. It is with respect to how information and communication technologies are *used* that their economic and cultural values are either realized or fail to materialize.

The era of the network information appliance parallels the growth of the 'network' concept in a variety of other contexts. For instance, renewed attention is being given to the roles of social networks in the creation and reproduction of knowledge, of networks of users in the process of innovation, and of networks of suppliers (local and global) in the competitive health of industries. In our view, the increasing importance of many kinds of networks reflects a growing recognition of the crucial role of interdependency in modern societies and economies. In Europe, concerns about the extent and nature of interdependencies not only have a long history, but they also have considerable contemporary significance. It is not surprising, therefore, that the new, networked era of information and communication technologies has been of special interest to Europe. Europeans not only were responsible for innovations that have contributed to this era, such as the World Wide Web, but also have been quick to embrace the idea of the information society. The term 'information society' implies the goal of achieving ubiquitous and accessible information resources as a foundation for economic growth and development. It also describes the increasing extent to which information is becoming a central feature of social and cultural life for people who are more literate and affluent, on average, than their ancestors.

As we emphasized in Ch. 1, the idea of the information society emerged alongside the initial formation of the European Union and became a centrepiece of the responses to the crises in employment and economic growth of the early 1990s. The vision of the European Union emphasized the role of 'trans-European' networks of all kinds as one means of extending linkages across borders and of achieving advantage from the geographic co-location of the Member States. The European information society has been, from its origins, a transnational construction. Like other emerging European institutions, however, it is a construction that aggregates national diversity into a loose structure where the boundaries between national and supra-national initiatives are fluid and provide a productive tension for consultation and consensus formation. Although each Member State has articulated its own perspective on, and approach to, information society developments, within each of the countries the value of a common perspective on the broad outlines defining a European information society is recognized.

The close association between the formation of the European Union and the concept of a European information society has played a major role in the search for common agreements about the components of the information society. The result has been the development of four 'cornerstones' of policy—the principles of liberalization, harmonization, cohesion, and shared development frameworks. The last of these is our terminology for the many initiatives that have been taken to promote and enhance co-ordination in areas that are not directly associated with the first three principles. These include the funding of Research, Technology, Development and Demonstration programmes and the establishment of consultative processes and organizations, such as the Information Society Forum or the High Level Expert Group. We have argued that each of the four principles has been of substantial value in promoting the development of a healthy and inclusive realization of the information society concept, but we have raised criticisms about how these principles are employed or executed in practice. These criticisms are linked to, and motivated by, the three main themes in this book.

The first of the major themes concerns the lack of attention in both the policy and academic communities to the issues surrounding the individual and collective use of information and communication technologies. In our view this neglect is the result of several interrelated habits of thought. The first is the presumption that any particular configuration in the use of information and communication technologies and services reflects the most appropriate configuration, given technical and economic constraints, and the current state of knowledge of producers and users. This habit of thought is a variety of technological determinism. It leads to the view that both policy intervention and research and analysis should occur 'after the fact'; in other words, policy actions or research should be undertaken after the consequences of technological development have been realized. Contributing to this habit of thought is the faith that the economic system, particularly under competitive conditions, will deliver the best possible outcomes and that any alternative to reliance on market mechanisms will necessarily deliver inferior results.

We have contested this habit of thought with regard to technological evolution and the faith that market processes will operate in the manner assumed in textbook economics. Regarding the emergence of particular technological outcomes, we have analysed the way in which many technological outcomes are mediated by deliberative processes rather than by technological necessity. The determination of technical compatibility standards, the regulatory interpretation of interconnection obligations, the use of hardware identification for copyright protection, and the governance of electronic payment systems, are all instances in which the technological outcomes are a reflection of deliberations that have led to public or private choices between competing technologies or to the rules that will make particular technologies and services viable.

With respect to the faith in competitive market outcomes, we have illustrated how some of the most basic assumptions underlying textbook economic analysis do not hold for many information society markets. Individuals do not, in any meaningful sense, have pre-existing preferences for the consumption of particular services or for investment in specific skills. The markets for information, as well as for many information and communication technologies, are subject to increasing returns because 'first copy' costs are fixed and shared among subsequent copies, yielding ever-declining costs. Increasing returns mean that a company, technology, or market configuration may achieve substantial competitive advantage as a result of its starting position, or quirks in the markets it serves, rather than as a result of its inherent superiority. Although some information society markets are experiencing freer, and more open entry conditions, many resources in the information and communication infrastructure are either non-reproducible, often due to intellectual property right restrictions, or are very costly to reproduce. This allows firms to create, or maintain, positions of advantage that impede normal competitive processes. Thus, we conclude that neither technological nor economic mechanisms can be relied upon to produce the best possible, or even necessarily a desirable, outcome. This is not a new conclusion and it is surprising that it needs to be emphasized in the context of information society developments, especially in the light of experience with market power in telecommunication and computer markets over the past thirty years.

Our purpose in disputing the applicability of doctrines of technological necessity and perfect competition is to open the door to new approaches in the conduct of social science investigations of information society issues. We have exemplified the value of incorporating concepts of cumulativeness and incremental processes in the analysis of information society developments. Thus, we have argued that the analysis of processes of diffusion should take account of the different rates of learning within target user communities (Ch. 2), the availability of complementary technologies supporting the spread of a new technological system (Ch. 3), and the influence of improvements in rival technologies (Ch. 4). We also have indicated how *institutions* (formal rules as well as norms and practices) shape technological and market outcomes. The institutional features of the information society include the creation, extension, and maintenance of trust (Chs. 5, 6, and 8), the implications of specific formal rules for market development (Chs. 6 and 7), and the inclusion or exclusion of the user in the technological design and improvement process (Ch. 2). We emphasize, however, that our view of the incremental, cumulative, and institutional processes does not preclude a major role for the specific features of technological developments. In Ch. 3, we have shown how innovations in the local area network play a large part in information society developments, as do the mobile and optical technologies discussed in Ch. 4, the copy protection technologies in Ch. 7, and the cryptographic techniques in Ch. 8. An account of information society developments that makes technological developments entirely subsidiary to economic and institutional influences is as likely to produce errors as one that relies upon the inevitability of technological and market developments.

The second major theme in this book concerns the role of the incumbent, insurgent, and virtual community strategies and constituencies in influencing information society developments. Our decision to organize the book around this theme was taken because we believe that it is the most concise way to characterize the nature of the rivalry for control of information society developments. Our approach is grounded in economic logic with respect to market dynamics and rational decision-making. It is also informed by political economy, which takes account of the role of power and the distributional outcomes of economic processes.

Our theory of incumbency is derived from the tradition of imperfect competition in which a principal source of market power is the control of fixed, and difficult to reproduce, assets.[2] The nature and extent of these assets continues to be fraught with controversy, particularly for those who believe that even a little market competition is effective in disciplining anti-competitive behaviour.[3] Intellectual property rights, the ownership of 'essential' facilities, such as the local loop, and long-established market positions, however, often establish a basis for 'incumbent' market power.[4]

Our theory of insurgency draws upon the theory of monopolistic competition,[5] and more contemporary theories of the role of technology in creating product differentiation.[6] It is influenced by an understanding of the unique features of information goods and markets where 'winner takes all' contests are not only possible but are treated as an objective of firm strategy in recent work.[7] The coupling of network externalities and economies of scale defines the insurgent strategy. The aim of creating market conditions that promote this strategy is, in our view, one of the most significant economic developments influencing the future of the information society.

Our theory of the virtual community strategy is influenced by several writers on information society developments who pursue sociologically informed approaches.[8] Virtual community strategies are directed at intensifying and deepening the relationships within a particular community of users and these communities may or may not include a 'producer'. When a producer is part of the community, the virtual community is organized around the intensification and deepening of producer–user relationships. However, in many virtual communities, the members of the community are themselves co-producers of the information content. For example, research communities involve networks of users, many or all of whom are co-producers of the information content of the virtual community. A virtual community may have one or more strong players, and includes situations where the community is organized around a producer who may be the central hub of the network. Many other virtual community network architectures are possible.

Our view that the virtual community strategy offers a particularly attractive avenue for European information society development is influenced by the importance attributed to small and medium-sized enterprises in creating employment

---

[2] e.g. Bain (1956), J. M. Clark (1923), and Robinson (1932).

[3] e.g. Bork (1978).

[4] See Mansell (1993) for a consideration of the complex issues of market power arising in telecommunication equipment markets.

[5] e.g. Chamberlin (1938).

[6] e.g. Sutton (1998).

[7] e.g. Shapiro and Varian (1998).

[8] We draw particularly on Mitchell (1996) and on the insights developed by van Dijk (1999); Gelder and Thornton (1997); Harasim (1993); Silverstone (1999); and M. A. Smith and Kollock (1999).

opportunities and the significance of the Third Sector (Ch. 9) for European economies and societies. We have attempted to trace the technological, economic, and institutional implications of each of these three strategies for the organizations that embrace them.

Our approach offers both a normative and positive view of the different strategies. We have been careful to stress that our normative conclusions about these strategies are related to particular markets. We do not reach the general conclusion that the ascendancy of any one of the strategies is inherently, or generally, supportive of, or inimical to, the public interest. Each can deliver undesirable outcomes from the standpoint of social well-being and each may be preferred under particular circumstances. As the incumbent strategy is associated with the accumulation of market power it may be regarded as problematic. However, market power has a specific role in creating incentives to innovate and to achieve systemic integration, both of which are desirable from a collective or social viewpoint. While liberalization eventually may deliver a more competitive market, we question whether attempting to build an information and communication infrastructure in a fully liberalized market will deliver an appropriate level of co-ordination and investment. This scepticism is reflected in our analysis of the market for home access to the infrastructure in Ch. 4 and in our analysis of European market liberalization policies in Ch. 6. It also informs our conclusions in Ch. 4 regarding the slowing pace of technological innovation in mobile telecommunication systems.

The risks associated with the accumulation of market power may be just as great in the case of insurgency where first-mover advantages may lead to the emergence of an incumbent position based upon strategic dominance over market development rather than upon ownership of specific assets. The existence of an insurgent strategy is a powerful force for innovation as we have illustrated in the cases of the deployment of local area networks, the demise of Integrated Services Digital Networks as a model for universal broadband access (Ch. 3), and the introduction of electronic payment systems (Ch. 8). The *potential* role of an insurgent strategy is even more significant where it is influencing both the evolution of the market for augmented mobile applications and optical technology for multimedia applications (Ch. 4), and the search for a successful strategy for developing electronic commerce (Ch. 5). Institutional issues, including the regulation of interconnection and interoperability (Ch. 6), and the rules governing data reuse (Ch. 8), also affect the potential of insurgent strategies. Our analysis raises concerns about insurgent strategies because they are often linked to 'winner take all' strategies at a global level. Therefore, they contribute to the potential for the exclusion of European producers from important growth markets in the information society. The advantages of the North American market in supporting the development of insurgent strategies are well recognized and they often produce outcomes that benefit Europeans. At the same time, however, insurgent strategies may become a means of foreclosing or dominating markets, as was concluded in the Microsoft antitrust case 'findings of fact'.[9]

We have emphasized the value of virtual community strategies throughout this

---

[9] See United States District Court for the District Of Columbia (1999).

book for several reasons. Public policy actions are influenced by whether constituencies are discernible and have identifiable interests. Unfortunately, virtual community constituencies and interests are often obscured by the drama surrounding the rivalry between incumbent and insurgent strategies. This is unfortunate because of the particular advantages that virtual community strategies offer for the development of an inclusive information society that is responsive to a wide range of social needs and aspirations. The value of electronic and other information and communication infrastructures stems not only from the commodification of information goods and services, but also from the processes of social exchange involved in the pursuit of cultural, education, religious, and political goals.

Our most intense criticism of policies that tilt the playing-field against these activities is presented in our consideration of the evolution of copyright protection (Ch. 7). We suggest that the actions that are being taken to strengthen intellectual property rights ignore other social interests in the development of the information and communication infrastructure. From our viewpoint, the imposition of a single model of copyright protection for the production of all forms of information that adheres to expression *regardless of the creator's preference*, is inappropriate. While the case of copyright protection is the most flagrant instance of ignoring virtual community interests in the information society, it is not the only one. The evolution of standards-making organizations (Ch. 6), which is also influenced by government policy, has yet to produce an effective means of representing small users or of representing the interests of future market participants. Virtual community interests also play an important, but not yet fully considered, role in the evolution of the institutions governing electronic commerce (Ch. 5) and electronic payment systems (Ch. 8) where private sector decisions may impose substantial costs on small and medium-sized enterprises.

The significance of virtual community strategies is not being taken into account sufficiently in the socio-economic research that is being conducted to assess the implications of the information society. In this case, a major problem is the lack of funding for the examination of important issues, such as the role of the electronic information systems in the evolution of libraries,[10] the formation and operation of research communities,[11] or the role of the Third Sector or civic nets (Ch. 9). Our partial examination of virtual community developments in Ch. 2 is illustrative of the still exploratory quality of the work in this field. In the absence of more extensive socio-economic research on virtual community strategies in Europe, we expect that there will be many unintended and unwanted consequences in the implementation of information society policies.

Virtual community strategies also play an important economic role in the information society. Information and communication infrastructures in general, and the Internet in particular, provide a means for small producers of goods and services,

---

[10] Many of the European studies such as those by Brophy, Allred, and Allred (1995); Danmarks Biblioteksskole (1996); and Gristock and Mansell (1997) are largely exploratory in nature.

[11] An indication of the range of issues that need deeper consideration is given in National Research Council (1997).

including those that are information-based, to gain access to markets. The Internet has the potential to assist in the intensification and deepening of supplier and customer relationships and to provide an unprecedented level of personal service through the growth of new intermediaries (Ch. 5). The development of an understanding of how this process works and the provision of guides for those venturing into this territory have only just begun. In our view, work needs to progress at a much more rapid pace if it is to support the cultural, linguistic, and social diversity of Europe.

As the preceding discussion indicates, the interaction between incumbent, insurgent, and virtual community strategies and constituencies is both a political and economic process. We have attempted to lay the foundations for a deeper consideration of these issues in which institutional, technological, social, and economic influences shape the relative strength of alternative strategies. In our view, socially appropriate outcomes will arise from competition between these approaches only if attention is devoted to establishing policies that avoid premature or persistent control of one strategy to the exclusion of the other two. We, therefore, advocate policies that will maintain a pro-competitive environment both among the players and the models for competition supporting the evolution of the information society. The achievement of this requires a consideration of competing interests in the tradition of political economy rather than approaches that are predicated on a presumption that unalloyed market outcomes will necessarily produce the most appropriate outcomes.[12]

The third theme in this book concerns the consequence of inclusion in and exclusion from information society developments. The preceding two themes, that is, the importance of a detailed examination of the use of information and communication technologies and the significance of the rivalry between incumbent, insurgent, and virtual community strategies and constituencies, address many of the actual and potential shortcomings of the implementation of the principles of liberalization and harmonization. The consequences of inclusion and exclusion, however, involve the third cornerstone of European information society policy, that is, cohesion. The concern in Europe about cohesion is a consequence of the effort to achieve the social and economic integration of a sundry collection of countries, each of which is comprised of diverse regions and ethnic groups. Concerns about the issue of cohesion are not limited to the issues of nationality or cultural identity. They also include fears about potentially divisive stratification by other criteria, such as economic wealth, social privilege, gender, and disability. A distinguishing feature of European policies for the information society is that the issue of social and economic cohesion has been, and remains, present throughout the policy debates. We have argued that the construction of the information society is, in a very fundamental sense, a process of social development in which gaining access to skills and pertinent knowledge is essential for meaningful participation in the information society. These issues are important because information society developments involve access to resources for education, health, and culture, as well as the increasing use of information and communication technologies in the workplace.

---

[12] This view is similar to that developed by Machlup (1952) or Commons (1957), who considered the problem of market power from institutional and legal viewpoints.

Cohesion is shaped by whether individuals are included in, or excluded from, participating in information society developments. We have shown in Ch. 2 that the process of inclusion is complex and that many of the aspects contributing to this process can be understood by separate consideration of the issues of skills and access to infrastructure. It is certainly possible, in principle, to address either in isolation. For example, it is possible to teach the literacy or numeracy skills that are prerequisites for the effective use of information and communication technologies without access to these technologies. It is also feasible to provide access to the information and communication infrastructure without encouraging the development of the skills needed to make effective use of this access. However, there is evidence to suggest that the outcomes of these approaches will be unsatisfactory. The competent use of information and communication technologies requires the accumulation of experience that cannot be achieved effectively without access. For most users, there is little value in simply having access to an information or communication medium. Access generally must be complemented by assistance in unlocking and realizing its potential for meeting users' needs and aspirations. In the first instance, therefore, our concern is with the social institutions that support the development of skills and access. Although people of all ages and abilities may develop the capacity to participate in the information society, our immediate concern is with the availability of access and training in schools. Substantial progress is being made in this area, but much remains to be done. The largest part of the problem lies in developing the skills needed by teachers and others involved in schools to support the use of information and communication technologies. Reductions in the cost of hardware and software tools, as well as in the cost of telecommunication network access, are likely to continue, reducing one of the barriers to the acquisition of relevant technologies.

The biggest investment will continue to be the human costs incurred in building skills and knowledge and in introducing organizational change. Some readers may be sceptical of the priority that we assign to this issue and consider that education has much weightier responsibilities than achieving the capacity to use the tools of the Information Age. Our contention, however, is that these technologies will have an ever-expanding influence on the way that knowledge is produced and used, on the nature of communication and work processes, and on a growing variety of social relationships and interactions. This is not for better or worse, but for better *and* worse, in that many valuable skills and capabilities are likely to be displaced or temporarily submerged by these developments. Just as we argued that these opportunities should be extended to people involved with education institutions as teachers or students, they should also become available increasingly to people who are not currently involved in formal education through engagement with the process of 'lifelong learning'.

Realizing these opportunities will involve a reconsideration of the issues surrounding universal access. In Chs. 2 and 6 we observed that those concerned with universal access policies have been moving towards the idea that access to the information and communication infrastructure should become more affordable and effective. We have emphasized that attention should be devoted especially to investments in the skills and access available through public institutions, such as libraries, where it is possible to mitigate some of the problems of social exclusion. We have argued that the design of information and communication technology artefacts and services should incorporate a more inclusive perspective of the user community, taking into account how the elderly and disabled will be able to benefit. Each of these developments will assist in reducing the potential for exclusion. However, we also note that this area suffers, along with virtual community developments, from insufficient research. We have been able to rely only upon the crudest indicators of the extent and nature of the use of information and communication technologies in schools and cultural institutions. Although there has been some progress towards a better understanding of the availability and use of information and communication technologies in recent years, the entire field of inquiry remains heavily influenced by the *ex post* counting of the diffusion of particular types of technologies rather than efforts to assess the characteristics and qualities of user skills and experience.

Our aim in this book has been to articulate a viewpoint on the development of the information society that avoids several key pitfalls in social science examinations of the process of technological change. Foremost among these pitfalls is a doctrine of technological determinism, which maintains that there is an inevitable path of development that follows from the elaboration of the intrinsic and implicit features of a technology. We also have attempted to steer clear of another pitfall in which technological development is regarded as being so heavily influenced by the processes of social construction that no significant trends or consequences can be discerned. The other pitfalls and traps that abound in the attempt to characterize and order the complex developments associated with the information society are numerous. Those that we *have* fallen prey to will become more apparent over time.

In reviewing our work with a view to the future we can identify three areas of potential change that would be of particular significance for our argument. The first is with regard to our scepticism about the speed at which business-to-consumer electronic commerce will develop and provide a stronger foundation for home use of the Internet and a much greater demand for higher capacity data communication services to the home. Substantial investments are being made in the attempt to open retail Internet outlets. These may become fashionable because of people's desires to participate in the novel and exciting developments they represent. If these outlets were to develop at a rate far in excess of our speculations, this would confound not only our own expectations, but those of many other people about the extent to which Europeans insist upon a tangible and personal interaction with the 'shopping' experience and with the artefacts they interact with in their everyday lives. Very rapid development of Internet retail outlets would provide new possibilities for extending the infrastructure and would substantially enlarge the constituency for policies aimed at accelerating the diffusion of the information and communication infrastructure to the home, potentially establishing a better balance between business and home use of information resources.

We have expressed our concern about the relatively slow pace at which schools and cultural institutions in Europe are gaining access to the Internet. There are already important exceptions in the experience of the United Kingdom where there has been considerable investment and attention given to exactly this issue. To the extent that other European countries will come to regard more rapid action in this area as a priority, substantial progress could be made in a relatively short time. This is an area where we would be delighted to have our expectations confounded. Broader access to Internet resources is the best prospect for the next generation of European citizens to have access to the skills and knowledge that are rapidly becoming an integral part of the businesses in which most of them will be employed. Broader access to the information and communication infrastructure would also reduce the extent to which extreme divisions between information 'have' and 'have not' communities emerge for those of all ages or social status in Europe.

The third area where our expectations might be confounded is in the development of effective infrastructures and services for the home use of advanced information services, such as the Internet. As we have observed, the principal barriers preventing such infrastructures and services from coming into existence are uncertainty about demand coupled with the fragmentation of markets offering delivery and services. These conditions, along with a suitable technological solution, are the starting or initial conditions needed for the emergence of a successful insurgent strategy. There are many potential technologies waiting in the wings including those for augmenting the capacity of the local telecommunication infrastructure, the extension of digital broadcasting services, and the creation of wireless broadband networks. Our expectation is that none of these technologies will be taken up sufficiently rapidly to amass the lead required for achieving a successful insurgent strategy. This expectation could be confounded by events. Nevertheless, even if our expectations in each of these three areas were to be confounded, the main elements of our conclusions would stand.

A principal aim of social science investigation is to illuminate processes that would otherwise be obscured by common habits of thought or belief. Our analysis has demonstrated the value of shifting the perspective away from the supply of new technologies and from a concern with the economic determinants of diffusion and assessments of social and economic impact. Instead, we have developed our analysis with a focus on uses and users and on the economic, social, technological, and institutional issues surrounding participation in the information society. We have been critical of many of the consequences of the moves towards the information society including the growing possibility of social exclusion (Ch. 2), the potentially disruptive effects of electronic commerce for small and medium-sized enterprises (Ch. 5), the likelihood of growing problems associated with privacy (Ch. 8), and the potential for a significant challenge to existing means of tax collection (Ch. 9).

Some readers may conclude that we have taken the inevitability and desirability of the information society as assumptions. The information society and the technologies accompanying it are the harbingers of fundamental change. The opportunities to use these technologies to restructure the way that people gain access to information and engage in communication in support of their interests and ambitions are so numerous that we are confident in our prediction that we stand only at the beginning of the Information Age. In this respect, information societies are inevitable. With respect to the desirability of this transformation, this book represents a dialogue between a sceptic and an enthusiast with a frequent exchange of roles. We have argued that the information society should offer equal opportunity for all Europeans to participate, but there will not be equality in the outcome. Some people will receive extraordinary benefits from the development of the information society and will feel comfortable with, and even welcome, the changes that it brings to their lives. Other people will be excluded regardless of the efforts that are made to include them due to temperament, belief, or simply preference, just as there are many Europeans who live pre-industrial lifestyles, some out of choice and many out of necessity. Our aim, and it is one that we believe that policy-makers and other people in Europe share, is to strive for an information society in which exclusion is the choice made *by* the individual rather than *for* him or her.

References

Abegglen, J. C., and Stalk Jr., G. (1985), *Kaisha: The Japanese Corporation*, New York: Basic Books.

Academy, The (1998), 'Divx Debuts in San Francisco and Richmond', *The Academy Advancing High Performance Audio & Video*, http://www.avacademy.com/news/stories/06_06_98_02.html, 3, accessed 1 Sept. 1999.

Aderton, S., and Delaney, J. (1995), 'IP: The Impact of Telco Services and Revenues (Volume 1)', London: Ovum.

Agre, P. E., and Rotenberg, M. (eds.) (1997), *Technology and Privacy: The New Landscape*, Cambridge, Mass.: MIT Press.

Akerlof, G. (1970), 'The Market for Lemons: Quality Uncertainty and the Market Mechanism', *Quarterly Journal of Economics*, 84: 488–500.

Amendola, G., and Ferraiuolo, A. (1994), 'Regulating Mobile Communications', International Telecommunications Society Tenth Annual Conference, Beyond Competition, Sydney, 3–6 July.

Amusao, C., and Fluss, D. (1999), 'Spending to Save Money: Interactive Service Web Sites', *Gartner Group Research Note*, 2 Aug., http://gartner12.gartnerweb.com/public/static/home/home.html accessed 2 Aug. 1999.

Analysys Ltd (1995a), 'The Costs, Benefits and Funding of Universal Service in the UK', London: Final Report (95200) prepared for OFTEL, 19 July.

——(1995b), 'USO in a Competitive Telecoms Environment', Cambridge: Analysys Ltd.

——(1997a), 'The Impact of Liberalisation on the Single Integrated Information Market', Brussels: Analysys report prepared for European Commission DG XV.

——(1997b), 'The Future of Universal Service in Telecommunications in Europe', Cambridge: Analysys Ltd, Final Report for European Commission DGCIII/A1.

Andersen Consulting (1996), 'Electronic Publishing, Strategic Development for the European Publishing Industry towards the Year 2000', n.p.: Andersen Consulting.

Anderson, C. (1997), 'A Survey of Electronic Commerce: In Search of the Perfect Market', *The Economist*, 10–16 May, pp. 1–26.

Armington, P. S. (1969), 'A Theory of Demand for Products Distinguished by Place of Production', *International Monetary Fund Staff Papers*, 159–76.

Arroio, A. C. (1999), 'Technological Opportunities for Brazilian Social Development: An Examination of Low Earth Orbit Satellite Deployment', SPRU, University of Sussex, unpublished D.Phil. thesis, Brighton.

Arrow, K. J., and Debreu, G. (1954), 'The Existence of an Equilibrium for a Competitive Economy', *Econometrica*, XXII: 265–90.

Arthur, B. (1996), 'Increasing Returns and the New World of Business', *Harvard Business Review*, July/Aug., pp. 100–9.

ASSENT (1999a), 'Working Towards Knowledge Society Telematics Applications—Programme Level Report: An Assessment of the Results of the Fourth Framework Telematics Application Programme, Report prepared for the European Commission DGXIII C/E', Brighton: The ASSENT (Assessment of Telematics) Project Consortium SU2101, principal responsibility of SPRU University of Sussex, Project SU 2101—Deliverable D09.02. Part B (6), 1 July.

——(1999b), 'Working Towards Knowledge Society Telematics Applications—Telematics and the Disabled and Elderly Sector: An Assessment of the Results of the Fourth Framework Telematics Application Programme, Report prepared for the European Commission DGXIII C/E', Brighton: The ASSENT Project Consortium SU2101, principal responsibility of Fraunhofer-Institut für Systemtechnik und Innovationsforschung (FhG-ISI).

——(1999c), 'Working Towards Knowledge Society Telematics Applications—Urban and Rural Areas Sector: An Assessment of the Results of the Fourth Framework Telematics Application Programme, Report Prepared for the European Commission DGXIII C/E', Brighton: The ASSENT Project Consortium SU2101, principal responsibility of ZEUS EEIG and SPRU, Project SU 2101—Deliverable D09.02. Part B, 1 July.

Association for Computing Machinery US Public Policy Committee (1994), 'Cryptography in Public: A Brief History', in L. Hoffman (ed.), *Building Big Brother: The Cryptography Policy Debate*, New York: Springer Verlag, 41–50.

AT&T (1997), 'AT&T and Mondex Announce Electronic Cash for the Internet', *Press Release*, 12 Mar.

Ayre, J., Callaghan, J., and Hoffos, S. (1994), *The Multimedia Yearbook 1995*, London: Interactive Multimedia Publications Ltd.

Babbage, C. (1835), *On the Economy of Machinery and Manufactures*, 4th edn., London: Charles Knight, repr. 1986 by A. M. Kelley, Fairfield, NJ.

Bailey, J. (1997), 'Economics and Internet Interconnection Agreements', in L. McKnight and J. Bailey (eds.), *Internet Economics*, Cambridge, Mass.: MIT Press, 155–68.

Bain, J. S. (1956), *Barriers to New Competition*, Cambridge, Mass.: Harvard University Press.

Bainbridge, D. I. (1994), *Intellectual Property*, 2nd edn., London: Pitman.

Baldwin, T. F., McVoy, D. S., and Steinfield, C. (1995), *Convergence: Integrating Media, Information and Communication*, Thousand Oaks, Calif.: Sage.

Balenson, D. (1996), 'Trusted Information Systems World-wide Survey of Cryptographic Products—Status March '96', *TIS Website*, http://www.tis.com/crypto/survey.html accessed 15 October 1997.

Bar, F., Cohen, S., Cowhey, P., DeLong, B., Kleeman, M., and Zysman, J. (1999), 'Defending the Internet Revolution in the Broadband Era: When Doing Nothing is Doing Harm', Berkeley: Berkeley Round Table on the International Economy (BRIE), University of California at Berkeley, E-conomy Working Paper No. 12, Aug.

Barbetta, G. P. (1996), *Senza scopo di lucro: Il settore non-profit in Italia*, Bologna: Il Mulino.

Barling, B., and Stark, H. (1995), 'Business-to-Business, Electronic Commerce—Opening the Market (Volume 1)', London: Ovum.

Bell, D. (1973), *The Coming of Post-Industrial Society: A Venture in Social Forecasting*, New York: Basic Books.

Bengtsson, I. B., and Wihdén, B.-M. (1997), 'No Time to Rest Once You Reach the Top', Stockholm: Research and Development in Ericsson Contact in Depth, http://www.ericsson.com/SE/kon_con/tema_indepth/indepth/id15_97/t_2.html accessed 21 Aug. 1999.

Bennahum, D. S. (1988), 'The Hot New Medium is . . . Email', *Wired*, 6 Apr., pp. 104–5.

Bernard, J. (1997a), 'The Internet Opportunity: A US Perspective', Paris: Technology Investment Partners, FAIR Working Paper, Feb.

——(1997b), 'Technical Infrastructure and Services Trends', Paris, Technology Investment Partners: FAIR Working Paper No. 30, Mar.

——(1998), 'The Computerization of Public Networks: An Opportunity and a Challenge for the European Telecom Industry', Paris: Technology Investment Partners, FAIR Working Paper No. 49, Apr.

Bernard, J., Cattaneo, G., Mansell, R., Morganti, F., Silverstone, R., and Steinmueller, W. E. (1997), 'The European Information Society at the Crossroads', Summary of the 2nd Year's Activities in the ACTS FAIR Project AC093, Brighton: SPRU.

Bernard, J., Cattaneo, G., Mansell, R., Silverstone, R., and Steinmueller, W. E. (1996), 'The Way Forward: Advanced Communication, Economic Growth and Social Development in Europe', Summary of the 1st Year's Activities in the ACTS FAIR Project AC093, Brighton: SPRU.

Besen, S. M., and Raskind, L. J. (1991), 'An Introduction to the Law and Economics of Intellectual Property', *Journal of Economic Perspectives*, 5(1): 3–27.

Bethesda Research Institute (1984), 'Study of Local Bypass—Final Survey Results', New York: Submitted to New York State Public Service Commission, Case No. 28710, 19 June.

Bianchi, A., and Kluzer, S. (1997), 'The Information Society and Regional Development in Europe', Milan: Centre for Urban and Regional Development Studies (CURDS), University of Newcastle and Databank Consulting, FAIR Working Paper No. 27, Mar.

Bicknell, D. (1995), 'Encryption Rules Put BT Disc on Export Black List', *Computer Weekly*, 7 Dec., p. 2.

Bigham, F. (1997), 'Telecom Costing in Canada: The Story and the Lessons', in W. H. Melody (ed.), *Telecom Reform: Principles, Policies and Regulatory Practices*, Lyngby: Technical University of Denmark, 247–72.

Bijker, W., and Law, J. (1992), *Shaping Technology/Building Society: Studies in Sociotechnical Change*, Cambridge, Mass.: MIT Press.

BIPE Conseil, IFO Institute, and LENTIC Institute (1997), 'Effects on Employment of the Liberalisation of the Telecommunications Sector', Brussels: A report for European Commission DG V and DG XIII by BIPE Conseil in partnership with IFO Institute, Munich and LENTIC Institute in Liege, Jan.

Blackman, C. R. (1995), 'Universal Service: Obligation or Opportunity?', *Telecommunications Policy*, 19(3): 171–6.

Blair, T. (1999), 'Speech by the Rt Hon Tony Blair MP at the Confederation of British Industry Conference '99', London: Confederation of British Industry News Release, Nov.

Blum, D. C. (1996), 'State and Local Taxing Authorities: Taking More Than Their Fair Share of the Electronic Information Age', *The John Marshall Journal of Computer and Information Law*, 3: 493–522.

Boczkowski, P. (1999), 'Understanding the Development of Online Newspapers', *New Media and Society*, 1(1): 101–26.

Boekhoudt, A. H., and te Spenke, G. (1996), 'Virtual World, Real Tax Problems', *International Tax Review*, 7: 9–11.

Boisot, M. H. (1995), *Information Space: A Framework for Learning in Organizations, Institutions and Culture*, London: Routledge.

——(1998), *Knowledge Assets: Securing Competitive Advantage in the Information Economy*, Oxford: Oxford University Press.

Booz Allen & Hamilton (1997), 'Enabling the Information Society', The Hague: Prepared for the Informal Council of Industry Ministers, 31 Jan.–2 Feb.

Bork, R. H. (1978), *The Antitrust Paradox*, New York: Basic Books.

Borland, J. (1998), 'Governors Vote to Support Net Taxes', *Net Insider*, 24 Feb.

Borrows, J. D., Bernt, P. A., and Lawton, R. W. (1994), 'Universal Service in the United States: Dimensions of the Debate, Discussion Paper No. 124', Bad Honnef: Wissenschaftliches Institut für Kommunikationsdienste.

Bourdieu, P. (1977a), *Outline of a Theory of Practice*, Cambridge: Cambridge University Press.

——(1977b), *Reproduction in Education, Society and Culture*, London: Sage.

—— (1986), *Distinction: A Social Critique of the Judgement of Taste*, London: Routledge & Kegan Paul.

Branscomb, A. (1993), 'Jurisdictional Quandaries for Global Networks', in L. M. Harasim (ed.), *Global Networks*, Cambridge, Mass.: MIT Press, 83–104.

—— (1994), *Who Owns Information? From Privacy to Public Access*, New York: Basic Books.

Branscomb, L. M., and Keller, J. H. (eds.) (1996), *Converging Infrastructures: Intelligent Transportation and the National Information Infrastructure*, Cambridge, Mass.: MIT Press.

Brophy, P., Allred, J., and Allred, J. (1995), 'Open Distance Learning in Public Libraries: Final Report', Brussels: PROLIB/ODL 10117 by the University of Central Lancashire, Centre for Research in Library & Information Management prepared for the European Commission, DG XIII, Library Networks and Services.

Brown, D., and Capelli, W. (1996), 'Electronic Cash Opportunities for Banks and IT Suppliers', London: Ovum.

Business Week (1996*a*), 'New Tolls on the Information Highway? State Sees Bit Revenues in Cyberspace', *Business Week*, 12 Feb., pp. 9–10.

—— (1996*b*), 'Survey Conducted by ActivMedia', *Business Week*, 23 Sept., pp. 22–5.

—— (1996*c*), 'The Tax Man Cometh to Cyberspace', *Business Week*, 9 Dec., pp. 21–2.

Calhoun, G. (1992), *Wireless Access and the Local Telephone Network*, Norwood, NJ: Artech House.

Callon, M. (1992), 'The Dynamics of Techno-Economic Networks', in R. Coombs, R. Saviotti, and V. Walsh (eds.), *Technological Change and Company Strategies: Economic and Sociological Perspectives*, New York: Harcourt Brace Javanovich, 72–102.

Cargill, C. (1989), *Information Technology Standardization: Theory, Process, and Organizations*, Maynard, Mass.: Digital Press.

Castells, M. (1989), *The Informational City: Information Technology, Economic Restructuring, and the Urban-Regional Process*, Oxford: Basil Blackwell.

—— (1996), *The Information Age: Economy, Society and Culture*, I. *The Rise of the Network Society*, Oxford: Blackwell.

—— (1997), *The Information Age: Economy, Society and Culture*, II. *The Power of Identity*, Oxford: Blackwell.

—— (1998), *The Information Age: Economy, Society and Culture*, III. *End of Millennium*, Oxford: Blackwell.

Cattaneo, G., Grazzini, F., and Kluzer, S. (1997), 'Opportunities for Economic and Employment Growth in the Evolution towards the Information Society', Milan: FAIR Working Paper No. 29, Mar.

Cattaneo, G., Kluzer, S., Melloni, S., and Tardia, T. (1996), 'Review of Developments in Advanced Communication Markets', Milan: Databank, FAIR Working Paper No. 1, Oct.

Cattaneo, G., Mansell, R., Steinmueller, W. E., Soete, L., and Bernard, J. (1998), 'Building the European Information Society', Summary of the 3rd Year's Activities in the ACTS FAIR Project AC093, Nov., Milan: Databank.

Cave, M. (1994), 'The Lean Controller: The New Patterns of Regulation', *Demos*, 4: 16–18.

—— (1997), 'Cost Analysis and Cost Modelling for Regulatory Purposes: UK Experience', in W. H. Melody (ed.), *Telecom Reform: Principles, Policies and Regulatory Practices*, Lyngby: Technical University of Denmark, 273–342.

Cave, M., and Cowie, C. (1996), 'Regulating Conditional Access in European Pay Broadcasting', Solomon, Md.: Telecommunications Policy Research Conference, 5–7 Oct.

—— (1998), 'Not Only Conditional Access: Towards a Better Regulatory Approach to Digital TV', *Communications & Strategies*, 30(3rd Quarter): 77–101.

Cawson, A., Haddon, L., and Miles, I. (1995), *The Shape of Things to Consume: Delivering Information Technology into the Home*, Aldershot: Avebury.

Centre for the Study of Financial Innovation (1997), *The Internet and Financial Services*, London: City and Financial Publishing.

Chamberlin, E. (1938), *The Theory of Monopolistic Competition*, Cambridge, Mass.: Harvard University Press.

Chaum, D. (1992), 'Achieving Electronic Privacy', *Scientific American*, Aug.: 96–101.

Chesbrough, H., and Teece, D. (1996), 'When is Virtual Virtuous?: Organising for Innovation', *Harvard Business Review*, Jan./Feb.: 65–73.

Chiariglione, L. (1996), 'MPEG and Multimedia Communications', Turin: CSELT.

Christensen, K. J., Haas, L. C., Noel, F. E., and Strole, N. C. (1995), 'Local Area Networks—Evolving from Shared to Switched Access', *IBM Systems Journal*, 34(3): 347–74.

Cigler, J. D., Burritt, H. C., and Stinnett, S. E. (1996), 'Cyberspace: The Final Frontier for International Tax Concepts?', *The Journal of International Taxation*, 8: 340–50.

Claisse, G. (1997), 'The Multimedia Galaxy: Patterns and Future Prospects for Household Equipment', Milan: A report for Telecom Italia, published in 1998 as 'La Galassia Multimediale Logiche e prospective di equipaggiamento delle famiglie', in *Telecommunicando in Europa, A Cura di Leopoldina Furtunati Collana di Sociologia*, Milan: Franco Angeli.

Clark, J. M. (1923), *The Economics of Overhead Costs*, Chicago: University of Chicago Press.

Clark, T. (1998), 'Digicash Files Chapter 11', CNET News.Com, 4 Nov., http://news.cnet.com/news/0-1003-200-334992.htm accessed 20 Sept. 1999.

Coase, R. H. (1937), 'The Nature of the Firm', *Economica*, 4(Nov.): 386–405.

Cohen, R. B. (1996), 'An Economic Model of Future Changes in the US Communications and Media Industries', Washington, DC: Consultancy R. B. Cohen.

Collaborative Open Group on Ethics (1995), 'Internet Ethical Issues: Report from Ethics COG', Ethics COG.

Collins, R., and Murroni, C. (1996), *New Media, New Policies: Media and Communications Strategies for the Future*, Cambridge: Polity.

Common Law Institute of Intellectual Property Rights (1994), 'Digitisation and the Challenge to Copyright', London: Common Law Institute of Intellectual Property Rights, 28 Apr.

Commons, J. R. (1957), *The Legal Foundations of Capitalism*, Madison: University of Wisconsin Press.

Communications Media Center at New York Law School (1998a), 'Internet Tax Moratorium Approved by US Senate Finance Committee', *Bulletin*, 28 July, http://www.cmcnyls.edu/bulletin.htm accessed 15 Aug. 1999.

——(1998b), 'US Lawmakers Compromise on Moratorium on Internet Taxation', *Bulletin*, 21 Mar., http://www.cmcnyls.edu/bulletin.htm accessed 15 Aug. 1999.

Comparetto, G., and Ramirez, R. (1997), 'Trends in Mobile Satellite Technology', *Computer*, Feb., pp. 12–14.

Computer Science and Telecommunications Board (CSTB) (1994), *Realising the Information Future: The Internet and Beyond*, Washington, DC: National Academy.

——(1996), *The Unpredictable Certainty: Information Infrastructure Through 2000*, Washington, DC: National Academy.

Confidea USA (1996), 'Evoluzione e prospettive del mercato del lavoro negli Stati Uniti', Turin: Fondazione Giovanni Agnelli.

Cooke, P., and Morgan, K. (1998), *The Associational Economy: Firms, Regions and Innovation*, Oxford: Oxford University Press.

Copyright Clearance Agency (1999), 'Copyright Clearance Service Reaches £1 Million', London: Copyright Clearance Agency.

Copyright Licensing Agency (1998), 'White Paper on CLA's Proposals for Licensing Digitisation in Higher Education', London: Copyright Licensing Agency.

Cordell, A. J., Ide, T. R., Soete, L., and Kamp, K. (1997), *The New Wealth of Nations: Taxing Cyberspace*, Toronto: Between the Lines.

Cornford, C., Gillespie, A., and Richardson, R. (1996), 'Regional Development in the Information Society: A Review and Analysis', Newcastle upon Tyne: Paper prepared for the EU High Level Expert Group on the Social and Societal Aspects of Information Society, Centre for Urban and Regional Development Studies (CURDS), University of Newcastle.

Correa, C. M. (1994), 'The TRIPS Agreement: New International Standards for Intellectual Property Rights', Buenos Aires: Latintrade/UNCTAD, Dec.

Cowan, R., David, P. A., and Foray, D. (1999), 'The Explicit Economics of Knowledge Codification and Tacitness', Maastricht, Oxford, and Paris: University of Maastricht, All Souls College, and University of Paris-Dauphine/CNRS, paper prepared under the European Commission TSER Programme's TIPIK Project for presentation to the TIPIK Workshop in Strasbourg, at BETA, University of Louis Pasteur, forthcoming in *Industrial and Corporate Change*, May.

Cowhey, P. (1990), 'The International Telecommunications Regime: The Political Roots of Regimes for High Technology', *International Organization*, 44(2): 169–99.

Credé, A. (1997a), 'An Examination of Credit Risk Assessment and Cash Handling Procedures in Commercial Banks', SPRU University of Sussex, unpublished D.Phil. thesis, Brighton.

——(1997b), 'Information Society Security: Trust, Confidence and Technology: ICTs, Information Production and Tacit Authentication', Brighton: FAIR Working Paper No. 26, Feb.

Cusumano, M. A., and Yoffie, D. B. (1998), *Competing on Internet Time: Lessons from Netscape and its Battle with Microsoft*, New York: Free Press.

D'Amico, M. A. (1997), 'WIPO Proposals: What Me Worry?', *Digital Media*, 6(6): 3 pages at http://lawcrawler.findlaw.com/MAD/wipo.html accessed 1 Sept. 1999.

Danmarks Biblioteksskole (1996), 'Public Libraries and the Information Society—A Study', Copenhagen: Danmarks Biblioteksskole.

Databank Consulting (1997), 'Evolution of the Internet and the WWW in Europe', Milan: Databank Consulting with the support of IDATE and TNO, study for the European Commission DG XIII.

Datamation (1997), 'Survey', *Datamation*, 17 Oct.: 12–14.

Datapro (1994), *Voice Security Devices: Overview*, New York: McGraw Hill.

Date, C. J. (1995), *An Introduction to Database Systems*, 6th edn., New York: John Wiley & Sons.

David, P. A. (1975), 'The Mechanization of Reaping in the Ante-Bellum Midwest', in P. A. David (ed.), *Technical Choice, Innovation and Economic Growth*, Cambridge: Cambridge University Press, 195–232.

——(1987), 'Some New Standards for the Economics of Standardization in the Information Age', in P. Dasgupta and P. Stoneman (eds.), *Economic Policy and Technological Performance*, Cambridge: Cambridge University Press, 206–39.

——(1993), 'Intellectual Property Institutions and the Panda's Thumb: Patents, Copyrights, Trade Secrets in Economic Theory and History', in M. B. Wallerstein, M. E. Mogee, and R. A. Schoen (eds.), *Global Dimensions of Intellectual Property Rights in Science and Technology*, Washington, DC: National Academy, 19–61.

David, P. A., and Foray, D. (1994), 'Markov Random Fields, Percolation Structures and the

Economics of EDI Standards Diffusion', in G. Pogorel (ed.), *Global Telecommunication Strategies and Technical Change*, Amsterdam: Elsevier, 135–70.

David, P. A., and Greenstein, S. (1990), 'The Economics of Compatibility Standards: An Introduction to Recent Research', *Economics of Innovation and New Technology*, 1(1): 3–41.

David, P. A., and Shurmer, M. (1996), 'Formal Standards-Setting for Global Telecommunications and Information Services: Towards an Institutional Regime Transformation?', *Telecommunications Policy*, 20(10): 789–815.

David, P. A., and Steinmueller, W. E. (1990), 'The ISDN Bandwagon is Coming, But Who Will be There to Climb Aboard?: Quandaries in the Economics of Data Communication Networks', *Economics of Innovation and New Technology*, 1(1–2): 43–62.

—— (1996), 'Standards, Trade and Competition in the Emerging Global Information Infrastructure Environment', *Telecommunications Policy*, 20(10): 817–30.

—— (2000), 'Understanding the Puzzles and Payoffs of the IT Revolution: The "Productivity Paradox" after Ten Years', in P. A. David and W. E. Steinmueller (eds.), *Productivity and the Information Technology Revolution*, London: Harwood Academic (forthcoming).

Davies, A. (1996), 'Innovation in Large Technical Systems: The Case of Telecommunications', *Industrial and Corporate Change*, 5(4): 1143–80.

De Bony, E. (1997), 'US, European Officials Rally Against Activation of Net Taxes', *Online News Story*, 2 Oct.

Denning, D. (1996), 'The Future of Cryptography (Revised Version)', Canberra: Joint Australian/OECD Conference on Security, Privacy and Intellectual Property Protection in the Global Information Infrastructure.

Department of Commerce (1999), 'The Emerging Digital Economy II', Washington, DC: Department of Commerce, June.

Department of Commerce and the National Security Agency (1996), 'A Study of the International Market for Computer Software with Encryption—Prepared for the Interagency Working Group on Encryption and Telecommunications Policy', Washington, DC: Department of Commerce.

Department of Trade and Industry (1996), 'IT for ALL: A Survey into Public Awareness of Attitudes Toward and Access to Information and Communication Technology', London: DTI, Information Society Initiative.

—— (1997a), 'The Guide to How IT Can Help You', London: DTI, Information Society Initiative.

—— (1997b), 'The UK R&D Scoreboard, 1997', London: DTI.

—— (1998a), 'The Latest Findings Concerning Attitudes Towards IT', London: DTI, Information Society Initiative.

—— (1998b), 'Our Competitive Future: Building the Knowledge Driven Economy, The 1998 Competitiveness White Paper', London: DTI, Dec.

—— (1998c), 'Strategic Export Controls', London: DTI, presented to Parliament by the President of the Board of Trade by Command of Her Majesty, July.

—— (1999a), 'Annex 1, List Referred to in Article 2 of Decision 94/942/CFSP and Article 3(1) of Regulation (EC) No. 381/94, Incorporating UK National Controls from Dual-Use and Related Goods (Export Control) Regulations 1996, List of Dual-Use Goods', London: DTI, EU & UK National Controls, ANX1_A02.DOC, 18 Apr., 14 July.

—— (1999b), 'Category 5—Telecommunications and "Information Security"', London: DTI, EU & UK National Controls, CAT5_A01.DOC, 18 Apr.

—— (1999c), 'Export License', London: DTI, mimeo, Nov. 1999.

Department of Trade and Industry and Home Office (1999a), 'Building Confidence in Electronic Commerce: A Consultation Document', London: DTI and Home Office, 5 Mar.

—— (1999b), 'A Report for the DTI Summarising Responses to "Building Confidence in Electronic Commerce: A Consultation Document"', London: DTI and Home Office.

Dervin, B., and Shields, P. (1990), 'Users: The Missing Link in Technology Research', Communication Technology Section Meeting, International Association for Mass Communication Research, Yugoslavia, Lake Bled, Aug. 25–31.

Dibona, C., Stone, M., and Ockman, S. (eds.) (1999), *Open Sources: Voices from the Open Source Revolution*, Cambridge: O'Reilly & Associates.

Diebold, J. (1959), *Automation: Its Impact on Business and Labor*, Washington, DC: Planning Pamphlet No. 106, National Planning Association.

Digital Video Express (1999), 'Digital Video Express, LP to Discontinue Operations', *Digital Video Express Official Website* http://www.divx.com accessed 24 Aug. 1999.

van Dijk, J. (1999), *The Network Society*, London: Sage.

Downes, T. A., and Greenstein, S. M. (1998), 'Do Commercial ISPs Provide Universal Access?', Medford, Mass. and Evanston, Ill.: Tufts University and Northwestern University, paper prepared for the Telecommunication Policy Research 1998 Conference, 2 Dec. at http://skew2.kellogg.nwu.edu/~greenste/research/ accessed 27 Aug. 1999.

Drucker, P. F. (1993), *Post-Capitalist Society*, New York: Harper Business Books.

Dryden, J. (1997), 'Policy Implications of the Development and Impacts of the Information Society', in A. Dumort and J. Dryden (eds.), *The Economics of the Information Society*, Luxembourg: Office for Official Publications of the European Communities, 272–6.

DuBoff, R. (1967), 'The Introduction of Electrical Power in American Manufacturing', *Economic History Review*, 20(3): 509–18.

—— (1983), 'The Telegraph and the Structure of Markets in the United States, 1845–1890', *Research in Economic History*, 8: 253–77.

Dumort, A., and Dryden, J. (eds.) (1997), *The Economics of the Information Society*, Luxembourg: Office for Official Publications of the European Communities.

Dumort, A., and Riché-Magnier, M. (1997), 'Employment and Labour in the Information Society', in A. Dumort and J. Dryden (eds.), *The Economics of the Information Society*, Luxembourg: Office for Official Publications of the European Communities, 161–9.

Dunahoo, C., and Carlisle, J. F. (1997), ' Cybertax 1.0: The U.S. Treasury Paper on Electronic Commerce', *Tax Notes International*, 8: 693–9.

Dutton, W. H. (ed.) (1996), *Information and Communications Technologies: Visions and Realities*, Oxford: Oxford University Press.

Dutton, W. H. (1999), *Society of the Line: Information Politics in the Digital Age*, Oxford: Oxford University Press.

Dyson, E. (1997), *Release 2.0: A Design for Living in the Digital Age*, London: Viking.

e-cash Technologies Inc. (1999), 'Press Release', Seattle: e-cash Technologies Inc., http://ecashtechnologies.com/hp.htm accessed 22 Oct. 1999.

Economist, The (1995a), 'The Accidental Superhighway', Special Issue.

—— (1995b), 'The Internet Survey', 1 July.

—— (1996a), 'The Economics of the Internet—Too Cheap to Meter?', 19 Oct.

—— (1996b), 'Taxed in Cyberspace', 13 July.

—— (1996c), 'Why the Net Should Grow Up', 19 Oct.

—— (1997a), 'Disappearing Taxes: The Tap Runs Dry', 31 May.

—— (1997b), 'The Disappearing Taxpayer', 31 May.

Electronic Frontier Foundation (1999a), 'Challenging US Export Controls on Encryption:

Background to Bernstein v. US Department of Justice', Washington, DC: Electronic Frontier Foundation, http://www.eff.org/bernstein accessed 24 Sept. 1999.

Electronic Frontier Foundation (1999b), 'Recent News, Encryption Policy News', Washington, DC: Electronic Frontier Foundation, http://www.eff.org, accessed 24 Sept. 1999.

Eliasson, G. (1990), *The Knowledge-Based Information Economy*, Stockholm: Almqvist & Wiksell.

——(1991), 'Modeling the Experimentally Organized Economy: Complex Dynamics in an Empirical Micro-Macro Model of Endogenous Economic Growth', *Journal of Economic Behavior and Organization*, 16(1/2): 153–82.

Employment Horizon (1996), 'Provisional Directory of Projects: Working Document, Volume 2, The Disadvantaged', Brussels: DG V Industrial Relations and Social Affairs, European Commission.

ETNO (1993), 'ETNO Report on Draft Directive SYN 288', Brussels: European Public Telecommunications Network Operators' Association (ETNO).

——(1994), 'ETNO Reflection Document on Amended Commission Proposal for an EP and Council Directive Concerning the Protection of Personal Data and Privacy, in Particular ISDN and Digital Mobile Networks, COM (94)128 final—COD 288—13/6/94', Brussels: European Public Telecommunications Network Operators' Association (ETNO).

Eurocities (1996), 'Eurocities—The European Association of Metropolitan Cities', no city named: Eurocities, http://www.eena.org/dacor/profiles/eurocity.html accessed 12 Sept. 1999.

European Commission (1983), 'Telecommunications (Communication from the Commission to the Council)', Brussels: European Commission, COM(83)329 final, 9 June.

——(1987), 'Towards a Dynamic European Economy: Green Paper on the Development of the Common Market for Telecommunication Services and Equipment', Brussels: European Commission, COM(87) final, 30 June.

——(1988a), 'Commission Directive of 16 May on Competition in the Markets in Telecommunication Terminal Equipment', Brussels: European Commission 88/301/EEC, OJ L 131/73, 16 May.

——(1988b), 'Green Paper on Copyright and the Challenge of Technology: Copyright Issues Requiring Immediate Action', Brussels: COM(88)172 final, 7 June.

——(1990a), 'Commission Directive of 28 June 1990 on Competition in the Markets for Telecommunications Services', Brussels: European Commission, 90/388/EEC, OJ L 192/10, 24.7.90, 24 July.

——(1990b), 'Commission Green Paper on the Development of European Standardization: Action for Faster Technological Integration in Europe', Brussels: European Commission COM(90)456 final.

——(1991), 'Standardization in the European Economy', European Commission, COM(91)521, Brussels, 16 Dec.

——(1993a), 'Communication from the Commission to the Council, the European Parliament and the Economic and Social Committee. Developing Universal Service for Telecommunications in a Competitive Environment. Proposal for a Council Resolution on Universal Service Principles in the Telecommunications Sector', Brussels: European Commission COM(93)543, 15 Nov.

——(1993b), 'Growth, Competitiveness, and Employment: The Challenges and Ways Forward into the 21st Century. White Paper', Brussels: European Commission, COM(93)700 final.

——(1994a), 'Commission Statement Concerning Council Resolution on Universal Service in the Telecommunications Sector', Brussels: European Commission, O J 16/2/94, 16 Feb.

——(1994b), 'Communication from the Commission: Green Paper on the Liberalisation of

Telecommunications Infrastructure and Cable Television Networks: Part One—Principle and Timetable', Brussels: European Commission, COM(94)440 final, 25 Oct.

—— (1994c), 'Communication from the Commission to the Council and European Parliament Regarding Measures to be taken Regarding the Consultancy on the Green Paper on Pluralism and Media Concentration in the Internal Market, Assessment of the Need for a Community Action', Brussels: European Commission COM(94)353, 5 Oct.

—— (1994d), 'Council Resolution of 7 February 1994 on Universal Service Principles in the Telecommunications Sector', Brussels: European Commission, OJ 16.2.94, 94/C48/01, 7 Feb.

—— (1994e), 'Europe's Way to the Information Society. An Action Plan. Communication from the Commission to the Council and the European Parliament and to the Economic and Social Committee and the Committee of Regions', Brussels: European Commission, COM(94)347 final, 19 July.

—— (1995a), 'Commission Directive 95/51/EC Amending Directive 90/388/EEC with Regard to the Abolition of the Restrictions on the Use of Cable Television Networks for the Provision of Already Liberalised Telecommunications Services', Brussels: European Commission, OJ No. L 256/49, 26 Oct.

—— (1995b), 'Communication on Wider Use of Standardisation to Support EU Policy', Brussels: European Commission COM(95)412, 30 Oct.

—— (1995c), 'Directive 95/46/EC of the European Parliament and of the Council of 24 October 1995 on the Protection of Individuals with Regard to the Processing of Personal Data and on the Free Movement of Such Data', Brussels: European Commission, OJ No. L 281/31, 24 Oct.

—— (1995d), 'First Annual Report from the Commission to the Council, the European Parliament and the Economic and Social Committee on Progress in Implementing the Action Plan for the Introduction of Advanced Television Services in Europe', Brussels: European Commission, COM(95)263, 16 July.

—— (1995e), 'Green Paper on Copyright and Related Rights in the Information Society', Brussels: European Commission COM(95)382 final, 19 July.

—— (1995f), 'Green Paper on Innovation', Brussels: European Commission COM(95)688.

—— (1995g), 'Green Paper on the Liberalisation of Telecommunications Infrastructure and Cable Television Networks (Part II)', Brussels: European Commission, 25 Jan.

—— (1995h), 'Opinion of the Commission pursuant to Article 189 b(2)(d) of the EC Treaty on the European Parliament's amendments to the Council's Common Position Regarding the Proposal for a European Parliament and Council Directive on the Use of Standards for the Transmission of Television Signals', Brussels: European Commission COM(95)319 final—COD 476, 6 July.

—— (1995i), 'An Overview of the Programme and Projects', Brussels: Advanced Communications Technologies and Services (ACTS), European Commission DG XIII.

—— (1995j), 'Proposal for a European Parliament and Council Directive on Interconnection in Telecommunications with Regard to Ensuring Universal Service and Interoperability through Application of the Principles of Open Network Provision (ONP)', Brussels: European Commission COM (95)379 final, 19.07.1995, 19 July.

—— (1996a), 'Advanced Communications in Europe, 1996 Strategic Audit of Advanced Communications Developments in Europe', Brussels: European Commission, 4 July.

—— (1996b), 'Communication of the Commission to the Council, the European Parliament, the Economic and Social Committee and the Committee of the Regions on the Information Society: From Corfu to Dublin', Dublin: European Commission, 13 Sept.

European Commission (1996*c*), 'Communication to the Commission, Background Paper for the Information Society Council of Ministers Meeting in Dublin', Dublin: European Commission, 8 Oct.

—— (1996*d*), 'Communication to the European Parliament, the Council, the Economic and Social Committee and the Committee of the Regions—Illegal and Harmful Content on the Internet COM (96)487', Brussels: European Commission, 16 Oct.

—— (1996*e*), 'Communication to the European Parliament, the Council, the Economic and Social Committee and the Committee of the Regions on Universal Service for Telecommunications in the Perspective of a Fully Liberalised Environment', Brussels: European Commission COM(96)73, 12 Mar.

—— (1996*f*), 'Council Resolution of 21 November 1996 on New Policy Priorities regarding the Information Society, OJ No. C 376', Brussels: European Commission, 12 Dec.

—— (1996*g*), 'Directive 89/552/EEC on Television without Frontiers', Brussels: European Commission OJ No. L 298 17 Oct., proposal for an amendment dated 31 May 1995 COM(95) 86 final; Modified Proposal COM(96)200 of 7 Apr. 1996; Common Position of 8 July 1996 and Communication from the Commission and the Parliament SEC(96) 1292 on the Common Position, 8 July.

—— (1996*h*), 'Draft Communication from the European Commission to the Council, the European Parliament, the Economic and Social Committee, and Committee of the Regions on "Europe at the Forefront of the Global Information Society: Rolling Action Plan"', Brussels: European Commission, 26 Nov.

—— (1996*i*), 'Employment in Europe 1996', Luxembourg: European Commission DG V (Employment, Industrial Relations and Social Affairs), COM(96)485, Office for Official Publications of the European Communities.

—— (1996*j*), 'Extended Report of the Meeting with the British, Italian and German Internet Service Providers Association (ISPA)', Brussels: European Commission, 12 July.

—— (1996*k*), 'Green Paper on the Protection of Minors and Human Dignity in Audiovisual and Information Services', Luxembourg: European Commission, INFO2000, OJ No. C 93/1, 24 Oct.

—— (1996*l*), 'Legal Protection for Encrypted Services in the Internal Market: Consultation on the Need for Community Action—Commission Green Paper', Brussels: European Commission, COM(96)76 final, 6 Mar.

—— (1996*m*), 'Living and Working in the Information Society: People First—Green Paper', Brussels: European Commission, COM(96)389, 22 July.

—— (1996*n*), 'Networks for People and their Communities: Making the Most of the Information Society in the European Union', Brussels: First Annual Report to the European Commission from the Information Society Forum, June.

—— (1996*o*), 'Networks for People and their Communities: Making the Most of the Information Society in the European Union—Supplement containing Working Groups' Reports', Brussels: First Annual Report to the European Commission from the Information Society Forum, June.

—— (1996*p*), 'Proposal for a European Parliament and Council Directive on the Application of Open Network Provision (ONP) to Voice Telephony and on Universal Service for Telecommunications in a Competitive Environment (replacing European Parliament and Council Directive 95/62/EC)', Brussels: European Commission, 11 Sept.

—— (1996*q*), 'Report of the Task Force—Educational Software and Multimedia', Luxembourg: European Commission.

—— (1996*r*), 'Standardization and the Global Information Society: The European Approach',

Communication from the Commission to the Council and the Parliament, Brussels: European Commission COM (96)359, 24 July.

—— (1997*a*), 'Directive 95/47/EEC On the Use of Standards for the Transmission of Television Signals', Brussels: European Commission.

—— (1997*b*), 'Directive 97/33/EC of the European Parliament and the Council of 30 June 1997 on Interconnection in Telecommunications with regard to Ensuring Universal Service and Interoperability through Application of the Principles of Open Network Provision', Brussels: European Commission OJ No. L 199, 26.7.1997, 30 June.

—— (1997*c*), 'Employment in Europe 1997', Luxembourg: European Commission DGV (Employment, Industrial Relations and Social Affairs), Office for Official Publications of the European Communities.

—— (1997*d*), 'A European Initiative in Electronic Commerce', Brussels: European Commission, COM(97)157.

—— (1997*e*), 'Green Paper—Partnership for a New Organisation of Work', Brussels: European Commission COM(97)128.

—— (1997*f*), 'Green Paper on the Convergence of the Telecommunications, Media and Information Technology Sectors, and the Implications for Regulation, Towards an Information Society Approach', Brussels: European Commission COM(97)623, 3 Dec.

—— (1997*g*), 'Information Society Forum 1997 Report', Brussels: Information Society Forum.

—— (1997*h*), 'Note for the Attention of Mr A. Larsson, Director General DGV, Mr J. Currie, Director General DGXXI, Bit Tax Proposal and Bit Tax Proposal Analysis by DGXIII', Brussels: European Commission, Directorate General XIII, Ref DGXIII/A/003843, 20 Apr.

—— (1997*i*), 'Proposal for a European Parliament and Council Directive on the Application of Open Network Provision (ONP) to Voice Telephony and on Universal Service for Telecommunications in a Competitive Environment (replacing EP and Council Directive 95/62/EC)', Brussels: European Commission General Secretariat of the Council, Working Document No. 4/97, 10 Mar.

—— (1998*a*), 'The Commission Adopts a Green Paper on Tackling the Problem of Counterfeiting and Piracy in the Single Market', Brussels: European Commission, 22 Oct.

—— (1998*b*), 'Commission's Recommendation on Interconnection in a Liberalised Telecommunications Market, Part 1—Interconnection Pricing C(98)50', Brussels: European Commission, 8 Jan.

—— (1998*c*), 'Communication from the Commission to the Council, the European Parliament, the Economic and Social Committee and the Committee of the Regions on the Implementation of the Telecommunication Regulatory Package', Brussels: European Commission, http://europaeu.int/comm/dg04/libera/en/com9705.htm accessed 6 April 2000.

—— (1998*d*), 'Directive on Data Protection in the Telecommunications Sector Adopted by the Council and European Parliament on 15 December 1997', Brussels: European Commission, 97/66/EC, OJ No. L 24, 30 Jan.

—— (1998*e*), 'The European Employment Strategy: Investing in People', Brussels: European Commission Employment & Social Affairs, Employment & European Social Fund.

—— (1998*f*), 'Green Paper Combating Counterfeiting and Piracy in the Single Market', Brussels: European Commission EC569/98, 15 Oct.

—— (1998*g*), 'Job Opportunities in the Information Society: Exploiting the Potential of the Information Revolution', Brussels: European Commission, Report to the European Council COM (1998)590 final.

—— (1998*h*), 'OII Guide to Intellectual Property Rights in Electronic Information Interchange', Brussels: I*M Europe, Info 2000, Apr.

European Commission (1998*i*), 'Proposal for a Council Regulation (EC) Setting Up a Community Regime for the Control of Exports of Dual-Use Goods and Technology', Brussels: European Commission, COM(1998)257 final, OJ 21 Dec., 98/C 399/01.

—— (1998*j*), 'Proposal for a Directive on Copyright and Related Rights in the Information Society', Brussels: European Commission COM(97)628 OJ No. C 108, 10 Dec.

—— (1998*k*), 'Proposal for a European Parliament and Council Directive on a Common Framework for Electronic Signatures', Brussels: European Commission, COM(1998)297 final, 98/0191 (COD).

—— (1998*l*), 'Proposal for a European Parliament and Council Directive on Certain Legal Aspects of Electronic Commerce in the Internal Market', Brussels: European Commission COM(1998)586 final, 18 Nov.

—— (1998*m*), 'Public Sector Information: A Key Resource for Europe—Green Paper on Public Sector Information in the Information Society', Brussels: European Commission COM (1998)585 final.

—— (1998*n*), 'Third Report on the Implementation of the EU Telecommunications Regulatory Package', DN: IP/98/165', Brussels: European Commission, 18 Feb.

—— (1999*a*), 'Amended Proposal for a European Parliament and Council Directive on Certain Legal Aspects of Electronic Commerce in the Internal Market', Brussels: European Commission, COM(1999)427 final, 98/0325 (COD), presented to the Commission pursuant to Article 250 (2) of the EC-Treaty.

—— (1999*b*), 'Amended Proposal for a European Parliament and Council Directive on Copyright and Related Rights in the Information Society', Brussels: European Commission COM(99) 250 final, 97/0359 (COD), 21 Apr.

—— (1999*c*), 'Communication to the European Parliament, the Council, the Economic and Social Committee and the Committee of the Regions—The Convergence of Telecommunications, Media and Information Technology Sectors, and the Implications for Regulation—Results of the Public Consultation on the Green Paper COM(97)623', Brussels: European Commission COM(1999)108 final, 10 Mar.

—— (1999*d*), 'ESIS Basic Facts, European Overview', Brussels: European Survey of the Information Society, Information Society Project Office (ISPO), European Commission, http://www.ispo.cec.be/isis/ accessed 13 Aug. 1999.

—— (1999*e*), 'Green Paper on the Protection of Minors and Human Dignity in the Context of New Electronic Services COM(97)570fin', Brussels: European Commission, 11 Apr.

—— (1999*f*), 'Results of the Public Consultation on the Convergence of the Telecommunications, Media and Information Technology Sectors', Brussels: European Commission DN: IP/99/164.

European Commission High Level Expert Group (1996), 'Building the European Information Society for Us All—Interim Report, First Reflections of the High Level Expert Group', Luxembourg: Office for Official Publications of the European Communities.

—— (1997), 'Building the European Information Society For Us All: Final Policy Report of the High Level Expert Group, Directorate General for Employment, Industrial Relations and Social Affairs', Luxembourg: Office for Official Publications of the European Communities.

European Commission Information Market Observatory (IMO) (1994), 'EU Electronic Information Supply Industry: Statistics in Perspective', Luxembourg: European Commission IMO Working Paper 94/5.

European Commission Information Society Forum (1999), 'Opinion on the Green Paper of the Commission on Public Sector Information in the Information Society', Brussels: Information Society Forum, European Commission, May.

European Council (1981), 'Convention for the Protection of Individuals with Regard to Automatic Processing of Personal Data', Luxembourg: European Treaty Series No. 108, Jan.

—— (1990), 'Council Directive of 28 June 1990 on the Establishment of the Internal Market for Telecommunications Services through the Implementation of Open Network Provision', Brussels: 90/387/EEC, OJ 24.7.1990 No. L 192: 1–9, 24 July.

—— (1991), 'Council Directive of 14 May 1991 on the Legal Protection of Computer Programs', Brussels: 91/250/EEC, OJ No. L 122/42, 14 May.

—— (1992*a*), 'Council Directive of 5 June 1992 on the Application of Open Network Provision to Leased Lines', Brussels: OJ No. L 165, 19.06.92, 5 June.

—— (1992*b*), 'Council Directive of 19 November 1992 on Rental Right and Lending Right and on Certain Rights Related to Copyright in the Field of Intellectual Property', Brussels: Council of the European Communities, 92/100/EEC, 27 Nov.

—— (1992*c*), 'Council Resolution of 19 December 1991 on the Development of the Common Market for Satellite Communications Services and Equipment', Brussels: European Commission, (92/C8/01), OJ 14.01.1992 No. C8: 1–2. c, 14 Jan.

—— (1993*a*), 'Council Directive of 27 September on the Co-ordination of Certain Rules Concerning Copyright and Certain Rights Related to Copyright Applicable to Satellite Broadcasting and Cable Retransmission', Brussels: Council of the European Communities, 93/83/EEC, 6 Oct.

—— (1993*b*), 'Council Directive of 29 October 1993 Harmonising the Term of Protection of Copyright and Certain Related Rights', Brussels: Council of the European Communities, 93/98/EEC, 29 Oct.

—— (1993*c*), 'Council Resolution of 22 July 1993 on the Review of the Situation in the Telecommunications Sector and the Need for Further Development in that Market', Brussels: (93/C213/01), OJ 06.08.1993 No. C213: 1–3, 22 July.

—— (1994), 'Council Resolution of 7 February 1994 on Universal Service Principles in the Telecommunications Sector (94/C48/01)', Brussels: European Commission, OJ 16.02.94, 7 Feb.

—— (1996*a*), 'Council Decision Adopting a Multiannual Community Programme to Stimulate the Development of a European Multimedia Content Industry and to Encourage the Use of Multimedia Content in the Emerging Information Society', Brussels: European Commission, 4245/1/96, No. 95/0156 (CNS) http://www.echo.lu/info2000/mmrcs/en/info_cns.html accessed 2 Sept. 1999.

—— (1996*b*), 'Directive 96/9/EC of the European Parliament and of the Council of 11 March 1996 on the Legal Protection of Databases', Brussels: European Commission, OJ No. L 77, 27 Mar.

European Information Technology Observatory (EITO) (1996), 'European Information Technology Observatory 1996', Frankfurt: EITO.

—— (EITO) (1997), 'European Information Technology Observatory 1997', Frankfurt: EITO.

—— (EITO) (1999), 'European Information Technology Observatory 1999', Frankfurt: EITO.

European Music Office (1996), 'The Economic Importance of Music in the EU', Brussels: European Music Office report for DGX.

European Round Table of Industrialists (1994), 'Building the Information Highways to Re-engineer Europe. A Message from Industrial Users', Brussels: European Round Table of Industrialists.

EURORIM Project (1997*a*), 'Demand Forecasts at National and EU Level on a Computer-Based Model Taking Usage Costs into Account, EURORIM Deliverable D303—AC219', Brussels: EURORIM Report Prepared for the European Commission.

EURORIM Project (1997*b*), 'A Report on Commercialisation Evolution of Multimedia Services', Brussels: EURORIM Report Prepared for the European Commission. EURORIM Deliverable D305—AC219 Eurorim Web Server at http://www.swt.iao.fhg.de/eurorim accessed 9 Aug. 1999.

Eurostat (1995), *Eurostat Yearbook '95: A Statistical Eye on Europe 1983–1993*, Luxembourg: Office of the Official Publications of the European Communities.

Evans, J. E. (1998), 'New Satellites for Personal Communications', *Scientific American*, Apr., pp. 60–7.

Experian (1999*a*), 'Experian—the New Name for Information Systems', News Release, Nottingham: Experian, http://www.experian.com/corporate/press_releases/060297.html accessed 14 Nov. 1999.

——(1999*b*), 'Experian Extends Consumer Information for Marketeers', News Release, Nottingham: Experian, http://www.experian.com/corporate/press_releases/021899a.html accessed 14 Nov. 1999.

Fancher, C. H. (1996), 'Smart Cards', *Scientific American*, Aug., pp. 24–9.

Farrell, J., and Saloner, G. (1987), 'Competition, Compatibility and Standards: The Economics of Horses, Penguins, and Lemmings', in L. Gabel (ed.), *Product Standardization and Competitive Strategy, Advanced Series in Management*, Amsterdam, Oxford, and Tokyo: North Holland, xi. 1–21.

Federal Communications Commission (1996*a*), 'Joint Board Adopts Universal Service Recommendations, CC Docket 96-45, News Report No. DC 96-100', Washington, DC: Federal Communications Commission, 7 Nov.

——(1996*b*), 'Recommended Decision in the Matter of Federal-State Joint Board on Universal Service, CC Docket No. 96-45', Washington, DC: Federal Communications Commission, 8 Nov.

——(1998*a*), 'In the Matter of Federal-State Joint Board on Universal Service, Report to Congress', Washington, DC: Federal Communications Commission, FCC 98-67, 10 Apr.

——(1998*b*), 'Report in Response to Senate Bill 1768 and Conference Report on H.R. 3579, Report to Congress', Washington, DC: Federal Communications Commission, FCC 98-85, 8 May.

——(1999*a*), 'FCC Adopts Order Addressing Dial-Up Internet Traffic', Washington, DC: Federal Communications Commission, News Release, 25 Feb.

——(1999*b*), 'In the Matter of Changes to the Board of Directors of the National Exchange Carrier Association, Inc., Federal-State Joint Board on Universal Service, Fifth Order of Reconsideration in CC Docket No 97-21 Eleventh Order on Reconsideration in CC Docket No. 96-45 and Further Notice of Proposed Rulemaking', Washington, DC: Federal Communications Commission, 28 May.

——(1999*c*), 'In the Matter of Federal-State Joint Board on Universal Service, Twelfth Order on Reconsideration in CC Docket No. 96-45', Washington, DC: Federal Communications Commission, 28 May.

——(1999*d*), 'In the Matter of Implementation of Local Competition Provisions in the Telecommunications Act of 1996, Inter-Carrier Compensation for ISPP-Bound Traffic, Declaratory Ruling in CC Docket No. 96-98 and Notice of Proposed Rulemaking in CC Docket No. 99-68', Washington, DC: Federal Communications Commission, 25 Feb.

——(1999*e*), 'In the Matter of Inquiry Concerning the Deployment of Advanced Telecommunications Capability to All Americans in a Reasonable and Timely Fashion, and Possible Steps to Accelerate Such Deployment Pursuant to Section 706 of the Telecommunications Act of 1996, CC Docket No. 98-146', Washington, DC: Federal Communications Commission, 2 Feb.

—— (1999*f*), 'No Consumer Per-Minute Charges to Access ISPs', Washington, DC: Federal Communications Commission, Fact Sheet, Feb.

Ferbrache, D. (1996), 'The Nature of the Hacking Threat to Open Networks', London: Paper presented at 'Security, is IT Safe' IEE Conference, Savoy Place, 28 June.

Ferge, Z., and Miller, S. (1993), 'Social Reproduction and the Dynamics of Deprivation', in Z. Ferge and S. Miller (eds.), *Dynamics of Deprivation*, Aldershot: Gower, 296–314.

Ferné, G., Hawkins, R. W., and Foray, D. (1996), 'The Economic Dimension of Electronic Data Interchange (EDI)', Geneva and Paris: International Organization for Standardization (ISO) and Organization for Economic Co-operation and Development (OECD).

Foley, T. (1999*a*), 'Satcom Investors Take Action as Stocks Tumble', *Communications Week International*, 228: 31.

—— (1999*b*), 'Satellite Gets Tied up with Cable', *Communications Week International*, 224: 6–7.

Folio and Copyright Clearance Center (1995), 'Folio Corporation and Copyright Clearance Center Create First Solution for Electronic Copyright Protection', Danvers, Mass.: Copyright Clearance Center/Folio Infobase Technology.

Foray, D. (1995), 'The Economics of Intellectual Property Rights and the Systems of Innovation: The Inevitable Diversity', in J. Hagedoorn (ed.), *Technical Change and the World Economy*, London: Edward Elgar, 109–33.

Forrester Research (1996), 'Will the Web Kill EDI?': Forrester Network Strategy Report No. 10(3), Feb.

Foschini, E. (1997), 'Attivi e Interattivi: Esperienze di Utilizzo delle Reti Informatiche in Istruzione', Milan: available at http://arci01.bo.cnr.it/~foschini/ accessed 4 July 1999.

Fost, D. (1998), 'Latest Video War Erupts—It's DVD vs Divx, Two New Ways to Watch Movies at Home', *San Francisco Chronicle*, 13 Aug. http://www.sfgate.com/cgi-bin/ accessed 24 Aug. 1999.

—— (1999), 'Divx's Death Pleases Opponents', *San Francisco Chronicle*, 18 June http://www.sfgate.com/cgi-bin/ accessed 24 Aug. 1999.

Franklin, J. (1997), 'Employment Projections', Washington DC: Bureau of Labor Statistics, http://bls.gov.news.release/ecopro.table4.htm accessed 16 Sept. 1999.

Fraunhofer-Gesellschaft (1999), 'MPEG Audio Layer-3', *Fraunhofer ISS-A Layer 3 Info*, http://www.iis.fhg.de/amm/techinf/layer3/index.html accessed 12 Aug. 1999.

Freeman, C. (1987), *Technology Policy and Economic Performance: Lessons from Japan*, London: Pinter.

—— (1994), 'The Economics of Technical Change, Critical Survey', *Cambridge Journal of Economics*, 18(5): 463–514.

Freeman, C., and Perez, C. (1988), 'Structural Crises of Adjustment, Business Cycles and Investment Behaviour', in G. Dosi, C. Freeman, R. Nelson, G. Silverberg, and L. Soete (eds.), *Technical Change and Economic Theory*, London: Pinter, 38–66.

Freeman, C., and Soete, L. (1994), *Work for All or Mass Unemployment? Computerised Technical Change into the Twenty-First Century*, London: Pinter.

—— (1997), *The Economics of Industrial Innovation*, 3rd edn., London: Pinter/Cassel.

Freund, B., König, H., and Roth, N. (1997), 'Impact of Information Technology on Manufacturing', *Technology Management*, 13(3): 215–28.

Frieden, K. A., and Porter, M. E. (1996), 'The Taxation of Cyberspace (Briefing on State Tax Issues Related to The Internet and Electronic Commerce)': Arthur Andersen, Andersen Worldwide SC, June.

Froomkin, A. M. (1995), 'The Metaphor is the Key: Cryptography, The Clipper Chip, and the

Constitution', *University of Pennsylvania Law Review*, 709: http://www-swiss.ai.mit.edu/b095/articles/froomkin-metaphor/copyright.htm accessed 24 Sept. 1999.

Fulk, J., and Steinfield, C. (1990), *Organizations and Communication Technology*, Thousand Oaks, Calif.: Sage.

Galasyn, J. P. (1996), 'Big Brother is Closing In', *Computer Privacy Digest*, 8(10): 1–2.

Gandy, O. H. (1993), *The Panoptic Sort: A Political Economy of Personal Information*, Westview, Col.: Westview.

Gann, D., Barlow, J., and Venables, T. (1999), *Digital Futures: Making Homes Smarter*, Coventry: Chartered Institute of Housing for the Joseph Rowntree Foundation.

Garcia, D. L. (1995), 'Networking and the Rise of Electronic Commerce: The Challenge for Public Policy', *Business Economics*, 30(4): 7–14.

Garnham, N. (1994), 'Whatever Happened to the Information Society?', in R. Mansell (ed.), *The Management of Information and Communication Technologies: Emerging Patterns of Control*, London: Aslib, 42–51.

—— (1997), 'Universal Service', in W. H. Melody (ed.), *Telecom Reform: Principles, Policies and Regulatory Practices*, Lyngby: Technical University of Denmark, 207–12.

Gelder, K., and Thornton, S. (eds.) (1997), *The Subcultures Reader*, London: Routledge.

General Accounting Office (1986), 'Telephone Communications: Bypass of the Local Telephone Companies', Washington, DC: GAO.

German Institute for Economic Research (DIW) (1996), 'Multimedia: Forecasts of Employment Growth in the Media and Communications Sector Often Exaggerated', *Economic Bulletin*, 33(4): 2–3.

Gervais, D. J. (1996), 'Digital Technology and the "Copyright Industries"', *Copyright World*, 22–9.

Geuna, A., and Steinmueller, W. E. (1997), 'Joining the Information Society: Internet Access Issues for Europeans', Brighton: SPRU, University of Sussex, FAIR Working Paper No. 17, Feb.

Gibbons, M., Limoges, C., Nowotny, H., Schwartzman, S., Scott, P., and Trow, M. (1994), *The New Production of Knowledge: The Dynamics of Science and Research in Contemporary Societies*, London: Sage.

Gibson, W. (1984), *Neuromancer*, New York: Ace Books.

Giga Information Group (1999), 'Global Annual Cost Savings from Electronic Commerce will Reach $1.25 trillion by 2002', *Giga Information Group News Release*, 5 Aug. at http://www.gigaweb.com/marketing/gpr/ecomm_trillion.htm accessed 22 Aug. 1999.

Gilder, G. (1994), *Telecosm*, New York: Simon & Schuster.

Gillespie, A. (1996), 'Regions in the Global Information Society: Assessing Today's Experience', Brussels: Paper presented at the RESTPOR '96 Conference on Global Comparison of Regional RTD & Innovation Strategies for Development and Cohesion.

Gilster, P. (1993), *The Internet Navigator: The Essential Guide to Network Exploration for the Individual Dial-up User*, New York: Wiley.

Global Information Networks Conference (1997a), 'Industrial Declaration', Bonn: Ministerial Conference, 6–8 July.

—— (1997b), 'Realising the Potential, Theme Paper', Bonn: Ministerial Conference, 6–8 July.

Goolsbee, A. (1999), 'In a World Without Borders: The Impact of Taxes on Internet Commerce', Chicago: Graduate School of Business, University of Chicago, original Nov. 1998, revised July 1999 at http://gsbwww.uchicago.edu/fac/austan.goolsbee/research/intertax.pdf accessed 9 Sept. 1999.

Gouldner, A. (1979), *The Future of Intellectuals and the Rise of the New Class*, New York: Seabury.

de Gournay, C., Tarrius, A., and Missaoui, L. (1997), 'The Structure of the Use of Communications by "Travelling Managers"', in L. Haddon (ed.), *Communications on the Move: The Experience of Mobile Telephony in the 1990s*, Brussels: European Commission CTST248 Report of the Mobile Phone Workgroup, 51–72.

Government of France (1999), 'Décret no 99-200 du 17 mars 1999 définissant les catégories de moyens et de prestation de cryptologie dispensées de toute formalité préalable', Paris: Service d'Information du gouvernement (SIG), France, http://www.internet.gov/francais/textesref/cryptodecret99200.htm accessed 24 Sept. 1999.

Graham, C., Lewin, D., Milne, C., Moroney, J., and Skouby, E. (1996), 'The Consumer in the Information Society', London: Ovum.

Graham, I., Spinardi, G., Webster, J., and Williams, R. (1993), 'The Dynamics of EDI Standards/Development', Edinburgh: Research Centre for Social Science, The University of Edinburgh, The Edinburgh PICT Working Paper Series, No. 45.

Greenstein, L. (1995), 'Frame Relay and Frame-Based ATM: A Comparison of Technologies—White Paper', Frame Relay Forum, June.

Greguras, F., and Wong, S. J. (1995), 'Multimedia Content and the Super Highway: Rapid Acceleration or Foot on the Brake?', Palo Alto, Calif.: Law Firm of Fenwick & West.

Griliches, Z. (1957), 'Hybrid Corn: An Exploration in the Economics of Technological Change', *Econometrica*, 25: 501–22.

Gristock, J., and Mansell, R. (1997), 'Distributed Library Futures: IT Applications for 2000 and Beyond', Brighton: Report for the Institute of Development Studies, prepared by the Science Policy Research Unit, University of Sussex, 14 Nov.

Guerin-Calvert, M. E. (1989), 'Vertical Integration as a Threat to Competition: Airline Computer Reservation Systems', in J. E. Kwoka and L. J. White (eds.), *The Antitrust Revolution*, Glenview, Ill.: Scott, Foresman, and Co., 338–70.

Haas, P. M. (1992), 'Introduction: Epistemic Communities and International Policy Coordination', *International Organization*, 46(1): 1–36.

Haddon, L. (1998), 'New Dimensions of Social Exclusion in a Telematic Society', Brighton: Graduate Research Centre in Culture and Communication, University of Sussex, FAIR Working Paper No. 45, Mar.

Haddon, L., and Silverstone, R. (1993), 'Teleworking in the 1990s: A View from the Home', Brighton: SPRU University of Sussex, CICT Report Series No. 10, July.

——(1995), 'Lone Parents and their Information and Communication Technologies', Brighton: SPRU University of Sussex, CICT Report No. 12, Jan.

——(1996), 'The Young Elderly and their Information and Communication Technologies', Brighton: SPRU University of Sussex, CICT Report No. 13, Mar.

Hadfield, G. K. (1988), 'The Economics of Copyright: An Historical Perspective', Palo Alto, Calif.: Stanford Law School, paper prepared for ASCAP Copyright Law Symposium, 1989.

Hagedoorn, J., and Schakenraad, J. (1992), 'Leading Companies and Networks of Strategic Alliances in Information Technologies', *Research Policy*, 21: 163–90.

Hailsham, L. R. H. (ed.) (1987), *Offences against Decency and Morality, Hallsbury's Laws of England*, 4th edn., London: Butterworth & Co.

Hall, J. (1999), 'Reducing Environmental Impacts through the Procurement Chain', SPRU—Science and Technology Policy Research, University of Sussex, unpublished D.Phil. thesis, Brighton.

Handy, C. (1990), *The Age of Unreason*, London: Arrow Books.

Harasim, L. M. (ed.) (1993), *Global Networks: Computers and International Communication*, Cambridge MA: MIT Press.

Hardesty, D. (1999a), 'Future Taxation of E-Commerce', San Fransisco: E-Commerce Tax News, Markle, Stuckey, Hardesty, and Bott, 2 May, http://www.mbhh.com/services accessed 15 Aug. 1999.

——(1999b), 'NTA Issues Report on E-Commerce Tax Policy', San Fransisco: E-Commerce Tax News, Markle, Stuckey, Hardesty, and Bott, 30 Aug. http://www.mbhh.com/services accessed 9 Sept. 1999.

Harris, M. (1979), *Cultural Materialism: The Struggle for a Science of Culture*, New York: Random House.

Hart, T. C. (1998), 'A Dynamic Universal Service for a Heterogeneous European Union', *Telecommunications Policy*, 22(10): 839–52.

Häußermann, H., and Petrowsky, W. (1989), 'Das Telefon im Alltagvon Arbeitslosen', *Telefon und Gesellschaft*, 1(Volker Spiess, Berlin): 116–34.

Hawkins, R. W. (1996), 'Standards for Communication Technologies: Negotiating Institutional Biases in Network Design', in R. Mansell and R. Silverstone (eds.), *Communication by Design: The Politics of Information and Communication Technologies*, Oxford: Oxford University Press, 157–86.

——(1997a), 'The Changing Nature of Technical Regulation in Telecommunication Networks', in W. H. Melody (ed.), *Telecommunication Reform: Principles and Regulatory Practices*, Lyngby: Technical University of Lyngby, 197–206.

——(1997b), 'Emerging Technology Clusters for New Electronic Services', Brighton: SPRU, University of Sussex, FAIR Working Paper No. 19, Feb.

——(1998a), 'Creating a Positive Environment for Electronic Commerce in Europe', Brighton: SPRU University of Sussex, FAIR Working Paper No. 36, Mar.

——(1998b), 'Standardisation and Industrial Consortia: Implications for European Firms and Policy', Brighton: SPRU, University of Sussex, FAIR Working Paper No. 38, Mar.

Hawkins, R. W., Mansell, R., and Steinmueller, W. E. (1997), 'Green Paper—Mapping and Measuring the Information Technology, Electronics and Communications Sector in the United Kingdom', Brighton: Report prepared for the Office of Science and Technology, Technology Foresight Panel on Information Technology, Communications and Electronics, SPRU, Final Version, Aug.

——(1999), 'Towards Digital Intermediation in the Information Society', *Journal of Economic Issues*, XXXIII(2): 383–91.

Hawkins, R. W., Molas-Gallart, J., and Walker, W. (1996), 'The Impact of CALS and CALS Principles on UK Industry Supply Chains', Brighton: Report to the Department of Trade and Industry by the Science Policy Research Unit, University of Sussex, 7 Feb.

Henningsson, N. (1999a), 'Bluetooth Unites Data and Telecom', *Contact Technology*, May, p. 11.

——(1999b), 'Voice and Flexibility Key for Third Generation', *Contact Online*, http://www.ericsson.com/SE/kon_con/contact/teknik/te_09.html accessed 11 Aug. 1999, reporting Kjell Gustafsson view.

Herman, R., Ardekani, S. A., and Ausabel, J. H. (1989), 'Dematerialisation', *Technology and Environment*, Washington: National Academy, 50–69.

High-Level Group on the Information Society (1994), 'Europe and the Global Information Society: Recommendations to the European Council', Brussels: European Commission.

Hill, R. (1995), 'What is the Smallest Copyrightable Element in a Multimedia Work?', *Computers and Law (Society for Computers and Law)*, Aug./Sept.: 15–18.

Hills, M. (1997), *Intranet as Groupware*, New York: John Wiley & Sons.

von Hippel, E. (1978), 'Users as Innovators', *Technology Review*, 80(3): 31–9.

von Hippel, E., and Urban, G. L. (1988), 'Lead User Analyses for the Development of New Industrial Products', *Management Science*, 34(5): 569–82.

Hjelm, J. (1998), 'Final Report on Advanced Mobile Multimedia Applications, Project OnThe-Move (AC034)', Stockholm: Report prepared for the European Commission, DG XIII, ACTS Programme by Ericsson Radio Systems User Application Lab.

Hobday, M. (1995), *Innovation in East Asia: The Challenge to Japan*, Cheltenham: Edward Elgar.

Hoeren, T. (1995), 'An Assessment of Long-term Solutions in the Context of Copyright and Electronic Delivery Services and Multimedia Products', Brussels: European Commission/DG Telecommunications, Information Market and Exploitation of Research.

Hoffman, L. J. (ed.) (1994), *Building in Big Brother: The Cryptography Policy Debate*, New York: Springer Verlag.

Home Affairs Committee (1994), 'First Report: Computer Pornography', London: HMSO Report 126.

House of Commons (1993), 'Computer Pornography: The Government Reply to the First Report From the Home Affairs Committee, Session 1993–94, HC 126', London: HMSO.

Hoynes, M. F. (1999), 'The Impact of the Internet on Consumer Purchasing and Implications for Independent Booksellers', *Bookweb.org Industry Newsroom*, 6 Aug., http://www.bookweb.org/home/news/btw/2244.html accessed 22 Aug. 1999.

Huart, O. (1996), 'USO Costs in France', Paris: ICC Conference, Générales des Eaux.

Hugenholtz, B. (1995), 'Copyright Problems of Electronic Document Delivery', Brussels: European Commission.

Hughes, T. P. (1987), 'The Evolution of Large Technological Systems', in W. E. Bijker, T. P. Hughes, and T. J. Pinch (eds.), *The Social Construction of Technological Systems: New Directions in the Sociology and History of Technology*, Cambridge MA: MIT Press, 51–82.

Hulsink, W. (1996), 'Intellectual Property Rights in Europe's Digital Era: The Coordination Problems of Creative and Collecting Societies', Brighton: FAIR Working Paper No. 10, Nov.

Huston, G. (1999), 'Interconnection, Peering and Settlements', New York: based in part on G. Huston, ISP Survival Guide, John Wiley & Sons (1998), http://www.telstra.net/gih/peerdocs/peer.html accessed 25 Sept. 1999.

Hutchison, I. (1996), 'The Value-Added Tax Information Exchange System and Administrative Cooperation Between the Tax Authorities of the European Community', *Information Technology and Innovation in Tax Administration, Kluwer Law International*, issue edited by G. P. Jenkins, pp. 101–13.

I*M Europe (1996), 'Legal Issues, Intellectual Property—Technical Devices', Brussels: European Commission.

ICO (1999), 'ICO Files Voluntary Chapter 11 Petition to Facilitate Financing of Global Telecommunications Systems', London: ICO, 27 Aug., http://www.ico.com/press/releases/199908/990827.htm accessed 10 Sept.

Industry Canada (1997), 'Preparing Canada for the Digital World: Final Report of the Information Highway Advisory Council', Ottawa: Communications Branch.

Information Infrastructure Task Force (1995), 'Intellectual Property and the National Information Infrastructure', Washington, DC: The Report of the Working Group on Intellectual Property Rights.

Information Society Trends (1997), 'Editorial Contribution', *Information Society Trends*, 28 Jan.–11 Feb.

Infotech Research (1998), 'Web Site Listings', http://www.infotecresearch.com accessed 15 September 1999: Infotech Research.

Inland Revenue and HM Customs and Excise (1998), 'Electronic Commerce: UK Policy on Taxation Issues', London: Inland Revenue and HM Customs and Excise, 6 Oct.

Innis, H. A. (1951), *The Bias of Communication*, Toronto: University of Toronto Press.

INRA (International Research Associates) (1999), 'Measuring Information Society', Brussels: INRA, 16 Mar., available from http://www.ispo.cec.be/polls/EB98.htm accessed 15 September 1999.

Institute for Information Studies (ed.) (1993), *The Knowledge Economy—The Nature of Information in the 21st Century*, Nashville: Institute for Information Studies.

Inteco (1994), 'The Interactive Home', London: Inteco.

——(1996), 'Data published on the Internet', Inteco, http://www.inteco.com/data3.html and /data2.html accessed 24 July.

Intelligent Home Newsletter (1993), 'What are They Saying about Home Automation', *Intelligent Home Newsletter*, 4(3), 5.

International Data Corporation (1997), 'Wide Area Networking In Europe', London: IDC.

——(1999), 'IDC European IT Forum: Europe to See Surge in E-Business', not provided: International Data Corporation (IDC) News Service, http://www.idcresearch.com/Events/press/EVT091399PR.htm accessed 20 Sept. 1999.

International Federation of the Phonographic Industry (IFPI) (1994), *Practical Guide*, 2nd edn., London: International Federation of the Phonographic Industry.

International Organization for Standardization/International Electrotechnical Commission (1990), 'A Vision for the Future: Standards Needs for Emerging Technologies', Geneva: ISO/IEC.

International Record Industry Association (1996), 'The Recording Industry in Numbers', London: International Record Industry Association.

International Telecommunication Union (1998), 'World Telecommunication Development Report: Universal Access', Geneva: International Telecommunication Union.

——(1999), 'Challenges to the Network—Internet for Development', Geneva: International Telecommunication Union.

International Working Group on Data Protection in Telecommunication (1996), 'Data Protection on the Internet: Report and Guidance "Budapest Draft"', Budapest: International Working Group on Data Protection in Telecommunication.

Internet Service Providers Association (ISPA) (1996), 'Code of Practice', London: ISPA.

Irwin, M. R. (1984), *Telecommunications America: Markets Without Boundaries*, Westport, Conn.: Quorum Books.

Jansen, E., and Mansell, R. (1998), 'A Case of Electronic Commerce: The On-line Music Industry—Content, Regulation and Barriers to Development', Brighton: SPRU FAIR Working Paper No. 40, Mar.

Jasanoff, S. (1987), 'Contested Boundaries in Policy-Relevant Science', *Social Studies of Science*, 17: 195–230.

Jeong, B. S. (1999), 'Analysis of the Linux System, A New Entrant in the Operating System Market: Technological Innovations and Business Models', unpublished SPRU M.Sc. Dissertation, University of Sussex, Brighton.

Jorde, T. M., and Teece, D. J. (1989), 'Innovation, Cooperation and Antitrust: Balancing Competition and Cooperation', *High Technology Law Journal*, 4(1): 1–131.

Jospin, L. (1999), 'Discours et interventions, Conférence de presse de Monsieur Lionel Jospin, Premier ministre, à l'issue due Comité interministériel pour la société de l'information Hôtel de Matignon', Paris: Speech presented at a Conference on the Information Society, http://www.premier-ministre.gouv.fr/PM/D190199.HTM, 19 Jan., accessed 24 Sept. 1999.

Justice and Home Affairs Council of the European Union (1998), 'Formal Conclusions on Encryption and Law Enforcement', Brussels: Justice and Home Affairs Council of the European Union, European Council Doc. No. 8856/98 (PRESSE 170/G).

Kahin, B. (ed.) (1996), *Building Information Infrastructures—Issues in the Development of the National Research and Education Network*, New York: McGraw-Hill.

Kahin, B., and Keller, J. (eds.) (1996), *Public Access to the Internet*, Cambridge, Mass.: MIT Press (A Publication of the Harvard Information Infrastructure Project).

Kahin, B., and Nesson, C. (eds.) (1995), *Borders in Cyberspace*, Cambridge, Mass.: MIT Press.

Kahin, B., and Wilson III, E. J. (eds.) (1997), *National Information Infrastructure Initiatives: Vision and Policy Design*, Cambridge, Mass.: MIT Press.

Kahn, D. (1983), *The Codebreakers*, London: Sphere Books.

Kalakota, R., and Whinston, A. (1997), *Electronic Commerce: A Manager's Guide*, New York: Addison-Wesley Longman Inc.

Kalil, T. (1995), 'Public Policy and the National Information Infrastructure', *Business Economics*, 30(4): 15–20.

Kamata, H. (1996), 'OECD Work on Cryptography Policy Guidelines', Paris: Paper prepared for the OECD Workshops on the Economics of the Information Society, Seoul.

Kaplinsky, R. (1994), *Easternisation: The Spread of Japanese Management Techniques to Developing Countries*, London: Frank Cass.

Katz, M., and Shapiro, C. (1985), 'Network Externalities, Competition and Compatibility', *American Economic Review*, 75(3): 424–40.

——(1986), 'Technology Adoption in the Presence of Network Externalities', *Journal of Political Economy*, 94: 822–41.

Kelly, K. (1994), *Out of Control: The New Biology of Machines, Social Systems and the Economic World*, Reading, Mass.: Addison-Wesley.

——(1998), *New Rules for the New Economy*, London: Fourth Estate.

Kiessling, T., and Blondeel, Y. (1999), 'The Impact of Regulation on Facility-Based Competition in Telecommunications', *Communications & Strategies*, 34(2nd Quarter): 19–44.

Kizza, J. M. (1998), *Civilizing the Internet: Global Concerns and Efforts Towards Regulation*, Jefferson, NC: McFarland.

Klaes, M. (1997), 'Sociotechnical Constituencies, Game Theory, and the Diffusion of Compact Discs: An Inter-Disciplinary Investigation into the Market for Recorded Music', *Research Policy*, 25: 1221–34.

Kling, R., Crawford, H., Rosenbaum, H., Sawyer, S., and Weisband, S. (1999), 'Information Technologies in Human Contexts: Learning from Organizational and Social Informatics', Bloomington, Ind.: Manuscript prepared by Center for Social Informatics, Indiana University.

Kluzer, S. (1997), 'The Role of the Third Sector in the Information Society Development Implications for Advanced Communications', Milan: Databank FAIR Working Paper No. 12, Jan.

Kluzer, S., and Farinelli, M. (1997), 'A Survey of European Cities' Presence on the Internet', Milan: Databank FAIR Working Paper No. 31, Mar.

Kluzer, S., and Hounsome, P. (1998), 'The Networked Society in the Making in Two European Regions: Emilia-Romagna and Wales', Milan: Databank FAIR Working Paper No. 48, Mar.

Kobayashi, K. (1980), 'Telecommunications and Computers: An Inevitable Marriage', *Telephony*, 28 Jan., pp. 78–86.

Kokuryo, J., and Takeda, Y. (1995), 'The Role of Platform Business as Intermediaries of Electronic Commerce', Tokyo: Paper presented at the Hitosubashi Organisation Science Conference on Asian Research Organisations.

Kollock, P. (1999), 'The Economies of Online Cooperation: Gifts and Public Goods in Cyberspace', in M. A. Smith and P. Kollock (eds.), *Communities in Cyberspace*, London: Routledge, 220–39.

Koops, B.-J. (1999), 'Overview per Country', Crypto Law Survey, Version 15.0, July 1999, http://cwis.kub.nl/~frw/people/koops/cls2.htm accessed 24 Sept. 1999.

KPMG (1996), 'Public Policy Issues Arising from Telecommunications and Audiovisual Convergence', London: European Commission.

Kreile, R., and Becker, J. (1996), 'Multimedia und die Praxis der Lizenzierung von Urheberrechten', *Gewerblicher Rechtschutz und Urheberrecht (Internationaler Teil)*, 6: 677–92.

Lamberton, D. M. (ed.) (1971), *The Economics of Information and Knowledge*, Harmondsworth: Penguin.

Lamberton, D. M. (1984), 'The Economics of Information and Organization', *Annual Review of Information Science and Technology*, 19: 3–30.

Lane, R. E. (1991), *The Market Experience*, Cambridge: Cambridge University Press.

Lanham, R. (1993), *The Electronic Word: Democracy, Technology and the Arts*, Chicago: University of Chicago Press.

—— (1995), 'Digital Literacy', *Scientific American*, 273(3): 198–200.

Latour, B., and Woolgar, S. (1986), *Laboratory Life: The Construction of Scientific Facts*, Princeton, NJ: Princeton University Press.

Leadbeater, C. (1999), *Living on Thin Air: The New Economy*, London: Viking.

Leebaert, D. (ed.) (1998), *The Future of the Electronic Market-place*, Cambridge, Mass.: MIT Press.

Leer, A. C. (1995), 'Information Transaction in the Global Information Market (GIM): Strategic and Regulatory Issues Concerning the Cross-border Trade of Information Assets', Luxembourg: Report prepared for the European Commission, EC DGXIII, Oct.

—— (1996), *It's a Wired World—The New Networked Economy*, Oslo and Brussels/Luxembourg: Scandanavian University Press and European Commission, DGXIII.

Legal Advisory Board (1995), 'The Information Society: Copyright and Multimedia', Luxembourg: Legal Advisory Board.

Leiner, B. M., Cerf, V. G., Clark, D. D., Kahn, R. E., Kleinrock, L., Lynch, D., Postel, J., Roberts, L. G., and Wolff, S. (1998), *A Brief History of the Internet*, http://www.iso.org/internet-history: 20 Feb., accessed 16 Aug. 1999.

Leiss, W. (1976), *The Limits to Satisfaction: An Essay on the Problem of Needs and Commodities*, Toronto: University of Toronto Press.

Levy, D. A. L. (1997), 'The Regulation of Digital Conditional Access Systems: A Case Study in European Policy Making', *Telecommunications Policy*, 21(7): 661–76.

Levy, S. (1994), 'The Cypherpunks vs. Uncle Sam', in L. Hoffman (ed.), *Building Big Brother—The Cryptography Policy Debate*, New York: Springer-Verlag, 266–83.

Ling, R., Julsrud, T., and Krogh, E. (1997), 'The Goretex Principle: The Hytte and Mobile Telephones in Norway', in L. Haddon (ed.), *Communications on the Move: The Experience of Mobile Telephony in the 1990s*, Brussels: European Commission COST248 Report of the Mobile Phone Workgroup, 97–119.

Lips, A. M. B., Frissen, P. H. A., and Prins, J. E. J. (1998), 'Regulatory Review through New Media in Sweden, the UK and the USA: Convergence or Divergence of Regulation?', *The EDI Law Review*, 5: 123–257.

Lipsey, R. (1995), 'A Structuralist View of Technical Change and Economic Growth', Toronto: Canadian Institute for Advanced Research, Reprint 38.

Lipsey, R., and Lancaster, K. (1956), 'The General Theory of the Second Best', *Review of Economic Studies*, XXIV(Oct.): 11–32.

LlwybrPathway Project (1998), 'The Llwybr.Pathway Annual Report 1998', Machynlleth: Llwybr.Pathway Project Partnership.

Lunaria (1996), 'Lavori Scelti: Come Creare Occupazione nel Terzo Settore', Roma: Lunaria—

Gruppo di Lavoro sul Terzo Settore, in collaboration with the Forum Permanente del Terzo Settore.

Lundvall, B.-Å., and Johnson, B. (1994), 'The Learning Economy', *Journal of Industry Studies*, 1(2): 23–42.

Lynd, R. S., and Lynd, H. M. (1929), *Middletown: A Study of American Culture*, New York: Harcourt, Brace.

Lyon, D. (1988), *The Information Society: Issues and Illusions*, Cambridge: Polity.

—— (1994), *The Electronic Eye: The Rise of the Surveillance Society*, Cambridge: Polity.

Macdonald, S. (1998), *Information for Innovation: Managing Change from an Information Perspective*, Oxford: Oxford University Press.

Machlup, F. (1952), *The Political Economy of Monopoly: Business, Labor and Government Policies*, Baltimore: The Johns Hopkins Press.

—— (1962), *The Production and Distribution of Knowledge in the US Economy*, Princeton, NJ: Princeton University Press.

MacKenzie, D. (1992), 'Economic and Sociological Explanation of Technical Change', in R. Coombs, P. Saviotti, and V. Walsh (eds.), *Technological Change and Company Strategies: Economic and Sociological Perspectives*, London: Academic Press, 25–48.

—— (1996), *Knowing Machines: Essays on Technical Change*, Cambridge, Mass.: MIT Press.

MacKinnon, C. (1987), *Feminism Unmodified: Discourses on Life and Law*, Cambridge: Harvard University Press.

McKnight, L. W., and Bailey, J. P. (eds.), (1997), *Internet Economics*, Cambridge, Mass.: MIT Press.

MacLean, D. (1996), 'Global Mobile Personal Communications by Satellite: Regulatory Risk vs. Sovereignty Risk at the ITU World Telecommunications Forum', London: Mobile Satellite Communications Global Conference, Kensington Close Hotel, 17–19 June.

McLuhan, M. (1964), *Understanding Media: The Extensions of Man*, New York: McGraw-Hill.

McWilliams, B. (1997), 'Out-of-State Customers May Pay Sales Tax', *PC World News Radio*, 6 Nov.

Mansell, R. (1986), 'The Telecommunications Bypass Threat: Real or Imagined?', *Journal of Economic Issues*, 20(1): 145–64.

—— (1993), *The New Telecommunications: A Political Economy of Network Evolution*, London: Sage.

—— (1994), 'Negotiating the Management of ICTs: Emerging Patterns of Control', in R. Mansell (ed.), *The Management of Information and Communication Technologies: Emerging Patterns of Control*, London: ASLIB, 336–47.

—— (1995), 'Standards, Industrial Policy and Innovation', in R. Hawkins, R. Mansell, and J. Skea (eds.), *Standards, Innovation and Competitiveness: The Politics and Economics of Standards in Natural and Technical Environments*, Cheltenham: Edward Elgar, 213–27.

—— (1996a), 'Communication by Design?', in R. Mansell and R. Silverstone (eds.), *Communication by Design: The Politics of Information and Communication Technologies*, Oxford: Oxford University Press, 15–43.

—— (1996b), 'Telecommunications in the UK: Controlling the Information Society Gateways', *Telematics and Informatics*, 13(2/3): 141–56.

—— (1997), 'Strategies for Maintaining Market Power in the Face of Rapidly Changing Technologies', *Journal of Economic Issues*, XXXI(4): 969–89.

—— (1998), 'Citizen Expectations: The Internet and the Universal Service Challenge', *Intermedia*, 26(Mar.): 4–7.

Mansell, R., and contributors (eds.) (1988), *New Telecommunications Services: Videotex Development Strategies*, Paris: OECD.

Mansell, R., and Hawkins, R. W. (1991), 'Mobile Communication Systems: Issues and Prospects', Sharing Spectrum in the Digital Age, WARC 92, London.

Mansell, R., and Jenkins, M. (1992*a*), 'Electronic Trading Networks and Interactivity: The Route to Competitive Advantage? Case Study Report', Science Policy Research Unit, University of Sussex.

——(1992*b*), 'Electronic Trading Networks and Interactivity: The Route Towards Competitive Advantage?', *Communications & Strategies*, 2(6): 63–85.

Mansell, R., and Silverstone, R. (eds.) (1996), *Communication by Design: The Politics of Information and Communication Technologies*, Oxford: Oxford University Press.

Mansell, R., and Steinmueller, W. E. (1995), 'Intellectual Property Rights: The Development of Information Infrastructures for the Information Society, Final Report prepared for the Scientific and Technological Options Assessment Programme of the European Parliament', Maastricht: MERIT.

——(1996*a*), 'Intellectual Property Rights in the Information Society', *Science and Public Affairs*, Autumn: 18–21.

——(1996*b*), 'Securing Electronic Networks', Brighton: SPRU University of Sussex, FAIR Working Paper No. 7, Mar. (reissued Nov.) with David Sayers.

——(1996*c*), 'The Way Forward: Socio-Economic and Policy Issues and Advanced Communication Technologies and Services', Brighton: Report for the CEC on ACTS FAIR Project AC093, Analysis of ACTS-SEP Matrix Issues—Part C: Techno-Economic and Socio-Political Analysis of Infrastructure and Service Deployment.

Mansell, R., and Wehn, U. (eds.) (1998), *Knowledge Societies: Information Technology for Sustainable Development*, Oxford: Published for the United Nations Commission on Science and Technology for Development by Oxford University Press.

Mansfield, E. (1963), 'Intrafirm Rates of Diffusion of an Innovation', *Review of Economics and Statistics*, 45(Nov.): 348–59.

Margaris, P., and Mansell, R. (1998), 'Global Mobile Personal Communication Systems: Bridging the Compatibility Gap in International Mobile Telephony', Brighton: SPRU FAIR Working Paper No. 39, Mar.

Marshall, T. H. (1973), *Class, Citizenship and Social Development*, London: Greenwood, first pub. in 1964, Garden City, NY: Doubleday.

Marsland, V. (1998), 'EU Attempts Greater Copyright Harmonization', *IP Worldwide*, May/June(http://www.ljextra.com/copyright/0506_eucpharmony.html accessed 19 Aug. 1999): 7.

Martin, J. (1973), *Design of Man–Computer Dialogues*, New York: Prentice Hall.

Marvin, C. (1988), *When Old Technologies Were New: Thinking About Electric Communication in the Late Nineteenth Century*, Oxford: Oxford University Press.

Mazda, X., and Mazda, F. (1999), *The Focal Illustrated Dictionary of Telecommunications*, Oxford: Focal.

Meijers, H. (1998), 'Fiscal Impacts of the Growing Use of Advanced Communications Technologies and Services: A Quantitative Analysis', Maastricht: MERIT FAIR Working Paper No. 34, Mar.

Melbin, M. (1978), 'Night as Frontier', *American Sociological Review*, 43(1): 3–22.

Melody, W. H. (1977), 'Mass Media: The Economics of Access to the Market-place of Ideas, Business and the Media: A National Symposium', Atlanta, Georgia, 7 Sept.

——(1981), 'The Economics of Information as Resource and Product', in D. J. Wedemeyer (ed.), *Proceedings of the Pacific Telecommunications Conference*, Honolulu: Pacific Telecommunications Council, pp. C7: 5–9.

——(1994), 'The Information Society: Implications for Economic Institutions and Market Theory', in E. A. Comor (ed.), *The Global Political Economy of Communication*, New York: St. Martin's Press, 21–36.

Mercer, R. A. (1996), 'Overview of Enterprise Network Developments', *IEE Communications*, Jan., pp. 30–7.

Metcalfe, B. (1995), 'Predicting the Internet's Catastrophic Collapse and Ghost Sites Galore in 1996', *InfoWorld Electronic Opinons*, 4 Dec., http://www.infoworld.com accessed 21 Aug.

——(1998), 'Internet Bottlenecks: There's an Element of Truth behind a Game-Show Door', *InfoWorld Electronic Opinons*, 27 Apr., http://www.infoworld.com accessed 21 Aug.

——(1999), 'Linux's '60s Technology, Open-sores Ideology Won't Beat Y2K, But What Will?', *InfoWorld Electronic Opinons*, 21 June, http://www.infoworld.com accessed 21 Aug.

Metcalfe, J. S., and Miles, I. (1994), 'Standards, Selection and Variety: An Evolutionary Approach', *Information Economics and Policy*, 6(3/4): 243–68.

Micelli, S. (1997), 'Networks Without Technology: The Diffusion of ICT in Italy's North East SMEs', Bologna: Paper presented at the Conference on Networking and Small and Medium Sized Enterprises, 19–20 June.

Miles, I. (1996), 'Service Firms and Innovation—Telematics and Beyond', Manchester: PREST, Commissioned by United Nations University Institute for New Technology as a background paper for the United Nations Commission on Science and Technology for Development, Working Group on Information Technology and Development.

Miles, I., and Thomas, G. (1995), 'User Resistance to New Interactive Media: Participants, Processes and Paradigms', in M. Bauer (ed.), *Resistance to New Technology*, Cambridge: Cambridge University Press, 255–75.

Millard, J. (1996), 'Advanced Communications and Regional Development: Overview of European Experience, Presentation', Brussels: European Telework Development Project presented at the ACTS Meets the Regions Workshop, 6 Nov.

Millard, J., and O'Shea, M. (1996), 'FORA Working Group C Final Report, Developing an Integrated Strategy for Telematics in Rural Areas', Brussels: European Commission.

Miller, D. (1995), *Acknowledging Consumption: A Review of New Studies*, London: Routledge.

Miller Freeman Entertainment Ltd. (1997), 'MBI World Report 1997', London: Music Business International.

Milne, C. (1990), 'Universal Telephone Service in the UK: An Agenda for Policy Research and Action', *Telecommunications Policy* (Oct.): 365–71.

Mitchell, W. J. (1996), *City of Bits: Space, Place and the Infobahn*, Cambridge, Mass.: MIT Press.

Molas-Gallart, J., and Walker, W. (1992), 'Military Innovation's Growing Reliance on Civil Technology: A New Source of Dynamism and Structural Change', in W. A. Smit, J. Grin, and L. Voronkov (eds.), *Military Technological Innovation and Stability in a Changing World: Politically Assessing and Influencing Weapon Innovation and Military Research and Development*, Amsterdam: VU University Press, 15–26.

Molho, I. (1997), *The Economics of Information: Lying and Cheating in Markets and Organizations*, Oxford: Blackwell.

Molina, A. (1995), 'Sociotechnical Constituencies as Processes of Alignment: The Rise of a Large-Scale European Information Technology Initiative', *Technology in Society*, 17(4): 385–412.

Moltzen, E. (1998), 'Will Politics Spoil a Tax-Fee Internet?', *Computer Reseller*, 9 Mar.

Monopolies and Mergers Commission (1994), 'The Supply of Recorded Music: A Report on the Supply in the UK of Pre-recorded Compact Discs, Vinyl Discs and Tapes Containing Music', London: Monopolies and Mergers Commission, June.

Morrell, L. (1997), 'Recorded Delivery', *Internet World*, Mar., pp. 25–30.

Mosco, V. (1982), *Pushbutton Fantasies: Critical Perspectives on Videotex and Information Technology*, Norwood, NJ: Ablex.

Mueller, M. L. (1997), *Universal Service: Competition, Interconnection, and Monopoly in the Making of the American Telephone System*, Cambridge, Mass.: MIT Press and AEI Press.

Murroni, C. (1996), 'Future Directions in Telecom Legislation: The UK: Notes for a Presentation at the Centre for Tele-Information', Lyngby: Technical University of Denmark, 29 Jan.–2 Feb.

Muter, P., and Maurutto, P. (1991), 'Reading and Skimming from Computer Screens and Books: The Paperless Office Revisited?', *Behaviour and Information Technology*, 10(4): 257–66.

Narendran, P. (1997), 'Making the World Safe for SMDS: ATM Challenges to Traditional Telecommunication Management', MERIT: Maastricht and London: Ovum, FAIR Working Paper No. 22, Feb.

National Information Infrastructure Task Force (1995), 'Intellectual Property and the National Information Infrastructure: The Report of the Working Group on Intellectual Property Rights', Washington, DC: National Information Infrastructure Task Force, Task Force on Intellectual Property Rights.

National Research Council (1997), *Bits of Power: Issues in Global Access to Scientific Data*, Washington, DC: National Academy Press.

Negroponte, N. (1995), *Being Digital*, London: Hodder & Stoughton.

Neice, D. (1996), 'Information Technology and Citizen Participation', Ottawa: Department of Canadian Heritage SRA 167, Aug.

——(1998a), 'ICTs and Dematerialisation: Some Implications for Status Differentiation in Advanced Market Societies', Brighton: SPRU University of Sussex, FAIR Working Paper No. 43, Mar.

——(1998b), 'Measures of Participation in the Digital Techno-Structure', Brighton: SPRU University of Sussex, FAIR Working Paper No. 44, Mar.

——(2000), 'Access to Digital Technologies: Implications for Social Status', unpublished D.Phil. thesis, SPRU, University of Sussex, Brighton, forthcoming.

Nelkin, D. (ed.) (1992), *Controversy: The Politics of Technical Decisions*, Thousand Oaks, Calif.: Sage.

Nelson, R., and Winter, S. (1982), *An Evolutionary Theory of Economic Change*, Cambridge: Harvard University Press.

NERA and Denton Hall (1997), 'Issues associated with the Creation of a European Regulatory Authority for Telecommunications, Report for the European Commission, DGXIII', London: NERA and Denton Hall, Mar.

Network Wizards (1999a), 'Distribution by Top-Level Domain Name by Host Count', Network Wizards, July, http://isc.org/WWW-9907/dist-bynum.html accessed 29 Oct.

——(1999b), 'Internet Domain Survey', Network Wizards, July, http://www.isc.org/ds/WWW-9907/report.html accessed 29 Oct.

NEXUS Europe—Centre for Urban and Regional Development Studies—University of Newcastle (1996), 'An Assessment of the Social and Economic Cohesion Aspects of the Development of the Information Society in Europe. Volume II. "The Gap": The Capacity of Cohesion Regions to Access and Participate in the Information Society', Dublin and Newcastle: Research Report for EC DG XIII.A.7 and DG XVI European Commission.

Nishiyama, S. (1982), 'The Impact of New Electronic Technologies: Direction, Channels, Speed', in H. Giersch (ed.), *Emerging Technologies: Consequences for Economic Growth, Structural Change, and Employment—Symposium 1981*, Tübingen: J. C. B. Mohr (Paul Siebeck), 309–23.

Noble, D. F. (1986), *Forces of Production: A Social History of Industrial Automation*, New York: Oxford University Press.

——(1998), *The Religion of Technology: The Divinity of Man and the Spirit of Invention*, New York: Alfred A. Knopf.

Nourouzi, A., and May, A. (1996), 'LEOs, MEOs and GEOs: The Market Opportunity for Mobile Satellite Services', London: Ovum Consulting.

O'Connor, R. M. (1994), 'Towards a New Policy for ITC Standards', Genval, Belgium: Conference on ICT Standards Policy, Genval, Belgium, 28–30 Nov. 1994.

OECD (1981), 'Guidelines on the Protection of Privacy and Transborder Flows of Personal Data', Paris: OECD.

——(1985), 'Declaration on Transborder Data Flows', Paris: OECD.

——(1992*a*), *Convergence Between Communications Technologies: Case Studies from North America and Western Europe*, Paris: OECD, Information Computers and Communication Policy Report No. 28.

——(1992*b*), 'Guidelines for the Security of Information Systems', Paris: OECD.

——(1995), *Universal Service Obligations in a Competitive Telecommunications Environment*, Paris: OECD, Information, Computers and Communication Policy Report No. 38.

——(1996*a*), 'Access and Pricing for Information Infrastructure Services: Communication Tariffication, Regulation and the Internet', Dublin: OECD, 20–1 June.

——(1996*b*), 'Global Information Infrastructures—Global Information Society (GII-GIS): Statement of Policy Recommendations made by the ICCP Committee', Paris: OECD/ GD(96)93.

——(1997*a*), 'Cryptography Policy: The Guidelines and the Issues', Paris: OECD.

——(1997*b*), 'Dismantling the Barriers to Global Electronic Commerce', Turku, Norway: OECD Conference on Electronic Commerce, http://www.oecd.org/dsti/sti, accessed 2 Aug. 1999.

——(1997*c*), 'Information Infrastructures: Their Impact and Regulatory Requirements', Paris: OECD/GD(97)18 OECD ICCP.

——(1998*a*), 'Consumer Protection in the Electronic Marketplace', Paris: OECD DSTI/ CP(98)13/Final.

——(1998*b*), 'Ministerial Declaration on Consumer Protection in the Context of Electronic Commerce', Ottawa: OECD Ministerial Meeting, 7–9 Oct. 1998, published by OECD, 22 Dec.

——(1998*c*), 'Ministerial Declaration on the Protection of Privacy in Global Networks', Ottawa, 7–9 October', Ottawa: OECD DSTI/REG(98)10/Final.

——(1999*a*), *The Economic and Social Impacts of Electronic Commerce: Preliminary Findings and Research Agenda*, Paris: OECD.

——(1999*b*), 'Inventory of Instruments and Mechanisms Contributing to the Implementation and Enforcement of the OECD Privacy Guidelines on Global Networks', Paris: DSTI/ ICCP/REG(98)12/final.

——(1999*c*), 'Joint OECD-Private Sector Workshop on Electronic Authentication, Background paper on Electronic Authentication Technology and Issues', Stanford and Menlo Park, Calif.: OECD.

——(1999*d*), *OECD Communications Outlook 1999*, Paris: OECD.

Office of Technology Assessment (1986), 'Intellectual Property Rights in an Age of Electronics and Information', Washington DC: Office of Technology Assessment, US Congress, Government Printing Office, OTA-CIT-302, Apr.

Office of Telecommunications (1994), 'Households without a Telephone: Market Research', London: Office of Telecommunications, Dec.

Office of Telecommunications (1995a), 'Universal Telecommunications Services. Consultative Document on Universal Service in the UK from 1997', London: Office of Telecommunications.

—— (1995b), 'Beyond the Telephone, the Television and the PC', London: Office of Telecommunications.

—— (1999), 'Market Information Update', London: Office of Telecommunications.

Orzech, D. (1999), 'XML is Here to Stay', *Datamation*, July,
    http://www.datamation.com/apdev/9907XML1.html accessed 6 Apr. 2000.

Overby, B. A. (1996), 'Identification and Validation of a Societal Model of Usenet', San Jose, Calif.: San Jose, State University.

Ovum Consulting (1995), 'Multimedia Publishing: Market Opportunities', London: Ovum.

—— (1997), 'Cable Modems—Stealing the Broadband Market', London: Ovum.

Oxbrow, N., Kibby, P., and While, M. (1997), 'European Multimedia Market Information: An Analysis of Supply and Demand', London: TFPL.

Oxman, J. (1999), 'The FCC and the Unregulation of the Internet', Washington, DC: Federal Communications Commission, Office of Plans and Policy Working Paper No. 31.

van de Paal, G. (1997), 'CD-ROMs and Advanced Communications: Substitutes or Complements?', Maastricht: MERIT FAIR Working Paper No. 20, Feb.

van de Paal, G., and Steinmueller, W. E. (1998), 'Multimedia Platform Technologies as a Means of Building Consumer Demand for Data Communication Services', Maastricht: MERIT FAIR Working Paper No. 41, Mar.

Paltridge, S. (1996), 'How Competition Helps the Internet', *OECD Observer*, 201: 25–7.

Passamonti, L., and Lucchi, G. (1998), 'Preliminary Estimate of the Multiplier Effects of Electronic Commerce on EU Economy and Employment', Milan: Databank FAIR Working Paper No. 47, Mar.

Passamonti, L., Sisti, L., and Cattaneo, G. (1997), 'Review of Advanced Communications Markets Developments', Milan: Databank, FAIR Working Paper No. 32, Nov.

Pauwels, C. (1998), 'Integrating Economies, Integrating Policies: The Importance of Antitrust and Competition Policies within the Global Audiovisual Order', *Communications & Strategies*, 30(2nd Quarter): 103–32.

Pearce, D. W. (ed.) (1994), *The MIT Dictionary of Modern Economics*, 4th edn., Cambridge, Mass.: MIT Press.

Pearsall, J., and Trumble, B. (eds.) (1996), *The Oxford English Reference Dictionary*, 2nd edn., Oxford: Oxford University Press.

Peha, J. M. (1999), 'Tradeable Universal Service Obligations', *Telecommunications Policy*, 23(5): 363–74.

Pender, L. (1999), 'XML Deployment Push', *PC Week Online*, 2 Aug.,
    http://www.zdnet.com/pcweek/stories/news/0,4153,410812,00.html accessed 18 Aug. 1999.

Perez, C. (1983), 'Structural Change and the Assimilation of New Technologies in the Economic and Social System', *Futures*, 15(4): 357–75.

Petit, P., and Soete, L. (1996), 'Technical Change and Employment Growth in Services: Analytical and Policy Challenges', Paris: Paper for TSER project Technology, Economic Integration and Social Cohesion, presented at the Workshop on Technology and (Un)employment, Skills and Social Cohesion, 22–3 Nov.

PIRA International (n.d.), 'MMRCS Executive Summary, Multimedia Rights Clearance Systems, INFO2000, a report prepared for the European Commission INFO2000 programme', Leatherhead: PIRA International MMRCS Strategic Analysis.

Plutarch (1928), *Plutarch's Lives*, London: Heinemann.

Polanyi, M. (1966), *The Tacit Dimension*, London: Routledge & Kegan Paul.

Policy Studies Institute and PIRA International (1996), 'European Information Trends 1996', Brussels: European Commission.

Porter, M. E. (1985), *Competitive Advantage: Creating and Sustaining Superior Performance*, Toronto: Collier Macmillan Canada.

Putnam, H. B. (1995), 'Interconnection: Regulatory Issues', London: International Telecommunication Union, ITU Regulatory Colloquium No. 4.

Quah, D. T. (1996), 'The Invisible Hand and the Weightless Economy', London: LSE Centre for Economic Performance, Occasional Paper 12, Programme on National Economic Performance, Apr.

Qvortrup, L., and Bianchi, A. (1996), 'Barriers and Strategies to Effective Participation in the Information Society in Cohesion Regions', Brussels: NEXUS Europe, CURDS, CCS, Study Assessing the Social and Economic Cohesion Aspects of the Development of an Information Society in Europe: Study for DG XIII/A.7-DG XVI, Vol. 3 for the European Commission.

Raab, C., and Bennett, C. J. (1995), 'Taking the Measure of Privacy on the Information Highway, Paper prepared for PICT International Conference on The Social and Economic Implications of Information and Communication Technologies', London: Programme on Information and Communication Technology (PICT), 10–12 May.

Reed, C. (1996), *The Legal Regulation of Internet Banking*, London: Internet Law Project.

Reed, C., and Davies, L. (1995), *Digital Cash: The Legal Implications*, London: Internet Law Project.

Reich, R. B. (1991), *The Work of Nations: Preparing Ourselves for 21st-Century Capitalism*, New York: Simon & Schuster.

Reisman, R. R. (1995), 'CD-ROM/Online Hybrids. The Missing Link', *CD-ROM Professional*, 8(4): 22–3.

Rejane-Legey, L., and Maculan, A.-M. (1999), 'Adoption and Diffusion of EDI in the Brazilian Market', Rio de Janeiro: University of Rio de Janeiro, Science and Technology Programme Working Paper, Nov.

Retail Banking Research Ltd. (1995), 'Payment Cards in Europe', London: Retail Banking Research Ltd.

Rheingold, H. (1993), *The Virtual Community: Homesteading on the Electronic Frontier*, Reading, Mass.: Addison-Wesley.

Ricardo, D. (1821), *The Principles of Political Economy and Taxation*, 1973 edn., London: J. M. Dent & Sons.

Rice, R. E. (1993), 'Media Appropriateness: Using Social Presence Theory to Compare Traditional and New Organizational Media', *Human Communication Research*, 19(4): 451–84.

——(1999), 'Artifacts and Paradoxes in New Media', *New Media and Society*, 1(1): 24–32.

Richardson, R., and Gillespie, A. (1996), 'Advanced Communications and Employment Creation in Rural and Peripheral Regions: A Case Study of the Highlands and Islands of Scotland', *The Annals of Regional Science*, 30: 91–110.

Rifkin, J. (1995), *The End of Work—The Decline of the Global Labor Force and the Dawn of the Post-Market Era*, London: G. P. Putnam's Sons.

Robinson, J. (1932), *The Economics of Imperfect Competition*, London: Macmillan.

Rogers, D. (1993), *The Future of American Banking—Managing for Change*, New York: McGraw-Hill.

Rogers, E. M. (1983), *Diffusion of Innovations*, 3rd edn., London: Free Press.

Rohlfs, J. (1974), 'A Theory of Interdependent Demand for a Communications Service', *Bell Journal of Economics*, 5(1): 16–37.

Romeo, A. (1975), 'Interindustry and Interfirm Differences in the Rate of Diffusion of an Innovation', *Review of Economics and Statistics*, 57(3): 311–19.

Romer, P. (1993a), 'Idea Gaps and Object Gaps in Economic Development', *Journal of Monetary Economics*, 32(3): 543–73.

——(1993b), 'Ideas and Things', *The Economist*, 11 Sept., pp. 6–7.

Rosenberg, N. (1976), *Perspectives on Technology*, Cambridge: Cambridge University Press.

——(1994), *Exploring the Black Box: Technology, Economics and History*, Cambridge: Cambridge University Press.

Roth, J. P. (ed.) (1988), *CD-ROM Applications and Markets*, Westport, Conn.: Meckler.

Ruggles, M. A. (1994), *The Audience Reflected in the Medium of Law: A Critique of the Political Economy of Speech Rights in the United States*, Norwood, NJ: Ablex.

Salamon, L. S., and Anheier, H. (1994), *The Emerging Sector: An Overview, Institute for Policy and Social Studies*, Baltimore: Johns Hopkins University.

Samarajiva, R. (1985), 'Property Rights and Information Markets: Policy Issues Affecting News Agencies and Online Databases', unpublished Ph.D. thesis, Department of Communication, Simon Fraser University.

——(1994), 'Privacy in Electronic Public Space: Emerging Issues', *Canadian Journal of Communication*, 19(1): 87–99.

——(1996a), 'Consumer Protection in the Decentralized Network', in E. Noam (ed.), *Private Networks Public Objectives*, Amsterdam: Elsevier, 287–306.

——(1996b), 'Surveillance by Design: Public Networks and the Control of Consumption', in R. Mansell and R. Silverstone (eds.), *Communication by Design: The Politics of Information and Communication Technologies*, Oxford: Oxford University Press, 129–56.

——(1997), 'Connecting to Things or to People? Access Reconsidered', Amsterdam: Paper presented at the Opening Conference of the Amsterdam School of Communications Research at the Royal Dutch Academy of Arts and Sciences, 18–19 Sept.

Samuelson, P. (1995), 'The Copyright Grab', *Wired*, 2 Jan., pp. 135–6.

Sayers, D. (1997a), 'Electronic Payment Systems—A Horizontal or a Vertical Future?', Brighton: SPRU University of Sussex, FAIR Working Paper No. 16, Feb.

——(1997b), 'Erosion of Privacy and Security in Public Telecommunications Networks—The Growing Significance of Tele-Metadata in Advanced Communication Services', Brighton: SPRU University of Sussex, FAIR Working Paper No. 13, Feb.

Scannell, E. (1998), 'Taming the Wild Web', *InfoWorld*, 13 Apr., pp. 4–5.

Schmidt, S. K., and Werle, R. (1992), 'The Development of Compatibility Standards in Telecommunications: Conceptual Framework and Theoretical Perspective', in M. Dierkes and U. Hoffman (eds.), *New Technology at the Outset: Social Forces in the Shaping of Technological Innovations*, Frankfurt: Campus, pp. 301–28.

——(1998), *Co-ordinating Technology: Studies in the International Standardization of Telecommunications*, Cambridge, Mass.: MIT Press.

Schneider, V., Charon, J.-M., Miles, I., Thomas, G., and Vedel, T. (1991), 'The Dynamics of Videotex Development in Britain, France and Germany: A Cross-National Comparison', *European Journal of Communication*, 6: 187–212.

Schneideran, A. (1999), 'Three Myths about Government, Markets, and The Net: A Special Report on the Clinton Administration's Plans for Global Electronic Commerce', *ENODE*, 2(4): 7–8.

Schneier, B. (1996), *Applied Cryptography: Protocols, Algorithms and Source Code in C*, New York: John Wiley & Sons.

Schoechle, T. D. (1995), 'Privacy on the Information Superhighway: Will My House be My Castle?', *Telecommunications Policy*, 19(6): 435–52.

Schumpeter, J. A. (1954), *A History of Economic Analysis*, ed. E. B. Schumpeter, New York: Oxford University Press.

SCIENTER (1998), 'Multimedia Educational Software Observatory (MESO), Final Report, Volume 1—European Overview, Revised Synthesis', Brussels: A study funded by European Commission, DGXXII, Nov.

Scitovsky, T. (1986), *The Joyless Economy*, New York: Oxford University Press.

Scott, J. (1996), *Stratification & Power: Structures of Class, Status and Command*, London: Polity.

Seeley, J. R., Sim, R. A., and Loosley, E. W. (1956), *Crestwood Heights: A Study of the Culture of Suburban Life*, New York: Basic Books.

Shapiro, C., and Varian, H. (1998), *Information Rules: A Strategic Guide to the Network Economy*, Cambridge, Mass.: Harvard Business School Press.

Shurmer, M., and Swann, G. M. P. (1995), 'An Analysis of the Process Generating De Facto Standards in the PC Spreadsheet Software Market', *Journal of Evolutionary Economics*, 5(2): 119–32.

Silverstone, R. (1999), *Why Study the Media?*, London: Sage.

Silverstone, R., and Haddon, L. (1996a), 'Design and the Domestication of Information and Communication Technologies: Technical Change and Everyday Life', in R. Mansell and R. Silverstone (eds.), *Communication by Design: The Politics of Information and Communication Technologies*, Oxford: Oxford University Press, 44–74.

—— (1996b), 'Television, Cable and AB Households: A Report for Telewest plc', Brighton: Graduate Research Centre in Culture and Communication, University of Sussex.

—— (1997), 'The Role of AC Services in Preventing Social Exclusion in the Emerging Information Society', Brighton: Graduate Research Centre in Culture and Communication, University of Sussex, FAIR Working Paper No. 28, Mar.

Silverstone, R., and Hartmann, M. (1998), 'Methodologies for Media and Information Technology Research in Everyday Life', Brighton: The European Media Technology and Everyday Life Network (EMTEL), Working Paper No. 5, Graduate Research Centre in Culture and Communication, University of Sussex.

Silverstone, R., and Hirsch, E. (eds.) (1992), *Consuming Technologies: Media and Information in Domestic Spaces*, London: Routledge.

Silverstone, R., and Mansell, R. (1996), 'The Politics of Information and Communication Technologies', in R. Mansell and R. Silverstone (eds.), *Communication by Design: The Politics of Information and Communication Technologies*, Oxford: Oxford University Press, 213–27.

Simon, H. A. (1955), 'A Behavioral Model of Rational Choice', *Quarterly Journal of Economics*, 69: 99–118.

Sipior, J. C., and Ward, B. T. (1995), 'The Ethical and Legal Quandary of Email Privacy', *Communications of the ACM*, 38(12): 48–54.

Sirbu, M. (1989), 'Telecommunications Standards, Innovation and Industry Structure', Washington, DC: International Institute of Communication, Telecommunications Forum.

Skouby, K. E. (1997), 'The Industry, the Markets and the Services', in W. H. Melody (ed.), *Telecom Reform: Principles, Policies and Regulatory Practices*, Lyngby: Technical University of Denmark, 97–105.

—— (1998), 'ACTS Service Integration for Interactive Multimedia (SII) Chain, Guideline G9,

Electronic Commerce': AMUSE and EURORIM Projects, European Commission ACTS Programme, ed. K. E. Skouby.

Smart Storage (1999), 'CD Technology: The Standard for Secondary Storage—A White Paper', no city: Available from Special Interest Group on CD/DVD Application & Technology (SIGCAT) at http://www.sigcat.org/articles/white/smart1.htm accessed 30 Oct. 1999.

Smith, G. J. H. (1996), *Internet Law and Regulation*, London: Financial Times Law and Tax.

Smith, K. (1995), 'Interactions in Knowledge Systems: Foundations, Policy Implications and Empirical Mapping', Canary Islands: Systems of Innovation Research Network Workshop, 20–2 Jan.

Smith, M. A., and Kollock, P. (eds.) (1999), *Communities in Cyberspace*, London: Routledge.

Smith System Engineering Ltd. (1997), 'Feasibility of Censoring and Jamming Pornography and Racism in Informatics', Guildford: Smith System Engineering Ltd. (The Smith Group), Final Report prepared for the European Parliament, Scientific and Technological Options Assessment Programme, July.

Soete, L., and Kamp, K. (1996), 'The "Bit Tax": The Case for Further Research', *Science and Public Policy*, 23(6): 353–60.

—— (1997), 'Taxing Consumption in the Electronic Age', *Intermedia*, 25(4): 19–22.

—— (1998), 'Fiscal Issues in the Growth of Electronic Commerce', Maastricht: MERIT, University of Maastricht, FAIR Working Paper No. 33, June.

Sørensen, K. H. (1998), 'Learning Technology, Constructing Culture: Socio-technical Change as Social Learning', Dragvoll: Centre for Technology and Society, Norwegian University of Science and Technology, Paper prepared for the Social Learning in Multimedia (SLIM) project funded by the European Commission, http://www.ed.ac.uk/~rcess/SLIM/public/phase1/knut.html accessed 14 Mar. 1999.

Spectrum Strategy (1996), 'Development of the Information Society: An International Analysis', London: A report by Spectrum Strategy Consultants for the Department of Trade and Industry, HMSO, Oct.

Srivastava, L., and Mansell, R. (1998), 'Electronic Cash and the Innovation Process: A User Paradigm', Brighton: SPRU University of Sussex, FAIR Working Paper No. 35, Mar.

Steele, R. (1993), 'Mobile Communications in the 21st Century', in D. E. N. Davies, C. Hilsum, and A. W. Rudge (eds.), *Communications After AD2000*, London: Chapman & Hall, pp. 135–47.

Steering Committee on Research Opportunities Relating to Economic and Social Impacts of Computing and Communications (1998), 'Fostering Research on the Economic and Social Impacts of Information Technology: Report of a Workshop', Washington DC: The Steering Committee and Computer Science and Telecommunications Board, Commission on Physical Sciences, Mathematics, and Applications, National Research Council.

Stefik, M., Barlow, J. P., Lessig, L., and Mann, C. C. (1998), 'Roundtable on Life, Liberty, and the Pursuit of Copyright?', *Atlantic Unbound*, 29 Sept., pp. 10–17, see http://www.theatlantic.com/unbound/forum/copyright/ accessed 24 Aug. 1999.

Steinmueller, W. E. (1992a), 'The Economics of Alternative Integrated Circuit Manufacturing Technology: A Framework and Appraisal', *Review of Industrial Organisation*, 7: 327–49.

—— (1992b), 'The Economics of Production and Distribution of User-Specific Information via Digital Networks', in C. Antonelli (ed.), *The Economics of Information Networks*, Amsterdam: North Holland, 173–94.

—— (1996), 'The US Software Industry: An Analysis and Interpretive History', in D. C. Mowery (ed.), *The International Computer Software Industry*, Oxford: Oxford University Press, 15–52.

—— (1998), 'Virtual Communities Developments: Globally and in the ACTS and Telematics Application Programmes', Maastricht: MERIT, University of Maastricht, FAIR Working Paper No. 46, Mar.

—— (1999), 'Paths to Convergence: The Roles of Popularisation, Virtualisation and Inter-mediation', in E. Bohlin, K. Brodin, A. Lundgren, and B. Thorngren (eds.), *Convergence in Communications and Beyond*, Amsterdam: Elsevier, forthcoming 2000.

Stoneman, P. (1983), *The Economic Analysis of Technological Change*, Oxford: Oxford University Press.

Strassmann, P. A. (1985), *Information Payoff: The Transformation of Work in the Electronic Age*, New York: Free Press.

—— (1990), *The Business Value of Computers*, New Canaan, Conn.: Information Economics Press.

Strate, L., Jacobson, R., and Gibson, S. B. (eds.) (1996*a*), *Communication and Cyberspace: Social Interaction in the Electronic Environment*, Cresskill, NJ: Hampton.

—— (eds.) (1996*b*), *Surveying the Electronic Landscape: An Introduction*, Cresskill, NJ: Hampton.

Summerton, J. (ed.) (1994), *Changing Large Technical Systems*, Boulder, Col.: Westview.

Sutton, J. (1998), *Technology and Market Structure: Theory and History*, Cambridge, Mass.: MIT Press.

Swankin, D. A. (1990), 'How Due Process in the Development of Voluntary Standards Can Reduce the Risk of Anti-Trust Liability', Washington, DC: National Institute of Standards and Technology (NIST), Feb.

Taaffe, J. (1999), 'Nor.Web Turns Off Powerline Service', *Communications Week International*, 20 Sept., p. 4.

Takeyama, L. (1994), 'The Shareware Industry: Some Stylised Facts and Estimates of Rates of Returns', *Economics of Innovation and New Technology*, 3(2): 161–72.

Tapscott, D. (1995), *The Digital Economy: Promise and Peril in the Age of Networked Intelligence*, New York: McGraw-Hill.

Telecommunication Technology Committee (TTC) (1995), 'Survey Report on Telecommunication-Related Forums' Activities', Tokyo: Telecommunication Technology Committee.

ter Weel, B. (1997), 'Cybertax', Maastricht: MERIT Working Paper No. 2/97-019, October.

TFPL Publishing Ltd (1996), 'Facts and Figures 1996', London: TFPL Publishing Ltd.

—— (1997), 'TFPL Multimedia, and CD-ROM Directory on CD-ROM, 1997 Edition', TFPL Publishing Ltd.

Tournier, J.-L. (1995), 'The Future of Collective Administration of Authors' Rights', Luxembourg: European Commission, Legal Advisory Board.

Townsend, P. (1987), 'Conceptualising Poverty', in Z. Ferge and S. Miller (eds.), *Dynamics of Deprivation*, Aldershot: Gower, 31–44.

Treanor, P. (1996), 'Why Telecity Projects are Wrong', http://www.inter.nl.net/users/Paul.Treanor accessed 14 Mar. 1997.

Trebing, H. M. (1997), 'Emerging Market Structures and Options for Regulatory Reform in Public Utility Industries', in W. H. Melody (ed.), *Telecom Reform: Principles, Policies and Regulatory Practices*, Lyngby: Technical University of Denmark, 29–40.

Tremblay, G. (1995), 'The Information Society: From Fordism to Gatesism', *Canadian Journal of Communication*, 20: 461–82.

Tuck, B. (1996), 'Electronic Copyright Management Systems: A Discussion Paper', London: Conference Proceedings: Electronic Copyright Management Systems Workshop.

Turing, A. M. (1950), 'Computing Machinery and Intelligence: Can Machines Think?', *Mind*, 59: 433–60.

Turkle, S. (1999), 'Commodity and Community in Personal Computing', in D. A. Schon, B. Sanyal, and W. J. Mitchell (eds.), *High Technology and Low-Income Communities: Prospects for the Positive Use of Advanced Information Technology*, Cambridge, Mass.: MIT Press, 337–48.

Turner, B. (1989), 'Status Politics in Contemporary Capitalism', in R. J. Holton and B. S. Turner (eds.), *Max Weber on Economy and Society*, London: Routledge, 131–59.

Tyler, M., and Joy, C. (1997), *1.1.98: Telecommunications in the New Era: Competing in the Single Market*, London: Multiplex.

United Kingdom Government (1994), 'The Data Protection Act 1994', London: HMSO.

—— (1998), 'Data Protection Act 1998', London: Data Protection Registrar, http://www.legislation.hmso.gov.uk/acts/acts98/19980029.htm accessed 6 Apr. 2000.

—— (1999), 'The Telecommunications (Data Protection and Privacy) Regulations 1999', London: UK Government Statutory Instrument 1999 No. 2093.

United Nations (1976), 'International Covenant on Civil and Political Rights', New York: United Nations.

—— (1990), 'Guidelines for the Regulation of Computerised Personal Data Files Adopted by the UN General Assembly on 14 December', Geneva: United Nations, 14 Dec.

United Nations Conference on Trade and Development (1996), 'The TRIPS Agreement and Developing Countries', New York/Geneva: Prepared by the UNCTAD Secretariat, UNCTAD/ITE/1.

United Nations Educational Scientific and Cultural Organization (1994), *UNESCO Statistical Yearbook 1994*, Geneva: United Nations.

—— (1997), *World Information Report 1997/98*, edited Y. Courrier and A. Lange, Geneva: UNESCO.

United States (1993), 'National Information Infrastructure: Agenda for Action—Realizing the Information Future', Washington DC: Information Infrastructure Task Force.

United States District Court for the District Of Columbia (1999), 'Findings of Fact, US vs. Microsoft Corporation, Civil Action No. 98-1232 (TPJ)', Washington DC: United States District Court for the District Of Columbia, US District Judge Thomas Penfield Jackson.

United States Congress (1996), 'Telecommunications Act of 1996', Washington DC: United States Congress, Pub. L. No. 104-104, 110 Stat. 56 codified at 47 U.S.C. § 151 *et seq.* (1996 Act).

—— (1998), 'Digital Millennium Copyright Act (DMCA) of 1998', Washington DC: Pub. L. No. 105-304 112 Stat. 2860.

Universal Mobile Telecommunication Forum (UMTS) Forum (1998), 'The Path Toward UMTS—Technologies for the Information Society', Report 2, UMTS Forum, http://www.umts-forum.org/reports.html accessed 18 Aug. 1999.

—— (1999), 'The Future Mobile Market: Global Trends and Developments with a Focus on Western Europe', Cambridge: Report prepared by Analysys Ltd., Report No. 8, http://www.umts-forum.org/reports.html accessed 19 Aug.

Vaitilingam, R. (ed.) (1998), *Europe's Network Industries: Conflicting Priorities—Telecommunications*, London: Centre for Economic Policy Research.

Venturelli, S. (1998), *Liberalizing the European Media: Politics, Regulation, and the Public Sphere*, Oxford: Clarendon.

Viswanath, K., Samarajiva, R., and Park, E. (1994), 'Covering Telecommunication Privacy: A Study of National and Local Press Coverage of the Policy Process', AIERI/IAMCR Scientific Conference, Seoul, Korea, 3–8 July.

Waldman, S. (1997), 'Making a Net Profit: The Battle Lines are Drawn for On-line Music Retail', *Music Week*, 12 July, p. 8.

Walker, W., Graham, M., and Harbor, B. (1988), 'From Components to Integrated Systems: Technological Diversity and Interactions between the Military and Civilian Sectors', in P. Gummett and J. Reppy (eds.), *The Relations Between Defence and Civil Technologies*, Dordrecht: Kluwer, 17–37.

Wallenstein, G. (1990), *Setting Global Telecommunication Standards: The Stakes, the Players and the Process*, Norwood, Mass.: Artech House.

Walz, J. (1999), 'Statement from Iridium North America Regarding Iridium LLC's Voluntary Chapter 11 Bankruptcy Filing', Arizona: Iridium, 13 Aug., http://www.iridium.com/corporate/news/1999/docs/991308b.html accessed 10 Sept.

van Warrebey, G. (1998), *Read My Lips: The Latest University Findings on Subliminal Advertising & Sales*, Sparta, NJ: Lehigh.

Washington State Department of Revenue (1993), 'Information on Washington's Tax Structure: Real Estate Transactions and Use Tax', Olympia, Wash.: Washington State Department of Revenue, Feb.

Watkins, T. (1988), 'Dual-Use Technologies: Diffusion Structures and International Policy Convergence, Working Paper', Cambridge Mass.: Harvard University.

Webster, F. (1995), *The Information Society*, London: Routledge.

Wehn, U. (1996), 'International Governance of Cryptography', Brighton: SPRU University of Sussex, FAIR Working Paper No. 9, Nov.

Wernick, I. K., Herman, R., Govind, S., and Ausabel, J. H. (1996), 'The Liberation of the Environment', *Daedalus*, 125(3): 171–98.

Wessels, B. (1999), 'The Cultural Dynamics of Innovation', unpublished D.Phil. thesis, SPRU, University of Sussex, Brighton.

Williams, B. (1979), *Report of the Committee on Obscenity and Film Censorship, Home Office*, London: HMSO Cmd. 7772.

Williams, M. R. (1985), *A History of Computing Technology*, Englewood Cliffs: Prentice-Hall.

Williams, R., and Slack, R. S. (eds.) (1999), *Europe Appropriates Multimedia: A Study of the National Uptake of Multimedia in Eight European Countries and Japan, Report No. 42*, Trondheim: Norwegian University of Science and Technology, Centre of Technology and Society.

Williamson, O. E. (1975), *Markets and Hierarchies: Analysis and Antitrust Implications*, New York: Free Press.

—— (1985), *The Economic Institutions of Capitalism*, New York: Free Press.

—— (1995), 'Hierarchies, Markets and Power in the Economy: An Economic Perspective', *Industrial and Corporate Change*, 4(1): 21–49.

Williamson, O. E., and Winter, S. G. (eds.) (1991), *The Nature of the Firm: Origins, Evolution, and Development*, Oxford: Oxford University Press.

Wood, J. (1993), 'Mobile Communications: New User Perspectives', Kenilworth: SPRU, University of Sussex, Paper presented at the PICT National Conference, Kenilworth, 19–21 May.

Woolgar, S. (1996), 'Technologies as Cultural Artefacts', in W. H. Dutton (ed.), *Information and Communication Technologies: Visions and Realities*, Oxford: Oxford University Press, 87–102.

World Intellectual Property Organization (1979), 'Berne Convention for the Protection of Literary and Artistic Works of September 9, 1886 completed at Paris on July 24 1971, as amended on September 28, 1979', Geneva: WIPO Publication No. 287(E).

—— (1996a), 'Information on World Intellectual Property Organisation', Geneva: WIPO, 7 Apr.

World Intellectual Property Organization (1996*b*), 'WIPO Copyright Treaty', Geneva: WIPO adopted by the Diplomatic Conference on 20 Dec.

—— (1996*c*), 'WIPO Performances and Phonograms Treaty', Geneva: WIPO adopted by the Diplomatic Conference on 20 Dec.

World Trade Organization (1999), 'An Overview of the Agreement on Trade-Related Aspects of Intellectual Property Rights (TRIPS Agreement)', Geneva: World Trade Organization.

Worthington, S. (1995), 'The Cashless Society', *International Journal of Retail and Distribution Management*, 23(7): 31–40.

—— (1996), 'Plastic Payment Cards—Where are They Now and Where are They Going?', *EFMA Newsletter*, 141: 3.

Xavier, P. (1997), 'Universal Service and Public Access in the Networked Society', *Telecommunication Policy*, 21(9): 829–43.

Young, M. (1961), *Family and Kinship in East London*, Harmondsworth: Penguin.

Zakon, R. H. (1999), 'Hobbes' Internet Timeline v4.2', Internet Society http://infor.isoc.org/guest/zakon/Internet/History/HIT.html accessed 6 Apr. 2000.

Zona Research (1996), 'Internet and Intranet: 1996 Markets, Opportunities and Trends', Redwood City, Calif.: Zona Research.

Zuboff, S. (1988), *In the Age of the Smart Machine*, New York: Basic Books.

Subject Index

Name Index